Praise for *The Success Principles*™

Canfield's principles are simple, but the results you'll achieve will be extraordinary!
—Anthony Robbins, author of *Awaken the Giant Within* and *Unlimited Power*

If you could only read one book this year, you have it in your hands.
—Harvey Mackay, author of the *New York Times* number one bestseller *Swim with the Sharks Without Being Eaten Alive*

When Jack Canfield writes, I listen. This is Jack's finest piece of writing and will impact your life forever.
—Pat Williams, senior vice president of the NBA's Orlando Magic

Jack Canfield is a Master of his medium, giving people who are hungry for more life the wisdom, insights, understanding, and inspiration they need to achieve it. Great book, great read, great gift for anyone committed to becoming a Master of Life!
—Michael E. Gerber, author of *The E-Myth* books

In one book, *The Success Principles* gives you the basic strategies for success plus the advanced strategies that will help you become a success master. I have personally learned a lot from Jack Canfield and I trust you will, too.
—John Gray, Ph.D., author of *Men Are from Mars, Women Are from Venus*

Before you can change your life, you must first change your thinking. Jack and Janet have created an inspirational and motivational road map for your personal success! My real estate home-study course has helped thousands become confident, successful real estate investors. I am convinced *The Success Principles* will change the way you think, the way you act, and help you change your life in ways you never dreamed possible! I would not only recommend this book to my students, but also to anyone committed to being successful—beyond their wildest dreams! I urge you to read this wonderful book. It will absolutely help you to change your life for the better!
—Carleton Sheets, creator of the "No Down Payment Real Estate" home-study course

Canfield and Switzer have put their methods to success in an illuminating and easy-to-read book. Jack's teaching is highly effective and this new book will be the gift to give this year.
—Ken Blanchard, coauthor of *The One Minute Manager*® and *Customer Mania!*®

In *The Success Principles,* Jack Canfield reveals the specific methodology and results-oriented principles required for success and ultimate achievement. Whether you need to boost sales at the office, expand creativity, or create more balance in your life, this book will pave the way to achieving your highest success!
—Peter Vidmar, two-time Olympic gold medalist in gymnastics and member of the U.S. Olympic Hall of Fame

The Success Principles will inspire and empower you to lead a more fulfilling life. Get ready for some changes with this book!
—Kathy Smith, a leading force in American fitness and wellness

Jack's message is simple, powerful, and practical. If you work the principles, the principles work. A must-read for those who want to create the successful life about which they dream.
—Andrew Puzder, president and CEO of CKE Restaurants, Inc., Carl's Jr., Hardee's, and La Salsa

What a great book! Jack Canfield's *The Success Principles* is a reference book for everyone who is interested in actually having the life they have dreamed about. Keep this book with you, use it as a guide and inspiration to help you achieve your highest potential and the inner peace that you desire. You need this book.
—Marilyn Tam, former president of Reebok Apparel Products Group and author of *How to Use What You've Got to Get What You Want*

If you thought you knew everything about how to be successful in business, wait until you read what's inside *The Success Principles*. From start-up entrepreneurs to the world's most powerful CEOs, this book can and will teach anyone how to be more successful and much happier doing what they love to do.
—John Assaraf, RE/MAX Indiana, *New York Times* and *Wall Street Journal* bestselling author of *The Street Kid's Guide to Having It All*

Page for page the best system for achieving anything you want. Get ready for the ride of your life. I couldn't put it down!
—Marcia Martin, former vice president of EST and transformational coach

Jack Canfield's amazing ability to be extremely articulate, understandable, and approachable makes *The Success Principles* not only an amazing blueprint for success, but also a pure joy to read.   —Jim Tunney, Ed.D., former NFL referee, educator, and author of *It's the Will, Not the Skill*

I have witnessed firsthand Jack Canfield's tenacity in using the principles within this book. It is because of this determination and his beliefs in these principles that the Chicken Soup for the Soul® book series was born. *The Success Principles* is not only an amazing book that will give you the guide to outstanding achievement, but it in itself is proof that the principles work.
—Peter Vegso, president of Health Communications, Inc., and publisher of Chicken Soup for the Soul®

Most of us know what we want out of life, but only a handful of us have learned how to get it. Now *The Success Principles* not only gives you the road map, it hands you the keys to the ignition and puts gas in your tank! Get yourself some cookies and don't put this book down till you've mastered its message.
—Wally Amos, author of *The Cookie Never Crumbles*

My good friend Jack Canfield is one of the most insightful speakers and teachers in the world today. After you have spent time with him, internalizing his ideas and insights, you will be changed in a positive way for the rest of your life.
—Brian Tracy, one of America's leading authorities on the development of human potential and personal effectiveness and author of *Success Is a Journey, Million Dollar Habits,* and *The Traits of Champions*

By bringing your actions in line with Jack's core principles and values, you can achieve any success you seek, including inner peace. Jack has written the road map to that end in *The Success Principles.* All you have to do is follow it.
—Hyrum W. Smith, vice chairman and founder of FranklinCovey

In today's super-competitive marketplace, high achievers are those people who follow a systematic approach to their success. Now in the best success classic to come along in decades, *The Success Principles* catalogs and explains these systems in simple language with step-by-step instructions, and features inspiring stories of others who have traveled the path before you. If your goal is greater accomplishment, more money, more free time, and less stress, read and apply the proven principles in this book.
—Les Brown, author of *Live Your Dreams* and *Conversations on Success*

What a great collection of "successful" thoughts and ideas . . . some simple, some profound, and all "essential" in today's complex world . . . a must-read!
—Steven Stralser, Ph.D., managing director of and clinical professor at the Global Entrepreneurship Center, Thunderbird: The Garvin School of International Management, and author of *MBA in a Day: What You Would Learn in Top-Tier Schools of Business—If You Only Had the Time*

After you read *The Success Principles,* you will approach your short- and long-term goals in a completely new and exciting fashion. This book outlines the tools you need to get everything you want out of life and more! Canfield and Switzer's own success is evidence that these principles work and can be easily applied to any goal.
—Rita Davenport, former president of Arbonne International

Success is something almost everyone wants, and many spend a lifetime hoping for. Some never find it while others realize it early in life. No matter where you are in your life, stop and read this magnificent book by Jack Canfield and Janet Switzer. Maybe you're already there, or are trying to get there, or are lost somewhere between the desire for and the realization of personal success. When you've finished *The Success Principles: How to Get from Where You Are to Where You Want to Be,* you'll immediately know where you are, where you want to be, and how to get there. This is a work that should become a textbook and required reading before earning "adulthood."
—Dave Liniger, chairman of the board of RE/MAX International

Jack Canfield has done it again! In *The Success Principles,* he explains with great ease and compassion the time-tested techniques employed by high achievers from every walk of life—techniques that can take you as far as you dare to dream. No matter what your definition of "success" is, this book is going to get you there!
—Jeff Liesener, president of High Achievers Network

If you've ever wanted Jack Canfield to personally mentor you in achieving your highest vision, this book is the next best thing to having him as your personal guide. It's packed with information, inspiration, and—most important—understanding. Along with his proven strategies, Jack's support, compassion, and integrity shine through.
—Marshall Thurber, cofounder of the Excelerated Business School and Money and You

The success principles in this book are so simple to follow but at the same time so powerful. They are essential to achieving your goals. Jack has a way of making learning entertaining and fun. This book is a true winner!
—Kathy Coover, cofounder and executive vice president of Isagenix International

In a world filled with dubious paths to success, *The Success Principles* identifies the proven steps today's biggest names and brightest stars use to achieve their ideal future. I can't think of a better way to get from where you are to where you want to be. —Bill Harris, director, Centerpointe Research

If you have a big vision and big plans, read *The Success Principles* and take action on what you learn. After all, you deserve to have more of what you want out of life.
—H. Ronald Hulnick, Ph.D., president of the University of Santa Monica

A unique blend of lessons and techniques with true-life anecdotes and humor make *The Success Principles* a great read. Educational, humorous, and very down-to-earth, this book uses Jack Canfield's ability to motivate and inspire without an overly "hyped" attitude. These success principles offer great value to any reader.
—Christen Brown, president of On Camera Entertainment and author of *Star Quality*

No matter what your idea of success is, Jack Canfield can help you get there. *The Success Principles* is life's reference book for the young and old alike. Transform your dreams of success into reality. Buy this book today.
—Gary T. Van Brunt, vice chairman of Discount Tire Co.

The Success Principles proves once and for all that personal achievement is not an accident of birth or privilege. Rather, it's the result of thinking, and of doing—of planning, and of follow-through. But most important, the power to achieve is a *skill* that can be *taught*—and no one teaches it more superbly than Jack Canfield.
—Catherine B. Reynolds, chairman of the board of the Catherine B. Reynolds Foundation

This book is a must-read! Canfield and Switzer explain the specific, step-by-step formulas all of us can use to achieve more success in our careers and personal lives. If making more money, playing a bigger game, and achieving your dream lifestyle are what you want, *The Success Principles* delivers it masterfully.
—Gay Hendricks, Ph.D., author of *Conscious Living* and coauthor (with Dr. Kathlyn Hendricks) of *Conscious Loving*

No matter where you are with your life, *The Success Principles* gives you proven strategies and time-tested systems to create a brighter future. Join the ranks of today's highest achievers in reading and applying what this impressive new success classic tells you. Then plan to get a copy for a friend.
—Paul R. Scheele, author of *Natural Brilliance, Genius Code, Abundance for Life,* and *The PhotoReading Whole Mind System*

This book is a brilliantly written, masterful distillation of the leading principles and processes available today for creating real success in your life.
—Hale Dwoskin, author of the *New York Times* bestseller
The Sedona Method: Your Key to Lasting Happiness, Success, Peace, and Emotional Well-being

Success in all areas of your life can be yours! Follow Jack Canfield's principles and strategies to achieve any goal! *The Success Principles* offers a detailed yet understandable guide to achieving more of what YOU want. It's enjoyable and effective. Read it today!
—Erin Saxton, Eleven Communications

Reading *The Success Principles* is as close as possible to having Jack Canfield as your personal coach. Jack has the ability to blend intelligence and compassion, making the book very approachable. The book's principles and stories of others who have used these principles is effective and inspiring. This dynamic book will be spoken of for years to come!
—George R. Walther, author of *Heat Up Your Cold Calls*

If you are looking for a magic bullet to improve your life, your career, and your relationships, *The Success Principles* delivers it in spades. But don't just buy this impressive new classic and put it on a shelf. Read its proven strategies, apply its time-tested systems, then get ready to join the ranks of the world's highest achievers!
—Raymond Aaron, Canada's number one business and investment coach

What a great collection of "successful" thoughts and ideas . . . some simple, some profound, and all "essential" in today's complex world. A must-read! I used the principles in this book to propel my website from 100 visitors a month to over 5,000 visitors a month.
—Zev Saftlas, author of *Motivation That Works* and founder of empoweringmessages.com

Jack Canfield's *The Success Principles* intertwines strategies for success with proven examples and stories. The book should be a must-read for everyone who is looking to attain new heights in his or her life. Is there a way to make this required reading for future generations? I wish I had this information twenty years ago!
—Arielle Ford, author of *Hot Chocolate for the Mystical Soul*

Canfield and Switzer have created a book that is alive with intellect, compassion, and humor. This is one of the best books on success I have ever read! If you have a dream that you have not yet attained, let Jack Canfield lead the way. You will be happy you did.
—Bill Cirone, superintendent of Santa Barbara County Office of Education

If expanding your opportunities, creating new alliances, helping more people, and getting more out of every minute of your life are your goals, *The Success Principles* can bring you these results. I loved it!
—John Demartini, CEO of Demartini Seminars and founder of the Concourse of Wisdom

Successful people know the most significant investment you can make is in yourself. *The Success Principles* helps you master the skill sets that will attract great people, great opportunities, and great fortune into your life. Let this investment pay off for you. —Cynthia Kersey, author of *Unstoppable* and *Unstoppable Women*

If ever there was a book that uncovered the secret strategies of today's highest achievers, *The Success Principles* is it. Easy, understandable, applicable. It's the best success tool to come along in years.
—Bill Bauman, Ph.D., Bill Bauman Seminars and Mentoring

Finally, a book that lives up to what it claims. *The Success Principles* really does take your life to the next level and helps you achieve anything you've ever dreamed of. Using the principles that have made Jack Canfield and the many other successful men and women within this book, you, too, can attain amazing achievement. Read this book today! —Tom Hill, founder of the Eagle Institute and author of *Living at the Summit: A Life Plan*

If you're looking for a winning plan for success, look no further than Jack Canfield's *Success Principles*. —Suzanne de Passe, television producer

Jack Canfield is a true master. He understands what it takes to lead a successful life, and in *The Success Principles* he puts all the key elements together in one place for the rest of the world to see. —T. Harv Eker, author of *Secrets of the Millionaire Mind*

I have been a student of Jack Canfield for over a decade and have used the principles he teaches in this book to accelerate my own success and the success of the people I train and manage at the Henry Ford Museum. This book has my highest recommendation. It will change your life.
—Jim Van Bochove, director of workforce development at the Henry Ford: America's Greatest History Attraction

Jack Canfield's *Success Principles* brilliantly and succinctly imparts the tried and true formula for living a successful, fulfilled life. You will find inspiration and motivation on every page.
—Debbie Ford, number one *New York Times* bestselling author of *The Dark Side of the Light Chasers* and *The Best Year of Your Life*

Jack Canfield has, with diamond-like clarity, crafted the ultimate success manual. It's the manual I wish I'd had when I began my quest for the best.
—Master Mary Louise Zeller, "Ninja Grandma," twelve-time national and five-time international gold medalist in Olympic-style tae kwon do

Whether you are a budding entrepreneur, have been in business for decades, or have just graduated high school, Jack Canfield's *The Success Principles* is a must-read. The book takes you step-by-step through the stages of success and achievement and will propel you to your next level (and most likely far beyond that, too)! Jack's down-to-earth style and straightforward language allow the everyday person to enjoy this incredibly thorough, comprehensive, and intelligent book.
—Linda Distenfield, president, and Ira Distenfield, CEO of We The People

I still play *The Success Principles* in my car during "drive-time university." In three short years, I went from the edge of bankruptcy to owning a seven-person real estate company producing in the top two percent of all agents in Arizona. I built a respected real estate law firm and have now partnered in a land acquisition and development company. The foundation of my success is directly traced to the lessons I've learned from this book.
—Jason Wells, Tempe, Arizona

Once I read *The Success Principles,* I bought copies for my husband's dental staff. As a result, we decided to open a dental-assisting school to produce excellent dental assistants who would easily get jobs. Now I buy a copy of the book for every student and talk about key principles at our graduation ceremony. *The Success Principles* offers everything they need to be successful in every area of their lives.
—Helen Hussey, Arlington, Washington

In the two years since reading *The Success Principles,* I received an offer to work as the head of the psychology department at a prominent institute in Qatar; went on a fabulous long holiday to Thailand, the UK, and India; became part owner of an apartments-and-suites property; published my first book with Hay House Publishers; created an effective plan to manage my finances, tithing, and wealth—and became a millionaire in the process.
—Dr. A Moosani, Mumbai, Maharastra, India

For 10 years I worked as a doctor in different countries and fields of medicine, but although that sounds exciting, I was never truly happy in hospital jobs, which made me feel miserable and drained. *The Success Principles* made me realize I could say "no" and taught me to "inquire within" about what felt right for me. When I saw an ad on the Internet from the air ambulance looking for a flight doctor, it sounded like such a fantastic opportunity, even though I wasn't sure they'd be interested in me. I applied anyway—and was hired. It's by far the best job I have ever had!
—Johanna Gnad, Vienna, Austria

After a 34-year hiatus from competitive amateur wrestling, I decided to compete in the Veteran's Nationals just two months away. With my son as a coach, I used visualization, modified my diet, worked out vigorously, and kept my eye on the prize. Even when our flight got rerouted and we arrived at 2:00 A.M., I still persevered. On just a few hours of sleep, I practiced my affirmation and visualized winning. Several hours later I was the Freestyle National Champion.
—Skip Mondragon, Evans, Georgia

This book was the catalyst that reunited my family and saved my marriage! I was on the road to divorce—I'd separated from my husband and moved across the country. As I write this, my husband and I have reconciled and our family is back together. I've shared the book and what I've learned with my husband and children, and even lead a weekly "Jack Meeting" for our office. I feel so fulfilled sharing what I've learned with others.
—Carole Murphy, Columbus, Ohio

My son is a very bright individual, but never found his place in the education system. As he struggled through his first year in university, I gave him a copy of *The Success Principles.* He read your book and, soon after, left university to pursue his dream to become an entrepreneur. That was five years and two companies ago. Thank you.
—Janet Barlow, Ajax, Ontario, Canada

When I immigrated to Germany five years ago, I was living on 500 euros a month, afraid of the future. I found *The Success Principles* in one of the houses where I worked as a babysitter—and within two months of starting to follow the principles, I got a job as a consultant that paid 200 euros per day—or 4,000 euros per month. A year later, wanting to pursue my Ph.D., I got a scholarship to attend university that 200 other students had applied for.
—Maria Fernanda Valdes, Berlin, Germany

By following *The Success Principles,* I was able to fulfill my lifelong dream of traveling around the world. I have now traveled to six of the seven continents and 40+ countries and have helped many children and families along the way. In 2013, I was on the road for almost nine months out of the year, traveling through South and Central America, Europe, Africa, and the Middle East. It was an amazing year!
—Antoinette Bernardo, Brooklyn, New York

I was near suicidal after a layoff and a tough season of self-employment. After reading *The Success Principles,* I committed to writing a book, winning a Toastmaster contest, and finding a mentor who would take me to the next level. Within 24 months, I completed my book *Live a More Excellent Life,* finished in the top 20 of the Toastmaster's International Speech Contest out of 35,000 contestants, and am now a certified professional speaker, trainer, and coach.
—J. Loren Norris, Euless, Texas

After reading *The Success Principles,* I was able to turn my life around. I went from being $30,000+ in debt to saving my business from failure, paying off my debt, and creating substantial savings for a new home and retirement—all in just under a year!
—Jenny Cleary, Chicago, Illinois

Jack has returned my self-esteem and courage to pursue my dreams. Today, I am financially independent and own a company that helps people design their lives. I do seminars with thought leaders to audiences of 800 to 1,000 people. I am well respected in my community and PTA president at my son's school. All of this was possible because Jack gave me back what I had lost: MY POWER.
—Puja Gupta, Chennai, India

Because of the "Reject Rejection" principle, I became a pastry chef after being told it was impossible since I hadn't apprenticed at a young age—and because I have three small children and a husband with a demanding career. I kept knocking on doors until one opened up—and I'm proud to say that I now work at the best French patisserie in Calgary, Canada. Thank you!
—Mariko Tancon, Calgary, Alberta, Canada

The Success Principles

Jack Canfield

cocreator of
Chicken Soup for the Soul

with Janet Switzer

20th ANNIVERSARY EDITION

The Success Principles

How to Get from Where You Are to Where You Want to Be

Thorsons

Thorsons
An imprint of HarperCollins*Publishers*
1 London Bridge Street
London SE1 9GF

www.harpercollins.co.uk

HarperCollins*Publishers*
Macken House, 39/40 Mayor Street Upper
Dublin 1, D01 C9W8, Ireland

First published by Thorsons 2005
This revised edition published 2025

1 3 5 7 9 10 8 6 4 2

© Jack Canfield 2025

Jack Canfield asserts the moral right to be identified as the author of this work

Jack Canfield is a registered trademark of Self Esteem Seminars, LP. The Success Principles is the common law trademark of Self Esteem Seminars, LP. Chicken Soup for the Soul is a registered trademark of Chicken Soup for the Soul Publishing, LLC. All rights reserved.

Designed by Ellen Cipriano

A catalogue record of this book is available from the British Library

ISBN 978-0-00-875739-7
SELF-HELP

Printed and bound in India by Thomson Press India Ltd.

All rights reserved. No part of this publication may be reproduced, stored in a retrieval system, or transmitted, in any form or by any means, electronic, mechanical, photocopying, recording or otherwise, without the prior written permission of the publishers.

Without limiting the author's and publisher's exclusive rights, any unauthorised use of this publication to train generative artificial intelligence (AI) technologies is expressly prohibited. HarperCollins also exercise their rights under Article 4(3) of the Digital Single Market Directive 2019/790 and expressly reserve this publication from the text and data mining exception.

This book is produced from independently certified FSC® paper to ensure responsible forest management.

For more information visit: www.harpercollins.co.uk/green

This book is dedicated to the millions of readers, students, fans, and followers of The Success Principles *over the past two decades, and to the countless individuals who have helped me validate these methods during the 50 years of my teaching, speaking, and training career. I applaud you. I congratulate you. You humble me. You inspire me.*

This book is also dedicated to my wife Inga, who has stood by me while I wrote the first version of this book and twice revised it for days on end over the years.

Life is like a combination lock; your job is to find the right numbers, in the right order, so you can have anything you want.
BRIAN TRACY

If we did all the things we are capable of doing, we would literally astound ourselves.
THOMAS A. EDISON

CONTENTS

Foreword	xix
Introduction	xxix

I. The Fundamentals of Success

1.	Take 100% Responsibility for Your Life	3
2.	Be Clear Why You're Here	23
3.	Decide What You Want	30
4.	Believe It's Possible	42
5.	Believe in Yourself	48
6.	Use the Law of Attraction	59
7.	Unleash the Power of Goal-Setting	76
8.	Chunk It Down	90
9.	Success Leaves Clues	95
10.	Release the Brakes	97
11.	See What You Want, Get What You See	109
12.	Act As If	125
13.	Take Action	135
14.	Just Lean Into It	145
15.	Experience Your Fear and Take Action Anyway	152
16.	Be Willing to Pay the Price	165
17.	Ask! Ask! Ask!	176
18.	Reject Rejection	185
19.	Use Feedback to Your Advantage	194
20.	Commit to Constant and Never-Ending Improvement	205
21.	Keep Score for Success	209
22.	Practice Persistence	213

23. Practice the Rule of 5	221
24. Exceed Expectations	224

II. Transform Yourself for Success

25. Drop Out of the "Ain't It Awful" Club . . . and Surround Yourself with Successful People	231
26. Acknowledge Your Positive Past	237
27. Keep Your Eye on the Prize	247
28. Clean Up Your Messes and Your Incompletes	250
29. Complete the Past to Embrace the Future	256
30. Face What Isn't Working	267
31. Embrace Change	272
32. Transform Your Inner Critic into an Inner Coach	275
33. Transcend Your Limiting Beliefs	288
34. Develop Four New Success Habits a Year	292
35. 99% Is a Bitch; 100% Is a Breeze	296
36. Learn More to Earn More	299
37. Stay Motivated with the Masters	307
38. Fuel Your Success with Passion and Enthusiasm	311

III. Build Your Success Team

39. Stay Focused on Your Core Genius	319
40. Redefine Time	324
41. Build a Powerful Support Team and Delegate to Them	330
42. Just Say No!	335
43. Become a Leader Worth Following	341
44. Create a Network of Mentors and Others Who Will Up-Level You	353
45. Hire a Personal Coach	368
46. Mastermind Your Way to Success	374
47. Inquire Within	380

IV. Create Successful Relationships

48. Be Hear Now	395
49. Have a Heart Talk	400

50.	Tell the Truth Faster	405
51.	Speak with Impeccability	415
52.	When in Doubt, Check It Out	421
53.	Practice Uncommon Appreciation	426
54.	Keep Your Agreements	433
55.	Be a Class Act	439

V. Success and Money

56.	Develop a Positive Money Consciousness	447
57.	You Get What You Focus On	455
58.	Pay Yourself First	461
59.	Master the Spending Game	470
60.	To Spend More, First Make More	477
61.	Give More to Get More	489
62.	Find a Way to Serve	496

VI. Success in the Digital Age

63.	Master the Technology You Need	503
64.	Brand Yourself with an Online Persona	522
65.	Use Social Media in a Way That Enhances Your Reputation	536
66.	Use the Exponential Power of Crowdfunding	544
67.	Connect with People Who Can Expand Your Vision	553

Afterword: Empower Yourself by Empowering Others	557
The Success Principles *Free Success Tools*	567
Bring the Power of Change to Your Organization:	
The Success Principles *Keynote, Workshop, and Training*	569
Suggested Reading and Additional Resources for Success	571
About the Authors	573
Acknowledgments	577
Permissions	581
Index	585

FOREWORD

Twenty years ago, Janet Switzer and I envisioned a time when *The Success Principles* would be read in dozens of languages and followed in more than 100 countries—a time when individuals from every walk of life and groups of every kind would use it as a guidebook for dreaming bigger dreams, planning bigger outcomes, taking action in a bigger way, and enjoying the kind of expanded, abundant lifestyle that, for them, never seemed possible before.

We envisioned a time when educators, corporate managers, and small-group leaders would take up our challenge to advance the message of *The Success Principles* by training others in these human-potential basics—a time when we could look back, with pride, at the millions of lives that had been touched by the universal message and proven principles in this book.

I'm happy to say that time is now.

Over the past 20 years, not only has *The Success Principles* spread to 112 countries in 41 languages, but the feedback and success stories we've received in return have been gratifying—and humbling. Men, women, teens, students, athletes, entrepreneurs, stay-at-home parents, rising corporate stars, and other achievers have become dedicated to creating lives of abundance, joy, professional fulfillment, and personal accomplishment.

They are proof positive that these principles work—if you work the principles.

Through countless stories and heartwarming reports, I've watched this phenomenon unfold, as readers moved beyond today's culture of resignation and mediocrity to create the exciting, compelling life of their dreams.

They have overcome their own limitations—whether physical challenges, economic hardship, past failures, or simply their own limiting beliefs—to achieve astounding success.

At one time, perhaps just like you, they wondered how a single book could change their lives.

Doug Wittal, a builder from Kamloops, British Columbia, Canada, doubled his income within a year of applying what he learned, then doubled it again 12 months later. He began enjoying substantially more free time and built four magnificent homes so he and his family could spend summers and winters in temperate climates.

Days before talking to Doug, we heard from Miriam Laundry—a mom who dreamed of bringing self-esteem concepts to more than 100,000 children, changing lives and communities around the globe. Not only did she surpass her goal in less than a year, she attained a Guinness World Records® title for her accomplishment.

Sean Gallagher, a successful Irish entrepreneur, appeared for three seasons on the hit television show Dragon's Den (Shark Tank in the U.S.), and later fulfilled his most audacious goal when he stood for election to become the President of Ireland. He's now a highly sought after speaker and writer helping to inform and inspire the next generation of Irish business leaders.

Justin Bendel—an aspiring orchestral musician—used *The Success Principles* to visualize playing at a world-class concert hall whose picture he'd had for years. Though he didn't know the name of the concert hall in the photo, he pasted it to his vision board anyway. Soon after, he received a fully paid scholarship to pursue graduate studies in music and, within his first year of grad school, was chosen to play with the university orchestra at Carnegie Hall in New York—the concert hall in the photograph he had pasted on his vision board.

Using *Principle 24: Exceed Expectations,* 25-year-old Canadian franchisee Natalie Peace built one of her juice-bar locations to record revenues, then sold it for the highest amount ever received for that franchise. She's since earned her MBA and now (among other things) teaches business administration classes to fourth-year university students—recommending *The Success Principles* as a powerful textbook for future entrepreneurs.

After one of my readers—a successful Malaysian businessman—was incarcerated under extremely harsh conditions in China, his wife convinced the guards to pass along his tattered, dog-eared, and marked-up copy of *The Success Principles* so he could stay motivated during his 20-month ordeal. He not only reread it hundreds of times but also used it to transform himself into an even more motivated, excited, and fearless person who—since his release—has launched a successful information technology business, started two restaurants, and acquired a portfolio of international properties with a group of real-estate investors.

Pavel Popiolek—Czech Republic's leading importer of computer equipment with a $600 million business to manage—used what he learned in *The Success Principles* to balance his life and work, making time for his true passion—competitive cycling. So far, he's won the Val d'Aran UCI World Cycling Tour race in the Pyrenees, qualified for the World Master's Cycling Championship, and been profiled in *Men's Health* magazine.

Of course, beyond business success and professional accomplishment are those readers whose entire lives have changed because they implemented the principles in this book.

Heather O'Brien Walker, who sustained a devastating brain injury in a warehouse accident at work, first heard *The Success Principles* from her hospital bed as her fiancé read them aloud during Heather's 30 days of rehabilitation. Though she couldn't walk or talk—or even function normally—she began to visualize her wedding day and made *walking down the aisle* her breakthrough goal. The process of learning to walk again was grueling. But today, Heather has not only recovered but she also shares her message of overcoming adversity through speaking engagements and her book, *Don't Give Up, Get Up.*

Akshay Nanavati, an ex-Marine who was diagnosed with post-traumatic stress disorder upon his return from Iraq, is using the principles to beat the condition. He has since written a book endorsed by the Dalai Lama, run many ultramarathons, including running the length of eight countries, and now as a professional adventurer, he is currently training for a never-before-accomplished 110-day, 1,700-mile, solo, coast-to-coast ski crossing of Antarctica. Despite losing the tips of two fingers to frostbite on one of his training expeditions, he leveraged the success principles to continue on his mission undeterred—not only as a way to inspire others but also to give himself the inspiration to get up and take action every day.

And Lewis Pugh of Great Britain—who was the first person to complete a long-distance swim in every ocean of the world—has, over a period of 37 years, pioneered swims in the most hostile waters on Earth, including the Antarctic, the North Pole, and the Himalayas, and developed an understanding of the beauty and fragility of life and its many ecosystems. Millions have viewed his talks at TEDGlobal, and in 2015, after campaigning tirelessly, he helped establish the largest Marine Protected Area in the world. In 2013, the United Nations appointed the maritime lawyer as Patron of the Oceans. And yes, he's a *Success Principles* reader, too.

With stories like these—and thousands more that have poured in—when it came time to prepare the *20th Anniversary Edition* of *The Success Principles,* I quickly realized that I could produce an entire companion book filled with just the inspiring and fascinating stories we've received from readers over the last decade. Countless others have used what they learned to become bestselling authors, start businesses, purchase investment properties, get married, lose weight, achieve professional honors, get job promotions, travel the world, get out of debt, raise amazing kids, and so much more.

But while many of these readers knew exactly what they wanted to achieve when they picked up their copy of *The Success Principles*, many more didn't. For some readers, achievement seemed so far away that their only "want" was for life to simply get better.

Forrest Willett was one of those readers.

At 31 years old, Forrest's life was right on track. He owned three homes and seven businesses. He'd been married for seven years to a beautiful woman and had a two-year-old son. He was on top of the world. That is, until his world turned upside down. *Literally.* He was in an automobile accident that threw his car end-over-end three times, leaving him with a catastrophic brain injury.

Suddenly, Forrest found himself incapable of doing even the simplest tasks—with his beautiful wife now teaching him to brush his teeth and comb his hair. Although he knew he was lucky to be alive, he began to spiral faster and faster into a deep pit of depression, anger, and despair.

In the beginning, like a stroke survivor, he had difficulty conversing on even the most basic level. His humiliation rendered him housebound, and soon, fatigue and apathy dominated his existence. For hours, Forrest lay on the sofa, sleeping or watching television. The doctors, his speech therapist, his occupational therapist, his physical therapist—essentially all of the experts—told him that returning to a productive life with the promise of success wasn't possible. So Forrest gave up all hope of ever having a normal existence—let alone a life that fulfilled his dreams.

Then one day, as he lay in bed, numbly surfing the TV channels, the words, "If you want to get from where you are, to where you want to be . . ." caught his attention. Forrest sat up enough to focus on what the news anchor was saying. "Jack Canfield was coming up next" to discuss his book *The Success Principles.* With the smallest spark of hope ignited, Forrest bought the book they were talking about—the first edition of *The Success Principles,* which was over 400 pages. At the time, Forrest was just learning to read his son's books—a 35-year-old man reading books for a kindergartener. His speech therapist thought a 400-page book was being overly ambitious. But Forrest was more than ready to get from where he was to where he wanted to be.

And so, he began his journey.

In the beginning, reading even a single page was slow and laborious. Though he was motivated, Forrest began to wonder if his therapist had been right. Maybe he *was* being overly ambitious.

Then, several months after starting to work his way through *The Suc-*

cess Principles—and a full five years after the accident—he got his biggest wake-up call. At his son Hunter's seventh birthday party, Forrest was out in the yard with the boy and a group of his friends as Hunter opened his presents. Picking a round-shaped package from the pile, Hunter ripped the wrapping paper off to reveal a baseball. Smiling with delight, he immediately threw it at the ground. Naturally, the ball landed with a thud and rolled a couple of feet into the dirt. Hunter picked it up and hurled it at the ground again, where it once more rolled away from him. Before he could try again, the friend who had given him the baseball, shouted, "Hunter, baseballs don't bounce!"

In that moment, Forrest was thunderstruck as the impact of his absence hit him like a ton of bricks. *How could his son know about such things? They had never thrown a baseball together.*

Forrest realized he had spent more time with his negative thoughts than with his own son—essentially abandoning him, as well as his wife. He knew that if he didn't take charge of his life, it would end up in pieces. He'd find himself divorced, homeless, or worse.

The spark inside him turned into a blaze. He went back to the first of the Success Principles, *Take 100% Responsibility for Your Life,* and tackled it in earnest.

In his case, taking 100% responsibility for his life meant he had to stop the negative self-talk: no more "Poor Forrest " and "Why did this happen to me?" Without that constant negative soundtrack to distract him, Forrest could see that he hadn't been an active participant in his own rehabilitation. He had been letting his physical therapist stretch him—then wondered why he wasn't getting stronger. He'd sat there passively listening while his speech therapist read to him—then complained that his reading skills weren't getting any better.

Now Forrest started to believe that his life could be different, that he could *make it* different. And that's when things really started to change.

Almost immediately, his self-awareness began to grow. Things that had gone over his head for so long finally registered. Where were all his friends? The answer was as painful as it was clear: He'd abandoned them, in the same way he'd abandoned his family. Everyone had stopped calling long ago, pushed away by Forrest's negativity—and he'd been too self-absorbed to care. Just noticing these things was a success in itself, Forrest reminded himself. He was making progress.

Next, he decided to give up blaming and complaining—not an easy task. It had become so habitual that Forrest didn't even realize he was doing it. So he asked the people around him to help him become aware when he slipped back into his old ways. In fact, his wife and therapists had a sign: If

Forrest began to blame or complain, they let him know by pulling on their ear. When he saw that, he'd stop whatever he was saying in midsentence, take a deep breath, and consider his next words more carefully.

Not that speaking—positively *or* negatively—was easy for him. Forrest still hadn't fully regained his speech faculties, and sometimes he was unable to find the words he needed, or he stuttered. Because of this, he didn't want to go to the grocery store or post office in case he ran into someone he knew. To counter this, he focused on Principle 22: "Practice Persistence." Each day he read *The Success Principles* for twenty minutes and practiced stepping out of his comfort zone. Day after day, he practiced a little more and went a little further.

One of his steps out of his comfort zone took him to a local coffee shop. For years, Forrest had put his head down and walked past the coffee shop, keeping his eyes glued to the cement. But this day he walked in—reminding himself of Principle 15: "Experience Your Fear and Take Action Anyway." Unfortunately, he was met right away by his worst fear. An old acquaintance recognized him and called out.

Although he was cringing with embarrassment inside, Forrest stayed calm and walked over and sat down. He explained as best he could what had been happening. He was amazed to find it actually felt good to stand up for himself. In the coming days, Forrest tried this with others, and with time talking got easier. He discovered there were people around him who were willing to support him—especially now that Forrest was willing to support himself.

He also saw that he wasn't alone in dealing with life's fears and challenges. Everyone he talked to seemed to have struggles and pain of their own. This insight helped him to overcome the shame he'd been carrying for so long.

As time passed, he could hardly believe the new successes he was having. Within a year of applying the principles, Forrest was doing all of the things his doctors had said he'd never do again. He returned to school. He got off all medications, both for pain and depression. He started volunteering. He started turning every negative into a positive.

And he's been doing that ever since.

Today, it's hard to believe there was a time, not that long ago, that Forrest couldn't speak fluently—nor read or write very well. But he turned that around so completely that he wrote a book about his experiences! And while he never would have believed it possible during the dark days, today he loves public speaking and believes he's found the work he was meant to do. He's thrilled to travel and speak to groups around the world.

Reading *The Success Principles* also shifted Forrest's thinking about success in general. Before the accident, "success" to him meant more money and more things—a bigger house, a bigger boat, opening more businesses, owning more stuff. After the accident, he'd given up on ever attaining *any* success, however you define it.

Today, thanks to *The Success Principles,* he's learned the profound truth that having all the stuff in the world doesn't mean anything if you're not truly living—which Forrest now knows means giving and receiving love. If currency were counted in friends and love, Forrest would be the richest man in the world.

While Forrest Willett used *The Success Principles* to define and achieve success for himself, how *you* define success is solely in *your* power. For you, "success" might be a substantial income, effortless financial reward, and the luxuries of a high-net-worth lifestyle. It may be professional recognition or achievement in your hobby or philanthropic endeavors. It may be healthy, happy, and engaged children—or a family life that provides day-after-day enjoyment and bliss. Or it may be entrance onto the world stage for a project or subject matter you are passionate about. Whatever *your* definition of success, rest assured that you hold in your hands the road map to achieving it.

EVEN WHEN YOU'RE SKEPTICAL, THE PRINCIPLES ALWAYS WORK

One of my favorite stories over the last 20 years is from a reader in the Philippines who, at first, was skeptical but who committed to applying the principles anyway—for just one year.

On the last stop of a six-city Asian tour conducting *Success Principles* workshops, a young man named John Calub approached me at a book signing in Manila's largest shopping mall. He was writing a newspaper column about successful people for the biggest newspaper in the Philippines, and asked me for an interview. At the end of a very engaging hour, I told him that he was a great interviewer and asked how long he had been doing it. With a sense of pride, he replied that I was his very first interviewee.

He went on to say that, up until recently, he and two partners had owned and operated three successful restaurants, but that bickering between the partners had eventually led to the failure of the business. John was now homeless, broke, and sleeping on couches in his friends' apartments. He had taken public transportation to the book signing because he no longer owned a car. And all the money he had in the world was the $3.00 cash left in his pocket.

When I heard this, and because I liked John, I bought him a copy of

The Success Principles from the bookstore and offered him a free seat in the next day's workshop. Giving him $20 to buy some food, I extracted a promise that, if he liked it, he would write a feature article about the workshop.

Two and a half years later, I returned to Manila to conduct another workshop. As I was getting ready to begin, I noticed a well-dressed man in a blue blazer and gold Doc Marten shoes followed by an entourage of ten people all wearing the same polo shirt with a bright logo on it. I was curious, so I walked over to the group, and—to my surprise and delight—the man in the blue blazer was John Calub!

He told me that he had become one of the most successful businessmen in Manila. When John related the story of how he'd accomplished his success, I was so moved that I asked John to share it—in his own words.

> Sitting in the seminar, with my arms crossed tightly across my chest, I listened carefully as Jack Canfield described his principles for success. At first I was very skeptical. He had crazy ideas—like cutting out pictures, pasting them on a board and looking at it every day, then *feeling* as though you already had what you wanted. My rational mind said, *What a joke. Like looking at some pictures is going to help me get what I want.*
>
> At one point, Jack even talked about Dr. Masaru Emoto's famous experiment with water crystals and showed pictures of how water can be affected by thoughts, words, and feelings. Though I was intrigued, I still wasn't convinced.
>
> With my mind full of doubts and questions, I returned home from the seminar and thought more about what Jack had shared. It soon dawned on me: Jack was a very, very successful guy who had used these principles—and here I was totally broke. *Who would you listen to?* I asked myself. Besides, I had lost everything—I had nothing else to lose.
>
> I decided to read the book he had given me and diligently follow the principles for one year.
>
> Every week I worked with a different principle. I began using visualization and even created one of those "crazy" dream boards I'd been so skeptical about.
>
> The first image I cut out was a picture of a BMW—my dream car. At the time, I was so far away from affording any car, let alone a BMW. To get around, I walked or rode in a Jeepney, a very crowded mode of public transportation in the Philippines. Soon, however, I used the principle to turn my doubt into trust. It worked! And within a year, I bought my first BMW.
>
> Another principle I discovered was Principle 2: "Be Clear Why You're Here." When I was younger, I bounced from job to job—just to make a

living and pay my bills. Then, during the seminar, Jack led us through an exercise to identify our deepest passion. I not only realized I have a love for teaching, but I began to identify it as my true gift and purpose. To begin taking action on this purpose, I created a breakthrough goal at the seminar to become the Philippines' leading success coach.

I launched a series of seminars—teaching the principles I had learned from Jack. I started coaching and began consulting for different companies. My income quickly rose, and soon I was earning over a million pesos—which in the Philippines is a lot of money! Next, I combined my interest in travel with my passion for teaching and began conducting seminars around the world.

Today, my training company is the biggest profit center of all the companies I own. Before, I hadn't been doing what I loved—so my success was hit-or-miss. Now I'm so enthusiastic about teaching these principles that people flock to see me—I've even earned seven-figures in one day!

Jack has helped me see that you really can have it all. My first vision board was created in 2006, and since then I've achieved more than 70% of what I set out to do. Because of *The Success Principles,* I'm the highest paid motivational speaker in the country and am well on my way to becoming the Philippines' number one success coach. If I can go from broke to becoming a star in my field just by living these principles, anyone can.

I've also seen the results in the lives of my clients as thousands of my countrymen have achieved *their* dreams. Many were living a hand-to-mouth existence but are now on their way to becoming multi-millionaires. We are all living proof that the principles always work, if you always work the principles.

John Calub experienced the power of *The Success Principles*—and you, too, will see changes in your life when you apply these classic principles along with the new insights contained in this *20th Anniversary Edition.*

I salute you. I congratulate you. I welcome you on this journey.

To your success,
Jack Canfield

INTRODUCTION

If a man for whatever reason has the opportunity to lead an extraordinary life, he has no right to keep it to himself.
JACQUES-YVES COUSTEAU
Legendary underwater explorer and filmmaker

If a man writes a book, let him set down only what he knows. I have guesses enough of my own.
JOHANN WOLFGANG VON GOETHE
German poet, novelist, playwright, and philosopher

This is not a book of good ideas. This is a book of timeless principles used by successful men and women throughout history. I have studied these success principles for over 50 years and have applied them to my own life. The phenomenal level of success that I now enjoy is the result of applying these principles day in and day out since I began to learn them in 1968.

My success includes being the author and editor of more than 200 books—including 60 *New York Times* bestsellers with over 500 million copies in print in 50 languages around the world; holding a Guinness World Record title for having seven books on the May 24, 1998, *New York Times* bestsellers list; earning a multimillion-dollar net income every year for the past 30 years; living in a beautiful California estate; appearing on every major talk show in America (from *Oprah* and *Montel* to *Larry King Live* and *Good Morning America*); having a weekly newspaper column read by millions every week; commanding speaking fees of $25,000 to $60,000 a talk; speaking to Fortune 500 companies all over the world; being the recipient of numerous professional and civic awards; having outrageous relationships with my amazing wife and wonderful children; and having achieved a steady state of wellness, balance, happiness, and inner peace.

I get to socialize with CEOs of Fortune 500 companies; movie, television, and recording stars; celebrated authors; and the world's finest spiritual teachers and leaders. I have given speeches to members of Congress, professional athletes, corporate managers, and sales superstars in many of the best resorts and retreat centers in the world—from the Four Seasons Resort in the British West Indies to the finest hotels in Acapulco and Cancun. I enjoy skiing in Idaho, California, and Utah; go river rafting in Colorado; and hike in the mountains of California and Washington. Plus I get to vacation in the world's finest resorts in Hawaii, Australia, Thailand, Morocco, France, Bali, and Italy. All in all, life is a real kick!

Yet like most of you reading this book, my life started out in a very average way. I grew up in Wheeling, West Virginia, where my dad worked in a florist's shop, making $8,000 a year. My mother was an alcoholic and my father was a workaholic. I worked during the summers to make ends meet (as a lifeguard at a pool and at the same florist's shop as my father). I went to college on a scholarship and worked serving breakfast in one of the dorms to pay for books, clothes, and dates. Nobody handed me anything on a silver platter. During my last year of graduate school, I had a part-time teaching job that paid me $120 every two weeks. My rent was $79 a month, so that left $161 to cover all my other expenses. Toward the end of the month, I ate what became known as my 21¢ dinners—a 10¢ can of tomato paste, garlic salt, and water over an 11¢ bag of spaghetti noodles. I know what it is like to be scraping by on the bottom rungs of the economic ladder.

After graduate school, I started my career as a high school history teacher in an all-black school on the South Side of Chicago. And then I met my mentor, W. Clement Stone. Stone was a self-made multimillionaire who hired me to work at his foundation, where he trained me in the fundamental success principles that I still operate from today. My job was to teach these same principles to others. Over the years, I have gone on from my time with Mr. Stone to interview hundreds of successful people—Olympic and professional athletes, celebrated entertainers, bestselling authors, business leaders, political leaders, successful entrepreneurs, and top salespeople. I have read literally thousands of books, attended hundreds of seminars, and listened to thousands of hours of audio programs to uncover the universal principles for creating success and happiness. I then applied those principles to my own life. The ones that worked are the principles I have taught in my speeches, seminars, and workshops to well over 2 million people in all 50 U.S. states . . . and in more than 50 countries around the world.

These principles and techniques have not only worked for me but they have also helped hundreds of thousands of my students achieve breakthrough success in their careers, greater wealth in their finances, greater aliveness and joy in their relationships, and greater happiness and fulfillment in their lives. My students have started successful businesses, become self-made millionaires, achieved athletic stardom, received lucrative recording contracts, starred in movie and television roles, won political offices, had huge impact in their communities, written bestselling books, been named teacher of the year in their school districts, broken all sales records in their companies, written award-winning screenplays, become presidents of their corporations, been recognized for their outstanding philanthropic contributions, created highly successful relationships, and raised unusually happy and successful children.

THE PRINCIPLES ALWAYS WORK IF YOU ALWAYS WORK THE PRINCIPLES

All of these same results are possible for you. I know for a fact that you, too, can attain unimagined levels of success. Why? Because the principles and techniques always work—all you have to do is put them to work for you.

A few years before I wrote this book, I was interviewed on a television show in Dallas, Texas. I had made the claim that if people would use the principles I was teaching, they could double their income and double their time off in less than two years. The woman interviewing me was highly skeptical. I gave her a copy of one of my audio programs and told her that if she used the principles and techniques for two years and she didn't double her income and double her time off, I would come back on her show and write her a check for $1,000. If they did work, she had to ask me back and tell her viewers the principles had worked. A short nine months later, I ran into her at the National Speakers Association convention in Orlando, Florida. She told me that not only had she *already* doubled her income but she had also moved to a bigger station with a substantial pay increase, had started a public speaking career, and had already finished and sold a book—all in just nine months!

The fact is that anyone can consistently produce these kinds of results on a regular basis. All you have to do is decide what you want, believe you deserve it, and practice the success principles in this book.

The fundamentals are the same for all people and all professions—even if you're currently unemployed. It doesn't matter if your goals are to be the top salesperson in your company, get straight As in school, lose weight, buy your dream home—or become a world-class professional athlete, rock star, award-winning journalist, multimillionaire, or successful entrepreneur.

The principles and strategies are the same. And if you learn them, assimilate them, and apply them with discipline every day, they will transform your life beyond your wildest dreams.

"YOU CAN'T HIRE SOMEONE ELSE TO DO YOUR PUSH-UPS FOR YOU"

As motivational philosopher Jim Rohn so aptly put it, "You can't hire someone else to do your push-ups for you." You must do them yourself if you are to get any value out of them. Whether it is exercising, meditating, reading, studying, learning a new language, creating a mastermind group, setting measurable goals, visualizing success, repeating affirmations, or practicing a new skill, *you* are going to have to do it. No one else can do these things for you. I will give you the road map, but you will have to drive the car. I will teach you the principles, but you will have to apply them. If you choose to put in the effort, I promise you the rewards will be well worth it.

HOW THIS BOOK IS STRUCTURED

To help you quickly learn these powerful principles, I have organized this book into six sections. Part I, "The Fundamentals of Success," consists of 25 chapters that contain the absolute basics you must do to get from where you are to where you want to be. You'll start by exploring the critical importance of taking 100% responsibility for your life and your results. From there, you'll learn how to clarify your life purpose, your vision for your ideal life, and what you truly want to achieve.

Next we'll look at how to create an unshakable belief in yourself and your dreams. Then I'll help you turn your vision into a set of concrete goals and an action plan for achieving them. I'll also teach you how to harness the incredible power of affirmations and visualization—two of the greatest success secrets of all Olympic athletes, top entrepreneurs, world leaders, and high achievers. The next few chapters have to do with taking those necessary but sometimes scary action steps that are required to make your dreams come true.

Part II, "Transform Yourself for Success," addresses the important inner work you'll need to do—work that will help you remove any mental and emotional blocks you may have to success. It's not enough to *know* what to do. You also need to understand the methodology for removing self-defeating beliefs, fears, and habits that are holding you back. Like driving your car with the emergency brake on, these blocks can significantly slow your progress. You must learn how to release the brakes, or you will always experience life as a struggle and fall short of your intended goals.

Part III, "Build Your Success Team," reveals how to build different kinds of support teams so you can spend your time focusing exclusively on your core genius. You'll also learn how to redefine time, utilize the benefits of a personal coach, and access your *own* inner wisdom—an untapped but ultrarich resource.

In Part IV, "Create Successful Relationships," I'll teach you a number of principles, as well as some very practical techniques, for building and maintaining successful relationships. In this day of strategic alliances and power networks, it's literally impossible to build large-scale, long-lasting success without world-class relationship skills, including in social media.

Next, because so many people equate success with money, and because money is vital to our survival and the quality of our life, Part V is entitled "Success and Money." I'll teach you how to develop a more positive money consciousness, how to ensure that you have plenty of money to live the lifestyle you want, both now and after you retire, and the importance of tithing and service in guaranteeing your financial success.

Finally, in Part VI, because technology is so important today, I've honed down the most important principles that successful people follow in "Success in the Digital Age"—a look at how to master only the technology you need, how to "brand" yourself and develop a unique voice online, how to use social media to connect and develop valuable relationships, and how to use crowdfunding, crowdsourcing, and other Internet-based strategies to find the people and resources that can help you reach your most important goals.

HOW TO READ THIS BOOK

Everyone learns differently, and you probably know how you learn best. And though there are many ways that you can read this book, I'd like to make a few suggestions that previous readers have found helpful.

You may want to read this book through once just to get a feel for the total process before you start the work of creating the life you truly want. The principles are presented in an order that builds one upon the other. They are like the numbers in a combination lock—you need all the numbers, and you need them in the right order. It doesn't matter what color, race, gender, or age you are. If you know the combination, the lock has to open for you.

As you are reading, I strongly encourage you to underline and highlight everything that feels important to you. Make notes in the margin about the things you'll put into action. Then review those notes and highlighted sections again and again. Repetition is the key to real learning. Every time you reread portions of this book, you'll literally "re-mind" yourself of what you need to do to get from where you are to where you want to be. As you'll discover, it takes repetitive exposure over time to a new idea before that idea becomes a natural part of your way of thinking and being.

You may also discover that you're already familiar with some of the principles here. That's great! But ask yourself, *Am I currently practicing them?* If not, make a commitment to put them into action—now!

Remember, the principles only work if *you* work the principles.

The second time you read through this book, you'll want to read one chapter at a time, then take whatever time necessary to put into practice that principle and the techniques that accompany it. If you're already doing some of these things, keep doing them. If not, start now.

Like many of my past students and clients, you, too, may find yourself resisting taking some of the suggested action steps. But my experience has shown that the ones you most resist are the ones you most need to embrace. Remember, reading this book is not the same as doing the work, any more than reading a book on weight loss is the same as actually eliminating certain foods, eating fewer calories, and exercising more.

You might find it useful to connect with one or two other people who would like to join you as accountability partners (see page 375) and ensure that each of you actually implements what you learn. True learning only occurs when you assimilate and apply the new information—when there is a *change in your behavior.*

A WARNING

Of course, any change requires sustained effort to overcome years' worth of internal and external resistance. Initially you may find yourself getting very excited about all this new information. You may feel a newfound sense of hope and enthusiasm for the new vision of your life as it can be. This is good. But be forewarned that you may also begin to experience other feelings, as well. You may feel frustration at not knowing about all of this earlier, anger at your parents and teachers for not teaching you these important concepts at home and at school, or anger at yourself for having already learned many of these things and not having acted on them.

Just take a deep breath and realize that this is all part of the process of your journey. Everything in the past has actually been perfect. Everything in your past has led you to this transformative moment in time. Everyone—including you—has always done the best they could with what they knew at the time. Now you are about to know more. Celebrate your new awareness! It is about to set you free.

You may also find that there will be times when you wonder, *Why isn't all of this working faster? Why haven't I already achieved my goal? Why aren't I rich already? Why don't I have the man or woman of my dreams by now? When am I going to achieve my ideal weight?* Success takes time, effort, perseverance, and patience. If you apply all of the principles and techniques covered in this book, you *will* achieve your goals. You will realize your dreams. But it won't happen overnight.

Finally, it's natural in the pursuit of any goal to come upon obstacles, to feel temporarily stuck on a plateau. This is normal. Anyone who has ever played a musical instrument, participated in a sport, or practiced a martial art knows that you hit plateaus where it seems as though you're making no progress whatsoever. That's when the uninitiated often quit, give up, drop out, or take up another instrument or sport. But the wise have discovered if they just keep practicing their instrument, sport, or martial art (or, in your case, the success principles in this book), eventually they make what feels like a sudden leap to a higher level of proficiency. Be patient. Hang in there. Don't give up. You *will* break through. I promise you—the principles *always* work.

Okay, let's get started.

It's time to start living the life you've imagined.
HENRY JAMES
American-born author of 20 novels, 112 stories, and 12 plays

PART ONE

The Fundamentals of Success

*Learn the fundamentals
of the game and stick to them.
Band-Aid remedies never last.*

JACK NICKLAUS
Legendary professional golfer

PRINCIPLE 1

TAKE 100% RESPONSIBILITY FOR YOUR LIFE

You must take personal responsibility. You cannot change the circumstances, the seasons, or the wind, but you can change yourself.

JIM ROHN
America's foremost business philosopher

One of the most pervasive myths in the American culture today is that we are *entitled* to a great life—that somehow, somewhere, someone (certainly not us) is responsible for filling our lives with continual happiness, exciting career options, nurturing family time, and blissful personal relationships simply because we exist.

But the real truth—and the one lesson this whole book is based on—is that there is only one person responsible for the quality of the life you live.

That person is *you*.

If you want to be successful, you have to take 100% responsibility for everything that you experience in your life. This includes the level of your achievements, the results you produce, the quality of your relationships, the state of your health and physical fitness, your income, your debts, your feelings—everything!

This is not easy.

In fact, most of us have been conditioned to blame something outside of ourselves for the parts of our life we don't like. We blame our parents, our bosses, our friends, our coworkers, our spouse, the weather, the economy, the government, our astrological chart, our lack of money—anyone or anything we can pin the blame on. We never want to look at where the real problem is—*ourselves*.

There is a wonderful story told about a man who is out walking one night and comes upon another man down on his knees looking for something under a street lamp. The passerby inquires as to what the other man is looking for. He answers that he is looking for his lost key. The passerby offers to help and gets down on his knees and helps him search for the key. After an hour of fruitless searching, he says, "We've looked everywhere for it and we haven't found it. Are you sure that you lost it here?"

The other man replies, "No, I lost it in my house, but there is more light out here under the streetlamp."

It is time to stop looking outside yourself for the answers to why you haven't created the life and results you want, for it is you who creates the quality of the life you lead and the results you produce.

You—no one else!

To achieve major success in life—to achieve those things that are most important to you—you must assume 100% responsibility for your life. Nothing less will do.

100% RESPONSIBILITY FOR EVERYTHING

As I mentioned in the Introduction, when I was only one year out of graduate school, I had the good fortune to work for W. Clement Stone. He was a self-made multimillionaire worth $600 million at the time. Stone was also America's premier success guru. He was the publisher of *Success Magazine,* author of *The Success System That Never Fails,* and coauthor with Napoleon Hill of *Success Through a Positive Mental Attitude.*

When I was completing my first week's orientation, Mr. Stone asked me if I took 100% responsibility for my life.

"I think so," I responded.

"This is a yes or no question, young man. You either do or you don't."

"Well, I guess I'm not sure."

"Have you ever blamed anyone for any circumstance in your life? Have you ever complained about anything?"

"Uh . . . yeah . . . I guess I have."

"Don't guess. Think."

"Yes, I have."

"Okay, then. That means you don't take one hundred percent responsibility for your life. Taking 100% responsibility means you acknowledge that you create everything that happens to you. It means you understand that *you* are the cause of all of your experiences. If you want to be really successful, and I know you do, then you will have to give up blaming and complaining and take total responsibility for your life—that means all your results, both your successes *and* your failures. That is the prerequisite for creating a life of success. It is only by acknowledging that you have created everything up until now that you can take charge of creating the future you want.

"You see, Jack, if you realize that you have created your current conditions, then you can uncreate them and re-create them at will. Do you understand that?"

"Yes, sir, I do."

"Are you willing to take one hundred percent responsibility for your life?"

"Yes, sir, I am!"

And I did.

YOU HAVE TO GIVE UP ALL YOUR EXCUSES

Ninety-nine percent of all failures come from people who have a habit of making excuses.

GEORGE WASHINGTON CARVER
Chemist who discovered over 325 uses for the peanut

If *you* want to create the life of your dreams, then *you* are going to have to take 100% responsibility for your life as well. That means giving up all your excuses, all your victim stories, all the reasons why you can't and why you haven't up until now, and all your blaming of outside circumstances. You have to give them all up forever.

You have to take the position that you have always had the power to make it different, to get it right, to produce the desired result. For whatever reason—ignorance, lack of awareness, fear, needing to be right, the need to feel safe—you chose not to exercise that power. Who knows why? It doesn't matter. The past is the past. All that matters now is that from this point forward you choose—that's right, it's a choice—to act as if you are 100% responsible for everything that does or doesn't happen to you.

If something doesn't turn out as planned, you will ask yourself, *How did I create that? What was I thinking? What were my beliefs? What did I say or not say? What did I do or not do to create that result? How did I get the other person to act that way? What do I need to do differently next time to get the result I want?*

A few years after I met Mr. Stone, Dr. Robert Resnick, a psychotherapist in Los Angeles, taught me a very simple but very important formula that made this idea of 100% responsibility even clearer to me. The formula is:

$$E + R = O$$
(Event + Response = Outcome)

The basic idea is that every outcome you experience in life (whether it is success or failure, wealth or poverty, health or illness, intimacy or estrangement, joy or frustration) is the result of how you have responded to an earlier event or events in your life.

If you don't like the outcomes you are currently getting, there are two basic choices you can make.

1. **You can blame the event (E) for your lack of results (O).** In other words, you can blame the economy, the weather, the lack of money, your lack of education, racism, gender bias, the current administration in Washington, your parents, your wife or husband, your boss's attitude, your employees, the system or lack of systems, and so on. If you're a golfer, you've probably even blamed your clubs and the course you played on. No doubt all these factors do exist, but if they were *the* deciding factor, nobody would ever succeed.

    Jackie Robinson would never have played major league baseball, Barack Obama would never have become president of the United States, Sidney Poitier and Denzel Washington would never have become movie stars, Dianne Feinstein and Barbara Boxer would never have become U.S. senators, Bill Gates would never have founded Microsoft, and Steve Jobs would never have started Apple Computers. For every reason why it's not possible, there are hundreds of people who have faced the same circumstances and succeeded.

    Lots of people overcome these so-called limiting factors, so it can't be the limiting factors that limit you. It is not the external conditions and circumstances that stop you—it is you! We stop ourselves! We think limiting thoughts and engage in self-defeating behaviors. We defend our self-destructive habits (such as drinking, smoking, and not getting enough sleep) with indefensible logic. We ignore useful feedback, fail to continuously educate ourselves and learn new skills, waste time on the trivial aspects of our lives, engage in idle gossip, eat unhealthy food, fail to exercise, spend more money than we make, fail to invest in our future, avoid necessary conflict, fail to tell the uncomfortable truth, don't ask for what we want—and then wonder why our lives don't work.

2. **You can instead simply change your responses (R) to the events (E)—the way things are—until you get the outcomes (O) you want.** You can change your thinking, change your communication, change the pictures you hold in your head (your images of yourself and the world), and change your behavior—the things you do. That is all you really have any control over anyway. Unfortunately, most of us are so run by our habits that we never change our behavior. We get stuck in our conditioned responses—to our spouses and our children, to our colleagues at work, to our customers and our clients, to our students, and to the world at large. We are a bundle of conditioned reflexes that operate outside of our control. You have to regain control of your thoughts, your images, your dreams and daydreams, and your behavior. Everything you think, say, and do needs to become intentional and aligned with your purpose, your values, and your goals.

IF YOU DON'T LIKE YOUR OUTCOMES, CHANGE YOUR RESPONSES

Let's look at some examples of how this works.

I remember living in Los Angeles during a terrible earthquake. Two days later, I watched as a CNN reporter interviewed people commuting to work. The earthquake had damaged one of the main freeways leading into the city. Traffic was at a standstill, and what was normally a one-hour drive had become a two- to three-hour drive.

The CNN reporter knocked on the window of one of the cars stuck in traffic and asked the driver how he was doing.

He responded angrily, "I hate California. First there were fires, then floods, and now an earthquake! No matter what time I leave in the morning, I'm going to be late for work. This sucks!"

Then the reporter knocked on the window of the car behind him and asked the second driver the same question. This driver was all smiles. He

"What do we make where I work? Mostly we make excuses."

replied, "It's no problem. I left my house at five A.M. I don't think under the circumstances my boss can ask for more than that. I have lots of music and my Spanish-language lessons with me. I've got my cell phone. I have coffee in a thermos, my lunch—I even brought a book to read. So I'm fine."

Now, if the earthquake or the traffic (the *event*) were really the deciding variables, then everyone should have been angry. But everyone wasn't. It was their individual *response* to the traffic that gave them their particular *outcome*. It was thinking negative thoughts or thinking positive thoughts, leaving the house prepared or leaving the house unprepared that made the difference. It was all a matter of attitude and behavior that created their completely different experiences.

I'VE HEARD THERE'S GOING TO BE A RECESSION; I'VE DECIDED NOT TO PARTICIPATE

A friend of mine owns a Lexus dealership in Southern California. When war in the Middle East broke out, people stopped coming in to buy Lexuses. My friend and his sales team knew that if they didn't change their response (R) to the event (E) of nobody coming into the showroom, they were going to slowly go out of business. Their normal response (R) would have been to continue placing ads in the newspaper and on the radio, then wait for people to come into the dealership. But that wasn't working. The outcome (O) they were getting was a steady decrease in sales. So they tried a number of new things. The one that worked was driving a fleet of new cars out to where the rich people were—the country clubs, marinas, polo grounds, parties in Beverly Hills, Westlake Village, and Lake Sherwood—and then inviting them to take a spin in a new Lexus.

Now think about this . . . have you ever test-driven a new car and then got back into your old car? Remember that feeling of dissatisfaction you felt as you compared your old car to the new car you had just driven? Your old car was fine up until then. But suddenly you knew there was something better—and you wanted it. The same thing happened with these folks. After test-driving the new car, a high percentage of the people bought or leased a new Lexus.

The dealership had changed their response (R) to an unexpected event (E)—the war—until they got the outcome (O)—increased sales—that they wanted. They actually ended up selling more cars per week than before the war broke out.

EVERYTHING YOU EXPERIENCE TODAY IS THE RESULT OF CHOICES YOU HAVE MADE IN THE PAST

Everything you experience in life—both internally and externally—is the result of how you have responded to a previous event.

Event: You are given a $400 bonus.
Response: You spend it on a night on the town with friends.
Outcome: You are broke.

Event: You are given a $400 bonus.
Response: You invest it in your mutual fund.
Outcome: You have an increased net worth.

You have control over only three things in your life—the thoughts you think, the images you visualize, and the actions you take (your behavior). How you use these three things determines everything you experience.

If you don't like what you are producing and experiencing, you have to change your responses. Change your negative thoughts to positive ones. Change what you daydream about. Change your habits. Change what you read. Change your friends. Change how you talk to yourself and others.

IF YOU KEEP ON DOING WHAT YOU'VE ALWAYS DONE, YOU'LL KEEP ON GETTING WHAT YOU'VE ALWAYS GOT

Twelve-step programs such as Alcoholics Anonymous define *insanity* as "continuing the same behavior and expecting a different result." It ain't gonna happen! If you are an alcoholic and you keep on drinking, your life is not going to get any better. Likewise, if you only continue your current behaviors, your life is not going to get any better, either.

The day you change your responses is the day your life will begin to get better! If what you are currently doing would produce the "more" and "better" that you are seeking in life, the more and better would have already shown up! If you want something different, you are going to have to *do* something different!

YOU HAVE TO GIVE UP BLAMING

All blame is a waste of time. No matter how much fault you find with another, and regardless of how much you blame him, it will not change you.

WAYNE DYER
Coauthor of *How to Get What You Really, Really, Really, Really Want*

You will never become successful as long as you continue to blame someone or something else for your lack of success. If you are going to be a winner, you have to acknowledge the truth—it is *you* who took the actions, thought the thoughts, created the feelings, and made the choices that got you to where you now are. It was you!

You are the one who ate the junk food.
You are the one who didn't say no!
You are the one who took the job.

You are the one who stayed in the job.
You are the one who chose to believe them.
You are the one who ignored your intuition.
You are the one who abandoned your dream.
You are the one who bought it.
You are the one who didn't take care of it.
You are the one who decided you had to do it alone.
You are the one who trusted him.
You are the one who said yes to the dogs.

In short, you thought the thoughts, you created the feelings, you made the choice, you said the words, and that's why you are where you are now.

YOU HAVE TO GIVE UP COMPLAINING

The man who complains about the way the ball bounces is likely the one who dropped it.

LOU HOLTZ
The only coach in NCAA history to lead six different college teams to postseason bowl games, and winner of a national championship and "coach of the year" honors

Let's take a moment to really look at complaining. In order to complain about something or someone, you have to believe that something better exists. You have to have a reference point of something you prefer that you are not willing to take responsibility for creating. Let's look at that more closely.

If you didn't believe there was something better possible—more money, a bigger house, a more fulfilling job, more fun, a more loving partner—you couldn't complain. So you have this image of something better and you know you would prefer it, but you are unwilling to take the risks *required to create it*. Complaining is an ineffective response to an event that does not produce a better outcome.

Think about this . . . people only complain about things they can do something about. We don't complain about the things we have no power over. Have you ever heard anyone complain about gravity? No, never. Have you ever seen an elderly person all bent over with age walking slowly down the street with the aid of a walker complaining about gravity? Of course not.

But why not? If it weren't for gravity, people wouldn't fall down the stairs, planes wouldn't fall out of the sky, and we wouldn't break any dishes. But nobody complains about it. And the reason is because gravity just exists. There is nothing anyone can do about gravity, so we just accept it. We know that complaining will not change it, so we don't complain about it. In fact, because it just is, we use gravity to our advantage. We build aqueducts down mountainsides to carry water to us, and we use drains to take away our waste.

Even more interesting is that we choose to play with gravity, to have fun with it. Almost every sport we play uses gravity. We ski, skydive, high-jump, throw the discus and the javelin, and play basketball, baseball, and golf—all of which require gravity.

The circumstances you complain about are all situations you can change—but you have chosen not to. You can get a better job, find a more loving partner, make more money, move to where the jobs are, live in a nicer house, and eat healthier food. But all of these things would require you to change.

Refer to the list on pages 10–11. You could:

Learn to cook healthier food.
Say no in the face of peer pressure.
Quit and find a better job.
Take the time to conduct due diligence.
Trust your own gut feelings.
Go back to school to pursue your dream.
Take better care of your possessions.
Reach out for help.
Ask others to assist you.
Take a self-development class.
Sell or give away the dogs.

But why don't you simply do those things? It's because they involve risks. You run the risk of being unemployed, left alone, or ridiculed and judged by others. You run the risk of failure, confrontation, or being wrong. You run the risk of your mother, your neighbors, or your spouse disapproving of you. Making a change might take effort, money, and time. It might be uncomfortable, difficult, or confusing. And so, to avoid risking any of those uncomfortable feelings and experiences, you stay put and complain about it.

As I stated before, complaining means you have a reference point for something better that you would prefer but that you are unwilling to take the risk of creating. Either accept that you are making the choice to stay where you are, take responsibility for your choice, and stop complaining . . . or . . . take the risk of doing something new and different to create your life exactly the way you want it.

If you want to get from where you are to where you want to be, of course you're going to have to take that risk.

So make the decision to stop complaining, to stop spending time with complainers, and get on with creating the life of your dreams.

Pete Carroll, the former coach of the NFL Seattle Seahawks football team, which won the 2014 Super Bowl, has three rules for his team: (1) ALWAYS protect the team; (2) no whining, no complaining, and no excuses; and (3) be early. These are the rules of a Super Bowl championship team. They are worth adapting.

THE $2.00 GAME

Here's an exercise you can do in your home or your office. It's one we do in ours and in our seminars. Find a large jar or a fishbowl and label it No Blaming, No Complaints, No Excuses. Every time you or someone in your group catches themselves blaming someone else, complaining about something, or making an excuse for their lack of results, the offender has to put $2.00 in the jar—not as punishment, but as a technique to deepen everyone's awareness that these behaviors have a cost.

YOU'RE COMPLAINING TO THE WRONG PERSON

Have you ever noticed that people almost always complain to the wrong person—to someone who can't do anything about their complaint? They go to work and complain about their spouse; then they come home and complain to their spouse about the people at work. Why? Because it's easier; it's less risky. It takes courage to tell your spouse that you are not happy with the way things are at home. It takes courage to ask for a behavioral change. It also takes courage to ask your boss to plan better so that you don't end up working every weekend. But only your boss can do anything about that. Your spouse can't.

Learn to replace complaining with making requests and taking action that will achieve your desired outcomes. That is what successful people do. That is what works. If you find yourself in a situation you don't like, either work to make it better or leave. Do something to change it or get the heck out. Agree to work on the relationship or get a divorce. Work to improve working conditions or find a new job. Either way, you will get a change. As the old adage says, "Don't just sit there (and complain), do something." And remember, it's up to you to make the change, to do something different. The world doesn't owe you anything. You have to create it.

YOU EITHER CREATE OR ALLOW EVERYTHING THAT HAPPENS TO YOU

To be powerful, you need to take the position that you create or allow everything that happens to you. By *create,* I mean that you directly cause something to happen by your actions or inactions. If you walk up to a man in a bar who is bigger than you and has obviously been drinking for a long time, and say to him, "You are really ugly and stupid," and he jumps off the bar stool, hits you in the jaw, and you end up in the hospital—you created that. That's an easy-to-understand example.

Here's one that may be harder to swallow: You work late every night. You come home tired and burned out. You eat dinner in a coma and then sit down in front of the television to watch a basketball game. You're too tired and stressed out to do anything else—like go for a walk or play with the kids. This goes on for years. Your wife asks you to talk to her. You say, "Later! I'm watching the game!" Three years later, you come home to an empty house and a note that says she has left you and taken the kids. You created that one, too!

Other times, we simply allow things to happen to us by our inaction and our unwillingness to do what is necessary to create or maintain what we want:

- You didn't follow through on your threat to take away privileges if the kids didn't clean up after themselves, and now the house looks like a war zone.
- You didn't demand he join you in counseling or leave the first time he hit you, so now you're still getting hit.
- You didn't attend any sales and motivational seminars because you were too busy, and now the new kid just won the top sales award.
- You didn't make the time to take the dogs to obedience training, and now they're out of control.
- You didn't take time to maintain your car, and now you're sitting by the side of the road with your car broken down.
- You didn't go back to school, and now you are being passed over for a promotion.

Realize that you are not the victim here. You stood passively by and let it happen. You didn't say anything, make a demand, make a request, say no, try something new, or leave.

YELLOW ALERTS

Be aware that nothing ever just "happens" to you. Just like the "yellow alerts" in the *Star Trek* television series and movies, you almost always receive advance warnings—in the form of telltale signs, comments from others, gut instinct, or intuition—that alert you to the impending danger and give you time to prevent the unwanted outcome.

You are getting yellow alerts all the time. There are *external* yellow alerts:

He keeps coming home later and later with alcohol on his breath.
The client's first check bounced.
He screamed at his secretary.
His mother warned you.
Your friends told you.

And there are *internal* yellow alerts:

That feeling in your stomach
That fleeting thought that just maybe . . .
That intuition that said . . .
That fear that emerged
That dream that woke you up in the middle of the night

We have a whole language that informs us:

Clues, inklings, suspicions
The handwriting on the wall
I had a feeling that . . .
I could see it coming for a mile.
My gut feeling told me.

These alerts give you time to change your response (R) in the $E + R = O$ equation. However, too many people ignore the yellow alerts because paying attention to them would require them to do something that is uncomfortable. It is uncomfortable to confront your spouse about the cigarettes in the ashtray that have lipstick on them. It is uncomfortable to speak up in a staff meeting when you are the only one who feels that the proposed plan won't work. It is uncomfortable to tell someone you don't trust them.

So you pretend not to see and not to know because it is easier, more convenient and less uncomfortable, avoids confrontation, keeps the peace, and protects you from having to take risks.

LIFE BECOMES MUCH EASIER

Successful people, on the other hand, face facts squarely. They do the uncomfortable and take steps to create their desired outcomes. Successful people don't wait for disasters to occur and then blame something or someone else for their problems.

Once you begin to respond quickly and decisively to signals and events as they occur, life becomes much easier. You start seeing improved outcomes both internally and externally. Old internal self-talk such as *I feel like a victim; I feel used; nothing ever seems to work out for me* is replaced with *I feel great; I am in control; I can make things happen.*

External outcomes such as "Nobody ever comes to our store; we missed our quarterly goals; people are complaining that our new product doesn't work" are transformed into "We have more money in the bank; I lead the division in sales; our product is flying off the shelves."

SIMPLE ISN'T NECESSARILY EASY

Though this principle is simple, it is not necessarily easy to implement. It requires concentrated awareness, dedicated discipline, and a willingness to experiment and take risks. You have to be willing to pay attention to what you are doing and to the results you are producing. You have to ask yourself, your family, your friends, your colleagues, your managers, your teachers, your coaches, and your clients for feedback. "Is what I'm doing working? Could I be doing it better? Is there something more I should be doing that I am not? Is there something I am doing that I should stop doing? How do you see me limiting myself?"

Don't be afraid to ask. Most people are afraid to ask for feedback about how they are doing because they are afraid of what they are going to hear. There is nothing to be afraid of. The truth is the truth. You are better off knowing the truth than not knowing it. And once you know, you can do something about it. You cannot improve your life, your relationships, your game, or your performance without feedback.

Slow down and pay attention. Life will always give you feedback about the effects of your behavior if you will just pay attention. If your golf ball is always slicing to the right, if you're not making sales, if you're getting Cs in all your college courses, if your children are mad at you, if your body is tired and weak, if your house is a mess, or if you're not happy—this is all feedback. It is telling you that something is wrong. This is the time to start paying attention to what is happening.

Ask yourself: How am I creating or allowing this to happen? What am I doing that's working that I need to be doing more of? Should I do more practicing, meditating, delegating, trusting, listening, asking questions, keeping my eye on the ball, advertising, saying "I love you," controlling my carbohydrate intake?

Or: What am I doing that's not working? What do I need to be doing less of? Am I talking too much, watching too much television, spending too much money, eating too much sugar, drinking too much, being late too often, gossiping, putting other people down?

You can also ask yourself: What am I not doing that I need to try and see if it works? Do I need to listen more, exercise, get more sleep, drink more water, ask for help, do more marketing, read, plan, communicate, delegate, follow through, hire a coach, volunteer, or be more appreciative?

This book is full of proven success principles and techniques you can immediately put into practice in your life. You will have to suspend judgment, take a leap of faith, act as if they are true, and try them out. Only then will you have firsthand experience about their effectiveness for your life. You won't know if they work unless you give them a try. And here's the rub—no one else can do this for you. Only you can do it.

But the formula is simple—do more of what is working, do less of what isn't, and try on new behaviors to see if they produce better results.

PAY ATTENTION... YOUR RESULTS DON'T LIE

The easiest, fastest, and best way to find out what is or isn't working is to pay attention to the results you are currently producing. You are either rich or you are not. You either command respect or you don't. You are either golfing par or you are not. You are either maintaining your ideal body weight or you are not. You are either happy or you are not. You either have what you want or you don't. It's that simple. Results don't lie!

You have to give up any excuses and justifications and come to terms with the results you are producing. If you are under quota or overweight, all the great reasons in the world won't change that. The only thing that will change your results is to change your behavior. Prospect more, get some sales training, change your sales presentation, change your diet, consume fewer calories, and exercise more frequently—these are things that will make a difference. But you have to first be willing to look at the results you are producing. The only starting point that works is reality.

So start paying attention to what is so. Look around at your life and the people in it. Are you and they happy? Is there balance, beauty, comfort, and ease? Do your systems work? Are you getting what you want? Is your net worth increasing? Are your grades satisfactory? Are you healthy, fit, and pain-free? Are you getting better in all areas of your life? If not, then something needs to happen, and only you can make it happen.

Don't kid yourself. Be ruthlessly honest with yourself. Take your own inventory.

FROM VICTIM TO VICTORY

Raj Bhavsar was born to be a gymnast. It was the natural career choice for a kid who—at the age of four—lived to climb up things, including trees and furniture, and jump off them. His parents, worried that he'd hurt himself and destroy their house, signed him up for gymnastics classes at a nearby gym. Raj quickly fell in love with the sport, and by the age of 10, he wanted to be the best at this sport that he loved and represent his country in the Olympics.

He began focusing intensely on becoming a better gymnast, and soon the success began to show. He started winning first and second place at competitions and was a five-time Texas champion by the time he entered high school.

His high school and college years were a blur of awards and championships: regional state champion, national champion, senior national team, and then placement in two medal-winning championship teams. In his mind, he was unstoppable.

In 2004, Raj was competing for a spot in the U.S. Olympic gymnastics team. Of the 12 routines he'd done, 11 of them had been perfect. Everybody agreed that he was a shoo-in. Elated, he was thinking, *Greece, here I come!*

But at the conclusion of the trials, when they read off the names of the Olympians, his wasn't on the list. Then he heard the words, "Raj Bhavsar, alternate." In that moment, his whole world—everything he'd been working toward for a decade and a half—was shattered. His expectations were sky-high and tangled up in his self-worth, so when they weren't met on that awful day in 2004, he came down to earth with a crash. For the next few years, he burned with one desire: to find out why he'd been denied. He needed to find someone to blame.

Although Raj went to Greece as an alternate, it was a bittersweet experience watching his teammates work together and compete day after day. Unofficially, he was part of the team, yet it was clear he wasn't really one of them. He never had a chance to compete, and he returned from the trip disillusioned and lost.

Back at home, he did some serious soul-searching. He asked himself,

Do I truly enjoy gymnastics? Do I love the competition regardless of the scores and the accolades? His answer was *Yes!* So he decided to recommit himself to being a gymnast, and this time to throw himself into the sport—not just to win competitions, but for the art of it, and the love of it.

Unfortunately, without the intense drive to win, his performance suffered. At the 2007 U.S. Nationals, held nine months before the 2008 Olympic team was selected, he bombed. His performance was rocky, and for the first time in nine years, he didn't even make the national team. He had to own up to the truth: What he was doing wasn't working.

A few days later, a friend of his, a 2000 Olympian himself, handed Raj a book and said, "You need to read this." Raj took it from him and saw on the cover a picture of a white-haired guy with a big smile and the words: *How to Get from Where You Are to Where You Want to Be.* He thought, *No book can get me where I want to be; my problem is different.* But when his coach recommended the same book a few days later, Raj decided to give it a chance.

I'll let Raj tell the rest of the story:

> The book was *The Success Principles,* and the first thing I learned was that, to be successful, you have to take 100% responsibility for everything that happens in your life. This was a tough one to swallow considering I had been convinced—for years—that life had played against me. Soon, however, I realized that harboring resentment and dwelling on "what happened" had gotten me nowhere. Suddenly, instead of continuing to look for someone to blame, I began to turn that energy inward and examine how my own mindset of fear and negativity had contributed to my recent performance. *Where was my fear coming from, and what was causing these negative thoughts in my head?*
>
> I had always thought that fear meant I was broken—but Jack taught me that successful people experience fear and negativity on a daily basis yet still choose to move forward toward their goals. Negative thoughts, rejection, fear—they're just part of the process! Suddenly, these thoughts became challenges to overcome, rather than huge roadblocks or evidence of my failure. I was on a whole new course.
>
> My coach saw the light go on in me. It was like a switch was flipped, he said. Working with him on a new training plan, I recommitted to my dream of being an Olympian—but now I also wanted to be an Olympian in *life.*
>
> I created a vision board and mind map—not only to help me visualize success but also to break down my huge, lofty, overwhelming Olympic goal into areas of daily focus that I could manage. When the

2008 Olympic tryouts were held, I sailed through the competition. I felt happy, clear, and on top of my game. I nailed all my routines. With all the work I'd done on myself, I was confident they would name me to the team this time.

But when they named the final team members, my name wasn't called. *What?!*

In a cruel repeat of 2004, I heard, "Raj Bhavsar, alternate."

When a reporter from NBC asked me how I felt about being named an alternate a second time, I answered with one sentence, "There is no external event that can defeat my sense of inner accomplishment."

Still, I was honestly baffled that—after all I had done—my dream was still outside my grasp. While a part of me was ready to give up on being an Olympian, something inside me said, "Keep the dream alive! There's no way this is over."

The next morning, I called the USA Gymnastics officials and reconfirmed that I'd be honored to be an alternate. For the next week, I trained hard and stayed ready. Then it was announced that Paul Hamm—the 2004 Olympic gold medalist and a member of the Olympic team for 2008—had made the decision to withdraw due to injuries. The committee would decide which one of the three alternates would be chosen to replace him. Waiting for the decision was probably the most excruciating, yet exciting, 24 hours of my entire life.

The next day at the gym, my coach, my sports performance counselor, and I were on the phone to USA Gymnastics when the president of the organization came on the line to give us the official announcement. As he started his announcement—saying how happy they were about the decision and on and on—inside I was begging, *Just say the name! Is it me or not?*

"At this time," he finally said, "we'd like to announce the new member of the 2008 Olympic team . . . Raj Bhavsar."

With a shout, Raj fell to his knees. Then, smiling and crying at the same time, he stood up and hugged his coach. He hugged his counselor. He hugged everyone.

But Raj also knew the road ahead would be difficult. With Paul Hamm out, not a single member of the team had any Olympic experience. Sports media—even people in the gymnastics community—had written off the team, doubting they could make it into the finals. That was when Raj committed to doing whatever he could to keep their outlook positive.

The night before the competition, he assembled all six team members and urged them to commit to caring for one another as human beings first—athletes second. In that moment, each knew that his teammates had his back. The next morning, the team walked onto the competition floor with their heads held high and, in a stunning upset—with the entire arena chanting *"USA! USA!"*—Raj and his teammates edged out the Germans to win the Olympic bronze medal.

PRINCIPLE 2

BE CLEAR WHY YOU'RE HERE

*Decide upon your major definite purpose in life
and then organize all your activities around it.*

BRIAN TRACY
One of America's leading authorities on the development
of human potential and personal effectiveness

I believe each of us is born with a life purpose. Identifying, acknowledging, and honoring this purpose is perhaps the most important action that successful people take. They take the time to understand what they're here to do—and then they pursue that with passion and enthusiasm.

WHAT WERE YOU PUT ON THIS EARTH TO DO?

I discovered long ago what I was put on this earth to do. I determined my true purpose in life, my "right livelihood." I discovered how to inject passion and determination into every activity I undertake. And I learned how purpose can bring an aspect of fun and fulfillment to virtually everything I do.

Now I'd like to help uncover the same secret for you.

You see, without a purpose in life, it's easy to get sidetracked on your life's journey. It's easy to wander and drift, accomplishing little.

But with a purpose, everything in life seems to fall into place. To be "on purpose" means you're doing what you love to do, doing what you're good at, and accomplishing what's important to you. When you are truly and passionately on purpose, the people, resources, and opportunities you need naturally gravitate toward you. The world benefits, too, because when you act in alignment with your true life purpose, which may at first glance seem selfish, all of your actions automatically serve others.

SOME PERSONAL LIFE PURPOSE STATEMENTS

My life purpose is *to inspire and empower people to live their highest vision in a context of love and joy in harmony with the highest good of all concerned.* I inspire people to live their highest vision by collecting and disseminating inspiring stories through the *Chicken Soup for the Soul*® series and in my inspirational keynote speeches. I empower people to live their dreams by writing practical self-help books like this one, *Tapping Into Ultimate Success,* and *The Power of Focus;* by designing courses for high school and college students; and by conducting seminars for individuals and corporations that teach powerful tools for creating one's ideal life both at work and at home.

Here are the life purpose statements of some of my friends. It is important to note that they have all become self-made millionaires through the fulfillment of their life purpose.

- To inspire and empower people to achieve their destiny[*]
- To uplift humanity's consciousness through business[†]
- To humbly serve the Lord by being a loving, playful, powerful, and passionate example of the absolute joy that is available to us the moment we rejoice in God's gifts and sincerely love and serve all of his creations[‡]
- To leave the world a better place than I found it, for horses and for people, too[§]

Once you know what your life purpose is, you can organize all of your activities around it. Everything you do should be an expression of your purpose. If an activity didn't align with your purpose, you wouldn't work on it. Period.

WHAT'S THE "WHY" BEHIND EVERYTHING YOU DO?

Without purpose as the compass to guide you, your goals and action plans may not ultimately fulfill you. You don't want to get to the top of the ladder only to find you had it leaning against the wrong wall.

---

[*] Robert Allen, coauthor of *The One Minute Millionaire.*
[†] DC Cordova, cofounder of the Excellerated Business School.
[‡] Anthony Robbins, author of *Personal Power* and *Get the Edge,* entrepreneur, and philanthropist.
[§] Monty Roberts, author of *The Man Who Listens to Horses.*

When Julie Marie Carrier was a child, she was a very big fan of animals. As a result, all she ever heard growing up was "Julie, you should be a vet. You're going to be a great vet. That's what you should do." So when she got to Ohio State University, she took biology, anatomy, and chemistry, and started studying to be a vet. A Rotary Ambassadorial Scholarship allowed her to spend her senior year studying abroad in Manchester, England. Away from the family and faculty pressures back home, she found herself one dreary day sitting at her desk, surrounded by biology books and staring out the window, when it suddenly hit her: *You know what? I'm totally miserable. What am I doing? I don't want to be a vet!*

Julie then asked herself, *What is a job I would love so much that I'd do it for free but that I could actually get paid for? It's not being a vet. That's not the right job.* Julie thought back over all the things she'd done in her life and what had made her the most happy. Suddenly it hit her—it was all of the youth leadership conferences that she had volunteered at, and the communications and leadership courses she had taken as elective courses back at Ohio State.

How could I have been so ignorant? she thought. *Here I am in my fourth year at school and just finally realizing I'm on the wrong path. But it's been right here in front of me the whole time. I just never took the time to acknowledge it until now.*

Buoyed by her new insight, Julie spent the rest of her year in England taking courses in communications and media performance. When she returned to Ohio State, she was eventually able to convince the administration to let her create her own program in "leadership studies." And while it took her two years longer to finally graduate, she went on to become a senior management consultant in leadership training and development for the Pentagon. She also won the Miss Virginia USA contest, which allowed her to spend much of the year speaking to kids all across Virginia plus launch a national speaking career to empower youth with messages of leadership and character. By the way, Julie was able to do this at only 26 years old—a testament to the power that clarity of purpose can create in your life.

Today Julie has reached over a million young people as one of the top national youth leadership speakers for student conferences, high schools, colleges, and youth programs worldwide. You may have seen her on NBC's *Today* show or *Fox News,* in the *New York Times,* or as a success coach for teens and young women featured on a goal-setting TV show on MTV (Julie has even received an Emmy nomination!).

The good news is that you don't have to go all the way to England to discover what you are really here to do. You can simply complete two simple exercises that will help you clarify your purpose.

YOUR INNER GUIDANCE SYSTEM IS YOUR JOY

It is the soul's duty to be loyal to its own desires.
It must abandon itself to its master passion.

DAME REBECCA WEST
Bestselling author

You were born with an inner guidance system that tells you when you are on or off purpose by the amount of joy you are experiencing. The things that bring you the greatest joy are in alignment with your purpose. To begin to home in on your purpose, here are a couple of exercises. The first is to make a list of the times you have felt most joyful and alive. What are the common elements of these experiences? Can you figure out a way to make a living doing these things?

Pat Williams is the former senior vice president of the NBA's Orlando Magic basketball team. He has also written more than 70 books and is a professional speaker. When I asked him what he felt the greatest secret to success was, he replied, "Figure out what you love to do as young as you can, and then organize your life around figuring out how to make a living at it." For young Pat, it was sports—more specifically, baseball. When his father took him to his first baseball game in Philadelphia, he fell in love with the game. He learned to read by reading the sports section of the *New York Times*. He knew he wanted to grow up and have a career in sports. He devoted almost every waking moment to it. He collected baseball cards, played sports, and wrote a sports column for the school newspaper.

Pat went on to have a career in the front office of the Philadelphia Phillies baseball team, then with the Philadelphia 76ers basketball team. When the NBA considered granting an expansion team franchise to Orlando, Pat was there to lead the fight. Now in his eighties, Pat has enjoyed 50-plus years doing what he loves, and he has enjoyed every minute of it. Once you are clear about what brings you the greatest joy, you will have a major insight into your purpose.

The second exercise is a simple but powerful way to create a compelling statement of your life purpose that can guide your behavior. Take time now to complete the following exercise.

THE LIFE PURPOSE EXERCISE*

1. List two of your unique personal qualities, such as *enthusiasm* and *creativity*.

   _____   _____

2. List one or two ways you enjoy expressing those qualities when interacting with others, such as *to support* and *to inspire*.

   _____   _____

3. Assume the world is perfect right now. What does this world look like? How is everyone interacting with everyone else? What does it feel like? Write your answer as a statement, in the present tense, describing the ultimate condition, the perfect world as you see it and feel it. Remember, a perfect world is a fun place to be.

   EXAMPLE: *Everyone is freely expressing their own unique talents. Everyone is working in harmony. Everyone is expressing love.*

   _____
   _____
   _____

4. Combine the three prior subdivisions of this paragraph into a single statement (see example on the next page).

---

*There are many ways to approach defining your purpose. I learned this version of the life purpose exercise from the late Arnold M. Patent, spiritual coach and author of *You Can Have It All*.

EXAMPLE: *My purpose is to use my creativity and enthusiasm to support and inspire others to freely express their talents in a harmonious and loving way.*

_____
_____
_____

Here are some examples of life purpose statements that people in my recent workshops have written:

- To use my humor, creativity, and knowledge to inspire, uplift, and empower people in recovery to stay sober. (Recovery coach and author)
- To inspire and empower small business owners to systematize for easier revenue generation. (Small-business consultant and author)
- To inspire people to have faith in themselves and believe in their natural genius. (Educator)
- To raise healthy, prosperous children who make a difference in the world. (Full-time homemaker)
- To create a world in which people are living ecologically sustainable, spiritually fulfilling, and socially just lives. (Environmentalist and social activist)
- To use my vast knowledge of integrative medicine to educate, inspire, and empower people to live longer and healthier lives. (Holistic medical doctor)
- To live every day to the fullest, and give back as much as possible, while appreciating someone special every day. (Contractor and home builder)
- To live my life with integrity and compassion while serving others, and to always value the unexpected. (Fireman)

STAYING ON PURPOSE

Once you have determined and written down your life purpose, read it every day, preferably in the morning. If you are artistic or strongly visual by nature, you may want to draw or paint a symbol or picture that represents your life purpose and then hang it somewhere (on the refrigerator, opposite your desk, near your bed) where you will see it every day. This will keep you focused on your purpose.

As you move forward in the next few chapters to define your vision and your goals, make sure they are aligned with and serve to fulfill your purpose.

Another approach to clarifying your purpose is to set aside some time for quiet reflection—using meditation to inquire within (see Principle 47). After you become relaxed and enter into a state of deep self-love and peacefulness, ask yourself, *What is my purpose for living?* or *What is my unique role in the universe?* Allow the answer to simply come to you. Let it be as expansive as you can imagine. The words that come need not be flowery or poetic; what is important is how inspired the words make you feel.

If you really want to go deep with this exercise, you can do two more exercises we do in my Breakthrough to Success Training. The first is the Passion Test. It is a sample exercise you can go through alone or with a partner. The process can be found in the book *The Passion Test* by Janet and Chris Attwood (Plume, 2008).

The other exercise, which many people find to be the most powerful, is the Life Purpose Guided Visualization—part of my *Awakening Power* set of meditations on CD.*

"All of my professors told us the key to success is doing something you love. I love living at home with you and mom."

---

*This six-CD program contains 11 guided visualizations narrated by myself and Dr. Deborah Sandella. You can order this audio program at jackcanfield.com.

PRINCIPLE 3

DECIDE WHAT YOU WANT

The indispensable first step to getting the things
you want out of life is this: Decide what you want.

BEN STEIN
Actor and author

Once you have decided why you're here, you have to decide what you want to do, be, and have. What do you want to accomplish? What do you want to experience? And what possessions do you want to acquire? In the journey from where you are to where you want to be, you have to decide where you want to be. In other words, what does success look like to you?

One of the main reasons why most people don't get what they want is they haven't *decided* what they want. They haven't defined their desires in clear and compelling detail.

EARLY CHILDHOOD PROGRAMMING OFTEN GETS IN THE WAY OF WHAT YOU WANT

Inside of every one of us is that tiny seed of the "you" that you were meant to become. Unfortunately, you may have buried this seed in response to your parents, teachers, coaches, and other adult role models as you were growing up.

You started out as a baby knowing exactly what you wanted. You knew when you were hungry. You spit out the foods you didn't like and avidly devoured the ones you did. You had no trouble expressing your needs and wants. You simply cried loudly—with no inhibitions or holding back—until you got what you wanted. You were fed, changed, and held. As you got older, you crawled around and moved toward whatever held the most interest for you. You were clear about what you wanted, and you headed straight toward it with no fear.

So what happened? Somewhere along the way, someone said . . .

Don't touch that!
Stay away from there.
Keep your hands to yourself.
Eat everything on your plate whether you like it or not!
You don't really feel that way.
You don't really want that.
You should be ashamed of yourself.
Stop crying. Don't be such a baby.

As you got older, you heard . . .

You can't have everything you want simply because you want it.
Money doesn't grow on trees.
Can't you think of anybody but yourself?!
Stop being so selfish!
Stop doing what you're doing and come do what I want you to do!

DON'T LIVE SOMEONE ELSE'S DREAMS

After many years of these kinds of sanctions, most of us eventually lost touch with the needs of our bodies and the desires of our hearts—and somehow got stuck trying to figure out what other people wanted us to do. We learned how to act and how to be to get *their* approval. As a result, we now do a lot of things we don't want to do but that please a lot of other people:

- We go to medical school because that is what Dad wanted for us.
- We get married to please our mother.
- We get a "real job" instead of pursuing a dream career in the arts.
- We go straight into graduate school instead of taking a year off and backpacking through Europe.

In the name of being sensible, we end up becoming numb to our own desires. It's no wonder that when we ask many teenagers what they want to do or be, they honestly answer, "I don't know." There are too many layers of "should's," "ought to's," and "you'd better's" piled on top of and suffocating what they really want.

So how do you reclaim yourself and your true desires? How do you get back to what you really want with no fear, shame, or inhibition? How do you reconnect with your real passion? You start on the smallest level by honoring your preferences in every situation—no matter how large or small. Don't think of them as petty. They might be inconsequential to someone else, but they are not to you.

STOP SETTLING FOR LESS THAN YOU WANT

If you are going to reown your power and get what you really want out of life, you will have to stop saying, "I don't know; I don't care; it doesn't matter to me"—or the current favorite of teenagers, "Wha*tev*er." When you are confronted with a choice, no matter how small or insignificant, act as if you have a preference. Ask yourself, *If I did know, what would it be? If I did care, which would I prefer? If it did matter, what would I rather do?*

Not being clear about what you want and making other people's needs and desires more important than your own is simply a habit. You can break it by practicing the opposite habit.

THE YELLOW NOTEBOOK

Many years ago, I took a workshop with self-esteem and motivational expert Chérie Carter-Scott, author of *If Life Is a Game, These Are the Rules.* As the 24 of us entered the training room on the first morning, we were directed to take a seat in one of the chairs facing the front of the room. There was a spiral-bound notebook on every chair. Some were blue, some were yellow, some were red. The one on my chair was yellow. I remember thinking, *I hate yellow. I wish I had a blue one.*

Then Chérie said something that changed my life forever: "If you don't like the color of the notebook you have, trade with someone else and get the one you want. You deserve to have everything in your life exactly the way you want it."

Wow, what a radical concept! For 20-some years, I had not operated from that premise. I had settled, thinking I couldn't have everything I wanted.

So I turned to the person to my right and said, "Would you mind trading your blue notebook for my yellow one?"

She responded, "Not at all. I prefer yellow. I like the brightness of the color."

I now had my blue notebook. Not a huge success in the greater scheme of things, but it was the beginning of reclaiming my birthright to acknowledge my preferences and get exactly what I want. Up until then, I would have discounted my preference as petty and not worth acting on. I would have continued to numb out my awareness of what I wanted. That day was a turning point for me—the beginning of allowing myself to know and act on my wants and desires in a much more powerful way.

MAKE AN "I WANT" LIST

One of the easiest ways to begin clarifying what you truly want is to make a list of 30 things you want to do, 30 things you want to have, and 30 things you want to be before you die. This is a great way to get the ball rolling.

Another powerful technique to unearth your wants is to ask a friend to help you make an "I Want" list. Have your friend continually ask, "What do you want? What do you want?" for 10 to 15 minutes, and jot down your answers. You'll find the first wants aren't all that profound. In fact, most people usually hear themselves saying, "I want a Mercedes. I want a big house on the ocean." And so on. However, by the end of the 15-minute exercise, the real you begins to speak: "I want people to love me. I want to express myself. I want to make a difference. I want to feel powerful" . . . wants that are more true expressions of your core values.

MAKE A "20 THINGS I LOVE TO DO" LIST

What often stops people from expressing their true desire is they don't think they can make a living doing what they love to do.

"What I love to do is hang out and talk with people," you might say.

Well, Oprah Winfrey has made a living hanging out and talking with people for 40 years. And my friend Diane Brause, who is an international tour guide, makes a living hanging out and talking with people in some of the most exciting and exotic locations in the world.

Tiger Woods loves to play golf. Ellen DeGeneres loves to make people laugh. Caitlin Clark loves to play basketball. Ryan Gosling loves to act. I love to read and share what I have learned with others in books, speeches, and workshops. It is possible to make a living doing what you love.

Make a list of 20 things you love to do, and then think of ways you can make a living doing some of those things. If you love sports, you could play sports, be a sportswriter or photographer, or work in sports management as an agent or in the front office of a professional team. You could be a coach, a manager, or a scout. You could be a broadcaster, a camera operator, or a team publicist. There are myriad ways to make money in any field that you love.

For now, just decide what you would like to do, and in the following chapters I'll show you how to be successful and make money at it.

CLARIFY YOUR VISION OF YOUR IDEAL LIFE

The theme of this book is how to get from where you are to where you want to be. To accomplish this, you have to know two things—where you are and where you want to get to. Your vision is a detailed description of where you want to get to. It describes in detail what your destination looks like and feels like. To create a balanced and successful life, your vision needs to include the following seven areas: work and career, finances, recreation and free time, health and fitness, relationships, personal goals, and contribution to the larger community.

At this stage in the journey, it is not necessary to know exactly how you are going to get there. All that is important is that you figure out where "there" is. If you get clear on the what, the how will show up.

YOUR INNER GLOBAL POSITIONING SYSTEM

The process of getting from where you are to where you want to be is like using the GPS (Global Positioning System) technology in your car or smartphone. For the system to work, it simply needs to know where you are now and where you want to go. The navigation system figures out where you are by the use of an onboard computer that receives signals from multiple satellites and calculates your exact position. When you type in your destination, the navigational system plots a perfect course for you. All you have to do is follow the instructions.

Success in life works the same way. All you have to do is decide where you want to go by clarifying your vision, then lock in the destination through goal-setting, affirmations, and visualization, and then start moving in the right direction. Your inner GPS will keep unfolding your route as you continue to move forward. In other words, once you clarify and stay focused on your vision, the exact steps will keep appearing along the way. Once you are clear about what you want and keep your mind constantly

"I'm wealthy beyond my wildest dreams! Unfortunately, my dreams were never very wild."

focused on it, the how will keep showing up—sometimes just when you need it and not a moment earlier.

HIGH ACHIEVERS HAVE BIGGER VISIONS

The greater danger for most of us is not that our aim is too high and we miss it, but that it is too low and we reach it.

MICHELANGELO
Renaissance sculptor and painter who spent four years lying on
his back painting the ceiling of the Sistine Chapel

I want to encourage you not to limit your vision in any way. Let it be as big as it is. When I interviewed Dave Liniger, "chairman of the board" of RE/MAX, the country's largest franchise real estate company, he told me, "Always dream big dreams. Big dreams attract big people." General Wesley Clark, the former Supreme Allied Commander of NATO forces in Europe, once told me, "It doesn't take any more energy to create a big dream than it does to create a little one." My experience is that one of the few differences between the super-achievers and the rest of the world is that the super-achievers simply dream bigger. John F. Kennedy dreamed of putting a man on the moon. Martin Luther King Jr. dreamed of a country free of prejudice and injustice. Bill Gates dreams of a world in which every home has a computer that is connected to the Internet. Buckminster Fuller dreamed of a world where everybody had access to electrical power.

These high achievers see the world from a whole different perspective—as a place where amazing things can happen, where billions of lives can be improved, where new technology can change the way we live, and where the world's resources can be leveraged for the greatest possible mutual gain. They believe anything is possible, and they believe they have an integral part in creating it.

When Mark Victor Hansen and I first published *Chicken Soup for the Soul®*, what we called our "2020 vision" was also a big one—to sell one billion *Chicken Soup* books and to raise $500 million for charity (through tithing a portion of all of our profits) by the year 2020. We were, and continue to be, very clear about what we want to accomplish. As of 2025, we have sold more than 600 million copies in 51 languages. We didn't accomplish our vision by 2020, but the vision inspired us to take massive action and the numbers keep climbing every year.

If you limit your choices only to what seems possible or reasonable, you disconnect yourself from what you truly want, and all that is left is a compromise.

ROBERT FRITZ
Author of *The Path of Least Resistance*

DON'T LET ANYONE TALK YOU OUT OF YOUR VISION

There are people who will try to talk you out of your vision. They will tell you that you are crazy and that it can't be done. My friend Monty Roberts, author of *The Man Who Listens to Horses,* which spent 58 weeks on the *New York Times* bestsellers list, calls these people dream-stealers. Don't listen to them.

When Monty was in high school, his teacher gave the class an assignment to write about what they wanted to do when they grew up. Monty wrote that he wanted to own a 200-acre ranch and raise Thoroughbred racehorses. His teacher gave him an F and explained the grade reflected that he deemed Monty's dream unrealistic. No boy who was living in a camper on the back of a pickup truck would ever be able to amass enough money to buy a ranch, purchase breeding stock, and pay the necessary salaries for ranch hands. When he offered Monty the chance of rewriting his paper for a higher grade, Monty told him, "You keep the F. I'm keeping my dream."

Today Monty's 154-acre Flag Is Up Farms in Solvang, California, raises Thoroughbred racehorses and trains hundreds of horse trainers in a more humane way to "join up" with and train horses.* His work has produced 8 national champions in the show rings of the world and more than 300 international stakes winners in Thoroughbred racing.

THE VISION EXERCISE

Create your future from your future, not your past.

WERNER ERHARD
Founder of EST training and the Landmark Forum

The following exercise is designed to help you clarify your vision. Start by putting on some relaxing music and sitting quietly in a comfortable environment where you won't be disturbed. Then, close your eyes and ask your subconscious mind to give you images of what your ideal life would look like if you could have it exactly the way you want it, in each of the following categories:

1. First, focus on the financial area of your life. What is your ideal annual income and monthly cash flow? How much money do you have in savings and investments? What is your total net worth?

    Next... what does your home look like? Where is it located? Does it have a view? What kind of yard and landscaping does it have? Is there a pool or a stable for horses? What does the furniture look like? Are there paintings hanging in the rooms? Walk through your perfect house, filling in all of the details.

---

*To learn more about Monty and his work, go to montyroberts.com or read one of his books: *The Man Who Listens to Horses, Shy Boy, Horse Sense for People,* and *From My Hands to Yours.*

At this point, don't worry about how you'll get that house. Don't sabotage yourself by saying, "I can't live in Malibu because I don't make enough money." Once you give your mind's eye the picture, your mind will solve the "not enough money" challenge.

Next, visualize what kind of car you are driving and any other important possessions your finances have provided.

2. Next, visualize your ideal job or career. Where are you working? What are you doing? With whom are you working? What kind of clients or customers do you have? What is your compensation like? Is it your own business?
3. Then, focus on your free time, your recreation time. What are you doing with your family and friends in the free time you've created for yourself? What hobbies are you pursuing? What kinds of vacations do you take? What do you do for fun?
4. Next, what is your ideal vision of your body and your physical health? Are you free of all disease? Are you pain free? How long do you live? Are you open, relaxed, in an ecstatic state of bliss all day long? Are you full of vitality? Are you flexible as well as strong? Do you exercise, eat good food, and drink lots of water? How much do you weigh?
5. Then, move on to your ideal vision of your relationships with your family and friends. What is your relationship with your spouse and family like? Who are your friends? What do those friendships feel like? Are those relationships loving, supportive, empowering? What kinds of things do you do together?
6. What about the personal arena of your life? Do you see yourself going back to school, getting training, attending personal growth workshops, seeking therapy for a past hurt, or growing spiritually? Do you meditate or go on spiritual retreats with your church? Do you want to learn to play an instrument or write your autobiography? Do you want to run a marathon or take an art class? Do you want to travel to other countries?
7. Finally, focus on the community you've chosen to live in. What does it look like when it is operating perfectly? What kinds of community activities take place there? What charitable, philanthropic, or volunteer work? What do you do to help others and make a difference? How often do you participate in these activities? Who are you helping?

You can write down your answers as you go, or you can do the whole exercise first and then open your eyes and write them down. In either case, make sure you capture everything in writing as soon as you complete the exercise.

Every day, review the vision you have written down. This will keep your conscious and subconscious minds focused on your vision, and as you apply the other principles in this book, you will begin to manifest all the different aspects of your vision.

SHARE YOUR VISION FOR MAXIMUM IMPACT

When you've finished writing down your vision, share your vision with a good friend whom you can trust to be positive and supportive. You might be afraid that your friend will think your vision is too outlandish, impossible to achieve, too idealistic, unrealistic, or materialistic. Almost everyone has these thoughts when they think about sharing their vision. But the truth is, most people, deep down in their hearts, want the very same things you want. Everyone wants financial abundance, a comfortable home, meaningful work they enjoy, good health, time to do the things they love, nurturing relationships with their family and friends, and an opportunity to make a difference in the world. But too few of us readily admit it.

You'll find that, when you share your vision, some people will want to help you make it happen. Others will introduce you to friends and resources that can help you. You'll also find that each time you share your vision, it becomes clearer and feels more real and attainable. And most important, every time you share your vision, you strengthen your own subconscious belief that you can achieve it.

FROM LIVING AT THE MISSION TO LIVING HIS MISSION

In July 2010, Logan Doughty was sitting outside a homeless shelter, awaiting intake into a long-term no-frills recovery program. He had recently hit rock bottom due to alcohol and drugs. His parents and siblings wouldn't take him in, and he couldn't control his drinking or his temper long enough for anyone to do anything more than show him the door. He was emotionally spent, physically tired, and seriously stressed.

As the months went by at the Rescue Mission, his head slowly began to clear. And with the help of a 12-step program, plus kind (but strict) Christian souls, he began to believe he *might* recover from this devastating chapter in his life.

Eventually his family invited him over occasionally and actually enjoyed having him around. At Christmas that year, his sister Alice gave him a copy of *The Success Principles*. He thought the gift was sort of corny, but he thanked her nonetheless and added it to his stack of books to read.

Logan writes:

I respect my sister, so I knew this book wouldn't be garbage. But honestly, I was far from sold. I thought, *You can tell the guy's rich. How can he know what I'm going through?*

To my surprise, Jack seemed like a real guy. He wasn't born rich, and he satisfied my cynical side by explaining in painstaking detail the process by which normal people could actually change their lives.

I read the book every day and even did the exercises Jack suggests. Then on March 26, 2011, at 9:11 P.M., I had an "AHA!" moment—one that will stay with me forever. As I read the chapter "Decide What You Want," I realized that in the past, I would think up ways to make money—but rarely did I focus on what *I enjoyed most* and *what I wanted to do*.

With great excitement, I began to create my list: *(1) Exercise, (2) Kung-fu, (3) Ride my bike, (4) Teach self-defense....* When I jotted down *(10) Encourage people,* things suddenly clicked into place. I instantly knew what I wanted to do—create and teach a self-defense system that would encourage and empower people! I even realized that I was uniquely suited to help others in this very specific way.

For years I'd been a serious martial artist, and some time ago I'd started developing a self-defense program for women. But with my descent into alcoholism, the discipline and honor that is so vital to the martial artist had drained away along with my self-respect. In doing Jack's "20 Things I Love to Do" exercise, I discovered that my martial arts experience—combined with my newfound energy and focus—made it possible for me to teach self-defense for a living. In fact, I was exceptionally qualified to stand up in front of a group of women and speak to them with authority and understanding. I had witnessed what happened to women on the street and in shelters—I'd seen how the strong prey on the weak. Without that experience, I'd just be an academic—someone who'd studied the martial arts but had never applied them in real life situations, under duress and trauma.

I realized that my unique experience, skills, and wants could all align in a single activity where I could actually make a living! It was like being struck by a thunderbolt.

Six months after affirming his true wants, Logan left the Rescue Mission with a completely different perspective. No longer does he feel like a victim. Instead, he constantly looks for how the world will do him good. He treats others with compassion, tolerance, and patience. Armed with nothing but a bicycle, clothes, and the newfound knowledge that he could change his environment, Logan started a small but successful yard-cleaning business and, within months, became the mission's senior self-defense instructor, teaching volunteers and staff how to deal with disruptive and potentially dangerous behavior at the facility.

Today, he has a thriving career teaching corporate groups and medical teams in the art of nonviolent crisis intervention, and he's written a book, *Fearless: A Woman's Guide to Personal Self-Protection*. As Logan puts it, "I owe so much of this success to *The Success Principles*. Now I know who I am and where I'm going. And that can never be taken away."

PRINCIPLE 4

BELIEVE IT'S POSSIBLE

The number one problem that keeps people from winning in the United States today is lack of belief in themselves.

ARTHUR L. WILLIAMS
Founder of A.L. Williams Insurance Company,
which was sold to Primerica for $90 million

Napoleon Hill, the author of *Think and Grow Rich,* once said, "Whatever the mind can conceive and believe, it can achieve." In fact, the mind is such a powerful instrument, it can deliver to you literally everything you want. But you first have to *believe* that what you want is possible. And belief is a choice. It is simply a thought you choose to think over and over until it becomes automatic.

YOU GET WHAT YOU EXPECT

Scientists used to believe that humans responded to information flowing into the brain from the outside world. But today, they're learning instead that we respond to what the brain, on the basis of previous experience, expects to happen next.

Researchers at Baylor College of Medicine, for example, recently studied the outcome of arthroscopic knee surgery on patients with painful, worn-out knees who were given one of two types of arthroscopic surgery—either scraping out the knee joint or washing it out. Their results were then compared to patients who had unknowingly received a "pretend" surgery where doctors made tiny incisions in the knee as if to insert their surgical instruments, then did nothing.

Two years later, patients who underwent the pretend surgery reported equal improvement in pain relief and knee function as those patients who had received an actual surgery. The brain *expected* the imaginary surgery to improve the knee, and it did. This is known as the placebo effect.

Why does the brain work this way? Neuropsychologists who study expectancy theory say it's because we spend our whole lives becoming conditioned. Through a lifetime's worth of events, our brain actually learns what to expect next—whether it eventually happens that way or not. And because our brain expects something will happen a certain way, we often achieve exactly what we anticipate.

This is why it's so important to hold positive expectations in your mind. When you replace your old negative expectations with more positive ones—when you begin to believe that what you want is possible—your brain will actually take over the job of accomplishing that possibility for you. Better than that, your brain will actually expect to achieve that outcome.

"YOU GOTTA BELIEVE"

You can be anything you want to be, if only you believe with sufficient conviction and act in accordance with your faith; for whatever the mind can conceive and believe, the mind can achieve.

NAPOLEON HILL
Bestselling author of *Think and Grow Rich*

When Philadelphia Phillies pitcher Tug McGraw—father of legendary country singer Tim McGraw—struck out batter Willie Wilson to earn the Phillies the 1980 World Series title, *Sports Illustrated* captured an immortal image of elation on the pitcher's mound—an image few people knew was played out *exactly as McGraw had planned it.*

When I had the opportunity to meet Tug one afternoon in New York, I asked him about his experience on the mound that day.

"It was as if I'd been there a thousand times before," he said. "When I was growing up, I would pitch to my father in the backyard. We would always get to where it was the bottom of the ninth in the World Series with two outs and three men on base. I would always bear down and strike them out." Because Tug had conditioned his brain day after day in the backyard, the day eventually arrived where he was living that dream for real.

McGraw's reputation as a positive thinker had begun seven years earlier during the New York Mets' 1973 National League championship season, when Tug coined the phrase "You gotta believe" during one of the team's meetings. That Mets team, in last place in the division in August, went on to win the National League pennant and reach game seven of the World Series, where they finally succumbed to the Oakland A's.

Another example of his always optimistic "You gotta believe" attitude was the time, while he was a spokesman for the Little League, that he said, "Kids should practice autographing baseballs. This is a skill that's often overlooked in Little League." And then he smiled his infectious smile.

BELIEVE IN YOURSELF AND GO FOR IT

Sooner or later, those who win are those who think they can.

RICHARD BACH
Bestselling author of *Jonathan Livingston Seagull*

Tim Ferriss, the author of *The 4-Hour Workweek,* believed in himself. In fact, he believed so strongly in his abilities that he won the national San Shou kickboxing title just six weeks after being introduced to the sport.

As a prior all-American and judo team captain at Princeton, Tim had always dreamed of winning a national title. He had worked hard. He was good at his sport. But repeated injuries over multiple seasons had continually denied him his dream.

So when a friend called one day to invite Tim to watch him in the national Chinese kickboxing championships six weeks away, Tim instantly decided to join him in the competition.

Because Tim had never been in any kind of striking competition before, he called USA Boxing and asked where the best trainers could be found. He traveled to a tough neighborhood in Trenton, New Jersey, to learn from boxing coaches who had trained gold medalists. And after four grueling hours a day in the ring, he put in more time conditioning in the weight room. To make up for his lack of time in the sport, Tim's trainers focused on exploiting his strengths instead of making up for his weaknesses.

Tim didn't want to merely compete. He wanted to win.

When the competition day at last arrived, Tim defeated three highly acclaimed opponents before making it to the finals. As he anticipated what he would have to do to win in the final match, he closed his eyes and visualized defeating his opponent in the very first round.

Later, Tim told me that most people fail not because they lack the skills or aptitude to reach their goal, but because they simply don't believe they can reach it. Tim believed. And he won.

BELIEVE, EVEN WHEN YOU DON'T KNOW HOW THE REQUIREMENTS WILL BE MET

Jason McDougall believed it was possible. As a wholesaler who was shipping goods to the historic Canadian department-store chain Fields, his gut told him something was wrong at the retail giant. Wondering if the chain might be for sale, Jason cold-called the head of the company and asked him to dinner—never doubting the general manager would say yes.

When the dinner conversation eventually turned to the question of a buyout, the general manager replied, "If ever there was a time to buy, it would be now."

What followed was 90 days of frantic activity for Jason—putting the deal together and coming up with the cash. For Jason and his small company, the transaction was like a minnow swallowing a whale. Not only was the retail chain 30 times the size of Jason's business, but Jason also had no idea where the money would come from. His biggest bank loan up to that point had been just $5,000.

Yet still he believed, with utter conviction, that he would eventually own Fields stores.

Even when the first nonrefundable deposit was due—$150,000 that Jason didn't have—his unwavering belief led him to attend a Thursday-night business function where an old friend offered to give Jason the cash by Friday morning's deadline.

At another stage, Jason found himself $400,000 short in making a $1 million deposit—with a deadline that was just two hours away. Using his internal guidance and steadfast belief, Jason came up with the money just minutes before the deadline passed. And just 25 days later, when another $12 million was due, Jason miraculously assembled two banks and six private investors—one of whom rushed through the paperwork—in order to meet the funding deadline.

At each stage of the transaction, as larger and larger nonrefundable deposits were due, Jason had absolute faith that the deal would happen. It had to. In fact, it was either bring in the cash or lose not only the deal but also all the money he'd paid up to that point.

How did Jason maintain this unwavering belief in the face of incredible odds? He followed his own guiding philosophy that, if a thing is supposed to happen, it will. If God had put him on this path, he said, the transaction was meant to be. Of course, the fact that each deadline was met through remarkable and serendipitous means only galvanized Jason's belief that this deal was destined to close. Each small success along the way made him believe even more that victory was on the horizon.

By the time the transaction was eventually completed six months later, Jason had raised tens of millions of dollars, bought an established company that was an institution in Canada, saved hundreds of jobs, and created a sizable new business for himself.

All because he believed it was possible.

You must find a place in yourself where nothing is impossible.

DEEPAK CHOPRA
Author of *The Seven Spiritual Laws of Success*

IT'S NOT WHAT YOU DON'T KNOW THAT HOLDS YOU BACK; IT'S WHAT YOU DO KNOW THAT ISN'T TRUE

In 1983, a 61-year-old scrawny and socially awkward potato farmer named Cliff Young entered the Sydney to Melbourne Ultramarathon, which was considered one of the world's most difficult physical challenges—544 miles (875 kilometers) of flats and hills that would take six or seven days to complete. The runners were allowed to eat and sleep as they chose, and the winner would win $10,000. When Cliff showed up in overalls and rain boots, the other runners, who were much younger and dressed in the latest Nike, Reebok, and Adidas running gear, made fun of him. The race officials were worried that Cliff might die of a heart attack, but Cliff assured them that he had grown up on a farm where they couldn't afford horses or four-wheel drives, and that whenever a storm was coming in he'd often run for two to three days without sleep in order to round up his family's 2,000 sheep on their 2,000-acre ranch.

When the race started, all the other runners took off at a high speed, leaving Cliff in the dust. Cliff, however, started with a slow loping pace and style that would later come to become known as the Cliff Young shuffle. Now the race officials were sure Cliff would collapse and die somewhere along the route.

But Cliff had a secret that no one knew about—including him. You see, Cliff had never met another long-distance runner before. He had never talked to a coach. He had never read *Runner's World* magazine or a book on long-distance running. He therefore didn't know you are supposed to sleep for six or seven hours a night during a long-distance endurance race. That first night Cliff slept for only two hours. By running while the others slept, he took the lead the first night and maintained it for the remainder of the race. The next day he ran nonstop for 23 hours, pausing to sleep for only one hour.

Running with virtually no sleep for the entire race, Cliff crossed the finish line 10 hours ahead of the next finisher. He had covered 544 miles in 5 days, 15 hours, and 4 minutes—the equivalent of almost four marathons a day—shattering the previous race record by more than two days.

Cliff's story illustrates that sometimes it isn't what you don't know that stops your success. It's what you do know that isn't true. It is wise to question all of your assumptions about how things are done and be open to new possibilities.

PRINCIPLE 5

BELIEVE IN YOURSELF

You weren't an accident. You weren't mass produced. You aren't an assembly-line product. You were deliberately planned, specifically gifted, and lovingly positioned on the Earth by the Master Craftsman.

MAX LUCADO
Bestselling author

If you are going to be successful in creating the life of your dreams, you have to believe that you are capable of making it happen. You have to believe you have the right stuff, that you are able to pull it off. You have to believe in yourself. Whether you call it self-esteem, self-confidence, or self-assurance, it is a deep-seated belief that you have what it takes—the abilities, inner resources, talents, and skills to create your desired results.

BELIEVING IN YOURSELF IS AN ATTITUDE

Believing in yourself is a choice. It is an attitude you develop over time. Although it helps if you had positive and supportive parents, the fact is that most of us had run-of-the-mill parents who inadvertently passed on to us the same limiting beliefs and negative conditioning they grew up with.

But remember, the past is the past. There is no useful payoff for blaming your parents for your current level of self-confidence. It's now *your* responsibility to take charge of your own self-concept and your beliefs. You must choose to believe that you can do anything you set your mind to—anything at all—because, in fact, you can. It might help you to know that the latest brain research now indicates that with enough positive self-talk and positive visualization combined with the proper training, coaching, and practice, anyone can learn to do almost anything.

Of the hundreds of super-successful people I have interviewed for this and other books, almost every one of them told me, "I was not the most gifted or talented person in my field, but I chose to believe anything was possible. I studied, practiced, and worked harder than the others, and that's how I got to where I am." If a 20-year-old Texan can take up the luge and become an Olympic athlete, a college dropout can become a billionaire, and a dyslexic student who failed three grades can become a bestselling author and television producer, then you, too, can accomplish anything if you will simply believe it is possible.

If you assume in favor of yourself and act as if it is possible, then you will do the things that are necessary to bring about the result. If you believe it is impossible, you will not do what is necessary, and you will not produce the result. Either way, it becomes a self-fulfilling prophecy.

THE CHOICE OF WHAT TO BELIEVE IS UP TO YOU

Consider the case of Victor Serebriakoff, the son of a Russian émigré, who grew up in a London slum. Believing that he had no chance of ever finishing school or finding meaningful employment, Victor's teachers labeled him a dunce and told him he should drop out of school. Succumbing to the destiny that others had prescribed for him, Victor dropped out of school when he was 15 and became an itinerant worker, moving from one dead-end job to another, often living on the streets with no aspirations other than merely surviving.

When he was 32, Victor joined the British army, which gave him an intelligence test that revealed he was mentally gifted with an IQ of 161. He was a genius! Astonished by the results, Victor nevertheless decided to believe them. Once he learned that he was a genius, he decided to act like a genius. While he was in the army, he got assigned to the education corps to train recruits. When he left the army, he got a job at a timber company and eventually became the manager of a group of woodworking factories. He also became a highly respected timber technologist and revolutionized the timber industry by inventing a machine for grading timber and by introducing the metric system to the trade. He later became the chairman of a national timber standards commission and held several valuable sawmill-related patents.

One day his wife, Mary, spotted an advertisement for a society that was looking for people of high intelligence. Victor took the entrance test for Mensa and easily surpassed the group's only requirement for membership—an IQ of 140 or more. Again he scored 161, putting him in the "exceptionally gifted" category. Several years later this former dropout was elected chairman of Mensa International.

So what made the difference in Victor's life? It wasn't that he suddenly became smart. The truth is that he was smart all along. The intellectual potential was always there. What changed was the way he chose to see himself. When he was 15, he chose to believe his teachers, who saw him as stupid. When he was 32, he chose to believe the army's IQ test that said he was a genius, and he released the innate potential that had always been there.

Victor's story is an awesome demonstration of the power of choosing to believe in yourself and your capabilities. What potential is lying dormant in you that could be released if you just chose to believe in yourself and your abilities?

I am looking for a lot of men who have an infinite capacity to not know what can't be done.

HENRY FORD
Founder and CEO of the Ford Motor Company

YOU HAVE TO GIVE UP "I CAN'T"

The phrase "I can't" is the most powerful force of negation in the human psyche.

PAUL R. SCHEELE
Cofounder, Learning Strategies Corporation

If you are going to be successful, you need to give up the phrase "I can't" and all of its cousins, such as "I wish I were able to." The words *I can't* actually disempower you. They actually make you weaker when you say them. In my seminars, I use a technique called *applied kinesiology* to test people's muscle strength as they say different phrases. I have them put their left arm out to their side, and I push down on it with my left hand to see what their normal strength is. Then I have them choose something they think they can't do, such as *I can't play the piano,* and say it out loud. I then push down on their arm again. It is always weaker. Then I have them say, "I can do it" (I can play the piano), and their arm is stronger.

Your brain is designed to solve any problem and reach any goal that you give it. The words you think and say actually affect your body. We see this in toddlers, for example. When you were a toddler, there was no stopping you. You thought you could climb up on anything. No barrier was too big for you to attempt to overcome. But little by little, your sense of invincibility was conditioned out of you by the repetition of limiting beliefs, emotional hits, (and sometimes even physical abuse) that you received from your family, friends, and teachers, and by the decisions you made in response to that, until you no longer believe you can.

You must take responsibility for removing *I can't* from your vocabulary. I once attended a Tony Robbins seminar in which we learned to walk on burning coals. When we began, we were all afraid that we would not be able to do it—that we would burn the soles of our feet. As part of the seminar, Tony had us write down every other *I can't* that we had—*I can't find the perfect job, I can't be a millionaire, I can't find the perfect mate*—and then we threw them onto the burning coals and watched them go up in flames. Two hours later, 350 of us walked on the burning coals without anybody getting burned. That night we all learned that just like the belief that we couldn't walk on burning coals without getting burned was a lie, every other limiting belief about our abilities was also a lie.

When George Dantzig was a graduate student in mathematics at UC Berkeley, he arrived late for a graduate-level statistics class and found two problems written on the blackboard that he assumed had been assigned for homework, so he wrote them down. Not knowing that they had been written on the board as two examples of famous "unsolvable" statistics problems, he set out to solve them.

Dantzig would later recount that the problems "seemed to be a little harder than usual," but a few days after he copied them down, he handed in the completed solutions for the problems, still believing they were part of an assignment that was overdue.

Dantzig said, "If I had known that the problems were not homework, but were in fact two famous unsolved problems in statistics, I probably would not have thought positively, would have become discouraged, and would never have solved them."

Dantzig's story is a wonderful example of how, when you pursue your goals without any limiting beliefs about what you can accomplish, you can create unexpected and extraordinary results.

DON'T WASTE YEARS BELIEVING YOU CAN'T

On the other hand, there is the story of Catherine Lanigan. All through her childhood and teens she was considered a gifted writer.

In college she entered the school of journalism. During the second semester of her freshman year, she was recommended for a creative writing seminar—usually reserved for seniors—to be taught by a visiting professor from Harvard. When she wrote her first short story, the professor called her into his office to discuss her story. He was the quintessential English professor: horn-rimmed glasses, tweed coat, 6 foot 6. He said, "Come in, Miss Lanigan, sit down." He took her manuscript, threw it across his desk, and said, "Frankly, Miss Lanigan, your writing stinks."

She was devastated.

He said, "I have no idea how you got into my class. You have no concept of plot structure or characterization. There is no way you'll ever make a dime as a writer, but you are a fortunate young woman, because I have caught you at the crossroads of your life. Your parents are spending all their money on your education and you need to change your major."

Because it was too late in the semester for her to drop the course, he said, "I know you're coming to the class with a 4.0 and I know you have declared your bid to graduate summa cum laude [with highest honors]. I'll make a bargain with you. I'll get you through the class and I'll give you a B if you'll promise never to write again." Not seeing another choice, she took the bargain.

Later that night, she took her short story and a metal waste can, went to the top of her dorm, burned the manuscript, and declared to the winter night sky, "I vow I will never believe in dreams. I will deal only with reality." She then changed her major to education.

For 14 years Catherine didn't write. But one summer when she was in San Antonio, she noticed a group of writers and journalists sitting around one of the tables by the pool of her hotel. Summoning up her courage, she walked over to them and said, "I want you to know that I really admire what you do as journalists, seeking out news stories. My secret dream was to be a writer." One of the older guys turned around and said, "Is that right? Because if you wanted to be a writer, you would be a writer."

Catherine replied, "I have it on good authority that I have no talent whatsoever." He asked who told her that, and she told him the story of the professor. He gave her his card and told her to call him if she did any writing. She said she wasn't going to write, to which he replied, "Oh yes, you are."

She thought about it, went home, wrote a book, and sent it to him.

Three months later, he called and said that he liked it and had sent it to his agent, who would call in a half hour. The agent did call and said, "Catherine, you are startlingly talented." Catherine signed a contract with the agency, and within three weeks, had two publishing companies bidding on the book. Since then, Catherine has published 33 books, including *Romancing the Stone* and *Jewel of the Nile*, both of which were made into blockbuster movies starring Michael Douglas and Kathleen Turner.

Think about this for a moment: Catherine lost the first 14 years of what was to become a lucrative and creative writing career because she believed the professor who told her she couldn't write. Don't ever let someone else tell you what you are not capable of. With training, determination, and hard work you can eventually do anything you set your mind to. Remember, your beliefs are a choice. So make the choice to believe in yourself no matter what anyone else says.

IT'S NEVER TOO LATE

It's never too late—never too late to start over, never too late to be happy.

JANE FONDA
Academy Award–winning actress

One of the most common excuses people use to avoid the risk of going for their dreams is "I'm too old. It's too late for me. I didn't start soon enough." Well, it's not true. Consider this.

Julia Child, one of the most famous chefs in history, didn't even learn to cook until she was almost 40 and didn't launch *The French Chef,* the popular television show that would make her a household name, until she was 51.

Susan Boyle was an unknown 48-year-old amateur when in the spring of 2009, she skyrocketed onto the international stage by belting out "I Dreamed a Dream" from *Les Misérables* on *Britain's Got Talent*. Since then she has recorded eight albums which have sold over 25 million copies, received two Grammy nominations, and amassed an estimated net worth of more than £31 million ($40 million U.S.).

Ray Kroc was 52, after spending 17 years of his adult life as a paper cup salesman and approximately another 17 peddling a machine that could make five milk shakes at once, when he met the McDonald brothers, who owned a few great hamburger restaurants in California and convinced them to let him help them franchise their operation on a national scale.

Seven years later Ray convinced them to sell out their shares and went on to become a billionaire.

Elizabeth Jolley had her first novel published at the age of 56. In one year alone she received 39 rejection letters, but she finally had 15 novels and four short-story collections published to great success.

Doris Haddock was 89 in 1999, when she began walking the 3,200 miles (5,150 kilometers) between Los Angeles and Washington, D.C., to raise awareness for the issue of campaign finance reform. Granny D, as she became known, walked 10 miles a day on her journey, relying on the kindness of strangers for her housing and meals over the 14 months that her walk took. At the age of 94, she even made a bid for a seat in the U.S. Senate, making her one of the oldest candidates ever to run for a major public office.

Anna Mary Robertson Moses, better known to the world as Grandma Moses, is one of the biggest names in American folk art, yet she didn't even pick up a brush until she was 76. She painted for another 25 years, which was long enough to allow her to see the canvases she had originally sold for $3 sell for more than $10,000. Today some of her paintings sell at auction for more than $1,000,000.

In 2007, 95-year-old Nola Ochs graduated from Fort Hays State University in Kansas, with a degree in history, making her the oldest person to graduate with a college degree, breaking the record, according to Guinness World Records, which had previously belonged to Mozelle Richardson, who received a journalism degree from the University of Oklahoma at age 90 in 2004. Three years later Nola went on to receive her master's degree, making her the oldest recipient of a master's degree at age 98. On her hundredth birthday Nola started writing her first book, *Nola Remembers.*

And then, as if there were some kind of new competition, in 2011, Leo Plass graduated at 99 years old with an associate's degree from Eastern Oregon University, setting a world record for the oldest man to get a college degree. It's clear that it's never too late to do anything.

FROM NURSING SHOES TO RUNNING SHOES

When Helen Klein was 55 years old, her husband, Norm, came to her and asked her to train with him for a 10-mile run. She had been smoking for 25 years and had never run a mile in her life, but she agreed to try it out. However, panting and exhausted after running two laps on a track they had marked off in their backyard, she wasn't so sure. But she decided to continue, and each day she ran one lap farther. Ten weeks later she finished last, but she completed the 10-mile race.

Spurred on by this success, Helen entered other "short" races, but realized she was not blessed with amazing speed, so she decided to try longer, slower marathons. Since then she has run more than 60 marathons and 140 ultramarathons. Here are a few highlights from Helen's remarkable achievements.

At age 66, she ran five 100-mile mountain trail events within 16 weeks. In 1991, she ran across the state of Colorado in 5 days and 10 hours, setting the world record for the 500K. She also holds a world age-group record in the 100-mile run. In 1995, at age 72, Helen ran 145 miles across the Sahara and also completed the 370-mile Eco-Challenge, in which she rode 36 miles on horseback, hiked 90 miles through broiling desert heat, negotiated 18 miles through freezing, water-filled canyons, mountain-biked 30 miles, rappelled down a 440-foot cliff, climbed 1,200 feet straight up, paddled 90 miles on a river raft, hiked another 20 miles, and finally, canoed 50 miles to the finish line. She also broke the world marathon record for the 80- to 85-year-old class completing the 26.2-mile run in 4 hours and 31 minutes.

Remember that Helen had never run before the age of 55. Her story is proof that it really is never too late to start.

Another example of starting late and achieving inspiring results in the running world is the story of Mathea Allansmith, who started running in 1977 at the age of 46 when a coworker suggested she start running two miles a day. Mathea took her advice, and soon she was running 5K races and eventually completed the Boston Marathon in 1982. Then, in 2022, at the age of 92 years old, after running a staggering 36 miles of training runs every week, she completed the Honolulu Marathon, making her the oldest woman to ever complete a marathon. Just one more example of anything is possible if you believe it and act on that belief.

YOU'RE NEVER TOO YOUNG TO START

On the flip side of the coin, many people stop themselves by telling themselves they are too young to start or that they don't have enough experience yet to pursue their dreams. That is also a false notion. Consider this:

When I was speaking at the California Women's Conference, I met 12-year-old Ryan Ross, whom the media has dubbed "Tiny Trump." When he was three years old, he started a chicken-and-egg business in his back-

Encumbered by a low self-image, Bob takes a job as a speed bump.

yard. He had 60 chickens and sold a dozen eggs for $3. He was making $15 a day. When he got tired of selling eggs, he started his next venture—a lawn-mowing business. He charged his customers $20 an hour, but because he was too young to operate a lawn mower, he paid older kids to do the work for $15 an hour, giving him a $5-an-hour profit. His next business was a power-washing business for which he charged $200 an hour and paid someone $100 an hour to do the work.

At the age of five, Ryan was already investing his profits in buying real estate in his hometown of Toronto, Ontario, and in British Columbia. By the time he was eight, he owned six buildings and had a personal net worth of a million dollars. Ryan also engages in philanthropy that feeds and clothes families in Third World countries. He told me he was having lunch with the real Donald Trump the following week.

When Alec Greven was nine years old, HarperCollins published his first book, *How to Talk to Girls,* which started out as a project for school. In the year after it came out, he appeared on *The Ellen DeGeneres Show, Late Night with Conan O'Brien,* and *The Tonight Show with Jay Leno.* Within the first three months, the book made it onto the *New York Times* bestsellers list. A year later, he published three more books: *How to Talk to Moms, How to Talk to Dads,* and *How to Talk to Santa.* A year after that, at roughly 11 years old, he published *Rules for School.* His books are now available in 17 countries.

And then there's the story of Ryan Hreljac. When he was six years old, he was shocked to learn that children in Africa had to walk many miles every day just to fetch water. So Ryan decided he needed to build a well for a village in Africa. By doing household chores and speaking at churches and schools on clean water issues, Ryan was able to raise enough money to get his first well built in northern Uganda by the time he was eight. Ryan's determination led to his founding the Ryan's Well Foundation, which has raised millions of dollars and has completed more than 1,000 water projects and 1,120 latrines in 16 countries, bringing access to clean water and sanitation to more than 1,400,000 people. When Ryan was 23, he completed his studies in international development and political science at University of King's College in Halifax on the east coast of Canada and still remains active with the foundation as speaker and its executive director.

And when Jaylen Bledsoe was just 13 years old, he started his own tech company, Bledsoe Technologies, specializing in web design and other IT services. In two years, he grew the company from just two employees to 150 contracted workers and expanded it into a global enterprise now worth $3.5 million. There are very few adults who can say they grew their business into a multimillion-dollar business in just two years!

By the age of 12, Brianna and Brittany Winner had completed their first novel, *The Strand Prophecy,* which was distributed nationally through Barnes & Noble. By the end of the tenth grade, these identical twins had completed four novels, a screenplay, a guide to writing, and a comic book. And get this: They are both dyslexic.

DON'T ASSUME YOU NEED A COLLEGE DEGREE

Here's another statistic showing that belief in yourself is more important than knowledge, training, or schooling: 20% of America's millionaires never set foot in college, and 16 of the 492 Americans listed as billionaires in 2014 never got their college diplomas; *two never even finished high school!* So although education and a commitment to lifelong learning are essential to success, a formal degree isn't a requirement. This is true even in the high-tech world of the Internet. Larry Ellison, CEO of Oracle, dropped out of the University of Illinois and at the time of this writing was worth $107 billion. Mark Zuckerberg dropped out of Harvard after founding Facebook and now has a net worth of $64 billion. And Bill Gates dropped out of Harvard and later founded Microsoft. Today he is considered by Forbes to be one of the richest men in the world, with a net worth of more than $129 billion.

Even former Vice President Dick Cheney dropped out of college. So when you realize that a former vice president, several of the richest people in America, and many $20-million-a-movie actors, as well as many of our greatest musicians and athletes, are all college dropouts, it's clear that you can start from anywhere and create a successful life for yourself.*

WHAT OTHERS THINK ABOUT YOU IS NONE OF YOUR BUSINESS

*You have to believe in yourself when no one else does.
That's what makes you a winner.*

VENUS WILLIAMS
Olympic gold medalist and professional tennis champion

If having others believing in you and your dream was a requirement for success, most of us would never accomplish anything. You need to base your decisions about what *you* want to do on *your* goals and desires—not the goals, desires, opinions, and judgments of your parents, friends, spouse, children, and coworkers. Quit worrying about what other people think about you and follow your heart.

I like Dr. Daniel Amen's 18/40/60 Rule: When you're 18, you worry about what everybody is thinking of you; when you're 40, you don't give a darn what anybody thinks of you; when you're 60, you realize nobody's been thinking about you at all.

Surprise, surprise! Most of the time, nobody's thinking about you at all! They are too busy worrying about their own lives, and if they are thinking about you at all, they are wondering what you are thinking about them. Meanwhile, all that time you are wasting—worrying about what other people think about your ideas, your goals, your clothes, your hair, and your home—could all be better spent focusing on doing the things that will achieve *your* goals.

---

*From "Some Billionaires Choose School of Hard Knocks," June 29, 2000, Forbes.com, 2003; "The 25 Richest People in the World 2023," Forbes.com, 2023; list of college dropout billionaires from Wikipedia.

PRINCIPLE 6

USE THE LAW OF ATTRACTION

*What you radiate outward in your thoughts, feelings,
mental pictures, and words, you attract into your life.*

CATHERINE PONDER
Author of *The Dynamic Laws of Prosperity*

One of the most powerful forces in the universe surrounds us, affects us, and can be used to positively impact our future. Like gravity, it's not something we can turn on and off. It just *is*. And like gravity, we can choose to fight it, complain about it, or harness its tremendous benefits—just as successful people do.

I'm talking about the *Law of Attraction*.

For centuries, most people didn't know it existed until, in 2006, a documentary movie and book called *The Secret* was released that featured me and many of my colleagues as teachers of this powerful law. I've consciously used the Law of Attraction to create personal success and business milestones throughout my life. And interestingly, the key practices for harnessing its power are many of the same principles and practices you're reading about in this book, *The Success Principles*—behaviors like taking 100% responsibility for the outcomes in your life, believing it's possible, visualizing your desired results, creating a vision board, repeating affirmations, acting as if, maintaining a positive expectancy, practicing forgiveness, meditating, practicing uncommon appreciation, and developing a positive money consciousness.

Since *The Secret* and the Law of Attraction have become so much a part of our culture, let's take a few moments to discover what it is, how it works and—most important—how you can use it to create the life and results you want.

Stated in its most basic form, the Law of Attraction says, *What you think about, talk about, believe strongly about, and feel intensely about, you will bring about.*

Throughout history, the greatest minds and spiritual teachers have been pointing us to this truth. Consider the following:

- "What things soever ye desire, when ye pray, believe that ye receive them, and ye shall have them."—Mark 11:24 (King James Version of the Bible)
- "All that we are is a result of what we have thought."—Buddha
- "A man is but the product of his thoughts. What he thinks he becomes."—Gandhi
- "The empires of the future are the empires of the mind."—Winston Churchill
- "We become what we think about all day long."—Ralph Waldo Emerson
- "Until you make the unconscious conscious, it will direct your life and you will call it fate."—Carl Jung

These great thinkers knew the power that our thoughts have over our lives—from impacting what we have, to creating everything we experience, even to determining our place in the world. How can mere thoughts control so many aspects of our life?

BECAUSE OUR THOUGHTS ARE MADE UP OF ENERGY, THEY CAN IMPACT OUR PHYSICAL WORLD

Today, scientists know that everything found in the universe is made up of energy. This goes for both physical and nonphysical objects. Of course, basic chemistry tells us that a physical object, such as a building, a tree, or this book, is made up of billions of individual atoms—little energy bundles that interact and bond with other atoms into many forms including water, metals, plants, soil, plastics, wood pulp, and other raw materials used to manufacture physical objects.

Nonphysical things—including thoughts—are also made up of energy and, as such, can also "bond" and interact with aspects and objects of our physical world. It's well known, for instance, that our brain waves (literally, our thoughts) are a form of intense energy that can be easily detected with standard medical equipment—and that can interact with our physical world as any other form of energy would.

What do I mean by "interact with our physical world"?

Well, have you ever thought about a distant friend, only to get a phone call from her minutes later? Have you ever driven down a highway wondering whether you'll get a speeding ticket—only to see flashing red lights in your rearview mirror? That's your brain waves interacting with your physical reality. Luckily, it's possible to use your thoughts to stimulate positive outcomes, too. If you've ever desired something intensely for months, only to suddenly receive it through serendipitous means—or step into a situation where it was provided to you—that was also your thoughts, intention, and desire impacting your experience.

The world as we have created it is a process of our thinking.
It cannot be changed without changing our thinking.

ALBERT EINSTEIN
Physicist and winner of the Nobel Prize

Albert Einstein studied this phenomenon in 1935 when he experimented with *quantum mechanics*—the idea that energetically activating a particle on one side of the universe created an instantaneous response in a "partner" particle elsewhere in the universe. Columbia University professor Brian Greene explains it this way: "According to quantum theory and the many experiments that bear out its predictions, the quantum connection between two particles can persist *even if they are on opposite sides of the universe.*" In other words, something that happens over here can be entwined with something that happens over there.★

A number of other documented experiments have also proven that thoughts can rapidly travel through space and either be picked up by others or have an effect on matter. The book *Thoughts Through Space*† recounts an experiment in 1937 by Arctic explorer Sir Hubert Wilkins and Harold Sherman—a student of mental powers who had long been interested in the phenomenon of mind-to-mind communication. The experiment began when a group of Russian fliers crashed on a shelf of ice on the Alaskan side of the North Pole. The Russian government commissioned Sir Hubert Wilkins to organize and lead an aerial search in the region to find and rescue them—if they were still alive.

While in New York prior to his departure, Sir Hubert met Harold Sherman, and—seeing an unusual opportunity to put mind-to-mind communication to a scientific test—they decided to collaborate on a six-month

---

★Brian Greene is a professor of physics and mathematics at Columbia University. His book *The Fabric of the Cosmos* was the basis for a mini-series on PBS Television's NOVA program.
†*Thoughts Through Space* by Sir Hubert Wilkins and Harold Sherman (Charlottesville, VA: Hampton Roads Publishing, 2004).

experiment. It was agreed that Wilkins, once his expedition was underway, would (as an experiment separate from his rescue mission) transmit "thought-messages" at prearranged times directly to Sherman in New York. Both men would keep written records of each session, with Wilkins noting his thoughts as the "sender" and Sherman recording his mental impressions in his role as the "receiver." Both written records were regularly given to third parties so the results couldn't be altered later.

When Wilkins returned to the United States at the end of his expedition and showed his diary of thought-messages sent to Sherman, an amazing 80% of Sherman's "readings" were accurate—proving that thought-messages were successfully sent and received across 3,400 miles!

A more recent experiment conducted by astronaut Edgar Mitchell during his Apollo 14 mission in 1971 established that thoughts could travel at least 250,000 miles—the distance from the Earth to the moon. While in outer space, Mitchell, who holds a doctorate degree in science, transmitted a telepathic message to four individuals on Earth. Three of them received the message correctly. According to the story, one of those to whom the message was transmitted was Olof Jönsson, an engineer and a psychic, who was living in Chicago. At a prearranged time from inside his space capsule, Mitchell arranged a sequence of cards containing different symbols such as a cross, a star, a wave, a circle, and a square—and Jönsson tried to picture the unknown cards from 250,000 miles away. Not only did Jönsson get all of the symbols correct, he also saw them in the correct order.

Dozens of scientists have produced thousands of papers in the scientific literature offering sound evidence that thoughts are capable of profoundly affecting all aspects of our lives. As observers and creators, we are constantly remaking our world at every instant. Every thought we have, every judgment we hold, however unconscious, is having an effect.

LYNNE McTAGGART
Author of *The Field, The Intention Experiment,* and *The Bond*

Today, scientists have advanced to studying not just transmission of thought but also *bio-entanglement physics*—discovering how to harness these energy connections to bring desired results into our physical reality.

While *The Secret* and the Law of Attraction have had their share of critics over the years, I think humankind is just beginning to understand the power of thought and the theory of *entanglement*—literally that our mind is energetically "entangled" with the physical universe, and as such, can activate the universe to deliver whatever is on our mind.

THE LAW OF ATTRACTION RELIES ON THE FACT THAT EVERYTHING IS IN A CONSTANT STATE OF VIBRATION

Another fact that's widely known by scientists is that the Earth—and everything on Earth, including you—is vibrating at a specific frequency that's unique to that object or person. From the smallest atomic particle to the largest skyscraper, everything ever created is in a constant state of vibration—literally, in energetic motion.

Scientists also know that the Earth's vibrational frequency can fluctuate under intense energy—not only in areas of extreme weather *but also around worldwide events such as terrorist attacks, natural disasters, and other instances of extreme human emotion*. It's not much of a stretch to realize that—through our own intense emotions—we, too, can raise, lower, and even match the vibrational frequencies of objects, situations, experiences, and people we want to attract into our existence. In fact, one of the main precepts of the Law of Attraction is that the level of vibrational frequency and the flow of energy is controlled by thought. Through your deliberate thoughts, you can bring yourself into vibrational harmony with (and attract) anything you desire. As bestselling author Lynne McTaggart writes: *Where attention goes, energy flows. Where intention goes, energy flows.**

A major focus of *The Secret* is how to use the power of intention—that is, deliberate thought—to manifest what you want in life. It's a three-step process: ask, believe and receive.

STEP ONE: ASK FOR WHAT YOU WANT, NOT FOR WHAT YOU DON'T WANT

Every day, you send out requests to the universe—as well as to your subconscious mind—in the form of thoughts: literally, what you think about, read about, talk about, and give your attention to. This includes the books and magazines you read, the television shows and movies you watch, the

---

*To learn more about the power of intention, read *The Intention Experiment: Using Your Thoughts to Change Your Life and the World* by Lynne McTaggart (New York: Atria Books, 2008).

emails you answer, the websites you visit, the blogs you read, and the music you listen to. Unfortunately, much of this thought is random, contradictory, nonproductive, and certainly not deliberate—it happens without our conscious awareness or intention.

Even worse, we send negative requests to the universe when we criticize ourselves, complain about things, and focus on the lack of abundance in our lives. Similarly, when you blame, find fault, or judge someone or something, you're also focusing on a negative experience that you don't want. The same is true when you worry. I often refer to worrying as negative goal-setting. You're creating pictures in your mind of what you don't want.

Because the Law of Attraction states that you'll attract into your life whatever you give your energy, focus, and attention to—wanted or unwanted—you must become more deliberate about what you think and feel. The Law of Attraction also states that each thought or feeling you offer carries with it a vibrational frequency—to which the universe responds by giving you more of whatever you are vibrating. It doesn't care whether that request is good for you or not; it simply responds to your vibration.

The problem is that, most of the time, you're not aware of the vibration you are offering. You are simply responding to things outside of yourself—current events, the news, how people treat you, the stock market, how much money you make, how your children are doing in school, and whether or not "your" team wins. You're responding by feeling positive or negative. Unfortunately, when you merely respond unconsciously to what is currently happening around you—never offering deliberate thought about what you want in your future—you can stay "stuck" in your current condition forever. This is why most people's lives never seem to change. They get stuck in a cycle of re-creating the same reality over and over because the universe faithfully responds to the negative vibration they are sending out.

Compare that with offering positive thoughts instead—feeling excited, enthusiastic, passionate, happy, joyful, loving, appreciative, abundant, prosperous, relaxed, and peaceful. These are thoughts that give off positive vibrations. By contrast, feeling bored, anxious, worried, confused, sad, lonely, hurt, angry, resentful, guilty, disappointed, frustrated, overwhelmed, stressed out, or depressed gives off negative vibrations.

The Law of Attraction responds either way, and brings you more of what you are vibrating. This is shocking to most people. To learn that the life they're living now is the result of the thoughts and vibrations they've offered in the past is revolutionary. Even more exciting is learning that to create the future of your dreams, you need only change your thoughts and vibrations from this day forward.

How would you be feeling if you already had those things and lifestyle experiences you desire—the perfect job, the perfect relationship, world travel, the amount of money that you want to have?

Start Intentionally Creating Your Future

To become more intentional about the thoughts you offer the universe, you'll need to decide what you want—but also practice feeling those emotions you'll experience when you have it.★ Perhaps you want to change career, move to another state, win a major professional award, have your own TV show, or recover from a major illness. How would you feel once you've "arrived" at your goal? What would you be doing throughout your day? Who would you be spending time with?

The more you focus on and talk about what you DO want (instead of what you don't want), the faster you will manifest your dreams and goals. Think of your mind as a GPS system, like the one on your smartphone or in your car. With every picture you visualize, you're "inputting" the destination you want to get to. Every time you express a preference for something, you are expressing an intention. A table by the window, front-row seats at a conference, first-class tickets, a room with an ocean view, a loving relationship—these images and thoughts are all sending requests to the universe.

Use Words That Focus the Universe on What You Want

Of course, how you state your goals is very important to this focusing process. Instead of saying, *I want to get out of debt*—which keeps your mind focused on the debt you have now—say, *I am living a life of abundance and wealth.* Words like these keep you in a positive state of thought.

Be similarly careful when you talk with other people about your current situation. Talking about "the way things are" and describing what's going on in your "current reality" actually creates more of the same in your future. By thinking about and voicing opinions about your current situation, you're actually *prescribing* the future, rather than simply *describing* the present.

The difference between the two was dramatically brought home to me

---

★ To help you decide what you want, see Principle 3: "Decide What You Want." To learn how to practice the emotional joy and satisfaction of having, being, and doing what you want, see Principle 12: "Act As If."

a few years ago when Mark Victor Hansen and I flew to New York to be inducted into the Ardath Rodale Hall of Fame in recognition for the positive impact of our *Chicken Soup for the Soul®* books. On the flight to New York, I sat next to a man who spent the entire trip talking about how terrible the world was—the government, the economy, crime, corruption, pollution, how ungrateful and out of control teenagers were, and on and on. He was an unhappy man.

But when Mark and I went out for a late dinner after the awards ceremony, all we could talk about were all the wonderful things that were happening in our lives—our recent successes, the projects we were working on, how we could help each other, who we wanted to introduce each other to, the recent insights we were having, what we were grateful for, and all the other positives in our life.

Having a positive outlook, using future-thinking language, and being in a state of expectancy about the good that's coming into your life is the best way to "ask" the universe to deliver the very things, people, and experiences you want.

Replace Negative Images and Thoughts with Positive Ones

In the same way that you can write the script for your exciting future life, you can prevent the things you *don't want* by keeping your mind off of them. Whenever you see things you don't want, make a conscious decision not to think about them, write about them, talk about them, push against them, or join groups that focus on them.

Whenever you catch yourself worrying or focusing on lack, quickly replace these negative thoughts with pictures, feelings, and emotions of you enjoying what you *do want*. This is intentional daydreaming—a great use of the power of visualization (something I discuss later in Principle 11).

Whenever you slip into judging yourself—or someone or something else—realize that you're focusing on what you don't want. Take action to shift your thinking. Civil rights leader Dr. Martin Luther King's greatest speech was not titled "I Have a Complaint"—it was called "I Have a Dream." And when Mother Teresa was asked why she didn't participate in anti-war demonstrations, she said, "I will never do that, but as soon as you have a pro-peace rally, I'll be there." These great leaders knew that to be against something—to focus on your opposition to it—just creates more of it.

This is why meditation, mindfulness, and paying attention are so important.

You will become more powerful in creating what you *do want* when you learn to focus your attention and monitor your thoughts. Replace negative thoughts that produce feelings of resignation, hopelessness, depression, guilt, fear, and anger with more positive thoughts that produce feelings of happiness, contentment, love, acceptance, hope, peace, and joy.

Ask for What You Want. Then Let the Universe Worry About How You'll Get It.

As I mentioned in Principle 3: "Decide What You Want," your only job is to focus on what you want. Don't worry about how to get it. That's the universe's job, and—as we'll see—it's phenomenally good at aligning the people, situations, money, resources, and other things necessary to bring about your desired goals.

Be more intentional by deciding exactly what you want. Focus your thoughts. They will attract to you the people, things, and experiences that match the content and vibration of your thoughts.

Just like the GPS system I mentioned earlier, when you present your goals to the universe and its powerful technology, you will be surprised and dazzled by what it delivers. This is where the magic and miracles truly happen. It's the same for Christians and other people of faith who are willing to turn their dreams, fears, and desires over to God.

"My thoughts are not your thoughts," says the Lord in Isaiah 55:8, "nor are your ways My ways. For as the heavens are higher than the Earth, so are My ways higher than your ways."

STEP TWO: BELIEVE THAT YOU'LL GET WHAT YOU WANT, THEN TAKE ACTION

Our intentions attract the elements and forces, the events, the situation, the circumstances, and the relationships necessary to fulfill the intended outcome. We don't need to become involved in the details—in fact, trying too hard may backfire. Let the nonlocal intelligence synchronize the actions of the universe to fulfill your intentions for you.

DEEPAK CHOPRA
Physician, speaker, and author of *The Seven Spiritual Laws of Success*

What does it mean to *believe* you'll get what you want? It means maintaining a positive expectancy, going about your day with certainty—knowing that you've put your future in the hands of powers that are greater than yours.

It's deciding with conviction that what you want *will absolutely happen*.

This is not always easy. Many people have limiting beliefs which keep them from allowing abundance and happiness into their lives. If this describes you, realize that you must first change your limiting beliefs into thoughts that you are deserving, worthy, lovable, desirable, and capable—as well as smart enough, strong enough, attractive enough, rich enough, good enough, and "enough" in every other way that matters to you. I've written a simple strategy in Principle 33: "Transcend Your Limiting Beliefs" to help you eliminate any beliefs that are holding you back. And if you need to turn your inner critic into an inner coach, see Principle 32 for ways to overcome negative thoughts that can block the positive expectancy that is so critical to the Law of Attraction at work.

Of course, once you believe that you'll get what you want, the second part of the equation is to take action. Taking the actions that would create your desired result *affirms your belief* that what you want is within reach. It adds to your expectation.

Some of the actions you'll take are what I call "obvious actions"—like enrolling in biochemistry and anatomy classes in college if your goal is to become a doctor, or changing your diet if your goal is to lose weight. You don't need to wait for the universe to deliver a unique set of circumstances to you—it's obvious what you must do, and those opportunities are readily available to you.

Then, there are what I call "inspired actions." These are the actions you take when you receive inner guidance, an intuitive hit, a hunch, or a gut feeling—like when you respond to a random thought such as *I don't know why, but I have this urge to call my college roommate,* or *I'm feeling this strong need to attend that conference.* Many people, during their visualization or meditation time, keep paper and pencil nearby to capture these ideas. Most of the time, you won't see the whole plan. But with a strong enough belief, you can move forward and take action anyway, watching for other action steps to appear.

SHE FOLLOWED HER INSPIRATION

By thought, the thing you want is brought to you; by action, you receive it.

WALLACE D. WATTLES
Author of *The Science of Getting Rich*

When Jeanette Maw was four months into a new job as a 401(k) sales rep for a large national bank, management announced that if the sales team

THE FUNDAMENTALS OF SUCCESS

didn't turn things around soon and create some impressive numbers fast, all of them would be out of jobs.

Up until that time, they had followed very prescribed steps for making a sale—make a certain number of cold calls each day, set up a certain number of meetings each week, and use a list of responses to potential objections.

These were sales strategies that had been tried and proven many times for others, but it wasn't working for their team. And now the team was spending too much of its time discussing what was going wrong, whose fault it was, and why things weren't working.

After learning their jobs were on the line if they didn't produce results in a hurry, Jeanette threw out her pipeline and script sheet and decided to try something else.

She remembered hearing about a journal writing technique in which if you wrote a page a day about what you wanted as if you already had it, by the time you got to the end of your book, you would have what you want. Jeanette didn't have a lot of time, so she pulled out the smallest book she could find—a 2" × 3" notebook, about 25 pages long. It took all of two minutes to fill her first page.

She wrote about how excited prospects were to talk with her. How they loved her product and couldn't wait for her to implement it. She wrote about the instant excellent rapport she felt, and how the product she offered really was the perfect solution for their company.

After making her first entry, she checked in with herself about what felt good to do next. The answer was "Lunch!"

She hadn't had a real lunch since her first week on the job. Her lunch "hour" since then had consisted of literally running down the hall to the vending machine. Then she would run back to her desk and eat her unhealthy fare between calls to business owners.

On this day, however, she followed her inner guidance and decided on a better lunch. It felt truly luxurious to actually leave the building, sit at an outside table, and enjoy her favorite Greek food on a spring day. After she enjoyed a delicious meal, she kicked her feet up on the table and threw leftover pita bread to the sparrows nearby.

When she was good and ready, she meandered back to the office. It was in the elevator, on the way back to her cubicle, that a stranger introduced himself to her and asked who she was. "I'm Jeannette, and I sell small business 401(k)s for the bank."

He couldn't believe his ears! He insisted she follow him to his office, which is where he showed her a desk littered with 401(k) sales literature from a variety of vendors. He said he hadn't been able to make heads or tails of any of it, and had no idea her bank sold 401(k)s to small businesses. She shared her sales material. He was elated. It was exactly what he wanted. He asked how soon she could put this in place for his company.

In a bit of a daze, she let him introduce her to his Human Resources director. He instructed his Human Resources director to sign whatever Jeannette needed as soon as possible. He wanted this plan in place immediately!

Within two hours of her first entry in her journal, she was already experiencing amazing success. Her colleagues and manager were equally astounded. This never happened.

Jeanette attributed the happy result to giving up the "supposed to" actions that management had given them, and instead doing what "felt good."

KNOW WHEN TO TAKE INSPIRED ACTION

As the Law of Attraction goes to work on your goals, you'll find that numerous ideas, strategies, and inspirations will come into your awareness. These might be flashes of insight that come up during visualization or meditation time. Sometimes the opportunity will appear in the form of an unexpected phone call or a new acquaintance who brings you details of a "lucky break." At other times, it will be an unusual monetary transaction, rebate, or other financial boost that brings you the money you need to take the first step toward your goal. Yet again, it might be merely an impulse, an inspired idea, or a strategy that briefly comes to mind that you write down.

I call these *inspired ideas.* They're not random ideas you'd like to try or strategies you think might work. They're approaches you've never considered before that could only have come to mind because of your use of the Law of Attraction.

Whatever appears, your task is to recognize these opportunities for what they are, then act quickly while the associated energy is in your favor. It's not enough to simply think positive thoughts. When a chance appears, you must take action.

When Janet Switzer wanted to sell her own book, *Instant Income,* shortly after *The Success Principles* was first released, she set the intention to land a publishing deal from a prominent New York publisher, then spent days writing an elaborate book proposal—knowing with certainty that an opportunity to take action would appear. Within two weeks, Janet got a call from the former Chairman and CEO of Time Warner Book Group who had recently retired and started his own literary agency. A friend had mentioned Janet's latest project to him, and he had called to discuss representing her. Because Janet was prepared with her book proposal, was clear about what she wanted, and recognized the lucky break for what it was, she took action and quickly signed on as one of the CEO's first clients. Within weeks, Janet was in New York meeting with America's biggest publishing houses—and sold her book for a major advance just a few days later.

In the beginning, as you start intentionally creating your future, it may seem like these inspirations and opportunities are swift to appear and overwhelming in number. You may not trust them all, and you'll probably feel like they're seriously impacting your to-do list. So how can you distinguish the truly inspired ideas, prioritize them, then accomplish all of them if you're supposed to take *immediate* action? How can you discern which actions are the most important and which can be left until later?

One way is to use an exercise called *somatic decision making,* sometimes referred to as *the sway test.* It's based on the idea that our bodies instinctively know what's right for us and can therefore help us decide by considering our different options. To start the process, stand with your feet together and your arms relaxed at your sides. Close your eyes and simply ask your body, "What is a YES answer?" Wait until your body automatically leans forward or backward. Then ask your body, "What is a NO answer?" If it leans in the opposite direction, you have successfully calibrated your body's answers. When you've determined which direction means "yes" for you—and which way means "no"—you can begin to test the accuracy of the calibration by asking your body some standard questions that you already know the answer to, such as, *Is my name Jack? Do I live in Dallas, Texas? Am I wearing a blue shirt?*

Once you have determined that you can trust the answers you are getting, you can begin to ask your body questions about the inspired ideas you've received. *Should I bring on Jonathan as a partner in the business? Should I marry Doug? Should I buy the boat that Marcus called about today?*

Another way to discern between the many inspired ideas you receive is to simply see which ones keep coming up for you. When I first got the idea to form the Transformational Leadership Council, I didn't take action right away. In fact, it was months before I could take the necessary steps. But the idea kept popping into my head at odd moments—newly embellished with specific ideas about who to invite as members, what the organization's goals should be, where we would meet for annual meetings, and so on. I couldn't get these thoughts out of my head. The same thing happened with the first *Chicken Soup for the Soul®* book. I got so many messages that I knew I simply *had to take action on the idea.*

STEP THREE: RECEIVE WHAT YOU WANT BY BECOMING A VIBRATIONAL MATCH FOR IT

Remember I said that everything on Earth vibrates at a specific frequency? In order to receive that which you are intending, you must become a "vibrational match" for what you want to attract into your life. You are like a radio station that is broadcasting on a specific frequency. If you want to listen to jazz, you have to tune your dial to a station that broadcasts jazz, not one that plays heavy metal. If you want more abundance and prosperity in your life, you have to tune the frequency of your thoughts and feelings to ones of abundance and prosperity.

The easiest way to become a *vibrational match* is to focus on creating positive emotions of love, joy, appreciation, and gratitude throughout your day. You can also *practice feeling the emotions you would be experiencing* if you already had what you wanted. You can also create these emotions through the thoughts that you think. In fact, your thoughts are creating feelings all the time, so it's important to catch yourself when your emotions turn negative—striving to replace them with what *The Law of Attraction* authors Esther and Jerry Hicks call a "better feeling thought."★

For example, thinking you don't have enough money to pay your mortgage will create negative feelings of fear and hopelessness—even guilt and shame for not being able to provide for your family. Instead of giving energy to these negative thoughts, shift your thinking to positive ones such as, *I will find a way*—or by visualizing yourself easily paying the mortgage on time.

At first, this process may seem foreign to you, but the truth is you can, over time, learn to choose only uplifting, inspiring, motivational, and empowering thoughts. It is simply a habit that—with intention and discipline—can be developed.

Use Affirmations to Create a Vibrational Match

Another way to bring yourself into vibrational alignment with what you want is to use affirmations—something I discuss in great detail in Principle 10: "Release the Brakes." An affirmation is a statement of your goal or desire—now realized in present time. They are statements you can write down, then repeat regularly, to bombard your subconscious mind with the

---

★*The Law of Attraction: The Basics of the Teachings of Abraham* by Esther and Jerry Hicks (Carlsbad, CA: Hay House, 2006).

thoughts, images, and feelings you would be experiencing if your goal was already complete.

Affirmations sound like this: *I am so happy and grateful that I live in a 4,000-square-foot oceanfront home on Ka'anapali Beach.* Or *I'm so happy and grateful that I am effortlessly depositing $20,000 a month into my bank account.*

When you use affirmations to visualize your goals as already complete, you keep yourself in that heightened state of joy that is required to maintain a vibrational match to what you want. Resentment that you *don't have* what you want, on the other hand, keeps you out of vibrational alignment. It's simply impossible to receive or allow what you want when you are bitter, blaming, judging, or feeling guilty. These feelings *push away* what you want.

If the only prayer you ever say in your entire life is thank you, it would be enough.

MEISTER ECKHART
German theologian and philosopher

Create a Vibrational Match Through Appreciation and Gratitude

The two most powerful feelings for quickly manifesting your goals are *appreciation* and *gratitude*. Think about it. If you had whatever it is you are wanting, you would feel appreciation and gratitude for having received it. So not only is appreciation a great feeling to focus on, but gratitude is also a powerful mindset for attracting more of what you want. You can get into the habit of appreciation by making it a daily discipline. Set aside five to ten minutes a day to focus on appreciation. Make a list in your journal of all the things you are grateful for—that's how I first started.

You can also practice appreciation and gratitude through meditation.

Yet another technique is an exercise that Esther and Jerry Hicks call the "Rampage of Appreciation"—where you simply look around you and gently notice something that pleases you. Hold your attention on it while you think about how wonderful, beautiful, or useful it is. If it's an item you own, appreciate the fact that it is already in your life. Continue observing it until you feel your appreciation expanding. When you do this, you are telling the universe, "Give me more of this, please." Eventually, choose another object to appreciate—then another and another.

In my longer workshops, I will send people out of the training room on a silent rampage of appreciation, with instructions to focus on all the things in the environment that are serving them. I tell them to feel appreciation not just for the carpet—which makes the room more attractive, makes the sound more pleasing, and makes walking on the floor more comfortable—but also to appreciate the hotel staff who vacuumed the carpet, the people who made the carpet, the people who installed the carpet, the people who made the dyes, the sheep that gave up their wool, the sheep farmers who sheared the sheep, and so on. People always return from this exercise with a smile on their face and joy in their heart—feeling much happier than when they left the room.

You might want to take a short break now from reading this book and do a rampage of appreciation wherever you are. Notice how it makes you feel.

The key here is to develop a practice of appreciation and begin to continually look for things to appreciate in your life. This goes for appreciating the positive aspects of all the people you meet, too. As you learn to focus on what is good about them (rather than what is wrong with them), you'll be amazed at how your relationship with them will change.

Appreciating and being in a state of gratitude gives power to the old saying *What you think about and thank about, is what you will bring about.*

When I was on the *Oprah Winfrey Show* with several other teachers who appeared in the movie *The Secret,* there was a couple in the front row of the studio audience who shared that before watching *The Secret* they had not been happy in their relationship for a very long time. The woman said that after watching the movie she decided to focus on the positive aspects of her husband rather than on all his faults and the things about him that irritated her. She also started writing him notes about what she appreciated about him and leaving them on the kitchen counter where he would find them in the morning. Some days she would even attach a $5 bill with a note that said, "I love you. This is for your first cup of coffee at Starbucks to get your day off to a good start." She said that over the course of just a few weeks, the love and romance had come back into their relationship. You could tell it was true by the way they were holding hands as they were sitting snuggled next to each other and smiling like a couple of high school sweethearts.

Attention to what-is only creates more of what-is. In order to effect true positive change in your experience, you must disregard how things are— as well as how others are seeing you—and give more of your attention to the way you prefer things to be. With practice, you will change your point of attraction and will experience a substantial change in your life experience.

ESTHER AND JERRY HICKS
Coauthors of *The Law of Attraction*

PRACTICE AND YOU WILL CHANGE YOUR POINT OF ATTRACTION

As I said earlier, there are many principles and practices regarding implementing a conscious approach to utilizing the Law of Attraction throughout this book. However, if you wish to explore the Law of Attraction more deeply, I recommend starting with these four books. There is a much more extensive list in the "Suggested Reading and Additional Resources for Success" section at jackcanfield.com/tsp-resources.

- *Jack Canfield's Key to Living the Law of Attraction* by Jack Canfield and D.D. Watkins (Deerfield Beach, FL: Health Communications Inc., 2007)
- *The Law of Attraction* by Esther and Jerry Hicks (Carlsbad, CA: Hay House, 2006)
- *The Secret* by Rhonda Byrne (New York: Atria Books/Beyond Words, 2006)
- *Life Lessons for Mastering the Law of Attraction* by Jack Canfield, Mark Victor Hansen, Jeanna Gabellini, and Eva Gregory (Deerfield Beach, FL: Health Communications Inc., 2008)

And if you haven't seen the movie *The Secret,* I highly recommend you watch it. While its documentary format is far from that of a Hollywood blockbuster, it's the easiest way I know to get a quick and powerful overview of the Law of Attraction.

Once you discover its power, you'll want to make the Law of Attraction a regular part of your life—a mindset you live with every day.

PRINCIPLE 7

UNLEASH THE POWER OF GOAL-SETTING

If you want to be happy, set a goal that commands your thoughts, liberates your energy, and inspires your hopes.

ANDREW CARNEGIE
The richest man in America in the early 1900s

Once you know your life purpose, determine your vision, and clarify what your true needs and desires are, you have to convert them into specific, measurable goals and objectives—and then act on them with the certainty that you will achieve them.

Experts on the science of success know the brain is a goal-seeking organism. Whatever goal you give to your subconscious mind, it will work night and day to achieve.

THE AWESOME POWER OF GOAL-SETTING

For as long as I can remember, trainers have cited a study on goal-setting done at Yale in which only 3% of the graduating class had written specific goals for their future. Twenty years later, those 3% were found to be earning an astounding 10 times more than the group that had no clear goals. The trouble is, this "study" turns out to be merely an urban myth—as extensive reviews of available research literature by Dr. Gail Matthews and Dr. Stephen Kraus revealed that no such study had ever been done!★

However, as a result of this finding, Dr. Matthews decided to conduct a study of her own that focused on how goal achievement is influenced by

---

★Dr. Gail Matthews is a psychology professor at Dominican University and Dr. Stephen Kraus is a social psychologist who received his Ph.D. from Harvard University.

writing down one's goals, committing to goal-directed actions, and being held accountable for those actions.

A total of 267 participants ranging in age from 23 to 72 were recruited from the United States, Europe, Australia, and Asia, and included a variety of entrepreneurs, educators, health care professionals, artists, attorneys, bankers, marketers, human services providers, managers, vice presidents, and directors of nonprofits. The participants were randomly assigned to one of five groups.

Group 1 was simply asked to think deeply about their goals—what they wanted to accomplish over the next four weeks—but not to write them down.

Groups 2, 3, 4, and 5 were asked to write down their goals.

Group 3 was asked to also formulate a list of action commitments.

Group 4 was asked to formulate a list of action commitments and then send their list of goals and action commitments to a supportive friend.

Group 5 was asked to do all of the above, and provide a weekly progress report to a friend.

At the end of four weeks, the participants were asked to rate their progress and the degree to which they had accomplished their goals. The participants in Group 1 accomplished only 43% of their goals, while participants in Group 5 achieved 76% of their goals. That's a 33% increase over Group 1. The complete results are summarized in the chart below.

	Group 1	Group 2–3	Group 4	Group 5
Think about goals	✓	✓	✓	✓
Write down goals		✓	✓	✓
Share with a friend			✓	✓
Weekly **progress report** to friend				✓
Success Rate	43%	56%	64%	76%

This study provides empirical evidence for the importance and effectiveness of three essential success principles: (1) writing down your goals; (2) making a public declaration of your goals; and (3) being accountable to another person—such as a coach, an accountability partner, or a mastermind group—for the achievement of your goals.

Also, consider this: According to a study conducted by David Kohl, professor emeritus at Virginia Tech, 80% of Americans report that they don't have goals. Some 16% say they do have goals, but they don't write them down. Less than 4% take the time to write down their goals, and less than 1% review them regularly. This small percentage of Americans, who write down their goals and review them regularly, earn nine times more over the course of their lifetimes, than those who don't set goals. This study alone should motivate you to write down your goals.

HOW MUCH, BY WHEN?

To make sure a goal unleashes the power of your subconscious mind, it must meet two criteria: *how much* (some measurable quantity such as pages, pounds, dollars, square feet, or points) and *by when* (a specific time and date). It must be stated in a way that you and anybody else could measure it. *I will lose 10 pounds* is not as powerful as *I will weigh 135 pounds by 5 P.M. on June 30*. The second is clearer, because anybody can show up at 5 o'clock on June 30 and look at the reading on your scale. It will either be 135 pounds or less or not.

Be as specific as possible with all aspects of your goals—include the make, model, color, year, and features . . . the size, weight, form, and any other details. Remember, vague goals produce vague results.

A GOAL VERSUS A GOOD IDEA

When there are no criteria for measurement, it is simply something you want, a wish, a preference, a *good idea*. To engage your subconscious mind, a goal or objective has to be measurable. Here are a few examples to give you more clarity:

GOOD IDEA	GOAL OR OBJECTIVE
I would like to own a nice home on the ocean.	I will own a 4,000-square-foot house on Pacific Coast Highway in Malibu, California, by noon, April 30, 2032.
I want to lose weight.	I will weigh 185 pounds by 5 P.M., January 1, 2027.
I need to treat my employees better.	I will acknowledge a minimum of six employees for their contribution to the department by 5 P.M., this Friday.

WRITE IT OUT IN DETAIL

One of the best ways to get clarity and specificity on your goals is to write them out in detail—as if you were writing specifications for a work order. Think of it as a request to God, Source, the universal mind, or the quantum field. Include every possible detail.

If there is a certain house you want to own, write down its specifics in vivid colorful detail—the location, landscaping, furniture, artwork, sound system, and floor plan. If a picture of the house is available, get a copy of it. If it's an ideal fantasy that doesn't yet exist in physical form, take the time to close your eyes and fill in all of the details. Then provide a date by which you expect to own it.

When you write it all down, your subconscious mind will know what to work on. It will know which opportunities to home in on to help you reach your goal.

When you create your goals, be sure to write down some big ones that will stretch you and require you to grow to achieve them. It's a good thing to have some goals that make you a little uncomfortable. Why? Because the ultimate goal, in addition to achieving your material goals, is to become a *master* at life. And to do this, you will need to learn new skills, expand your vision of what's possible, build new relationships, and learn to overcome your fears, considerations, and roadblocks.

CREATE A BREAKTHROUGH GOAL

In addition to turning every aspect of your vision into a measurable goal, and all the quarterly and weekly and daily goals that you routinely set, I also encourage you to set what I call a breakthrough goal that would represent a quantum leap for you and your career. Most goals represent incremental improvements in your life. They are like plays that gain you 4 yards in the game of football. But what if you could come out on the first play of the game and throw a 50-yard pass? That would be a quantum leap in your progress down the field. Just as there are plays in football that move you far up the field in one move, there are plays in life that will do the same thing. They include accomplishments such as losing 60 pounds, writing a book, appearing on *Oprah,* winning a gold medal at the Olympics, creating a killer website, getting your master's or doctoral degree, getting elected president of your union or professional association, or hosting your own radio show. The achievement of that one goal would change everything.

Wouldn't that be a goal worth pursuing with passion? Wouldn't that be something to focus on a little each day until you achieved it?

If you were an independent sales professional, for example, and knew you could get a better territory, a substantial bonus commission, and maybe even a promotion once you landed a certain number of customers, wouldn't you work day and night to achieve that goal?

And if you were a stay-at-home mom whose entire lifestyle and finances would change if you earned an extra $1,000 or $2,000 a month through participating in a network marketing company, wouldn't you pursue every possible opportunity until you achieved that goal?

That's what I mean by a breakthrough goal—something that changes your life, brings you new opportunities, gets you in front of the right people, and takes every activity, relationship, or group you're involved in to a higher level.

What would a breakthrough goal be for you? Writing a bestselling book was a breakthrough goal for me and Mark Victor Hansen. *Chicken Soup for the Soul*® took us from being known in a couple of narrow fields to being recognized internationally. It created greater demand for our audio programs, speeches, and seminars. The additional income it produced allowed us to improve our lifestyle, secure our retirement, hire more staff, take on more projects, and have a larger impact on the world.

REREAD YOUR GOALS THREE TIMES A DAY

Once you've written down all your goals, both large and small, the next step on your journey to success is to activate the creative powers of your subconscious mind by reviewing your list two or three times every day. Take time to read your list of goals. Read the list (out loud with passion and enthusiasm if you are in an appropriate place) one goal at a time. Close your eyes and picture each goal as if it were already accomplished. Take a few more seconds to feel what you would feel if you had already accomplished each goal.

Following this daily discipline of success will activate the power of your desire. It increases what psychologists refer to as "structural tension" or cognitive dissonance in your brain. Your brain wants to close the gap between your current reality and the vision of your goal. By constantly repeating and visualizing your goal as already achieved, you will be increasing this structural tension. This will increase your motivation, stimulate your creativity, and heighten your awareness of resources that can help you achieve your goal.

Make sure to review your goals at least twice a day—in the morning upon awakening, and again at night before going to bed. I write each of mine on a 3" × 5" index card. I keep the pack of cards next to my bed and then I go through the cards one at a time in the morning and again at night. When I travel, I take them with me.

Put a list of your goals in your daily planner or calendar system. You can also create a pop-up or screen saver on your computer, tablet, or smartphone that lists your goals. The objective is to constantly keep your goals in front of you.

Legendary tennis player Serena Williams has often talked about the power of setting clear goals and how her own goals played a crucial role in her remarkable career. Early in her career, Serena wrote down her goals on a piece of paper—goals like winning Grand Slam titles, becoming the world's #1 ranked player, and achieving many other milestones in the world of tennis. But Serena didn't just keep these goals to herself; she carried the piece of paper with her everywhere she went, not only to serve as a constant reminder of her aspirations but also to fuel her determination. While Serena faced various challenges and setbacks throughout her career—including injuries and tough competition—she continued to carry her written goals as a source of motivation. In fact, the physical presence of her goals in written form became a tangible representation of her dreams and ambitions. Of course, over the years, Serena has achieved unparalleled success, surpassing many of the goals she originally wrote down. Carrying those written aspirations served as a powerful tool in propelling her toward greatness in the world of tennis.

CREATE A GOALS BOOK

Another powerful way to speed up the achievement of your goals is to create a Goals Book. Buy a three-ring binder, a scrapbook, or a journal. Then create a separate page for each of your goals. Write the goal at the top of the page and then illustrate it with pictures, words, and phrases that you cut out of magazines, catalogs, and travel brochures that depict your goal as already achieved. As new goals and desires emerge, simply add them to your list and your Goals Book. Review the pages of your Goals Book at least once every day.

CARRY YOUR MOST IMPORTANT GOAL IN YOUR WALLET

When I first started working for W. Clement Stone, he taught me to write my most important goal on the back of my business card and carry it in my wallet at all times. Every time I would open my wallet, I would be reminded of my most important goal.

When I met Mark Victor Hansen, I discovered that he, too, used the same technique. After finishing the first *Chicken Soup for the Soul*® book, we wrote "I am so happy selling 1.5 million copies of *Chicken Soup for the Soul*® by December 30, 1994." We then signed each other's cards and carried them in our wallets. I still have mine in a frame behind my desk.

Though our publisher laughed and told us we were crazy, we went on to sell 1.3 million copies of the book by our target date. Some might say, "Well, you missed your goal by 200,000 copies." Perhaps, but not by much . . . and that book went on to sell well over 10 million copies in 47 languages around the world. Believe me . . . I can live with that kind of "failure."

WRITE YOURSELF A CHECK

Around 1990, when Jim Carrey was a struggling young Canadian comic trying to make his way in Los Angeles, he drove his old Toyota up to Mulholland Drive. While sitting there looking at the city below and dreaming of his future, he wrote himself a check for $10 million, dated it Thanksgiving 1995, added the notation "for acting services rendered," and carried it in his wallet from that day forth. The rest, as they say, is history. Carrey's optimism and tenacity eventually paid off, and by 1995, after the huge box office success of *Ace Ventura: Pet Detective, The Mask,* and *Dumb & Dumber,* his asking price had risen to $20 million per picture. When Carrey's father died in 1994, he placed the $10 million check into his father's coffin as a tribute to the man who had both started and nurtured his dreams of being a star.

ONE GOAL IS NOT ENOUGH

If you are bored with life, if you don't get up every morning with a burning desire to do things—you don't have enough goals.

LOU HOLTZ
The only coach in NCAA history to ever lead six different
college teams to postseason bowl games, and a man who also won
national championship and "coach of the year" honors

Lou Holtz, the legendary football coach of Notre Dame, is also a legendary goal-setter. His belief in goal-setting comes from a lesson he learned in 1966 when he was only 28 years old and had just been hired as an assistant coach at the University of South Carolina. His wife, Beth, was eight months pregnant with their third child, and Lou had spent every dollar he had on a down payment on a house. One month later, the head coach who had hired Lou resigned, and Lou found himself without a job.

In an attempt to lift his spirits, his wife gave him a book—*The Magic of Thinking Big* by David Schwartz. The book said that you should write down all the goals you want to achieve in your life. Lou sat at the dining room table, turned his imagination loose, and before he knew it, he had listed 107 goals he wanted to achieve before he died. These goals covered every area of his life and included having dinner at the White House, appearing on *The Tonight Show,* meeting the pope, coaching at Notre Dame, leading his team to a national championship, and shooting a hole in one in golf. So far Lou has achieved 102 of those goals, including shooting a hole in one—not once, but twice!

Take the time to make a list of 101 goals *you* want to achieve in your life. Write them in vivid detail, noting where, when, how much, which model, what size, and so on. Put them on 3" × 5" cards, on a goals page, or in a Goals Book. Every time you achieve one of your goals, check it off and write *victory* next to it. I made a list of 109 major goals that I wanted to achieve before I died, and I have already achieved 68 of them in only

24 years, including traveling to Africa, flying in a glider, learning to ski, attending the summer Olympic games, writing a children's book, and appearing in a movie.*

CONSIDERATIONS, FEARS, AND ROADBLOCKS

It's important to understand that as soon as you set a goal, three things are going to emerge that stop most people—but not you. If you know that these three things are simply part of the process, then you can treat them as what they are—just things to handle—rather than letting them stop you.

These three obstacles to success are *considerations, fears,* and *roadblocks.*

Think about it. As soon as you say you want to double your income next year, within moments considerations such as *I'll have to work twice as hard* or *I won't have time for my family* or *My wife's going to kill me* begin to emerge. You might have thoughts such as *My territory is maxed out—I can't see how I could possibly get the buyers on my current route to buy any more product from me.* If you say you're going to run a marathon, you might hear a voice in your head say, *You could get hurt,* or *You'll have to get up two hours earlier every day.* It might even suggest that you're too old to start running. These thoughts are called *considerations.* They are all the reasons why you shouldn't attempt the goal—all the reasons why it is impossible to achieve.

But surfacing these considerations is a good thing. They have been there in your subconscious mind, stopping you all along. Now that you have brought them into your conscious awareness, you can deal with them, confront them, and move past them.

Fears, on the other hand, are feelings. You may experience a fear of rejection, a fear of failure, or a fear of making a fool of yourself. You might be afraid of getting physically or emotionally hurt. You might be afraid that you will lose all the money you have already saved. These fears are not unusual. They are just part of the process. Knowing that in advance helps you move through them.

Finally, you'll become aware of *roadblocks.* These are purely external circumstances—well beyond just thoughts and feelings in your head. A roadblock may be that nobody wants to join you on your project. A roadblock might be that you don't have all the money you need to move forward. Perhaps you need other investors. Roadblocks might be that your

---

*You can read my "101 Goals List" at jackcanfield.com/tsp-resources.

state or national government has rules or laws that prohibit what you want to do. Maybe you need to petition the government to change the rules.

Stu Lichtman, a business turnaround expert, took over a well-known shoe company in Maine that was in such bad shape financially it was virtually doomed to go out of business. The business owed millions of dollars to creditors and was short the $2 million needed to pay them. As part of the proposed turnaround, Stu negotiated the sale of an unused plant near the Canadian border that would bring the company $600,000. But the state of Maine had a lien on the plant that would have taken all of the proceeds. So Stu went to the governor of Maine to inform him of the company's dilemma. "We can either go bankrupt," he said, "in which case nearly one thousand Maine residents will soon be out of work and on the unemployment rolls, costing the government millions of dollars," or the company and the government could together pursue Stu's plan of keeping the company alive, helping to keep the state's economy going, keeping nearly 1,000 people employed, and turning the company around in preparation for a takeover by another company. But the only way to achieve that goal was to overcome—you guessed it—the *roadblock* of the state's lien on the plant. Instead of letting that lien stop him, Stu decided to talk to the person who could remove the roadblock. In the end, the governor decided to cancel the lien.

Of course, you may not encounter roadblocks that require you to approach a governor—but then again, depending on how large your goal is, you very well might!

Roadblocks are simply obstacles that the world throws at you—it rains when you're trying to put on an outdoor concert, your wife doesn't want to move to Kentucky, you don't have the financial backing you need, and so on. Roadblocks are simply real-world circumstances that you need to deal with in order to move forward. They are just things that you will need to handle.

Unfortunately, when these considerations, fears, and roadblocks come up, most people see them as a stop sign. They say, "Now that I'm thinking that, feeling this, and finding out about that, I think I won't pursue this goal after all." But I'm telling you not to see considerations, fears, and roadblocks as stop signs but rather as a normal part of the process that will always appear. When you remodel your kitchen, you resign yourself to a little dust and disturbance as part of the price you will have to pay. You simply learn to deal with it. The same is true of considerations, fears, and roadblocks. You just learn to deal with them.

In fact, they're supposed to appear. If they don't, it means you haven't set a goal that's big enough to stretch you and grow you. It means there's no real potential for self-development.

Learn to welcome considerations, fears, and roadblocks when they appear, because many times they are the very things that have been holding you back in life. Once you can see these subconscious thoughts, feelings, and obstacles, once you are aware of them, you can face them, process them, and deal with them. When you do, you become better prepared for the next venture you want to undertake.

MASTERY IS THE GOAL

You want to set a goal that is big enough that in the process of achieving it you become someone worth becoming.

JIM ROHN
Self-made millionaire, success coach, and philosopher

Of course, the ultimate benefit of overcoming these considerations, fears, and roadblocks is not the material rewards that you enjoy but the personal development that you achieve in the process. Money, cars, houses, boats, attractive spouses, power, and fame can all be taken away—sometimes in the blink of an eye. But what can never be taken away is who you have become in the process of achieving your goal.

To achieve a big goal, you are going to have to become a bigger person. You are going to have to develop new skills, new attitudes, and new capabilities. You are going to have to stretch yourself, and in so doing, you will be stretched forever.

On October 20, 1991, a devastating fire roared through the scenic hills above Oakland and Berkeley, California, igniting one building every 11 seconds for over 10 hours, completely destroying more than 3,700 homes and apartments. A friend of mine who is also an author lost everything he owned, including his entire library, files full of research, and a nearly complete manuscript of a book he was writing. Though he was certainly devastated for a short period of time, he soon realized that although everything he owned was indeed lost in the fire, who he had become inside—everything he had learned and all the skills and self-confidence he had developed writing and promoting his books—was all still inside of him and could never be burned up in a fire.

You can lose the material things, but you can never lose your *mastery*—what you learn and who you become in the process of achieving your goals.

I believe that part of what we're on Earth to do is become masters of many skills. Christ was a spiritual master who turned water into wine, who healed people, who walked on water, and who calmed storms. He said that you and I, too, could do all these things *and more*. We definitely have that potential.

Even today, in a town square in Germany, stands a statue of Christ, its hands blown off during the intensive bombing of World War II. Though the townspeople could have restored the statue decades ago, they learned this more important lesson—instead placing a plaque underneath that reads "Christ hath no hands but yours." God needs our hands to complete His tasks on Earth. But to become masters and do this great work, we all have to be willing to go through the considerations, fears, and roadblocks.

THE POWER OF A GOAL

Things do not happen; things are made to happen.

JOHN F. KENNEDY
The 35th president of the United States

When I was conducting a workshop in Chennai, India, I had the great fortune to meet CK and Veena Kumaravel. Their story illustrates the awesome power of committing to a goal.

When CK and Veena's children started attending school, Veena decided she wanted to do something to earn 60,000 rupees ($1,300) a month. Veena could have easily landed a job or stayed at home as a homemaker, but she was resolute in her desire to be self-employed. She knew she wanted to be her own boss, but she hadn't yet identified what she wanted to do.

One of the techniques I teach that can help you decide what to do with your life is to think about what irritates or frustrates you—then see whether you can create a livelihood there. If something is bothering you, chances are it's probably bothering others, too. I simply suggested that Veena follow that age-old rule of business: "Find a need and fill it."

Veena realized she had long been irritated by the lack of good-quality, affordable beauty salons where they lived. Attractive salons were found only in India's five-star hotels—and were both expensive and intimidating for most local people. At the other end of the spectrum were the local beauty parlors and barbershops with standards of hygiene that were far below par. Veena and CK soon realized there was a need for a quality, value-focused salon in Chennai that could serve both men and women.

Having made the decision to start such a salon, the next challenge was to find skilled staff and managers. Veena was not a beautician, hairdresser, or makeup artist—and CK knew even less about the industry. They solved this first challenge by hiring the manager of the salon at the Taj—the leading five-star hotel in India—who then hired the rest of the staff.

Their next challenge—usually the most critical faced by all first-generation entrepreneurs—was to find start-up money. CK quickly approached what he calls the three Fs—family, friends, and fools—and was able to collect enough to open their first Naturals Unisex Salon and Spa on Khader Nawaz Khan road in Chennai. Eventually, they achieved Veena's original monthly income goal of 60,000 rupees, and even opened a second salon. But they decided to think even bigger.

By opening four more salons, Veena concluded, they could turn Naturals into a salon chain. One after another, however, the bankers they met with said no.

Taking their cue from *The Success Principles*—which taught that "no" means "next!"—they asked again and again, until the fifty-fourth banker—impressed by this dedicated husband-and-wife team doing business together—said yes to their loan request of $130,000.

With the addition of the new salons, the Naturals brand was visible and growing. This success inspired Veena and CK to franchise their business. So they advertised in two major newspapers—expecting 500 inquiries or more. When just 334 people responded—and only 32 filled out the preliminary paperwork—Veena and CK could identify no one who was actually serious about becoming a franchisee. At the time, beauty salons were considered taboo, and what's more, Naturals was not a big multinational brand.

Their solution to the challenge? Find prospective franchisees who would co-invest and partner with Veena and CK on each salon location—providing a level of confidence for franchisees who would operate the salon.

Soon, the Naturals chain nearly doubled to 13 locations from this winning formula of adding franchisees. By 2014, the chain had grown to 376 salons. And by 2024, there were 800 Naturals salons across India—as well as in Sri Lanka, Singapore, Dubai, and Qatar, where millions of people from India live and work. Veena and CK also added ancillary services to the salons and new brands to their company, such as Nails & Beyond, Happy Feet reflexology, BAE retail outlets, and even a Naturals beauty academy. "The influence of *The Success Principles* on our journey is very significant,"

CK reflects, noting that the principle of E + R = O and Chapter 18: Reject Rejection were transformational.

Today, however, what gives CK and Veena the greatest satisfaction is that they've created 440 financially successful women entrepreneurs—80% of whom started out as stay-at-home housewives. Even more important, they have created 13,400 jobs.* CK told me that his goal is to erase the word *housewife* from the dictionary and create 2,000 successful women entrepreneurs, 6,000 salons, and 1,000,000 jobs by December 31, 2030.

---

*During one of my trips to Chennai, the Kumaravels invited me to attend the opening of one of their new salon spas. What an experience! The salon was clean, brightly lit, and very welcoming—as were all the staff—and the level of positive energy was unmistakable. But the thing that deeply moved me was that several of the staff were visually challenged. The Kumaravels had discovered that, due to their heightened sense of touch, these young men and women make the best foot reflexology and massage therapists. And now they employ a large number of these young men and women who would otherwise be relegated to a life of poverty and neglect. You can read more about their salons at naturals.in.

PRINCIPLE

8

CHUNK IT DOWN

The secret of getting ahead is getting started. The secret of getting started is breaking your complex, overwhelming tasks into small, manageable tasks, and then starting on the first one.

MARK TWAIN
Celebrated American author and humorist

Sometimes our biggest life goals seem so overwhelming. We rarely see them as a series of small, achievable tasks. But in reality, breaking down a large goal into smaller tasks—and accomplishing them one at a time—is exactly how any big goal gets achieved. So after you have decided what you really want and have set measurable goals with specific deadlines, the next step is to determine all of the individual action steps you will need to take to accomplish your goal.

HOW TO CHUNK IT DOWN

There are several ways to figure out the action steps you will need to take to accomplish any goal. One is to consult with people who have already done what you want to do and ask what steps they took. From their experience, they can give you all of the necessary steps, as well as advice on what pitfalls to avoid. Another way is to purchase a book, a manual, or an online course that outlines the process. Yet another way is to start from the end and look backward. You simply close your eyes and imagine that it is now the future and you have already achieved your goal. Then just look back and see what you had to do to get to where you now are. What was the last thing you did? And then the thing before that, and then the thing before that, until you arrive at the first action you had to start with.

Remember that it is okay to not know how to do something. It's okay to ask for guidance and advice from those who do know. Sometimes you can get it free, and sometimes you have to pay for it. Get used to asking, "Can you tell me how to . . . ?" and "What would I have to do to . . . ?" and "How did you . . . ?" Keep researching and asking until you can create a realistic action plan that will get you from where you are to where you want to go.

What will you need to do? How much money will you need to save or raise? What new skills will you need to learn? What resources will you need to mobilize? Who will you need to enroll in your vision? Who will you need to ask for assistance? What new disciplines or habits will you need to build into your life?

A valuable technique for creating an action plan for your goals is called mind mapping.

USE MIND MAPPING

Mind mapping is a simple but powerful process for creating a detailed to-do list for achieving your goal. It lets you determine what information you'll need to gather, who you'll need to talk to, what small steps you'll need to take, how much money you'll need to earn or raise, which deadlines you'll need to meet, and so on—for each and every goal.

When I began creating my first educational program—a breakthrough goal that led to extraordinary gains for me and my business—I used mind mapping to help me "chunk down" that very large goal into all the individual tasks I would need to complete in order to produce a finished album.*

The original mind map I created for my audio program is on page 91. To mind-map your own goals, follow these steps as illustrated in the example:

1. **Center circle:** In the center circle, jot down the name of your stated goal—in this case, *Create an Educational Audio Program*.
2. **Outside circles:** Next, divide the goal into the major categories of tasks you'll need to accomplish to achieve the greater goal—in this case, *Title, Studio, Topics, Audience,* and so on.
3. **Spokes:** Then, draw spokes radiating outward from each minicircle and label each one (such as *Write Copy, Color Picture for Back Cover,* and *Arrange Lunch*). On a separate line connected to

---

*For the best primer on mind mapping, see *Mind Map Mastery: The Complete Guide to Learning and Using the Most Powerful Thinking Tool in the Universe* by Tony Buzan (London: Watkins Publishing, 2018).

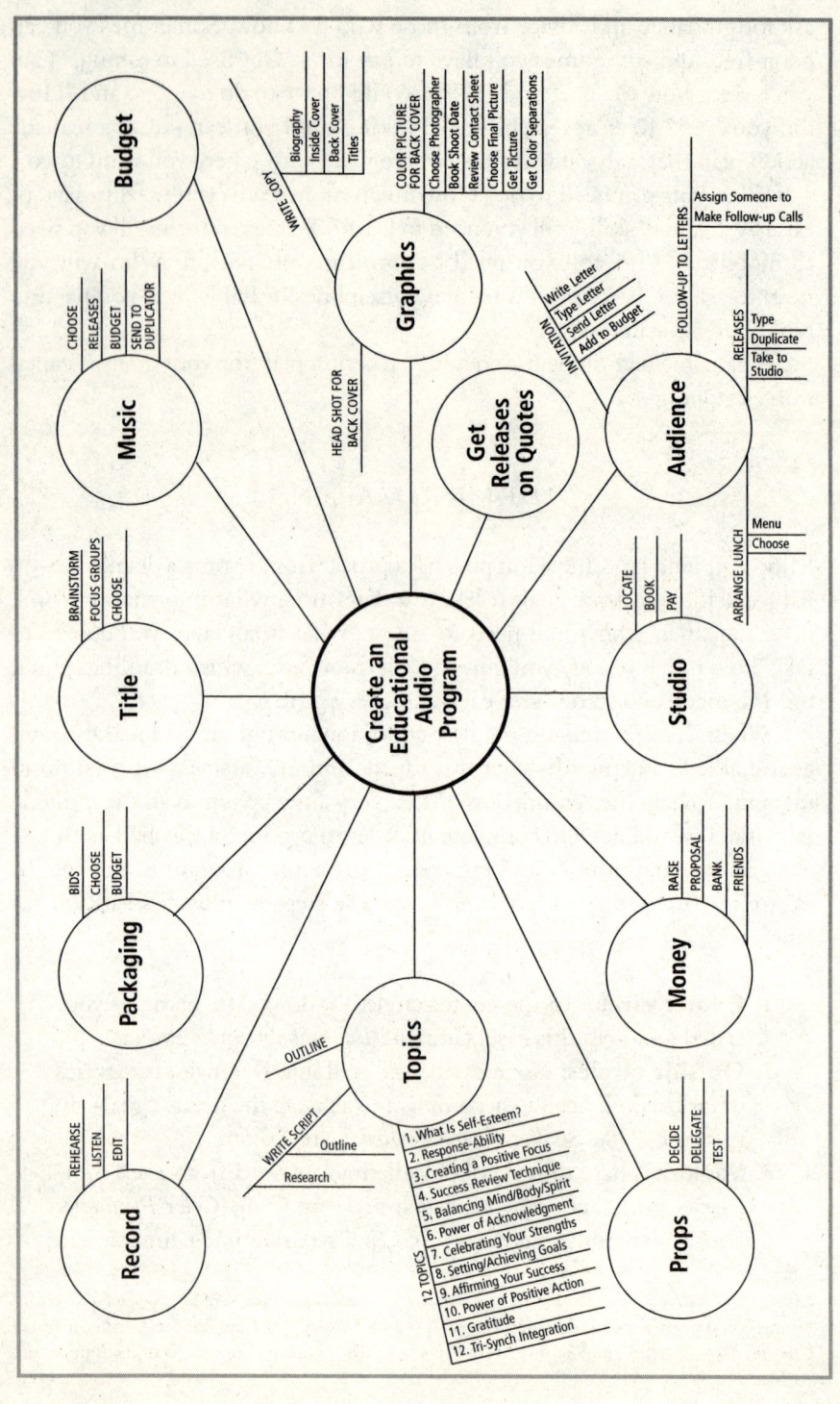

the minicircle, write every single step you'll need to take. Break down each one of the more detailed task spokes with action items to help you create your master to-do list.

NEXT, MAKE A DAILY TO-DO LIST

Once you've completed a mind map for your goal, convert all of the to-do items into daily action items by listing each one on your daily to-do lists and committing to a completion date for each one. Schedule them in the appropriate order into your calendar, then do whatever it takes to stay on schedule.

DO FIRST THINGS FIRST

The goal is to stay on schedule and complete the most important item first. In his excellent book, *Eat That Frog! 21 Great Ways to Stop Procrastinating and Get More Done in Less Time,* Brian Tracy reveals not just how to conquer procrastination but also how to prioritize and complete all of your action items.

In his unique system, Brian advises goal-setters to identify the one to five things you must accomplish on any given day, and then pick the one you absolutely must do first. This becomes your biggest and ugliest frog. If you know you have to eat a big ugly frog before the end of the day, you don't want to spend the whole day dreading eating it. The simplest thing is to eat it first and get it over with. He then suggests you accomplish that most important task first—in essence, eat that frog first—and, by so doing, make the rest of your day much, much easier. It's a great strategy. But unfortunately, most of us leave the biggest and ugliest frog for last, hoping it will go away or somehow become easier. It never does. However, when you accomplish your toughest task early in the day, it sets the tone for the rest of your day. It creates momentum and builds your confidence, both of which move you farther and faster toward your goal.

PLAN YOUR DAY THE NIGHT BEFORE

One of the most powerful tools high achievers use for chunking things down, gaining control over their life, and increasing their productivity is to plan their next day the night before. There are two major reasons why this is such a powerful strategy for success:

1. If you plan your day the night before—making a to-do list and spending a few minutes visualizing exactly how you want the day to go—your subconscious mind will work on these tasks all night long. It will think of creative ways to solve any problem, overcome any obstacle, and achieve your desired outcomes. And if we follow the basic precepts of quantum physics, it will also send out waves of energy that will attract the people and resources to you that are needed to accomplish your goals.*
2. By creating your to-do list the night before, you can start your day running. You know exactly what you're going to do and in what order, and you've already pulled together any materials you need. If you have five telephone calls to make, you would have them written down in the order you plan to make them, with the phone numbers next to the person's name and all the support materials at hand. By midmorning, you would be way ahead of most people, who waste the first half hour of the day clearing their desk, making lists, finding necessary paperwork—in short, just *getting ready* to work.

USE THE ACHIEVERS FOCUSING SYSTEM

A valuable tool that will really keep you focused on achieving all of your goals in the seven areas we explained in your vision (see pages 37–38) is the Achievers Focusing System developed by Les Hewitt of the Achievers Coaching Program. It is a form you can use to plan and hold yourself accountable for 13 weeks of goals and action steps. You can download a copy of the form and instructions on how to use it for free at jackcanfield.com/tsp-resources.

---

*See *The Seven Spiritual Laws of Success: A Practical Guide to the Fulfillment of Your Dreams* by Deepak Chopra (San Rafael, CA: Amber-Allen, 1995); *The Spontaneous Fulfillment of All Desire: Harnessing the Infinite Power of Coincidence* by Deepak Chopra (New York: Harmony Books, 2003); *The Power of Intention: Learning to Co-Create Your World Your Way* by Wayne W. Dyer (Carlsbad, CA.: Hay House, 2004); *The 11th Element: The Key to Unlocking Your Master Blueprint for Wealth and Success* by Robert Scheinfeld (Hoboken, NJ: John Wiley & Sons, 2003); *The Secret* by Rhonda Bryne (New York: Atria Books, 2006); and *Ask and It Is Given* by Esther and Jerry Hicks (Carlsbad, CA: Hay House, 2010).

PRINCIPLE 9

SUCCESS LEAVES CLUES

Long ago, I realized that success leaves clues, and that people who produce outstanding results do specific things to create those results. I believed that if I precisely duplicated the actions of others, I could reproduce the same quality of results that they had.

ANTHONY ROBBINS
Author of *Unlimited Power*

One of the great things about living in today's world of abundance and opportunity is that almost everything you want to do has already been done by someone else. It doesn't matter whether it's losing weight, running a marathon, starting a business, becoming financially independent, triumphing over breast cancer, becoming a social-media influencer, or hosting the perfect dinner party—someone has already done it *and left clues* in the form of books, manuals, audio and video programs, university classes, online courses, seminars, and workshops.

WHO'S ALREADY DONE WHAT YOU WANT TO DO?

If you want to retire a millionaire, for instance, there are hundreds of books, ranging from *The Automatic Millionaire* to *The Millionaire Next Door*, and workshops like Doria Cordova's Money and You.* If you want to have a better relationship with your spouse, you can read John Gray's *Men Are from Mars, Women Are from Venus;* attend a couples workshop; or take one of Gay and Katie Hendricks's seminars.

For virtually everything you want to do, there are books and courses

---

*You can access an updated and ever-expanding list of these kinds of resources at jackcanfield.com/tsp/resources.

on how to do it. Better yet, just a phone call away are people who've already successfully done what you want to do and who are available as teachers, facilitators, mentors, advisors, coaches, and consultants.

Here are three ways you can begin to seek out clues: (1) Seek out a teacher, coach, mentor; a manual, book, audio program, or an Internet resource to help you achieve one of your major goals. (2) Seek out someone who has already done what you want to do, and ask the person if you can interview him or her on how you should proceed. (3) Ask someone if you can shadow them for a day and watch them work. Or offer to be a volunteer, assistant, or intern for someone you can learn from.

WHY PEOPLE DON'T SEEK OUT CLUES

When I was preparing to go on a morning news show in Dallas, I asked the station's makeup artist what her long-term goals were. She said she'd always thought about opening her own beauty salon, so I asked her what she was doing to make that happen.

"Nothing," she said, "because I don't know how to go about it."

I suggested she offer to take a salon owner to lunch and ask how she had opened her own salon.

"You can do that?" the makeup artist exclaimed.

You most certainly can. In fact, you have probably thought about approaching an expert for advice but rejected the idea with thoughts such as, *Why would someone take the time to tell me what they did? Why would they teach me and create their own competition?* Banish those thoughts. You will find that most people love to talk about how they built their business or accomplished their goals. But unfortunately, like the makeup artist in Dallas, most of us don't take advantage of all the resources available to us. Why?

- It never occurs to us. We don't see others using these resources, so we don't do it either. Our parents didn't do it. Our friends aren't doing it. Nobody where we work is doing it.
- It's inconvenient. We'd have to drive across town to a meeting. We'd have to take time away from television, family, or friends.
- Asking others for advice or information puts us up against our fear of rejection. We are afraid to take the risk.
- Connecting the dots in a new way would mean change, and change—even when it's in our best interest—is uncomfortable.
- Connecting the dots means hard work, and frankly, most people don't want to work that hard.

PRINCIPLE

10

RELEASE THE BRAKES

Everything you want is just outside your comfort zone.
ROBERT ALLEN
Coauthor of *The One Minute Millionaire*

Have you ever been driving your car and suddenly realized you've left the emergency brake on? Did you push down harder on the gas to overcome the drag of the brake? No, of course not. You simply released the brake . . . and with no extra effort you started to go faster.

Most people drive through life with their psychological emergency brake on. They hold on to negative images about themselves or suffer the mental and emotional effects of powerful experiences they haven't yet resolved and released. They stay in a comfort zone entirely of their own making. They maintain inaccurate beliefs about reality or harbor guilt and self-doubt. And when they try to achieve their goals, these negative images and preprogrammed comfort zones always cancel out their good intentions—no matter how hard they try.

Successful people, on the other hand, have discovered that instead of using increased willpower as the engine to power their success, it's simply easier to "release the brakes" by letting go of and replacing their limiting beliefs, by changing their self-images, and by releasing negative emotions like fear, resentment, anger, guilt, and shame.

GET OUT OF YOUR COMFORT ZONE

Think of your comfort zone as a prison you live in—a largely self-created prison. It consists of the collection of *can'ts, musts, must nots,* and other unfounded beliefs formed from all the negative thoughts and decisions you have accumulated and reinforced during your lifetime.

Perhaps you've even been *trained* to limit yourself.

DON'T BE AS DUMB AS AN ELEPHANT

A baby elephant is trained at birth to be confined to a very small space. Its trainer will tie its leg with a rope to a wooden post planted deep in the ground. This confines the baby elephant to an area determined by the length of the rope—the elephant's comfort zone. Though the baby elephant will initially try to break the rope, the rope is too strong, and so the baby elephant learns that it can't break the rope. It learns that it has to stay in the area defined by the length of the rope.

When the elephant grows up into a five-ton colossus that could easily break the same rope, it doesn't even try because it learned as a baby that it couldn't break the rope. In this way, the largest elephant can be confined by the puniest little rope.

Perhaps this also describes you—still trapped in a comfort zone by something as puny and weak as the small rope that controls the elephant, except your rope is made up of the limiting beliefs and images that you received and took on when you were young. If this describes you, the good news is that you can change your comfort zone. How? There are four different ways:

1. You can use affirmations and positive self-talk to affirm already having what you want, doing what you want, and being the way you want.
2. You can create powerful and compelling new internal images of having, doing, and being what you want.
3. You can use the revolutionary technique called Tapping Therapy.
4. You can simply change your behavior.

All four of these approaches will shift you out of your old comfort zone.

STOP RE-CREATING THE SAME EXPERIENCE OVER AND OVER!

An important concept that successful people understand is that you are never *stuck*. You just keep re-creating the same experience over and over by thinking the same thoughts, maintaining the same beliefs, speaking the same words, and doing the same things.

Too often, we create an endless loop of reinforcing behavior, which keeps us trapped in a constant downward spiral. Our limiting thoughts create images in our mind, and those images govern our behavior, which in turn reinforces that limiting thought. Imagine thinking that you are going to forget your talking points when you have to give a presentation at work. The thought stimulates a picture of you forgetting a key point. The image creates an experience of fear. The fear clouds your clear thinking, which makes you forget one of your key points, which reinforces your self-talk that you can't speak in front of groups. *See, I knew I would forget what I was supposed to say. I can't speak in front of groups.*

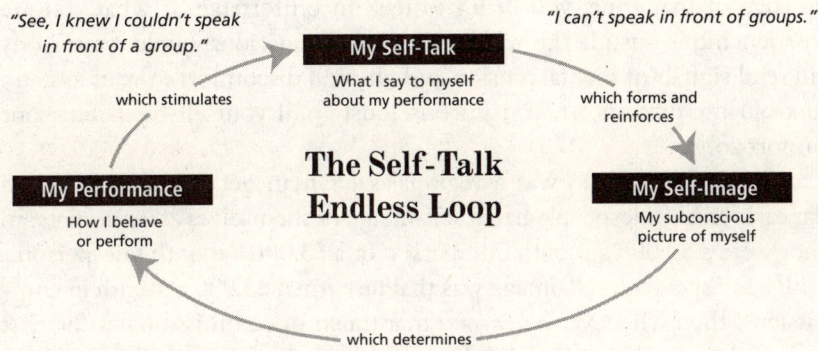

As long as you keep complaining about your present circumstances, your mind will focus on it. By continually talking about, thinking about, and writing about the way things are, you are continually reinforcing those very same neural pathways in your brain that got you to where you are today. And you are continually sending out the same vibrations that will keep attracting the same people and circumstances that you have already created.

To change this cycle, you must focus instead on thinking, talking, and writing about the reality you want to create. You must flood your unconscious with thoughts and images of this new reality.

The significant problems we face cannot be solved by the same level of thinking that created them.

ALBERT EINSTEIN
Physicist and winner of the Nobel Prize

WHAT'S YOUR FINANCIAL TEMPERATURE?

Your comfort zone works the same way the thermostat in your home works. When the temperature in the room approaches the edge of the thermal range you have set, the thermostat sends an electrical signal to the furnace or the air conditioner to turn it on or off. As the temperature in the room begins to change, the electrical signals continue to respond to the changes and keep the temperature within the desired range.

Similarly, you have an internal psychological thermostat that regulates your level of performance in the world. Instead of electrical signals, your internal performance regulator uses discomfort signals to keep you within your comfort zone. As your behavior or performance begins to approach the edge of that zone, you begin to feel uncomfortable. If what you are experiencing is outside the self-image you unconsciously hold, your body will send signals of mental tension and physical discomfort to your system. To avoid the discomfort, you unconsciously pull yourself back into your comfort zone.

My stepfather, who was a regional sales manager for NCR, noticed that each of his salespeople had a self-image of themselves as a salesperson. They were a $2,000 a month salesperson or a $3,000 a month salesperson.

If a salesperson's self-image was that he earned $3,000 a month in commissions, then whenever he earned that much in commissions in the first week of the month, he would slack off for the rest of the month.

On the other hand, if it were near the end of the month and he had only earned $1,500 in commissions, he would put in 16-hour days, work weekends, create new sales proposals, and do everything possible to get to the $3,000 level for that month.

No matter what the circumstance, a person with a $36,000 self-image would always produce a $36,000 income. To do anything else would make them uncomfortable.

I remember one year my stepfather was out selling cash registers on New Year's Eve. He was out well past midnight with the intention of selling two more cash registers so that he would qualify for the annual trip to Hawaii awarded to all salesmen who hit their yearly quota. He had earned the trip for several years running, and his self-image would not allow him to lose out that year. He sold those machines and made the trip. It would have been outside of his comfort zone to do anything less.

Imagine the same scenario in relation to your savings account. Some people are comfortable as long as they have $2,000 in their savings account. Others are uncomfortable if they have any less than eight months' income salted away. Still others are comfortable with no savings and credit card debt of $25,000.

If the person needing eight months' income in savings to feel comfortable is hit with an unexpected medical expense of $16,000, he will curtail his spending, work overtime, have a garage sale—whatever it takes to get his savings back up to the previous level. Likewise, if he suddenly inherits money, he is likely to spend enough of it to stay in that same savings comfort zone.

No doubt you have heard that most lottery winners lose, spend, squander, or give away all of their newfound money within a few years of winning it. In fact, 80% of lottery winners in the United States file for bankruptcy within five years! The reason is because they failed to develop a millionaire mindset. As a result, they subconsciously re-create the reality that matches their previous mindset. They feel uncomfortable with so much money, so they find some way to get back to their old familiar comfort zone.

We have a similar comfort zone for the kinds of restaurants we eat in, the hotels we stay in, the kind of car we drive, the houses we live in, the clothes we wear, the vacations we take, and the type of people we associate with.

If you have ever walked down Fifth Avenue in New York or Rodeo Drive in Beverly Hills, you have probably experienced walking into a store and immediately feeling as if you didn't belong there. The store was just too upscale for you. You felt out of place. That's your comfort zone in operation.

CHANGE YOUR BEHAVIOR

When I first moved to Los Angeles, my new boss took me shopping for clothes at a very upscale men's shop in Westwood. The most I had previously ever paid for a dress shirt was $35 at Nordstrom. The cheapest shirt in this store was $95! I was stunned and broke out in a cold sweat. While my boss purchased many things that day, I bought one Italian designer shirt for $95. I was so far out of my comfort zone, I could hardly breathe. The next week, I wore the shirt and was amazed by how much better it fit, how much better it felt, and how much better I looked wearing it. After a couple more weeks of wearing it once a week, I really fell in love with it. Within a month, I bought another one. Within a year, shirts like that were all I wore. Slowly my comfort zone had changed because I'd gotten used to something better even though it cost more. Today I often pay $300 for custom-made shirts.

When I was on the faculty of the Million Dollar Forum and Income Builders International—two organizations dedicated to teaching people how to become millionaires—all of the trainings were held at the Ritz-Carlton Hotel in Laguna Beach, California, the Hilton Hotel on the

Big Island of Hawaii, and other high-end luxury resort hotels. The reason was to get the participants used to being treated in a first-class way. It was part of stretching their comfort zones—changing the image of who they thought they were. Every training concluded with a black-tie dinner dance. For many of the participants, it was the first time they had ever attended a black-tie affair—another comfort zone stretch.

CHANGE YOUR SELF-TALK WITH AFFIRMATIONS

I've always believed in magic. When I wasn't doing anything in this town, I'd go up every night, sit on Mulholland Drive, look out at the city, stretch out my arms, and say, "Everybody wants to work with me. I'm a really good actor. I have all kinds of great movie offers." I'd just repeat these things over and over, literally convincing myself that I had a couple of movies lined up. I'd drive down that hill, ready to take the world on, going, "Movie offers are out there for me, I just don't hear them yet." It was like total affirmations, antidotes to the stuff that stems from my family background.*

JIM CARREY
Actor

One way to stretch your comfort zone is to bombard your subconscious mind with new thoughts and images—of a big bank account, a trim and healthy body, exciting work, interesting friends, memorable vacations—of all your goals as already complete. The technique you use to do this is called *affirmations*. An affirmation is a statement that describes a goal in its already completed state, such as "I am enjoying watching the sunset from the lanai of my beautiful beachfront condo on the Ka'anapali coast of Maui" or "I am celebrating feeling light and alive at my perfect body weight of one thirty-five."

THE NINE GUIDELINES FOR CREATING EFFECTIVE AFFIRMATIONS

To be effective, your affirmations should be constructed using the following nine guidelines:

---

*From an interview in *Movieline*, July 1994.

1. **Start with the words *I am*.** The words *I am* are the two most powerful words in the language. The subconscious takes any sentence that starts with the words *I am* and interprets it as a command—a directive to make it happen.

2. **Use the present tense.** Describe what you want as though you already have it, as though it is already accomplished.

   Wrong: I am going to get a new red Porsche 911.
   Right: I am enjoying driving my new red Porsche 911.

3. **State it in the positive. Affirm what you want, not what you don't want.** State your affirmations in the positive. The unconscious does not hear the words *no,* or *not.* This means that the statement "Don't slam the door" is heard as "Slam the door." The unconscious thinks in pictures, and the words "Don't slam the door" evoke a picture of slamming the door. The phrase "I am no longer afraid of flying" evokes an image of being afraid of flying, while the phrase "I am enjoying the thrill of flying" evokes an image of enjoyment.

   Wrong: I am no longer afraid of flying.
   Right: I am enjoying the thrill of flying.

4. **Keep it brief.** Think of your affirmation as an advertising jingle. Act as if each word costs $1,000. It needs to be short enough and memorable enough to be easily remembered.

5. **Make it specific.** Vague affirmations produce vague results.

   Wrong: I am driving my new red sports car.
   Right: I am driving my new red Porsche 911.

6. **Include an action word ending with *-ing*.** The active verb adds power to the effect by evoking an image of doing it right now.

   Wrong: I express myself openly and honestly.
   Right: I am confidently expressing myself openly and honestly.

7. **Include at least one dynamic emotion or feeling word.** Include the emotional state you would be feeling if you had already

achieved the goal. Some commonly used words are *enjoying, joyfully, happily, celebrating, proudly, calmly, peacefully, delighted, enthusiastic, lovingly, secure, serenely,* and *triumphant.*

Wrong: I am maintaining my perfect body weight of 178 pounds.
Right: I am feeling agile and great at 178!

Note that the last one has the ring of an advertising jingle. The subconscious loves rhythm and rhymes.

8. **Make affirmations for yourself, not others.** When you are constructing your affirmations, make them describe your behavior, not the behavior of others.

Wrong: I am watching Johnny clean up his room.
Right: I am effectively communicating my needs and desires to Johnny.

9. **Add *or something better*.** When you are affirming getting a specific situation (job, opportunity, vacation), material object (house, car, boat), or relationship (husband, wife, child), always add the words "or something (someone) better." Sometimes our criteria for what we want come from our ego or from our limited experience. Sometimes there is someone or something better that is available for us, so let your affirmations include this phrase when it is appropriate.

Example: I am enjoying living in my beautiful beachfront villa on the Ka'anapali coast of Maui or somewhere better.

Lately, for creating affirmations, I have been using this simple form that was taught by Bob Proctor. It combines all of the above elements and is easy to remember.

I am so happy and grateful now that _____.

Examples would be:

I am so happy and grateful now that I am earning $150,000 a year.

I am so happy and grateful now that I am driving my new Porsche Macan.

I am so happy and grateful now that I am living at my perfect body weight of 145 pounds or less.

I am so happy and grateful now that money is coming to me in increasing amounts through multiple sources on a continuous basis.

HOW TO USE AFFIRMATIONS AND VISUALIZATION

1. Review your affirmations one to three times a day. The best times are first thing in the morning, in the middle of the day to refocus yourself, and around bedtime.
2. If appropriate, read each affirmation out loud.
3. Close your eyes and visualize yourself as the affirmation describes. See it as if you were looking out at the scene from inside of yourself. In other words, don't see yourself standing out there in the scene; see the scene looking out through your eyes as if you were actually living it.
4. Hear any sounds you might hear when you successfully achieve what your affirmation describes—the sound of the surf, the roar of the crowd, the playing of the national anthem. Include other important people in your life congratulating you and telling you how pleased they are with your success.
5. Feel the feelings that you will feel when you achieve that success. The stronger the feelings, the more powerful the process. (If you have difficulty creating the feelings, you can affirm "I am enjoying easily creating powerful feelings in my effective work with affirmations.")
6. Say your affirmation again, and then repeat this process with the next affirmation.

OTHER WAYS TO USE AFFIRMATIONS

1. Post 3" × 5" index cards with your affirmations around your home.
2. Hang pictures of the things you want around your house or your room. You can put a picture of yourself in the picture.

3. Repeat your affirmations during "wasted time" such as waiting in line, exercising, and driving. You can repeat them silently or out loud.
4. Record your affirmations and listen to them while you work, exercise, drive, or fall asleep.
5. Have one of your parents make a recording of encouraging things you would like to have heard from them when you were growing up or words of encouragement and permission you would currently like to hear.
6. Repeat your affirmations in the first person ("I am . . ."), second person ("You are . . ."), and third person ("He/she is . . ." or "Your name is. . .").
7. Put your affirmations on your screen saver on your computer, tablet, or smartphone, so you'll see them every time you use your computer.

AFFIRMATIONS WORK

I first learned about the power of affirmations in my twenties when W. Clement Stone challenged me to set a goal that was so far beyond my current circumstances it would literally astound me if I achieved it. Though I thought Stone's challenge had merit, I didn't really apply it to my life in a serious way until several years later when I decided to make the jump from earning $25,000 a year to making $100,000 or more.

The first thing I did was to craft an affirmation after one I'd seen by Florence Scovell Shinn. My affirmation was

> God is my infinite supply and large sums of money come to me quickly and easily under the grace of God for the highest good of all concerned. I am happily and easily earning, saving, and investing $100,000 a year.

Next, I created a huge replica of a $100,000 bill, which I affixed to the ceiling above my bed. On awakening, I would see the bill, close my eyes, repeat my affirmation, and visualize what I would be enjoying if I were living a $100,000-a-year lifestyle. I envisioned the house I would live in, the furnishings and artwork I would own, the car I would drive, and the vacations I would take. I also created the feelings I would experience once I had already attained that lifestyle.

Soon I awoke one morning with my first $100,000 idea. It occurred to me that if I could sell 400,000 copies of my book, *100 Ways to Enhance Self-Concept in the Classroom,* on which I received a 25¢-per-copy royalty, I would earn a $100,000 income. I added to my morning visualizations the image of my book flying off bookstore shelves and my publisher writing me a $100,000 check. Not long after, a freelance journalist approached me and wrote an article about my work for the *National Enquirer.* As a result, thousands of additional copies of my book were sold that month.

Almost daily, more and more money-making ideas flowed into my mind. For instance, I took out small ads and sold the book on my own—making $3.00 per copy instead of just 25¢. I started a mail-order catalog of mine and others' books on self-esteem and made even more money from these same buyers. The University of Massachusetts saw my catalog and invited me to sell books at a weekend conference, helping me generate more than $2,000 in two days—and introducing me to another strategy for making $100,000 a year.

At the same time I was visualizing greater book sales, I also got the idea to generate more income from my workshops and seminars. When I asked a friend who did similar work how I could charge higher fees, he revealed he was *already* charging more than double what I was being paid! With his encouragement, I tripled my speaking fee and discovered the schools that were hiring me to speak had budgets even higher than that.

My affirmation was paying off big time. But if I hadn't set the goal to make $100,000 and been diligent about affirming and visualizing it, I never would have raised my speaking fees, started a mail-order bookstore, attended a major conference, or been interviewed for a major publication.

As a result, my income that year skyrocketed from $25,000 to over $92,000!

Of course, I missed my $100,000 goal by $8,000, but I can assure you I wasn't depressed about it. On the contrary, I was ecstatic. I had almost quadrupled my income in less than a year, using the power of visualization and affirmations coupled with the willingness to act when I had an "inspired idea."

After our $92,000 year, my wife asked me, "If affirmations worked for $100,000, do you think they would also work for $1 million?" Using a new affirmation—"I am happily depositing my million-dollar royalty check from my bestselling book"—along with visualization, I achieved that goal, too, and have continued to make $1 million or more every year since.

DON'T WAIT 30 YEARS TO USE THIS STRATEGY

Joe Newberry heard me tell this story at a business networking breakfast in the 1980s. But he didn't get around to putting his own $100,000 bill on the ceiling until 30 years later.

It was June and he was looking for ways to boost his income. When he saw me retell that story in the movie *The Secret,* he rushed home to put his own $100,000 bill above his bed, where he would see it each morning when he woke up. By September, people were calling to hire him as a consultant. Soon after, he was representing two recording labels and negotiating deals for major artists.

And in January, he flew to New York to pitch Barnes & Noble—as one of dozens of other sales representatives pitching that day—asking them to place an order for the recorded works he represented. After chatting pleasantly with the Barnes & Noble buyer about her kids and family, Joe watched in amazement as she pulled out the necessary paperwork and wrote him an order on the spot.

It wasn't the modest order Joe had expected, however.

As he headed for the elevator and looked at the paperwork in his hand, he quickly calculated his commissions on the far more substantial order she had written. To the penny, he had just earned $100,000!

PRINCIPLE 11

SEE WHAT YOU WANT, GET WHAT YOU SEE

Imagination is everything. It is the preview of life's coming attractions.
ALBERT EINSTEIN
Physicist and winner of the Nobel Prize

Visualization—or the act of creating compelling and vivid pictures in your mind—may be the most underutilized success tool you possess because it greatly accelerates the achievement of any success in three powerful ways.

1. Visualization activates the creative powers of your subconscious mind.
2. Visualization focuses your brain by programming its *reticular activating system* (RAS) to notice available resources that were always there but were previously unnoticed.
3. Visualization, through the Law of Attraction, magnetizes and attracts to you the people, resources, and opportunities you need to achieve your goal.*

When you perform any task in real life, researchers have found, your brain uses the same identical processes it would use if you were only vividly visualizing that activity. In other words, your brain sees no difference whatsoever between visualizing something and actually doing it.

This principle also applies to learning anything new. Research at Harvard University found that students who visualized in advance performed tasks with nearly 100% accuracy, whereas students who didn't visualize achieved only 55% accuracy.

Visualization simply makes the brain achieve more. And though none

---
*The Law of Attraction basically states that whatever you think about, talk about, fantasize about, and feel strongly about, you will attract into your life.

of us were ever taught this in school, sports psychologists and peak performance experts have been popularizing the power of visualization since the 1980s. Almost all Olympic and professional athletes now employ the power of visualization.

Jack Nicklaus, the legendary golfer with 73 major tournament victories and $5.7 million in winnings, once said, "I never hit a shot, not even in practice, without having a very sharp, in-focus picture of it in my head. It's like a color movie. First I 'see' where I want it to finish, nice and white and sitting high on the bright green grass. Then the scene quickly changes, and I 'see' the ball going there: its path, trajectory, and shape, even its behavior on landing. Then there's sort of a fade-out, and the next scene shows me making the kind of swing that will turn the previous images into reality."

HOW VISUALIZATION WORKS TO ENHANCE PERFORMANCE

When you visualize your goals as already complete each and every day, it creates a conflict (structural tension) in your subconscious mind between what you are visualizing and what you currently have. Your subconscious mind works to resolve that conflict by turning your current reality into the new, more exciting vision.

This conflict, when intensified over time through constant visualization, actually causes three things to happen:

1. It programs your brain's RAS to start letting into your awareness anything that will help you achieve your goals.
2. It activates your subconscious mind to create solutions for getting the goals you want. You'll start waking up in the morning with new ideas. You'll find yourself having ideas in the shower, while you are taking long walks, and while you are driving to work.
3. It creates new levels of motivation. You'll start to notice you are unexpectedly doing things that take you to your goal. All of a sudden, you are raising your hand in class, volunteering to take on new assignments at work, speaking out at staff meetings, asking more directly for what you want, saving money for the things that you want, paying down a credit card debt, or taking more risks in your personal life.

Let's take a closer look at how the RAS works. At any one time, there are about 11 million bits of information streaming into your brain—most of which you cannot attend to, nor do you need to. So your brain's RAS filters most of them out, letting into your awareness only those signals that can help you survive and achieve your most important goals.

So how does your RAS know what to let in to your awareness and what to filter out? It lets in anything that will help you achieve the goals you have set and are *constantly* visualizing and affirming. It also lets in anything that matches your beliefs and images about yourself, others, and the world.

The RAS is a powerful tool, but it can only look for ways to achieve the exact pictures you give it. Your creative subconscious doesn't think in words—it thinks in pictures. So how does all this help your effort to become successful and achieve the life of your dreams?

When you give your brain specific, colorful, and vividly compelling pictures to manifest—it will seek out and capture all the information necessary to bring that picture into reality for you. If you give your mind a $10,000 problem, it will come up with a $10,000 solution. If you give your mind a $1 million problem, it will come up with a $1 million solution.

If you give it pictures of a beautiful home, an adoring spouse, an exciting career, and exotic vacations, it will go to work on achieving those. By contrast, if you are constantly feeding it negative, fearful, and anxious pictures—guess what?—it will work to achieve those, too.

THE PROCESS FOR VISUALIZING YOUR FUTURE

The process of visualizing for success is really quite simple. All you have to do is close your eyes and see your goals as already complete.

If one of your objectives is to own a nice house on the lake, then close your eyes and see yourself walking through the exact house you would like to own. Fill in all of the details. What does the exterior look like? How is it landscaped? What kind of view does it have? What do the living room, kitchen, master bedroom, dining room, family room, and den look like? How is it furnished? Go from room to room and fill in all of the details.

Make the images as clear and bright as possible. This goes for any goal you make—whether it's in the area of work, play, family, personal finances, relationships, or philanthropy. Write down each of your goals and objectives, then review them, affirm them, and visualize them every day.

Then, each morning when you awake and each night before you go to bed, read through the list of goals out loud, pausing after each one to close your eyes and re-create the visual image of that completed goal in your mind. Continue through the list until you have visualized each goal as complete and fulfilled. The whole process will take between 10 and

15 minutes, depending on how many goals you have. If you meditate, do your visualization right after you finish meditating. The deepened state you have achieved in meditation will heighten the impact of your visualizations.

ADDING SOUNDS AND FEELINGS TO THE PICTURES

To multiply the effect many times over, add sound, smells, tastes, and feelings to your pictures. What sounds would you be hearing, what smells would you be smelling, what tastes would you be tasting, and—most important—what emotions and bodily sensations would you be feeling if you had already achieved your goal?

If you were imagining your dream house on the beach, you might add in the sound of the surf lapping at the shore outside your home, the sound of your kids playing on the sand, and the sound of your spouse's voice thanking you for being such a good provider.

Then add in the feelings of pride of ownership, satisfaction at having achieved your goal, and the feeling of the sun on your face as you sit on your deck looking out at a beautiful sunset over the ocean.

"Don't disturb Daddy. He's busy visualizing unparalleled success in the business world and, by extension, a better life for us all."

FUEL YOUR IMAGES WITH EMOTION

By far, these feelings and emotions are what propel your vision forward. Researchers know that when accompanied by intense emotions, an image or scene can stay locked in the memory forever.

I'm sure you remember exactly where you were when the World Trade Center collapsed on September 11, 2001, when the U.S. Capitol was invaded on January 6, 2021, or perhaps when Hamas led surprise attacks against Israel on October 7, 2023. Your brain remembers it all in great detail because not only did your brain filter information you needed for survival during these tense moments but also the images themselves were created with intense emotion. These intense emotions actually stimulate the growth of additional spiny protuberances on the dendrites of brain neurons, which ultimately creates more neural connections, thus locking in the memory much more solidly. You can bring this same emotional intensity to your own visualizations by adding inspiring music, real-life smells, deeply felt passion, even loudly shouting your affirmations with exaggerated enthusiasm. The more passion, excitement, and energy you can muster, the more powerful your ultimate results will be.

VISUALIZATION WORKS

Olympic gold medalist Peter Vidmar describes his use of visualization in his successful pursuit of the gold:

> To keep us focused on our Olympic goal, we began ending our workouts by visualizing our dream. We visualized ourselves actually competing in the Olympics and achieving our dream by practicing what we thought would be the ultimate gymnastics scenario.
>
> I'd say, "Okay, Tim, let's imagine it's the men's gymnastics team finals of the Olympic Games. The United States team is on its last event of the night, which just happens to be the high bar. The last two guys up for the United States are Tim Daggett and Peter Vidmar. Our team is neck and neck with the People's Republic of China, the reigning world champions, and we have to perform our routines perfectly to win the Olympic team gold medal."
>
> At that point we'd each be thinking, *Yeah, right. We're never going to be neck and neck with those guys. They were number one at the Budapest world championships, while our team didn't even win a medal. It's never going to happen.*

But what if it did happen? How would we feel?

We'd close our eyes and, in this empty gym at the end of a long day, we'd visualize an Olympic arena with 13,000 people in the seats and another 200 million watching live on television. Then we'd practice our routines. First, I'd be the announcer. I'd cup my hands around my mouth and say, "Next up, from the United States of America, Tim Daggett." Then Tim would go through his routine as if it were the real thing.

Then Tim would go over to the corner of the gym, cup his hands around his mouth, and, in his best announcer voice, say, "Next up, from the United States of America, Peter Vidmar."

Then it was my turn. In my mind, I had one chance to perfectly perform my routine in order for our team to win the gold medal. If I didn't, we'd lose.

Tim would shout out, "Green light," and I'd look at the superior judge, who was usually our coach Mako. I'd raise my hand, and he'd raise his right back. Then I'd turn, face the bar, grab hold, and begin my routine.

Well, a funny thing happened on July 31, 1984.

It was the Olympic Games, men's gymnastics team finals in Pauley Pavilion on the UCLA campus. The 13,000 seats were all filled, and a television audience in excess of 200 million around the world tuned in. The United States team was on its last event of the night, the high bar. The last two guys up for the United States just happened to be Tim Daggett and Peter Vidmar. And just as we visualized, our team was neck and neck with the People's Republic of China. We had to perform our high bar routines perfectly to win the gold medal.

I looked at Coach Mako, my coach for the past 12 years. As focused as ever, he simply said, "Okay, Peter, let's go. You know what to do. You've done it a thousand times, just like every day back in the gym. Let's just do it one more time, and let's go home. You're prepared."

He was right. I had planned for this moment and visualized it hundreds of times. I was prepared to perform my routine. Rather than seeing myself actually standing in the Olympic arena with 13,000 people in the stands and 200 million watching on television, in my mind I pictured myself back in the UCLA gym at the end of the day with two people left in the gym.

When the announcer said, "From the United States of America, Peter Vidmar," I imagined it was my buddy Tim Daggett saying it. When the green light came on, indicating it was time for the routine, I imagined that it wasn't really a green light but that it was Tim shouting, "Green light!" And when I raised my hand toward the superior judge from East Germany, in my mind I was signaling my coach, just like I had signaled him every day at the end of hundreds of workouts. In the gym, I always visualized I was at the Olympic finals. At the Olympic finals, I visualized I was back in the gym.

I turned, faced the bar, jumped up, and grabbed on. I began the same routine I had visualized and practiced day after day in the gym. I was in memory mode, going yet again where I'd already gone hundreds of times. I quickly made it past the risky double-release move that had harpooned my chances at the world championships. I moved smoothly through the rest of my routine and landed a solid dismount, where I anxiously waited for my score from the judges.

With a deep voice the announcement came through the speaker, "The score for Peter Vidmar is 9.95." "Yes!" I shouted. "I did it!" The crowd cheered loudly as my teammates and I celebrated our victory.

Thirty minutes later, we were standing on the Olympic medal platform in the Olympic arena with 13,000 people in the stands and over 200 million watching on television, while the gold medals were officially draped around our necks. Tim, me, and our teammates stood proudly wearing our gold medals as the national anthem played and the American flag was raised to the top of the arena. It was a moment we visualized and practiced hundreds of times in the gym. Only this time, it was for real.

VISUALIZATION HELPED HER WALK AGAIN

The first time Heather O'Brien Walker heard about positive self-talk and visualization was when she saw me in the film *The Secret*.

"I was glued to the screen," she told me, "when you told the story of how visualization had brought you so much success." Heather was hooked. But how could she create images that were just as powerful, she wondered.

She chose to combine the principle of visualization with her experience in Hollywood—where she had worked among many of Hollywood's greatest stars including Elizabeth Taylor, Tom Cruise, Drew Barrymore, Bruce Willis, Patrick Swayze, and Demi Moore. She knew that people in the film industry are masters at creating compelling images that pull you into another world. In fact, Heather had already seen stunning visual images flicker across the screen and take moviegoers on emotional journeys that literally changed the way they looked at life.

She decided to create her own moving images—"mind movies" she called them—with positive self-talk in place of the musical score. Over the years, these movies had been very effective in helping Heather overcome obstacles. At the same time, she had also developed a mantra that she repeated during trying times—"Don't give up, get up!"

Ironically, Heather had no idea that her mantra and "mind movies" would literally become critical to her very survival.

In July 2011, as Heather was joyfully planning the details of her upcoming wedding, she also landed an executive position with a luxury retailer—overseeing a staff of 30 cosmetics consultants, 50 vendors, and millions of dollars in product. Barely a month into her new job, Heather tripped over a cardboard box filled with trash that someone had carelessly left in a stockroom walkway. As she fell violently forward, Heather struck the front of her head—first on a heavy metal shelf, knocking her unconscious, and then again as she fell face-first onto the concrete floor.

Her fiancé, TW, frantically rushed to the hospital upon being notified.

And, as Heather awakened in the hospital ICU, she knew something serious had happened to her. The entire room was spinning and lurching like a carnival ride. Her head felt like it was being crushed in a vice, and there was an ear-piercing ringing in her head. She could barely see shapes and objects, yet the light in the room was blinding. Thunderous sounds surrounded her, too—as if someone had turned up the volume full blast in her ears. As she struggled to sit up and make sense out of it all, she made a terrifying discovery . . . she couldn't move her legs.

Heather later learned that she had suffered a traumatic brain injury—and that the blows to her head would effect the functioning of her entire body from that day forward. She couldn't feel her legs—or even move them without physically picking them up using special straps that felt like lead weights. She couldn't even sit up because the dizziness and disorientation made her feel ill. When she tried to speak, her words came out garbled and slurred. She couldn't recall details or follow a conversation.

To make matters worse, her doctors were not encouraging about her recovery. People who had sustained similar trauma, they said, were living out their lives in nursing homes unable to function outside of bed. And some would just slip into a coma and pass away.

It was then that Heather knew the only person responsible for bringing about her recovery would be herself.

Immediately, she began building a new "mind movie"—this time focused on her recovery. The problem was that she was attempting to use her brain to heal herself, when her brain was the very thing that had been so deeply injured! As much of a challenge as it was, however, she knew that visualization would be an essential asset to her recovery.

For the next month, Heather worked hard on her therapy and replaying her "mind movie." She desperately wanted to go home, but was warned that—most likely—she'd never be completely free of the vast array of symptoms she suffered. Eventually, still unable to walk, care for herself, or doing anything on her own, Heather was released to the full-time care of her fiancé.

TW had to bathe her, dress her, feed her, take her to the bathroom, and manage all her medications and therapy—all while trying to run his business.

Then Heather was dealt another devastating blow.

One week after being released from the hospital, on the way home from a doctor's appointment, she and TW were hit by a reckless and impaired driver, causing a second traumatic brain injury as Heather's air bag deployed and sent her head crashing into the passenger window. Considering her existing injuries, Heather was lucky to be alive. And, as if that weren't enough adversity to handle, TW was also seriously injured—sustaining a broken foot and a severe back injury that would later require several surgeries.

The next several weeks were some of the darkest days they had ever faced. Yet Heather continually replayed her "mind movie" and used her "Don't give up, get up" mantra.

One day shortly after the car accident, TW approached Heather with an idea. He had an inspiration for a new "mind movie," he told her—planning their wedding and officially setting the date. At first, Heather was aghast. In fact, she was angry that TW would even suggest such a thing!

"Wheeling down the aisle in a wheelchair, in pain, trying to recite garbled words—with the very great possibility that I will lose track of what I'm saying?!" she exclaimed. "No way. Making a complete fool of myself is not what I had in mind for our wedding."

As Heather recounted the story . . .

> I will never forget TW, gently taking hold of the armrests of my wheelchair, pulling me close to him and looking me directly in the eye saying, in his usual joking manner, "You are going to be Mrs. Walker, so it's kind of important for you to get up and get yourself WALKing again quickly. You will walk down that aisle by yourself."
>
> Always great at making me laugh, but understanding the seriousness

behind the joke, I looked right back into his eyes and—as if my heart was the one who responded—I said, "I believe it."

I concentrated many times a day on re-playing a new "mind movie"—that of my barefoot beach wedding where I saw myself walking down the aisle toward the gently splashing waves, feeling the sand between my toes and the breeze on my face—all as my mantra played in the background, *Don't give up, get up.*

I am proud to say that on April 14, 2012—seven months after sustaining my second brain injury—TW and I were married in a beautiful beach ceremony where I did indeed walk down the aisle by myself... just as I had heard and seen in my "mind movie" thousands of times before.

Today, Heather shares her story through keynote speeches, workshops, and coaching sessions with clients from around the world. She's also published her story in a new book called *Don't Give Up, Get Up!*

At the limit of her perseverance, Heather recovered through the power of visualization.

WHAT IF I DON'T SEE ANYTHING WHEN I VISUALIZE?

Some people are what psychologists refer to as *eidetic visualizers.* When they close their eyes, they see everything in bright, clear, three-dimensional Technicolor images. Most of us, however, are noneidetic visualizers. That means you don't really *see* an image as much as you just *think* it. This is perfectly okay. It still works just as well. Do the visualization exercise of imagining your goals as already complete twice a day, every day, and you will still get the same benefit as those people who claim to actually see the image.

USE PRINTED PICTURES TO HELP YOU

If you have trouble seeing your goals, use pictures, images, and symbols you collect to keep your conscious and subconscious mind focused on your goals. For example, if one of your goals is to own a new Lexus LS 500, you can take your camera down to your local Lexus dealer and ask a salesperson to take a picture of you sitting behind the wheel.

If your goal is to visit Paris, find a poster of the Eiffel Tower—then cut out a picture of yourself and place it at the base of the Eiffel Tower as if it were a photograph taken of you in Paris. Several years ago I did this with a picture of the Sydney Opera House, and within a year I was in Sydney, Australia, standing in front of it.

If your goal is to be a millionaire, you might want to write yourself a check for $1,000,000 or create a bank statement that shows your bank account or your stock portfolio with a $1,000,000 balance.

Mark Victor Hansen and I created a mock-up of the *New York Times* bestsellers list with the original *Chicken Soup for the Soul*® in the number one spot. Within 15 months, that dream became a reality. Four years later, we achieved a *Guinness* World Record for having seven books on the *New York Times* bestsellers list at the same time.

USE VISION BOARDS

Once you have found or created these images, you can place them—one to a page—in a three-ring binder that you review every day. Or you could create a *vision board*—a collage of all these images that you place somewhere where you will see them every day.

To create your vision board, scour through magazines and catalogs, research online image libraries, or snap photos of your own that resonate with your goals. To use the example of the Lexus LS 500 mentioned above, you can simply go to Google, type in Lexus LS 500, and then click on IMAGES. Hundreds of pictures of that car will appear. Click on the one you want and then print it. I actually find most of my images that way.

You can also select images, headlines, words, or numbers that both represent your desired goals as already achieved and also evoke strong emotions in you, such as joy, pride, excitement, and confidence. Not all images need to be the same size. In fact, your biggest goals could justify larger images or words.

To create the collage itself, opt for a backing board in a soothing hue, like serene blue, or choose a more vibrant color to promote optimism and motivation. Once you've arranged and glued down the images, place your vision board in a prominent location, such as on your bedroom wall or in your office space, ensuring that you'll see it every day. I also recommend taking a few moments every day to really stop and look at the images on your vision board and imagine what it would feel like to actually have already acquired or achieved everything on it.

I find it interesting that when NASA was working on putting a man on the moon, they had a huge picture of the moon covering the entire wall, from floor to ceiling, of their main construction area. Everyone was clearly visualizing the goal, and they reached that goal two years ahead of schedule!

VISION BOARDS AND GOAL BOOKS MADE THEIR DREAMS COME TRUE

In 1995, John Assaraf created a vision board and put it up on the wall in his home office. Whenever he saw a materialistic thing he wanted or a trip he wanted to take, he'd get a photo of it and glue it to the board. Then he'd see himself already enjoying the object of his desire.

In May 2000, having just moved into his new home in Southern California a few weeks earlier, he was sitting in his office one morning when his five-year-old son Keenan came in and sat on a couple of boxes that had been in storage for over four years. Keenan asked his father what was in the boxes. When John told him his vision boards were in the boxes, Keenan replied, "Your vision whats?"

John opened one of the boxes to show Keenan a vision board. John smiled as he looked at the first board and saw pictures of a Mercedes sports car, a watch, and some other items, all of which he had acquired by then.

But as he pulled out the second board, he began to cry. On that board was a picture of the house he had just bought and was living in! Not a house *like* it but *the* house! The 7,000-square-foot house that sits on six acres of spectacular views, with a 3,000-square-foot guest house and office complex, a tennis court, and 320 orange trees—that very home was a home he had seen in a picture that he had cut out of *Dream Homes* magazine four years earlier!

THE MAGIC OF VISUALIZING

Create a vision of who you want to be, and then live into that picture as if it were already true.

ARNOLD SCHWARZENEGGER
Actor, body builder, film producer, and former governor of California

When Kabir Khan was six years old, he found his life's calling the night he saw the world's greatest magician, David Copperfield, perform on television. For days, all he could talk about was the magic show. A few weeks later his parents bought him a magic kit that had a device in it that made coins vanish. He spent hours in his room practicing. When he turned 11, his mother bought him a full set of magic equipment, and he started performing at birthday parties and his school.

As the years passed, his goals became more ambitious. He longed to train with the best magicians in the world, all of whom were in America. But how could he get there? His family didn't have a lot of money and they expected him to pursue a normal career. So after high school, he attended college and studied marketing. But he also kept his dream alive by performing regularly at one of the large hotels in Kuala Lumpur.

Then for his twentieth birthday, he received a copy of *The Success Principles*.

From the very first page, he was hooked, and when he learned that I was coming to speak in Kuala Lumpur, he knew he had to come see me.

At the training, he heard me talk about writing down your goals, creating a vision board, using affirmations, and taking 100% responsibility for your life. These were all things he had read about in *The Success Principles*, but for some reason he'd been holding back from putting them into action. Now he dove in!

One of the principles I teach is "Act As If." Act as if you are already where you want to be. This means thinking like, dressing like, acting like, and feeling like the person who has already achieved your goal. So he asked himself, *If I were already a world-famous magician, how would I act? What would I wear? Where would I shop?* Thinking that David Copperfield would go only to the best stores, he took the train to the high-end mall, where he saw a shop displaying beautiful watches of all types.

One watch, made by a Swiss company called Fortis, really attracted him. The clerk said it was a watch that the Russian astronauts wore. As soon as he placed it on his wrist, he fell in love with the feel of it; it was so solid and well made. But it cost $3,000! He didn't have that kind of money.

Using his cell phone, he took a picture of the watch, still on his wrist. At home, he printed out the photo and pasted it on his vision board. Remembering my instructions, he made a point to look at the picture of the Fortis on his wrist each day.

About six months after my workshop, Kabir found a group willing to pay for him to go to magic school in America! But his joy was short-lived, because after more consideration, the group decided that he was too young. They told him he should finish college and then come back and ask again. He was devastated and humiliated. He'd told all his friends that he was going to America. Now what would he say?

He stayed at home for a few days, feeling terrible. Then he read in the paper that I was scheduled to give another talk in Kuala Lumpur the very next day. He immediately went to the hotel where he thought I'd be staying and sat in the lobby for six hours, holding his copy of *The Success Principles* and scanning each new arrival coming through the door. Finally, he saw me come in, walked over to me, held up the book, and said, "Jack, I need your help." Recognizing him from my last visit, I invited him up to my suite to talk.

When he finished telling me his story, I said, "You've done well, Kabir, but you need to refine your goals. Don't say, 'I want to study magic in America.' Say, 'I *am* studying magic in America.' Change your vision board to reflect this. Use images and phrases that create the feeling of already having what you want."

I reminded him of Principles 17 and 18, "Ask! Ask! Ask!" and "Reject Rejection." "Remember, there are a million people out there. If you don't get your yes—you just haven't asked the right person yet."

After my pep talk, he began asking everyone he could think of to sponsor him: businessmen, community leaders, even the prime minister! He was relentless. And to keep himself accountable, he emailed me regularly with progress reports. (Remember the research on the importance of being accountable to another person? See page 77.)

Not long afterward, a successful Chinese businessman named Mr. Wong offered to pay Kabir's way to America. After meeting with Kabir's family, Mr. Wong handed Kabir a check for 80,000 Ringgit ($23,000 U.S.)—20,000 Ringgit more than the amount he'd put on his vision board! With that money, he was able to go to the United States and attend magic school for a year, graduating with a certificate and an even fiercer desire to become a world-famous magician—the Malaysian David Copperfield!

Back in Kuala Lumpur, he began performing regularly throughout Malaysia and eventually all over the Middle East and Asia. He was steadily gaining momentum toward his goal, but to really hit the big time, he knew he'd have to perform in the United States—specifically at the Magic Castle in Hollywood and at a club or hotel in Las Vegas.

Now, the Magic Castle is a very prestigious venue for a magician. Only handpicked magicians are allowed to perform there before its elite audience. His experience with Mr. Wong's check had convinced him of the power of visualizing, so he had a friend make a mock-up of a newspaper article with the headline MALAYSIAN MAGICIAN TO PERFORM IN HOLLYWOOD. In the article, he included a photo of himself and the news that he'd been invited to perform at the Magic Castle in Hollywood and also in Las Vegas.

He put this "article" on his vision board and read it every day, making a point to experience the same feelings of gratitude and exhilaration he'd have if it were real. It got so that just walking by his vision board would fill his heart with joy.

The picture of the Fortis on his wrist was also still pinned to his vision board, and Kabir included it in his daily visualization, too. He had continued to save money toward purchasing it, and when he finally had the amount he needed, he set off to buy the watch. But when he walked into the shop, his heart stopped—the whole Fortis display was gone! The salesman told him that the watches weren't selling well in Malaysia, so they'd stopped stocking them. Seeing his disappointment, the man said, "Hold on a sec. Let me just look in the back." He returned with a pile of watches he said they offered in private shows and dumped them on the counter. There it was! His watch! He picked it up and put it on.

The clerk told him that, because it was discontinued, he would give him a big discount. So he paid just $1,000 for his dream watch!

Then, after a year of visualizing and practicing other techniques from *The Success Principles,* he received an invitation to perform at The Magic Castle. He also booked a few engagements in some Las Vegas nightclubs. All that was missing now were enough funds to travel to the United States; his fees wouldn't cover all his expenses—even using the money he'd saved on the watch. Determined not to let this opportunity slip away, he racked his brain for ways to raise the money.

That's when he had a brilliant idea. He picked up the phone and called the Fortis sales representative for Singapore, who had heard about Kabir's enthusiasm for his Fortis and his persistence in getting it. In fact, he had long considered Kabir an unofficial Fortis ambassador, having inspired a number of people to purchase one.

"Mr. Michael," Kabir said, "it's confirmed! I'm going to be the first Malaysian magician to perform in Hollywood and Las Vegas! This could be a great opportunity for Fortis. Would you like to sponsor my U.S. tour?" Mr. Michael contacted the Fortis executives in Switzerland and called him back the next day to tell him they had agreed to sponsor him! He was going to the USA!

The trip was fantastic and performing onstage at The Magic Castle and in Las Vegas was every bit as exciting and fulfilling as he had imagined it would be. But one of the most satisfying moments of all happened before he even left Malaysia. Looking online, he couldn't believe his eyes when he saw an article about his upcoming trip on Yahoo News. He had been reading his made-up headline for months and there it was, but this time for real: MALAYSIAN MAGICIAN TO PERFORM IN HOLLYWOOD. He had done it! And quickly too—he was only 26 years old.

The fact that he was the first ever Malaysian magician to be personally invited to perform in Hollywood and Las Vegas, along with his record of 21 straight shows in Hollywood, earned him an honorary award by the Malaysian Book of Records.

Kabir continues to perform internationally and even gave a recent command performance for the Sheikh of Dubai—but there's more. Mr. Wong and he are now business partners and have several exciting and lucrative projects together, including the iconic Revolving Restaurant at the famous Kuala Lumpur Tower, the sixth highest restaurant in the world!

When Kabir first learned magic, one of his favorite tricks was to make money disappear. Years later, he credits *The Success Principles* for teaching him another kind of magic, the kind that makes money—and fame, success, and happiness—appear! Today he tells his audiences, "Magic is believing anything can happen."

START NOW

Set aside time each and every day to visualize every one of your goals as already complete. This is one of the most vital things you can do to make your dreams come true. Some psychologists are now claiming that one hour of visualization is worth seven hours of physical effort. That's a tall claim, but it makes an important point—visualization is one of the strongest tools in your success toolbox. Make sure you use it.

You don't need to visualize your future achievements for a whole hour. Just 10 to 15 minutes is plenty. Azim Jamal, a prominent speaker in Canada, recommends what he calls "the Hour of Power"—20 minutes of visualization and meditation, 20 minutes of exercise, and 20 minutes of reading inspirational or informational books. Imagine what would happen to your life if you did this every day.

PRINCIPLE 12

ACT AS IF

Believe and act as if it were impossible to fail.

CHARLES F. KETTERING
Inventor with over 140 patents and honorary doctorates
from nearly 30 universities

One of the great strategies for success is to act as if you *already are where you want to be*. This means thinking like, talking like, dressing like, acting like, and feeling like the person who has already achieved your goal. Acting as if sends powerful commands to your subconscious mind to find creative ways to achieve your goals. It programs the *reticular activating system* (RAS) in your brain to start noticing anything that will help you succeed, and it sends strong messages to the universe that this end goal is something you really want.

START ACTING AS IF

The first time I noticed this phenomenon was at my local bank. There were several tellers working there, and I noticed that one in particular always wore a suit and tie. Unlike the other two male tellers who just wore a shirt and a tie, this young man looked like an executive.

A year later, I noticed he had been promoted to his own desk where he was taking loan applications. Two years later, he was a loan officer, and later he became the branch manager. I asked him about this one day, and he replied that he always knew he would be a branch manager, so he studied how the manager dressed and started dressing that way. He studied how the manager treated people and started interacting with people the same way. He started acting as if he were a branch manager long before he ever became one.

*To fly as fast as thought, to be anywhere there is, you must
first begin by knowing that you have already arrived.*

RICHARD BACH
Bestselling author of *Jonathan Livingston Seagull*

BECOMING AN INTERNATIONAL CONSULTANT

In the late '70s, I met a seminar leader who had just returned from Australia. I decided that I, too, wanted to travel and speak around the globe. I asked myself what I would need to become an international consultant. I called the passport office and asked them to send me an application. I purchased a clock that showed all the international time zones. I had business cards printed with the words *international consultant* on them. Finally, I decided that Australia would be the first place I would like to go, so I went to a travel agency and got a huge travel poster featuring the Sydney Opera House, Ayers Rock, and a kangaroo-crossing sign. Every morning while I ate my breakfast, I looked at that poster on my refrigerator and imagined being in Australia.

Less than a year later, I was invited to conduct seminars in Sydney and Brisbane. As soon as I started acting as if I were an international consultant, the universe responded by treating me like one—the powerful Law of Attraction at work.

The Law of Attraction simply states that what you think about, you will bring about. The more you create the vibration—the mental and emotional states—of already having something, the faster you attract it to you. This is an immutable law of the universe and critical to accelerating your rate of success.

ACTING AS IF IN THE PGA

A heartwarming example of the power of acting as if is the story of Fred Couples and Jim Nantz, who started out as two kids who loved golf and had very big dreams. Fred's goal was to someday win the Masters Tournament, and Jim's was to someday work for CBS Sports as an announcer. When Fred and Jim were suitemates in college at the University of Houston, they used to playact the scene where the winner of the Masters is escorted into Butler Cabin to receive his green jacket and be interviewed by the CBS announcer. Fourteen years later, the scene they had rehearsed many times in Taub Hall at the University of Houston played out in reality as the whole world was watching. Fred Couples won the Masters and was taken by tournament officials into Butler Cabin, where he was interviewed by none other than CBS Sports announcer Jim Nantz. After the cameras stopped rolling, the two embraced each other with tears in their eyes. They always knew it was going to be the Masters that Fred won, and that Jim would be there to cover it for CBS—the amazing power of acting as if with unwavering certainty.

THE MILLIONAIRE COCKTAIL PARTY

In my Breakthrough to Success seminars, we do a role-playing exercise called the Millionaire Cocktail Party. Everyone stands up and socializes with the other participants as if they were all at an actual cocktail party. However, they must act as if they have already achieved all of their financial goals in life. They act as if they have already achieved their lifestyle goals, too—their dream house, their vacation home, their dream car, their dream career—as well as any personal, professional, or philanthropic goals that are important to them.

Everyone suddenly becomes more animated, alive, enthusiastic, and outgoing. People who seemed shy a few minutes earlier reach out and assertively introduce themselves to others. The energy and volume level of the room soars. People excitedly tell each other about their achievements, invite each other to their vacation homes in Hawaii and the Bahamas, and discuss their recent safaris in Africa and their philanthropic missions to Third World countries.

After about five minutes, I stop the exercise and ask people to share how they are feeling. People report feeling excited, passionate, positive, supportive, generous, happy, self-confident, and content.

I then ask them to look at the fact that their inner feelings—both emotional and physiological—were different, even though in reality their outer circumstances were still the same. They had not actually become millionaires in the real world, but *they had begun to feel like millionaires simply by acting as if they were.*

THE PARTY THAT COULD CHANGE YOUR LIFE

In 1986, I attended a party that deeply impacted the lives of all of us who attended. It was a "come as you will be in 1991 party" held on the *Queen Mary* in Long Beach, California. Those of us who attended were to envision where we would like to be in 1991—five years into the future.

When we arrived, we were to act as if it really were 1991 and our vision had already come true. We were to dress the part, talk the part, and bring any props that demonstrated that our dream had already come true—books written, awards earned, and large paychecks received. We were to spend the evening bragging about our accomplishments, talking about how happy and fulfilled we were, and discussing what we were going to do next. We were to stay in character the entire night.

When we arrived, we were met by 20 college students who had been hired to play the part of adoring fans and paparazzi. Cameras flashed and fans screamed our names, asking for autographs.

I went as a bestselling author with several reviews of my number one *New York Times* bestseller to show people. A man who came as a multimillionaire dressed as a beach bum—his vision of retirement—spent the evening handing out real lottery tickets to everyone at the party. A woman brought a mock edition of *Time* magazine with her face on the cover for winning an international award for making advances in the peace movement.

A man who wanted to retire and spend his life as a sculptor showed up in a leather sculptor's apron with a hammer and chisel and safety goggles and pictures of sculptures he had made. A man who wanted to become a successful stock trader spent the entire evening answering his cell phone, talking animatedly and then commanding, "Buy five thousand shares" or "Sell ten thousand shares." He had actually hired someone to call him every 15 minutes during the party just to carry off his "act as if"!

A woman who was just embarking on a writing career and had yet to sell a book arrived carrying mock-ups of three books she had written. In the spirit of everyone supporting everyone else's dream, people told her that they had seen her on *Oprah* and the *Today* show. That woman was Susan Jeffers, who did go on from that transformational evening to publish 17 successful books, including the internationally acclaimed *Feel the Fear and Do It Anyway*.

And the same thing happened to me. I went on to write, compile, and edit more than 200 books, including more than 40 *New York Times* bestsellers. That party, where we maintained our future personas for over four hours, flooded our subconscious with powerful images of having already achieved our aspirations. These vivid experiences, infused with the positive emotions generated by the events of the evening, strengthened the positive neural pathways in our brains that in some cases forged, and in other cases deepened, our new self-images of being super-successful.

And it worked. All those who attended that party have gone on to realize the dreams they acted out that night and much, much more.

Make the commitment to throw a "Come As You'll Be" party for your closest circle of friends, your company, your business associates, your graduating class, or your mastermind group. Since this book was first published, many small companies and large corporations have built a "Come As You'll

Be" party into their in-house trainings, conferences, and sales meetings. Why not build it into yours? Think of the creative energy, awareness, and support it will release.

You can use the invitation below:

COME AS YOU WILL BE ... IN 2030!

Join us for a celebration that will stretch your imagination and catapult you into your own future.

When: _____

Where: _____

Given by: _____

RSVP to: _____

Arrive as who you will be 5 years from now. Dress in your very best. Speak only in the present tense the entire evening, as if it were already 2030, all your goals have been achieved, and all your dreams have already come true.

You will be videotaped as you arrive. Bring props to show everyone what you have achieved in the years between, such as bestselling books you've written, magazine covers you've been on, awards you've won, and photographs or scrapbooks of your achievements. Throughout the evening, you will have the opportunity to applaud others in their achievements and to receive congratulations.

SERGIO'S STORY

Sergio Sedas Gersey is a professor of robotics at the Tecnológico de Monterrey in Monterrey, Mexico. While attending my Breakthrough to Success training, he attended his first Come As You'll Be Party. Here's his story:

> In the first two days of the seminar, I set some goals that I wanted to achieve in my life:
>
> - To be a guest speaker at a TED conference
> - To write a book on Context-Based Learning (a new educational model I was developing)
> - To take my wife to Greece
> - To own a house by the lake
> - To start a tech museum
> - To develop a national program that would help youngsters develop self-confidence and a sense of purpose
>
> All of these appeared to be distant dreams. I lacked the money, the time, and the experience. And I had even had to cancel my family's last scheduled vacation.
>
> Regardless, as I prepared for my Come As You'll Be Party, I wanted to play the game full-out. My wife helped me pick out some pictures for a mock photo album that would be my prop to show people my accomplishments—pictures of the Greek Islands, pictures of Rome, a picture of a house by a lake. She even Photoshopped my picture on top of a TED conference stage. I was ready.
>
> I was a little nervous when I arrived, but I approached a group of people I knew. One of my new friends came dressed as an Olympics coach; she shared that she was coaching a league of minors that got into the Olympics. Soon it was my turn. "What have you been up to?" they asked.
>
> "Well," I began, "I just came back from giving a talk at a TED conference, and I got my book, *Context-Based Learning,* published. Oh, and I took my family on a vacation. We went to Greece and Rome." And I thanked them for coming to stay with us at our lake house, which I described clearly: a main house with two adjacent houses full of bunk beds—one for girls and one for boys.
>
> The party went on for hours, and I shared my "accomplishments of the last five years" with nearly a hundred people. Eventually it was time to eat, and slowly people began to leave the foyer and cross the line into a ballroom where dinner was waiting for us. I really did not want to go. I felt comfortable in the future, and I was afraid I would go back in time

the moment I crossed the line. But it was time to go. Yet when I crossed the line, I was confused. What was real? What was my imagination? I wasn't sure anymore.

A year and a half later, I was invited to speak at a TEDx conference in Chennai, India. My topic was "Context-Based Learning: Learning Through Understanding." A couple of months later, I submitted a paper on "Context-Based Learning and Learning Through Understanding" to a conference on Education Innovation and received the Best Paper Award.

But that is not all. A friend of mine from Greece invited me to start a nonprofit organization called Better Life Day in Mexico. Our first conference was in Athens in June. I needed to go to Athens to see what it was all about. With perfect timing, extra money came my way, so I invited my wife to go with me.

Just as I was about to purchase the plane tickets, my wife suggested, "Why not go via Rome and stop by Santorini—one of the Greek Islands?"

WOW! Everything that I had talked about at the Come As You'll Be Party was happening.

Three years have passed since then. My national program to generate self-confidence and a sense of purpose in youngsters is also now a reality. It is being taught and migrated into 33 campuses nationwide. I am now an international speaker and trainer. And yes, at the end of each seminar we hold a Come As You'll Be Party.

A couple of weeks ago, I picked up the photo album my wife had made for that very first Come As You'll Be Party. As I looked through it, one particular picture stood out. It was the picture my wife had composed of me—on stage in front of the TED logo. Side by side, it's the spitting image of an actual picture someone took of me speaking at TEDx in India!

ACTING AS IF IN THE CLASSROOM

Trisha Jacobson, a health teacher in Conway, New Hampshire, decided to conduct an experimental two-week Success Principles curriculum with a group of her eighth graders. For the last day, she planned a Come As You'll Be Party, similar to what she had experienced at several of my trainings. Here's what happened.

> I called it a Come As You'll Be As An Adult Party and encouraged the kids to come all dressed up and ready to act out their ideal adult lives and greet their classmates as if they hadn't seen each other since the eighth grade.

On Friday morning, as the party started, a group of kids gathered in the middle of the room—smiling, high-fiving, and hugging each other as if they hadn't seen each other in years and sharing their stories about their cool jobs, houses, cars, and families.

Mariah, one of the popular girls, showed up in high heels and a sparkly outfit, with a plastic microphone, and announced that she was a popular singer/songwriter and had just come off a promotional tour of her new album. She spoke of her mansion house, her hot new husband, and her sports car.

Jeff wore his school baseball jersey and told me he had just been drafted by the New York Yankees. He was still dating his middle school crush and saw marriage in the near future. He talked about his busy travel schedule, his record-breaking batting average, and the new car he was going to buy.

Ian was a sportscaster at a local TV station, married with three kids, a dog, and a moderate life in New Hampshire.

Justin bought the family farm and was enjoying a simple life with his family.

Audrey, who was still Mariah's best friend, was now her personal assistant and traveled with her on tour to take care of all the details and keep her friend organized.

Brian was an aeronautical design engineer who worked from his high-tech home office, complete with a wall-to-wall big-screen TV, where he spent his spare time playing video games with friends. He had designed an amazing piece of equipment and was on his way to catch a plane to the Kennedy Space Station to witness the launch.

The energy in the room was electric! Except in the corner to my right . . . where two kids were sitting by themselves. Matt wore a shirt and tie and sat quietly at his desk looking at his binder. Emily was dressed in a navy blue business suit that was a couple of sizes too big for her. She was reading her book in silence.

When I walked over to check in with Matt, he explained that he was an accountant. He had a house, a wife, two kids, a dog, and a nice car. He had a couple of good friends, he liked being quiet, and he spent a lot of time working with numbers, which he really enjoyed.

Emily was reluctant to share her story with me at first, but then told me that she had borrowed her mom's business suit. She told me that she had a hard time acting as if it was the future, but she knew she wanted to be an attorney, just like her mom. She also told me she wanted to get better at meeting people because she got teased a lot at school for being so shy.

Matt, who was listening to my conversation with Emily, told us that he was also pretty shy and got teased a lot about being a geek.

In a moment of divine inspiration, I asked them if they would like me to introduce them to some people who needed their services. They looked perplexed, but got up and followed me over to where the crowd had gathered and the others were still acting out their roles.

I walked over to where Mariah, the up-and-coming rock star, and Jeff, the baseball star, were standing. "Mariah, it's so good to see you again!" I said. "I heard your album and it was awesome! I'm thinking that you could probably use a good accountant and a good lawyer now that you're so successful. Meet my friends Matt and Emily. He's an accountant and she's a lawyer."

Jeff immediately reached over, shook Matt's hand, and said, "Dude, can you take a look at my new contract?" while Mariah asked Emily about what it was like to be a lawyer.

I got goose bumps as I watched what unfolded over the next several minutes. Jeff and Mariah connected Matt and Emily to their classmates and promoted their accounting and legal services to anyone they thought would need them. The bell rang; the students grabbed their binders, thanked me for having such a fun party, and were on their way to their next class.

I was in shock... but that was nothing compared to what I witnessed the following Monday. As I was walking down the hallway to class, I heard someone call my name. I turned around to see Mariah, Emily, and Audrey coming toward me, arm in arm with big smiles, as if they had been friends forever.

As I walked into the classroom, Jeff and Matt were sitting near Matt's desk making plans for Matt to help Jeff with his math homework after school.

Although I had experienced the power of the Come As You'll Be Party several times before, I had never anticipated the impact such an activity could have on young people. In literally half an hour, connections were made, perspectives were changed, shyness was overcome, and an appreciation for each other's unique gifts and talents was discovered.

POSITIVE EMOTIONS BECOME "IMPRINTED" IN YOUR SUBCONSCIOUS MIND

The purpose of the Come As You'll Be Party is to create an emotionally charged experience of what it will be like when you have made it—when you have achieved your dreams. When you spend an evening living out the lifestyle you want and deserve, you lay down powerful blueprints in your subconscious mind that will later support you in perceiving opportunities, creating powerful solutions, attracting the right people, and taking the necessary actions to achieve your dreams and goals.

Be clear that one party like this is not enough by itself to change your entire future. You will still have to do other things to make it happen. However, it is one more piece in an overall system of powerful "acting as if" strategies that will support you in the creation of your desired future.

BE, DO, AND HAVE EVERYTHING YOU WANT...STARTING NOW

You can begin right now to act as if you have already achieved any goal you desire, and that outer experience of acting as if will create the inner experience—the millionaire mindset, as it were—that will take you to the actual manifestation of that experience.

Once you choose what it is you want to be, do, or have, all you have to do is start acting as if you already are being, doing, or having it. How would you act if you already were a straight-A student, top salesperson, highly paid consultant, rich entrepreneur, world-class athlete, bestselling author, internationally acclaimed artist, sought-after speaker, or celebrated actor or musician? How would you think, talk, act, carry yourself, dress, treat other people, handle money, eat, live, travel, and so forth?

Once you have a clear picture of that, start being it—now!

Successful people exude self-confidence, ask for what they want, and say what they don't want. They think anything is possible, take risks, and celebrate their successes. They save a portion of their income and share a portion with others. You can do all of those things now before you ever become rich and successful. These things don't cost money, just intention. And as soon as you start acting as if, you will start drawing to you the very people and things that will help you achieve it in real life.

Remember, the proper order of things is to start now and *be* who you want to be, then *do* the actions that go along with being that person, and soon you will find that you easily *have* everything you want in life—health, wealth, fulfilling relationships, and social impact.

PRINCIPLE 13

TAKE ACTION

Things may come to those who wait,
but only the things left by those who hustle.

ABRAHAM LINCOLN
The 16th president of the United States

What we think or what we know or what we believe is, in the end,
of little consequence. The only consequence is what we do.

JOHN RUSKIN
English author, art critic, and social commentator

The world doesn't pay you for what you know; it pays you for what you do. There's an enduring axiom of success that says, "The universe rewards action." Yet as simple and as true as this principle is, it's surprising how many people get bogged down in analyzing, planning, and organizing when what they really need to do is take action.

When you take action, you trigger all kinds of things that will inevitably carry you to success. You let those around you know that you are serious in your intention. People wake up and start paying attention. People with similar goals become aligned with you. You begin to learn things from your experience that cannot be learned from listening to others or from reading books. You begin to get feedback about how to do it better, more efficiently, and more quickly. Things that once seemed confusing begin to become clear. Things that once appeared difficult begin to be easier. You begin to attract others who will support and encourage you. All manner of good things begin to flow in your direction once you begin to take action.

TALK IS CHEAP!

Over the years of teaching and coaching people in my company and in my seminars, I have found that the one thing that seems to separate winners from losers more than anything else is that winners take action. They simply get up and do what has to be done. Once they have developed a plan, they start. They get into motion. Even if they don't start perfectly, they learn from their mistakes, make the necessary corrections, and keep taking action, all the time building momentum, until they finally produce the result they set out to produce . . . or something even better than they conceived of when they started.

To be successful, you have to do what successful people do, and successful people are highly action-oriented. Once you have created a vision, set goals, broken them down into small steps, visualized and affirmed your success, and chosen to believe in yourself and your dreams, it's now time to take action. Enroll in the course, get the necessary training, make those sales calls, call the travel agent, start writing that book, start saving for the down payment on your home, join the health club, sign up for those piano lessons, or write that proposal.

NOTHING HAPPENS UNTIL YOU TAKE ACTION

If your ship doesn't come in, swim out to meet it.

JONATHAN WINTERS
Grammy Award–winning comedian, actor, writer, and artist

To demonstrate the power of taking action in my seminars, I hold up a $100 bill and ask, "Who wants this $100 bill?" Invariably, most of the people in the audience will raise their hands. Some will wave their hands vigorously back and forth; some will even shout out "I want it" or "I'll take it" or "Give it to me." But I just stand there calmly holding out the bill until they *get it*. Eventually, someone jumps out of her seat, rushes to the front of the room, and takes the bill from my hand.

After the person sits down—now $100 richer for her efforts—I ask the audience, "What did this person do that no one else in the room did? She got off her butt and took action. She did what was necessary to get the money. And that is exactly what you must do if you want to succeed in life. You must take action, and, in most cases, the sooner the better." I then ask,

"How many of you thought about getting up and just coming and taking the money, but you stopped yourself?"

I then ask them to remember what they told themselves that stopped them from getting up.

The usual answers are

"I didn't want to look like I wanted it or needed it that badly."
"I wasn't sure if you would really give it to me."
"I was too far back in the room."
"Other people need it more than I do."
"I didn't want to look greedy."
"I was afraid I might be doing something wrong, and then people would judge me or laugh at me."
"I was waiting for further instructions."

I then point out that whatever things they said to stop themselves are the same things that they say to stop themselves in the rest of their lives.

One of the universal truths in life is, "How you do anything is how you do everything." If you are cautious here, you are probably cautious everywhere. If you hold yourself back for fear of looking foolish here, you probably hold yourself back for fear of looking foolish elsewhere. You have to identify those patterns and break through them. It's time to stop holding yourself back and just go for the gold.

RUBEN GONZALEZ GOES FOR OLYMPIC GOLD

Ever since third grade, Ruben Gonzalez had wanted to be an Olympic athlete. He respected the Olympians because they were an example of what he believed in—they are willing to commit to a goal, risk adversity in the pursuit of it, and fail and keep trying until they succeed.

But it was not until he was in college and saw Scott Hamilton compete in the 1984 Sarajevo Games that he actually made the decision to train for the Olympics. Ruben said to himself, *If that little guy can do it, I can do it too! I'm going to be in the next Olympics! It's a done deal. I just have to find a sport.*

After doing a little research on Olympic sports, Ruben decided he needed to pick a sport that would build on his strengths. He knew that he was a good athlete but not a great athlete. His strength was perseverance. He never quit anything. In fact, he had earned the nickname Bulldog in high school. He figured he had to find a sport so tough, a sport with so many broken bones, that there would be lots of quitters. That way maybe he could rise to the top on the attrition rate! He finally settled on the luge.

Next he wrote *Sports Illustrated* (this was before the Internet) and asked, "Where do you go to learn how to luge?" They wrote back, "Lake Placid, New York. That's where they had the Olympics in 1936 and 1980. That's where the track is." Ruben picked up the phone and called Lake Placid.

"I'm an athlete in Houston and I want to learn how to luge so I can be in the Olympics in four years. Will you help me?"

The guy who answered the phone asked, "How old are you?"

"Twenty-one years old."

"Twenty-one? You're way too old. You're ten years too late. We start them when they're ten years old. Forget it."

But Ruben couldn't forget it, and he started to tell the man his life story to buy some time until he thought of something. Along the way he happened to say that he was born in Argentina.

All of a sudden, the man on the other end of the phone got excited. "Argentina? Why didn't you say so? If you'll go for Argentina, we'll help you." It turns out the sport of luge was in danger of being dropped from the Olympics because there weren't enough countries competing on the inter-

"I wondered why there was such a bad smell in here."

national level. "If you'll go for Argentina and somehow we can get you into the top fifty ranked lugers in the world in four years, which is what you'll need to make it into the Olympics, it would add one more country to the sport of luge, and that would make it a stronger sport. If you make it, you'd be helping the U.S. team." Then he added, "Before you come all the way to Lake Placid, you have to know two things. Number one: If you want to do it at your age and you want to do it in only four years, it will be brutal. Nine out of every ten guys quit. Number two: Expect to break some bones."

Ruben thought, *Great! This works right into my plan. I'm not a quitter. The harder it is, the easier it is for me.*

A few days later Ruben Gonzalez was walking down Main Street in Lake Placid looking for the U.S. Olympic Training Center. A day later, he was in a beginner's class with 14 other aspiring Olympians. The first day was miserable, and he even thought of quitting, but with the help of his friend Craig, he recommitted to his Olympic dream and, though all 14 of the other aspirants eventually quit before the end of the first season, Ruben finished the summer training.

Four grueling years later, Ruben Gonzalez realized his dream when he walked into the opening ceremonies of the 1988 Calgary Winter Olympics. He returned again in Albertville in 1992 and Salt Lake City for the 2000 Winter Games. Ruben Gonzalez, because he took immediate and persistent action on his dream, will always be a "three-time Olympian." And as many Olympians do, Ruben has gone on to have a successful career as a motivational speaker.

SUCCESSFUL PEOPLE HAVE A BIAS FOR ACTION

Most successful people I know have a low tolerance for excessive planning and talking about it. They are antsy to get going. They want to get started. They want the games to begin. A good example of this is my friend Bob Kriegel's son Otis. When Otis came home for the summer with his new girlfriend after his freshman year in college, they both began looking for jobs. While Otis just picked up the phone and started calling around to see who might need someone, his girlfriend spent the first week writing and rewriting her résumé. By the end of the second day, Otis had landed a job. His girlfriend was still rewriting her résumé. Otis just got into action. He figured if someone asked for a résumé, he'd deal with it then.

Planning has its place, but it must be kept in perspective. Some people spend their whole lives waiting for the perfect time to do something.

There's rarely a "perfect" time to do anything. What is important is to just get started. Get into the game. Get on the playing field. Once you do, you will start to get feedback that will help you make the corrections you need to make to be successful. Once you are in action, you will start learning at a much more rapid rate.

READY, FIRE, AIM!

Most people are familiar with the phrase "Ready, aim, fire!" The problem is that too many people spend their whole life aiming and never firing. They are always getting ready, getting it perfect. The quickest way to hit a target is to fire, see where the bullet landed, and then adjust your aim accordingly. If the hit was two inches above the target, lower your aim a little. Fire again. See where it is now. Keep firing and keep readjusting. Soon you are hitting the bull's-eye. The same is true for anything.

When we started marketing the first *Chicken Soup for the Soul*® book, it occurred to me that it would be a good idea to give away free excerpts from the book to small and local newspapers in exchange for them printing a box at the end of the story telling people that the story was excerpted from *Chicken Soup for the Soul*®, which was available at their local bookstore or by calling our 800 number. I had never done this before, so I wasn't sure if there was a correct way to submit a story to a newspaper or magazine, so I just sent off a story from the book entitled "Remember, You Are Raising Children, Not Flowers!" that I had written about my neighbor and his son, along with a cover letter to the editor of *L.A. Parent* magazine. The letter read:

Jack Bierman
L.A. Parent

Dear Jack,
 I would like to submit this article for publication in *L.A. Parent*. I have enclosed a brief bio. I would like you to print the little blurb I included on my new book *Chicken Soup for the Soul*® with my article. If you would like a copy of the book, I would be more than happy to send one to you!
 Thank you for your time.

Sincerely,
Jack Canfield

A few weeks later, I received the following letter back:

Dear Jack:

I was annoyed by your fax. How dare you tell me to include "the little blurb on your book." How could you assume I'd be interested in this little bit of unsolicited word processing. Then I read the article. Needless to say, I'll run your little blurb and then some!

I was moved by this exercise and am sure it will touch the hearts of our 200,000-plus readers from here to San Diego.

Has it ever appeared anywhere in my demographic? If so, where? I look forward to working with you on raising children, not flowers.

Best regards,
Jack Bierman, Editor in Chief

I had not known how to submit a proper query letter to an editor. There was an accepted format that I was unaware of. But I took action anyway. In a subsequent phone call, Jack Bierman generously taught me the correct way to submit an article to a magazine. He gave me feedback on how to do it better next time. Now I was in the game and I was learning from my experience. Ready, fire, aim!

Within a month I had submitted that same article to over 50 local and regional parenting magazines all across the United States. Thirty-five of them published it, introducing *Chicken Soup for the Soul*® to over 6 million parents.

DO IT NOW!

My mentor, W. Clement Stone, used to hand out lapel pins that said "Do it now." When you have an inspired impulse to take action, do it now. Ray Kroc, the founder of McDonald's, said, "There are three keys to success: 1. Being at the right place at the right time. 2. Knowing you are there. 3. Taking action."

On March 24, 1975, Chuck Wepner, a relatively unknown 30-to-1 underdog, did what no one thought he could do—he went 15 rounds with the world heavyweight champion Muhammad Ali. In the ninth round, he reached Ali's chin with a right hand, knocking the champion to the ground—shocking both Ali and the fans watching the fight. Wepner was only seconds away from being the world's heavyweight champion. However, Ali recovered and went on to win the 15-round bout and retain his title.

Over a thousand miles away, a struggling actor named Sylvester Stallone watched the fight on a newly purchased television set. Though Stallone had contemplated the idea of writing a screenplay about a down-and-out fighter getting a title shot before he saw the Ali–Wepner fight, he didn't think it was plausible. But after seeing Wepner, whom most people didn't know, fighting the most well-known fighter of all time, all he thought was *Get me a pencil.* He began to write that night, and three days later, he had completed the script for *Rocky,* which went on to win three Oscars, including one for best picture, thus launching Stallone's multimillion-dollar movie career.

Imagination means nothing without doing.

CHARLIE CHAPLIN
Actor, comedian, and filmmaker

GIVE ME A BREAK!

A story is told of a man who goes to church and prays, "God, I need a break. I need to win the state lottery. I'm counting on you, God." Having not won the lottery, the man returns to church a week later and once again prays, "God, about that state lottery . . . I've been kind to my wife. I've given up drinking. I've been really good. Give me a break. Let me win the lottery."

A week later, still no richer, he returns to pray once again. "God, I don't seem to be getting through to you on this state lottery thing. I've been using positive self-talk, saying affirmations, and visualizing the money. Give me a break, God. Let me win the lottery."

Suddenly the heavens open up, light and heavenly music flood into the church, and a deep voice says, "My son, give me a break! Buy a lottery ticket!"

FAIL FORWARD

No man ever became great or good except through many and great mistakes.

WILLIAM E. GLADSTONE
Former prime minister of Great Britain

Many people fail to take action because they're afraid to fail. Successful people, on the other hand, realize that failure is an important part of the learning process. They know that failure is just a way we learn by trial and error. Not only do we need to stop being so afraid of failure but we also need to be willing to fail—even eager to fail. I call this kind of instructive failure "failing forward." Simply get started, make mistakes, listen to the feedback, correct, and keep moving forward toward the goal. Every experience will yield more useful information that you can apply the next time.

This principle is perhaps demonstrated most compellingly in the area of start-up businesses. For instance, venture capitalists know that most businesses fail. But in the venture capital industry, a new statistic is emerging. If the founding entrepreneur is 55 years or older, the business has a 73% better chance of survival. These older entrepreneurs have already learned from their mistakes. They're simply a better risk because through a lifetime of learning from their failures, they have developed a knowledge base, a skill set, and a self-confidence that better enables them to move through the obstacles to success.

You can never learn less; you can only learn more.
The reason I know so much is because I have made so many mistakes.

BUCKMINSTER FULLER
Mathematician and philosopher who never graduated from college
but received 46 honorary doctorates

One of my favorite stories is about a famous research scientist who had made several very important medical breakthroughs. He was being interviewed by a newspaper reporter, who asked him why he thought he was able to achieve so much more than the average person. In other words, what set him so far apart from others?

He responded that it all came from a lesson his mother had taught him when he was two years old. He'd been trying to take a bottle of milk out of the refrigerator, when he lost his grip and spilled the entire contents on the kitchen floor. His mother, instead of scolding him, said, "What a wonderful mess you've made! I've rarely seen such a huge puddle of milk. Well, the damage is already done. Would you like to get down and play in the milk before we clean it up?"

Indeed, he did. And, after a few minutes, his mother continued, "You know, whenever you make a mess like this, eventually you have to clean it up. So, how would you like to do that? We could use a towel, sponge, or mop. Which do you prefer?"

After they were finished cleaning up the milk, she said, "What we have here is a failed experiment in how to carry a big bottle of milk with two tiny hands. Let's go out in the backyard, fill the bottle with water, and see if you can discover a way to carry it without dropping it." And they did.

What a wonderful lesson!

The scientist then remarked that it was at that moment that he knew he didn't have to be afraid to make mistakes. Instead, he learned that *mistakes are just opportunities for learning something new*—which, after all, is what scientific experiments are all about.

That bottle of spilled milk led to a lifetime of learning experiences—experiences that were the building blocks of a lifetime of world-renowned successes and medical breakthroughs!

PRINCIPLE 14

JUST LEAN INTO IT

A journey of 1,000 miles begins with one step.
ANCIENT CHINESE PROVERB

Oftentimes, success happens when you just lean into it—when you make yourself open to opportunities and are willing to do what it takes to pursue it further—without a contract, without a promise of success, without any expectation whatsoever. You just start. You lean into it. You see what it feels like. And you find out if you want to keep going—instead of sitting on the sidelines deliberating, reflecting, and contemplating.

LEANING INTO IT CREATES MOMENTUM

One of the most extraordinary benefits of just leaning into it is that you begin creating momentum—that unseen energy force that brings more opportunity, more resources, and more people who can help you into your life at seemingly just the right time for you to benefit the most from them.

Many of the best-known acting careers, entrepreneurial pursuits, philanthropic projects, and other "overnight successes" happened because someone responded favorably to the question "Have you ever considered . . . ?" or "Could I convince you to . . . ?" or "Would you be willing to take a look at . . . ?" They leaned into it.

You can't cross a sea by merely staring into the water.
RABINDRANATH TAGORE
1913 Nobel laureate for literature

BE WILLING TO START WITHOUT SEEING THE WHOLE PATH

Take the first step in faith. You don't have to see the whole staircase. Just take the first step.

MARTIN LUTHER KING JR.
Legendary civil rights leader; Nobel Peace Prize recipient

Of course, just leaning into a project or opportunity also means you must be willing to start without necessarily seeing the entire pathway from the beginning. You must be willing to lean into it and see how it unfolds.

Often we have a dream and because we can't see how we're going to achieve it, we are afraid to start, afraid to commit ourselves because the path is unclear and the outcome is uncertain. But leaning into it requires that you be willing to explore—to enter unknown waters, trusting that a port will appear.

Simply start, then keep taking what feel like logical next steps, and the journey will ultimately take you to where you want to go—*or even someplace better.*

SOMETIMES YOU DON'T EVEN HAVE TO HAVE A CLEAR DREAM

From as early as she could remember, Jana Stanfield wanted to be a singer. She didn't know where her dream would eventually lead her, but she knew she had to find out. She leaned into it and took some singing lessons—then eventually got a job singing weekends at the local country club. She leaned into it a little more, and at 26 years old, she packed her bags for Nashville, Tennessee, to pursue her dream of becoming a songwriter and recording artist.

Three long years she lived and worked in Nashville, seeing hundreds of more brilliant, talented, and deserving performers than there were record deals to be had. Jana began to see the music industry as a room full of slot machines that paid out just enough to keep you playing. A producer loves your work, an artist considers your song for her next album, and maybe a record company tells you you're great—but rarely do the slot machines pay off with the big jackpot, the coveted recording contract.

After several years of working at a record promotion company to learn the business "from the inside out," Jana had to face facts: There were no guarantees—she could play the slots forever and grow old in Nashville.

Finally, she admitted to herself that continuing to try to get a record deal was like pounding her head against a wall. She didn't realize at the time that often when you lean into it, roadblocks are put in your path to force you onto a different path—a path that may be truer to your real purpose.

For every failure, there's an alternative course of action. You just have to find it. When you come to a roadblock, take a detour.

MARY KAY ASH
Founder of Mary Kay Cosmetics

LOOKING FOR HER UNDERLYING MOTIVATION

Jana had learned what many achievers have: that even when you can't move forward, you can turn right or you can turn left, but you have to keep moving. She discovered through some personal development courses that sometimes, in the rush to fulfill our dreams, we get caught up in what we think is the only form that will satisfy that dream—in Jana's case, a recording contract.

But as Jana would soon learn, there are many ways to accomplish your goal if you know what you're really pursuing. Because underneath her desire to land a record deal was a deeper motivating need, the real motivation for her dream—to use her music to uplift, inspire, and offer hope to people.

I want to combine music, comedy, storytelling, and motivation with what I'm here for, she wrote in her journal. *I am an artist and my art is unfolding before me. The roadblock that blocked my path has been lifted.*

Emboldened by this new insight, Jana began to play anywhere people would let her. "Where two or more are gathered, I will bring my guitar" became her motto. She played in living rooms, driveways, schools, churches, anywhere she could.

"I'M NOT LOST, I'M JUST EXPLORING"

But Jana was still at a loss to figure out how to combine her talents in a way that would be helpful to people and pay her a modest income. There was no one out there already doing what she wanted to do—combining music, comedy, storytelling, and motivation. There was no career path already laid out to follow, no footsteps to walk in. She was charting new territory. She didn't know where she was going or what form it would ultimately take, but she kept leaning into it.

KEEP LEANING AND THE PATH WILL APPEAR

Jana began to work odd jobs—always leaning into it—trying to figure out how to turn her passion for her art and her desire to help people into something she could make a living from. *I'm willing to use my gifts to make this world a better place,* she wrote in her journal. *I don't know exactly how to use my gifts to do this, but I have let God know that I am ready.*

Again she leaned into it. Jana called churches, saying, "If you would let me come and sing two songs in your service, it will give you a chance to get to know me and how I might be helpful. Then in a few months, maybe you'd like to have me come back and do a concert in the afternoon."

THE TURNING POINT

After just two or three songs, church members would approach her and ask if she had her songs on tape. There was one song, "If I Had Only Known," that people requested more than any other. They'd say, "I noticed a lot of people crying when you played that song. I've had a loss that's so painful that I can't cry here at church because I don't know if I can put myself back together once I start. Would you make me a copy of this song so I can have it when I'm alone and really feel the feelings you're bringing to me?"

Jana spent a lot of time making cassettes and mailing them to people, but all the while, her friends kept telling her to make an album. "You've got all these demos of songs you recorded when you were trying to get a record deal," they said. "Just take your demos and make an album."

Jana thought, *Oh, I couldn't do that. It wouldn't be a real album with a real record company. It wouldn't really count. It would just show what a failure I've been.* But her friends kept after her, and eventually Jana leaned into it one more time.

She paid an engineer $100 to put together 10 of her songs, which she playfully referred to as "a compilation of my top 10 most rejected songs." She made the covers at Kinko's and reproduced 100 cassettes, which she now laughingly recalls she thought would be "a lifetime supply." As she traveled from living room to living room and tiny church to tiny church, she set out her cassettes on a card table and sold them after her performance.

Then came the turning point.

"My husband went with me to a church in Memphis," Jana recalls. "They didn't feel comfortable having a card table with my cassettes inside the church, so they put my card table out on their new parking lot. It had just been repaved—and in 95-degree weather, the asphalt was hot and black and gooey. After the parking lot finally emptied, we got in the car and turned on the air-conditioning and began counting what we'd earned."

To Jana's amazement, she had sold $300 worth of cassettes—$50 more than she earned all week working a freelance TV job she had taken to help make ends meet. Holding that $300 in her hand made Jana realize, for the first time, that she *could* support herself doing what she loved to do.

Today, Jana's company Keynote Concerts* produces more than 50 motivational concerts a year for groups all over the world. She started her own recording company, Relatively Famous Records, which produced nine of Jana's CDs and has sold well over 100,000 copies. Jana's songs have been recorded by Reba McEntire, Andy Williams, Suzy Bogguss, John Schneider, and Megon McDonough. She's opened for Kenny Loggins and toured with author Melody Beatty. Her "heavy mental" music has been featured on *Oprah, 20/20, Entertainment Tonight,* and radio stations coast to coast, as well as in the movie *8 Seconds.*

Jana Stanfield achieved her dream of becoming a songwriter and recording star—all because she leaned into it and trusted the path that appeared. You, too, can get from where you are to where you want to be if you'll just trust that if you lean into it, the path will appear. Sometimes it will be like driving through the fog, where you can only see the road 10 yards ahead of you. But if you keep moving forward, more of the road will be revealed, and eventually, you will arrive at the goal.

Pick an area of your life—career, financial, relationship, health and fitness, recreation, hobby, or contribution—that you would like to explore and just lean into it.

START NOW!...JUST DO IT!

Of course, there is no perfect time to start. If you are into astrology and you want to contact your astrologer about an auspicious date to get married, open your store, launch a new product line, or begin a concert tour, okay—that's fine. I can understand that. But for everything else, the best strategy

---

*You can learn more about Jana's work and her CDs at jana-stanfield.com. And if you want to experience five minutes of pure joy and encouragement, go to YouTube and watch her video "If I Were Brave" by Jana Stanfield (sponsored by Awesome Women Hub).

is just to jump in and get started. Lean into it. Don't keep putting things off waiting for 12 doves to fly over your house in the sign of a cross before you begin. Just start.

You want to be a public speaker? Fine. Schedule a free talk for a local service club, school, or church group. Just having a date will put the pressure on you to start researching and writing your speech. If that's too big of a stretch, then join Toastmasters or take a speech class.

You want to be in the restaurant business? Go get a job in a restaurant and start learning the business. You want to be a chef? Great! Enroll in a cooking school. Take action and get started—today! You do not have to know everything to get going. Just get into the game. You will learn by doing.

First you jump off the cliff and you build wings on the way down.
RAY BRADBURY
Prolific American author of science fiction and fantasy

Don't get me wrong here. I am a big proponent of education, training, and skill building. If you need more training, then go and get it. Sign up for that class or that seminar now. You may need a coach or a mentor to get where you want to go. If so, then go get one. If you're afraid, so what? Feel the fear and do it anyway. The key is to just get started. Quit waiting until you are *perfectly* ready. You never will be.

I started out my career as a history teacher in a Chicago high school. I was far from the perfect teacher on my first day of teaching school. I had a lot to learn about classroom control, effective discipline, how to avoid getting conned by a slick student, how to confront manipulative behavior, and how to motivate an unmotivated student. But I had to start anyway. And it was in the process of teaching that I learned all of those other things.

MOST OF LIFE IS ON-THE-JOB TRAINING

Some of the most important things can only be learned in the process of doing them. You do something and you get feedback—about what works and what doesn't. If you don't do anything for fear of doing it wrong, poorly, or badly, you never get any feedback, and therefore you never get to learn and improve.

When I started my first business, a retreat and conference center in

Amherst, Massachusetts, called the New England Center for Personal and Organizational Development, I went to a local bank to get a loan. The first bank I went to told me I needed to have a business plan. I didn't know what that was, but I went and bought a book on how to write a business plan. I wrote one up and took it to the bank. They told me there were a bunch of holes in my plan. I asked what they were, and they told me. I went back and rewrote the plan, filling in the areas I had left out or that were unclear or unconvincing. I then went back to the bank. They said the plan was good, but they wanted to pass. I asked them who might be willing to fund the plan. They gave me the names of several bankers in the area they thought might respond favorably. Again I went off to bank after bank. Each one gave me more feedback until I had honed the plan and my presentation to the point where I did finally obtain the $20,000 loan that I needed.

When Mark Victor Hansen and I first released *Chicken Soup for the Soul*®, I thought it would be a good idea to sell the book in bulk quantity to some of the larger network marketing companies, thinking they could give them or resell them to their sales force to motivate them to believe in their dreams, take more risks, and therefore achieve greater success in selling. I got a list of all the companies that belonged to the Direct Marketing Association, and I started cold-calling the sales directors of the larger companies. Sometimes I couldn't get the sales director to take my call. Other times I was told, "We're not interested." Several times I was actually hung up on! But eventually, after getting better at getting through to the right decision maker and properly discussing the book's potential benefits, I made several significant sales. A few of the companies liked the book so much they later hired me to speak at their national conventions. All because I leaned into it.

Was I a little scared making cold calls? Yes. Did I know what I was doing when I started? No. I had never tried to sell mass quantities of books to anyone before. I had to learn as I went. But the most important point is that I just got started. I got into communication with the people I wanted to serve; found out what their dreams, aspirations, and goals were; and explored how our book might help them in achieving their objectives. Everything unfolded because I was willing to take a risk and jump into the ring.

You, too, have to begin—from wherever you are—to start taking the actions that will get you to where you want to be.

PRINCIPLE 15

EXPERIENCE YOUR FEAR AND TAKE ACTION ANYWAY

We come this way but once. We can either tiptoe through life and hope that we get to death without being too badly bruised or we can live a full, complete life achieving our goals and realizing our wildest dreams.

BOB PROCTOR
Self-made millionaire, radio and TV personality, success trainer, and featured teacher in the movie and book *The Secret*

As you move forward on your journey from where you are to where you want to be, you are going to have to confront your fears. Fear is natural. Whenever you start a new project, take on a new venture, or put yourself out there, there is usually fear. Unfortunately, most people let fear stop them from taking the necessary steps to achieve their dreams. Successful people, on the other hand, feel the fear along with the rest of us but don't let it keep them from doing anything they want to do—*or have to do.* They understand that fear is something to be acknowledged, experienced, and taken along for the ride. They have learned, as author Susan Jeffers suggests, "to feel the fear and do it anyway."★

WHY ARE WE SO FEARFUL?

Millions of years ago, fear was our body's way of signaling us that we were out of our comfort zone. It alerted us to possible danger, and gave us the burst of adrenaline we needed to run away. Unfortunately, though this response was useful in the days when saber-toothed tigers were chasing us, today most of our threats are not all that life-threatening.

★ I consider *Feel the Fear and Do It Anyway* by the late Susan Jeffers to be a must-read book. I endorsed her book saying, "Should be required for every person who can read!"

Today, fear is more of a signal that we must stay alert and cautious. We can feel fear, but we can still move forward anyway. Think of your fear as a two-year-old child who doesn't want to go grocery shopping with you. You wouldn't let a two-year-old's mentality run your life. Because you must buy groceries, you'll just have to take the two-year-old along with you. Fear is no different. In other words, acknowledge that fear exists but don't let it keep you from doing important tasks.

YOU HAVE TO BE WILLING TO FEEL THE FEAR

Some people will do anything to avoid the uncomfortable feeling of fear. If you are one of those people, you run an even bigger risk of never getting what you want in life. Most of the good stuff requires taking a risk. And the nature of a risk is that it doesn't always work out. People do lose their investments, people do forget their lines, people do fall off mountains, people do die in accidents. But as the old adage so wisely tells us, "Nothing ventured, nothing gained."

In 2009, Peter Douglas was a self-sufficient successful businessman, rancher, and self-described "cowboy" who had pulled himself up by the bootstraps his whole life. As the result of a mistake made by the anesthesiologist during what was supposed to be a "routine shoulder surgery," he found himself unable to grab his own bootstraps, much less pull on them. He woke up to discover that both his arms were totally paralyzed from the shoulders down.

For the first time in his life, without the use of his hands, Peter felt helpless, which he describes as "that feeling you get when you KNOW that you have to do something, but you just can't do it." After years of rehab, Peter still has only limited fine motor skills in his hands. He has some triceps and forearm movement; and he can move his arms with difficulty, but as he describes it, his thumbs "are not exactly opposable anymore."

For the years following his surgery, he didn't go anywhere without his wife or someone else to help him. And he definitely wouldn't consider traveling by himself. The thought of being alone in a strange place terrified him. What if he needed help? What if he couldn't open his hotel room door by himself?

What if?

Then one day he decided enough was enough. Realizing that he was letting the fear of the unknown dictate his life and where he went, he finally made the decision to travel on his own. But each step of the way he knew he would have to face and experience the fear of the next complication, obstacle, or stumbling block that might eventually cause him to throw up his hands (in theory at least) and say, "That's it! I'm going home!" But he was determined to work through the fear. And what he discovered is that, as he faced each fear, a solution appeared. Here's what Peter told me:

Fear: I was afraid of the check-in at the airport. I didn't know if I'd have enough strength to swipe my credit card at the check-in kiosk. *Solution:* I asked the people at the airlines to help, and they were more than happy to assist.

Fear: I was nervous about getting the seat belt buckled in. I wasn't sure I'd have enough grasp in my hand to do the task. *Solution:* The flight attendants were kind and helpful with the seat belt.

Fear: I didn't know how I'd get things set up in my hotel room. *Solution:* Once I was in my room, the bell captain helped me unwrap the soap, set up the room, pull the curtains, unfold the covers, and unpack my luggage.

Fear: I didn't know how I would get myself dressed flying solo. I still hadn't been able to get any of my clothes buttoned on my own. *Solution:* My wife packed all my shirts prebuttoned, so I simply had to slip them on over my head. My pants had Velcro, so I could fasten them myself. My socks had loops that I could grab and pull. BUT . . . there were still two buttons on my shirt that needed to be buttoned. Again, I *asked* for help. The first time I asked a hostess to do it, she was taken aback. But now it's amazing—if I am at the hotel for several days, the hostess will watch for me and step right up to help.

Fear: I was afraid to eat by myself. I still can't cut meat and I have difficulty with most flatware. *Solution:* I traveled with a special fork that allows me to feed myself. And now that I've traveled on my own several times, I can't tell you how many times people have offered to wash the fork for me and take special care of it.

What I learned is that we have everything around us we need to erase fear. Just look to your left and to your right at the people around you. Are they strangers? Doesn't matter. There are amazing people at every step of my journey who don't just assist me; they literally jump at the chance to help another human being!

The only way to find out if you can do something is to ACTUALLY DO IT. As Peter says, "It takes a little bit of trust, but the only way you will ever find out if you can fly solo is to experience your fear and take the leap and trust that you will be okay." Peter still experiences some anxiety when he travels on his own, but most of the fear is gone and has been replaced with gratitude for all the assistance people continue to offer him.

The reason I know Peter's story is that after facing the fact that he would never rope cattle again, he decided he would like to pursue a career as a public speaker and a trainer. Having heard me speak and after reading in *The Success Principles* that "success leaves clues," he decided to attend my Train-the-Trainer program. As a result, he wrote a book called *Cowboy Leadership,* delivered speeches, and created a seminar and a workshop all based on his "Saddle Up Philosophy."

FANTASIZED EXPERIENCES APPEARING REAL

Another important aspect to remember about fear is that, as humans, we've also evolved to the stage where almost all of our fears are now self-created. We frighten ourselves by fantasizing negative outcomes to any activity we might pursue. Luckily, because we are the ones doing the fantasizing, we are also the ones who can stop the fear by facing the actual facts, rather than giving in to our imaginations. We can choose to be sensible. Psychologists like to say that *fear* means

Fantasized
Experiences
Appearing
Real

To help you better understand how we actually bring unfounded fear into our lives, make a list of the things you are afraid to *do*. This is not a list of things you are afraid *of,* such as being afraid *of* spiders, but things you're afraid to *do,* such as being afraid to pick up a spider. For example, *I am afraid to*

- Ask my boss for a raise
- Ask Sally for a date
- Go skydiving
- Leave my kids home alone with a sitter
- Leave this job that I hate
- Ask my friends to look at my new business opportunity
- Delegate any part of my job to others

Now go back and restate each fear using the following format:

I want to _____, and I scare myself by imagining _____.

The key words are *I scare myself by imagining.* All fear is self-created by imagining some negative outcome in the future. Using some of the same fears listed above, the new format would look like this:

- I want to ask my boss for a raise, and I scare myself by imagining he would say no and be angry with me for asking.
- I want to ask Sally for a date, and I scare myself by imagining that she would say no and I would feel embarrassed.
- I want to leave this job I hate in order to pursue my dream, and I scare myself by imagining I would go bankrupt and lose my house.
- I want to ask my friends to look at my new network marketing business opportunity, and I scare myself by imagining they will think I am only interested in making money off them.
- I want to delegate parts of my work to others, and I scare myself by imagining that they won't do it as well as I would.

Can you see that you are the one creating the fear?

HOW TO GET RID OF FEAR

I have lived a long life and had many troubles, most of which never happened.

MARK TWAIN
Celebrated American author and humorist

One way to actually *disappear* your fear is to ask yourself what you're imagining that is scary to you, and then replace that image with its positive opposite.

When I was flying to Orlando recently to give a talk, I noticed the woman next to me was gripping the arms of her seat so tightly her knuckles were turning white. I introduced myself, told her I was a trainer, and said I couldn't help but notice her hands. I asked her, "Are you afraid?"

"Yes."

"Would you be willing to close your eyes and tell me what thoughts or images you are experiencing in your head?"

After she closed her eyes, she replied, "I just keep imagining the plane not getting off the runway and crashing."

"I see. Tell me, what are you headed to Orlando for?"

"I'm going there to spend four days with my grandchildren at Disney World."

"Great. What's your favorite ride at Disney World?"

"It's a Small World."

"Wonderful. Can you imagine being at Disney World in one of the gondolas with your grandchildren in the It's a Small World attraction?"

"Yes."

"Can you see the smiles and the looks of wonder on your grandchildren's faces as they watch all the little puppets and figures from the different countries bobbing up and down and spinning around?"

"Uh-huh."

At that point I started to sing, "It's a small world after all; it's a small world after all . . ."

Her face relaxed, her breathing deepened, and her hands released their grip on the arms of the seat.

In her mind, she was already at Disney World. She had replaced the catastrophic picture of the plane crashing with a positive image of her desired outcome, and instantly her fear disappeared.

You can use this same technique to disappear any fear that you might ever experience.

REPLACE THE PHYSICAL SENSATIONS FEAR BRINGS

Another technique that works for relieving fear is to focus on the *physical sensations* you're currently feeling—sensations you're probably just identifying as fear. Next, focus on those feelings you would *like* to be experiencing instead—courage, self-confidence, calm, joy.

Fix these two different impressions firmly in your mind's eye, then slowly shuttle back and forth between the two, spending about 15 seconds in each one. After a minute or two, the fear will dissipate and you will find yourself in a neutral, centered place.

REMEMBER WHEN YOU TRIUMPHED IN THE FACE OF FEAR

Did you ever learn to dive off a diving board? If so, you probably remember the first time you walked to the edge of the board and looked down. The water looked a lot deeper than it really was. And considering the height of the board and the height of your eyes above the board, it probably looked like a *very* long way down.

You were scared. But did you look at your mom or dad or the diving instructor and say, "You know, I'm just too afraid to do this right now. I think I'll go do some therapy on this, and if I can get rid of my fear, I'll come back and try again . . ."?

No! You didn't say that.

You felt the fear, somehow mustered up courage from somewhere, and jumped into the water. You felt the fear and did it anyway.

When you surfaced, you probably swam like crazy to the side of the pool and took a few well-earned deep breaths. Somewhere, there was a little rush of adrenaline, the thrill of having survived a risk, plus the thrill of jumping through the air into the water. After a minute, you probably did it again, and then again and again—enough to where it got to be really fun. Pretty soon, all of the fear was gone and you were doing cannonballs to splash your friends and maybe even learning how to do a backflip.

If you can remember that experience or the first time you drove a car or the first time you kissed someone on a date, you've got the model for everything that happens in life. New experiences may feel a little scary. That's the way it works. But every time you face a fear and do it anyway, you build up that much more confidence in your abilities.

SCALE DOWN THE RISK

Anthony Robbins says, "If you can't, you must, and if you must, you can." I agree. It is those very things that we are most afraid to do that provide the greatest liberation and growth for us.

If a fear is so big that it paralyzes you, scale down the amount of risk. Take on smaller challenges and work your way up. If you're starting your first job in sales, call on prospects or customers you think will be the easiest to sell to first. If you're asking for money for your business, practice on those lending sources whom you wouldn't want to get a loan from anyway. If you're anxious about taking on new responsibilities at work, start by asking to do parts of a project you're interested in. If you're learning a new sport, start at lower levels of skill. Master those skills you need to learn, move through your fears, and then take on bigger challenges.

WHEN YOUR FEAR IS REALLY A PHOBIA

Some fears are so strong that they can actually immobilize you. If you have a full-blown phobia, such as fear of flying or fear of being in an elevator, it can seriously inhibit your ability to be successful. Fortunately, there is a simple solution to most phobias. The Five-Minute Phobia Cure, developed by Dr. Roger Callahan, is easy to learn and can be self-administered as well as facilitated by a professional.

I learned about this magical technique from Dr. Callahan's book and video and have used it successfully in my seminars for more than 15 years.* The process uses a simple but precise pattern of tapping on various acupressure points of the body while you simultaneously imagine the object or experience that stimulates your phobic reaction. It acts in much the same way as a virus in a computer program by permanently interrupting the "program" or sequence of events that occur in the brain between the initial sighting of the thing you are afraid of (such as seeing a snake or stepping into an airplane) and the physical response (such as sweating, shaking, shallow breathing, or weak knees) you experience.

When I was leading a seminar for real estate agents, a woman revealed that she had a phobia about walking up stairs. In fact, she had experienced it that very morning, when in response to her request for directions to the seminar, the bellman had pointed to a huge staircase leading to the grand ballroom. Fortunately, there was also an elevator, so she made it to the seminar. If there hadn't been, she would have turned around and driven home. She admitted that she had never been on the second floor of any home she had ever sold. She would pretend she had already been up there, tell the prospective buyers what they would find on the second floor, on the basis of her reading of the listing sheet, and then let them explore it on their own.

I did the Five-Minute Phobia Cure with her and then took all 100 people out to the same hotel stairway that had petrified her earlier in the day. With no hesitation, heavy breathing, or drama, she walked up and down the stairs twice. It is that simple.

---

*If you have a phobia that is holding you back, visit rogercallahan.com for a free guide and other self-help materials. You can also schedule private consultations or find a practitioner near you at tftpractitioners.net.

TAKE A LEAP!

Come to the edge, He said.
They said: We are afraid.
Come to the edge, He said.
They came. He pushed them,
And they flew . . .

GUILLAUME APOLLINAIRE
Avant-garde French poet

All the successful people I know have been willing to take a chance—a leap of faith—even though they were afraid. Sometimes they were terrified, but they knew if they didn't act, the opportunity would pass them by. They trusted their intuition and they simply went for it.

Progress always involves risk; you can't steal
second base and keep your foot on first.

FREDERICK WILCOX
American author

Mike Kelley lives in paradise and owns several companies under the umbrella of Beach Activities of Maui. With only a year of college under his belt (he never did return to get his degree), Mike left Las Vegas at age 19 for the islands of Hawaii and ended up selling suntan lotion by the pool at a hotel in Maui. From these humble beginnings, Mike went on to create a company with 175 employees and over $5 million in annual revenues that provides catamaran and scuba diving excursions for tourists, plus concierge services and business centers for many of the island's hotels.

Mike credits much of his success to always being willing to take a leap when needed. When Beach Activities of Maui was attempting to expand its business, there was an important hotel whose business he wanted, but a competitor had held the contract for over 15 years. To maintain a competitive edge, Mike always reads the trade journals and keeps an ear open to what is happening in his business. One day he read that this hotel was changing general managers, and the new general manager who would be coming in lived in Copper Mountain, Colorado. This got Mike thinking: Because it's so hard to get through all of the gatekeepers to secure a meeting with a general manager, maybe he should try to contact him before he actually moved to Hawaii. Mike wrestled with what would be the best way to contact him. Should he write a letter? Should he call him on the phone? As he pondered these options, his friend Doug suggested, "Why don't you just hop on a plane and go see him?"

Always one to take action and take it now, Mike quickly put together a pro forma and a proposal and hopped on a plane the next night. After flying all night, he arrived in Colorado, rented a car, and drove the two hours out to Copper Mountain, showing up unannounced at the new general manager's office. Mike explained who he was, congratulated the general manager on his new promotion, told him that he looked forward to having him in Maui, and asked for a few moments to tell him about Beach Activities of Maui and what it could do for his hotel.

Mike didn't get the contract during that first meeting. But the fact that a young kid was so confident in himself and his business that he would take a leap of faith, jump on a plane, fly all the way to Denver—then drive out into the middle of Colorado on the off chance that he would be able to meet in person—left such a huge impression on the general manager that, when he did finally get to Hawaii, he awarded Mike the contract, which was worth hundreds of thousands of dollars to Mike's bottom line over the ensuing 15 years.

TAKING A LEAP CAN TRANSFORM YOUR LIFE

Authority is 20% given and 80% taken . . . so take it!
PETER UEBERROTH
Organizer of the 1984 Summer Olympics and commissioner
of Major League Baseball, 1984–1988

Multimillionaire Dr. John Demartini is a resounding success by anyone's standards. He owns several homes in Australia. He spent over 60 days a year for several years circumnavigating the globe with his wife in their $3 million luxury apartment onboard the $550 million ocean liner *World of ResidenSea*—a residence they purchased after selling their Trump Tower apartment in New York City.

The author of 54 training programs and 13 books and a featured teacher in the movie *The Secret,* John spends the year traveling the world speaking and conducting his courses on financial success and life mastery.

But John didn't start out rich and successful. At age seven, he was found to have a learning disability and was told that he would never read, write, or communicate normally. At 14, he dropped out of school, left his Texas home, and headed for the California coast. By 17, he had ended up in Hawaii, surfing the waves of Oahu's famed North Shore, where he almost died from strychnine poisoning. His road to recovery led him to Dr. Paul Bragg, a 93-year-old man who changed John's life by giving him one simple affirmation to repeat: "I am a genius and I apply my wisdom."

Inspired by Dr. Bragg, John went to college, earned his bachelor's degree from the University of Houston, and later earned his doctoral degree from the Texas Chiropractic College.

When he opened his first chiropractic office in Houston, John started with just 970 square feet of space. Within nine months, he'd more than doubled that and was offering free classes on healthy living. When attendance grew, John was ready to expand again. It was then that he took a leap that changed his career forever.

"It was Monday," John said. "The shoe store next door had vacated over the weekend." *What a perfect lecture hall,* John thought as he quickly phoned the leasing company.

When no one called him back, John concluded they weren't going to rent the space soon, so he took a leap.

"I called a locksmith to come out and open up the place," John said. "I thought the worst thing they would do was charge me rent."

He quickly transformed the space into a lecture hall and within days was holding free talks there on a nightly basis. Because the space was located right next to a movie theater, he added a loudspeaker so moviegoers could hear his lectures as they walked to their cars. Hundreds began attending classes and eventually became patients.

John's practice grew rapidly. Yet nearly six months went by before the property manager came to investigate.

"You've got a lot of courage," the manager said. "You remind me of me." In fact, he was so impressed with John's daring, he even gave John six months' free rent! "Anybody that has the courage to do what you did deserves it," he told him. The manager later invited John down to his office, where he offered him a quarter of a million dollars a year to come work for him. John turned it down because he had other plans, but it was a huge validation of his courage to act.

Taking a leap helped John build a thriving practice, which he later sold to begin consulting full time with other chiropractors.

"Taking that leap opened up a doorway for me," John said. "If I'd held back . . . if I had been cautious . . . I wouldn't have made the breakthrough that gave me the life I live today."

Do you want to be safe and good, or do you want to take a chance and be great?
JIMMY JOHNSON
Coach who led the Dallas Cowboys football team to two
consecutive Super Bowl championships in 1992 and 1993

HIGH INTENTION . . . LOW ATTACHMENT

If you want to remain calm and peaceful as you go through life, you have to have high intention and low attachment. You do everything you can to create your desired outcomes, and then you let it go. Sometimes you don't get the intended result by the date that you want. That is life. You just keep moving in the direction of your goal until you get there. Sometimes the universe has other plans, and often they are better than the ones you had in mind. That is why I recommend adding the phrase "this or something better" to the end of your affirmations.

When I was vacationing with my family on a cruise in Tahiti one summer, my son Christopher and my stepson Travis, both 12 at the time, and I set out on a guided bicycle tour around the island of Bora-Bora with some other members from our cruise ship. My intention for the day was a bonding experience with my two sons. The wind was blowing really hard that day and the trip was a difficult one. At one point, Stevie Eller, who was struggling along with her 11-year-old grandson, took a nasty fall and badly cut her leg. Because there were only a few others in the back of the pack with us, we stayed behind to help her. There were no homes or stores and virtually no traffic on the far side of the island, meaning that there was no way to call for help, so after attempting some crude first aid, we decided to all push on together. Bored with the slow pace, my boys took off ahead, and I spent the next several hours pedaling and walking next to my new friend until we eventually reached a hotel where she called for a taxi and I rejoined my sons, who had stopped for a swim. That night Stevie and her husband, Karl, asked us to join their family for dinner.

It turned out that they were on the nominating committee for the International Achievement Summit sponsored by the Academy of Achievement. Its mission? To "inspire youth with new dreams of achievement in a world of boundless opportunity" by bringing together over 200 university and graduate student delegates from around the world to interact with contemporary leaders who have achieved the difficult or impossible in service to their fellow humans. After our time together, they decided to nominate me to become a member of the Academy and receive their Golden Plate Award, joining previous recipients such as former president Bill Clinton, Placido Domingo, George Lucas, U.S. senator John McCain, former prime minister of Israel Shimon Peres, and Archbishop Desmond Tutu. Because my nomination was accepted, I was able to attend the annual four-day event with some of the brightest young future leaders and some of the most interesting and accomplished people in the world in 2004, and will be able to attend future meetings when I want to.

Had I been totally attached to my original outcome of a day with my two sons and left Stevie to the care of others, I would have missed an even bigger opportunity that spontaneously came my way. I have learned over the years that whenever one door seemingly closes, another door opens. You just have to keep positive, stay aware, and look to see what it is. Instead of getting upset when things don't unfold as you anticipated, always remember to ask yourself the question, "What's the possibility that this is?"

PRINCIPLE 16

BE WILLING TO PAY THE PRICE

*If people knew how hard I had to work to gain my mastery,
it wouldn't seem wonderful at all.*

MICHELANGELO
Renaissance sculptor and painter who spent four years lying on
his back painting the ceiling of the Sistine Chapel

Behind every great achievement is a story of education, training, practice, discipline, and sacrifice. You have to be willing to pay the price.

Maybe that price is pursuing one single activity while putting everything else in your life on hold. Maybe it's investing all of your own personal wealth or savings. Maybe it's the willingness to walk away from the safety of your current situation.

But though many things are typically required to reach a successful outcome, the *willingness* to do what's required adds that extra dimension to the mix that helps you persevere in the face of overwhelming challenges, setbacks, pain, and even personal injury.

PAIN IS ONLY TEMPORARY...
THE BENEFITS LAST FOREVER

I remember back to the 1976 Summer Olympic Games, when the men's gymnastic competition captured the attention of the world. With the roar of the crowd in the background, Japan's Shun Fujimoto landed a perfect triple-somersault twist dismount from the rings to clinch the gold medal in team gymnastics. With his face contorted in pain and his teammates holding their breath, Fujimoto followed a near-flawless routine by achieving a stunning and perfect landing—on a *broken* right knee. It was an extraordinary display of courage and commitment.

Interviewed later about the win, Fujimoto revealed that even though he had injured his knee during the earlier floor exercise, it became apparent as the competition continued that the team gold medal would be decided by the rings apparatus—his strongest event. "The pain shot through me like a knife," he said. "It brought tears to my eyes. But now I have a gold medal and the pain is gone."

What was it that gave Fujimoto his extraordinary courage in the face of excruciating pain and the very real risk of serious injury? It was a willingness to pay the price—and probably a long history of paying the price, every day, on the road to simply winning a spot to compete in the Olympics.

PRACTICE, PRACTICE, PRACTICE!

When I played with Michael Jordan on the Olympic team, there was a huge gap between his ability and the ability of the other great players on that team. But what impressed me was that he was always the first one on the floor and the last one to leave.

STEVE ALFORD
Olympic gold medalist, NBA player, and
head basketball coach at the University of Nevada, Reno

Before Bill Bradley became a U.S. senator from New Jersey, he was an amazing basketball player. He was an all-American at Princeton University, won an Olympic gold medal in 1964, played in the NBA Championships with the New York Knicks, and was inducted into the Basketball Hall of Fame. How did he do so well at his sport? Well, for one thing, when he was in high school, he practiced for four hours a day every day.

In his memoir *Time Present, Time Past,* Bradley offers the following account of his self-imposed basketball-training regimen: "I stayed behind to practice after my teammates had left. My practice routine was to end by making 15 baskets in a row from each of five spots on the floor." If he missed a shot, he would start over from the beginning. He continued this practice all through his college and professional career.

He developed this strong commitment to practice when he attended summer basketball camps for high school players sponsored by the St. Louis Hawks' "Easy" Ed Macauley, where he learned the importance of practicing: "When you're not practicing, someone somewhere is. And when the two of you meet, given roughly equal ability, he will win." Bill took that advice to heart. The hours of hard work paid off. Bill Bradley scored over 3,000 points in four years of high school basketball.

OLYMPIC ATHLETES PAY THE PRICE

Work hard in silence. Let your success be the noise.

SIMONE BILES
Winner of 11 Olympic gymnastic medals and 30 world gymnastic titles

According to John Troup, writing in *USA Today,* "The average Olympian trains four hours a day at least 310 days a year for six years before succeeding. Getting better begins with working out every day. By 7:00 A.M. most athletes have done more than many people do all day.... Given equal talent, the better-trained athlete can generally outperform the one who did not give a serious effort, and is usually more confident at the starting block. The four years before the Olympics, Greg Louganis probably practiced each of his dives 3,000 times. Kim Zmeskal has probably done every flip in her gymnastics routine at least 20,000 times, and Janet Evans has completed more than 240,000 laps. Training works, but it isn't easy or simple. Swimmers train an average of 10 miles a day, at speeds of 5 mph in the pool. That might not sound fast, but their heart rates average 160 the entire time. Try running up a flight of stairs, then check your heart rate. Then imagine having to do that for four hours! Marathon runners average 160 miles a week at 10 mph."[*]

Consider the workout schedule of Michael Phelps—with 28 medals, the most decorated Olympic athlete of all time. He was usually at the pool by 6:30 A.M., where he would swim for an average of six hours a day—that's around eight miles a day. He swam six days a week including holidays. In addition to time in the pool, he lifted weights to add explosive speed to his regimen, spending an hour three days a week lifting weights, as well as an hour three days a week stretching his muscles.

Although most of you reading this will never become Olympic athletes, nor do you want to, you can become world class in whatever you do by putting in the disciplined effort to excel at your chosen trade, craft, or profession. To win at whatever game you choose to play, you need to be willing to pay the price.

---

[*] John Troup, *USA Today,* July 29, 1992.

> *It's not the will to win that matters—everyone has that.*
> *It's the will to prepare to win that matters.*
>
> PAUL "BEAR" BRYANT
> College football's winningest coach, with 323 victories, including
> 6 national championships and 14 Southeastern Conference titles

PRACTICE SPECIFIC THINGS CONSISTENTLY

> *Practice isn't the thing you do once you're good.*
> *It's the thing you do that makes you good.*
>
> MALCOLM GLADWELL
> Author of *Outliers: The Story of Success*

While many athletes, musicians, dancers, comedians, and other gifted people practice their sports skills, dance variations, and other routines on a regular basis, Dr. Christine Carter—a sociologist at UC Berkeley's Greater Good Science Center—says elite performers differ in their approach to practice time. Not only do top performers practice more than people of average talent, but they spend hours upon hours in what she calls "deliberate practice." Rather than merely plunking away at the keyboard because it is fun, they practice to reach specific objectives—such as to play a new piece that is just beyond their reach. In the beginning, Dr. Carter continues, they may also practice a new phrase or even a single measure again and again and again.*

While deliberate practice is rarely pleasurable, usually difficult, and quite often boring, an elite performer's willingness to practice in this goal-oriented way is what sets the world's best apart from people who are merely good at something. In other words, they don't just practice for fun—they practice specific things consistently over a long period of time. Consider this quote from Geoffrey Colvin, author of *Talent Is Overrated:*

---

*http://www.positivelypositive.com/2013/09/15/a-new-theory-of-elite-performance

What Really Separates World-Class Performers from Everybody Else:* "The reality that deliberate practice is hard can even be seen as good news. It means that most people won't do it. So your willingness to do it will distinguish you all the more."

What's more, numerous studies now show this commitment to *practicing toward a specific goal* is what helps elite performers overcome a lack of innate talent or prevail over deficiencies in their physical body—since consistent practice can actually help develop better physical characteristics such as perfect pitch, more flexible joints, higher octaves, and other attributes!

Legendary violinist Isaac Stern was once confronted by a middle-aged woman after a concert. She gushed, "Oh, I'd give my life to play like you!" "Lady," said Stern acidly, "that I did!"

DETERMINED TO BE AN ARTIST AT ANY COST

In the 1970s, Wyland was the classic starving artist who threw everything into his dream. He painted and he hustled. He would set up art shows at his local high school and sell original paintings for just $35, knowing that the only way he could develop as an artist was to sell his paintings for whatever he could get to earn enough money to buy the necessary supplies he needed to create more.

Then one day, in what was to become a defining moment for the young artist, Wyland's mother told him, "Art really isn't a job; it's a hobby. Now go out and get a real job." The next day she dropped him off at the Detroit Unemployment Bureau. But to Wyland's dismay, he was fired from three different jobs three days in a row. He couldn't keep his mind on the boring factory work—he wanted to be creative and paint. A week later, he built a studio in the basement and worked day and night creating a portfolio that eventually won him a full scholarship to art school in Detroit.

Wyland painted every moment he could, and he managed to sell some paintings, but for years he just managed to scrape by. But because he was determined that art was the only thing he wanted to do, he continued to work and hone his craft.

---

* I highly recommend reading *Talent Is Overrated* by Geoffrey Colvin (New York: Portfolio Trade, 2010), *The Talent Code: Greatness Isn't Born. It's Grown. Here's How* by Daniel Coyle (New York: Bantam, 2009), and *Outliers: The Story of Success* by Malcolm Gladwell (New York: Back Bay Books, 2011) to learn more about the power of deliberate practice.

One day, Wyland realized he had to go where other artists flourished and where new ideas were born. His destination was the well-known art colony of Laguna Beach, California, and with his dream fully alive, he moved into a cramped, tiny studio where he both worked and lived for several more years. Eventually, he was invited to participate in the annual art festival, where he learned to talk about his work and interact with collectors. Soon after, galleries in Hawaii discovered him but often sold his paintings without ever paying him, claiming their overhead was high. Out of the frustration of finally selling high-priced paintings only to have the money disappear, Wyland realized he had to own his own galleries. In his own galleries, he could control every aspect of selling his art—from how it was framed and hung to how it was sold and who it was sold by. Today, 36 years after opening his first gallery in Laguna Beach, he creates as many as 1,000 works of art a year (some of which sell for $200,000 apiece), creates artistic collaborations with the people at Disney, owns four homes in Hawaii, California, and Florida, and lives the life he always dreamed of.

Perhaps you, like Wyland, want to turn your hobby into your career. You can become hugely successful doing what you love if you are willing to pay the price. "In the beginning, you've got to kind of suffer," Wyland says, "giving in to everybody else. But there's nothing better than eventually achieving success on your own terms."

WILLING TO DO WHATEVER IT TAKES

Gordon Weiske found his passion at an early age. When he was six years old, his parents took him to see his first movie—*Close Encounters of the Third Kind*. Two hours later he knew that what he wanted to do with his life was make movies.

Growing up in Toronto, Canada, he made it through high school making short films with friends on outdated equipment, but they were enough to slap together a demo reel that got him accepted to a top film program at a Canadian university. He did well there until his third year, when he made a decision that threatened to derail him on the way to his dream.

With only three edit suites available for 150 students to edit their films on, he constantly found himself unable to book an edit suite.

That's when he made the choice to take matters into his own hands and stole a security pass card from one of his professors so he could sneak in and work from midnight to 5:00 A.M. to finish his film. For the first week everything went well. When week two rolled around, he invited two of his buddies to come in so they, too, could work on their film projects in the neighboring edit suites.

But in the third week, having finished their film projects, they decided to celebrate in their secret haven with their girlfriends and booze. At the height of the party, the campus police busted in on them, and Gordon was expelled from the university.

Gordon suddenly found himself with no degree and a pending trespassing charge. Still wanting to get into the film business, he gathered what little confidence he had left and went knocking at all the studio doors asking for a job. Any job! Even offering to work for free, he was met with the same old cliché: *"Don't call us, kid . . . we'll call you!"* Two weeks went by and his phone didn't ring once. And then it hit him. *If I'm going to make it in this business, I'm going to have to stand out from all the rest and never take no for an answer.*

At the time, Toronto hadn't quite hit major studio status yet, and most production offices were dirty old steel mills converted into soundstages. It's hard to imagine now, but it was so bad that whenever it would rain, film production would grind to a halt due to the echoing sound of raindrops pelting down on the tin-plated rooftops.

Knowing the grimy conditions, the second time Gordon visited each run-down studio and production office that had rejected him, he went armed with a bottle of Windex and a roll of paper towels—and asked for permission to clean their toilets. Some laughed, as they weren't sure if he was serious or not, while others gladly said yes—following it with, "But, kid . . . I'm still not going to hire you!"

Gordon did this every day for a week, each day religiously cleaning the dirtiest of dirty production office toilets that had once been graced by steelworkers. He encountered dirt on top of dirt, but Gordon worked until that porcelain shined. He also made sure to leave his phone number and name credit behind, because one thing he had learned about the film business is how important your name credit is. In fact, on the back of every stall door he attached the following sign to his film résumé:

WASHROOM CLEANED BY GORDON.
LOOKING TO GET MY FOOT IN THE WORLD OF FILM.
WILL WORK FOR FOOD!

Even though his film résumé and experience on paper was slim, he made sure his work spoke for him with the cleanest toilets in town. Think about it. What a perfect place to hang your résumé and get someone's undivided attention—while they are sitting on the toilet with nothing else to do but read what's hanging in front of them.

At the time—and unknown to Gordon—there was a team of Los Angeles producers scouting Toronto to see if the city was a suitable match for Boston, the setting for a film they were looking to shoot. It turned out that, in every production office they visited, they noticed a résumé inside the toilet stall. It actually became a game of theirs to look into each production office facility to see if Gordon's résumé was hanging there.

One night Gordon's phone rang and he was hired by the Los Angeles producers for two weeks, happily working for food and gas money as he ran errands for them. When the two weeks were up, they called him into their hotel room and shared the good news. The movie had just been given the green light and was going to be called *Good Will Hunting*. Even better news, the producers made Gordon the personal assistant to Matt Damon and Ben Affleck, who at the time were two relatively unknown actors, but were about to become superstars.

Because of his willingness to pay the price and do whatever it took, within a month of being expelled from film school and having his dreams crushed, he ended up working on an Academy Award–winning film that changed his life!

After the success of *Good Will Hunting,* Gordon went on to work on a long list of Hollywood blockbuster films for some of the industry's biggest names, including Steve Martin, Hugh Jackman, John Travolta, Charlize Theron, Gene Hackman, Michelle Pfeiffer, Helen Mirren, Forest Whitaker, and Morgan Freeman.

In 2011, Gordon was asked to join the DreamWorks development team working alongside his personal hero, Steven Spielberg—the director of *Close Encounters of the Third Kind,* the movie that had originally inspired Gordon's dream. Today Gordon is the president of CanWood Entertainment, a global entertainment company headquartered in Toronto, Canada.

And the sweetest part of the story? Not only has Gordon been invited many times to speak to the graduating class of the university that expelled him, they dismissed all trespassing charges!

PUTTING IN THE TIME

The big secret in life is that there is no secret. Whatever is your goal, you can get there if you are willing to work.

OPRAH WINFREY
Talk show host, actress, producer, author, and philanthropist

Part of paying the price is the willingness to do whatever it takes to get the job done—no matter what it takes, no matter how long it takes, no matter what comes up. It's a done deal. You are responsible for the results you intend. No excuses—just a world-class performance or an outstanding result that can be counted on. Consider this:

- Ernest Hemingway rewrote *A Farewell to Arms* . . . 39 times. This dedication to excellence would later lead him to win the Pulitzer and Nobel prizes for literature.
- M. Scott Peck received only a $7,500 advance for *The Road Less Traveled;* however, he was willing to pay the price to fulfill his dream. During the first year after it was published, he participated in 1,000 radio interviews to advertise and promote his book. He continued to do a minimum of one interview a day for the next 13 years, keeping the book on the *New York Times* bestsellers list for over 694 weeks, or more than 13 years (a record), and selling more than 10 million copies in over 20 languages.
- Michael Crichton created the Emmy Award–winning television series *ER*. His books have sold over 200 million copies in 30 languages, and 14 have been made into films, 7 of which he directed. His books and films include *Jurassic Park, The Andromeda Strain, Congo, Twister,* and *Westworld*. He is the only person to have had, at the same time, the number one book, the number one movie, and the number one television show in the United States. With all of his natural talent, Michael said, "Books aren't written—they're rewritten. . . . It is one of the hardest things to accept, especially after the seventh rewrite hasn't quite done it."

*Talent is cheaper than table salt. What separates the talented
individual from the successful one is a lot of hard work.*

STEPHEN KING
Bestselling author with over 50 books in print, many of which have
been made into movies, such as *Carrie, Cujo,* and *The Green Mile*

IT'S ABOUT BUILDING MOMENTUM

When a NASA rocket takes off from Cape Canaveral, it uses up a large portion of its total fuel just to overcome the gravitational pull of the Earth. Once it has achieved that, it can virtually coast through space for the rest of its journey. Likewise, an amateur athlete often puts in full training days with Spartan self-discipline for years. But after winning a gold medal or a world championship, offers for endorsements, spokesperson contracts, speaking engagements, retail merchandise deals, and other entrepreneurial opportunities often come pouring in, allowing them to slow down a bit and take advantage of the momentum they created earlier in their career.

Likewise, in any business or profession, once you have paid the price to establish yourself as an expert, a person of integrity who delivers high-quality results on time, you get to reap the benefits of that for the rest of your life. When I started speaking, no one had ever heard of me. As I delivered more and more speeches and seminars that delivered what the client wanted, my reputation grew. I had a file full of glowing testimonial letters and a track record of credibility that was built up over many years of giving free and low-fee talks until I had honed my craft. The same was true for writing books. It took many years to get good at it.

If you are involved in network marketing, you have to put in countless hours in the beginning, not getting paid what you are worth. You may work for months with no real income, but eventually the multiplier effect of your growing downline takes effect, and eventually you are making more money than you ever imagined possible.

Creating momentum is an important part of the success process. In fact, successful people know that if you are willing to pay the price in the beginning, you can reap the benefits for the rest of your life.

GOING THROUGH THE AWKWARD STAGE

Business consultant Marshall Thurber has said, "Anything worth doing well is worth doing badly in the beginning." Remember when you first learned to drive a car, to ride a bicycle, to play an instrument, or to play a sport? You understood in advance that you were going to be very awkward at first. You assumed that awkwardness was just part of what was required to learn that new skill that you wanted.

Well, not surprisingly, this initial awkwardness applies to anything you undertake, so you have to be willing to go through that awkward stage in order to become proficient. Children give themselves permission to do this. But sadly, by the time we're adults, we are so often afraid of making a mistake that we don't let ourselves be awkward, so we don't learn the way children do. We're so afraid of doing it wrong.

I didn't learn to ski until I was in my forties, and in the beginning, I was definitely not good at it. Over time, with lessons, I got better.

Even the first time I kissed a girl, it was awkward. But to gain a new skill or get better at *anything* you want to do, you have to be willing to keep on going in the face of looking foolish and feeling stupid for a time.

FIND OUT THE PRICE YOU HAVE TO PAY

Of course, if you don't know what the price is, you can't choose to pay it. Sometimes the first step is to investigate the steps that will be required to achieve your desired goal.

For example, many people—perhaps you—say they want to own a yacht. But have you ever researched how much money you would have to earn to buy one . . . or how much it costs to harbor the yacht in your local marina . . . or how much the monthly maintenance, fuel, insurance, and license cost? You may need to research what costs others have had to pay to achieve dreams similar to yours. You might want to make a list of several people who have already done what you want to do and interview them about what sacrifices they had to make along the way.

You may discover that some costs are more than you want to pay. You may not want to risk your health, your relationships, or your entire life savings for a certain goal. You have to weigh all of the factors. That dream job may not be worth your marriage, your kids, or a lack of balance in your life. Only you can decide what is right for you and what price *you* are willing to pay. It may be that what you want doesn't serve you in the long run. But if it does, find out what you need to do, and then set about doing it.

PRINCIPLE 17

ASK! ASK! ASK!

You've got to ask. Asking is, in my opinion, the world's most powerful and neglected secret to success and happiness.

PERCY ROSS
Self-made multimillionaire and philanthropist

History is filled with examples of incredible riches and astounding benefits people have received simply by asking for them. Yet surprisingly, asking—one of the most powerful success principles of all—is still a challenge that holds most people back. If you are not afraid to ask anybody for anything, then skip over this chapter. But if you are like most people, you may be holding yourself back by not asking for the information, assistance, support, money, and time that you need to fulfill your vision and make your dreams come true.

WHY PEOPLE ARE AFRAID TO ASK

Why are people so afraid to ask? They are afraid of many things, such as looking needy, looking foolish, and looking stupid. But mostly they're afraid of experiencing rejection. They are afraid of hearing the word *no*.

The sad thing is that they're actually rejecting themselves in advance. They're saying no to themselves before anyone else even has a chance to.

When I was a graduate student at the school of education at the University of Chicago, I participated in a self-development group with 20 other people. During one of the exercises, one of the men asked one of the women if she found him attractive. I was both shocked by the boldness of the question and embarrassed for the asker—fearing what he might get as a response. As it turned out, she said that she did. Emboldened by his success, I then asked her if she found *me* attractive. After this little exercise in "bold asking," several of the women told us that they found it unbelievable how scared men were when it came to asking women for a date. She said, "You reject yourself before you even give us a chance to. Take the risk. We might say yes."

Don't assume that you are going to get a no. Take the risk to ask for whatever you need and want. If they say no, you are no worse off than when you started. If they say yes, you are a lot better off. Just by being willing to ask, you can get a raise, a donation, a room with an ocean view, a discount, a free sample, a date, a better assignment, a more convenient delivery date, an extension, time off, or help with the housework.

HOW TO ASK FOR WHAT YOU WANT

There's a specific science to asking for and getting what you want or need in life, and Mark Victor Hansen and I have written a whole book about it. And though I recommend you learn more by reading our book *The Aladdin Factor,* here are some quick tips to get you started:

1. **Ask as if you expect to get it.** Ask with a positive expectation. Ask from the place that you have already been given it. It's a done deal. Ask as if you expect to get a yes.
2. **Assume you can.** Don't start with the assumption that you can't get it. If you are going to assume anything, assume you *can* get an upgrade. Assume you *can* get a table by the window. Assume that you *can* return it without a sales slip. Assume that you *can* get a scholarship, that you *can* get a raise, that you *can* get tickets at this late date. Don't ever assume against yourself.
3. **Ask someone who can give it to you.** Qualify the person. "Who would I have to speak to to get . . ." "Who is authorized to make a decision about . . ." "What would have to happen for me to get . . ."
4. **Be clear and specific.** In my seminars, I often ask, "Who wants more money?" I pick someone who raises a hand, and I give that person a dollar. I say, "You now have more money. Are you satisfied?"

    The person usually says, "No, I want more than that."

    So I give the person a couple of quarters, and ask, "Is that enough for you?"

    "No, I want more than that."

    "Well, just how much do you want? We could play this game of 'more' for days and never get to what you want."

The person usually gives me a specific number, and then I point out how important it is to be specific. Vague requests produce vague results. Your requests need to be specific. When it comes to money, you need to ask for a specific amount.

Don't say: I want a raise.
Do say: I want a raise of $500 a month.

When it comes to *when* you want something done, don't say "soon" or "whenever it's convenient." Give a specific date and time.

Don't say: I want to spend some time with you this weekend.
Do say: I would like to go out for dinner and a movie with you on Saturday night. Would that work for you?

When it comes to a behavioral request, be specific. Say exactly what you want the person to do.

Don't say: I want more help around the house.
Do say: I want you to wash the dishes every night after dinner and take out the garbage Monday, Wednesday, and Friday nights.

5. **Ask repeatedly.** One of the most important principles of success is persistence, not giving up. Whenever you're asking others to participate in the fulfillment of your goals, some people are going to say no. They may have other priorities, commitments, and reasons not to participate. It's not a reflection on you.

Just get used to the idea that there's going to be a lot of rejection along the way to your goal. The key is not to give up. When someone says no, you keep on asking. Why? Because when you keep on asking—even the same person again and again—you might get a yes . . .

On a different day
When the person is in a better mood

When you have new data to present
After you've proven your commitment to them
When circumstances have changed
When you've learned how to close better
When the person trusts you more
When you have paid your dues
When the economy is better

Kids understand this success principle perhaps better than anyone. They will ask the same person for the same thing over and over again without any hesitation. They eventually wear you down.

I once read a story in *People* magazine about a man who asked the same woman more than 30 times to marry him. No matter how many times she said no, he kept coming back—and eventually she said yes!

A TELLING STATISTIC

Herbert True, a marketing specialist at Notre Dame University, found that

- 44% of all salespeople quit trying to sell to a prospect after the first call
- 24% quit after the second call
- 14% quit after the third call
- 12% quit trying to sell their prospect after the fourth call

This means that 94% of all salespeople quit by the fourth call. But 60% of all sales are made *after* the fourth call. This revealing statistic shows that 94% of all salespeople don't give themselves a chance at 60% of the prospective buyers.

You may have the capacity, but you also have to have the tenacity! To be successful, you have to ask, ask, ask, ask, ask!

ASK, AND IT SHALL BE GIVEN TO YOU

A few years ago, Sylvia Collins flew all the way from Australia to Santa Barbara to take one of my weeklong seminars, where she learned about the power of asking. A year later, I received this letter from her.

I'm selling [real-estate] developments on the Gold Coast and work with a team of guys mostly in their twenties. The skills I've acquired through your seminars have helped me perform and be an active part of a winning team. I must tell you how having self-esteem and not being afraid to ask has impacted this office.

At a recent staff meeting, we were asked what we would like to do for our once-a-month team-building day. I asked Michael, the managing director, "What target would we have to reach for you to take us to an island for a week?"

Everyone went silent and looked at me; obviously it was out of everyone's comfort zone to ask such a thing. Michael looked around and then looked at me and said, "Well, if you reach . . . (and then he set a financial target), I'll take the whole team (ten of us) to the Great Barrier Reef!"

Well, the next month we reached the target and off we went to Lady Elliott Island for four days—airfare, accommodations, food, and activities all paid by the company. We snorkeled together, had bonfires on the beach, played tricks on each other, and had so much fun!

Afterwards, Michael gave us another target and said he would take us to Fiji if we reached it—and we reached that target in December!

ASK FOR AN UPGRADE

Patty Aubery, who has worked with me for more than 30 years now, tells the following story about the power of asking:

When I asked Jeff where he wanted to go for our honeymoon, he said, "Let's go to Maui. Make arrangements for something really special." So, I did! I reserved a beautiful suite at one of the nicest hotels on the island. When I told my husband where we were staying, he said, "Great. Did you ask if they have twenty-four-hour room service?"

I did ask, and they said it wasn't twenty-four, but it was until 2:00 A.M.

When we arrived at the hotel, we checked in and immediately went to our room. We were both dying of thirst and couldn't wait to crack open the minibar. That's when we realized there wasn't one! We weren't happy about it, but I decided nothing was going to ruin this special trip. We would just forget about it.

Then I decided to call room service. The person on the other end of the phone told me that room service was only available from 6:00 to 10:00 in the morning and from 6:00 to 10:00 in the evening! My husband was not happy, to say the least. I told him I would take care of the problem, and I went straight downstairs to see the manager.

When I met with the manager, I told her, "For $350 a day, I expect room service and a minibar. The brochure and the people I spoke with assured me I would have both."

She apologized and said, "But there is really nothing I can do. The kitchen is closed during those hours and there are no minibars on the property." She started to get agitated with me.

I went back to our room and told my husband what had happened. This might not seem like a big deal to the average person, but when someone guarantees me something like this, I expect it. My husband said, "Honey, look, it's our honeymoon! Let's not let this bother us." I couldn't help it. I wasn't going to settle.

I said, "Look, it's late. I'm going to go to bed, but in the morning, I am going back down there, and I am going to ask for the manager's manager. Working for Jack Canfield all these years has ingrained it into my head—*ask, ask, ask!* I mean after all, what are they going to do to me? Worst case, I have to spend a week in this suite without my minibar!"

The next morning my husband was almost embarrassed—he didn't even want to be present when I asked to see the "head manager." Well, the "head manager" ended up being the son of the owner. I introduced myself and stated my case. I said, "I made it very clear to your reservationist that having room service and a minibar was important to me, and that person assured me it was no problem. Now, I am here, and it is a problem. What I want is the following: A room that will be able to supply me with food and drinks twenty-four hours a day."

The manager then explained that the only rooms that had refrigerators were the villas on the water and they went for $895 per day. I then said, "Fine, that's where I would like to stay, and I would like it for the price of my suite." Five minutes later, he came out of his office and said, "Here are your keys for the villa, Mrs. Aubery. I hope you enjoy your stay."

I thought my husband was going to fall over when I told him what had happened. I said, "See, Jack is right. You have to ask, ask, ask!"

YOU HAVE NOTHING TO LOSE AND EVERYTHING TO GAIN BY ASKING

To be successful, you have to take risks, and one of the risks is the willingness to risk rejection. Here's an email I received from Donna Hutcherson, who heard me speak at her company's convention in Scottsdale, Arizona.

> My husband Dale and I heard you at the Walsworth convention in early January.... Dale came as one of the spouses.... He was particularly impressed by your mention of not having anything to lose by asking or trying. After hearing you speak, he decided to go for one of his lifetime goals (and heart's desire)—a head football coaching position. He applied for four openings within my sales territory and Sebring High School called him back the next day, encouraging him to fill out the application online. He did so right away and could hardly sleep that night. After two interviews he was chosen over 61 other applicants. Today Dale accepted the position as head football coach at Sebring High School in Sebring, Florida.
>
> Thank you for your vision and inspiration.

A year later, I heard from Donna again. Having taken over a program with back-to-back seasons of one win, nine losses, and a reputation for giving up, Dale led the Sebring High School team to a winning record—including four games where the team came from behind to win in the final three minutes of the game. Not only that, but Dale also coached the team to a county championship and the playoffs—for only the third time in the 78-year history of the school.

He was named County Coach of the Year and Sports Story of the Year. Most important, though, is that he changed the lives of the many players, staff, and students with whom he worked.

WILL YOU GIVE ME SOME MONEY?

In 1997, 21-year-old Chad Pregracke set out on a one-man mission to clean up the Mississippi River. He started with a 20-foot boat and his own two hands.

When Chad realized he would need more than his 20-foot boat—barges, trucks, and equipment—he asked state and local officials for help, only to be turned down. Not to be dissuaded, Chad grabbed a phone book, turned to the business listings, and called Alcoa—"because," he said, "it started with an A."

Armed only with his passionate commitment to his dream, Chad asked to speak to the "top guy." Eventually Alcoa gave him $8,400. Later, working his way through the As, he called Anheuser-Busch. As reported in *Smithsonian* magazine, Mary Alice Ramirez, the director of environmental outreach at Anheuser-Busch, remembers her first conversation with Chad this way:

"Will you give me some money?" Chad asked.

"Who are you?" replied Ramirez.

"I want to get rid of the garbage in the Mississippi River," Chad said.

"Can you show me a proposal?" Ramirez inquired.

"What's a proposal?" Chad replied.

Ramirez eventually invited Chad to a meeting and gave him a check for $25,000 to expand his Mississippi River Beautification and Restoration Project.*

More important than Chad's knowledge of fund-raising was his clear desire to make a difference, his unflagging enthusiasm, his complete dedication to the project—and his willingness to ask.

Eventually, everything Chad needed was secured through asking. He now has a board of directors made up of lawyers, accountants, and corporate officers. He has 12 full-time staff members and more than 120,000 volunteers and has raised millions of dollars in donations to support the work. He now has a fleet of five barges, three towboats, a crane, an excavator, five work boats, two skid steers, and six work trucks.

Over the years, he has cleaned up thousands of miles of shoreline on the Mississippi and 22 other rivers—removing over 13 million pounds of trash—but he's also drawn attention to the health and beauty of all rivers and the responsibility we all share in keeping them clean.† Chad's leadership and vision have earned him more than 40 awards and accolades, including the 2013 CNN Hero of the Year, the Jefferson Award for Public Service, and Mitchum's Hardest Working Person in America, as well as being honored at the Points of Light Tribute at the Kennedy Center, where he was given a standing ovation by all four living former U.S. presidents.

---

*"Trash Talker," *Smithsonian*, April 2003, pages 116–17.
†For more information about Chad's work, visit livinglandsandwaters.org.

START ASKING TODAY

Take time now to make a list of the things that you want that you don't ask for at home, school, or work. Next to each one, write down how you stop yourself from asking. What is your fear? Next, write down what it is costing you not to ask. Then write down what benefit you would get if you were to ask.

Take time to make a list of what you need to ask for in each of the following seven goal categories that I outlined in Principle 3 ("Decide What You Want"): financial, job and career, fun time and recreation, health and fitness, relationships, personal projects and hobbies, and contribution to the larger community.

Do you need to ask for: a raise, a loan, seed money, venture capital, feedback about your performance, a referral, an endorsement, time off to get additional training, someone to babysit your children, a massage, a hug, or help with a volunteer project?

PRINCIPLE 18

REJECT REJECTION

We keep going back, stronger, not weaker, because we will not allow rejection to beat us down. It will only strengthen our resolve. To be successful there is no other way.

EARL G. GRAVES
Founder and publisher of *Black Enterprise* magazine

If you are going to be successful, you are going to need to learn how to deal with rejection. Rejection is a natural part of life. You get rejected when you aren't picked for the team, don't get the part in the play, don't get elected, don't get into the college or graduate school of your choice, don't get the job or promotion you wanted, don't get the sale, don't get the raise you wanted, don't get the appointment you requested, don't get the date you asked for, don't get the permission you requested, or you get fired. You get rejected when your manuscript is rejected, your proposal is turned down, your new product idea is passed over, your fund-raising request is ignored, your design concept is not accepted, your application for membership is denied, or your offer of marriage is not accepted.

REJECTION IS A MYTH!

To get over rejection, you have to realize that rejection is really a myth. It doesn't really exist. It is simply a concept that you hold in your head. Think about it. If you ask Patty to have dinner with you and she says no, you didn't have anyone to eat dinner with before you asked her, and you don't have anyone to eat dinner with after you asked her. The situation didn't get worse; it stayed the same. It only gets worse if you go inside and tell yourself something extra like "See, Mother was right. No one will ever like me. I am the slug of the universe!"

If you apply to Harvard for graduate school and you don't get in, you weren't in Harvard before you applied, and you are not in Harvard after you applied. Again, your life didn't get worse; it stayed the same. You haven't really lost anything. And think about this—you have spent your whole life not going to Harvard; you know how to handle that.

The truth is, you never have anything to lose by asking, and because there is something to possibly gain, by all means ask.

SWSWSWSW

Whenever you ask anyone for anything, remember the following: SWSWSWSW, which stands for "some will, some won't; so what—someone's waiting." Some people are going to say yes, and some are going to say no. So what! Out there somewhere, someone is waiting for you and your ideas. It is simply a numbers game. You have to keep asking until you get a yes. The yes is out there waiting. As my coauthor Mark Victor Hansen is so fond of saying, "What you want wants you." You just have to hang in there long enough to eventually get a yes.

81 NOS, 9 STRAIGHT YESES

Because the program had so dramatically changed her life, a graduate of my "Self-Esteem and Peak Performance Seminar" was volunteering in the evenings to call people to enroll them in an upcoming seminar I was conducting in St. Louis. She made a commitment to talk to three people every night for a month. Many of the calls turned into long conversations with people asking tons of questions. She made a total of 90 phone calls. The first 81 people decided not to take the seminar. The next 9 people all signed up. She had a 10% success ratio, which is a good ratio for phone enrollments, but all 9 enrollments came in the last 9 calls. What if she had given up after the first 50 people and said, "This just isn't working. It's not worth the effort. Nobody is signing up." But because she had a dream of sharing with others the life-transforming experience that she had had, she persevered in the face of a lot of rejection, knowing that it was indeed a numbers game. And her commitment to the outcome paid off—she was instrumental in helping 9 people transform their lives.

If you're committed to a cause that evokes your passion and commitment, you keep learning from your experiences, and you stay the course to the end, you will eventually create your desired outcome.

Never give up on your dream. . . . Perseverance is all important. If you don't have the desire and the belief in yourself to keep trying after you've been told you should quit, you'll never make it.

TAWNI O'DELL
Author of *Back Roads,* an Oprah Book Club pick

JUST SAY "NEXT!"

Get used to the idea that there is going to be a lot of rejection along the way to your goals. The secret to success is to not give up. When someone says no, you say, *"Next!"* Keep on asking. When Colonel Harland Sanders left home with his pressure cooker and his special recipe for cooking Southern fried chicken, he received 1,009 rejections before he found someone to believe in his dream. Because he rejected rejection over 1,000 times, there are now more than 25,000 KFC outlets in 145 countries, and territories around the world.

If one person tells you no, ask someone else. Remember, there are over 5 billion people on the planet! Someone, somewhere, sometime will say yes. Don't get stuck in your fear or resentment. Move on to the next person. It is a numbers game. Someone is waiting to say yes.

CHICKEN SOUP FOR THE SOUL®

Success consists of going from failure to failure with no loss of enthusiasm.

WINSTON CHURCHILL
Former prime minister of the United Kingdom

In the fall of 1991, Mark Victor Hansen and I began the process of selling our first *Chicken Soup for the Soul*® book to a publisher. We flew to New York with Jeff Herman, our literary agent at the time, and met with every major publisher that would grant us a meeting. All of them said they weren't interested. "Collections of short stories don't sell." "There's no edge to the stories." "The title will never work." After that, we were rejected by another 20 publishers who had received the manuscript through the mail. After being rejected by more than 30 publishers, our agent gave the book back to us and said, "I'm sorry; I can't sell it for you." What did we do? We said, *"Next!"*

We also knew we had to think outside the box. After weeks of wracking our brains, we hit on an idea that we thought would work. We printed up a form that was a promise to buy the book when it was published. It included a place for people to write their name, address, and the number of books they pledged to buy.

Over a period of months, we asked everyone who attended our speeches or seminars to complete the form if they would buy a copy of the book when it was published. Eventually we had promises to buy 20,000 books.

The following spring, Mark and I attended the American Booksellers Association convention in Anaheim, California, and walked from booth to booth, talking to any publisher who would listen. Even with copies of our signed pledge forms to demonstrate the market for our book, we were turned down again and again. But again and again we said, *"Next!"* At the end of the second very long day, we gave a copy of the first 30 stories in the book to Peter Vegso and Gary Seidler, copresidents of Health Communications, Inc., a struggling publisher specializing in addiction-and-recovery books, who agreed to take it home and look it over. Later that week, Gary Seidler took the manuscript to the beach and read it. He loved it and decided to give us a chance. Those hundreds of "nexts" had paid off! After more than 140 rejections, that first book went on to sell 10 million copies, spawning a series of 250 bestselling books that have been translated into 43 languages with worldwide sales of 500 million books.

And those pledge forms? When the book was finally published, we stapled an announcement to the signed forms, sent them to the person at the address on the form, and waited for a check. Almost everyone who had promised to buy a book came through on his or her commitment. In fact, one entrepreneur in Canada bought 1,700 copies and gave one to every one of his clients.

This manuscript of yours that has just come back from another editor is a precious package. Don't consider it rejected. Consider that you've addressed it "to the editor who can appreciate my work" and it has simply come back stamped "not at this address." Just keep looking for the right address.

BARBARA KINGSOLVER
Bestselling author of *The Poisonwood Bible*

155 REJECTIONS DIDN'T STOP HIM

When 19-year-old Rick Little wanted to start a program in high schools that would teach kids how to deal with their feelings, handle conflict, clarify their life goals, and learn communication skills and values that would help them live more effective and fulfilling lives, he wrote a proposal and shopped it to over 155 foundations. He slept in the back of his car and ate peanut butter on crackers for the better part of a year. But he never gave up his dream. Eventually, the Kellogg Foundation gave Rick $130,000. (That's almost $1,000 for each no he endured.) Since that time, Rick and his team have raised over $100 million to implement the Quest program in 36 languages and more than 30,000 schools in 80 countries around the world. Three million kids per year are being taught important life skills because one 19-year-old rejected rejection and kept on going until he got a yes.

In 1989, Rick received a grant for $65,000,000, the second largest grant ever given in U.S. history, to create the International Youth Foundation. What if Rick had given up after the one hundredth rejection and said to himself, *Well, I guess this just isn't supposed to be?* What a great loss to the world and to Rick's higher purpose for being.

HE KNOCKED ON 12,500 DOORS

*I take rejection as someone blowing a bugle in my ear to
wake me up and get going, rather than retreat.*

SYLVESTER STALLONE
Actor, writer, and director

When Dr. Ignatius Piazza was a young chiropractor fresh out of school, he decided he wanted to set up offices in the Monterey Bay area of California. When he approached the local chiropractic association for assistance they advised him to set up shop somewhere else. They told him he wouldn't be successful because there were already too many chiropractors in the area. Undaunted, he applied the Next Principle. For months, he went from door to door early in the morning until sunset, knocking on doors. After introducing himself as the new young doctor in town, he asked a few questions:

"Where should I locate my office?"

"What newspapers should I advertise in to reach your neighbors?"

"Should I open early in the morning or stay open into the evening for those who have nine-to-five jobs?"

"Should I call my clinic Chiropractic West or Ignatius Piazza Chiropractic?"

And finally, he asked, "When I hold my open house, would you like to receive an invitation?" If people said yes, he wrote down their names and addresses and continued on . . . day after day, month after month. By the time he was done, he had knocked on over 12,500 doors and talked to over 6,500 people. He got a lot of nos. He got a lot of nobody-homes. He even got trapped on one porch—cornered by a pit bull—for a whole afternoon! But he also received enough yeses that during his first month in practice he saw 233 new patients and earned a record income of $72,000—in an area that "didn't need another chiropractor"!

Remember, to get what you want you are going to need to ask, ask, ask, and say *next, next, next* until you get the yes(es) you are looking for! Asking is, was, and always will be a numbers game. Don't take it personally, because it isn't personal.

SOME FAMOUS REJECTIONS

The girl doesn't, it seems to me, have a special perception or feeling which would lift that book above the "curiosity" level.

From the rejection slip for *The Diary of Anne Frank*

Everyone who has ever made it to the top has had to endure rejections. You just have to realize that they are not personal. Consider the following:

- Angie Everhart, who started modeling at the age of 16, was once told by model agency owner Eileen Ford that she would never make it as a model. Why not? "Redheads don't sell." Everhart later became the first redhead in history to appear on the cover of *Glamour* magazine, had a great modeling career, and then went on to appear in 27 films and numerous TV shows.
- Novelist Stephen King almost made a multimillion-dollar mistake when he threw his *Carrie* manuscript in the garbage because he was tired of the 30 rejections he had received. "We are not interested in science fiction which deals with negative utopias," he was told. "They do not sell." Luckily, his wife fished it out of the garbage. Eventually *Carrie* was printed by another publisher, sold more than 4 million copies, and was made into a blockbuster

film. Stephen King's net worth is now estimated to be $500 million.
- James Patterson is one of the great storytellers of our time. He is the creator of unforgettable characters and series—including Alex Cross, the Women's Murder Club, Jane Smith, and Maximum Ride—and of breathtaking true stories about the Kennedys, John Lennon, and Tiger Woods. Patterson has coauthored #1 bestselling novels with Bill Clinton and Dolly Parton, and in collaboration with Michael Crichton's widow, he completed Crichton's unfinished novel *Eruption*. He has received an Edgar Award, 10 Emmy Awards, the Literarian Award from the National Book Foundation, and the National Humanities Medal. His books have sold 425 million copies around the world, and several have been made into blockbuster movies. His net worth is estimated to be $850 million. What you may not be aware of is that his first novel, *The Thomas Berryman Number*, was turned down by 31 publishers. When it was finally published, it went on to win the Edgar Award for best first novel.
- In 1998, Google cofounders Sergey Brin and Larry Page approached Yahoo! and suggested a merger. Yahoo! could have snapped up the company for a handful of stock, but instead they suggested that the young Googlers keep working on their little school project and come back when they had grown up. Within five years, Google had an estimated market capitalization of $20 billion. At the time of this writing, Marketwatch.com reported Google's market capitalization (now Alphabet Inc.) at $1.78 trillion.
- Even the first Harry Potter book, *Harry Potter and the Philosopher's Stone,* was rejected by 12 publishers before it found a home. Because she didn't give up, J. K. Rowling is now one of the richest people in England with a net worth of $1 billion.
- Steven Spielberg applied and was rejected two times by the prestigious USC film school. He ended up at Cal State University in Long Beach. He later went on to produce and direct some of the greatest blockbuster movies of all time—*E.T., Lincoln, Saving Private Ryan, Jurassic Park, Jaws, The Color Purple,* and *Raiders of the Lost Ark*—ultimately giving Spielberg a net worth of $3 billion. Twenty-seven years later, after Spielberg had become famous, USC awarded him an honorary doctoral degree, and two years after that he became a trustee of the university.

SUSAN'S STORY

Twice in her life, Susan Mabet's entire future was changed by the generous acts of people who didn't even know her. The first time it happened was just days after she was born. Her birth mother did what may have been the only kind thing she could have done for her at the time; instead of abandoning her in the grassland to die, she placed her in a crowded market where she knew that she would be found. That simple act saved her life.

A woman named Monica found her. Monica had virtually no money and already had eight children to care for, but she couldn't turn away from Susan's cries. She picked her up and cared for her, and for weeks she brought her back to the market hoping to find her mother. Ultimately, she knew she never would. As poor as she was, Monica somehow found a way to make Susan her ninth.

While Monica's love for her saved her life and gave her the hope that she could grow up and become anything she desired, she also knew firsthand the realities of growing up as a girl in the Maasai Mara region of Kenya. Most girls were married off to older men while they were still girls. They'd get pregnant at an age when their young bodies were not meant to bear children, and many didn't survive childbirth.

For these girls, there was no time for studies. Their days were filled with walking for hours just to fetch filthy water for their family, and when they got home, new chores awaited them. The tiny fraction of girls in Kenya who were lucky enough to get an education seemed like the chosen few. Too few were able to escape that vicious cycle.

Yet from a young age, Susan knew that education was her only way out of a life that the vast majority of women in her village had known for generations. And her only hope was Kisaruni Secondary School—the first and only boarding school for girls near her village.

That first year, the newly built school funded by Cynthia Kersey's Unstoppable Foundation* announced that it could accept only 40 girls from the entire region. So Susan studied hard in primary school, and because she was at the top of all of her classes, she was confident and hopeful she would be accepted. She applied to Kisaruni and waited eagerly for the response. The last day of primary school, her heart was pounding because she knew she'd get the news of her future that day. When her teacher told her that she had not been accepted to Kisaruni, it felt like a death sentence.

The night before the doors were to open at Kisaruni that year, young

---

*To learn more about the Unstoppable Foundation and to support their work of educating children in Africa, visit unstoppablefoundation.org.

Susan lay awake—unable to sleep knowing that somewhere 40 girls were excitedly lying awake anticipating their first day at school. They were probably preparing their black and red school uniforms and looking forward to meeting new friends. But she had been condemned to a life of poverty in her village.

But Susan was not willing to let go of her dream of a better life that easily. The next morning, she set out on foot toward Kisaruni, miles away on a dusty path. As she approached the school, she could see the 40 lucky girls in their bright uniforms laughing and playing.

As Susan arrived, everyone turned to look at her. The principal approached her and asked why she was there. Though Susan was terrified, she bravely said she had been turned down by the school but needed to hear it directly from her because she simply couldn't believe it.

The principal gently explained that they had room for only 40 girls, that meant 40 beds, 40 desks, and 40 chairs. Unfortunately, Susan was the forty-first girl.

She tried not to cry. She tried to be brave. But the tears rolled down her dusty cheeks and she could not imagine how she would be able to walk home. As she gathered her strength to leave, the 40 girls began to surround her. One girl shouted, "Please don't make her go away. We'll move our beds together." Another girl pleaded, "I'll share my desk with her." Another shouted, "I'll share my books with her. Please don't make her go." The girls surrounded her in what felt like a circle of protection, not allowing her to move. She was stunned.

The girls' generosity that day allowed Susan to attend school that year. And later, when the Unstoppable Foundation and a generous donor heard of Susan's bravery—how she had refused to believe she couldn't go to school—they paid her tuition, making it possible for Susan to continue her studies and become Kisaruni's forty-first girl.

Let Susan's story of perseverance in the face of rejection inspire you to never count yourself out. Believe you will succeed, do everything in your power, and never give up.

PRINCIPLE 19

USE FEEDBACK TO YOUR ADVANTAGE

Feedback is the breakfast of champions.
KEN BLANCHARD AND SPENCER JOHNSON
Coauthors of *The One Minute Manager*

Once you begin to take action, you'll start getting feedback about whether you're doing the right thing. You'll get data, advice, help, suggestions, direction, and even criticism that will help you constantly adjust and move forward while continually enhancing your knowledge, abilities, attitudes, and relationships. But asking for feedback is really only the first part of the equation. Once you receive feedback, you have to be willing to respond to it.

THERE ARE TWO KINDS OF FEEDBACK

There are two kinds of feedback you might encounter—negative and positive. We tend to prefer the positive—that is, results, money, praise, a raise, a promotion, satisfied customers, awards, happiness, inner peace, intimacy, pleasure. It feels better. It tells us that we are on course, that we are doing the right thing.

We tend not to like negative feedback—lack of results, little or no money, criticism, poor evaluations, being passed over for a raise or a promotion, complaints, unhappiness, inner conflict, loneliness, pain. However, there is as much useful data in negative feedback as there is in positive feedback. It tells us that we are off course, headed in the wrong direction, doing the wrong thing. That is also valuable information.

In fact, it's so valuable that one of the most useful projects you could undertake is to change how you feel about negative feedback. I like to refer to negative feedback as information about "improvement opportunities." The world is telling me where and how I can improve what I am doing. Here is a place I can get better. Here is where I can correct my behavior to get even closer to what I want—more money, more sales, a promotion, a better relationship, better grades, or more success on the athletic field.

To reach your goals more quickly, you need to welcome, receive, and embrace all the feedback that comes your way.

ON COURSE, OFF COURSE, ON COURSE, OFF COURSE

There are many ways to respond to feedback, some of which work (they take you closer to your stated objectives), and some of which don't (they keep you stuck or take you even further from your goals).

When I conduct trainings on The Success Principles, I illustrate this point by asking for a volunteer from the audience to stand at the far side of the room. The volunteer represents the goal I want to reach. My task is to walk across the room to where he is standing. If I get to where he is standing, I have successfully reached my goal.

I instruct the volunteer to act as a constant feedback–generating machine. Every time I take a step, he is to say "On course" if I am walking directly toward him—and "Off course" if I am walking even the slightest bit off to either side.

Then I begin to walk very slowly toward the volunteer. Every time I take a step directly toward him, the volunteer says, "On course." Every few steps, I purposely veer off course, and the volunteer says, "Off course." I immediately correct my direction. Every few steps, I veer off course again and then correct again in response to his "Off course" feedback. After a lot of zigzagging, I eventually reach my goal . . . and give the person a hug for volunteering.

I ask the audience to tell me which feedback the volunteer gave more often—"On course" or "Off course." The answer is always "Off course." And here is the interesting part: I was off course more than I was on course, and I still got there . . . just by continually taking action and constantly adjusting to the feedback.

The same is true in life. All we have to do is to start to take action and then respond to the feedback. If we do that diligently enough and long enough, we will eventually get to our goals and achieve our dreams.

WAYS OF RESPONDING TO FEEDBACK THAT DON'T WORK

Though there are many ways you can respond to feedback, some responses simply don't work:

1. Caving in and quitting: As part of the seminar exercise I described above, I will repeat the process of walking toward my goal; however, in this round I will purposely veer off course, and when my volunteer keeps repeating "Off course" over and over, I break down and cry, "I can't take it anymore. Life is too hard. I can't take all this negative criticism. I quit!"

How many times have you or someone you know received negative feedback and simply caved in over it? All that does is keep you stuck in the same place.

Of course, it's easier not to cave in when you receive feedback if you remember that feedback is simply information. Think of it as correctional guidance instead of criticism. Think of the automatic pilot system on an airplane. The system is constantly telling the plane that it has gone too high, too low, too far to the right, or too far to the left. The plane just keeps correcting in response to the feedback it is receiving. It doesn't all of a sudden freak out and break down because of the relentless flow of feedback. Stop taking feedback so personally. It is just information designed to help you adjust and get to your goal a whole lot faster.

2. Getting mad at the source of the feedback: Once again, I will begin walking toward the other end of the room while purposely veering off course, causing the volunteer to say "Off course" over and over. This time I put one hand on my hip, stick out my chin, point my finger, and yell, "Bitch, bitch, bitch! All you ever do is criticize me! You're so negative. Why can't you ever say anything positive?"

Think about it. How many times have you reacted with anger and hostility toward someone who was giving you feedback that was genuinely useful? All it does is push the person and the feedback away.

3. Ignoring the feedback: For my third demonstration, imagine me putting my fingers in my ears and determinedly walking off course. The volunteer might be saying "Off course, off course," but I can't hear anything because my fingers are in my ears.

Not listening to or ignoring the feedback is another response that doesn't work. We all know people who tune out everyone's point of view but their own. They are simply not interested in what other people think. They don't want to hear anything anyone else has to say. The sad thing is, feedback could significantly transform their lives, if only they would listen and respond.

So, as you can see, when someone gives you feedback, there are three possible reactions that don't work: (1) crying, falling apart, caving in, and giving up; (2) getting angry at the source of the feedback; and (3) ignoring the feedback.

Crying and falling apart is simply ineffective. It may temporarily release whatever emotions you have built up in your system, but it takes you out of the game. It immobilizes you. It may stop the flow of "negative" feedback, but it doesn't get you the information you need to reach your goal. You can't win in the game of life if you are not on the playing field!

Getting angry at the person giving you the feedback is equally ineffective! It just makes the source of the valuable feedback attack you back or simply go away. What good is that? It may temporarily make you feel better, but it doesn't help you become more successful.

In my advanced trainings and in our Train-the-Trainer program, when everyone knows the other participants fairly well, I have the whole group stand up, mill around, and ask as many people as possible the following question: "How do you see me limiting myself?" After doing this for 30 minutes, people sit down and record what they have heard. You'd think that this would be hard to listen to for 30 minutes, but it is such valuable feedback that people are actually grateful for the opportunity to become aware of their limiting beliefs and behaviors—and replace them with more effective beliefs and behaviors. Everyone then develops an action plan for transcending their limiting behavior.

Remember, feedback is simply information. You don't have to take it personally. Just welcome it and use it. The most intelligent and productive response is to say, "Thank you for the feedback. Thank you for caring enough to tell me what you see and how you feel. I appreciate it."

BE WILLING TO ASK FOR FEEDBACK

Most people will not voluntarily give you feedback. They are as uncomfortable with possible confrontation as you are. They don't want to hurt your feelings. They are afraid of your reaction. They don't want to risk your disapproval. So to get honest and open feedback, you are going to need to ask for it . . . and make it safe for the person to give it to you. In other words, don't shoot the messenger. And don't argue with them. Just say, "Thank you."

A powerful question to ask your family members, friends, and colleagues is, "How do you see me limiting myself?" You might think that the answers would be hard to listen to, but most people find the information so valuable that they are grateful for what people tell them. Armed with this new feedback, you can create a plan of action for replacing your limiting beliefs and behaviors with more effective and productive beliefs and behaviors.

Most people are afraid to ask for corrective feedback because they are afraid of what they are going to hear. But you're better off knowing the truth than not knowing the truth. Once you know it, you can do something about it. You cannot fix what you don't know is broken. You cannot improve your life, your relationships, your game, or your performance without feedback.

When you avoid asking for feedback, you are the only one who is not in on the secret. The other person has usually already told their spouse, their friends, their parents, their business associates, and other potential customers what they are dissatisfied with. They should be telling you, but they are unwilling to do so for fear of your reaction. As a result, you are being deprived of the very thing you need to improve your relationship, your product, your service, your teaching, your managing, or your parenting. You must do two things to remedy this.

First, you must intentionally and actively solicit feedback. Ask your partner, your friends, your colleagues, your boss, your employees, your clients, your parents, your teachers, your students, and your coaches.

Second, you must be grateful for the feedback. Do not get defensive. Just say, "Thank you for caring enough to share that with me!" Remember, feedback is a gift that helps you become more effective. Be grateful for it.

Get your head out of the sand and ask, ask, ask! Then check in with yourself to see what fits for you, and put the useful feedback into action. Take whatever steps are necessary to improve the situation—including changing your own behavior.

THE MOST VALUABLE QUESTION YOU MAY EVER LEARN

In the 1980s, a multimillionaire businessman taught me a question that radically changed the quality of my life. If the only thing you get out of reading this book is the consistent use of this question in your personal and business life, it will have been worth the money and time you have invested. So what is this magical question that can improve the quality of every relationship you are in, every product you produce, every service you deliver, every meeting you conduct, every class you teach, and every transaction you enter into? Here it is:

> On a scale of 1 to 10, how would you rate the quality of our relationship (service/product) during the last week (two weeks/month/quarter/semester/season)?

Here are a number of variations on the same question that have served me well over the years:

> On a scale of 1 to 10, how would you rate the meeting we just had? me as a manager? me as a parent? me as a teacher? this class? this meal? my cooking? our sex life? this deal? this book?

Any answer less than a 10 gets this follow-up question:

> What would it take to make it a 10?

This is where the valuable information comes from. Knowing that a person is dissatisfied is not enough. Knowing in detail what will satisfy them gives you the information you need to do what is necessary to create a winning product, service, or relationship.

Make it a habit to end every project, meeting, class, training, consultation, installation, and consultation with the two questions.

MAKE IT A WEEKLY RITUAL

I ask my wife these same two questions every Sunday night. Here is a typical scenario:

"How would you rate the quality of our relationship this past week?"
"Eight."
"What would it take to make it a ten?"
"Come to bed at the same time with me at least four nights a week. Come in for dinner on time or call me and tell me you are going to be late. I hate sitting here waiting and wondering. Let me finish a joke I am telling without interrupting and taking over because you think you can tell it better. Put your dirty laundry in the clothes hamper instead of in a pile on the floor."

I ask my assistants this question every Friday afternoon. Here is one response I received one Friday:

"Six."
"Whoa! What would it take to make it a ten?"
"We were supposed to have a meeting this week to go over my quar-

terly review, but it got pushed aside by other matters. It makes me feel unimportant and that you don't care about me as much as the other people around here. The other thing is that I feel you are not using me enough. You are not delegating anything but the simple stuff to me. I want more responsibility. I want you to trust me more with the important stuff. This job has become boring and uninteresting. I want more of a challenge."

This was not easy to hear, but it was true and it led to two wonderful results. It helped me delegate more "important stuff" to her and thus cleared my plate, giving me more free time—and it also created a happier assistant who was able to serve me and the company better.

IT PAYS TO ASK

When Mark Victor Hansen and I decided to compile stories for *Chicken Soup for the African American Soul,* I asked Lisa Nichols to coauthor the book with us. Lisa was the founder and CEO of Motivating the Teen Spirit, which she started to empower teens to fall madly in love with themselves. In recent years, she has expanded her mission to include people of all ages, because she believes that all of us deserve to fall in love with the person we see in the mirror every morning. Lisa later went on to have a featured role in the movie *The Secret* and has authored several books of her own, including *No Matter What* and *Abundance Now.*

Over the course of working on two different books together, Lisa and I became close friends. She told me that one of the best things to come out of our relationship is the "On the scale of 1 to 10" question. After first hearing about this technique, she instantly began to use it with her son, Jelani, who was 11 years old at the time. She had been feeling really guilty about being separated from him so much due to her work. The first time she asked him to rate their relationship, Jelani gave it a 7. *Hmm,* she thought, *not terrible, but it sure could be better.* Taking a deep breath, she asked, "What would it take to make it a 10?"

He said, "I want to see you more. I want to travel with you."

She immediately took this to heart and committed to find a way to make it happen. First, she enrolled him in a private school, with the condition that Jelani be able to distance-learn while he traveled with her. The school administrators said, "We've never done that before."

Lisa told them, "I'm excited that we get to co-create a new possibility!"

The school agreed to try it, and for the next two years Jelani traveled with her whenever he wanted to. She'd show him her travel calendar six months in advance and he'd choose a place that he wanted to go. Eventually he said, "Mom, I'm ready to stay at home." They had handled that particular part of improving their relationship.

When Jelani was 17, she asked him the 1-to-10 feedback question while they were watching movies at home together. He said, "Oh, Mom, this again?"

She repeated the question.

He said, "I'd rate it a 9."

She asked, "What would it take to make it go from a 9 to a 10?"

He sat there and thought. Finally he said, "I can't think of anything. But it seems so weird to say it's a 10; that would make it perfect."

She said, "Okay, so if it's not perfect, what would make it a 10?"

Jelani said, "All I can think of is sitting on the couch, watching movies with you, our feet touching, and cooking with you. We're doing all that now, but it still feels weird to say it's a 10!"

In that moment, she felt her heart swell up with love. She told me, "I don't care how many stages I stand on, how many millions of people that I speak in front of, how much wealth I generate—the most important thing to me is the relationship I have with my son. It's beyond price. You gave me a tool to monitor my son's needs, his desires, what he's getting, and what he's *not* getting. For that, I'll be forever grateful."

HOW TO LOOK REALLY BRILLIANT WITH LITTLE EFFORT

Virginia Satir, the author of the classic parenting book *Peoplemaking,* was probably the most successful and famous family therapist who ever lived.

During her long and illustrious career, she was hired by the Michigan State Department of Social Services to provide a proposal on how to revamp and restructure the Department of Social Services so it would serve the client population better. Sixty days later, she provided the department with a 150-page report, which they said was the most amazing piece of work they had ever seen. "This is brilliant!" they gushed. "How did you come up with all these ideas?"

She replied, "Oh, I just went out to all the social workers in your system and asked them what it would take for the system to work better."

LISTEN TO THE FEEDBACK

Human beings were given a left foot and a right foot to make a mistake first to the left, then to the right, left again and repeat.

BUCKMINSTER FULLER
Engineer, inventor, and philosopher

Whether we ask or not, feedback comes to us in various forms. It might come verbally from a colleague. Or it might be a letter from the government. It might be the bank refusing your loan. Or it could be a special opportunity that comes your way because of a specific step you took.

Whatever it is, it's important to listen to the feedback. Simply take a step . . . and listen. Take another step and listen. If you hear "Off course," take a step in a direction you believe may be on course . . . and listen. Listen externally to what others may be telling you, but also listen internally to what your body, your feelings, and your instincts may be telling you.

Is your mind and body saying, "I'm happy; I like this; this is the right job for me," or "I'm weary; I'm emotionally drained; I don't like this as much as I thought; I don't have a good feeling about that guy"?

Whatever feedback you get, don't ignore the yellow alerts. Never go against your gut. If it doesn't feel right to you, it probably isn't.

IS ALL FEEDBACK ACCURATE?

Not all feedback is useful or accurate. You must consider the source. Some feedback is polluted by the psychological distortions of the person giving you the feedback. For example, if your drunk husband tells you, "You're a no-good @#*%!," that is probably not accurate or useful feedback. The fact that your husband is drunk and angry, however, *is feedback you should listen to.*

LOOK FOR PATTERNS

Additionally, you should look for patterns in the feedback you get. As my friend Jack Rosenblum likes to say: "If one person tells you you're a horse, they're crazy. If three people tell you you're a horse, there's a conspiracy afoot. If ten people tell you you're a horse, it's time to buy a saddle."

The point is that if several people are telling you the same thing, there is probably some truth in it. Why resist it? You may get to be "right," but the question you have to ask yourself is "Would I rather be right or be happy? Would I rather be right or be successful?"

I have an acquaintance who would rather be right than be happy and successful. He got mad at anyone who tried to give him feedback. "Don't you talk to me that way, young lady." "This is my business and I'll run it the way I want to." "I don't give a hoot what you think." He was a "my way or the highway" sort of person. He wasn't interested in anyone else's opinion or feedback. In the process, he alienated his wife, his two daughters, his clients, and all his employees. He ended up with two divorces, kids who didn't want to speak to him, and two bankrupt businesses. But he was "right." Don't *you* get caught in this trap. It is a dead-end street.

What feedback have you been receiving from your family, friends, members of the opposite sex, coworkers, boss, partners, clients, vendors, and your body that you need to pay more attention to? Are there any patterns that stand out? Make a list, and next to each item, write an action step you can take to get back on course.

WHAT TO DO WHEN THE FEEDBACK TELLS YOU YOU'VE FAILED

When all indicators say you've had a "failure experience," there are a number of things you can do to respond appropriately and keep moving forward:

1. Acknowledge you did the best you could with the awareness, knowledge, and skills you had at the time.

2. Acknowledge that you survived and that you can absolutely cope with any and all of the consequences or results.

3. Write down all the insights and lessons you learned from the experience in a file in your computer or in a journal. Read through this file often. Ask others involved—your family, employees, clients, team, and others—what they learned. Then make a list under the heading: "Ways to Do It Better Next Time."

4. Make sure to thank everyone for their feedback and their insights. If someone is hostile in the delivery of their feedback, remember that it is an expression of their level of fear, not your level of incompetence or unlovability. Just take in the feedback, use whatever is applicable and valuable for the future, and discard the rest.

5. Clean up any messes that have been created and deliver any communications that are necessary to complete the experience—including any apologies or regrets that are due. Do not try to hide the failure.

6. Take some time to go back and review your successes. It's important to remind yourself that you have had many more successes than you have had failures. You've done many more things right than you've done wrong.

7. Regroup. Spend some time with positive loving friends, family, and coworkers who can reaffirm your worth and your contribution.

8. Refocus on your vision. Incorporate the lessons learned, recommit to your original plan, or create a new plan of action, and then get on with it. Stay in the game. Keep moving toward the fulfillment of your dreams. You're probably going to make a lot of mistakes along the way. Just dust yourself off, get back on your horse, and keep riding.

PRINCIPLE 20

COMMIT TO CONSTANT AND NEVER-ENDING IMPROVEMENT

We have an innate desire to endlessly learn, grow, and develop. We want to become more than what we already are. Once we yield to this inclination for continuous and never-ending improvement, we lead a life of endless accomplishments and satisfaction.

CHUCK GALLOZZI
Author of *The 3 Thieves and 4 Pillars of Happiness*

In Japan, the word for constant and never-ending improvement is *kaizen*. Not only is this an operating philosophy for modern Japanese businesses, it is also the age-old philosophy of warriors, too—and it's become the personal mantra of millions of successful people.

Achievers—whether in business, sports, or the arts—are committed to continual improvement. If you want to be more successful, you need to learn to ask yourself, *How can I make this better? How can I do it more efficiently? How can I do this more profitably? How can we serve our customers better? How can I provide more value to more people? How can we do this with greater love?*

THE MIND-NUMBING PACE OF CHANGE

In today's world, a certain amount of improvement is necessary just to keep up with the rapid pace of change. New technologies are announced nearly every month. New manufacturing techniques are discovered even more often. New words come into use anytime a trend or fad catches on. And what we learn about ourselves, about our health, and about the capacity for human thought continues almost unabated.

Improving is therefore necessary simply to survive. But to thrive, as successful people do, a more dedicated approach to improvement is required.

IMPROVE IN SMALL INCREMENTS

Whenever you set out to improve your skills, change your behavior, or better your family life or business, beginning in small, manageable steps gives you a greater chance of long-term success. Doing too much too fast not only overwhelms you (or anyone else involved in the improvement), it can doom the effort to failure—thereby reinforcing the belief that it's difficult, if not impossible, to succeed. When you start with small, achievable steps you can easily master, it reinforces your belief that you can easily improve.

DECIDE WHAT TO IMPROVE ON

At work, your goal might be for your company to improve the quality of your product or service, your customer service program, your online marketing, or your advertising. Professionally, you might want to improve your computer skills, your sales skills, or your negotiating skills. At home you might want to improve your parenting skills, communication skills, or cooking skills. You could also focus on improving your health and fitness, your knowledge of investing and money management, or your musical ability. Or perhaps you want to develop greater inner peace through meditation, yoga, and prayer. Whatever your goal, decide where you want to improve and what steps you'll need to take to achieve that improvement.

Is it learning a new skill? Perhaps you can find that in a night class at the local community college. If it's improving your service to the community, perhaps you can find a way to spend an extra hour per week volunteering.

To keep yourself focused on constant and never-ending improvement, ask yourself every day, "How can I/we improve today? What can I/we do better than before? Where can I learn a new skill or develop a new competency?" If you do, you'll embark on a lifelong journey of improvement that will ensure your success.

YOU CAN'T SKIP STEPS

He who stops being better stops being good.

OLIVER CROMWELL
British politician and soldier (1599–1658)

One of life's realities is that major improvements take time; they don't happen overnight. But because so many of today's products and services promise overnight perfection, we've come to expect instant gratification—and we become discouraged when it doesn't happen. However, if you make a commitment to learning something new every day, getting just a little bit better every day, then eventually—over time—you will reach your goals.

Becoming a master takes time. You have to practice, practice, practice! You have to hone your skills through constant use and refinement. It takes years to have the depth and breadth of experience that produces expertise, insight, and wisdom. Every book you read, every class you take, every experience you have is another building block in your career and your life.

Don't shortchange yourself by not being ready when your big break appears. Make sure you have done your homework and honed your craft. Actors usually have to do a lot of preparation—acting classes, community theater, off-Broadway plays, bit parts in movies and television, more acting classes, voice lessons, accent training, dancing lessons, martial arts training, learning to ride a horse, more bit parts—until one day they are ready for the dream part that is ready for them.

Successful basketball players learn to shoot with their opposite hand, improve their foul-throw shooting, and work on their three-point shots. Artists experiment with different media. Airline pilots train for every kind of emergency in a flight simulator. Doctors go back to school to learn new procedures and obtain advanced certifications. They are all engaged in a process of constant and never-ending improvement.

Make a commitment to keep getting better and better every day in every way. If you do, you'll enjoy the feelings of increased self-esteem and self-confidence that come from self-improvement, as well as the ultimate success that will inevitably follow.

You will never change your life until you change something you do daily. The secret of your success is found in your daily routine.

JOHN MAXWELL
Leadership expert and author of more than 100 books

THE POWER OF THE SLIGHT EDGE

In his book *The Slight Edge,* Jeff Olson talks about the compound effect over time of doing just a little bit more or a little bit less of something. Whether it's doing a little *more* each day—20 push-ups, 20 minutes of meditation, 20 minutes of aerobics, 20 pages of reading, an extra hour of sleep, taking supplements—or a little *less* each day—an hour less of television, one less glass of wine, one less $4.00 latte, or one less hour surfing the Internet—over time these *little* changes make a *huge* difference in your results.

Think about these surprising facts. If you were to replace a sugary soft drink with a glass of water at lunch or during your afternoon break every day for a year, you would end up drinking almost 40 gallons of water, you'd avoid consuming close to 50,000 empty calories (the equivalent of fasting for 22 days, assuming you were eating 2,200 calories a day), and you'd save about $500 in expenses.

If you were to cut out an hour of watching television a day, that 365 hours would add up to nine 40-hour workweeks. That's like adding an extra two months of productive time to your life every year. In twelve years, that would equal having two extra years of focused time. Whether you use that time to focus on writing your books, practicing your instrument, improving your sports performance, learning a new language, making more sales calls, marketing on the Internet, reading, exercising, doing yoga, meditating, or deepening your relationships is up to you. But imagine the difference it would make over time.

PRINCIPLE 21

KEEP SCORE FOR SUCCESS

You have to measure what you want more of.

CHARLES COONRADT
Founder of the Game of Work

Remember when you were growing up and your mom or dad measured you every few months and kept track of your height on the wall near the pantry door? It was something visible that let you know where you stood in relation to the past and to your future goal (which was usually to be as tall as your mom or dad). It let you know you were making progress. It encouraged you to eat right and drink your milk to keep growing.

Well, successful people keep the same kind of measurements. They keep score of exciting progress, positive behavior, financial gain... anything they want more of.

In his groundbreaking book, *The Game of Work,** Charles Coonradt says that scorekeeping stimulates us to create more of the positive outcomes we're keeping track of. It actually reinforces the behavior that created these outcomes in the first place.

Think about it. Your natural inclination is always to improve your score. If you were to keep score on the five things that would advance your personal and professional objectives the most, imagine how motivated you would be each time the numbers improved in your favor.

**The Game of Work: How to Enjoy Work as Much as Play* by Charles A. Coonradt (Park City, Utah: Game of Work, 1997). Also recommended are Coonradt's other books, *Scorekeeping for Success* and *Managing the Obvious.*

MEASURE WHAT YOU WANT, NOT WHAT YOU DON'T WANT

We learn early in life that it's valuable to count what's valuable. We count the number of times we skip the rope, the number of jacks we pick up, the number of marbles we collect, the number of base hits we get in Little League, and the number of boxes of Girl Scout cookies we sell. Batting averages in baseball tell us the number of times we hit the ball, not the percentage of times we didn't. We keep score mostly of what is good, because that is what we want more of.

When Mike Walsh at High Performers International wanted to increase his bottom line, he started keeping track not just of the number of enrollments his company was getting—but also of how many cold calls employees were making, how many face-to-face appointments they set up, and how many of those appointments they turned into enrollments. As a result of this kind of scorekeeping, Mike saw a 39% increase in revenues in just six months.

USING CRITICAL DRIVERS TO KEEP SCORE IN BUSINESS

Once you start counting what you want more of in your business, you can start to develop benchmarks that you know will boost revenue, profits, and market share. In every business, there is a checklist of goals and targets that—when reached, surpassed, and improved upon—will continually drive revenue and increase profits. These targets are called *critical drivers*.

If you're in insurance or banking, for example, your critical drivers might be the number of cross-sells per customer or the number of loan originations. For a training company, an important critical driver would be the number of opt-ins for your free report. Whatever your critical drivers might be, the key is to inspire, motivate, and empower your team to continually identify, track, measure, and meet those benchmarks—even being accountable to meeting the critical drivers every week.

Once you get to that level of keeping score, you will see rapid progress happening in your business.*

---

*If you are looking to rapidly increase your business revenues, Janet Switzer has several programs that help business owners establish revenue-generation systems that include critical drivers so your staff stays focused on activity that increases profits and growth. To learn more, visit janetswitzer.com.

NOT JUST FOR BUSINESS OWNERS ANYMORE

When Tyler Williams joined a junior basketball league, his father, Rick Williams, coauthor of *Managing the Obvious,* decided to counteract the usual negative focus of youth sports by creating a "parent's scorecard" to keep track of what Tyler did right, rather than what he did wrong.

He tracked seven contributions his son could make to the team's success—points, rebounds, assists, steals, blocked shots, and so on—and awarded Tyler one point every time he made one of those positive plays. Whereas the statistics kept by the coaches centered chiefly on points and rebounds—the two traditional forms of measurement used in junior basketball—Tyler's dad's scorecard awarded points for virtually everything positive accomplished during a game.

It wasn't long before Tyler was sprinting over during timeouts to check on his contribution points. When they reached home after the game, Tyler would hustle to his bedroom, where he had a chart on the wall that plotted his progress. With a simple graph Tyler made himself, he could see where he was improving. As the season progressed, the line on his graph went steadily upward. Without a single harsh word from his coach or his dad, Tyler had turned into a better basketball player—and enjoyed the process besides.

KEEPING SCORE AT HOME

Of course, scorekeeping isn't just for business, sports, and school. It can be applied to your personal life, too. In the May 2000 issue of *Fast Company* magazine, Vinod Khosla, the founding CEO of Sun Microsystems, said

> It's great to know how to recharge your batteries. But it's even more important to make sure that you actually do it. I track how many times I get home in time to have dinner with my family; my assistant reports the exact number to me each month. I have four kids, ages 7 to 11. Spending time with them is what keeps me going.
>
> Your company measures its priorities. People also need to place metrics around their priorities. I spend about 50 hours a week at work, and I could easily work 100 hours. So I always make sure that, at the end of it all, I get home in time to eat with my kids. Then I help them with their homework and play games with them.... My goal is to be home for dinner at least 25 nights a month. Having a target number is key. I know

people in my business who are lucky if they make it home five nights a month. I don't think that I'm any less productive than those people.★

Decide where you need to keep score in order to manifest your vision and achieve your goals—then post your scores where you and any others playing the game can easily see them.

★"Don't Burn Out!" *Fast Company,* May 2000, page 106.

PRINCIPLE 22

PRACTICE PERSISTENCE

Most people give up just when they're about to achieve success. They quit on the one-yard line. They give up at the last minute of the game, one foot from a winning touchdown.

H. ROSS PEROT
American billionaire and former U.S. presidential candidate

Persistence is probably the single most common quality of high achievers. They simply refuse to give up. The longer you hang in there, the greater the chance that something will happen in your favor. No matter how hard it seems, the longer you persist the more likely your success.

IT'S NOT ALWAYS GOING TO BE EASY

Sometimes you are going to have to persist in the face of obstacles—oftentimes unseen obstacles—that no amount of planning or forethought could have predicted. Sometimes, you'll encounter what seem like overwhelming odds. And sometimes, the universe will test your commitment to the goal you're pursuing. The going may be hard, requiring you to refuse to give up while you learn new lessons, develop new parts of yourself, and make difficult decisions.

History has demonstrated that the most notable winners usually encountered heartbreaking obstacles before they triumphed. They won because they refused to become discouraged by their defeats.

B.C. FORBES
Founder of *Forbes* magazine

Hugh Panero, the cofounder and former CEO of XM Satellite Radio, is an example of amazing commitment and perseverance in the corporate sector. After two years recruiting investors ranging from General Motors and Hughes Electronics to DIRECTV and Clear Channel Communications, Panero's dream of becoming the world's largest subscription radio service nearly collapsed at the last minute when investors threatened to back out if an acceptable deal wasn't struck by midnight, June 6, 2001. After exhausting negotiations and shuttle diplomacy, Panero and his chairman of the board, Gary Parsons, secured commitments of $225 million just minutes before the deadline.

Less than a year later, the launch of one of XM's $200 million satellites was aborted just 11 seconds before liftoff when an engineer misread a message on his computer screen, forcing the company to wait for the next available launch date two months later!

Still, Panero persevered and finally scheduled the debut of XM Radio's 101 channels of programming for September 12, 2001. But when terrorists attacked the World Trade Center on the morning of September 11—just a day prior to the scheduled debut—Panero was forced to cancel the satellite's launch party and pull XM's inaugural TV ad featuring a rap star rocketing past a group of towering skyscrapers.

Panero's team urged him to postpone the company's launch for another year. Yet in the end, Panero held fast to his dream and debuted the service just two weeks later.

Today, through all the setbacks and delays, most of which make our own daily difficulties pale by comparison, the merged Sirius XM dominates the satellite radio business with more than 33 million subscribers paying every month to enjoy 145 channels of music plus 108 channels of premier sports, talk, comedy, children's and entertainment programming, and traffic and weather information.*

FIVE YEARS

"No" is a word on your path to "Yes." Don't give up too soon. Not even if well-meaning parents, relatives, friends, and colleagues tell you to get "a real job." Your dreams are your real job.

JOYCE SPIZER
Author of *Rejections of the Written Famous*

---

*See siriusxm.com for more information.

When Debbie Macomber decided to pursue her dream of becoming a writer, she rented a typewriter, put it on the kitchen table, and began typing each morning after the kids went off to school. When the kids came home, she moved the typewriter and made them dinner. When they went to bed, she moved it back and typed some more. For 2½ years, Debbie followed this routine. Supermom had become a struggling writer, and she was loving every minute of it.

One night, however, her husband, Wayne, sat her down and said, "Honey, I'm sorry, but you're not bringing in any income. We can't do this anymore. We can't survive on just what I make."

That night, her heart broken and her mind too busy to let her sleep, she stared at the ceiling in their darkened bedroom. Debbie knew—with all the responsibilities of keeping up a house and taking four kids to sports, church, and scouts—that working 40 hours a week would leave her no time to write.

Sensing her despair, her husband woke up and asked, "What's wrong?"

"I really think I could've made it as a writer. I really do."

Wayne was silent for a long time, then sat up, turned on the light, and said, "All right, honey, go for it."

So Debbie returned to her dream and her typewriter on the kitchen table, pounding out page after page for another 2½ years. Her family went without vacations, pinched pennies, and wore hand-me-downs.

But the sacrifice and the persistence finally paid off. After five years of struggling, Debbie sold her first book. Then another. And another. Until finally, today, Debbie has published more than 150 books, many of which have become *New York Times* bestsellers and four of which have become made-for-television movies. Over 170 million copies of her books are in print, and she has millions of loyal fans.

And Wayne? All that sacrifice in support of his wife paid off handsomely. He got to retire at age 50 and now spends his time building an airplane in the basement of their 7,000-square-foot mansion.

Debbie's kids got a gift far more important than a few summer camps. As adults, they realize what Debbie gave them was far more important—permission and encouragement to pursue their own dreams.

What could you accomplish if you were to follow your heart, practice this much daily discipline, and never give up?

NEVER GIVE UP ON YOUR HOPES AND DREAMS

Persistence and determination alone are omnipotent. The slogan "press on" has solved and always will solve the problems of the human race.

CALVIN COOLIDGE
The 13th president of the United States

Consider this:

- Admiral Robert Peary attempted to reach the North Pole seven times before he made it on try number eight.
- In its first 28 attempts to send rockets into space, NASA had 20 failures.
- Oscar Hammerstein had five flop shows that lasted less than a combined total of 6 weeks before *Oklahoma!*, which ran for 269 weeks and grossed $7 million.
- Oprah Winfrey was fired from an early television reporting job as "she was not deemed suitable for television."
- Tawni O'Dell's career as a writer is a testament to her perseverance. After 13 years, she had written six unpublished novels and collected 300 rejection slips. Finally, her first novel, *Back Roads*, was published after being chosen by Oprah Winfrey for the Oprah Book Club, and the newly anointed novel rose to number two on the *New York Times* bestsellers list, where it remained for eight weeks.

NEVER, NEVER, NEVER GIVE UP

During the Vietnam War, Texas computer billionaire H. Ross Perot decided he would give a Christmas present to every American prisoner of war in Vietnam. According to David Frost, who tells the story, Perot had thousands of packages wrapped and prepared for shipping. He chartered a fleet of Boeing 707s to deliver them to Hanoi, but the war was at its height, and the Hanoi government said it would refuse to cooperate. No charity was possible, officials explained, while American bombers were devastating Vietnamese villages. Perot offered to hire an American construction firm to help rebuild what Americans had knocked down. The government still wouldn't cooperate. Christmas drew near, and the packages were unsent.

Refusing to give up, Perot finally took off in his chartered fleet and flew to Moscow, where his aides mailed the packages, one at a time, at the Moscow central post office. They were delivered intact.* Can you see now why this man became the great success that he did? He simply refused to ever quit.

HANG IN THERE

It's always too soon to quit!

NORMAN VINCENT PEALE
Inspirational author

In 1992, screenwriter Craig Borten began writing the screenplay for *Dallas Buyers Club*. After drafting 10 different scripts for the movie, he spent most of the mid-1990s trying to sell it—but no one was willing to finance the production of the film.

According to an interview with Matthew McConaughey, who won an Academy Award for Best Actor in the starring role as AIDS patient Ron Woodroof, the film was turned down by potential backers 87 times before McConaughey eventually signed on 17 years later.

In 1996, the script got sold with Dennis Hopper to direct and Woody Harrelson to star—but the company that bought the script went bankrupt. The next year, Borten teamed up with screenwriter Melisa Wallack to revamp the script and sell it to Universal—this time with Marc Forster to direct and Brad Pitt to star—but Forster and Pitt never made the film.

Years later, after finally securing financing, director Gary Gillespie and actor Ryan Gosling agreed to do the film—but once more the financing fell apart. As a result, Universal decided the script was "not ready" and shelved the film for another nine years.

Eventually, due to a clause in their Writers Guild contract, Borten and Wallack managed to get back their rights to the script. And in 2009, nearly 20 years after the script was first conceived, Robbie Brenner—a producer who had been involved with the project almost from the beginning—convinced Matthew McConaughey to get involved.

But even after McConaughey lost 47 pounds for the role—and with filming scheduled to begin in just 10 weeks—the new investors backed out. With actors and crew secured and ready to move forward, the production

---

*Adapted from *David Frost's Book of Millionaires, Multimillionaires, and Really Rich People* (New York: Random House, 1984).

forged ahead and did the impossible: On a mere $5 million budget, they shot the entire film with one camera and 15-minute takes—in just 25 days.

Dallas Buyers Club was released in 2013 to universal acclaim by critics and audiences alike, and the tenacious commitment to see this film made eventually paid off in spades. Not only was it nominated for Best Picture at the Academy Awards, it earned nominations for Borten and Wallack for Best Original Screenplay at the 2014 Writers Guild of America Awards and at the Oscars—and went on to garner numerous Best Actor awards for McConaughey and Best Supporting Actor awards for Jared Leto.

By February 2014, the film had grossed more than $55 million worldwide.

30 YEARS IN THE MAKING

When screenwriter Allan Scott acquired the film rights to Walter Tevis's novel *The Queen's Gambit* in 1992, he could never have imagined it would take almost 30 years to get that movie made. Allan rewrote the script nine times, but studio after studio kept saying, "No one wants to watch a movie about chess."

Finally in 2019, Netflix decided to greenlight the project as a series, and in 2020 it became their number one show of the year after 62 million households tuned in to watch it within 28 days, making it the streaming platform's biggest scripted limited series in history, proving that perseverance does in fact pay off!

HE WOULDN'T GIVE UP HIS DREAM

We usually overestimate what we think we can accomplish in one year, but we grossly underestimate what we can accomplish in a decade.

ANTHONY ROBBINS
Motivational speaker and author of *Awaken the Giant Within*

Darrell Hammond started his career in acting in the seventies while attending the University of Florida. It was a rocky start because with his "fumbling speech" (the result of extreme child abuse by his mother), he was never cast in a role. He kept at it until eventually one theater professor took a chance on him and—because of Darrell's success in that and several subsequent roles—convinced him he should pursue a career in acting. After barely graduating with a 2.1 grade point average, Darrell followed his dream and moved to New York, but for the first several years he waited tables and got so drunk at times that he could barely make it to auditions.

Eventually, Darrell cut back on his drinking and started seriously studying acting at the prestigious Herbert Berghof Studio, which boasts alumni such as Robert De Niro, Matthew Broderick, Billy Crystal, Claire Danes, Whoopi Goldberg, Al Pacino, and Barbra Streisand. That led to some roles in plays off-Broadway and in regional theaters.

When he was 26, Darrell tried his hand at stand-up comedy, fell in love with it, and set a goal to be a cast member on *Saturday Night Live*. But it didn't happen overnight. Not even close. After not getting any traction in New York, he moved back to Florida and did voice-over work for the next few years. But he never gave up on his goal, and he committed to a program of self-improvement that helped him get through those years. He came up with the idea that if he could make one small improvement in his abilities, once a week, that would be 52 improvements a year.

He focused on this for five years and then moved back to New York City with the determination to become a successful stand-up comedian and attract the attention of the *Saturday Night Live* producers.

Starting in your thirties is late for stand-up, and Darrell thought he might be too old to make it, but he decided to try anyway because he didn't want to give up on his dream. He used to put pictures of Harriet Tubman, Martin Luther King Jr., and Mahatma Gandhi on his wall for inspiration. The reason? They were people who probably didn't have any evidence they could accomplish what they wanted to accomplish, but they kept on going anyway.

He continued to perform in the clubs around New York for the next seven years, during which time he had two failed auditions for *Saturday Night Live*. You'd think after seven years he would have given up. In fact, most people would have. But Darrell persisted, and finally, after seven long years, his persistence paid off. One night during his act at Carolines he threw in a short impression of President Bill Clinton. It just so happened that night that a producer from *Saturday Night Live* was in the audience, and he was looking for someone for the show that could do a good Bill Clinton impression. As a result, Darrell was invited to audition for Lorne Michaels, the creator of *Saturday Night Live*. Darrell said he had been preparing for that moment for 12 years. He was ready and he landed the role, finally fulfilling his ultimate dream.

Darrell went on to spend 14 years on the show, performing in more than 200 episodes, and became best known for his hilarious impressions of famous people such as Bill Clinton, Al Gore, Dick Cheney, and Donald Trump—as well as entertainers like Sean Connery and Jack Nicholson. Since he left the show in 2009 at 53 years of age (the oldest cast member in the history of the show), he has gone on to appear on Broadway and in numerous movies and television shows, including his own Comedy Central special. Darrell has had an extraordinary career because in the beginning he refused to give up.

HOW TO DEAL WITH OBSTACLES

For every failure, there's an alternative course of action. You just have to find it. When you come to a roadblock, take a detour.

MARY KAY ASH
Founder of Mary Kay Cosmetics

Whenever you confront an obstacle or run into a roadblock, you need to stop and brainstorm three ways to get around, over, or through the block. For every obstacle, come up with three different strategies for handling the potential obstacle. There are any number of ways that will work, but you will find them only if you spend time looking for them. Always be solution-oriented in your thinking. Persevere until you find a way that works.

Difficulties are opportunities to better things; they are stepping-stones to greater experience. . . . When one door closes, another always opens; as a natural law it has to, to balance.

BRIAN ADAMS
Author of *How to Succeed*

PRINCIPLE 23

PRACTICE THE RULE OF 5

Success is the sum of small efforts, repeated day in and day out.
ROBERT COLLIER
Bestselling author and publisher of *The Secret of the Ages*

When Mark Victor Hansen and I published the first *Chicken Soup for the Soul*® book, we were so eager and committed to making it a bestseller that we asked 15 bestselling authors ranging from John Gray (*Men Are from Mars, Women Are from Venus*) to Ken Blanchard (*The One Minute Manager*) and Scott Peck (*The Road Less Traveled*) for their guidance and advice. We received a ton of valuable information about what to do and how to do it. Next, we visited with book publishing and marketing guru Dan Poynter, who gave us even more great information. Then we bought and read John Kremer's *1001 Ways to Market Your Book*.

After all of that, we were overwhelmed with possibilities. To tell the truth, we became a little crazy. We didn't know where to start, plus we both had our speaking and seminar businesses to run.

FIVE SPECIFIC THINGS THAT MOVE YOU TOWARD YOUR GOAL

We sought the advice of Ron Scolastico, a wonderful teacher, who told us, "If you would go every day to a very large tree and take five swings at it with a very sharp ax, eventually, no matter how large the tree, it would have to come down." How very simple and how very true! Out of that we developed what we have called the Rule of 5. This simply means that every day, we do five specific things that will move our goal toward completion.

With the goal of getting *Chicken Soup for the Soul*® to the top of the *New York Times* bestsellers list, it meant having five radio interviews or sending out five review copies to editors who might review the book or calling five network marketing companies and asking them to buy the book as a motivational tool for their salespeople or giving a seminar to at least five people and selling the book in the back of the room. On some days we would simply send out five free copies to people listed in the *Celebrity Address Book*—people such as Harrison Ford, Barbra Streisand, Paul McCartney, and Steven Spielberg.

We made phone calls to people who could review the book, we wrote press releases, we called in to talk shows (some at 3:00 A.M.), we gave away free copies at our talks, we sent them to ministers to use as a source of talks for their sermons, we gave free "Chicken Soup for the Soul" talks at churches, we did book signings at any bookstore that would have us, we asked businesses to make bulk purchases for their employees, we got the book into the PXs on military bases, we asked our fellow speakers to sell the book at their talks, we asked seminar companies to put it in their catalogs, we bought a directory of catalogs and asked all the appropriate ones to carry the book, we visited gift shops and card shops and asked them to carry the book—we even got gas stations, bakeries, and restaurants to sell the book. It was a lot of effort—a minimum of five things a day, every day, day in and day out—for over two years.

LOOK WHAT A SUSTAINED EFFORT CAN DO

Was it worth it? Yes! The book eventually sold more than 10 million copies in the United States and Canada, was translated into 43 languages, and was published in more than 100 countries.

Did it happen overnight? No! We did not make a bestseller list until over a year after the book came out—a year! But it was the sustained effort of the Rule of 5 for over two years that led to the success—one action at a time, one book at a time, one reader at a time. But slowly, over time, each reader told another reader, and eventually, like a slow-building chain letter, the word was spread and the book became a huge success—what *Time* magazine called "the publishing phenomenon of the decade." It was less of a publishing phenomenon and more of a phenomenon of persistent effort—thousands of individual activities that all added up to one large success.

In *Chicken Soup for the Gardener's Soul,* Jaroldeen Edwards describes the day her daughter Carolyn took her to Lake Arrowhead to see a wonder of nature—fields and fields of daffodils that extend for as far as the eye can see. From the top of the mountain, sloping down for many acres across folds and valleys, between the trees and bushes, following the terrain, there are rivers of daffodils in radiant bloom—a literal carpet of every hue of the color yellow, from the palest ivory to the deepest lemon to the most vivid salmon-orange. There appear to be over a million daffodil bulbs planted in this beautiful natural scene. It takes your breath away.

As they hiked into the center of this magical place, they eventually stumbled on a sign that read: "Answers to the Questions I Know You Are Asking." The first answer was "One Woman—Two Hands, Two Feet, and Very Little Brain." The second was "One at a Time." The third: "Started in 1958."

One woman had forever changed the world over a 40-year period one bulb at a time. What might you accomplish if you were to do a little bit—five things—every day for the next 40 years toward the accomplishment of your goal. If you wrote 5 pages a day, that would be 73,000 pages of text—the equivalent of 243 books of 300 pages each. If you saved $5 a day, that would be $73,000, enough for four round-the-world trips! If you invested $5 a day, with compound interest at only 6% a year, at the end of 40 years, you'd have amassed a small fortune of around $305,000.

The Rule of 5. Pretty powerful little principle, wouldn't you agree?

PRINCIPLE 24

EXCEED EXPECTATIONS

It's never crowded along the extra mile.

WAYNE DYER
Coauthor of *How to Get What You Really, Really, Really, Really Want*

Are you someone who consistently goes the extra mile and routinely overdelivers on your promises? It's rare these days, but it's the hallmark of high achievers who know that exceeding expectations helps you stand above the crowd. Almost by force of habit, successful people simply do more. As a result, they experience not only greater financial rewards for their extra efforts but also a personal transformation, becoming more self-confident, more self-reliant, and more influential with those around them.

GO THE EXTRA MILE

Seattle-based Dillanos Coffee Roasters roasts coffee beans and distributes them to coffee retailers in almost all 50 U.S. states. Dillanos's mission statement is "Help people, make friends, and have fun." The company has six core values that guide all of their activities. They are so committed to these values that the entire staff reads the list in unison at the end of every staff meeting. Number two on the list is "Provide an 'extra mile' level of service, always giving the customer more than they expect." This means they treat every one of their customers like they'd treat a best friend—someone you'd go the extra mile for.

In 1997, one of those "friends," Marty Cox, who owned four It's a Grind Coffee Houses in Long Beach, California, was just an "average size customer," but Marty had big plans for the future. Dillanos founder and CEO David Morris wanted to help his "friend" fulfill this big dream. At the time, Dillanos shipped their beans by UPS. But in 1997 UPS went on strike, creating a threat to Marty's livelihood. How to get Marty's beans—the lifeblood of his business—from Seattle to Long Beach?

Dillanos considered the option of using the post office, but the company had heard through the grapevine that the post offices and FedEx were way overworked because of the UPS strike, and they didn't want to risk the beans arriving late. So Morris rented a trailer and drove his 800-pound coffee order to Marty's location, two weeks in a row. David made the 17-hour drive from Seattle to Long Beach, delivered Marty's one-week coffee supply, drove back, got more coffee, drove down there the next week, and delivered it again. That kind of commitment to go the extra mile—literally 2,320 miles round-trip—turned Marty into a loyal long-term customer. And what has that meant to Dillanos? In just six years, Marty's four stores grew into a 150-store franchise with retail operations in nine states. Marty is now Dillanos's biggest customer. Going the extra mile pays off!

As a result of going the extra mile for all of their customers, Dillanos has grown from a single 20-pound roaster in one 1,600-square-foot room roasting 200 pounds of coffee beans a month in 1992 to a 45,000-square-foot facility and 90 employees delivering well over 3.2 million pounds of coffee beans a year, with annual sales over $10 million and a growth rate that is on track to double every three years.

And in 2011, Dillanos was named Macro Roaster of the Year by *Roast Magazine*.

WHY GO THE EXTRA MILE?

*If you are willing to do more than you are paid to do,
eventually you will be paid to do more than you do.*

SOURCE UNKNOWN

So what's the payoff for you? When you give more than is expected, you are more likely to receive promotions, raises, bonuses, and extra benefits. You won't need to worry about job security. You'll always be the first hired and the last fired. Your business will make more money and attract lifelong loyal customers. You'll also find that you feel more satisfied at the end of each day.

But you have to start now for the rewards to begin appearing.

GIVE SOMETHING ABOVE AND BEYOND WHAT IS EXPECTED

If you want to really excel at what you do—really become a howling success in business, school, or life—do more than is required, always giving something extra, something that is not expected. A business that goes the extra mile earns the respect, loyalty, and referrals of its customers.

If you're focused on only your own needs, you may think that giving more than is expected is unfair. Why should you give extra effort without compensation or recognition? You have to trust that eventually it will get noticed and that you will receive the compensation and recognition that you deserve. Eventually, as the old saying goes, the cream always rises to the top. So will you and your company. You will earn an impeccable reputation, and that is one of your most valuable assets.

Here are a few more examples of giving more than is expected:

- A client pays you for an oil painting and you frame it for him at no extra charge.
- You sell someone a car and you detail it and fill it up with gas before you deliver it to him.
- You sell someone a house, and when she moves in she discovers a bottle of champagne and a gift certificate for $100 to a local gourmet restaurant.
- As an employee, you not only do all of your own work but you also work on your day off when another employee calls in sick, you take on new responsibilities without demanding more pay, you offer to train a new employee, you anticipate problems before they occur and prevent them, you see something that needs to be done and you act on it without waiting to be asked, and you constantly look for what else you can do to make a contribution and be of service. Instead of focusing on how you can get more, you focus on how you can give more.

What can you do to go the extra mile and give more value to your boss, more service to your clients and customers, or more value to your students? One way is to surprise people with more than they expect.

I know a car dealer in Los Angeles who provides a free car wash for all of his customers every Saturday at his dealership. Nobody expects it, and everyone loves it. It gets him lots of referral business because everyone is always talking about how satisfied they are with his service.

THE FOUR SEASONS ALWAYS GOES THE EXTRA MILE

The name *Four Seasons* is synonymous with knock-your-socks-off service. The hotel chain always goes the extra mile. If you ask for directions from hotel staffers, they never just tell you—they walk you there. They always treat everybody as if they are royalty.

Dan Sullivan tells the story about the man who was taking his daughter to San Francisco for the weekend, but realized that he didn't know how to braid her hair the special way her mother did it. When he called the Four Seasons to see if there was a staff person who could help him out, he was told that there was a woman on staff who was already assigned that job. It was something that management had anticipated that guests would someday need, and the hotel had it covered. Now that's going the extra mile.

Another hotel chain that is noted for its outstanding service is the Ritz-Carlton. When I arrived at my room during my last stay at the Ritz-Carlton in Chicago, there was a hot thermos of chicken noodle soup waiting on the desk. It had a little sign on it that read "Chicken Soup for Jack Canfield's Body." It was accompanied by a wonderful card from the manager saying how much he and his staff enjoyed the *Chicken Soup* books.

NORDSTROM GOES THE EXTRA MILE

Nordstrom is a chain of retail stores that is known for going the extra mile. Nordstrom's staff has always provided extraordinary service. Nordstrom salespeople have even been known to drop off merchandise to a customer on their way home from work.

Nordstrom also has a policy that you can return anything at any time. Does the policy get abused? Sure it does! But as a result of this policy, Nordstrom has an extraordinary reputation for quality customer service. It is part of the company's carefully guarded brand image. As a result, Nordstrom is very profitable.

Make a commitment to be world class like the Four Seasons, Ritz-Carlton, and Nordstrom by going the extra mile and exceeding expectations—starting today.

PART TWO

Transform Yourself for Success

The greatest revolution of our generation is the discovery that human beings, by changing the inner attitudes of their minds, can change the outer aspects of their lives.

WILLIAM JAMES
Harvard psychologist

PRINCIPLE

25

DROP OUT OF THE "AIN'T IT AWFUL" CLUB ... AND SURROUND YOURSELF WITH SUCCESSFUL PEOPLE

You are the average of the five people you spend the most time with.

JIM ROHN
Self-made millionaire and successful author

When Tim Ferriss, the bestselling author of *The 4-Hour Work Week,* was 12 years old, an unidentified caller left the above Jim Rohn quote on his answering machine. It changed his life forever. For days, he couldn't get the idea out of his mind. At only 12 years of age, Tim recognized that the kids he was hanging out with were not the ones he wanted influencing his future. So he went to his mom and dad and asked them to send him to private school. Four years at St. Paul's School set him on a path that led to a junior year abroad in Japan studying judo and Zen meditation; four years at Princeton University, where he became an all-American wrestler; a national kickboxing championship; and eventually starting his own company at the age of 23. Tim knew what every parent intuitively knows—that we become like the people we hang out with.

Why else are parents always telling their kids that they don't want them hanging out with "those kids"? It's because we know that kids (and adults!) become like the people they hang out with. That is why it is so important to spend time with the people you want to become like. If you want to be more successful, you have to start hanging out with more successful people.

There are lots of places to find successful people. Join a professional association. Attend your professional conferences. Join the chamber of commerce. Join the country club. Join the Young Presidents' Organization or the Young Entrepreneurs' Organization. Volunteer for leadership positions. Join civic groups like Kiwanis, Optimists International, and Rotary International. Volunteer to serve with other leaders in your church, temple, or mosque. Attend lectures, symposia, courses, seminars, clinics, camps, and retreats taught by those who have already achieved what you want to achieve. Fly first class or business class whenever you can.

YOU BECOME LIKE THE PEOPLE YOU SPEND THE MOST TIME WITH

Pay any price to stay in the presence of extraordinary people.
MIKE MURDOCK
Author of *The Leadership Secrets of Jesus*

John Assaraf is a successful entrepreneur who has seemingly done it all—including traveling the world for a year in his twenties, owning and operating a franchising company whose annual real estate revenues topped $3 billion, and helping to build Internet virtual tour pioneer Bamboo.com (now IPIX) from a team of six people to a team of 1,500 in just over a year, netting millions in monthly sales, and completing a successful initial public offering on the NASDAQ after just nine months.

John was a street kid who had been entangled in the world of drugs and gangs. When he landed a job working in the gym at the Jewish community center across the street from his apartment in Montreal, his life was changed by the powerful principle that you become like the people you spend the most time with. In addition to earning $1.65 an hour, he received access to the men's health club. John recounts that he got his early education in business in the men's sauna. Every night after work, from 9:15 to 10 P.M., you'd find him in the steamy hot room listening to successful businessmen tell their tales of success and failure.

Many of those successful men were immigrants who had come to Canada to stake their claim, and John was fascinated as much by their setbacks as by their successes. The stories of what went wrong with their businesses, families, and health gave him inspiration, because his own family was experiencing tremendous challenges and difficulties, and John learned that it was normal to have challenges—that other families also went through similar crises and still made it to the top.

These successful people taught John to never give up on his dreams. "No matter what the failure," they told him, "try another way; try going up, over, around, or through, but never give up. There's always a way."

John also learned from these successful men that it makes no difference where you are born, what race or color you are, how old you are, or whether you come from a rich family or a poor family. Many of the men in that sauna spoke broken English; some were single and some were divorced; some were happily married and some were not; some were healthy and others were in terrible shape; some had college degrees and some didn't. Some hadn't even been to high school. For the first time, John realized that success is not reserved just for those born into well-to-do families without challenges and to whom every advantage has been given. He realized that no matter what the conditions of your life, you could build a life of success. He was in the presence of men from all walks of life who had done it and freely shared their wisdom and experience with him.

Every night John attended his own private business school—in a sauna in a Jewish community center. You, too, need to be surrounded with those who have done it; you need to be surrounded with people who have a positive attitude, a solution-oriented approach to life—people who know that they can accomplish whatever they set out to do.

Confidence is contagious. So is lack of confidence.

VINCE LOMBARDI
Head coach of the Green Bay Packers who led them to six division titles, five NFL championships, and two Super Bowls

DROP OUT OF THE "AIN'T IT AWFUL" CLUB

There are two types of people—anchors and motors. You want to lose the anchors and get with the motors because the motors are going somewhere and they're having more fun. The anchors will just drag you down.

WYLAND
World-renowned marine artist

When I was a first-year history teacher in a Chicago high school, I quickly stopped going into the teachers' lounge, which I soon dubbed the "Ain't It Awful" Club. Worse than the haze of cigarette smoke that constantly hung over the room was the cloud of emotional negativity. "Can you believe what they want us to do now?" "I got that Simmons kid again this year in math. He's a holy terror." "There is no way you can teach these kids. They are totally out of control."

It was a constant stream of negative judgments, criticisms, blaming, and complaining. Not too long after, I discovered a group of dedicated teachers that hung out in the library and ate together at two tables in the teachers' lunchroom. They were positive and believed they could overcome and handle anything that was thrown at them. I implemented every new idea they shared with me, as well as a few more that I picked up from my weekend classes at the University of Chicago. As a result, I was selected by the students as teacher of the year in only my first year of teaching.

BE SELECTIVE

I just do not hang around anybody that I don't want to be with. Period. For me, that's been a blessing, and I can stay positive. I hang around people who are happy, who are growing, who want to learn, who don't mind saying sorry or thank you . . . and [are] having a fun time.

JOHN ASSARAF
Author of *The Street Kid's Guide to Having It All*

I'd like you to do a valuable exercise that my mentor W. Clement Stone did with me. Make a list of everyone you spend time with on a regular basis—your family members, coworkers, neighbors, friends, people in your civic organization, fellow members of your religious group, and so on.

When you've completed your list, go back and put a minus sign (–) next to those people who are negative and toxic, and a plus sign (+) next to those who are positive and nurturing. As you make a decision about each person, you might find that a pattern will begin to form. Perhaps your entire workplace is filled with toxic personalities. Or perhaps it's your friends who naysay everything you do. Or maybe it's your family members who constantly put you down and undermine your self-esteem and self-confidence.

I want you to do the same thing that Mr. Stone told me to do. Stop spending time with those people with a minus sign next to their name.

If that is impossible (and remember, nothing is impossible; it is always a choice), then severely decrease the amount of time you spend with them. You have to free yourself from the negative influence of others.

Are there people in your life who are always complaining and blaming others for their circumstances? Are there people who are always judging others, spreading negative gossip, and talking about how bad it is? Stop spending time with them as well.

Are there people in your life who, simply by calling you on the telephone, can bring tension, stress, and disorder to your day? Are there dream-stealers who tell you that your dreams are impossible and try to dissuade you from believing in and pursuing your goals? Do you have friends who constantly attempt to bring you back down to their level? If so, then it is time for some new friends!

AVOID TOXIC PEOPLE

Surround yourself with only people who are going to lift you higher.
OPRAH WINFREY
Billionaire talk-show host, actor, and founder of the OWN Network

Until you reach the point in your self-development where you no longer allow people to affect you with their negativity, you need to avoid toxic people at all costs. You're better off spending time alone than spending time with people who will hold you back with their victim mentality and their mediocre standards.

Make a conscious effort to surround yourself with positive, nourishing, and uplifting people—people who believe in you, encourage you to go after your dreams, and applaud your victories. Surround yourself with possibility thinkers, idealists, and visionaries.

SURROUND YOURSELF WITH SUCCESSFUL PEOPLE

One of the clients who hired me to teach these success principles to their salespeople is one of the leading manufacturers of optical lenses. As I mingled with the salespeople prior to the event, I asked each person I met if he or she knew who the top five salespeople in the company were. Most answered yes and quickly rattled off their names. That night I asked my audience of 300 people to raise their hands if they knew the names of the top five salespeople. Almost everyone raised a hand. I then asked them to raise their hands again if they had ever approached any of these five people and asked them to share their secrets of success. Not one hand went up.

Think about it! Everyone knew who the most effective people in the company were, but because of an unfounded fear of rejection, nobody had ever asked these sales leaders to share their secrets.

If you are going to be successful, you have to start hanging out with the successful people. You need to ask them to share their success strategies with you. Then try them on and see if they fit for you. Experiment with doing what they do, reading what they read, thinking the way they think, and so on. If these new ways of thinking and behaving work for you, adopt them. If not, drop them, and keep looking and experimenting.

Be around the light bringers, the magic makers,
the world shifters, the game shakers.
They challenge you, break you open,
uplift and expand you.
They don't let you play small with your life.
These heartbeats are your people.
These people are your tribe.

DANIELLE DOBY
Author, poet, and artist

PRINCIPLE 26

ACKNOWLEDGE YOUR POSITIVE PAST

*I look back on my life like a good day's work;
it is done and I am satisfied with it.*

GRANDMA MOSES
American folk artist who lived 101 years

Most people in our culture remember their failures more than their successes. One reason for this is the "leave 'em alone—pounce" approach to parenting, teaching, and management that is so prevalent in our culture. When you were a young child, your parents left you alone when you were playing and being cooperative, and then pounced on you when you made too much noise, were a nuisance, or got into trouble. You probably received a perfunctory "good job" when you got As but got a huge lecture when you got Cs and Ds, or, God forbid, an F. In school, most of your teachers marked the answers you got wrong with an X rather than marking the ones you got right with a check mark or a star. In sports, you got yelled at when you dropped the football or the baseball. There was almost always more emotional intensity around your errors, mistakes, and failures than there was around your successes.

Because the brain more easily remembers events that were accompanied by strong emotions, most people underestimate and underappreciate the number of successes they've had compared to the number of failures they've had. One of the ways to counteract this phenomenon is to consciously focus on and celebrate your successes.

One of the exercises I do in my corporate seminars is to have the participants each share a success they have had in the past week. It is always amazing to see how difficult this is for so many people. Many people don't think they have had any successes. They can easily tell you 10 ways they messed up in the last seven days but have a much harder time telling you 10 victories they had.

The sad truth is that we all have many more victories than failures—it's just that we set the bar too high for what we call a success. A participant in the GOALS (Gaining Opportunities and Life Skills) Program I developed to help get people off welfare in California actually asserted that he didn't have *any* successes. When I inquired about his accent, he told us that he had left Iran when the shah was toppled in 1979. He had moved his whole family to Germany, where he had learned German and become a car mechanic. More recently he had immigrated his whole family to the United States, had learned English, and was now in a program learning to be a welder—but he didn't think he had any successes!

When the group asked him what he thought a success was, he replied that it was owning a home in Beverly Hills and driving a Cadillac. In his mind, anything less than that was not an achievement. Slowly, with a little coaching, he began to see that he had many success experiences every single week. Simple things such as getting to work on time, getting into the GOALS Program, learning to speak English, providing for his family, and buying his daughter her first bicycle were all successes.

THE POKER CHIP THEORY OF SELF-ESTEEM AND SUCCESS

So why am I making such a big deal about acknowledging your past successes? The reason it is so important is because of its impact on your self-esteem. Imagine for a moment that your self-esteem is like a stack of poker chips. Then imagine that you and I are playing a game of poker and you have 10 chips and I have 200 chips. Who do you think is going to play more conservatively in this game of poker? Yes, you are. If you lose two bets of five chips, you're out of the game. I can lose five chips 40 times before I'm out of the game, so I am going to take more risks because I can afford to take the losses. Your level of self-esteem works the same way. The more self-esteem you have, the more risks you are willing to take.

Research has shown over and over again that the more you acknowledge your past successes, the more confident you become in taking on and successfully accomplishing new ones. You know that even if you fail, it won't destroy you, because your self-esteem is high. And the more you risk, the more you win in life. The more shots you take, the more chances you have of scoring.

Knowing that you have had successes in the past will give you the self-confidence that you can have more successes in the future. So let's look at some simple but powerful ways to build and maintain high levels of self-confidence and self-esteem.

BEGIN WITH NINE MAJOR SUCCESSES

Here is a simple way to begin an inventory of your major successes. (Consider having your spouse or family do this exercise, too.) Start by dividing your life into three equal time periods—for example, if you are 45 years old, your three time periods would be from birth to age 15, 16 to 30 years, and 31 to 45 years. Then list three successes you've had for each time period. To help you get started, I've listed my own below:

First Third: Birth to Age 23

1. Elected patrol leader in the Boy Scouts
2. Caught winning touchdown pass to win city championship game
3. Graduated from Harvard University

Second Third: Age 24–47

1. Earned my master's degree in education from the University of Massachusetts
2. Published my first book
3. Founded the New England Center for Personal and Organizational Development

Final Third: Age 47–70

1. Founded The Canfield Training Group
2. *Chicken Soup for the Soul*® hit number one on the *New York Times* bestsellers list
3. Achieved goal of having spoken professionally in all 50 states

CAN YOU LIST 100 SUCCESSES?

To really convince yourself that you're a successful person who can continue to achieve great things, the next step of this exercise is to make a list of 100 successes you've had in your life.

My experience is that most people do fine coming up with the first 30 or so; then it becomes a little more difficult. To come up with 100, you are going to have to list things like learning to ride a bicycle, singing a solo at church, getting your first summer job, the first time you got a hit in Little League, making the cheerleading squad, getting your driver's license, writing an article for your school newspaper, getting an A in Mr. Simon's history class, surviving basic training, learning to surf, winning a ribbon at the county fair, modifying your first car, getting married, having your first child, and leading a fund-raising campaign for your child's school. These are all things you probably take for granted now, but they all need to be acknowledged as successes you've had in life. If you are young, you may even need to resort to writing down things like "passed first grade, passed second grade, passed third grade," but that's okay. The goal is simply to get to 100.

CREATE A VICTORY LOG

Another powerful way to keep adding to that stack of poker chips is to keep a written record of your daily successes. It can be as simple as a running list in a spiral-bound notebook or a document on your computer, or it can be as elaborate as a leather-bound journal. By recalling and writing down your successes each day, you log them into your long-term memory, which enhances your self-esteem and builds your self-confidence. And later, if you need a boost of self-confidence, you can reread what you have written.

Peter Thigpen, a former vice president at Levi Strauss & Co., kept such a victory log on his desk, and every time he had a victory or a win, he wrote it down. When he was about to do something scary, such as negotiate for a multimillion-dollar bank loan or make a speech to the board of directors, he would read his victory log to build up his self-confidence. His list included entries such as *I opened up China as a market, I got my teenage son to clean up his room,* and *I got the board to approve the new expansion plan.*

When most people are about to embark on some frightening task, they have a tendency to focus on all the times they tried before and didn't succeed, which undermines their self-confidence and feeds their fear that they will fail again. Keeping and referring to your victory log keeps you focused on your successes instead.

Start your own victory log as soon as possible. If you want, you can also embellish it like a scrapbook with photos, certificates, memos, and other reminders of your success.

If many of your victories are featured on the Internet—for example, if you're an athlete, artist, author, or businessperson who appears in online news, photo galleries, interviews, or book reviews—you can make a digital scrapbook using Pinterest, the social-media and image-sharing app. Pinterest lets you collect links or "bookmarks" to photos, quotes, and written content featured anywhere on the Internet.

Simply start an account at Pinterest.com and begin "pinning" things you find online that talk about, portray, or visually capture your victories—such as news articles, blog posts, web pages, or photographs. Collect and organize these pins on your Pinterest board, which is created and controlled by you. If you like, you can share your victory log with friends and family—or with other Pinterest users who want to follow your board. And if you own a business and want to use some of your "victories" for promotional or public relations purposes, simply share your entire Pinterest board or share a subset of accomplishments by collecting them into themes or topics.

DISPLAY YOUR SUCCESS SYMBOLS

Researchers have discovered that what you see in your environment has a psychological impact on your moods, your attitudes, and your behavior. Your environment has a great deal of influence over you. But here's an even more important fact: You have almost total control over your immediate environment. You get to choose what pictures are hung on your bedroom or office wall, what memorabilia gets taped to your refrigerator or locker door, and what mementos you place on your desk or in your cubicle at work.

A valuable technique that will help build your self-esteem and motivate you to greater future success is the practice of surrounding yourself with awards, pictures, and other objects that remind you of your successes. These might include medals from your armed services days, a picture of you scoring the winning touchdown, a picture of you standing on the Great Wall of China, your wedding picture, a trophy, a framed copy of the poem you had published in the local newspaper, a letter of thanks, your college diploma, or your Eagle Scout badge or Girl Scout Gold Award.

Make a special place—a special shelf, the top of your dresser, the refrigerator door, a "victory wall" in a hallway you pass through every day—and fill it with your success symbols. Clean out that special drawer, those boxes in the closet, your files—then frame, laminate, polish, and display those symbols of your success so you will see them every day. This will have a powerful effect on your subconscious mind. It will subtly program you to see yourself as a winner—someone who has consistent successes in life! It will also convey this message to others. It will instill confidence in you and in others for you.

This is also a great thing to do for your children. Proudly display their success symbols as well—papers, ribbons, artwork, photographs of them in their baseball uniform or playing the violin, photographs of them enjoying themselves, trophies, medals, and other awards. If you have children living at home, frame their best artwork and hang it on the walls of the kitchen, their rooms, and the hallways in the house. When they see these framed and on the wall, it can be a major boost to their self-esteem.

THE MIRROR EXERCISE

You are a living magnet. What you attract into your life is in harmony with your dominant thoughts.

BRIAN TRACY
Leading authority on the development of human potential and personal effectiveness

Just as you acknowledge your big successes, you need to acknowledge your small daily successes, too. The Mirror Exercise is based on the principle that we all need acknowledgment, but the most important acknowledgment is the acknowledgment you give yourself.

The Mirror Exercise gives your inner child—which resides in your subconscious mind—the positive strokes it needs to pursue further achievements. It helps change any negative beliefs you have toward praise and accomplishment, and puts you in an achieving frame of mind. Do this exercise for a minimum of three months. After that, you can decide whether you want to continue. I know some very successful people who have been doing this every night for years.

Just before going to bed, stand in front of a mirror and appreciate yourself for all that you have accomplished during the day. Start with a few seconds of looking directly into the eyes of the person in the mirror—your mirror image looking back at you. Then address yourself by name and begin appreciating yourself *out loud* for the following things:

- Any achievements—business, financial, educational, personal, physical, spiritual, or emotional
- Any personal disciplines you kept—dietary, exercise, reading, meditation, prayer

- Any temptations that you did not give in to—eating dessert, lying, watching too much TV, staying up too late, drinking too much

Maintain eye contact with yourself throughout the exercise. When you're finished appreciating yourself, complete the exercise by continuing to look deep into your own eyes and saying, "I love you." Then stand there for another few seconds to really feel the impact of the experience—as if you were the one in the mirror who had just listened to all of this appreciation. The important thing during this last part is to not just turn away from the mirror feeling embarrassed or thinking of yourself or the exercise as stupid or silly.

Here is an example of what your exercise might sound like:

Jack, I want to appreciate you for the following things today: First, I want to appreciate you for going to bed on time last night without staying up too late watching TV, so that you got up bright and early this morning and had a really good conversation with Inga. And then you meditated for twenty minutes and worked out for 30 minutes before you took a shower. You ate a healthy low-fat, low-carbohydrate breakfast. You got to work on time and led a very good staff meeting with your support team. You did a great job of helping everyone listen to everybody's feelings and ideas. And you were great at drawing out the quiet ones.

Let's see . . . oh, and then you ate a really healthy lunch—soup and salad—and you didn't have the dessert that was offered. And you drank the ten glasses of water that you committed to drinking every day. And then . . . let's see . . . you finished editing the new Train-the-Trainer manual, and you got a really good start on scheduling the summer management training program. And then you filled in your Daily Success Focus Journal before you left work. Oh, and you appreciated Veronica for solving the problems with the travel schedule. It was great to see how she just lit up.

And when you got home, you called Oran and talked with your grandson on Skype. That was really special. And now you're going to bed at a good time again—and not staying up all night surfing the Internet. You were great today.

And one more thing, Jack—I love you!

It's not unusual to have a number of reactions the first few times you do this. You might feel silly, embarrassed, like crying (or actually begin crying), or just generally uncomfortable. Occasionally, people have even reported breaking out in hives, feeling hot and sweaty, or feeling a little light-headed. These are natural and normal reactions, as this is a very unfamiliar thing to be doing. We are not trained to acknowledge ourselves. In fact, we are mostly trained to do the opposite: *Don't toot your own horn. Don't get a swelled head. Don't get a stuffed shirt. Pride is a sin.* When you begin to act more positive and nurturing toward yourself, it is natural to have physical and emotional reactions as you release the old negative parental wounds, unrealistic expectations, and self-judgments. If you experience any of these things—and not all people do—don't let these things stop you. They are only temporary and will pass after a few days of doing the exercise.

When I first began to do this exercise, after just 40 days I noticed that all my negative internal self-talk had totally vanished, crowded out by the daily positive focus of the Mirror Exercise. I used to berate myself for things like misplacing my car keys or my glasses. That critical voice just simply disappeared. The same kind of thing can happen for you, but only if you take the time to actually do the exercise.

One note to remember: If you find yourself lying in bed realizing you haven't done the Mirror Exercise yet, get out of bed and do it. Looking at yourself in the mirror is a critical part of the exercise. And one last bit of advice: Be sure to let your spouse, children, roommate, or parents know in advance that you will be doing this exercise each evening for the next three months or more. You don't want them to walk in on you and think you've lost your mind! In fact, you are powerfully retraining your mind to focus on the positive while building up your stack of poker chips.

REWARD YOUR INNER CHILD

Inside all of us are three distinct and totally separate ego states that work in concert to make up our unique personality. We have a parentlike ego, an adult ego, and a childlike ego who act much the same way that parents, adults, and children do in real life.

Your adult ego state is the rational part of yourself. It gathers data and makes logical decisions devoid of emotion. It plans your schedule, balances your checkbook, figures out your taxes, and determines when to rotate your tires.

Your parentlike ego tells you to tie your shoes, brush your teeth, eat your vegetables, do your homework, exercise, meet your deadlines, and finish your projects. It has two sides to it. The negative side shows up as your inner critic—the part that judges you when you don't live up to its standards. The positive side shows up as the nurturing part of yourself that makes sure you're protected, taken care of, and provided for. It is also the part that validates, appreciates, and acknowledges you for doing a good job.

Your childlike ego, on the other hand, does what all children do—it whines, begs for attention, craves hugs, and acts out when it doesn't get its needs met. As we go through life, it's almost as if we have a three-year-old holding on to us who's constantly asking, *Why are we sitting at this desk? Why aren't we having more fun? Why am I still up at three in the morning? Why am I reading this boring report?*

As the parent of this "inner child," one of your most important tasks is to engage it and reward it for behaving while you get your work done.

If you had a three-year-old in real life, you might say, "Mommy has to finish this proposal in the next twenty minutes. But after Mommy's done, we'll go for an ice cream or play a video game." Your real-life three-year-old would probably answer, "Okay; I'll be good because I know I'm going to get something good at the end of it."

Well, not surprisingly, your inner child is no different. When you ask it to be still, let you finish your work, stay up late, and so on, it will behave as long as it knows there's a reward at the end for behaving. At some point, it needs to know it will get to read a novel, go to the movies, play with a friend, listen to music, go dancing, let loose, eat out, get a new "toy," or take a vacation.

A big part of creating more success in your life is rewarding yourself when you succeed. In reality, rewarding yourself for your successes keeps your inner child happy and compliant the next time it must behave while you work hard. It knows it can trust you to eventually deliver on your promises. If you don't, just like a real child, it will start to sabotage your efforts by doing things like getting sick, having accidents, or making mistakes that cost you a promotion or even your job, so that you are *forced* to take some time off. And that will only take you further away from the success you want to create.

A SENSE OF COMPLETION

Another reason to celebrate your successes is that you don't feel complete until you've been acknowledged. It gives you a sense of accomplishment and recognition. If you spend weeks producing a report and your boss doesn't acknowledge it, you are left feeling incomplete. If you send someone a gift and they don't acknowledge receiving it, you end up with this sense of incompletion—there's this little incomplete taking up space inside your mind. Your mind needs to complete the cycle, thus freeing up space that would be better used focusing on your goals.

Of course, even more important than just achieving a state of completion, the simple, enjoyable act of acknowledging and rewarding our successes causes your subconscious mind to say, *Hey, succeeding is cool. Every time we produce a success, we get to do something fun. Jack will buy us something we want or take us someplace neat. Let's have more of these successes, so Jack will take us out to play more.*

Rewarding yourself for your wins powerfully reinforces your subconscious mind's desire to want to work harder for you. It's just basic human nature.

PRINCIPLE 27

KEEP YOUR EYE ON THE PRIZE

It's easy to be negative and unmotivated, but it takes some work to be positive and motivated. While there's no off button for those relentless "tapes," there are things that you can do to turn down the volume and shift your focus from the negative to the positive.

DONNA CARDILLO, R.N.
Speaker, entrepreneur, humorist, and master motivator

Successful people maintain a positive focus in life no matter what is going on around them. They stay focused on their past successes rather than their past failures, and on the next action steps that will get them closer to the fulfillment of their goals rather than on all the other distractions that life presents to them. They are constantly proactive in the pursuit of their chosen objectives.

THE MOST IMPORTANT 45 MINUTES OF THE DAY

An important part of any focusing regimen is to set aside time at the end of the day—just before going to sleep—to acknowledge your successes, review your goals, focus on your successful future, and make specific plans for what you want to accomplish the next day.

Why do I suggest the *end* of the day? Because whatever you read, see, listen to, talk about, and experience during the last 45 minutes of the day has a huge influence on your sleep and your next day. During the night, your unconscious mind replays and processes this late-night input up to six times more often than anything else you experienced during the day. This is why cramming for school exams late at night can work and why watching a scary movie before bed will give you nightmares. This is also why reading good bedtime stories is so important for children—not just to get them to fall asleep, but because the repeated messages, lessons, and morals of the story become part of the fabric of the child's consciousness.

As you drift off to sleep, you enter into the alpha brain wave state of consciousness—a state in which you are very suggestible. If you drift off to sleep after watching the late news, that is what you'll be imprinting into your consciousness—war, crime, automobile accidents, rape, robbery, murder, gang wars, drive-by shootings, kidnappings, and corporate scandals.

Think how much better it would be to read an inspirational autobiography or a self-improvement book instead. Imagine the power of meditating, listening to a self-help audio program, or taking the time to plan your next day right before you go to sleep.

Here are two exercises that will keep you positively focused and moving forward at the end of the day.

THE EVENING REVIEW

This is a powerful exercise to help you more quickly install a new positive behavior (like punctuality), habit (like listening more), or quality (like patience or mindfulness). You'll be amazed at how fast this technique can lead to permanent change.

Sit with your eyes closed, breathe deeply, and give yourself *one* of the following directions:

- Show me where I could have been more effective today.
- Show me where I could have been more conscious today.
- Show me where I could have been a better (fill in your profession—manager, teacher, coach, salesperson, etc.) today.
- Show me where I could have been more loving today.
- Show me where I could have been more assertive today.
- Show me where I could have been more (fill in any quality or characteristic) today.

As you sit calmly in a state of quiet receptivity, you'll see that a number of events from the day will come to mind. Just observe them without any judgment or self-criticism. When no more events come to mind, take each incident and replay it in your mind *the way you would have preferred to have done it* had you been more conscious and intentional at the time. This creates a subconscious image that will help evoke the desired behavior the next time a similar situation occurs.

CREATE YOUR IDEAL DAY

Another powerful tool to keep you focused on creating your life exactly as you want it to be is to take a few minutes after you have planned your next day's schedule and visualize the entire day going exactly as you want it. Visualize everyone being there when you call them, every meeting starting and ending on time, all of your priorities being handled, all of your errands being completed with ease, making every sale, and so on. See yourself performing at your best in every situation you will encounter during the next day. This will give your subconscious all night to work on creating ways to make it all happen just as you have visualized it.

We also now know that every thought you think is broadcast out to the universe on what my friend and success coach Robert Scheinfeld calls the "innernet." So when you are visualizing your ideal day, you are also sending out your intention to the other people involved through what the physicists call the Quantum Field.

Get into the habit now of visualizing your ideal next day the night before. It will make a huge difference in your life.

PRINCIPLE

28

CLEAN UP YOUR MESSES AND YOUR INCOMPLETES

If a cluttered desk is the sign of a cluttered mind, what is the significance of a clean desk?

LAURENCE J. PETER
American educator and author

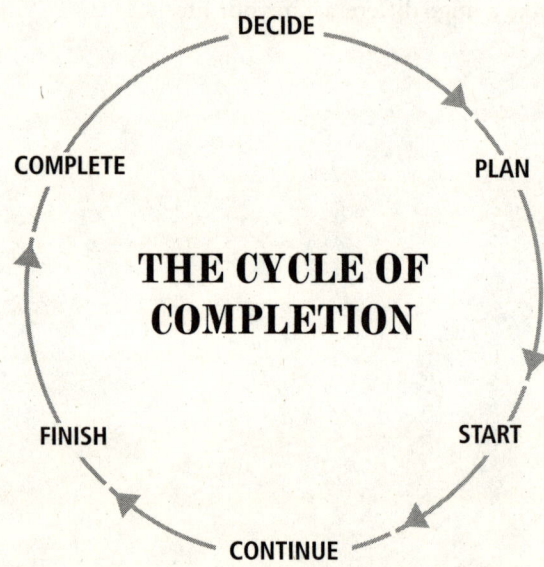

Take a look at the diagram above. It's called The Cycle of Completion. Each of these steps—Decide, Plan, Start, Continue, Finish, and Complete—is required to succeed at anything, to get a desired result, to finish. Yet how many of us never *complete*? We get all the way through the finishing stage—but leave one last thing undone.

Are there areas in your life where you've left uncompleted projects or failed to get closure with people? When you don't complete the past, you can't be free to fully embrace the present.

FAILING TO COMPLETE ROBS YOU OF VALUABLE ATTENTION UNITS

When you start a project or make an agreement or identify a change you need to make, it goes into your present memory bank and takes up what I call an "attention unit." We can only pay attention to so many things at one time, and each promise, agreement, or item on your to-do list leaves fewer attention units to dedicate to completing present tasks and bringing new opportunities and abundance into your life.

So why don't people complete? Often, incompletes represent areas in our life where we're not clear—or where we have emotional and psychological blocks.

For instance, you might have a lot of requests, projects, tasks, and other things on your desk you really want to say no to—but you're afraid of being perceived as the bad guy. So you put off responding in order to avoid saying no. Meanwhile the sticky notes and stacks of paper pile up and distract you. There may also be circumstances in which you have to make decisions that are difficult or uncomfortable. So rather than struggle with the discomfort, you let the incompletes pile up.

Some incompletions come from simply not having adequate systems, knowledge, or expertise for handling these tasks. Other incompletions pile up because of our bad work habits.

GET INTO COMPLETION CONSCIOUSNESS

Continually ask yourself, *What does it take to actually get this task completed?* Then you can begin to consciously take that next step of filing completed documents, mailing in the forms required, or reporting back to your boss that the project has been completed. The truth is that 20 things *completed* have more power than 50 things half completed. One finished book, for instance, that can go out and influence the world is better than 13 books you're in the process of writing. Rather than starting 15 projects that end up incomplete and take up space in the house, you'd be better off if you had started just 3 and completed them.

THE FOUR Ds OF COMPLETION

One way to take care of to-do items is something we've all seen in time management courses: the Four Ds. Do it, Delegate it, Delay it, or Dump it. When you pick up a piece of paper, decide then and there whether you'll ever do anything with it. If not, dump it. If you can take care of it within 10 minutes, do it immediately. If you still want to take care of it yourself, but know it will take longer, delay it by filing it in a folder of things to do later. If you can't do it yourself or don't want to take the time, delegate it to someone you trust to accomplish the task. Be sure to have the person report back when he or she finishes the task so that you know it is complete.

MAKING SPACE FOR SOMETHING NEW

In addition to professional incompletes, most households are also groaning under the weight of too much clutter, too many papers, worn-out clothes, unused toys, forgotten personal effects, and obsolete, broken, and unneeded items. In the United States, the entire ministorage industry has sprung up to help homeowners and small businesses store what they no longer can fit into their homes and offices.

But do we really need all this stuff? Of course not.

One of the ways to free up attention units is to free your living and work environments from the mental burden of all this clutter. When you clear out the old, you also make room for something new.

Take a look at your clothes closet, for instance. If you've got one of those where you can't put another thing into it—where you struggle to pull out a dress or shirt—that may be one reason why you don't have more new clothes. There's nowhere to put them. If you haven't worn something in six months and it's not a seasonal or a special-occasion item such as an evening gown or tuxedo, get rid of it.

If there's *anything* new that you want in your life, you've got to make room for it. I mean that psychologically as well as physically.

If you want a new man in your life, you've got to let go of (forgive and forget) the last one you stopped dating five years ago. Because if you don't, when a new man meets you, the unspoken message he picks up is, "This woman's attached to somebody else. She hasn't let go."

A woman in one of my seminars admitted that for years she kept piles of books and magazines on her bed—a collection that eventually covered over half the available sleeping space. When she also mentioned that she had suffered terribly from a broken romantic relationship, it was instantly obvious to me that covering half her bed with piles of reading material was her unconscious way of making sure there was no space for a man who might be romantically interested in her.

Not only had she failed to complete the past, the part of her that was afraid of being hurt again was making darn sure a similar unwanted future didn't show up either! After helping her see the connection between this self-imposed barrier and the lack of romance in her life, she used EFT tapping to release her fear of being hurt (see page 260), cleared the clutter off her bed, and made her bedroom inviting and welcoming again. Within months, she met a wonderful man who has become the love of her life.*

My good friend Martin Rutte once told me that whenever he wants to bring in new business, he thoroughly cleans his office, home, car, and garage. Every time he does, he starts getting calls and letters from people who want to work with him. Others find that doing spring cleaning helps them gain new clarity on problems, challenges, opportunities, and relationships.

When we don't throw away clutter and items we no longer need, it's as if we don't trust our ability to manifest the necessary abundance in our lives to buy new ones when we need them. But incompletes like this keep that very abundance from showing up. We need to complete the past so that our present has the space to show up more fully.

TWENTY-FIVE WAYS TO COMPLETE BEFORE MOVING FORWARD

How many things do you need to complete, dump, or delegate before you can move on and bring new activity, abundance, relationships, and excitement into your life? Use the checklist below to jog your thinking, make a list, and then write down how you'll complete each task.

Once you've made your list, choose four items and start completing them. Choose those that would immediately free up the most time, energy, or space for you—whether it's mental space or physical space.

At minimum, I encourage you to clean up one major incomplete every three months. If you want to really get the ball rolling, schedule a "completion weekend," and devote two full days to handling as many things on the following list as possible.

---

*By the way, if you are looking to attract a healthy and fulfilling relationship into your life, it is important to complete your past relationships both psychologically and energetically. *The Soulmate Secret: Manifest the Love of Your Life with the Law of Attraction* (New York: HarperOne, 2011) by Arielle Ford is an excellent resource that contains many exercises on letting go and completing your past relationships.

1. Former business activities that need completion
2. Promises not kept, not acknowledged, or not renegotiated
3. Unpaid debts or financial commitments (money owed to others or to you)
4. Closets overflowing with clothing never worn
5. A disorganized garage crowded with old discards
6. Haphazard or disorganized tax records
7. Checkbook not balanced or accounts that should be closed
8. "Junk drawers" full of unusable items
9. Missing or broken tools
10. An attic filled with unused items
11. A car trunk or backseat full of trash
12. Incomplete car maintenance
13. A disorganized basement filled with discarded items
14. Credenza packed with unfiled or incomplete projects
15. Filing left undone
16. Computer files not backed up or data needing to be converted for storage
17. Desk surface cluttered or disorganized
18. Family pictures never put into an album
19. Mending, ironing, or other piles of items to repair or discard
20. Deferred household maintenance
21. Personal relationships with unstated requests, resentments, or appreciations
22. People you need to forgive
23. Time not spent with people you've been meaning to spend time with
24. Incomplete projects or projects delivered without closure or feedback
25. Acknowledgments that need to be given or asked for

WHAT'S IRRITATING YOU?

Like incompletes, daily irritants are equally damaging to your success because they, too, take up attention units. Perhaps it's the missing button on your favorite suit that keeps you from wearing it to an important meeting or the torn screen on your patio door that lets in annoying insects. One of the best things you can do to move further and faster along your success path is to fix, replace, mend, or get rid of those daily irritants that annoy you and stay on your mind.

Talane Miedaner, the author of *Coach Yourself to Success,* recommends walking through every room of your house, your garage, and all around your property, jotting down those things that irritate, annoy, and bother you and then arranging to get each one handled. Of course, none of these may be urgent to your business or life-threatening to your family. But every time you notice them and wish they were different, they pull energy from you. They are subtly subtracting energy from your life instead of adding energy to your life. They are "expiring" you rather than "inspiring" you. Another negative psychological impact of not handling those incompletes and tolerating those things that irritate you is that it creates a state of resignation in you that affects your belief in your ability to achieve your bigger goals. Subconsciously your mind is thinking, *If I can't find a stapler when I want it and my filing system is dysfunctional, what makes me think I can start my own company or become a millionaire?*

CONSIDER HIRING A PROFESSIONAL ORGANIZER TO GET YOU STARTED

The mission of the National Association of Productivity & Organizing Professionals (NAPO) is to help you declutter your life and build systems to ensure that things stay that way. You may need someone who has a dispassionate eye to look beyond your attachments, familiarity, and fears and be neutral in a way you can't. Plus, NAPO members are experts in how to make things efficient and easy. It is their profession.*

For about the cost of several business lunches, you can hire an organizer from your local area for a day of work. Additionally, you can hire people to clean your home, as well as handle all the little irritants, maintenance chores, and other tasks you either don't want to do or aren't skilled enough to do.

If your finances don't allow for a professional organizer, ask a friend to help. Hire a neighborhood teen or the stay-at-home mom down the street. You can also read one of the many good how-to books and tackle things yourself. Just remember that you don't need to get it done all at once. Choose one each month. Just as cleaning up your incompletes is important to your successful future, there is literally no excuse for enduring the disorganization in your life.

---

*You can find organizers in your area (including outside the United States) by visiting the NAPO website at napo.net and clicking on "Find a Pro." Additionally, you can visit organizersincanada.com, which includes listings for residential and business services in Canada. Martha Ringer is the productivity coach who has helped me organize my desk and my work flow. In 2 days' time, my office looked like a brand-new place, and my work flow is now clean and efficient. You can read more about her and her work at martharinger.com.

PRINCIPLE 29

COMPLETE THE PAST TO EMBRACE THE FUTURE

None of us can change our yesterdays, but all of us can change our tomorrows.

COLIN POWELL
Former secretary of state of the United States
under President George W. Bush

Does this sound familiar? Some people go through life as if they have a big anchor behind them, weighing them down. If they could release it, they would be able to move faster and succeed more easily. Perhaps that's you—holding on to past hurts, past incompletes, past anger or fear. Yet releasing these anchors can often be the final step you need to complete your past and embrace the future.

I have known people who have forgiven their parents and doubled their income in the ensuing few months, as well as doubled their productivity and doubled their ability to achieve things. I've known others who have forgiven their aggressors for past harm and been relieved of actual physical ailments.

The truth is . . . we need to let go of the past to embrace the future. One method I use for this is called the Total Truth Process.

THE TOTAL TRUTH PROCESS AND TOTAL TRUTH LETTER

The Total Truth Process and the Total Truth Letter are two tools to help you release negative emotions from the past and come back to your natural state of love and joy in the present.*

---

*I want to thank John Gray and Barbara DeAngelis, who first taught me this process.

The reason I call it *total* truth is that often, when we're upset, we fail to communicate *all* our true feelings to the person we're upset with. We get stuck at the level of anger or pain and rarely move past it to emotional completion. As a result, it can be difficult to feel close to—or even at ease with—the other person after such an angry or painful confrontation.

The Total Truth Process helps you express all your true feelings, so you can recapture the caring, closeness, and cooperation that is your natural state.

The process is designed so as not to let you dump or discharge negative emotions onto another person but to allow you to move through the negative emotions and release them so that you can return to the state of love and acceptance that is your natural state of being, and from which joy and creativity can flow.

The Stages of the Total Truth Process

The Total Truth Process can be conducted verbally or in writing. Whichever method you choose, the goal is to express the anger, hurt, and fear, and then move toward understanding, forgiveness, and love.

If you do it verbally—always with the other person's permission—begin by expressing your anger, and then move through each stage all the way to the final stage of love, compassion, forgiveness, and appreciation. You can use the following prompts to keep you focused at each stage. For the process to be effective, you need to spend an equal amount of time on each of the six stages.

1. **Anger and resentment**
   I'm angry that . . .   I'm fed up with . . .
   I hate it when . . .   I resent . . .

2. **Hurt**
   It hurt me when . . .   I feel hurt that . . .
   I felt sad when . . .   I feel disappointed about . . .

3. **Fear**
   I was afraid that . . .   I get afraid of you when . . .
   I feel scared when . . .   I'm afraid that I . . .

4. **Remorse, regret, and accountability**
   I'm sorry that . . .   I'm sorry for . . .
   Please forgive me for . . .   I didn't mean to . . .

5. Wants
    All I ever want(ed) . . .   I want(ed) . . .
    I want you to . . .   I deserve . . .

6. Love, compassion, forgiveness, and appreciation
    I understand that . . .   I forgive you for . . .
    I appreciate . . .   Thank you for . . .
    I love you for . . .

If you're uncomfortable doing it verbally or if the other person cannot or will not participate, you can put your feelings in writing using the Total Truth Letter to express your true feelings.

The Total Truth Letter

Follow these steps when writing a Total Truth Letter:

1. Write a letter to the person who has upset you, with roughly equal portions of the letter expressing each of the feelings in the Total Truth Process.
2. If the other party is not someone who is likely to agree to cooperate with this process, you may choose to simply throw the letter away once you have completed it. Remember, the main purpose here is to *get you free* from the unexpressed emotions—not to necessarily change the other person.
3. If the person you are upset with is willing to participate, have him or her write a Total Truth Letter to you, too. Then exchange letters. Both of you should be present when you read the letters. Then discuss the experience. Avoid trying to defend your position. Make an effort to understand where the other person is coming from as you read their letter.

After some practice, you may find you can go through the six stages of the process quickly and less formally, but in times of great difficulty, you will still want to use the six stages as a guideline.

FORGIVE AND MOVE ON

*As long as you don't forgive, who and whatever it is
will occupy rent-free space in your mind.*

ISABELLE HOLLAND
Award-winning author of 28 books

Although it may seem unusual to mention forgiveness in a book on how to become more successful, the reality is that anger, resentment, and the desire for revenge can waste valuable energy that *could* be more effectively applied toward positive goal-directed action.

In light of the Law of Attraction, we have already discussed that you attract more of whatever feelings you are experiencing. Being negative, angry, and unforgiving about a past hurt only ensures that you'll continue to attract more of the same into your life.

FORGIVE AND BRING YOURSELF BACK TO THE PRESENT

In the world of business, in families, and in personal relationships, we, too, need to come from a place of love and forgiveness—to let go so that we can move on. You need to forgive a business partner who lied to you and hurt you financially. You need to forgive a coworker who stole credit for your work or gossiped about you behind your back. You need to forgive an ex-spouse who cheated on you, then got nasty during the divorce. You needn't condone their actions or ever trust them again. But you do need to learn whatever lessons there are, forgive the other person, and move on.

When you do forgive, it puts you back in the present—where good things can happen to you and where you can take action to create future gains for yourself, your team, your company, and your family. Staying mired in the past uses valuable energy and robs you of the power you need to forge ahead in the creation of what you want.

BUT IT'S SO HARD TO LET GO

I know how hard it can be to forgive and let go. I've been kidnapped and assaulted by a stranger, been physically abused by an alcoholic father, been the victim of reverse racism, had employees embezzle serious amounts of money from me, been sued in some blatantly frivolous lawsuits, and been taken advantage of in a number of business dealings.

But after each experience, I did the work of processing it and forgiving the other party because I knew that if I didn't, those past hurts would eat away at me and prevent me from focusing my full attention on enjoying the present and creating the future life I wanted.

With each experience, I also learned how to avoid letting it happen again. I learned how to better follow my intuition. I learned how to better protect myself, my family, and my hard-earned assets. And each time I finally released the experience, I felt lighter, freer, and stronger—with more energy to focus on the more important tasks at hand. There was no more negative self-talk. No more bitter recriminations.

Resentment is like drinking poison and then hoping it will kill your enemies.

NELSON MANDELA
Winner of the Nobel Peace Prize

Whatever hurts you are feeling, know that I've felt many of them, too.

But also know that *what can hurt you even more* is harboring the resentment, holding a grudge, and rerunning the same hatred over and over. The word *forgive* really means to *give* it up *for yourself*—not for them.

I've had people in my seminars who, when they finally *truly* forgive someone, release long-term migraine headaches within minutes, find immediate relief from chronic constipation and colitis, release their arthritis pain, improve their eyesight, and immediately experience a host of other physical benefits. One man actually lost six pounds in the next two days without changing his eating habits! I have also seen people subsequently create miracles in their careers and financial lives. Believe me, it is definitely worth the intention and the effort.

STEPS TO FORGIVING

The following steps are *all* integral to forgiving:

1. Acknowledge your anger and resentment.
2. Acknowledge the hurt and pain it created.

3. Acknowledge the fears and self-doubts that it created.
4. Acknowledge any part you may have played in letting the behavior or the event occur or letting it continue.
5. Acknowledge what you were wanting that you didn't get, and then put yourself in the other person's shoes and attempt to understand where he or she was coming from at that time, and what needs they were trying to meet—however inelegantly—by their behavior.
6. Let go and forgive the person.

If you're paying attention, you probably noticed that these steps involve the same six stages as the Total Truth Process.

MAKE A LIST

Make a list of anyone you feel has hurt you and how:

_____ hurt me by _____.

Then one by one, taking as many days as you need, go through the Total Truth Process with each person. You can do it as a written process or a verbal process where you pretend you are talking to the person who is sitting in an empty chair across from you. Make sure you take ample time to think about what must have been going on in each person's life at the time to make him or her do whatever they did to you.

Remember that all people (including you) are always doing the best they can to meet their basic needs with the awareness, knowledge, skills, and tools they have at the time. If they could have done better, they would have done better. As they develop more awareness of how their behavior affects others, and as they learn more effective and less harmful ways to meet their needs, they will behave in less harmful ways.

Think about it. No parent ever wakes up in the morning and says to his or her mate, "I've just figured out three more ways we can screw up the kids." Parents are always doing the best they can to be good parents. But the combination of their own psychological wounds, their lack of knowledge and parenting skills, and the pressures of their lives often converge to create behaviors that hurt us. It was not personal to you. They would have done the same thing to anyone who was in your shoes at that moment. The same is true for everyone else in your life . . . all the time.

IF THEY CAN DO IT, YOU CAN DO IT

In my search over the years for inspirational stories for the *Chicken Soup for the Soul*® books, I have found many stories of forgiveness that let me know that human beings can forgive anything—no matter how tragic or brutal.

In 1972, the Pulitzer Prize was awarded for a photograph of a young Vietnamese girl, her arms outstretched in terror and pain, running naked—her clothes having been seared from her body—and screaming from her village, which had just been bombed with napalm in the Vietnam War. That photo was reprinted thousands of times around the world and can still be found in high school history books. That day, Phan Thi Kim Phuc suffered third-degree burns over more than half of her body. After 17 operations and 14 months of painful rehabilitation, Kim miraculously survived. Having overcome her painful past through a process of forgiveness, she is now a Canadian citizen, a goodwill ambassador for the United Nations Educational and Scientific and Cultural Organization (UNESCO), and the founder of the KIM Foundation International, which helps innocent victims of war. Everyone who has ever met Kim comments on the amazing quality of peace that radiates from her.*

In 1978, Simon Weston joined the Welsh Guards in Great Britain. As part of the Falklands Task Force, he was aboard the *Sir Galahad* when it was bombed by Argentine planes. His face was badly disfigured, and he suffered burns over 49% of his body. He has undergone 70 operations since that fateful day and will still have to endure more. It would be easy for him to spend the rest of his life being bitter. Instead he says, "If you spend your life full of recriminations and bitterness, then you've failed yourself, failed the surgeons and nurses and everyone else, because you aren't giving anything back. Hatred can consume you, and it's wasted emotion."

Instead of drowning in a sea of bitterness, Simon has become an author, a motivational speaker, and the cofounder and vice president of Weston Spirit, a nonprofit organization that has worked with tens of thousands of young people whose lifestyles reflect a poverty of aspiration in the United Kingdom.

Like Simon and Kim, you can transcend and triumph, too.

---

*For more information on the work of the KIM Foundation International, visit kimfoundation.com.

TAPPING AWAY PAST HURTS

Of course, many of these past hurts get stored in the mind and even in the body—affecting all our future actions and decisions. For many people in my trainings, getting past their "past" is difficult, painful, and—until the last 20 years or so—very difficult, particularly if they have experienced violence, trauma, or abuse early in life.

But over the last 20 years, I've been using a little known but highly effective, drug-free, and noninvasive way to reduce or eliminate this post-traumatic stress with individuals I work with. It also helps reduce chronic pain, anxiety, phobias, and fears, limiting beliefs, plus many stress-related medical conditions. The technique is so powerful that it has been used with genocide victims in Rwanda and Bosnia, for disaster victims in Haiti—and is even used by a trainer of the British Special Forces in the Congo and with U.S. soldiers returning with post-traumatic stress disorder from the battlefield.

Called *Tapping Therapy,* it stimulates the body's own ability to release stored pain of any kind.* And the results are nothing short of miraculous.

For thousands of years, Eastern cultures have focused their methods for healing medical conditions on stimulating energy "meridians" or pathways throughout the body. These energy pathways send electrical impulses throughout the body to keep all systems working, but—in addition to moving and storing energy—it was discovered they also store emotions. Some healthcare professionals even believe that an illness or chronic pain in a specific area of the body is the result of a specific emotional pain stored in that meridian.

Thirty-four years ago, clinical psychologist Dr. Roger Callahan—the originator of Tapping Therapy—discovered that you could stimulate the instant release of these stored emotions by tapping along these meridians in acupressure-like fashion while focusing your mind on the past hurt or current stress (phobia, fear, or anxiety). He called his method Thought Field Therapy or TFT, and today Dr. Callahan's institute trains practicing therapists, healthcare professionals, and everyday people in how to use TFT both in clinical settings and at home.

Others, most notably Gary Craig and Nick Ortner, have brought TFT

---

*Dr. Roger Callahan, a psychologist and pioneer who developed advanced tapping sequences for various illnesses, founded an institute that trains Thought Field Therapy or the Callahan Techniques® for professional therapists, healthcare practitioners, early responders, and everyday people around the world. The Callahan organization distributes free guides at tappingtherapy.com and makes available private sessions plus audio instructions to eliminate phobias, anxiety, fear of flying, public speaking fear, and more.

to the masses as the Emotional Freedom Technique (EFT)* and Meridian Tapping Therapy.

My book *Tapping Into Ultimate Success*,[†] describes how to use tapping to free yourself from these stored anxieties, stresses, and emotional hurts, and focuses on helping you to better implement the principles in *this* book, *The Success Principles,* by tapping away any limiting beliefs, fears, and internal obstacles that arise when you are attempting to apply any of the principles.

The first part of the tapping protocol is to close your eyes, focus on the fear, anxiety, emotion, pain, or belief that you wish to release, and then determine on a scale of 1 to 10 (10 being high) how intense the feeling or belief is.

In the diagram, you'll see the nine tapping points depicted. The basic tapping sequence—to eliminate fears and negative beliefs and to neutralize negative events—then starts by tapping the "karate chop" spot on the heel of your hand 10 times, firmly enough to feel it, but not hard enough to bruise your hand. As you tap your hand, repeat aloud the belief, physical pain, or experience of hurt you are dealing with as you—most important—tune in to the *emotion* that belief or hurt brings forth. Follow your statement of the belief or hurt with the affirmation *I deeply and completely love and accept myself.* For example:

Even though I'm afraid to ask for a raise, I deeply and completely love and accept myself.

Or,

Even though I believe I don't deserve to be successful, I deeply and completely love and accept myself.

Once you've tapped the "karate chop" spot ten times, begin the EFT tapping sequence below while continuing to focus on the past hurt, limiting belief, emotion, stress, pain, or source of anxiety. Tap five to seven times firmly at each point. Accompany each tapping point with a statement that keeps you focused on the emotion. Like this:

---

*The Emotional Freedom Technique was created by Gary Craig in an attempt to simplify tapping sequences for use by nontherapists. You can get a quick overview of the technique at emofree.com and in the book *The Tapping Solution* by Nick Ortner (Carlsbad, CA: Hay House, 2013). Also check out Dawson Church's books and his website at eftuniverse.com.

†*Tapping Into Ultimate Success: How to Overcome Any Obstacle and Skyrocket Your Success* by Jack Canfield and Pamela Bruner (Carlsbad, CA: Hay House, 2012).

1. **Top of the Head:** *I'm afraid to ask for a raise.*
2. **Eyebrow:** *I'm afraid to ask for a raise.*
3. **Outside of Eye:** *I'm afraid he'll say no, and I'll be embarrassed.*
4. **Under the Eye:** *I'll be embarrassed.*
5. **Under the Nose:** *I'll be so embarrassed if he says no.*
6. **Chin:** *I'll be mortified if he says no.*
7. **Collarbone:** *I'm afraid to ask for a raise.*
8. **Under the Arm:** *I'll be so embarrassed.*

The exact words you say aren't important; what's important is that you are continually tuned in to your emotion. Additionally, you can tap the eyebrow, under the eye, collarbone, and under the arm spots on *either side of your body*. Repeat the sequence repeating your phrase again and again until you feel the intensity has dropped down to a 1 or is totally gone.

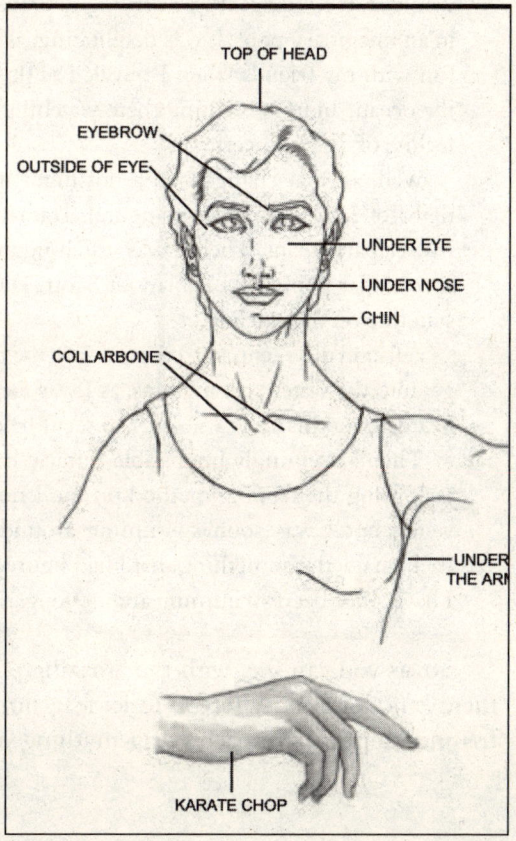

Tapping Therapy also works miraculously for serious phobias of all kinds. Actress and talk show host Kelly Ripa had a severe fear of flying—resulting from the trauma of watching airplanes hit the World Trade Center on September 11, 2001. When her producers wanted to tape the "Live with Regis and Kelly" show from Disneyland in California, she knew she needed to overcome her fear of flying in order to make the trip. Working with Dr. Callahan, who treated her with Tapping Therapy over the phone in New York, she was able to comfortably get on a plane and make the five-hour flight. Kelly was so delighted that she invited Dr. Callahan on the TV show to treat amusement-park guests for their fear of roller coasters. Seventeen people rode a whopper of a roller coaster just moments later—with most saying they wanted to ride again!

I have used tapping to help people in my seminars overcome the fear of flying, fear of public speaking, fear of singing in front of others, fear of heights, claustrophobia, and the fear of drowning. Here is what Sharon Worsley, one of my Train-the-Trainer students, posted on the Internet:

> Having been a swimmer when I was younger, I had two bad experiences where I nearly drowned at age 12 and 15. For the rest of my life I was not able to go back into the water. In fact, if I were to speak to you about swimming, I would start to get a physical reaction where my head would start to rise as if I was trying to prevent myself from going under in an imaginary pool. It was debilitating, as I was missing out on having fun with my friends when I traveled as they were enjoying the pool or the ocean, and I was sitting there watching them. Plus I didn't like this feeling of disempowerment.
>
> Well, all that changed on a hot night in June 2010. It was the last night of Jack Canfield's inaugural Train-the-Trainer program, where I was a participant. There I was watching my fellow attendees enjoy the spectacular pool at the Fairmont Scottsdale Princess while I had been standing on the sideline.
>
> A friend did eventually coax me into the pool somehow, but I couldn't get into the water past my hips, as I was feeling extremely anxious. Jack heard about this and came over to see if he could help me.
>
> Then a seemingly impossible miracle happened. Within minutes of Jack using the tapping method on me I not only went deeper into the water, but I was soon swimming around, including floating on my back unaided—something that I had figured would never happen again. I have since been swimming and no longer have any hesitation or fear.

So, as you can see, with the amazing power of this simple technique, there is no longer any reason to let fear, limiting beliefs, or past hurts and traumas stop you from achieving anything you want.

PRINCIPLE 30

FACE WHAT ISN'T WORKING

Facts do not cease to exist because they are ignored.
ALDOUS HUXLEY
Visionary writer

Our lives improve only when we take chances—and the first and most difficult risk we can take is to be honest with ourselves.
WALTER ANDERSON
Editor of *Parade* magazine for 20 years

If you are going to become more successful, you have to get out of denial and face what isn't working in your life. Do you defend or ignore how toxic your work environment is? Do you make excuses for your bad marriage? Are you in denial about your lack of energy, your excess weight, your ill health, or your level of physical fitness? Are you failing to acknowledge that sales have been on a consistent downward trend for the last three months? Are you putting off confronting an employee who is not delivering at an acceptable standard of performance? Successful people face these circumstances squarely, heed the warning signs, and take appropriate action, no matter how uncomfortable or challenging it might be.

REMEMBER THE YELLOW ALERTS

Remember E + R = O and the "yellow alerts" in Principle 1? Yellow alerts are all those little signals you get that something's not right. Your teen comes home late from school again. Strange notices show up in the company mail. A friend or neighbor makes an odd comment. Sometimes we choose to acknowledge these alerts and take action, but more often than not, we simply choose to ignore them. We pretend not to notice that something's amiss.

Why? Because to face what's not working in your life usually means you're going to have to do something uncomfortable. You might have to exercise more self-discipline, confront somebody, risk not being liked, ask for what you want, demand respect instead of settling for an abusive relationship, or maybe even quit your job. But because you don't want to do these uncomfortable things, you'll often defend tolerating a situation that doesn't work.

WHAT DOES DENIAL LOOK LIKE?

Though the bad situations in our lives can be uncomfortable, embarrassing, and painful, we often live with them or—worse—we hide them behind myths, widely accepted views, and platitudes. We don't even realize we are in denial. We use phrases such as these:

> It's just what guys do.
> You can't control teenagers these days.
> He's just venting his frustrations.
> It's got nothing to do with me.
> It's none of my business.
> It's not my place to say.
> I don't want to rock the boat.
> There's nothing I can do about it.
> Don't wash your dirty linen in public.
> Credit card debt like this is normal.
> I'll get fired if I say anything.
> Mom's church friends check on her.
> Luckily it's only marijuana.
> She's just at that age.
> I need these to help me relax.
> I have to work these long hours to get ahead.
> We just have to wait it out.
> I'm sure he is going to pay it back.

Occasionally, we'll even make up *reasons* why something that is not working *is working*, not realizing that if we would just acknowledge the bad situation sooner, it would often be less painful to resolve. It would be cheaper, the circumstances might be more beneficial, the problems would be easier to solve, we could be more honest with everyone concerned, we would feel better about ourselves, and we would certainly have more integrity. But we have to get past our denial.

Successful people, on the other hand, are more committed to finding out why things are going wrong and fixing them than they are to defending their own position or maintaining their ignorance.

In business, they look at the hard truth in real numbers rather than recalculating the numbers to look good to the stockholders. They want to know why someone didn't use their product or service, why the ad campaign didn't work, or why expenditures are unusually high. They are rational and in touch with reality. They are willing to look at what *is* and deal with it rather than hide it and deny it.

Doing more of what doesn't work won't make it work any better.
CHARLES J. GIVENS
Real estate investment strategist and author of *Wealth Without Risk*

KNOW WHEN TO HOLD THEM, KNOW WHEN TO FOLD THEM

A big part of getting out of denial is to get good at recognizing bad situations and then deciding to do something about them. It always amazes me how difficult recognition and decision is for most people—even when it comes to alcoholism and drug addiction. With many addicts, their marriages fail, their businesses fail, they lose their house, and even end up on skid row before they realize their addiction is not working for them.

Fortunately, most of our problems are less severe than drug addiction, but that doesn't make the recognition or decision any easier. Take your job, for instance. Are you in denial about what you would really like to be doing? Worse yet, do you constantly talk about how happy and fulfilled you are when you're not? Are you living a lie?

Workaholics are a perfect example of this kind of denial. A high-pressure schedule can't possibly work long term for anyone, but most workaholics will defend it with comments such as, "I'm making great money," "This is how I support my family," "It's how I get ahead," and "I have to do it to compete at the office." As we've explored already, defending and justifying a bad situation is really just a form of denial.

DENIAL IS BASED ON FEAR

Often denial is based on the notion that something even worse will happen if we stop our denial and take corrective action. In other words, we're *afraid* to face the truth.

Many a therapist can tell you that, in spite of overwhelming clues that their spouse is having an affair, many patients won't confront their spouse over it. They simply don't want to face the fact that the marriage might be over. They don't want to deal with the emotional stress and the physical inconvenience of a divorce. They don't want to deal with the financial upheaval or the possibility that they might have to move or get a job.

What are some of the situations *you* are afraid to deal with?

- Your teenager who is smoking or doing drugs?
- A supervisor who leaves early but dumps his late projects on you?
- A business partner who doesn't do his fair share of the work or spends too much money?
- Your house payment or expenses that are unmanageable?
- Your aging parents who now need full-time care?
- Your health, which is becoming a problem because of a poor diet or lack of exercise?
- A spouse who is never home, withdrawn, disrespectful, abusive, or super-critical?
- Not enough free time for yourself or your children?

Though many of the situations above may require drastic changes in how you live, work, and relate to others, remember that the solution to these problems isn't always to quit your job, get a divorce, fire the employee, or ground your teenager. It may be more productive to choose less extreme alternatives such as a discussion with your boss, marriage counseling, setting boundaries with your teens and siblings, scaling back your expenditures, or seeking competent professional help. Of course, these less drastic solutions still require you to face your fears and take action.

But you have to face what isn't working *first*.

The good news is that the more you face uncomfortable situations, the better you get at it. When you face just one thing that isn't working, the next time you have the slightest inkling, you are more likely to take action immediately. And the sooner you take action, the easier it is to clean up. Remember the old saying "A stitch in time saves nine"? It's true.

TAKE ACTION NOW

Take the time right now to make a list of what isn't working in your life. Start with the seven major areas where you would normally set goals—financial, career or business, free time or family time, health and appearance, relationships, personal growth, and making a difference. Ask your family, friends, employees, coworkers, class, group, coach, or team what they believe is not working.

Ask: *What's not working? How can we improve it? What requests can I make? What do you need from me? What do I/we need to do? What action steps can I/we take to get each of these situations to work the way I/we would like?*

Do you need to talk to someone? Call a repair person? Ask someone for help? Learn a new skill? Find a new resource? Read a book? Call an expert? Make a plan to fix it?

Choose one action you can take and then do it. Then keep taking another action and another action until you get the situation resolved.

PRINCIPLE 31

EMBRACE CHANGE

Change is the law of life. And those who look only to the past or present are certain to miss the future.

JOHN F. KENNEDY
The 35th president of the United States

Change is inevitable. At this very moment, for instance, your body and cells are changing. The Earth is changing. The economy, technology, how we do business, even how we communicate is changing. And though you can resist that change and potentially be swept away by it, you can also choose to cooperate with it, adapt to it, and benefit from it.

GROW OR DIE

In 1910, Florists' Telegraph Delivery—known today as FTD—was founded by 15 American florists who began using the telegraph to exchange orders and deliver flowers to customers' loved ones thousands of miles away. Gone were the days when a daughter or sister would go to the local florist and order a small bouquet. Family members were relocating to cities and towns far from home. And FTD flourished by identifying this trend and combining it with the telegraph, which represented a change in the way we communicate.

Around the same time, the American railroad industry began to see the automobile and the airplane as new technologies designed to transport people and goods from place to place. But unlike other industries who readily embraced these new machines, the railroad industry resisted, believing instead that they were in the railroad business—not the business of transporting goods and people. They didn't realize what they were up against. They didn't grow. Though businesses focusing on the railroads might have become automobile and aircraft businesses, they didn't. As a result, they almost died out.

WHERE DO YOU NEED TO GROW?

When change happens, you can either cooperate with it and learn how to benefit from it or you can resist it and eventually get run over by it. It's your choice.

When you embrace change wholeheartedly as an inevitable part of life, looking for ways to use new changes to make your life richer, easier, and more fulfilling, your life will work much better. You will experience change as an opportunity for growth and new experiences.

Several years ago, I was hired to consult with the Naval Sea Systems Command in Washington, D.C. They had just announced they were moving the entire command to San Diego, California, which meant that a lot of civil service jobs were going to be lost in that transition. My job was to conduct a seminar for all the nonmilitary personnel who would not be moving to California. And though the Naval Sea Systems Command had offered everyone jobs and transfers to San Diego (including reimbursement of all moving expenses) or assistance in locating a new job in the Washington, D.C., area, many of the employees had become almost frozen with fear and resentment.

Though nearly all of them looked at this change as a major disaster in their lives, I encouraged them to look at it as an opportunity—as something new. I taught them about E + R = O and how although the move to San Diego (E) was inevitable, their outcome (O)—whether or not they flourished afterward—was entirely dependent on their response (R) to the situation. "Perhaps you'll find a more empowering job in D.C.," I said, "or even get a job with better pay. Or maybe you would like to move to California where it's warm most of the year and new friends and adventures are awaiting you."

Slowly they began to move from panic and fear to realizing that things could indeed work out, maybe even for the better, if only they embraced this change as an opportunity to create something new and better for themselves.

HOW TO EMBRACE CHANGE

Realize that there are two kinds of change—*cyclical change* and *structural change*—neither of which you can control.

Cyclical change, such as the change we see in the stock market, happens several times a year. Prices go up and they go down. There are bull markets and corrections. We see seasonal changes in the weather, increased spending during the holidays, more travel in the summer, and so on. These are changes that happen in cycles, and we just accept them as a normal part of life.

But there are also structural changes—such as when the computer was invented and the Internet was created and both of these technologies completely changed how we live, work, get our news, and make purchases. Structural changes like these are the kinds of changes where there is no going back to doing things the way they were before. And these are the kinds of changes that can sweep you away if you resist them.

Like the Naval Sea Systems Command employees, FTD florists, or the railroad industry, will *you* embrace these structural changes and work to improve your life—or will you resist them?

Remember back to a time when you experienced a change but resisted. Perhaps it was a move, a job transfer, a change in suppliers, a change in technology in your company, a change in management, or even your teenager going off to college—a change you were going to have to deal with and you thought it was the worst thing in the world.

What happened once you surrendered to the change? Did your life actually improve? Can you look back now and say, "Wow, I'm glad that happened. Look at the good it eventually brought me."

If you can always remember that you've been through changes in the past—and that they've largely worked out for the best—you can begin to approach each new change with the excitement and anticipation you should. To help embrace any change, ask yourself the following questions:

What's changing in my life that I'm currently resisting?
Why am I resisting that change?
What am I afraid of with respect to this change?
What am I afraid might happen to me?
What's the payoff for my keeping things the way they are?
What's the cost I'm paying for keeping things the way they are?
What benefits might there be in this change?
What would I have to do to cooperate with this change?
What's the next step I could take to cooperate with this change?
When will I take this next step?

PRINCIPLE 32

TRANSFORM YOUR INNER CRITIC INTO AN INNER COACH

A man is literally what he thinks.
JAMES ALLEN
Author of *As a Man Thinketh*

Research indicates that, on average, people talk to themselves about 50,000 times a day. This includes you. Unfortunately, most of that self-talk is about yourself, and according to the psychological researchers, it is 80% negative—things such as *I shouldn't have said that. . . . They don't like me. . . . I'm never going to be able to pull this off. . . . I don't like the way my hair looks today. . . . That other team is going to kill us. . . . I can't dance. . . . I'm not a speaker. . . . I'll never lose this weight. . . . I can't ever seem to get organized. . . . I'm always late.*

Argue for your limitations, and sure enough, they're yours.
RICHARD BACH
Bestselling author of *Jonathan Livingston Seagull*

We also know from this research that these thoughts have a powerful effect on us. They affect our attitude, our motivation to act, our physiology, even our biochemistry. Our negative thoughts actually control our behavior. They make us stutter, spill things, forget our lines, break out in a sweat, breathe shallowly, feel anxious or scared—and taken to the extreme, they can even paralyze or kill us.

WORRIED HIMSELF TO DEATH

Many years ago, *Readers Digest* featured the true story of Nick Sitzman—a strong, healthy, and ambitious young railroad yardman. He had a reputation as a diligent worker and had a loving wife, two children, and many friends.

One midsummer day, the train crews were informed that they could quit an hour early in honor of the foreman's birthday. While performing one last check on some of the railroad cars, Nick was accidentally locked in a refrigerator boxcar. When he realized that the rest of the workmen had left the site, Nick began to panic.

He banged and shouted until his fists were bloody and his voice was hoarse, but no one heard him. With his knowledge of "the numbers and the facts," he predicted the temperature to be zero degrees. Nick's thought was, *If I can't get out, I'll freeze to death in here.* Wanting to let his wife and family know exactly what had happened to him, Nick found a knife and began to etch words on the wooden floor. He wrote, "It's so cold, my body is getting numb. If I could just go to sleep. These may be my last words."

The next morning, the crew slid open the heavy doors of the boxcar and found Nick dead. An autopsy revealed that every physical sign of his body indicated he had frozen to death. And yet the refrigeration unit of the car was inoperative, and the temperature inside indicated 55 degrees Fahrenheit. Nick had killed himself by the *power of his own thoughts.**

You, too, if you're not careful, can kill yourself with your limiting thoughts—not all at once like Nick Sitzman, but little by little, day after day, until you have slowly deadened your natural ability to achieve your dreams.

YOUR NEGATIVE THOUGHTS AFFECT YOUR BODY

We also know from polygraph (lie-detector) tests that your body reacts to your thoughts—changing your temperature, heart rate, blood pressure, breathing rate, muscle tension, and how much your hands sweat. When you are hooked up to a lie detector and are asked a question such as "Did you take the money?" your hands will get colder, your heart will beat faster, your blood pressure will go up, your breathing will get faster, your muscles will get tighter, and your hands will sweat if you did take the money and

---

*From *The Speaker's Sourcebook* by Glen Van Ekeren (Englewood Cliffs, NJ: Prentice-Hall, 1988).

you lie about it. These kinds of physiological changes occur not only when you are lying but also in reaction to every thought you think. Every cell in your body is affected by every thought you have.

Negative thoughts affect your body negatively—weakening you, making you sweat, and making you uptight. Positive thoughts affect your body in a positive way, making you more relaxed, centered, and alert. Positive thoughts cause the secretion of endorphins in the brain and reduce pain and increase pleasure.

STOMP THOSE ANTS

Psychiatrist Daniel G. Amen has named the limiting thoughts we hear in our head ANTs—Automatic Negative Thoughts. And just like real ants at a picnic, your ANTs can ruin your experience of life. Dr. Amen recommends that you learn to stomp the ANTs.* First you have to become aware of them; next you have to shake them off and stomp them by challenging them. Finally, you have to replace them with more positive and affirming thoughts.

Don't believe everything you hear—even in your own mind.
DANIEL G. AMEN, M.D.
Clinical neuroscientist, psychiatrist, and specialist in attention-deficit disorders

---

The key to dealing with any kind of negative thinking is to realize that you are ultimately in charge of whether to listen to or agree with any thought. Just because you think it—or hear it—doesn't mean it's true.

You want to constantly ask yourself, *Is this thought helping me or hurting me? Is it getting me closer to where I want to go, or taking me further away? Is it motivating me to action, or is it blocking me with fear and self-doubt?* You have to learn to challenge and talk back to the thoughts that are not serving you in creating greater success and happiness.

My friend Doug Bench, the author of *Revolutionize Your Brain*, recommends writing down every negative thought you think or say out loud and

---

*See *Change Your Brain, Change Your Life* by Daniel G. Amen, M.D. (New York: Three Rivers Press, 1998), for an illuminating look into how to use brain-compatible strategies to overcome anxiety, depression, obsessiveness, anger, and impulsiveness—all of which can severely block creating the life you want. The next few pages on stomping the ANTs draw heavily on Dr. Amen's insights.

every negative thought you hear anyone else say—for three whole days! (Make sure that two of the days are workdays and that one is a weekend day.)

Ask your spouse or partner, children, roommates, and fellow employees to catch you and impose a dollar fine every time they hear you uttering a negative thought. In a recent workshop I conducted, participants had to put $2 in a bowl every time they said anything that was blaming, justifying, or self-negating. It was amazing to see how fast the bowl filled up. However, as the four days went on, there were fewer and fewer automatic negative comments as everyone became more aware.

DIFFERENT TYPES OF NEGATIVE THOUGHTS

It is helpful to understand some of the different kinds of negative thoughts that might attack you. When you recognize these kinds of thoughts, realize they are irrational thoughts that need to be challenged and replaced. Here are some of the most common kinds of negative thoughts and how to eliminate them.

Always-or-Never Thinking

In reality, very few things are always or never. If you think something is always going to happen or you will never get what you want, you are doomed from the outset. When you use all-or-nothing words such as *always, never, everyone, no one, every time,* and *everything,* you are usually wrong. Here are some examples of always-or-never thinking:

> *I'll never get a raise.*
> *Everyone takes advantage of me.*
> *My employees never listen to me.*
> *I never get any time for myself.*
> *They're always making fun of me.*
>
> *I never get a break.*
> *No one ever cuts me any slack.*
> *Every time I take a risk, I get slammed.*
> *Nobody cares if I live or die.*

When you find yourself thinking always-or-never thoughts, replace them with what is really true. For example, you can replace *You always take advantage of me* with *I get angry when you take advantage of me, but I know that you have treated me fairly in the past and that you will again.*

Focusing on the Negative

Some people focus only on the bad and never on the good in a situation. When I was conducting trainings for high school teachers, I noticed that most of the teachers I met had a pattern of focusing on the negative. If they taught a lesson and 30 kids got it but 4 didn't, they would focus on the 4 who didn't get it and would feel bad, rather than focus on the 26 who did get it and feel good.

Learn to look for the positive. Not only will it help you feel better, but it will also be a critical component of your creating the success you want. Recently a friend of mine told me he had seen an interview with a multimillionaire on television who described the turning point in his career as the morning he asked all of his staff to talk about one good thing that had occurred during the past week. At first, all that came up were more complaints, problems, and difficulties. Finally, one employee commented that the UPS driver who delivered packages to the office had applied to college and was going back to school to get his degree, and how inspired he was by the man's commitment to further his education and pursue his dream in life. Slowly, one employee and then another came up with something else that was positive to share. Soon, this became a part of every meeting. Eventually, they had to end the meetings before every positive thing could be recounted. The entire attitude of the company changed from focusing on the negative to focusing on the good, and the business just took off and grew exponentially from that moment on.

You, too, can learn to play the Appreciation Game by looking for things to appreciate in every situation. A powerful exercise for building your appreciation muscle is to take a few minutes every morning to write down all the things you appreciate in your life. I recommend this as a daily ritual for the rest of your life. When you actively seek the positive, you become more appreciative and optimistic, which is a requirement for attracting more good and creating the life of your dreams. Look for the good.

As an example, my wife was recently in an automobile accident. She drove through an intersection where the traffic light was inoperative because of a power outage, and hit another car turning across her lane. She could have succumbed to a multitude of *automatic negative thoughts—What's wrong with me? I should have been paying better attention. I shouldn't have been out driving when the power was out.* Instead, she focused on the positive—*I'm so lucky to be alive and relatively unhurt. The other driver is alive and well. Thank God I was in such a safe car. I am so glad the police came as fast as they did. It's amazing how many people were there to help. This was a real wake-up call.*

Catastrophic Predicting

In catastrophic predicting, you create the worst possible scenario in your mind and then act as if it were a certainty. This could include predicting that your sales prospect won't be interested in your product, the person you are attracted to will reject your request to go out on a date, your boss won't give you a raise, or the plane you're flying on will crash. Replace "She'll probably laugh at me if I ask her out for a date" with "I don't know what she'll do. She might say yes."

Mind-Reading

You are mind-reading when you believe you know what another person is thinking even though he or she hasn't told you. You know you're mind-reading when you're thinking thoughts such as *He's mad at me. . . . She doesn't like me. . . . He's going to say no. . . . He's going to fire me.* Replace mind-reading with the truth: *I don't know what he is thinking unless I ask him. Maybe he's just having a bad day.*

Remember, unless you're a psychic, you can't read anyone else's mind. You don't ever know what they're really thinking unless they tell you or unless you ask them. Check out your assumptions by asking, "I'm imagining you might be mad at me. Are you?"

Remember the phrase "When in doubt, check it out!" to remind yourself to ask rather than assume you know.

Guilt-Tripping

Guilt happens when you think words such as *should, must, ought to,* or *have to.* Here are some examples: *I ought to spend more time studying for my bar exam. . . . I should spend more time at home with my kids. . . . I have to exercise more.* As soon as you feel like you *should* do something, you create an internal resistance to doing it.

I will not should on myself today.

SEEN ON A POSTER

You will be more effective if you replace guilt-tripping with phrases such as *I want to . . . It supports my goals to . . . It would be smart to . . . It's in my best interest to . . .* Guilt is never productive. It will stand in the way of achieving your goals. So get rid of this emotional barrier to success.

Labeling

Labeling is attaching a negative label to yourself or someone else. It is a form of shorthand that stops you from clearly making the finer distinctions that would help you be more effective. Some examples of negative labels are *jerk, idiot, arrogant,* and *irresponsible.* When you use a label like this, you are lumping yourself or someone else into a category of all the jerks or idiots you have ever known, and that makes it more difficult to deal with that person or situation as the unique person or experience they are. Challenge the thought *I am stupid* with *What I just did was less than brilliant, but I am still a smart person.*

All meaning is self-created.

VIRGINIA SATIR
Noted psychotherapist known for her contributions in
the fields of family therapy and self-esteem

Personalizing

You personalize when you invest a neutral event with personal meaning. *Kevin hasn't called me back yet. He must be mad at me.* Or *We lost the Vanderbilt account. It must be my fault. I should have spent more time on the proposal.* The truth is that there are many other possible explanations for other people's actions besides the negative reasons your automatic negative thoughts come up with. For example, Kevin may not have called you back because he is sick, out of town, or overwhelmed with his own priorities. You never really know why other people do what they do.

TALK TO YOURSELF LIKE A WINNER

*You are today where your thoughts have brought you;
you will be tomorrow where your thoughts take you.*

JAMES ALLEN
Author of *As a Man Thinketh*

What if you could learn to always talk to yourself like a winner instead of a loser? What if you could transform your negative self-talk into positive self-talk? What if you could silence your thoughts of lack and limitation and replace them with thoughts of unlimited possibility? What if you could replace any victim language in your thoughts with the language of empowerment? And what if you could transform your inner critic, who judges your every move, into a supportive inner coach who would encourage you and give you confidence as you faced new situations and risks? Well . . . all of that is possible with a little awareness, focus, and intention.

TRANSFORMING YOUR INNER CRITIC INTO YOUR INNER COACH

One of the most powerful exercises for retraining your inner critic is to teach it to tell you the *total* truth. (See Principle 29: "Complete the Past to Embrace the Future.") Just like your parents disciplined you for your own good, your inner critic really has your best interests in mind when it is criticizing you. It wants you to get the benefit of the better behavior. The problem is that it tells you only part of the truth.

When you were a little kid, your parents may have yelled at you and sent you to your room after you did something stupid like run out in front of a car. Their real communication was "I love you. I don't want you to get hit by a car. I want you to stay around so that you can grow up into a happy and healthy adult." But they delivered only half of the message: "What's wrong with you? Were you born without a brain? You know better than to run out into the street when there are cars coming. You're grounded for the next hour. Go to your room and think about what you just did." In their fear of losing you, they expressed only their anger. But underneath the anger were three more layers of message that never got delivered—fear, specific requests, and love. A complete message would look like this:

Anger:	I am mad at you for running out into the street without looking to see if any cars were coming.
Fear:	I am afraid that you'll get badly hurt or killed.
Requests:	I want you to pay more attention when you are playing near the street. Stop and look both ways before you walk or run out into the street.
Love:	I love you so much. I don't know what I would do without you. You are so precious to me. I want you to be safe and healthy. You deserve to have lots of fun and stay safe so you can continue to enjoy life to its fullest. Do you understand?

What a different message! You need to train your inner critic to talk to you the same way. You can practice this on paper or as a verbal exercise in which you talk to yourself out loud. I usually imagine talking to a clone of myself sitting in an empty chair opposite me.

Make a list of all the things you say when you are judging yourself. Include all of the things you tell yourself you *should* do, but you don't. A typical list might look like this:

You don't exercise enough.
You're gaining too much weight.
You're a fat slob—a real couch potato!
You drink too much alcohol and eat too many sweets.
You need to cut down on the carbs!
You need to watch less television and go to bed earlier.
If you got up earlier, you'd have more time to exercise.
You're lazy. Why don't you finish the things you start?!

Once you have completed your list, practice communicating the same information using the four-step process outlined above: (1) anger, (2) fear, (3) requests, and (4) love. Spend a minimum of one minute on each step. Make sure to be very specific in the requests stage. State exactly what you want yourself to do. "I want you to eat better" is too vague. Be more specific, such as "I want you to eat at least four servings of vegetables every day. I want you to stop eating French fries, sugar, and desserts. I want you to eat eggs and some kind of fruit for breakfast every day. I want you to eat whole grains like whole wheat and brown rice rather than white flour." The more specific you are, the more value you will receive from the exercise. If you do it out loud, which I recommend, *do it with as much emotion and passion as possible.*

Here's an example of what it might sound like using the list of judgments above:

Anger:	I am angry at you for not taking better care of your body. You are such a lazy slob! You drink too much and you eat too much. You don't have any self-discipline! All you do is sit around and watch TV. Your clothes don't fit, and you don't look good.
Fear:	If you don't change, I am afraid you are going to keep gaining weight until you are facing a real health risk. I am afraid your cholesterol is going to get so high that you might have a heart attack. I'm afraid that you could become diabetic. I am afraid that you are never going to change and then you are going to die young and never fulfill your dreams. I'm afraid that if you don't start eating better and taking better care of yourself, no one is going to be attracted to you. You might end up living alone for the rest of your life.
Requests:	I want you to join a health club and go at least three days a week. I want you to go for a twenty-minute walk

	the other four days. I want you to cut out one hour of television a day and devote that to exercise. I want you to stop eating fried foods and start eating more fresh fruits and vegetables. I want you to stop drinking sodas and start drinking more water. I want you to limit drinking alcohol to Friday and Saturday nights.
Love:	I love you. I want you to be around for a long time. I want you to have a wonderful relationship. You deserve to look good in your clothes and to feel good about yourself. You deserve to have all of your dreams come true. I want you to feel alive and energetic rather than tired and lethargic all the time. You deserve to live life fully and enjoy every moment of it. You deserve to be totally happy.

Whenever you hear a part of you judging yourself, simply reply, "Thank you for caring. What is your fear? . . . What specifically do you want me to do? . . . How will this serve me? . . . Thank you."

The first time I experienced this inner-critic to inner-coach process, it changed my life. After quitting my job at another training company, I had been working as a consultant and a professional speaker, but what I really wanted to do was start my own training company, train other trainers, open offices in other cities, and make a huge difference in the world. But it seemed like such an overwhelming commitment, and I was afraid of failure. What's worse, I had been regularly beating myself up for not having the courage to take the leap.

After completing the Turning Your Inner Critic into Your Inner Coach exercise, something shifted. I went beyond beating myself up to realizing how much I was missing out on by not taking the leap. I told myself clearly what I needed to do, and the following day, I outlined a business plan for the new company, asked my mother-in-law for a $10,000 loan, asked a friend to be my business partner, scheduled a meeting to draw up the incorporation papers, and began designing the letterhead. Less than three months later, I conducted my first weekend training in St. Louis for over 200 people. Less than a year later, I had offices in Los Angeles, St. Louis, Philadelphia, San Diego, and San Francisco. Since then, over 50,000 people have participated in my weekend and weeklong training programs.

By turning my inner critic into an inner coach, I was able to stop feeling like a failure and start engaging in the activities that made my dream a reality. I was able to move from someone who was using my energy against myself to someone who was using my energy to create what I wanted.

Do not let the seeming simplicity of this technique fool you. It is very powerful. But like everything else in this book, to obtain its value, you must use it. No one else can do it for you. Take 20 minutes now to do the Turn Your Inner Critic into Your Inner Coach exercise. Get all of you on your own side—working together for the greater good of your dreams and aspirations.

HOW TO SILENCE YOUR PERFORMANCE CRITIC

Have you ever taught a class, given a speech, made a sales presentation, competed in an athletic event, acted in a play, given a concert, or performed any kind of job, and then found yourself on the way home listening to that voice in your head telling you how you messed up, what you should have done differently, how you could have and should have done it better? I'm sure you have. And if you listen to that voice for very long, it can undermine your self-confidence, lower your self-esteem, and even demoralize and eventually paralyze you. Here is another simple but powerful method for redirecting your inner voice from one of judgment and criticism to one of correction and support.

Remembering again that the deepest underlying motivation of your inner critic is to help you be better at what you do, tell your inner critic to stop criticizing and berating you or you will stop listening to it. Tell that inner voice you are not willing to listen to any more character assassinations, name-calling, or browbeating—only specific steps you can take to do it better *the next time*. This eliminates put-downs and focuses the conversation on "improvement opportunities" for the next occasion. Now the inner critic becomes an inner coach that is simply pointing out ways to improve future results. The past is over, and there is nothing you can do to change it. You can only learn from it and improve your performance *the next time*.

Here is an example of what this might sound like taken from my own life. *IC* indicates that the inner critic/inner coach is talking.

IC: I can't believe it. What were you thinking? You tried to put way too much information in that seminar. You were talking way too fast, and you were rushed at the end. There's no way people could have assimilated all of that information! After all these years as a seminar leader, you'd think you'd know better than that!

Me: Hold on a minute. I'm not going to listen to you criticizing me. I just worked hard all day to give people the best experience that I knew how to create at the time. Now that I've done it, I am sure there are ways to improve it next time. If you have *specific* things you want me to do *next time,* then tell me. That is all I am interested in hearing about. I'm not interested in your judgments, just your ideas for how to make it better next time.

IC: All right. Next time pick just three or four major points to focus on and really drive those points home with examples, humor, and more interpersonal exercises so that people really integrate the material. You can't teach people everything you know in one day.

Me: You're right. Anything else?

IC: Yes. Make sure to include more interactive learning games in the afternoon when the energy is lower. That will make sure everyone stays alert and awake.

Me: Okay. Anything else?

IC: Yes. I think it would work better to take a ten-minute break every hour rather than a twenty-minute break every two hours. That'll help keep the energy higher and allow more time for people to integrate what they are learning.

Me: Good idea. Anything else?

IC: Yes. Make sure to integrate some physical activities throughout the day to keep the kinesthetic learners more engaged.

Me: Anything else?

IC: Yes. Make sure you give people two copies of the Achiever's Focusing Sheet next time—one to write on in the seminar and one to use as a photocopying master after they leave the seminar. Otherwise they can't really use it. You could also put a copy on your website that they could download for duplication.

Me: Good idea. Anything else?

IC: No. I think that's it.

Me: Okay. I've written all of that down. I will definitely incorporate these things into my next seminar. Thank you.

IC: You're welcome.

As you can see from the example, there are a lot of things that your inner coach observes about how to improve your performance in future situations. The problem—up until now!—is that it has been presenting the information as a judgment. Once you switch the conversation to a nonemotional discussion of improvement opportunities, the experience changes from a negative to a positive one.

And here's a valuable tip. Because research on memory tells us that a new idea lasts for only about 40 seconds in short-term memory and then it is gone, it is important to write down these ideas from your inner coach and put them in a file that you will review before your next performance. Otherwise, you may lose the benefit of the valuable feedback.

USE EFT TAPPING TO TRANSFORM YOUR INNER CRITIC

Another powerful way to transform your inner critic into an inner coach is to use the tapping technique outlined in my book *Tapping into Ultimate Success*. This specific tapping protocol is designed to turn your critic into a supportive ally by redefining its role.*

---

*See pages 121–26 of *Tapping into Ultimate Success: How to Overcome Any Obstacle and Skyrocket Your Results* by Jack Canfield and Pamela Bruner (Carlsbad, CA: Hay House, 2012).

PRINCIPLE

33

TRANSCEND YOUR LIMITING BELIEFS

Your subconscious mind does not argue with you. It accepts what your conscious mind decrees. If you say, "I can't afford it," your subconscious mind works to make it true. Select a better thought. Decree, "I'll buy it. I accept it in my mind."

DR. JOSEPH MURPHY
Author of *The Power of Your Subconscious Mind*

Many of us have beliefs that limit our success—whether they are beliefs about our own capabilities, beliefs about what it takes to succeed, beliefs about how we should relate with other people, or even common everyday myths that modern-day science or research studies have long since refuted. Moving beyond your limiting beliefs is a critical first step toward becoming more successful. You can learn how to identify those beliefs that are limiting you and then replace them with positive ones that support your success.

YOU ARE CAPABLE

One of the most prevalent and destructive limiting beliefs is the notion that somehow we are not capable of accomplishing our goals. Despite the best educational materials available, and despite decades of recorded knowledge about how to accomplish any task, we somehow choose to say instead, *I can't do that. I don't know how. There's no one to show me. I'm not smart enough.* And on and on.

Where does this come from? For most of us, it's a matter of early childhood programming. Whether they knew it or not, our parents, grandparents, and other adult role models told us, *No, no, honey. That's too much for you to handle. Let me do that for you. Maybe next year you can try that.*

We take this sense of inability into adulthood, where it gets reinforced through workplace mistakes and other "failures." But what if you decided to say instead, *I can do this. I am capable. Other people have accomplished this. If I don't have the knowledge, there's someone out there who can teach me.*

You make the shift to competence and mastery. The shift in thinking can mean the difference between a lifetime of "could have dones" and accomplishing what you really want in life.

YOU ARE CAPABLE AND WORTHY OF LOVE

Likewise, many people don't believe they are competent to handle life's challenges or are worthy of love—yet these two beliefs are the two main pillars of high self-esteem. Believing that you are *capable of handling anything that comes up in your life* means that you are no longer afraid of anything. And think about this—haven't you handled everything that has ever happened to you? Things that were far more difficult than you thought they would be? The death of a loved one, divorce, being broke? Loss of a friend, your job, your money, your reputation, your youth? These things were tough, but you handled them. And you can handle anything else that happens to you, as well. Once you get that, your confidence will soar.

Believing you are worthy of love means that you believe *I deserve to be treated well—with respect and dignity. I deserve to be cherished and adored by someone. I am worthy of an intimate and fulfilling relationship. I won't settle for less than I deserve. I will do whatever it takes to create that for myself.*

YOU CAN OVERCOME ANY LIMITING BELIEF

We suffer from other limiting beliefs, too. Do these sound familiar?

I'm not (smart, attractive, rich, old, or young) enough.
I'm not lovable.
I'm not worthy.
I'm not safe.
Life is hard.
They'd never pick me to head the new project.
Even if I don't like this job, I need the financial security.
Nothing I do is ever successful.
You can't get rich in this profession.
There aren't any good men left in this town.

HOW TO OVERCOME ANY LIMITING BELIEF

Here is a simple but powerful four-step process you can use to transform any limiting belief into an empowering belief.

1. Identify a limiting belief that you want to change. Start by making a list of any beliefs you have that might be limiting you. A fun way to do that is to invite two or three friends who would also like to accelerate their growth to join you to brainstorm a list of all the things you heard growing up from your parents, guardians, teachers, coaches—even well-meaning religious instructors such as the nuns in Catholic school—that might somehow still be limiting you. Here are some common ones and the limiting beliefs that grow out of them:

> Money doesn't grow on trees.
> *I'll never be rich.*
> Can't you do anything right?
> *I can't do anything right, so why even try?*
> Children should be seen and not heard.
> *I need to be quiet if I want to be loved.*
> Eat everything on your plate. The children in China are starving.
> *I should eat everything on my plate, even if I'm not hungry.*
> Boys don't cry.
> *It's not okay to share my feelings, especially my sadness.*
> Act like a lady.
> *It's not okay to act playful (silly, sexual, spontaneous).*
> The only person you ever think about is yourself.
> *It's not okay to focus on my own needs.*
> You're not smart enough to go to college.
> *I'm stupid. I'm not college material.*
> If you're not a virgin, nobody will want to marry you.
> *I am damaged goods and no one will ever love me.*
> People aren't interested in your problems.
> *I should hide what is really going on with me.*
> Nobody's interested in your opinion.
> *What I think is not important.*

When you are finished creating your list, pick a belief that you think is still limiting you and take yourself through the remaining three steps of the process.

2. Determine how the belief limits you.
3. Decide how you would rather be, act, or feel.
4. Create a turnaround statement that affirms or gives you permission to be, act, or feel this new way.

For example:

1. My negative limiting belief is *I have to do everything by myself. It's not okay to ask for help. It is a sign of weakness.*
2. The way it limits me is *I don't ask for help and I end up not meeting deadlines, staying up too late, and not making enough time for myself.*
3. The way I want to feel is *that it's okay to ask for help. It does not make me weak. It takes courage to ask for help. I ask for help when I need it, and I want to delegate to others some of the things I don't like doing and that are not the best use of my time.*
4. My turnaround statement is *It's okay to ask for help. I am worthy of receiving all the support I need.*

Here are some other examples of turnaround statements:

Negative: It's not okay to focus on my own needs.

Turnaround: My needs are just as important as everyone else's needs.

Negative: If I express my true feelings, people will think I am weak and take advantage of me.

Turnaround: The more I express my true feelings, the more people love, respect, and support me.

Negative: I can't do anything right, so why even try?

Turnaround: I can do many things right, and each time I try something new, I learn and get better.

Once you have created a new belief—your turnaround statement—you will need to implant it into your subconscious mind through constant repetition several times a day for a minimum of 30 days. Use the affirmation techniques we discussed in Principle 10: "Release the Brakes."

As Claude Bristol points out in his magnificent book *The Magic of Believing,* "This subtle force of repeated suggestion overcomes our reason. It acts directly on our emotions and our feelings, and finally penetrates to the very depths of our subconscious minds. It's the repeated suggestion that makes you believe."

PRINCIPLE

34

DEVELOP FOUR NEW SUCCESS HABITS A YEAR

The individual who wants to reach the top in business must appreciate the might and force of habit. He must be quick to break those habits that can break him—and hasten to adopt those practices that will become the habits that help him achieve the success he desires.

J. PAUL GETTY
Founder of Getty Oil Company, philanthropist, and, in the late 1950s, widely regarded as the richest man in the world

Psychologists tell us that up to 90% of our behavior is habitual. Ninety percent! From the time you get up in the morning until the time you retire at night, there are hundreds of things you do the same way every day. These include the way you shower, dress, eat breakfast, read the newspaper, brush your teeth, drive to work, organize your desk, shop at the supermarket, and clean your house. Over the years, you have developed a set of firmly entrenched habits that determine how well every area of your life works, from your job and your income to your health and your relationships.

The good news is that habits help free up your mind while your body is on automatic. This allows you to plan your day while you are in the shower and talk to your fellow passengers while you are driving your car. The bad news is that you can also become locked into habits that don't serve you—unconscious self-defeating behavior patterns that inhibit your growth and limit your success.

Whatever habits you have established up to this point are producing your current level of results. More than likely, if you want to create higher levels of success, you are going to need to drop some of your habits—not returning phone calls, staying up too late, watching too much television, making sarcastic comments, eating fast food every day, smoking, being late for appointments, spending more than you earn—and replace them with more productive habits—returning phone calls within 24 hours, getting 8 hours of sleep each day, reading for an hour a day, exercising four times a week, eating healthy food, being on time, and saving 10% of your income.

GOOD OR BAD, HABITS ALWAYS DELIVER RESULTS

Success is a matter of understanding and religiously practicing specific, simple habits that always lead to success.
ROBERT J. RINGER
Author of *Million Dollar Habits*

Your habits determine your outcomes. Successful people don't just drift to the top. Getting there requires focused action, personal discipline, and lots of energy every day to make things happen. The habits you develop from this day forward will ultimately determine how your future unfolds.

One of the problems for people with poor habits is that the results of their bad habits usually don't show up until much later in life. When you develop a chronic bad habit, life will eventually give you consequences. You may not like the consequences, but life will still deliver them. The fact is, if you keep on doing things a certain way, you will always get a predictable result. Negative habits breed negative consequences. Positive habits create positive consequences.

TAKE ACTION TO DEVELOP BETTER HABITS NOW

There are two action steps for changing your habits: The *first step* is to make a list of all the habits that keep you unproductive or that might negatively impact your future. Ask others to help you objectively identify what they believe are your limiting habits. Look for patterns. Also review this list of the most common unsuccessful habits below:

- Procrastinating
- Paying bills at the last minute
- Not delivering on promised documents and services in a timely way
- Letting receivables get overdue
- Arriving late for meetings and appointments
- Forgetting someone's name within seconds of being introduced

- Talking over others' comments, instead of listening
- Answering the telephone during family time or spouse time
- Handling mail more than once
- Working late
- Choosing work over time with your children
- Having fast-food meals more than two days a week

Once you have identified your negative habits, the *second step* is to choose better, more productive success habits and develop systems that will help support them.

For example, if your goal is to get to the gym every morning, one system you might put in place is to go to bed one hour earlier and set your alarm ahead. If you're in sales, you might develop a checklist of activities so that all prospects receive the same series of communications.

Maybe you want to get in the habit of completing your work by the close of business Friday, so you're free to spend weekends with your spouse and children. That's an excellent habit, *but what specifically will you do to adopt that new habit?* What activities will you engage in? How will you stay motivated? Will you develop a checklist on Monday of what must be accomplished by Friday afternoon to keep you on track? Will you spend less time chatting with coworkers at the water cooler? Email people their promised documents as you are talking on the phone with them? Take shorter lunches?

WHAT COULD YOU ACHIEVE IF YOU TOOK ON FOUR NEW HABITS A YEAR?

If you use these strategies to develop just four new habits a year, five years from now you'll have 20 new success habits that could bring you all the money you want, the wonderful loving relationships you desire, a healthier, more energized body, plus all sorts of new opportunities.

Start by listing four new habits you would like to establish in the next year. Work on one new habit every quarter. If you work diligently on building one new habit every 13 weeks, you won't overwhelm yourself with an unrealistic list of New Year's resolutions . . . and research now shows that if you repeat a behavior for 13 weeks—whether it is meditating for 20 minutes a day, flossing your teeth, reviewing your goals, or writing thank-you letters to your clients—it will be yours for life. By systematically adding one behavior at a time, you can dramatically improve your overall lifestyle.

Here are a couple of hints for making sure you follow through on your commitment to your new habit:

Put up signs to remind you to follow through on the new behavior. When I learned that even a little dehydration can decrease your mental acuity by as much as 30%, I decided to develop the habit that all of the health practitioners had been advising—drink ten eight-ounce glasses of water a day. I put signs that said "Drink water!" on my phone, my office door, my bathroom mirror, and my kitchen refrigerator. I also had my assistant remind me every hour.

Find an accountability partner. Another powerful technique to keep you focused on your new habit is to partner up with someone, keep score (see Principle 21), and hold each other accountable. Check in with each other at least once a week to make sure you are staying on track.

Commit 100%. Perhaps the most powerful way to stay on track is to follow the "no exceptions rule," which is explained in the next chapter.

PRINCIPLE

35

99% IS A BITCH;
100% IS A BREEZE

There is a difference between interest and commitment. When you're interested in doing something, you do it only when it's convenient. When you're committed to something, you accept no excuses, only results.

KEN BLANCHARD
Chief Spiritual Officer of the Ken Blanchard Companies and coauthor of over 60 books, including the classic bestseller *The One Minute Manager*

In life the spoils of victory go to those who make a 100% commitment to the outcome, to those who have a "no matter what it takes" attitude. They give it their all; they put everything they have into getting their desired result—whether it be an Olympic gold medal, the top sales award, a perfect dinner party, an A in microbiology, or their dream house.

What a simple concept this is—yet you'd be surprised how many people wake up every day and fight with themselves over whether or not to keep their commitments, stick to their disciplines, or carry out their action plans.

THE "NO-EXCEPTIONS RULE"

Successful people adhere to the "no exceptions rule" when it comes to their daily disciplines. Once you make a 100% commitment to something, there are no exceptions. It's a done deal. Nonnegotiable. Case closed!

If I make a 100% commitment to monogamy, for example, that's it. I never have to think about it again. There are no exceptions, no matter what the circumstances. It ends the discussion, closes that door, permits no other possibility. I don't have to wrestle with that decision every day. It's already been made. The die has been cast. All the bridges are burned. It makes life easier and simpler and keeps me on focus. It frees up tons of energy that would otherwise be spent internally debating the topic over and over and over, because all the energy I expend on internal conflict is now available to use for creating other achievement.

If you make the 100% commitment to exercise every day for 30 minutes, no matter what, then it is settled. You simply just do it. It doesn't matter if you are traveling, if you have a 7:00 A.M. television interview, if it's raining outside, if you went to bed late last night, if your schedule is full, or if you simply don't feel like it. You just do it anyway.

It's like brushing your teeth before you go to bed. You always do it, no matter what. If you find yourself in bed and you have forgotten, you get out of bed and brush them. It doesn't matter how tired you are or how late it is. You just do it.

Whether your discipline is to read for an hour, practice the piano five days a week, make two sales calls every day, learn a new language, practice typing, hit 200 golf balls, do 50 sit-ups, run six miles, meditate, pray, read the Bible, spend 60 quality minutes with your kids—or whatever else you need to do to achieve your goals—commit 100% to those daily disciplines that will get you there.

ONLY ON A FULL MOON

Sid Simon, one of my mentors, was a successful speaker, trainer, bestselling author, and poet who split his time between Hadley, Massachusetts, in the summer and Sanibel, Florida, in the winter. When I was a graduate student at the University of Massachusetts, Sid was the most popular professor in the Department of Education.

One of Sid's highest priorities is his health and fitness. At 87 years old, he still biked on a regular basis, took supplements, ate healthy foods, and— oh yes—he allowed himself a bowl of ice cream on the one day a month when there was a full moon.

When I attended Sid's seventy-fifth birthday celebration, over 100 of his family members, closest friends, and admiring former students came from all across the country to celebrate with him. Dessert was the standard birthday cake and ice cream. Only one problem, though—there wasn't a full moon. To cajole him into giving himself permission on this once-in-a-lifetime special occasion, four people who knew of Sid's commitment dressed as moon goddesses and entered the room carrying a huge full moon made out of cardboard and aluminum foil, so there would be a virtual full moon for Sid.

But even with all of that loving persuasion, Sid stood firm on his commitment and declined the ice cream. He knew if he broke his commitment

"I'm going to order a broiled skinless chicken breast, but I want you to bring me lasagna and garlic bread by mistake."

that one time, it would be that much easier to break it the next time he was offered ice cream. It would be easier to rationalize, justify, and explain away his commitment. Sid knew that a 100% commitment is actually easier to keep, and he was unwilling to undermine years of success for other people's approval. We all learned a lot about true self-discipline that night.

ONE FINAL REASON 100% IS SO IMPORTANT

This powerful 100% commitment also figures critically in other important areas—for instance, the workplace. Consider what a commitment to just 99.9% quality would mean in the following work situations. It would mean:

- Two unsafe landings at O'Hare International Airport each day
- 16,000 lost pieces of mail per hour
- 20,000 incorrectly filled drug prescriptions every year
- 500 incorrect surgical operations performed each week
- 22,000 checks deducted from the wrong account each hour
- Your heart failing to beat 32,000 times each year!

Can you see why 100% is such an important percentage? Just think how much better your life and the whole world would work if you were 100% committed to excellence in everything you do.

PRINCIPLE 36

LEARN MORE TO EARN MORE

If I am through learning, I am through.

JOHN WOODEN
Legendary UCLA basketball coach
who won 10 NCAA championships

People who have more information have a tremendous advantage over people who don't. And though you may think it takes years to acquire the knowledge you would need to become super-successful, the truth is that simple behaviors such as reading for an hour a day, turning television time into learning time, and attending classes and training programs can make it surprisingly easy to increase your knowledge—and substantially increase your level of success.

DECREASE YOUR TELEVISION AND STREAMING TIME

The sad reality is the average American watches television and on-demand content an astounding five hours a day. If you are one of these *average* folks, by the time you are 60 years old you will have wasted 12.5 years of your life watching television. That's almost one fifth of your life! Do you really want to spend one fifth of your life watching other people—the ones on television who are working—getting rich living out their dreams while you are vegging out on the couch?

In my very first meeting with my mentor, W. Clement Stone, he asked me to eliminate one hour of television a day. He went on to explain that cutting out just one hour of television a day creates an extra 365 hours per year to accomplish whatever is most important to you. That's over nine additional 40-hour workweeks—two months of additional time!

I asked him what he wanted me to do with that extra hour. "Anything productive," he said. "You can learn a new language, get superfit, spend quality time with your wife or children, learn to play a musical instrument, make more sales calls, or go back to school and get a degree. But what I most recommend is that you read for an hour a day. Read inspirational autobiographies of successful people. Read books on psychology, sales, finance, and health. Study the principles of successful living." And that is what I did.

In my life I've read more than 3,000 books, and that has made a huge difference in my success.

LEADERS ARE READERS

Self-made millionaire Dr. John Demartini made a list of all the Nobel Prize winners, then made a list of all the greats in those same fields—whether it was poetry, science, religion, or philosophy. He then proceeded to read their works and their biographies. Not surprisingly, John is also one of the brightest, wisest, and most financially successful people I have ever met. Reading pays off.

"You can't put your hand in a pot of glue without some of that glue sticking," says John. "So, too, you can't put your mind and heart into some of the works of these masters without some of it sticking. If you read about immortals, you increase the possibility of leaving an immortal effect. The result has been enormous for me."

The late Jim Rohn, one of America's foremost motivational philosophers, suggested using that one extra hour a day to read. He taught me that if you were to read one book a week, in 10 years you'd have read 520 books, and in 20 years, more than 1,000 books—enough to easily put you in the top 1% of experts in your field. Add to those the books from masters in related areas and you'd have an edge that others simply don't have.

LEARN TO READ FASTER TO READ MORE

If you read more slowly than you'd like, consider taking a course to increase not only your reading speed but also how fast you absorb the information. The best resource I've found is the PhotoReading Course developed by Paul Scheele. It's available as a weekend workshop in many cities around the world or as a self-study course from Learning Strategies Corporation. You can learn more about both the live and self-study at home courses at learningstrategies.com/photoreading.

A WEEKLY SYSTEM FOR GETTING SMART

Take a look at the extensive reading list I've included on the companion web page for this book at jackcanfield.com/tsp-resources. Reading books like these will help you achieve mastery in those areas of life that are most central to your happiness and fulfillment. They contain some of the best time-tested wisdom, information, methodologies, systems, techniques, and secrets of success that have ever been recorded. If you make a commitment to read one book a week, review what you have read, and apply at least one thing you learn from each book, you will be miles ahead of everyone else in creating an extraordinary life.

All of the books on this list are ones that have helped me attain the high level of success I have achieved. Many of them are timeless classics and should make up the core of your personal success library. Others contain the most recent breakthroughs in psychology, neuroscience, quantum physics, nutrition, and health.

If you can't yet afford to purchase your own books, borrow them from friends or your local library.

In addition to the list on the web page mentioned above, some of the best books out there are biographies and autobiographies of great people. By reading them, you will learn how to become great yourself.

And if you're going to watch television, I suggest you watch *Biography* on the A&E Television Network. I am always inspired by the lives of the people the program chronicles.

ATTEND SUCCESS RALLIES, CONFERENCES, AND RETREATS

I remember the first time I attended a success rally. Thousands of people were on hand to learn from many of the greatest speakers, trainers, and motivators of our day. You, too, can access these powerful learning experiences by attending rallies, conferences, and retreats—additionally benefiting from the excitement and inspiration of your fellow attendees and the networking that goes on at these events. Keep an eye out for ads in your local paper.

Another great resource that has developed in the last 10 years is an abundance of online summits. A summit usually consists of 8 to 24 experts speaking for 30 minutes apiece over one or more days. Just type the words *online summit* or *virtual summit* into your web browser and you will find them on lots of topics.

BE TEACHABLE

In a humble state, you learn better. I can't find anything else very exciting about humility, but at least there's that.

JOHN DOONER
Former chairman and CEO of the
Interpublic Group of Companies

While I was writing this book, I sat next to Skip Barber on a flight to Las Vegas. Skip trains people to drive high-performance cars under actual racing conditions. When I asked him what distinguishes his best students, he replied, "The ones who get it are teachable. They're open to learning. The ones who don't make it think they know everything already. You can't teach them anything."

To learn and grow in life, you need to be teachable, too. You need to let go of already knowing it all, needing to be right and looking good—and open yourself to being a learner. Listen to those who have earned the right to speak, who have already done what you want to do.

It is better to be prepared for an opportunity and not have one than to have an opportunity and not be prepared.

WHITNEY M. YOUNG JR.
American civil rights leader and
recipient of the Presidential Medal of Freedom

BE PREPARED WHEN OPPORTUNITY KNOCKS

In his book *Live Your Dreams,* Les Brown tells the story of how he dreamed of becoming a popular Miami disc jockey. "When I set out," he says, "I had no idea how I would do it, but I knew life would present the opportunities if I was prepared and in a position to take advantage of them."

Les shadowed his high school drama teacher, learning as much as he could about linguistics. Together, they worked on Les's speaking voice. Soon, Les began developing his own on-air style of patter, pretending at school that he was performing on the radio. He sought out mentors who could prepare him for the opportunity of being on the air. And after high school, though Les earned his wage as a city sanitation worker, his persistence landed him a job as a late-night gofer at a prominent Miami radio station.

Les immediately took advantage of the opportunity to learn even more. He absorbed all he could—hanging around the disc jockeys and engineers and practicing what he learned in a makeshift cardboard studio he created in his bedroom. His microphone was a hairbrush. Finally, one night, a deejay couldn't finish his show and Les had his chance to get on the air.

When the chance came, not only was Les prepared to be on the radio but he was also prepared to be *great* on the radio. The style, patter, dialogue, and broadcasting skills he had worked so hard to develop paid off instantly—Les was an immediate hit, and he was later promoted to fill-in deejay . . . then finally became a full-time disc jockey with his own radio show.

WHAT DO YOU NEED TO DO TO GET READY?

If you're an industry expert and believe your consulting business would skyrocket after presenting a workshop at the national convention, why not get prepared now . . . by writing your speaker's kit, joining Toastmasters, outlining and practicing your speech, and getting ready to be on the platform?

If you want a promotion at work, why not ask your boss what it takes to become promotable? Perhaps you need to go back to school and get your MBA. Or maybe you need one year of accounting experience. Or perhaps you need to learn the latest software programs. Do that, and when the next promotion comes around, you can say, "I'm ready!"

Do you need to learn a new foreign language? Could you develop advanced skills, more resources, or new contacts? Do you need to get your body into better physical shape? Should you expand your business skills, sales skills, or negotiating skills? Are you learning new skills on the computer—such as using PowerPoint, Keynote, graphic design suites, Photoshop, or Excel? Do you need to learn golf so that you can make business deals on the golf course? Would it improve your home life and marriage by taking dancing classes with your spouse? Are you learning to sail or play tennis? Do you need to learn to play a musical instrument, take acting classes, or learn how to write better to get where you want to go?

Whatever you need to do to get ready, start now by making a list of the top 10 things you could be doing to be ready when opportunity finds you. Take classes on your own time. Read books. Get new skills. Go to your industry's trade show. Dress the part. Look like a player before you're there.

As Les Brown's story teaches us, all it takes is passion, persistence, and the belief that someday the opportunity will come. Start getting ready now.

ATTEND HUMAN-POTENTIAL TRAININGS

Nothing changes until you do.

SOURCE UNKNOWN

If you suddenly discovered you were driving with the emergency brake on, would you push harder on the gas? No! You would simply release the brake and instantly go faster—without any additional expenditure of energy.

Most of us are going through life with the emergency brake on. It's time to release the limiting beliefs, emotional blocks, and self-destructive behaviors that are holding you back.

In addition to the techniques we've already covered in Principles 10 ("Release the Brakes"), 32 ("Transform Your Inner Critic into an Inner Coach"), and 33 ("Transcend Your Limiting Beliefs"), the two most powerful methods for releasing the brake are personal development training and individual therapy. If I were to attribute my success to any one thing, it would be the hundreds of personal development seminars I have attended over the past 50 years. All of us—including me—need outside influences to help us break through our habitual patterns and assist us in creating new ways of thinking and behaving.

INVEST IN YOUR TEAM'S EDUCATION

I recently saw this brilliant gem on the Internet: The CFO (chief financial officer) of a company asks the CEO, "What happens if we invest in developing our people and then they leave us?" The CEO responds, "What happens if we don't and they stay?"

"How are we supposed to get there?"

To stay competitive in today's world you must focus not only on your own learning and development but also on your team's development. Whether you are the CEO of a large corporation, the owner of a midsize company, a regional sales manager, a small entrepreneur, a school principal, or the leader of a network marketing downline, you have to make sure that everyone in your organization is constantly learning and growing—or you and your organization will ultimately be left behind.

In Japan, the average worker receives many more days of training a year than workers in America. This may be one of the reasons they have such a huge share of the American car, camera, and consumer electronics markets—including such popular brands as Toyota, Nissan, Mazda, Subaru, Lexus, Acura, Infiniti, Nikon, Fujifilm, Sony, Panasonic, and Sharp.

Why not invest in a lending library of books or provide access to online courses? Send people to trainings. Hire trainers to do in-house trainings, including both personal- and professional-development trainings.

Two resources that have transformed both individuals and workgroups—and in many cases, entire companies—are my Breakthrough to Success week-long training and my Train-the-Trainer program. At the live training program, Breakthrough to Success, thousands of people around the world have achieved their loftiest goals—from becoming bestselling authors to launching new businesses, doubling their incomes, tripling their time off, funding new charities, becoming the top salesperson, and so much more. Over several days, I help you get clear about what you want, help you overcome the obstacles that have been holding you back, and guide you as you write a step-by-step plan to take your life to the next level. Visit canfieldtrainings.com for information.

My Train-the-Trainer professional program for trainers, coaches, counselors, educators, and others develops you as a human-potential trainer who can bring *The Success Principles* exercises and transformational techniques to your office, classroom, therapy practice, or workshop audiences. I actually equip you with the skill-set, content, exercises, workshop design, training tools, and mindset necessary to get results with any group or individual. You can attend live sessions or study in the convenience of your home or office. Visit trainthetraineronline.com.

Finally, see the "Suggested Reading and Additional Resources for Success" page on our website at jackcanfield.com/tsp-resources. I've listed organizations and trainings that I've personally found most powerful—and most impactful—to my life and to the lives of my family, staff, clients, and students. Visit the websites of these organizations, call and talk to these companies, attend their guest events, and then make a decision to attend a few that feel right for you and your team.

COMMIT TO LIFELONG LEARNING

Realize that the amount of knowledge and information available in the world is growing at a mind-numbing pace. In fact, it has been said that all human knowledge has doubled in the last 10 years. Don't expect this trend to slow down.

More alarming, the information that allows you to be successful—to be on the cutting edge of your career and profession—is evolving at the same pace. That's why you *must* commit to lifelong self-improvement and learning—improving your mind, increasing your skills, and boosting your ability to assimilate and apply what you learn.

PRINCIPLE

37

STAY MOTIVATED WITH THE MASTERS

A successful person realizes his personal responsibility for self-motivation. He starts with himself because he possesses the key to his own ignition switch.

KEMMONS WILSON
Founder of Holiday Inn Hotels

So many of us today are trained—by the media, by our parents, by our schools, by our culture—to have limiting, "it's not possible, I don't deserve it" beliefs. This early conditioning is often so ingrained that it takes continual external motivation to overcome the decades of negative effects and move toward more success-oriented thoughts and attitudes.

Attending a weekend workshop isn't enough. Neither is reading a book or watching a training video. What truly successful people do is listen daily to audio programs from the world's most renowned motivational masters—in the car, at home, and at the office—even if it's just for 15 minutes each day.

LEARN VIRTUALLY ANYTHING YOU WANT OR NEED TO KNOW

The average person commutes 30 minutes each way to and from work. In five years, that's 1,250 hours in the car—enough time to give yourself the equivalent of a college education! Whether you're commuting by car or train, riding your bike, or going for a run, listening to audio or video recordings can give you the edge you need to excel in virtually any area of your life. You can keep yourself motivated, learn a language, learn management skills, learn sales and marketing strategies, learn better commu-

nication, learn about holistic health, and more. You can even discover the success secrets of the world's most powerful industrialists, business titans, real estate moguls, and entrepreneurs.

Just how motivating can the masters be in your life?

HOURS AND HOURS OF LISTENING

It all started when a coworker asked Elaine Fosse for help with a fundraiser for the Fort Lewis Family Support Group in Tacoma, Washington. But between working full time and finishing her B.A., Elaine had no extra time to spend in the kitchen making something for the group's upcoming bake sale. Instead, she opted to quickly make and bottle the brightly hued, homemade salad dressing for which she'd perfected the recipe two decades earlier. Packaging her batch of raspberry dressing into recycled sterilized bottles, Elaine added a cute label and topped the bottles with raffia ribbon.

Almost overnight, orders started to pour in. For the next 18 months, Elaine earned money for the troops by selling her dressing at additional bazaars and bake sales.

Knowing she had a high-end niche product that was great-tasting, low in calories—plus free of dairy, soy, salt, gluten, preservatives, and additives—she reasoned that her salad dressing was ready for a larger market. In fact, the dream of starting a business began to take form. But before

Elaine took the plunge, she wanted to test the waters further by selling at large farmers' markets in Bellevue, Washington, and Cannon Beach, Oregon—more than two hours' drive in each direction.

Maybe I can use the road time to gain insights on how to grow and expand my business, she thought.

In her search for audiobooks she discovered *The Success Principles* on CD at a Barnes & Noble. After listening to the first disc, she was hooked. Each time she left her driveway for the long trek, she'd pop a disc into the player, and by the time she reached the market, she would be energized.

More often than not, however, the weather in Washington and Oregon made standing under a tent miserable—as torrential rains blew in or 101-degree temperatures heated the pavement. Self-doubt, fright, and exhaustion sometimes crept in. But so did the lessons she'd learned from *The Success Principles*—lessons like feel the fear and do it anyway. Visualize. Act as if. Go the extra mile.

Instead of giving up, Elaine put those principles into action. She created beautiful displays. She put up great signage. She added fresh flowers to her table. She greeted every potential customer with a positive attitude and a smile. And each time her drive to the Bellevue Market took her past the local Whole Foods market, she'd tell herself, "My product is going to be on those shelves one day." Sometimes she'd even stop and walk the aisles, repeating out loud her positive affirmation in the face of so much competition.

Although she didn't know exactly how to get her dressings into Whole Foods, Elaine knew she didn't want to go into debt, hire a broker, or pay for shelf space. Instead, she expanded her line to include blackberry, cranberry, and marionberry salad dressings, as well as organic versions of each one—all the while, focusing on her Whole Foods dream.

Soon she was negotiating distribution in more than a dozen other stores and saw increasing online sales, too. And then it happened—a message on her answering machine: "This is Denise from the Whole Foods corporate office in Bellevue. I hear you have a product we're interested in."

It worked. It actually worked! Elaine thought to herself. *All those principles paid off!*

When Whole Foods invited her to "audition" her dressings, Elaine set up everything she needed to make a good impression and as she handed a sample to Denise she confided, "Seeing my dressings in Whole Foods is my goal, my dream."

Denise's eyes widened as she tasted Elaine's dressing. "Ohmigosh! And you have *seven* flavors?"

Elaine's dressings now stand proudly on the shelves of *all* Whole Foods stores in the Pacific Northwest.

> *Of course motivation is not permanent. But then neither is bathing,
> but it is something you should do on a regular basis.*
>
> ZIG ZIGLAR
> Motivational speaker and author of *See You at the Top*

WHERE TO GET THE BEST MOTIVATIONAL AUDIO PROGRAMS

You'll find my list of favorite motivational audio programs in the *Suggested Reading and Additional Resources for Success* on the companion website at jackcanfield.com/tsp-resources, where we constantly update the list of rec-

ommended audio programs on success, wealth-building, health, happiness, relationships, and more.

I also highly recommend five audio programs that I have produced to help you become more successful in every area of your life: *Maximum Confidence: 10 Steps to Extreme Self-Esteem*, *Self-Esteem and Peak Performance*, *The Aladdin Factor*, *The Success Principles: A 30-Day Journey from Where You Are to Where You Want to Be*, and *Effortless Success: Living the Law of Attraction*. They are all available at jackcanfield.com and Amazon.

PRINCIPLE

38

FUEL YOUR SUCCESS WITH PASSION AND ENTHUSIASM

Enthusiasm is one of the most powerful engines of success. When you do a thing, do it with all your might. Put your whole soul into it. Stamp it with your own personality. Be active, be energetic, be enthusiastic and faithful, and you will accomplish your object. Nothing great was ever achieved without enthusiasm.

RALPH WALDO EMERSON
American essayist and poet

Passion is something within you that provides the continual enthusiasm, focus, and energy you need to succeed. But unlike feel-good motivation derived from external sources, true passion has a more spiritual nature. It comes from within. And it can be channeled into amazing feats of success.

FILLED WITH PASSION

The word *enthusiasm* comes from the Greek word *entheos,* which means "to be filled with God." When you are filled with spirit, you are naturally inspired and passionate. Sometimes that passion expresses itself in a dynamic and energetic way, like the hustle of a champion athlete who is "on fire." Other times it expresses itself in a more peaceful and calm way, like the passion of Mother Teresa for ministering to the needs of the dying in Calcutta.

No doubt you know or have met people who are passionate about life and enthusiastic about their work. They can't wait to get up in the morning and get started. They are eager and energetic. They are filled with purpose and totally committed to their mission. This kind of passion comes from loving and enjoying your work. It comes from doing what you were born to do. It comes from following your heart and trusting your joy as a guide. Enthusiasm and passion come as a result of caring about what you do. If you love your work, if you enjoy it, you're already a success.

YOUR SUCCESS IS GUARANTEED

My son Kyle, aka El Kool Kyle, is a hip-hop artist in Berkeley, California. Though he's not made it big financially, in the past 20 years he has created 10 full-length CDs; performed at Woodstock '99; opened for KRS1 and Public Enemy; performed with Joan Baez, Jurassic 5, Dilated Peoples, and other major artists; sat in as a radio guest DJ; taught hip-hop at Richmond High School in California; been honored by the Mexican consulate for his contribution to cumbia music; and even cofounded a record label, Baylando Records, which has produced music for two Grammy-nominated groups.

He has doggedly pursued his dream and never given up on his art.

So even if he were never to make a lot of money or become a rap superstar outside of the Bay Area, Kyle is already successful. Because when you are happy doing what you love, you've already won. When you do something you love with passion and perseverance, you are already a success.

A PASSION FOR TEACHING

Hobart Elementary School is the third largest elementary school in the United States and is located in a gang- and drug-infested Los Angeles neighborhood. The fifth-grade students in teacher Rafe Esquith's classroom, who all speak English as a second language, score 50 points higher in math and reading than the students in the rest of the school. Their grasp and mastery of the English language is gained through learning and performing the plays of Shakespeare. To date, the Hobart Shakespeareans have performed 15 full-length plays to packed audiences, from the White House to the inner city. Among their passionate supporters are actors Sir Ian McKellen and Hal Holbrook.

When you walk into Rafe's classroom, you notice the large banner—THERE ARE NO SHORTCUTS—draped above the chalkboard. The nearby "Walls of Fame" feature school pennants from Stanford, Princeton, Yale, and UCLA, where many of his students have sought higher education.

School officials from all over the world sit in his classroom to observe the educational miracles at work. Not only was Rafe honored as Disney's National Teacher of the Year, but he is also the sole teacher in history to be presented with a National Medal of the Arts. Queen Elizabeth awarded him the highest tribute bestowed on a non-British citizen—he was named a Member of the British Empire.

What has fueled this devoted, visionary public-school teacher to work 12-hour days, 6 days a week, 52 weeks a year for 31 years? Passion and enthusiasm. There's nothing he loves more than bringing the joys of literature, theater, music, science, math, and plain old fun to hundreds of kids. The results? He infuses his students with their own joy for learning, boosting their self-esteem while boosting their academic performances. As Rafe puts it, "I'm a very ordinary fellow who made one smart move. I would not allow today's educational fiasco of systemized mediocrity and uniformity to crush me into the robot so many potentially good teachers become. I kept my own spirit and personal passions alive in my class, and as a lover of Shakespeare have passed on that excitement to eager young minds. In my school's neighborhood of failure and despair, success and excellence have become the standard rather than the exception to the rule. And best of all, the kids and I have a helluva good time working so hard and climbing to great heights. It's a wonderful life."*

HOW TO DEVELOP PASSION

How can you develop passion in the most important areas of your life?

Let's look at your career for a moment. That's the work that occupies the majority of your week. Recent Gallup polls and studies by Mercer report a full one third of Americans would be happier in another job. Ask yourself: *Am I doing what I love to do?*

If you aren't, and you had the choice to do anything you wanted to do, what would that be? If you believe you can't make money doing that, imagine that you just won the lottery. After buying your expensive mansion, a Rolls-Royce, and all the toys and travel you wanted, what would you do with your day? *What you're doing now or something different?*

The most successful people I've met love what they do so much, they

---

*If you want to read an inspirational story of passion and enthusiasm, get a copy of *There Are No Shortcuts* by Rafe Esquith or his *Teach Like Your Hair's on Fire*. For a real treat, watch Rafe's TED-ED presentation, "Ladies and Gentlemen, the Hobart Shakespeareans" on YouTube.

would actually do it for free. But they're successful because they've found a way to make a living doing what they love to do.

If you're not skilled enough to do the work you'd love to do, make time to educate yourself so you are. Do whatever it takes to prepare—working part time in your dream job or even volunteering as an intern—while still maintaining your current job.

Pay attention, too, to those times outside of the office when you feel the happiest, the most joyous, the most fully engaged, the most acknowledged and appreciated, and the most connected with yourself and others. What were you doing at those times? What were you experiencing? Those events are indicators of ways you can bring passion into your life outside your day-to-day work. It tells you what you would be happiest doing with your time.

HOW TO KEEP PASSION AND ENTHUSIASM ALIVE

Passion is a powerful tool for success and, as such, deserves to be an area you consistently work on.

Passion makes your days fly by. It helps you get more done in less time. It helps you make better decisions. And it attracts others to you. They want to be associated with you and your success.

So how can you maintain passion and enthusiasm every day? The most obvious is to spend more time doing what you love to do. As I have discussed in earlier chapters, that includes discovering your true purpose, deciding what you really want to do and have, believing you can do it and have it, deliberately creating your dream career, delegating as much as you can that is not your core genius, and taking concrete steps toward the attainment of your goals.

Another key to passion and enthusiasm is to reconnect with your original purpose for doing anything that you do. When you look underneath the surface of the things that feel like have-tos rather than want-tos, you'll almost always find that there is a deeper purpose that you are passionate about. You may not love the idea of sitting in a pediatrician's waiting room with your child, but when you get underneath it, aren't you passionate about your child's health and well-being? Ask yourself, *What is the why underneath what I am doing?* If you can get in touch with that, it is a lot easier to get enthusiastic about whatever it is that you *have* to do.

You'll discover that all of the things you feel like you have to do are really choices that you are making that serve some higher purpose such as feeding your family, creating security for your future, staying out of jail, or contributing to your health and longevity. Once you realize that these are choices you are making, you realize you can make one more choice, and that is the choice of your attitude. Even if you are trapped in an elevator with three strangers, you have a choice about your attitude. You can choose to be grumpy about not getting your work done, or you can see it as an opportunity to meet some new people on a deep level. The choice is up to you. Why not choose to do everything you do with joy and enthusiasm?

And here is one final thought. When you express your passion and enthusiasm, you will become a magnet to others, who will be attracted to your high level of energy. They will want to play with you, work with you, and support your dreams and goals. As a result, this extra manpower and the resources they bring means you will ultimately get more done in a shorter period of time.

PART THREE

Build Your Success Team

*Alone we can do so little;
together we can do so much.*

HELEN KELLER
American author, lecturer, and advocate for the blind

PRINCIPLE

39

STAY FOCUSED ON YOUR CORE GENIUS

*Success follows doing what you want to do.
There is no other way to be successful.*

MALCOLM S. FORBES
Publisher of *Forbes* magazine

I believe you have inside you a core genius—some one thing that you love to do and do so well that you hardly feel like charging people for it. It's effortless for you and a whole lot of fun. And if you could make money doing it, you'd make it your lifetime's work.

Successful people believe this, too. That's why they put their core genius first. They focus on it—and delegate everything else to other people on their team.

Compare that to the other people in the world who go through life doing everything, even those tasks they're bad at or that could be done more cheaply, better, and faster by someone else. They can't find the time to focus on their core genius because they fail to delegate even the most menial of tasks.

When you delegate the grunt work—the things you hate doing or those tasks that are so painful you end up putting them off—you get to concentrate on what you love to do. You free up your time so that you can be more productive. And you get to enjoy life more.

So why is delegating routine tasks and unwanted projects so difficult for most people? Most people are simply afraid to give up control or reluctant to spend the money to pay for help. Deep down, most people simply don't want to let go.

Others—possibly you—have simply fallen into the *habit* of doing everything themselves. "It's too time-consuming to explain it to someone," you say. "I can do it more quickly and better myself anyway." But can you?

DELEGATE COMPLETELY

If you're a professional earning $200 per hour and you pay a neighborhood kid $20 an hour to cut the grass, you save the effort of doing it yourself on the weekend and gain one extra hour when you could profit by $180. Of course, though one hour doesn't seem like much, multiply that by at least 20 weekends in the spring and summer and you discover you've gained 20 hours a year at $180 per hour—or an extra $3,600 in potential earnings.

Similarly, if you're a real estate agent, you need to list houses, gather information for the multiple listings, attend open houses, do showings, put keys in lockboxes, write offers, and make appointments. And if you're lucky, you eventually get to close a deal.

But let's say that you're the best closer in the area.

Why would you want to waste your time writing listings, doing lead generation, filling lockboxes, and making videos of the property when you could have a staff of colleagues and assistants doing all that, thus freeing you up to do more closing? Instead of doing just one deal a week, you could be doing three deals because you had delegated what you're less good at.

One of the strategies I use and teach is making complete delegations. It simply means that you delegate a task once and completely—rather than having to delegate it each time it needs to be done.

When I hired the gardener for my Santa Barbara estate, I said, "I want my grounds to look as close as possible to the grounds at the Four Seasons Biltmore in Montecito using the budget I'm providing you." When I go to the Four Seasons, I don't have to check whether the trees need to be trimmed or the automatic sprinklers are working. Someone else is in charge of that. Well, I want the same luxury at my home.

"With that as our operating principle," I said, "here's the budget. Take charge of the grounds. If I'm ever not happy, I'll let you know. If I'm not happy a second time, I'll find someone else. Does that feel like a workable agreement?"

My landscaper was, in fact, very excited. He knew he wouldn't be micromanaged, and I knew I wouldn't have to worry about it again—and I don't. See what I mean? Complete delegation.

When my niece came to stay with us one year while she attended the local community college, we made another complete delegation—the grocery shopping. We told her she could have unlimited use of our van if she would shop for the groceries every week. We provided her with a list of staples that we always want in the house (eggs, butter, milk, ketchup, and so on), and her job was to check every week and replace anything that was running low. In addition, my wife planned meals and let her know which items she wanted for the main courses (fish, chicken, broccoli, avocadoes, and so on). The task was delegated once and saved us hundreds of hours that year that could be devoted to writing, exercise, family time, and recreation.

BECOME A CON ARTIST DOING WHAT YOU LOVE TO DO

The biggest mistake people make in life is not trying to make a living at doing what they most enjoy.

MALCOLM S. FORBES

Strategic Coach Dan Sullivan once stated that all entrepreneurs are really con artists. They get other people to pay them to practice getting better at what they love to do.*

Think about it.

Ron Howard loves to make movies. People pay him big money to make movies. Every time he works on a film, he learns more about directing, producing, and filmmaking. He gets to practice and hang out with other filmmakers, all the while getting paid for it.

Anthony Robbins is a speaker and a trainer. He loves speaking and training. He has arranged his life so that people are constantly paying him large sums of money to do what he loves to do.

Or consider baseball great Aaron Judge of the New York Yankees. It takes him about one second to hit a home run—as long as it takes for the ball to meet the bat. He earns $40 million for about 98 seconds of batting time per year (he got 98 hits and 37 home runs in 2023 alone), so he has become really good at making the bat meet the ball. That's where he makes his money. That's where he puts all his time: practicing and getting ready for the bat to meet the ball. He has found his core genius and devotes the majority of his waking hours to perfecting his genius.

Of course, most of us are not on par with Ron Howard, Anthony Robbins, or Aaron Judge, but the fact is that we could learn a lot from their level of focus.

---

*I am grateful to Dan Sullivan for many of the ideas in this chapter and the next. You can learn more about his breakthrough coaching ideas at strategiccoach.com.

Many salespeople, for example, spend more time on account administration than they do on the phone making sales, when they *could* hire a part-time administrator (or share the cost with another salesperson) to do this time-consuming detail work.

Most female executives spend too much time running their household, when they could easily and inexpensively delegate this task to a cleaning service or part-time mother's helper, freeing themselves to focus more on their career or spend more time with their family.

Unfortunately, most entrepreneurs spend less than 30% of their time focusing on their core genius and unique abilities. In fact, by the time they've launched a business, it often seems entrepreneurs are doing everything *but* the one thing they went into business for in the first place.

Don't let this be your fate. Identify your core genius, then make complete delegations to free up more time to focus on what you love to do and do well.

DO WHAT YOU LOVE—THE MONEY WILL FOLLOW

Starting out to make money is the greatest mistake in life. Do what you feel you have a flair for doing, and if you are good enough at it, the money will come.

GREER GARSON
Academy Award winner for best actress

Diana von Welanetz Wentworth is someone who has always focused on her core genius while following her heart and has been wildly successful as a result. Her greatest pleasure was always to be cooking something and gathering people around the table to share at a deep level over food. She was always reaching for a deeper connection, what she calls "a sense of celebration at the table." So she started her career writing books about how to give a party and do everything ahead of time so you can actually be present and connect more deeply with the people you invite.

Then in May 1985, she went on a trip to the Soviet Union with a group of leaders in the human-potential movement, where she noticed that, for the most part, these leaders were all loners. Even though they were quite well known for their books and their impact in the world, they didn't know each other. When she returned, she realized that her life purpose had always been more about connection than food. She had just used food as a catalyst.

That realization led her to create the Inside Edge, an organization that hosted weekly breakfast meetings in Beverly Hills, Orange County, and San Diego, California, where nationally recognized people of vision came together to share their knowledge and wisdom on human potential, spirituality, consciousness, and world peace. Speakers included people such as Mark Victor Hansen and me, motivational expert Anthony Robbins, management consultant Ken Blanchard, actor Dennis Weaver, counselor the Reverend Leo Booth, and authors Susan Jeffers and Dan Millman. In addition to listening to an inspirational speaker, participants would network, encourage each other to dream bigger, and support each other's projects. Forty years later, members worldwide now meet online via Zoom meetings and virtual events.*

Diana has gone on to write and coauthor numerous books, including *The Chicken Soup for the Soul Cookbook,* once again integrating her love of food with her love of people sharing their ideas, wisdom, and stories.

Don't ask what the world needs. Ask yourself what makes you come alive and then do that. Because what the world needs is people who have come alive.

HOWARD THURMAN
Author, philosopher, theologian, and educator

---

*For more information on the Inside Edge, visit insideedge.org.

PRINCIPLE

40

REDEFINE TIME

The world is entering a new time zone, and one of the most difficult adjustments people must make is in their fundamental concepts and beliefs about the management of time.

DAN SULLIVAN
Cofounder and president of the Strategic Coach

The most successful people I know create superior results yet still maintain a balance among work, family, and recreation in their lives. To achieve this, they use a unique planning system that structures their time into three very different kinds of days that are prescheduled to assure the highest payoff for their efforts while still allowing abundant amounts of free time to pursue their personal interests.

Dan Sullivan, president of The Strategic Coach, created a great system that I use, called The Entrepreneurial Time System®★. It divides all of your time into three kinds of days: Focus Days, Buffer Days, and Free Days.

FOCUS DAYS®

A Focus Day is a day in which you spend at least 80% of your time operating in your core genius, or primary area of expertise—interacting with people or processes that give you the highest payoffs for the time you invest. To be successful, you must schedule more Focus Days and hold yourself accountable for producing the results.

In the previous chapter, we discussed your core genius—that one thing you love to do and do so well, you hardly feel like charging people for it. It's

---

★The Entrepreneurial Time System and Free Days, Focus Days, Buffer Days are registered trademarks of The Strategic Coach, Inc. All rights reserved. Used with written permission. Learn more at strategiccoach.com.

"It's come to my attention, Wycliff, that you're actually planning a life outside the office."

effortless for you and a whole lot of fun. And if you could make money doing it, you'd make it your lifetime's work. Your core genius is your natural talent, the area where you shine.

My areas of genius are speaking, training, conducting seminars, coaching, writing, and editing. I do these things easily and well—and when I do them in a focused way, they're the things I get paid the most money for. For me, a Focus Day would be a day in which I spend 80% of the time speaking or leading a seminar for a fee, writing or editing a book (like this one), developing a new audio or video program, or coaching someone to achieve a greater level of success.

For Janet Switzer, a Focus Day is consulting with clients on their revenue-generation systems, developing knowledge products, or speaking to a group of consultants and business owners about launching an authoring and thought-leader career.

Your Focus Day might be spent designing a new line of clothing, making sales calls, negotiating deals, producing a loan package to send to a mortgage lender, painting, performing, or writing a grant proposal for a nonprofit organization. You want to do whatever you can to increase your number of Focus Days.

BUFFER DAYS®

A Buffer Day is a day when you prepare and plan for a Focus or Free Day—either by learning a new skill, locating a new resource, training your support team, delegating tasks and projects to others, or traveling to a work site. Buffer Days ensure that your Focus Days are as productive as possible.

For me, a Buffer Day might be spent taking a seminar to improve my training skills, planning how to maximize sales of our books and online courses, rehearsing a new speech, reading potential stories for a new anthology book, or delegating a project to a member of my support team. Yours might be seeking out a mentor, developing a new sales presentation, writing a brochure, preparing your studio for a recording session, interviewing a new job candidate, training an assistant, attending an industry or professional convention, or writing an employee manual. The key is to group all your Buffer Day activities into the same day of the week (rather than spread them over several days), so you are not diluting your Focus Days and Free Days.

FREE DAYS®

A Free Day extends from midnight to midnight and involves no work-related activity of any kind. It's a day completely free of business meetings, business-related phone calls, cell phone calls, e-mails, or reading work-related journals and documents.

On a true Free Day, you're not available to your staff, clients, or students for any kind of contact except for *true* emergencies—injury, death, flood, or fire. The truth is that most so-called emergencies aren't emergencies at all. They're simply employees, coworkers, and family members who don't have—or haven't been given—enough training, responsibility, or authority to handle the unexpected situations that arise. You have to set clear boundaries, stop rescuing people, and trust that they can handle things by themselves. When you train your employer, staff, coworkers, and family not to bother you on your Free Days, it forces them to become more self-reliant. It also forces them to grow in ability and self-confidence. If you are consistent over time, people will eventually get the message. This is ultimately a good thing because it frees you up to have more Free Days *and* more Focus Days.

FREE MEANS SOME DAYS *WITHOUT* THE KIDS, TOO

The question often arises about what to do with the children. For the most part, you need to take some time away from your children on a regular basis. If you can't afford a babysitter, ask a trusted relative to take them. We've asked both aunts and uncles and our nieces. If they are unavailable or unwilling, trade with other parents: You take their little ones for a weekend and they take yours on a different weekend. And don't make the mistake of calling every hour to see how they're doing. Let go, trust, and take care of yourself for a change.

FREE DAYS HELP YOU WORK HARDER... AND SMARTER

The value of regular Free Days is that you come back to your work refreshed and ready to tackle it with renewed vigor, enthusiasm, and creativity. To become truly successful, you need these breaks to allow yourself some distance from your normal day-to-day life—so you can become more creative in solving problems and generating breakthrough ideas.

I believe everyone's ultimate goal should be 130 to 150 days off each year. If you took every weekend off—doing no work whatsoever—you would instantly enjoy 104 vacation days. And if you found another 48 Free Days in the form of long weekends, holiday weeks, two-week vacations, and other opportunities, you could easily enjoy 150 Free Days to rest, recharge, and rejuvenate with no laptops, no e-mails, no documents, and no contact with your staff, coworkers, or boss.

It may take you a while to work up to that number, perhaps even years, but the main thing is to constantly work to increase your number of Free Days every year.

USE YOUR VACATION TIME

According to the Travel Industry Association of America, the average vacation in 2022 was about four days. Even more alarming, the Families and Work Institute reports that more than one fourth of all American employees *did not even use* their vacation time. And a Harris Interactive survey found that 57% of Americans had unused vacation time—up to two weeks' worth—in 2011. Why? They were afraid that their job might not be there when they returned.

Compare that with the concept of Free Days, which actually makes you more rested, more productive, *and more valuable to your employer.* Jane Moyer, a former Xerox Business Services' role-model manager and now at Starbucks, summarized perfectly the value of Free Days in this interview with *Fast Company* magazine:

> . . . every October, I spend some time on Cape Cod. I rent a cabin that's two blocks from the ocean, and I stay there for a week. The cabin has no phone or television. I don't get in my car, I don't listen to the radio, and I don't read newspapers. For the first couple of days, I go through withdrawal, but then I adjust. I cook, I read, I walk on the beach. It's absolutely glorious. On my way home, when I start thinking about work again, I see things differently. Work seems much less cluttered. One of the amazing things about getting away is that it helps me understand what's important and what's not.★

START SCHEDULING

The key to getting more Free Days and Focus Days in your life is to sit down and schedule them. By jotting down how many Focus Days, Buffer Days, and Free Days you spend every month right now, you can work to increase the number of Focus Days and true 24-hour Free Days on your calendar, and reduce the number of Buffer Days. With this kind of schedule, you'll find yourself creating greater results at work, enjoying more fulfillment in your personal life, and experiencing more balance between the two.

Here are some other steps you might want to take to begin implementing The Entrepreneurial Time System:

1. List the three best Focus Days you have ever had. Write down any common elements. This will give you valuable clues as to how to create more perfect Focus Days. Plan for them.
2. Meet with your boss, staff, and coworkers to discuss how to create more Focus Days where you can focus 80% of your time on using your areas of brilliance to produce your best results.

★From *Fast Company,* May 2000, page 101.

3. Meet with your friends or family and discuss how to create more true Free Days in your life.
4. Schedule at least four vacations—they can be long weekends or longer—for the next year. These can be as simple as a weekend camping trip, a weekend in San Francisco taking in the sights, a trip to the wine country, a weekend at the shore, a fishing trip, or a week visiting friends in a nearby state, or it can include that dream-of-a-lifetime vacation you have always wanted to take to California, Hawaii, Florida, Mexico, Europe, or Asia. If you don't plan it, it won't happen, so sit down and make a plan.
5. List the three best Free Days you have ever had and look for the common elements in those. Schedule more of those elements into your planned Free Days.

As our world gets more complicated and more pressured, you will have to be increasingly more conscious and intentional to structure your time in a way that takes full advantage of your talents and maximizes your results and your income. Start now to control your time and your life. Remember, you are in charge.

PRINCIPLE 41

BUILD A POWERFUL SUPPORT TEAM AND DELEGATE TO THEM

The ascent of Everest was not the work of one day, nor even of those few unforgettable weeks in which we climbed.... It is, in fact, a tale of sustained and tenacious endeavor by many, over a long period of time.

SIR JOHN HUNT
Scaled Mount Everest in 1953

Every high achiever has a powerful team of key staff members, consultants, vendors, and helpers who do the bulk of the work while he or she is free to create new sources of income and new opportunities for success. The world's greatest philanthropists, athletes, entertainers, professionals, and others also have people who manage projects and handle everyday tasks—enabling them to do more for others, hone their craft, practice their sport, and so on.

THE TOTAL FOCUS PROCESS

To help you clarify what you should be spending your time on and what you should be delegating to others, do the following exercise. Your goal is to find the top one, two, or three activities that best use your core genius, bring you the most money, and produce the greatest level of enjoyment.

1. Start by listing all those activities that occupy your time... whether they're business-related, personal, or related to your civic organizations or volunteer work. List even small tasks such as returning phone calls, filing, or photocopying.

2. Next, choose from this list those one, two, or three things you are particularly brilliant at, your special and unique talents, those things very few other people can do as well as you. Also choose from this list the three activities that generate the most income for you or your company. Any activities that you are brilliant at *and* that generate the most income for you or your company are the activities where you'll want to focus the most time and energy.
3. Finally, create a plan for delegating everything else to other people. Delegating takes time, training, and patience, but over time you can keep chipping away at the low-payoff, nonessential tasks on your list until you are doing less and less of those and more and more of what you are really good at. That is how you create a brilliant career.

SEEK OUT KEY "STAFF MEMBERS"

If you're a business owner—and remember, becoming an entrepreneur early in life is one of the hallmarks of the most successful individuals throughout modern history—start looking for key staff members now or train your existing staff members on the tasks you identified above. If you're a one-person business, start looking for a dynamic number-two person who could handle your projects, run your programs, book your sales transactions, and completely take over other tasks while you concentrate on what you do best. You can hire them outright as employees or have them work part time on a contract basis as your company grows. I've seen many future achievers find a top-flight business manager months sooner than they expected, only to see their business grow exponentially once they made a deal to bring that person on board. Often you'll discover that once you put the word out, the right person was already circulating in your universe—you just didn't know it.

If philanthropic pursuits or community projects are your "business," there are volunteers you can "hire" to help you. Consider college interns, who may work solely for class credit. We have several in our company. Or perhaps a local foundation can offer you staff support for your project. You never know until you ask.

And if you are a stay-at-home mom or dad, your most valuable "staff" will be your house cleaner, the teenage helper down the street, your babysitter, and others who can help you get away for time by yourself and with your spouse. A neighbor or babysitter could also do grocery shopping, get your car washed, pick up the kids, or pick up the laundry and dry cleaning—all for $20 to $25 an hour. If you're a single parent, these folks are even more important to your successful future and should be chosen with great care.

WHY YOU NEED PERSONAL ADVISORS

Our world has become a very complex place. Just filing your tax return, planning for retirement, rewarding your employees—even buying a home—has become more complicated than ever. That's why every high achiever has a powerful team of personal advisors to turn to for assistance, advice, and support. In fact, this team is so critical, it pays to begin assembling the team early on in your success journey.

Regardless of whether you own a business, work for someone else, or stay home and raise your children, you need personal advisors to answer questions, help you plan, ensure that you make the most of life's efforts, and more. Your personal advisors can walk you through challenges and opportunities, saving you time, effort, and usually money. Your team of advisors should include your banker, your lawyers, a high-net-worth certified public accountant, your investment counselor, your doctor, nutritionist, personal trainer, and the leader of your religious organization.

In fact, if you run a business, this principle takes on a whole new meaning. Too many business owners, for example, don't even have an accountant. They run their entire business on accounting software and never have any outside expert checking their numbers. They never form relationships with outside consultants who can free them up to pursue their core competency and help them grow.

If you're a teenager or a college student, your team might be your parents, your best friends, your football coach, your counselor—people who believe in you. Often with teens, we find that their parents aren't really a part of their core group, but instead are part of the enemy. Sometimes this is the teen's perception, but sometimes it's actually the way things are. If your parents are dysfunctional, alcoholic, or abusive, or if they're simply not there because they're workaholics or divorced, you need a team of friends and other adults in your corner. Often, it's a parent of another teen in your neighborhood.

If you're a working mom, your core group should include a good babysitter or day care provider. Not only should you investigate them thoroughly, but you should also have a backup resource. You should have a good pediatrician, and dentist, too, plus others who can support you in raising healthy, happy children as you pursue your career.

Athletes have their coterie of coaches, chiropractors, nutritionists, and performance consultants. They have, as part of their support team, people who specialize in designing diets for their body type and for their sport. They find trustworthy advisors and build and maintain those relationships over time.

Once you determine who members of this support team are, you can begin to build and nurture those relationships. Make sure team members are clear about what you expect from them *and that you are clear about what they expect from you*. Is this a paid relationship? What kind of working relationship is preferable? How can both of you be there when the other person needs you? How can team members help you grow and succeed?

And finally, how can you keep in touch with them and best maintain this relationship? I recommend that you create a schedule of monthly, quarterly, or semiannual meetings with every member of your team.

ONCE YOU'VE CHOSEN YOUR TEAM MEMBERS, TRUST THEM

If you don't have an assistant, you are one.

RAYMOND AARON
Author of *Double Your Income Doing What You Love*

If you have chosen with care, you can begin to offload anything and everything that takes you away from focusing on your core genius—even "personal" projects.

When Raymond Aaron sold his home and decided to move into an apartment, he delegated the entire project to his assistant. He told her to find a one-bedroom luxury apartment near his office with an exercise facility on the main floor. "Find it, negotiate the lease, and bring me the contract to sign," he said. "Then hire a moving van, get a check from my office to pay the movers, pack up the fragile items, supervise the movers, and drive behind them to my new home." He even had her hire an advance cleaning crew, arrange the furniture with the movers, unpack boxes, put everything away—and call Raymond when the move was complete.

And where was Raymond while his assistant was moving his house? On vacation in Florida!

Though we often fear that if someone else performs tasks for us, the job won't be done as well—the reality is there are people who *love* to do what you hate to do. And they often do a much better job than you would or *could* yourself—at a cost that is much lower than you might think.

In fact, thanks to modern technology, these people don't necessarily need to live nearby in order to help you. Numerous trustworthy websites such as Upwork* and Freelancer.com† will connect you with virtual assistants and freelance professionals who can help you with a single project or ongoing work. Instead of working locally at your office or home, they work remotely and stay connected with you via email, telephone, Skype, Zoom, or other digital means.

What could a virtual assistant or virtual freelancer do for you? Write or edit reports, speeches, manuscripts, or proposals. Create a radio commercial, professionally record a telemarketing voice broadcast, or develop a YouTube video about your products or services. Do research of all kinds. Correct your vacation photographs using Adobe Photoshop, then compile them into a hardcover photo book at Shutterfly. Answer your telephone, handle your email, respond to your product inquiries, manage your social media—plus so much more. Additionally, micro-job websites such as Fiverr feature professionals who charge as little at $5 per project—a sum literally anyone can afford. There's no excuse anymore for doing everything yourself.

---

*Upwork is by far the best-known website for connecting with virtual workers, with millions of freelancers in 180 countries. Upwork even helps manage payment for services, so if there is ever any dispute, you have a middleman to help you.

†Freelancer.com is a website that also helps you outsource your contract work at a very low price. They seem to specialize more in the technical areas of website development, web design, computer programming, app development, data entry, Internet marketing, and search engine optimization, as well as copywriting and graphic design.

PRINCIPLE 42

JUST SAY NO!

*You don't have to let yourself be terrorized
by other people's expectations of you.*

SUE PATTON THOELE
Author of *The Courage to Be Yourself*

Our world is a highly competitive and overstimulating place, and more and more concentration is needed every day just to stay focused on completing your daily tasks and pursuing your longer-term goals. Because of the explosion of communications technology, we are more accessible to more people than ever before. Complete strangers can reach you by telephone, cell phone, text, regular mail, e-mail, and social media. They can reach you at home, at work, and on your smartphone. If you're not there, they can leave messages on your voice mail. If you are there, they can interrupt you with call waiting.

It seems everyone wants a piece of you. Your kids want rides or to borrow the car, your coworkers want your input on projects that are not your responsibility, your boss wants you to work overtime to finish a report he needs, your sister wants you to take her kids for the weekend, your child's school wants you to be a driver for next week's field trip, your mother wants you to come over and fix her screen door, your best friend wants to talk about his impending divorce, and a local charity wants you to head up the annual luncheon committee. And an endless array of telemarketers want you to subscribe to the local newspaper, contribute to the nearby wildlife sanctuary, or transfer all of your credit card debt over to their new card. Even your pets are clamoring for more attention.

We suffer under project and productivity overload at work—taking on more than we can comfortably deliver in an unconscious desire to impress others, get ahead, and keep up with others' expectations. Meanwhile, our top priorities go unaddressed.

To be successful in achieving your goals and creating your desired lifestyle, you will have to get good at saying no to all of the people and distractions that would otherwise devour you. Successful people know how to say no without feeling guilty. To them, "No" is a complete sentence.

DON'T JUST DELEGATE, ELIMINATE!

If you are going to increase your results and your income, as well as increase the amount of Free Days in your life, you are going to have to eliminate those activities, requests, and other time-stealers that don't have a high payoff.

You will have to structure your work so that you are focusing your time, effort, energies, and resources only on projects, opportunities, and people that give you a huge reward for your efforts. You are going to have to create strong boundaries about what you will and won't do.

Start by creating what Jim Collins, author of *Good to Great,* calls a "*stop doing*" list. Most of us are busy but undisciplined. We are active but not focused. We are moving, but not always in the right direction. By creating a stop-doing list as well as a to-do list, you bring more discipline and focus into your life.

Write your stop-doing list as soon as possible. Then make the things on your list "policies." People respond to policies. They understand a policy as a boundary. They will respect you more for being clear about what you won't do. For example, some of my "don't do" policies are:

- I don't give endorsements for books of fiction.
- I don't schedule more than five talks in one month.
- I no longer coauthor books with first-time authors. Their learning curve is too time-consuming and expensive.
- I don't take any calls on Tuesdays and Thursdays. Those are writing or product development days.
- I don't lend my books to other people. They rarely come back, and they are the source of my livelihood, so I don't lend them out.
- I don't lend money. I am not a bank.
- I don't discuss charitable contributions over the phone. Send me something in writing.

IF SAYING NO IS SO IMPORTANT, THEN WHY IS IT SO HARD TO SAY?

Why do we find it so hard to say no to everybody's requests? As children, many of us learned that *no* was an unacceptable answer. Responding with *no* was cause for discipline. Later, in our careers, *no* may have been the reason for a poor evaluation or failing to move up the corporate ladder.

Yet highly successful people say no all the time—to projects, to crazy deadlines, to questionable priorities, and to other people's crises. In fact, they view the decision to say no as equally acceptable as the decision to say yes.

"No, Thursday's out. How about never—is never good for you?"

Others say no but will offer to refer you to someone else for help. Still others claim their calendar, family obligations, deadlines, and even finances as reasons why they must decline requests. At the office, achievers find other solutions to their coworkers' repeated emergencies, rather than becoming a victim of someone else's lack of organization and poor time management.

"IT'S NOT AGAINST YOU; IT'S FOR ME"

One response that I have found helpful in saying no to crisis appeals or time-robbing requests from people is "It's not against you; it's for me."

When the local PTA chairman calls with yet another weekend fund-raising event that needs your dedication, you can say, "You know, my saying no to you is not against you or what you are trying to accomplish. It's a very worthy cause, but recently I realized I've been overcommitting myself outside my home. So even though I support what you're doing, the fact is I've made a commitment to spend more time with my family. It's not against you; it's for us." Few people can get angry at you for making and standing by this higher commitment. In fact, they'll probably respect you for your clarity and your strength.

There are lots of valuable techniques you can learn that will make it easier to say no without feeling guilty. I recommend you read one of the several good books that address this issue in greater depth than I have space for here. The two best books are *When I Say No, I Feel Guilty,* by Manuel J. Smith, and *How to Say No Without Feeling Guilty,* by Patti Breitman and Connie Hatch.

SAY NO TO THE GOOD SO THAT YOU CAN SAY YES TO THE GREAT

Good is the enemy of great.
JIM COLLINS
Author of *Good to Great, Built to Last,* and *Great by Choice*

What a simple concept this is, yet you'd be surprised how frequently even the world's top entrepreneurs, professionals, educators, and civic leaders get caught up in projects, situations, and opportunities that are merely good, while the great is left out in the cold, waiting for them to make room in their lives. In fact, concentrating on merely the good often prevents the great from showing up, simply because there's no time left in our schedules to take advantage of any additional opportunity.

Is this your situation—constantly chasing after mediocre prospects or pursuing misguided schemes for success when you could be holding at bay opportunities for astounding achievement?

THE PARETO PRINCIPLE: WHEN 20% EQUALS 80%

If you surveyed your life and jotted down those activities that brought you the most success, the most financial gain, the most advancement, and the most enjoyment, you would discover that about 20% of your activity produces about 80% of your success. This phenomenon is the basis for the Pareto Principle, often referred to as the "law of the vital few," named after the nineteenth-century economist who discovered that 80% of the land in Italy was owned by 20% of the population. Later researchers discovered that 80% of an enterprise's revenue usually comes from 20% of its customers.*

STOP MAJORING IN THE MINORS

Instead of dedicating yourself—and your time—to mundane, nonproductive, time-stealing activity, imagine how rapidly you would reach your goals and improve your life if you said no to those time-wasting activities and instead focused on the 20% of activity that would bring you the most benefit.

What if instead of watching television, mindlessly surfing the Internet, running unnecessary errands, and addressing problems you could have avoided in the first place, you used the extra time to focus on your family, your marriage, your business, your breakthrough goal, starting a new income stream, or other more productive activities?

SYLVESTER STALLONE'S "ROCKY" BEGINNING

Sylvester Stallone knows how to say no to the good. After finishing the very first *Rocky* screenplay, Stallone encountered several producers who were interested in making it into a movie. But even though that alone would have made Stallone a lot of money, he insisted on playing the lead role, too. Even though other actors such as James Caan, Ryan O'Neal, and Burt Reynolds were considered to play Rocky Balboa, Stallone said no, and after finding backers willing to finance a shoestring budget of under $1 million, Stallone completed filming on location in just 28 days.

---

*See *The 80/20 Principle: The Secret to Success by Achieving More with Less* by Richard Koch (New York: Currency, 1998) for an illuminating exploration of the application of the 80/20 Rule to accelerating the achievement of your personal success.

Rocky went on to become the sleeper hit of 1976, earning over $225 million dollars and garnering Oscars for best picture and best director, as well as acting and writing nominations for Stallone, who took full charge of his golden opportunities and turned Rocky Balboa—and later John Rambo—into industry franchises that have grossed over $2 billion in revenues worldwide.

What could show up in your life if you said no to the good?

HOW CAN YOU DETERMINE WHAT'S TRULY GREAT, SO YOU CAN SAY NO TO WHAT'S MERELY GOOD?

1. **Start by listing your opportunities—one side of the page for *good* and the other side for *great*.** Seeing options in writing will help crystallize your thinking and determine what questions to ask, what information to gather, what your plan of attack might be, and so on. It will help you decide if an opportunity truly fits with your overall life purpose and passion or if it's just life taking you down a side road.
2. **Talk to advisors about this potential new pursuit.** People who have traveled the road before you have vast experience to share and hard-headed questions to ask about any new opportunity you might be contemplating. They can talk to you about expected challenges and help you evaluate the cost factor—that is, how much time, money, effort, stress, and commitment will be required.
3. **Test the waters.** Rather than just take a leap of faith that the new opportunity will proceed as you expect, conduct a small test, spending a limited amount of time and money. If it's a new career you're interested in, first seek part-time work or independent consulting contracts in that field. If it's a major move or volunteer project you're excited about, see if you can travel for a few months to your dream locale or find ways to immerse yourself in the volunteer work for several weeks before committing 100%.
4. **And finally, look at where you spend your time.** Determine if those activities truly serve your goals or if saying no would free up your schedule for more focused pursuits.

PRINCIPLE 43

BECOME A LEADER WORTH FOLLOWING

*The most dangerous leadership myth is that leaders are born—
that there is a genetic factor to leadership. That's nonsense;
in fact, the opposite is true. Leaders are made rather than born.*

WARREN BENNIS
Founding chairman of the Leadership Institute at
the University of Southern California

Whether you own a business, teach school, manage a small group, coach an athletic team, or are working to advance a worthwhile cause, you need to enroll others in order to achieve the success you want. This not only requires you to hold a vision of what success is, it also requires you to practice leadership skills that will inspire others to want to help you reach that goal.

Because our success often requires the help of others, successful people—not surprisingly—are also successful leaders. They know how to communicate their vision in exciting and compelling terms. They've mastered the skill of motivating others to jump on board with full commitment. They recognize potential in their people, coach their team members to go above and beyond, and routinely acknowledge others' positive contribution. And while great leaders must demand accountability from the people they lead, they also hold *themselves* accountable for their contribution to the result.

In the process of leading, great leaders also transform their followers. They stimulate and inspire others to deliver extraordinary outcomes, of course. But they *also* help these followers *develop and grow into leaders themselves*. That's the true definition of great leadership.

Exceptional leaders aren't born that way. They become exceptional by developing a unique set of attitudes and skills that are both learnable and teachable.*

WHY BECOME A LEADER?

Becoming a leader gives you the opportunity to magnify your impact in the world. It allows you to leverage the hearts and actions of others toward the achievement of goals and objectives that you care about. It allows you to produce bigger results faster than you could ever do on your own. And while we're not all destined to become leaders on a level with John F. Kennedy, Mahatma Gandhi, Nelson Mandela, Steve Jobs, or Mother Teresa, we can all learn to develop our leadership skills for positive impact in our organizations and our local communities.

In fact, knowing how to be an effective leader will make you more successful in any role—whether you are climbing the corporate ladder, building a network marketing downline, working as a social change agent, coaching a Little League team, volunteering for a civic group, or simply organizing a church event. So let's take a look at some of the basics of becoming the kind of leader whom people will want to work with and follow.

Become the kind of leader that people would follow voluntarily; even if you had no title or position.

BRIAN TRACY
Author of *Maximum Achievement* and *The Ultimate Success Guide*

BEHAVIOR #1: KNOW YOUR OWN STRENGTHS AND WEAKNESSES

One of the most distinguishing qualities of a great leader is their dedication to understanding *themselves*. When you have a clear sense of who you are—your strengths and weaknesses—and know the impact your behavior has on others, your ability to lead others will improve.

---

*Kathleen Seeley is the leadership expert I consulted in developing this chapter. She trains many of the most forward-thinking companies in the world, and she is dedicated to helping leaders design sustainable, values-driven cultures. She is an executive coach, motivational speaker, and Associate Faculty Member in the School of Leadership at Royal Roads University in Victoria, British Columbia, Canada.

For one thing, self-awareness lets you be realistic about your ability to contribute (or detract) from the outcome of a project. If you know you're not the best graphic designer, for example, why impose your ideas on the company's brochure or website—especially when you could easily empower (and rely on) others to do this job better than you? Or if keeping your people accountable to meeting deadlines seems a constant headache—especially on top of your own duties—why not put systems in place that do the follow-up and reporting for you, such as weekly accountability meetings, project management software, calendar reminders, and more? And if you are shy, introverted, or downright fearful about negotiating anything, why not delegate that to people who love the game of bargaining for a great deal?

In fact, just as there are things *you* hate to do or aren't good at, there are people who *love* these tasks and are good at them because it's their passion. Knowing your strengths and weaknesses gives you the ability to discern when your skills will add value—or not—and keeps you open to delegating and listening to people with other points of view. Not only does this allow lots of creative ideas to emerge from your team, it simply makes your work easier because you'll never have to struggle with tasks you shouldn't be doing in the first place.

Knowing your own strengths and weaknesses also helps you keep your emotions in check during times of intense pressure or crisis. Self-awareness ensures you won't get swept away in the emotion of a situation—rather, you'll be able to respond with clear, compassionate, and fearless action. And by remaining calm, you also create a sense of safety for others—especially in times of crisis or rapid change.

All good leaders possess a heightened sense of awareness—an ability to read situations in which they find themselves and act accordingly. Great leaders take this one step further. They are not only aware; they are also self-aware.

LES MCKEOWN
Author of *Predictable Success: Getting Your Organization on the Growth Track—and Keeping It There*

Of course, the key to being self-aware as a leader is your *willingness* to be wrong, to not know everything, to recognize that you have certain biases, and to see where your opinions may be simply getting in the way. No one has all the answers, and great leaders admit there is always plenty to learn.

They also listen to feedback.

In fact, great leaders know that when you are *willing* to admit your own mistakes and genuinely listen to critical feedback—without rationalizing, justifying, or placing blame—you get to turn these moments into learning opportunities for yourself and "teachable moments" for your team. Instead of battles, you create a more open and collaborative culture among your team members—without the pressure or fear of anyone pretending to know it all. This kind of authenticity and transparency ultimately gives *others* permission to be open about their weaknesses, fears, and learning needs, too. No one will misrepresent their abilities to you, once you set a standard for openness.

BEHAVIOR #2: HOLD YOURSELF ACCOUNTABLE ... AND OTHERS, TOO

Essential to your success in leading others is a commitment to taking 100% responsibility for your own actions and results. When you consistently follow through on your own commitments, you begin to build others' trust in your leadership. To be trusted, you must be reliable, punctual—and a person who keeps your agreements.

Do you arrive at meetings on time? Do you deliver your part of projects completed and on deadline? Do you abide by promises made to your team members and others? Do you react in the same steady manner to every crisis? Do you soberly consider new opportunities in light of goals your team is already working on? These are the hallmarks of a leader who is responsible and consistent—versus one who is perpetually late, unprepared, emotional or continually led astray by the latest fad.

Of course, no one is perfect—including leaders. But while *perfection* might be desirable, *consistency* will be far more impactful because it builds integrity and reliability with your team. It makes you a trustworthy leader. Naturally, there will be times when you fall short on your promises or are unable to keep an agreement. In such cases, acknowledge your shortcomings to the team members involved and make plans to fix the problem—a move which will help you grow in integrity as a leader.

Taking 100% responsibility also extends to situations that do not turn out as planned, but that were under your control. In such cases, don't blame others for disappointing outcomes that you were in charge of or could have prevented. Instead, be accountable—reflect, learn, and adjust your behavior, so you can take responsibility for what happens *next*. If you blame others for missed targets or other failures of leadership, you will not only damage the trust of your team, you'll substantially reduce your personal power.

In addition to taking responsibility for your part of bad outcomes, you

"Sometimes it's smooth sailing, sometimes it gets rough and stormy and sometimes you sink to the bottom with your crew. That's why it's called leader*ship*."

must have the courage to hold others accountable for their actions and results. Accountability is a major factor in whether people feel empowered, perform effectively, take initiative, and act responsibly. But when people on your team are not creating the results you want, you must have the courage to confront what isn't working and engage the people involved in what can be a difficult and uncomfortable conversation about accountability and getting back on track with the goal. Don't shy away from these difficult conversations. Instead, have the courage to hold people accountable for their results.

BEHAVIOR #3: INSPIRE YOUR TEAM WITH A CLEAR, COMPELLING, CONTINUOUS VISION

The very essence of leadership is that you have to have a vision. It's got to be a vision you articulate clearly and forcefully on every occasion. You can't blow an uncertain trumpet.

REVEREND THEODORE HESBURGH
President Emeritus of the University of Notre Dame

To inspire others to work tirelessly to help accomplish your goal, you must first have a clear and compelling vision of the future. What will you and your team ultimately achieve? By when? What will everyone gain when the goal is reached? Is it honorable, beneficial, ethical, and uplifting? What's so compelling about it? What else will also be achieved as your team is striving for this major goal?

To get other people's buy-in, you'll also need to articulate who your team *will become* as they learn and grow on the path to achieving your vision. Your team must be able to see *themselves* in the future as better, smarter, stronger, more valued, and more confident. Defining that outcome—plus other benefits people will experience—is an important part of your clear and compelling vision.

Secondly, your belief in your vision must be unshakable. That means that you must believe it's not only possible—but also desirable, essential, and inevitable.

This kind of belief in your vision is simply a choice. You just choose to believe it and then communicate it with certainty.

President John F. Kennedy had a vision of the United States putting a man on the moon by "the end of the decade"—1970. Nelson Mandela had a vision of a South Africa without apartheid. Mahatma Gandhi had a vision of India without British rule achieved with nonviolence. Aung San Suu Kyi, an opposition leader in her home country of Myanmar (Burma) and the winner of the 1991 Nobel Prize for Peace, had a vision of her country governed by a democratically elected civilian government rather than a military dictatorship.

And in the world of business, Bill Gates had a vision of "a personal computer in every home and on every desk." Steve Jobs, creator of the iPod and iTunes, had a vision of revolutionizing the music industry and making it easy to download single songs and "put 1,000 songs in your pocket." Sara Blakely, the billionaire founder of Spanx, when she was going door-to-door selling fax machines in her twenties, had a vision of being the rich owner of Spanx, manufacturing and selling more comfortable and attractive hosiery products for women.

Every one of these great leaders communicated their vision with passion and conviction.

You, too, must be able to tell the story of your vision so convincingly that it captures the imagination, hearts, and hands of others. Your words must communicate the certainty of the goal—which will carry your team when they lose confidence in themselves and the process. You must also bring to the discussion your own natural passion and enthusiasm for the goal—something that cannot be faked and which is highly contagious.

One book that will help you tell powerful, compelling stories—ones that communicate your vision and enroll the people you need to achieve it—is *Tell to Win: Connect, Persuade, and Triumph with the Hidden Power of Story* by Peter Guber, former president of Sony Pictures Entertainment whose films have earned 155 Academy Awards nominations and generated more than $10.1 billion worldwide.* Not surprisingly, Guber says, the most successful companies and initiatives are built when leaders form personal and emotional connections with employees, partners, customers, volunteers, and suppliers who can help. Stories about your vision, your products, and even yourself produce that deep emotional reaction that is so important in creating a bond with others.

BEHAVIOR #4: LISTEN FOR POSSIBILITY

Once people are enrolled in the vision, a great leader will listen to his team—not only to hear their thoughts and input but also to make sure they feel heard. People want to know they make a difference and that their insights and opinions matter. When you develop your listening skills, you'll be more present in the moment, you'll be curious to hear other options, you'll be able to truly hear what emerges from a discussion, and you'll be open to a true dialogue with your team—instead of simply delivering orders or explaining the game plan.

This requires a willingness to be transformed by what you hear. But more important, it requires you to shift your focus from listening for "the right way or the wrong way" to listening for what is possible.

I call this "listening for possibility."

---

*Tell to Win: Connect, Persuade, and Triumph with the Hidden Power of Story by Peter Guber (New York: Crown Business, 2011).

There is no question that our culture rewards great speakers—people who can inspire and command an audience. But while being a passionate speaker can be a valuable skill, in the long run, *effective listening* may be a more valuable skill for leaders. In a meeting, when you're talking, you're merely repeating or reporting what you already know; nothing new is created. But when you listen intently, you can co-create new approaches, new outcomes, and new benefits from the ideas that you hear. If you find yourself formulating a response or improving on someone's idea while they are speaking, learn to be patient. Stop and truly listen. And let new possibilities emerge.

People don't need to be managed; they need to be unleashed.
RICHARD FLORIDA
Director of the Martin Prosperity Institute at the
University of Toronto's Rotman School of Management

One of my early models for effective leadership was Dr. Billy Sharp, the president of the W. Clement and Jesse V. Stone Foundation where I worked when I was 26. I admired his commitment to always be learning, his willingness to listen to the input of others, and his commitment to empower everyone on the staff to do the same. He always asked, "What do *you* think? What would *you* do? Why?" I vividly remember one day being asked to sit in on a meeting Dr. Sharp had scheduled with an expert on values. He knew that several of us had read this man's books and were interested in his work. Being only 26 at the time, it was a great thrill to be invited to sit in on a meeting with the president of the foundation and this well-known expert. When the three-hour meeting was over, and everyone else had left the room, I said to Dr. Sharp, "You asked this man question after question for several hours, and you never once talked about your research or the work we are doing here at the foundation. How come?"

He answered, "I already know what I know. I wanted to learn what he knew." That was a pivotal moment in my learning to be a better leader. It isn't about impressing others with how much I know. Ask more questions. Listen to *everybody*. Look for the underlying themes and patterns. Dr. Sharp taught me that it takes input from a lot of people to see the whole truth of any situation, to value curiosity, to be open to being changed during a dialogue, and to honor and appreciate everybody for their input.

Dr. Sharp communicated his belief in our ability to contribute by intently listening to each of our perspectives. He truly cared about our point of view. And because we felt valued, we always tried to do our best—to be worthy of his trust in us. As a result he got our best efforts.

Another reason to listen intently is that you'll often hear a story behind the story—that is, people's fears, insecurities, even judgments. When people feel they're not being heard or their true concerns are not being addressed, resentment builds to the point where people can become toxic to the rest of the team. While hearing the real story often takes empathy (an essential leadership skill), you should also listen for tension, disappointment, or indifference. Great leaders address these real problems as quickly as possible—which results in more committed and more engaged people working on your cause.

BEHAVIOR #5: COACH OTHERS TO TAKE A LEADERSHIP ROLE

The most essential work of the leader is to create more leaders.
MARY PARKER-FOLLETT
Social worker and pioneer in organizational theory and behavior

As a leader today, you will face increasing levels of uncertainty and complexity—that's just how the world works. You can't possibly know or control everything. So one way to overcome this is to coach your people to take a leadership role in their part of the project.

Instead of simply directing a preset plan, coaching people into action and helping them develop their own leadership skills means not only that you get to share decision making but also that you build a team of smart, self-confident, and self-directed people who can respond quickly to changing conditions and circumstances.

Growing a team of your own top-notch leaders simply makes your life easier.

And the most useful skill for growing other leaders is *coaching*. Through deep listening and skillful questioning, you can help others discover their own solutions to problems and opportunities. Instead of being the only person figuring out what to do next, when you use coaching to help others develop their own solutions, you are also helping them develop their own problem-solving skills. To any leader who has been bombarded with the simplest and most mundane problems to solve, this idea of empowering your people with their own leadership skills will be a relief.

So how can you coach your people to become leaders in their own right?

Start by asking your people to correctly define the problem. This gets them fully engaged in the process and helps them "take ownership" of the problem as one that *they* need to solve. Studies show that once a problem or challenge is *theirs,* it will be solved more efficiently and stay solved longer if you allow your team to create the solution. You provide direction only when they have reached the limits of their experience or training. Give people the tools and information they need to solve problems—then let them stretch.

One example of a series of coaching questions★ I often use with my people is something I call the "Difficult or Troubling Situation" exercise:

1. What is a difficult or troubling situation you are dealing with?
2. How are you creating or allowing it to happen?
3. What are you pretending not to know?
4. What is the payoff for keeping it like it is?
5. What would you rather be experiencing?
6. What actions will you take to create that?
7. By when will you take that action?

★You'll find this exercise in my book *Coaching for Breakthrough Success: Proven Techniques for Making Impossible Dreams Possible* by Jack Canfield and Dr. Peter Chee (New York: McGraw-Hill Professional, 2013).

Here's an example of what this series of questions might produce.

1. What is a difficult or troubling situation you are dealing with?
   Everyone seems to always come late to the meetings I run.
2. How are you creating or allowing it to happen?
   I have not made it clear that it is important to start on time. I usually wait for the people who are late to arrive so that the people who are there on time don't see any reason to be on time, and so they start coming late, too.
3. What are you pretending not to know?
   That people are not going to take the starting time seriously if I don't.
4. What is the payoff for keeping it like it is?
   I don't have to confront anyone about being late. I get to complain about how it is their fault.
5. What would you rather be experiencing?
   Getting the meetings started on time with a lot of positive energy.
6. What actions will you take to create that?
   —I'll send a memo stating that from now on we will start on time.
   —I'll find a way to reward people for being on time by showing a funny video from YouTube, maybe having a drawing for a $50 bill right at the beginning of the meeting for anyone who is on time. Make it fun and exciting to show up on time.
7. By when will you take that action?
   I'll write the memo today and have a drawing for a $50 bill at the next meeting.

This is just one example of the kind of question that gets people to take more responsibility for how they have created or allowed an unsatisfactory situation and how they can create more of what they want.

Ken Blanchard, author of *The One Minute Manager Meets the Monkey*,* writes that leaders often become overwhelmed by monkeys on their back—that is, projects and problems that don't belong to them. When a team member comes to you with a problem and you agree to do something about it, the monkey is off their back and onto yours. You've suddenly taken ownership of the problem.

Don't let this be your outcome. Coach your people to develop their own problem-solving and leadership skills instead, and let them solve more problems—thereby creating more time and space for you to focus on what *you* need to do to accomplish *your* vision.

---

*The One Minute Manager Meets the Monkey by Kenneth Blanchard, William Oncken Jr., and Hal Burrows (New York: Quill William Morrow, 1989).

BEHAVIOR #6: MAINTAIN AN ATTITUDE OF GRATITUDE

Whether you are leading a team of executives, athletes, community volunteers, school parents, or family game night, everyone needs to be acknowledged for what they do and who they are. Practicing gratitude and acknowledging others is the easiest way for a leader to build trust, enthusiasm, and commitment in those around you.

Numerous studies indicate that 80% of employees report that they are motivated to work harder when their employer shows appreciation for their work, while only 17% of people feel they are appreciated enough by their boss. And more than 50% of people would stay longer at their job if they felt more appreciation from their manager or boss.

So whether or not you feel you're too busy, too uncomfortable, or too unappreciated yourself, you need to schedule time and build in systems and rituals to appreciate people more often and more consistently. See Principle 53: "Practice Uncommon Appreciation" for details on how to more effectively appreciate people both at home and at work.

Developing an attitude of gratitude and appreciating the people you lead returns tremendous benefits. Scientists are now documenting the health benefits from practicing gratitude and are finding that those who consistently acknowledge and thank others have lower levels of stress, are more optimistic, and are less frequently drawn into anger, bitterness, and frustration. Gratitude and appreciation improves mood, makes you feel lighter, and helps you experience less stress. You simply cannot hold negative and positive emotions at the same time. Those around you will enjoy the same positive benefits, resulting in increased motivation, more involvement, and greater commitment to your project or cause.

So don't underestimate the power of a simple "thank-you" in every part of your life—be it at the dinner table or in the boardroom. My friend and coauthor of *The Power of Focus,* Les Hewitt, carries notecards with him at all times—then writes a sentence or two of appreciation or acknowledgment whenever he encounters extraordinary service or meets a valuable new business contact. He even carries postage stamps with him so that his note is often waiting for the new acquaintance upon their return to their office.

Begin cultivating your attitude of gratitude, and over time you'll not only transform your perspective but you'll also attract other like-minded, optimistic people into your life and your circle of influence.

PRINCIPLE 44

CREATE A NETWORK OF MENTORS AND OTHERS WHO WILL UP-LEVEL YOU

Study anyone who's great, and you'll find that they apprenticed to a master, or several masters. Therefore, if you want to achieve greatness, renown, and superlative success, you must apprentice to a master.

ROBERT ALLEN
Self-made multimillionaire and coauthor of *The One Minute Millionaire*

Despite some of the best information available on how to accomplish any task, most people still tend to ask their friends, neighbors, coworkers, and siblings for advice on key issues they may be facing. Too often, they ask the advice of others who have never triumphed over the specific hardship they are facing or who have never succeeded in their specific area of endeavor.

As I pointed out in Principle 9, success leaves clues. Why not take advantage of all the wisdom and experience that already exists by finding a mentor—or two or three—who have already been down the road you want to travel? All you have to do is ask.

One of the main strategies of the successful is that they constantly seek out guidance and advice from experts in their field. Set aside some time and make a list of the people you would like to ask to mentor you. Then approach them and ask for their help.

DETERMINE IN ADVANCE WHAT YOU WANT FROM A MENTOR

Though it may seem daunting at first to contact successful people and ask for ongoing advice and assistance, it's easier than you think to enlist the mentorship of those who are far ahead of you in the areas in which you'd like to succeed.

What mentors do more than anything, says famed speaker and bestselling author Les Brown, is help you see possibilities. In other words, mentors help you overcome "possibility blindness" both by acting as a role model for you and by conveying a certain level of expectation as they communicate with you.

When Les started his speaking career in the early 1980s, he sent a cassette tape of his earliest keynote speech to the late Dr. Norman Vincent Peale, the world-renowned speaker and publisher of *Guideposts* magazine. That cassette tape led to a long and fruitful relationship for Les, as Dr. Peale not only took Les under his wing and counseled him on his speaking style but also quietly opened doors and helped Les get important speaking engagements. Suddenly, though Les was a virtual unknown on the circuit, speakers' bureaus began calling him for bookings, even raising his rate to $5,000 per speech from the modest $700 Les had been charging.

As Les recounts the story, Norman Vincent Peale was the first person to tell Les he could make it big in the speaking industry.

"He spoke more to my heart than to my mind," said Les. "While I was doubting myself, my abilities, my lack of education, and my background, Dr. Peale said, 'You have the right stuff. You have everything it takes. Just continue to speak from your heart and you will do well.'"

That's when Les realized the value of having a mentor. And though their relationship consisted only of brief phone conversations and Les's occasionally trailing after Dr. Peale to learn his speaking style, in the end it meant more to both men than they knew at the time.

During his last public speech at age 95, Dr. Peale used one of his protégé's oft-repeated phrases: "Shoot for the moon because even if you miss, you'll land among the stars."

Perhaps like Les, you just need someone to open doors for you. Or perhaps you need a referral to a technical expert who can help you build a new service for your company. Maybe you simply need validation that the path you're pursuing is the right one. A mentor can help you with all of these things, but you need to be prepared to ask for specific advice.

DO YOUR HOMEWORK

One of the easiest ways to research the names and backgrounds of people who have been successful in your area of interest is to read industry magazines, search the Internet, ask trade association executive directors, attend trade shows and conventions, call fellow entrepreneurs, or approach others who operate in your industry or profession.

Look for mentors who have the kind of well-rounded experience you need to tackle your goal. When you start seeing a pattern of the same few people being recommended, you know you've identified your short list of possible mentors.

Janet Switzer regularly mentors people on how to grow their business. When Lisa Miller of CRA Management Group called Janet, she was just about to sign away a large percentage of her revenues to someone she thought would help her develop a new area of her business. Janet showed Lisa how to instantly accomplish the same goal without outside parties and even helped her land new business from existing clients, accelerating Lisa's company growth plan by four months and earning her hundreds of thousands of extra dollars.

To contact possible mentors like Janet and ensure a successful conversation once you do, make a list of specific points you'd like to cover in your first conversation, such as why you'd like them to mentor you and what kind of help you might be looking for. Be brief, but be confident, too.

The truth is that successful people like to share what they have learned with others. It is a human trait to want to pass on wisdom. Not everyone will take the time to mentor you, but many will if asked. You simply need to make a list of the people you would like to have as your mentor and ask them to devote a few minutes a month to you.

Some will say no, but some will say yes. Keep asking people until you get a positive response.

Les Hewitt, who founded the Achievers Coaching Program, coached the owner of a small trucking company who wanted to ask one of the major players in the trucking industry to be his mentor. The mentor was delighted to be asked, and he ended up helping the young man's company grow exponentially. His original script is one you might imitate:

> Hello, Mr. Johnston, my name is Neil. We haven't met yet. And I know you're a busy man, so I'll be brief. I own a small trucking business. Over the years, you have done a fantastic job building your business into one of the largest companies in our industry. I'm sure you had some real challenges when you were first starting out. Well, I'm still in those early stages, trying to figure everything out. Mr. Johnston, I would really appreciate it if you would consider being my mentor. All that would mean is spending ten minutes on the phone with me once a month, so I could

ask you a few questions. I'd really appreciate it. Would you be open to that?

If you are a small-business owner, or are contemplating starting a business, you should contact your local chapter of SCORE (Service Corps of Retired Executives). Working in partnership with the U.S. Small Business Administration, SCORE is an extensive, national network of over 10,000 retired and working volunteers providing free business counseling and advice as well as low-cost workshops as a public service to all types of businesses, in all stages of development, from idea to start-up to success. You can find one of their 250 chapter offices at score.org. Another source of free business advice and counseling for small-business owners is Small Business Development Centers, a service of the U.S. Small Business Administration. They have 62 offices across the country waiting to serve you. Find out more at sba.gov/sbdc.

VALUABLE ADVICE

Jason Dorsey was a typical college student when he unexpectedly met his first mentor, a local entrepreneur who had been asked to speak to his business class at the University of Texas. When Brad challenged the class by defining success as something greater than just making lots of money, Jason was intrigued and risked asking him to be his mentor.

During their first meeting, Brad asked Jason about his plans. He replied that he planned to finish college, work on the New York Stock Exchange, get an MBA, start his own business, and eventually retire at 40. Once retired, he planned to work with hard-to-reach youth to make sure they got a good education and a respectable job.

Hearing this, Brad asked Jason how old he would be by the time he got around to helping these young people. Jason guessed he'd be about 45. Then Brad asked a life-changing question: "Why wait twenty-five years to start doing what you really want to do? Why not start now? The longer you wait, the more difficult it might be for young people to relate to you."

Brad's observation made sense, but Jason was only 18 and living in a college dorm. He asked, "How do you think I could best help people my own age if I started now?"

"Write a book they will actually want to read," replied Brad. "Tell them your secrets for feeling good about yourself even when everyone else is so negative. Tell them what it takes to ask someone to be your mentor. Tell them why you have so many job opportunities and you're only 18 years old."

So on January 7, 1997, at 1:58 A.M., Jason started writing his book. Because he didn't know he couldn't do it, he completed the first draft of *Graduate to Your Perfect Job* just three weeks later. Jason published the book himself, started speaking at schools, and began mentoring other young people. By the time he was 25, he had spoken to over 500,000 people, been featured on NBC's *Today* show three times, and seen his first book become a course in over 1,500 schools. Jason is such a compelling speaker and motivator that soon the schools were hiring him to train their teachers and counselors as well. He is known as the Gen Y Guy, and his latest venture is a new company that helps executives and managers learn how to motivate and retain young employees. Best of all, Jason is still learning from his mentors—all five of them.

When Jason was only 26 years old, he won the Austin Under 40 Entrepreneur of the Year Award in the category of education. Today, at 47, Jason speaks worldwide—from India and Mexico to Norway and Egypt—to companies such as Mercedes-Benz, Four Seasons Hotels, SAS, and Visa. He's given over 1,000 speeches and seminars to audiences as large as 16,000 people, and he's written three more books—*Y-Size Your Business, Zconomy: How Gen Z Will Change the Future of Business and What to Do About It,* and *My Reality Check Bounced!*

Just think, if Jason had not taken the risk to ask a stranger to be his mentor, he probably would have just been graduating from his MBA program two years after already winning the Austin Under 40 Entrepreneur of the Year Award.

BE PREPARED TO RETURN THE FAVOR

Be prepared to give your mentors something in return. Even if it's something simple such as keeping them updated on industry information or calling with new opportunities that might benefit them, look for ways to give to your mentors. Help others, too. What a great reward to any mentor—to eventually have their former protégé out in the world mentoring others!

ASK SOMEONE WHO HAS ALREADY DONE IT

Success leaves clues.
ANTHONY ROBBINS
Motivational speaker and author of *Awaken the Giant Within*

When I was promoting the first edition of this book in 2005, I was scheduled to be on a morning news show in Dallas, Texas. While I was in the green room getting my makeup put on, I asked the makeup artist, as I often do with almost everyone I meet, "What is your dream goal?"

"Oh, I want to own my own salon," she replied.

"That's great. What are you doing to make that happen?"

"Nothing."

"That's a bad strategy," I said. "Why not?"

"I don't know what I have to do to own my own salon."

"Well," I said, "I have a radical idea that might help."

"What's that?" she asked.

"Why don't you go find someone who already owns their own salon and then ask them how they did it."

"Wow! That's a great idea," she exclaimed.

It never ceases to amaze me that people don't figure this out earlier, but at least you now know what to do when you don't know what to do. Go ask someone who has already done it.

HELP BREAKING THE WORLD RECORD

When 43-year-old Austrian skydiver Felix Baumgartner decided to break the records for the longest and fastest freefall, he asked retired U.S. Air Force Colonel Joseph Kittinger, the previous world record holder, who was now 84 years old, to help him break the record that Joe set in 1960.

Joe, willing to help someone younger break his own records, readily agreed. In addition to mentoring him, he also played the role of capcom (capsule communications) as Mission Control's primary point of radio contact with Felix during the ascent of the helium-filled balloon that lifted him 24 miles (39 km) above the Earth.

On October 14, 2012, Baumgartner jumped from 127,852 feet (about 24 miles) for the highest skydive ever—more than 4 miles higher than Kittinger's record-breaking jump of 19.5 miles in 1960. With Joe's help and supported by the Peak Performance Team at Red Bull, Baumgartner broke the records for the highest manned balloon flight, longest jump (9 minutes and 9 seconds), and fastest freefall at 833 miles per hour (1,357.64 km/h), achieving Mach 1.25 and becoming the first person to break the sound barrier outside a vehicle before landing safely in the desert of New Mexico after his death-defying 4-minute, 19-second freefall.

Despite the momentous day, there was one record Felix didn't shatter. After problems with his helmet fogging and falling faster than even he expected, he stuck with the contingency plan of pulling the chute early at 5,000 feet, which kept him from reaching the longest freefall record. But he said he was happy to leave that record intact for his mentor. Fifty-three years after he set it, the 4-minute, 36-second record still belongs to Joe Kittinger.

NETWORK YOUR WAY TO SUCCESS

Networking is the single most powerful marketing tactic to accelerate and sustain success for any individual or organization!

ADAM SMALL
Founder of Nashville Emerging Leaders

Aside from mentors, there are many other people who can also help you up-level your game—people who can be found through constant and proactive networking. In fact, one of the most important skills for success in today's world, especially for entrepreneurs and business owners, is networking. Jim Bunch, the creator of the Ultimate Game of Life, once stated, "Your network will determine your net worth." In my life this has proven to be true. The more time I have spent consciously building and nurturing my network of advisers, colleagues, clients, students, customers, and fans, the more successful I have become.

Business and careers are built on relationships, and relationships form when people meet and interact with each other over time in an authentic and caring way. And as I'm sure you are aware, statistics confirm over and over that people prefer to do business with people they know, like, and trust.

Here are some reasons to get more involved in networking if you are a business owner.

Generating referrals and increased business: The referrals that you get through networking are normally high quality and most of the time are even prequalified for you. Over time you can follow up on these referrals and turn them into clients. So you get much higher quality leads from networking than from other forms of marketing. This opportunity to increase sales is probably the biggest reason people network, but there are other advantages as well.

Expanding opportunities: When you get together with other motivated business owners, there is an opportunity for things like joint ventures, client leads, partnerships, speaking and writing opportunities, business or asset sales, investment opportunities, and much more to emerge.

Creating connections: The old adage "It's not WHAT you know, but WHO you know" is so true in business. If you want a really successful business, then you need to have a great source of relevant connections in your network that you can call on when you need them.

Networking will provide you with a great source of connections and really open the door to talk to influential people you might not otherwise be able to connect with. And remember, it's not just about the person you are directly networking with; that person will already have other complete networks he or she belongs to that you can tap into as well.

And, as we'll discuss in a moment, it's not just what you know or who you know, it's how well you know each other that counts.

Obtaining useful advice: Having like-minded business owners to talk to also gives you the opportunity to get advice on all sorts of things related to your business or even your personal life. Networking is a great way to tap into advice and expertise that you wouldn't otherwise be able to access.

I asked my friend Ivan Misner, whom CNN has called the father of modern networking, to share his VCP Process® of networking with you here, because it addresses one of the major mistakes people make when they network. Ivan is the founder and Chief Visionary Officer of BNI (Business Network International), the world's largest referral organization, with over 318,000 members in more than 11,000 chapters in 79 countries. BNI has fostered more than 5 million referrals a year, resulting in $22.1 billion dollars' worth of business generated for its members.

NETWORKING IS ALL ABOUT RELATIONSHIPS
BY DR. IVAN MISNER*

Speaking at a recent networking event attended by more than nine hundred people, I started my presentation by asking the audience: "How many of you came here today hoping to do a little business—maybe even make a sale?" The overwhelming majority of people raised their hands.

Then I asked, "How many of you are here today hoping to buy something?" No one raised a hand—not one single person!

This is the great disconnect about networking.

If you're attending networking events hoping to sell something, you're dreaming. Don't confuse direct selling with networking. Effective networking is all about developing relationships.

Of course, there will always be someone who says, "But, Ivan, I made a sale by attending a networking event!"—but for most people stumbling upon a new customer or making an on-the-spot sale happens about as often as a solar eclipse. And when most people at the event are also trying to sell (which means virtually no one is there to buy), you're crazy if you think the odds are in your favor to "sell" at a networking event.

So why go? You go because networking is more about farming than it is about hunting. It's about developing relationships with other business professionals. Sometimes you'll want to attend a networking event to increase your visibility; other times you go to establish further credibility with people you know; and sometimes you might attend simply to meet a longtime friend or associate, to further that business and move to profitability.

In any case, truly successful networkers focus more on moving through the VCP Process® than on closing deals.

VISIBILITY

The first phase of growing a relationship is visibility: You and another individual become aware of each other. In business terms, this individual—who is a potential source of future referrals or even a potential customer—has

---

*Dr. Ivan Misner is a *New York Times* bestselling author. He is the founder and Chief Visionary Officer of BNI (bni.com), the world's largest business networking organization, and is also the senior partner for the Referral Institute, an international referral training company. For more details on Dr. Misner—and his latest books, including *Networking Like a Pro, The 29% Solution, Who's in Your Room*, and *Work Your Network with the 4 Cs*—visit ivanmisner.com.

just become aware of the nature of your business, perhaps because of your public relations and advertising efforts, or perhaps through someone you both know. This person may observe you in the act of conducting business or relating with the people around you.

Soon, the two of you begin communicating and establishing links—perhaps a question or two over the phone about product availability. You may become personally acquainted and work on a first-name basis, but you know little else about each other. Form several of these types of relationships and you'll emerge with what's called a *casual-contact network,* a sort of de facto association based on one or more shared interests.

This visibility phase is important because it creates recognition and awareness. The greater your visibility, the more widely known you will be, the more information you will obtain about others, the more opportunities you will be exposed to, and the greater your chances will be of being accepted by other individuals or groups as someone to whom they can or should refer business.

Visibility must be actively maintained and developed; without it, you cannot move on to the next level . . . credibility.

CREDIBILITY

Credibility means being reliable and worthy of someone's confidence. Once you and your new acquaintance begin to form expectations of each other and those expectations are fulfilled, your relationship can enter the credibility stage. If each person is confident of gaining satisfaction from the relationship, then it will continue to strengthen.

Credibility grows when appointments are kept, promises are acted upon, facts are verified, and services are rendered. The old saying that results speak louder than words is true. Failure to live up to expectations—to keep both explicit and implicit promises—can kill a budding relationship before it has a chance to grow. What's worse, this failure can create visibility of a kind you don't want.

To determine how credible you are, people often turn to third parties. They ask someone they know who has known you longer, and perhaps even done business with you. Will she vouch for you? Are you honest? Are your products and services effective? Are you someone who can be counted on in a crunch?

PROFITABILITY

Of course, a mature networking relationship, whether business or personal, is where profitability occurs. Is it mutually rewarding? Do both partners gain satisfaction from it?

If it doesn't profit both partners to keep the relationship going, it probably will not endure.

So how long does it take to move through the various phases of a developing relationship?

It's highly variable. In fact, it's not always easy to determine when profitability has been achieved—a week? a month? one year?

In some cases—such as when an urgent need arises—you and the other person may proceed from visibility to credibility overnight. The same is true of profitability; it may happen quickly or it may take years—most likely, it's somewhere in between. Of course, much depends on the frequency and quality of your contact with each other but most especially on the desire of both parties to move the relationship forward.

This is why shortsightedness at any stage can hinder or even stop the full development of the relationship. Perhaps you're a customer who has networked and done business with a certain vendor off and on for several months—but to save pennies, you keep hunting around for the lowest price, ignoring the value this vendor provides you in terms of service, hours, goodwill, and reliability. Are you really profiting from the new relationship, or are you stunting its growth? Perhaps if you gave this vendor all your business, instead of continuing to shop around for better pricing, you could work out terms that would benefit both of you. Profitability is not found by bargain hunting. It must be cultivated, and, like farming, it takes patience.

What's another major benefit of the profitability stage of a relationship? Referrals coming to you from people with whom you've networked. When you've established an effective network, when you've entered the profitability stage of your relationships with many people, your finely tuned referral-generation system will send you referrals and customers as a result.

Profitability happens when there are benefits going both ways—whether referrals, information, support, or something else. Your ultimate goal should be a meaningful and *mutual* payoff in the relationship.

Of course, this profitability stage of a relationship isn't limited to making money from a new customer or client acquired through a referral. It may come in the form of a connection to someone who can help you launch a new initiative or otherwise grow your business. It may include access to a mentor or a professional adviser or a contact in another industry who can help you expand your market share or enter a new market. It might be the ability to delegate more of your workload, gain substantial free time for your hobby or personal interests—or spend more quality time with family members.

Janet Switzer, my business partner Patty Aubery, and I know the value of being connected to a robust and well-connected network. We've generated millions of dollars in business from the connections we have developed over the past 40 years. Between us, we've amassed over half a million blog readers, 2.5 million Facebook fans, and millions of customers, clients, and students who follow our Success Principles work. We've developed personal contact lists with hundreds of key individuals who can help out with advice, direction, a name, an idea, resources, marketing assistance, and more. My networks include the Transformational Leadership Council, the Association of Transformational Leaders, the National Council for Self-Esteem, the National Speakers Association, the Speakers and Authors Networking Group—plus connections to networks enjoyed by colleagues in the human-potential movement. At any time, Janet, Patty, and I can ask each other, *Who do we know who can help with this new initiative?*—confident that we can go to our contact list and get our needs and wants addressed within days. That's the real profitability of a network.

THE OPPORTUNITY TO NETWORK IS EVERYWHERE

Eighty percent of success is showing up.

WOODY ALLEN
Academy Award–winning director, screenwriter, actor, and comedian

You never know where you'll find your next connection. Early one spring morning Jean MacDonald stopped at a Dunkin' Donuts for coffee. The line was out the door, but longing for that caffeine fix, she decided to wait. While she was standing there, the woman in front of her commented, "With this kind of traffic, I should own one of these stores."

With that opening Jean started up a conversation and mentioned she was an entrepreneur who helped women look good and feel good. She went on to tell her she was with Mary Kay Cosmetics and that it was a wonderful opportunity. The woman in line told her she was a Girl Scout troop leader and she was looking for someone to come talk to the girls about skin care. Jean took her information and told her she'd be in touch.

Meanwhile, the woman behind them heard their conversation and told Jean she was a nurse and was interested in Mary Kay's hand-treatment products. She asked if Jean would come to her office and provide some pampering. Jean took her information, too.

But it didn't end there. The man behind her then joined in, telling Jean that his sister loved Mary Kay products, but she'd lost her representative. Jean took his sister's contact information, too.

Three strong leads, all just from chatting with people in line, and all before 7:30 A.M.

But the story doesn't end there, because at this point all Jean had were leads. Strong leads, but leads nonetheless.

Ninety-nine percent of all success in life is following up.

KENT HEALY
Coauthor of *The Success Principles for Teens*

Networking is so much more than just meeting people. It is following up and following through and continuing to connect and reconnect over and over again.

Jean connected with the Girl Scout leader, and she pampered 12 girls and several mothers. The troop leader loved what she did so much that she became a new consultant on her team.

The nurse was so pleased with the products that she met with Jean individually for a one-on-one appointment, and also became a new Mary Kay consultant.

Now, here is the kicker . . . the sister of the man she spoke with in line was the local mortician, and she told Jean she loved the look of the Mary Kay products on all her "customers." It turns out the products even gave luster and life to dead skin!!! Ultimately she introduced Jean to several of the local funeral homes, resulting in about $3,000 worth of product sales.

As a result of these connections, Jean's team became the leaders in the community for the Girl Scouts; they developed business with many nurses, doctor's offices, and funeral directors; and Jean's team earned their first Pink Cadillac.

The moral of this story is you never know where you'll find your next connection. And once you find that connection, you must follow up to get the results.

---

*The richest people in the world look for and build networks.
Everyone else looks for work!*

ROBERT KIYOSAKI
Author of *Rich Dad, Poor Dad: What the Rich Teach Their Kids
About Money That the Poor and Middle Class Do Not*

NETWORKING IS NOT JUST FOR BUSINESS OWNERS

On May 7, 2014, Miriam Laundry set a new Guinness World Records title for the "Largest Online Book Discussion in a 24-Hour Period" by reaching her personal goal of empowering 100,000 children. The Guinness World Records Adjudicator verified a total of 33,695 official comments. Unofficially there were 103,813 people from 29 different countries participating!

When Miriam looked back at her achievement, she said the success principle that helped her the most was networking.

During the last week of my Train-the-Trainer program, Miriam shared her breakthrough goal with a fellow participant. Her goal? To "empower 100,000 children to believe in themselves by June 1, 2014, through being read her children's book, *I CAN Believe in Myself.*" Her strategy for accomplishing this was to go for an official Guinness World Records title.

When the fellow trainer asked Miriam why she chose that project and that date, she explained that May 7 fell during Mental Health Awareness week in Canada, and her purpose for writing the book, which stemmed from losing her niece to suicide, was to teach positive mental health to children.

In a stunning coincidence, the trainer told her about a colleague of his who had founded the Winspiration Day Association, also celebrated every year on May 7! He quickly asked if he could pass along Miriam's book to his colleague, and a couple of months later Miriam got a call from Switzerland. It was the founder of the association who had been looking into her project and wanted to present her with the Winspiration Day Award for 2014!

The founder fully supported Miriam's official Guinness World Record attempt. He even put her in contact with an international company called Nikken, which asked her to speak with the managing director of Nikken

Europe. It seemed that everyone who heard about her goal wanted to help her.

The Nikken organization helped her finance the official Guinness World Record attempt—including paying the cost of making it an international event. Nikken hosted a global conference call with their offices in 26 countries, where they interviewed Miriam about her vision and her reasons for wanting to help children. The Nikken organization suggested she start a crowdfunding campaign where they could all contribute to help pay the CAD$15,000 costs associated with bringing a Guinness World Records Adjudicator to her city of St. Catharines, Ontario, Canada.

Overwhelmed by the outpouring of help, Miriam didn't fully realize the magnitude of support until she started receiving daily book orders from countries like Germany, Australia, Austria, the Philippines, Russia, the Netherlands, the United Kingdom, and many more.

The secret of her success, she says? NETWORKING!

And it all started with her being open to sharing her goals with others.

She reflects, "The most incredible thing to me is that, when you share your heartfelt purpose and vision with others, they want to jump on board and help.

"You never know whom you are talking to, who they know, and what their triggers are. Sharing my goal with that one participant resulted in me being awarded the prestigious Winspiration Day Award, the financial backing for my goal, the Guinness World Records title, and most important, having thousands of children being empowered, all learning the I CAN mentality all over the world!"

PRINCIPLE 45

HIRE A PERSONAL COACH

*I absolutely believe that people, unless coached,
never reach their maximum capabilities.*

BOB NARDELLI
Former CEO of Home Depot and Chrysler

You would never expect an athlete to reach the Olympic Games without a world-class coach. Nor would you expect a professional football team to enter the stadium without a whole team of coaches—head coach, offensive coach, defensive coach, and special teams coach. Well, over the years, coaching has moved into the business and personal realm to include coaches who have succeeded in your area of interest—and who can help you get from where you are to where you want to be faster and easier.

ONE OF THE MOST POWERFUL HABITS OF THE SUCCESSFUL

Of all the things successful people do to accelerate their trip down the path to success, working with a good coach is at the top of the list. A coach will help you clarify your vision and goals, overcome and support you through your fears, keep you focused, confront your unconscious behaviors and old patterns, expect you to do your best, help you live by your values, show you how to earn more while working less, and keep you focused on your core genius.

WORTH MORE THAN MONEY

I have had many coaches who have helped me achieve my goals—business coaches, writing coaches, marketing coaches, and personal coaches. But without a doubt, the coaching experience that most helped me leap forward in every area of my life was when I hired a coach to help me take my business to the next level.

What were the results? First and foremost, I immediately doubled my free time. I delegated more tasks, scheduled vacations rather than merely thought about them, and hired additional staff that ultimately positioned my business to earn more. And that was just in the first few months.

Not only did my business benefit but my family did, too.

For me, coaching wasn't just about making more money—although a big part of coaching is focused on making more money, managing it better, and settling on a financial plan that gives you the kind of freedom you want. It was about helping me make better decisions for myself and my business. The truth is, most coaching clients are smart—very smart. Yet, they still know the value of accessing someone who can be objective, honest, and constructive about the options they are facing.

WHY COACHING WORKS

Executive coaches are not for the meek. They're for people who value unambiguous feedback. If coaches have one thing in common, it's that they are ruthlessly results-oriented.

FAST COMPANY MAGAZINE

Regardless of whether the program is designed to achieve a specific business goal—say, increasing your real estate listings—or whether it is specifically designed to help you simply gain more clarity and progress in all aspects of your personal and professional life, a coach can help you . . .

- Determine your values, vision, mission, purpose, and goals
- Determine specific action steps to help you achieve those goals
- Sort through opportunities
- Maintain focus on your top priorities
- Achieve greater balance in your life while still accomplishing your business or career goals

As humans, we tend to do only some of what we are required to do, but virtually all of what we want to do. A personal coach can help you discover what you truly want to do—and can help you determine the steps and take the actions necessary to get there.

CANFIELD COACHING

Because of my personal success with coaching and my firm belief in the power of coaching to do the same for others, I developed my own coaching program to support people in implementing *The Success Principles*.

My experience has been that people often tend to shy away from the changes that would allow them to create the life of their dreams. The true value of coaching lies in how it assists you in making these changes. Whether it is replacing bad habits that have been holding you back or refining good habits into great ones, a coach knows how to help you get more from yourself and your environment. Our coaches offer accountability, encouragement, insight, motivation, and tough love, all of which accelerate you getting from where you are to where you want to be. They also help you move out of your comfort zone and build the daily disciplines of success needed to achieve your goals.

Graduates of our coaching programs have often accomplished more than they thought possible and in a shorter amount of time than they thought was realistic. For them, coaching multiplied both the size and speed of their success.

Here are a few excerpts from the thank-you letters I've received from graduates of our Canfield Coaching program.

> Since starting this journey, I have created a consistent flow of business, have built a stronger team of consultants, and continue to work toward my goal of becoming a director within my direct sales company. I have also created improved quality time with my two young boys, my husband and our family as a whole.—*Trish C., Ohiopyle, Pennsylvania*

> I read *The Success Principles* book and was really excited, but I had no idea how to absorb all the information. My coach has made it so manageable. I enjoy my daily rituals: meditating, affirmations, the Rule of 5, reviewing my day, planning for the next day and also the mirror exercise; these are all a normal part of my day now. My affirmations are beginning to truly materialize. I was so excited when my affirmation really happened in the exact way I visualized it. I have broken old habits and learned new

ones to improve my organization skills. I can now break down my goals into achievable tasks. I have the confidence to ask and seek advice or help whenever I need it. I now put myself first, and I don't feel guilty for saying no to people. . . . I can't believe how much my life has changed in such a short time.—*Sally-Ann D., Taupo, New Zealand*

Here's a typical success story.

When you offered me the opportunity to speak to one of your coaches, I had to think about it for a few hours. . . . I'd been wishing for a coach for years, but my shyness had stopped me from pursuing it. The timing couldn't have been more perfect. I was on the verge of going live with my new business and also had a few books in the works, but I knew that my blocks were preventing me from living up to my full potential. The time had come to break through the last few barriers, and I knew I was going to need one-on-one help to push me to the finish line. I took a deep breath, made the phone call, and said good-bye to my old defeatist ways.

The transformation that has taken place within me, thanks to you, your program, your excellent book, and my wonderful coach, is nothing short of astonishing. My coach immediately spotted that I was a perfectionist—something I had always been very proud of. But he helped me to see how my perfectionism was having a very negative effect on me and my performance, and steered me toward something much better: *excellence*.

I was on the verge of a total burnout. I was feeling completely overwhelmed by everything I felt I had to do, and I was drowning. Your book was a great help to me in this area. Your time management system has helped me to stay focused, use my time more effectively, and to rest without feeling guilty. I feel so much better now!

My copy of *The Success Principles* is completely dog-eared, I frequently refer to it, and I often find myself quoting it to others. The book is brilliant on its own, certainly, but the greatest benefit of having a coach to guide me through it was that I was forced to follow through. Someone was watching me and I could not chicken out and skip the things that made me feel uncomfortable. I did things that terrified me, like setting dates to goals—I thought my brain might explode, but I did it! I made scary phone calls. I learned to introduce myself to strangers and navigate social events. I asked people for help. I said "No." I learned to focus on my successes and to keep a log of them. I look in the mirror every day and tell myself what a wonderful person I am and what a great job I'm doing.

I find myself automatically doing things I've learned; they have become a habit. I find the things I've learned easily come to mind when I need them. It's like I now have a coach in my mind who speaks up and guides me whenever I need it! There is absolutely no comparison between the way I functioned four months ago and the way I live my life now. Everything is so much better!—*Pavanne V., Apeldoorn, Netherlands*

I have carefully assembled some of the best coaches in the entire industry and personally trained all of them. I know from the results that we have consistently produced for more than 6,000 people in 117 countries that they will also help you produce phenomenal results in every area of life. In short, they can help you change your life.

In the Canfield Coaching program, you will work one-on-one with your coach over the telephone or over Zoom, with a program customized to your needs and goals. Since the key to ongoing success is regular contact, over the course of your program, you'll work with your coach to develop goals, strategies, and a plan of action that is positive, desirable, and realistic.

To learn more and arrange a free phone session that will introduce you to coaching, go to jackcanfield.com/coaching.

COACHING FOR WRITERS

Without a doubt, one of the best things I've ever done to accelerate my success was to become a published author. You can share your ideas and influence with so many more people by writing and publishing a book. And being a published author gives you credibility. It establishes you as an expert. And for many people it serves as a brochure describing your work that other people pay for. And with today's myriad ebook and self-publishing options, it's easier than ever.

After two years of teaching disadvantaged teenagers in an inner-city high school and a Job Corps center, I wrote my first book, *100 Ways to Enhance Self-Concept in the Classroom,* in 1976. That book sold over 400,000 copies, which changed my career and my life almost overnight. I became a recognized authority in the education field and attracted a ton of paid speaking engagements. More important, I started hearing from teachers all across the country about how they were using my strategies to positively impact their students. That first book ultimately led to co-creating the *Chicken Soup for the Soul*® series, which now includes 46 *New York Times* bestsellers and more than 600 million copies sold around the world. And that really changed my life!

Since becoming an author changed my life in so many ways, one of my missions is to help others get their books out and share their messages with the world. To accomplish that I teamed up with Steve Harrison—who has helped more than 12,000 authors, including me with the *Chicken Soup* series, to successfully write and promote their books—to create the "Bestseller Blueprint," an online training course (including some live coaching calls) that provides step-by-step instruction on every aspect of writing, publishing, and marketing your book. In addition to my own proven methods, we've also included strategies and advice from such bestselling authors as Tim Ferriss (*The 4-Hour Workweek*), John Gray (*Men Are from Mars, Women Are from Venus*), Marci Shimoff (*Love for No Reason*), Ken Blanchard (*The One Minute Manager*), and many others.

You can access free author-training videos, which also preview the full course, by going to authorsuccess.com.

LEARN HOW TO COACH OTHERS

Finally, I believe everyone should learn to be a coach. If you know the basics steps and skills of coaching, it will make you a better parent, spouse, teacher, manager, network marketer, athletic coach, even a better friend. If you would like to add coaching to your skill set, a good resource is *Coaching for Breakthrough Success: Proven Techniques for Making Impossible Dreams Possible*,* a book I wrote with Dr. Peter Chee, the CEO of ITD World in Kuala Lumpur, Malaysia. The book details 30 principles that explain the role and benefits of coaching, and presents our Situational Coaching Model that covers the six paradigms for success—goals, exploration, analysis, releasing, decision, and action. It offers many techniques for helping people overcome barriers and achieve results.

---

*New York: McGraw-Hill, 2013.

PRINCIPLE 46

MASTERMIND YOUR WAY TO SUCCESS

When two or more people coordinate in a spirit of harmony and work toward a definite objective or purpose, they place themselves in position, through the alliance, to absorb power directly from the great storehouse of Infinite Intelligence.

NAPOLEON HILL
Author of *Think and Grow Rich*

We all know that two heads are better than one when it comes to solving a problem or creating a result. So imagine having a permanent group of five or six people who meet once every week or two for the purpose of problem solving, brainstorming, networking, encouraging, and motivating each other.

This process, called *masterminding,* is one of the most powerful tools for success presented in this book. I don't know anybody who has become super-successful who has not employed the principle of masterminding.

AN OLD IDEA THAT'S NEW AGAIN

Napoleon Hill first wrote about mastermind groups in 1937 in his classic book *Think and Grow Rich*. And all the world's richest industrialists—from the early twentieth century to today's modern icons of business—have harnessed the power of the mastermind group. It's the one concept achievers reference most when they credit any one thing with helping them become a millionaire.

Andrew Carnegie had a mastermind group. So did Henry Ford. In fact, Ford would mastermind with brilliant thinkers such as Thomas Edison and Harvey Firestone in a group they held at their winter mansions in Fort Myers, Florida.

They knew, as millions of others have discovered since, that a mastermind group can focus special energy on your efforts—in the form of knowledge, new ideas, introductions, a vast array of resources, and, most important, spiritual energy. And it's this spiritual aspect that Napoleon Hill wrote about extensively.

He said that if we are in tune with *the* mastermind—that is, God, Source, the universal power, Infinite Intelligence, or whatever term you use for the all-powerful creative life force—we have significantly more positive energy and power available to us, a power that can be focused on our success. Even the Bible talks about this: "For where two or three are gathered together in my name, there am I in the midst of them" (Matthew 18:20). "Mastermind," therefore, is both the creative power that comes to us from each other and the creative power that comes to us from above.

A PROCESS FOR ACCELERATING YOUR GROWTH

The basic philosophy of a mastermind group is that more can be achieved in less time when people work together. A mastermind group is made up of people who come together on a regular basis—weekly, biweekly, or monthly—to share ideas, thoughts, information, feedback, contacts, and resources. By getting the perspective, knowledge, experience, and resources of the others in the group, not only can you greatly expand your own limited view of the world but you can also advance your own goals and projects more quickly. By being part of an effective mastermind group, you will see opportunities you would not otherwise see and get help you would not otherwise get.

A mastermind group can be composed of people all drawn from your own industry or profession, or composed of people from a variety of walks of life. It can focus on business issues, personal issues, or both. But for a mastermind group to be powerfully effective, people must be comfortable enough with each other to tell the truth. Some of the most valuable feedback I have ever received has come from members of my mastermind group confronting me about overcommitting, selling my services too cheaply, focusing on the trivial, not delegating enough, thinking too small, and playing it safe.

Confidentiality is what allows this level of trust to build. Out in the world, we are usually managing our personal and corporate image. In a mastermind group, participants can let their hair down, tell the truth about their personal and business life, and feel safe that what is said in the group will stay in the group.

NEW THOUGHTS, NEW PEOPLE, NEW RESOURCES

When you form your mastermind group, consider bringing together people from different professional arenas and people who are "above" or "ahead" of you professionally or financially and who can introduce you to a network of people and resources you normally wouldn't have access to.

Though the benefits of masterminding with people outside your field may not seem obvious now, the truth is that we all tend to get stuck in our own field of expertise, seeing through the same narrow lens, and doing things the same way everyone else in our industry does. But when you assemble people from different industries, professions, or fields of study, you get lots of different perspectives on the same subject.

Henry Ford was an assembly-line expert. Thomas Edison was an inventor. Harvey Firestone was a corporate management genius. So their mastermind group brought together diverse talent that could lend different perspectives to one another's challenges, whether they were legal, financial, or relational.

Other mastermind groups have helped members start or salvage businesses, change jobs, become multimillionaires, become better parents, grow as teachers, become better advocates for social change, improve our environment, and more.

HOW TO ASSEMBLE A MASTERMIND GROUP

Regardless of your group's purpose, an important key is to choose people who are already where you'd like to be in your life—or who are at least a level above you. If your goal is to become a millionaire and you're currently making only $60,000 a year, you will be better served by gathering together with people who are already making more than you. If you're concerned that people who are already achieving at a higher level than you might not want to be involved in a group with you, remember that you're the one convening and facilitating the meeting. You are organizing, supporting, and building a forum for other people's growth and masterminding needs. Many people at a higher level will want to become involved simply because they'll get to play at a game they might never take the time to organize for themselves. They'd probably be delighted to mastermind with the other people you're going to invite—especially if some of the others are already playing at their level.

WHAT'S THE IDEAL SIZE FOR A MASTERMIND GROUP?

The ideal size of a mastermind group is five or six people. If it is any smaller, it loses its dynamics. If it is too much bigger, it gets unwieldy—meetings take longer, some people's needs may go unmet, and personal sharing is minimized. However, larger groups with as many as 20 people that periodically meet in person for a whole day or more can operate very successfully.

Another option to consider is to join a professionally facilitated mastermind group or to have your mastermind facilitated by a professional facilitator who takes responsibility for everything from call reminders to running the meetings according to the proven formula for success.

CONDUCTING A MASTERMIND MEETING

Mastermind meetings should be conducted weekly or every other week with all members of the group in attendance. They can be conducted in person, over the phone, or via Skype or Google Hangouts. About 60 to 90 minutes is an ideal length of time. If meetings are to be any longer than 60 minutes, it's important to have the full commitment of each group member to allocating that much time.

For the first few meetings, it's recommended that each member get the entire hour to familiarize the others with his or her situation, opportunities, needs, and challenges, while the other members ask clarifying questions, and brainstorm ways they can support that person. During later meetings, participants get a small amount of time (about 10 minutes each) to update the others, ask for help, and get feedback.

On an ongoing basis, each meeting should follow a proven format of steps to ensure that all participants get their needs met and therefore stay fully engaged. You'll find a complete kit for assembling a mastermind group and conducting mastermind meetings—complete with the seven steps and a helpful worksheet—at jackcanfield.com/tsp-resources.

SHE MASTERMINDED HER WAY TO SUCCESS

In 2010, Jill Douka of Athens, Greece, left my Breakthrough to Success training with the commitment to be part of a mastermind group she had formed with five other attendees from different countries.

When the economic downturn in Greece began affecting everyone locally, Jill found herself looking forward to "e-meeting" with her global mastermind group on Skype and Google Hangouts—spending one hour every other week not using the words *crisis, default, unemployment,* or *debt*.

Before long, Jill learned through her mastermind group about TEDx Chennai and ended up giving her first international speech there. On the plane trip home, an idea took shape in her mind: What if instead of just "*Ideas* Worth Spreading" (the wonderful concept of TED), Jill created a global platform that would spread *solutions?*

She could offer interactive workshops at one-day events, then upload the videos to YouTube so that people around the world could benefit from them.

With that concept, Better Life Day was born.

At first, with the economic crisis being so deep in Greece, and with local citizens actually protesting in the streets, Jill was embarrassed to discuss her idea of creating an event called Better Life Day with friends and colleagues in Athens. But when she discussed the idea with her mastermind group, they were ecstatic.

Jill recalls, "I will never forget the way they encouraged me to go ahead and create Better Life Day in Athens. I never would have gone ahead without their constant encouragement and support."

The first Better Life Day in Athens was jam-packed with 500 participants plus another 300 live streaming views, and was supported by 70 volunteers and 57 corporate sponsors. The feedback was unbelievable. People were walking through corridors of the venue as if they had been given happiness pills. The team got tons of emails and Facebook messages thanking them for the positive, solution-based outlook the event had given them. And the biggest gift of all was, because of the event, Jill met her husband!

The following November, Sergio Sedas, another Breakthrough to Success graduate and TEDx speaker, produced the second Better Life Day in Monterrey, Mexico, with more than 4,000 people participating in interactive solution-focused workshops given by presenters from the United States, Mexico, Canada, and Bermuda.

Throughout it all, Jill's mastermind group was there with ideas, encouragement, and solutions. Not bad for an investment of two hours a month.

"But above all," said Jill, "is the feeling that I have five souls with whom I can share my feelings, from complete devastation to overwhelming joy. That's priceless."

ACCOUNTABILITY PARTNERS

Instead of or in addition to being in a mastermind group, you might choose to work with what I call an accountability partner. The two of you agree to a set of goals that each is working toward and agree to talk regularly by phone to hold each other accountable for meeting deadlines, accomplishing goals, and making progress.

You agree to call each other at agreed-upon times (every day, every week, or every other week) to make sure you are both following through on your planned actions. Knowing that you'll be reporting to someone provides the extra motivation to get the job done. This is an especially useful relationship to develop if you're a solo entrepreneur and work from home. Knowing that you'll be talking to your accountability partner tomorrow morning makes it more likely you'll be productive today.

You can also ask your partner to share ideas, information, contacts, and resources. You can pitch your partner on your latest idea and ask for feedback: "What's your opinion? How would you proceed?" Your partner might agree to make a call for you, give you a contact name, or e-mail you some information he or she has already collected on that subject. It's important to remember that an accountability call is not a coaching call or social call. Accountability partnerships work best and last longest when calls are kept short and focused.

An accountability partner can also provide enthusiasm when yours is waning because of obstacles, distractions, setbacks, or failures. The key to a successful accountability relationship is choosing someone who is as excited about reaching his or her goal as you are about reaching yours—someone who is committed to your success and theirs.

PRINCIPLE

47

INQUIRE WITHIN

Brain researchers estimate that your unconscious database outweighs the conscious on an order exceeding ten million to one. This database is the source of your hidden, natural genius. In other words, a part of you is much smarter than you are. The wise people regularly consult that smarter part.

MICHAEL J. GELB
Author of *How to Think Like Leonardo da Vinci* and *Discover Your Genius*

According to an ancient legend, there was a time when ordinary people had access to all the knowledge of the gods. Yet time and again, they ignored this wisdom. One day, the gods grew tired of so freely giving a gift the people didn't use, so they decided to hide this precious wisdom where only the most committed of seekers would discover it. They believed that if people had to work to find this wisdom, they would use it more carefully.

One of the gods suggested that they bury it deep in the Earth.

No, the others said—too many people could easily dig down and find it.

"Let's put it in the deepest ocean," suggested one of the gods, but that idea was also rejected. They knew that people would one day learn to dive and thus would find it too easily.

One of the gods suggested hiding it on the highest mountaintop, but it was quickly agreed that people could climb mountains.

Finally, one of the wisest gods suggested, "Let's hide it deep inside the people themselves. They'll never think to look in there." And so it came to be—and so it continues today.

TRUST YOUR INTUITION

For most of us, our early education and training focused on looking outside of ourselves for the answers to our questions. Few of us have had any training on how to look inside, and yet most of the super-successful people I have met over the years are people who have developed their intuition and learned to trust their gut feelings and follow their inner guidance. Many practice some form of daily meditation to access this voice within.

Burt Dubin, at the time a successful real estate investor, now creator of the Burt Dubin Speaking Success System (serving speakers worldwide) knows all about trusting his intuition. For some time, he had been looking to buy a four-corner property in Kingman, Arizona. He knew it would be a good investment, but he had not been able to locate a property that was for sale. One night he went to bed as usual, only to be awakened at 3:00 A.M. with a clear inner message that he was to drive to Kingman, Arizona—now!

Burt found this strange because he had called a realtor in Kingman earlier that same day and was told there were no four-corner properties listed for sale. But having learned to trust his inner messages, Burt immediately got in his car and drove through the night, arriving at Kingman at 8:00 A.M. He went to Howard Johnson's, bought a paper, and turned to the real estate section, where he saw a four-corner property for sale. He went directly to the real estate office at 9:00 and had the property in escrow by 9:15.

But how was this possible? He had called the day before to find no four-corner properties for sale. But at 4:30 the previous day, a property owner had called from New York to sell his property; he needed the money. Because it was too late to get the property into the multiple listings, but knowing that the weekly paper didn't close until 5:00 P.M., the agent had called the paper and purchased an ad.

Because Burt had trusted his "still, small voice within," he managed to purchase this prime piece of real estate before anyone else even knew it was available.

When business magnate Conrad Hilton, founder of the Hilton Hotels Corporation, wanted to buy the Stevens Corporation at auction, he submitted a sealed bid for $165,000. When he awakened the next morning with the number 180,000 in his head, he swiftly changed his bid to $180,000, successfully securing the company and earning a $2 million profit. The next highest bid was $179,800!

Whether they are a real estate investor who hears a voice in the middle of the night, a detective who solves a dead-end case by following a hunch, an investor who just knows when to get out of the market, or a football linebacker who can sense what the quarterback's next play is going to be, successful people trust their intuition.

You, too, can use your intuition to make more money, make better decisions, solve problems quicker, unleash your creative genius, discern people's hidden motives, envision a new business, and create winning business plans and strategies.

EVERYONE HAS INTUITION—
IT'S JUST A MATTER OF DEVELOPING IT

All the resources we need are in the mind.

THEODORE ROOSEVELT
The 26th president of the United States

Intuition is not something relegated to certain people or to psychics. Everyone has it and everyone has experienced it. Have you ever been thinking about your old friend Jerry, and then the phone rings and it's Jerry on the line who was just thinking about you? Have you ever awakened in the middle of the night and knew something had happened to one of your children, only to find out later that it was the exact moment your son was in an automobile accident? Have you ever felt a burning sensation on the back of your neck, and then turned to see a man staring at you from across the room?

We've all experienced this kind of intuition. The trick is to learn how to tap into it at will to achieve greater levels of success.

USING MEDITATION TO ACCESS YOUR INTUITION

When I was 35, I attended a meditation retreat that permanently changed my life. For an entire week, we sat in meditation from 6:30 in the morning until 10:00 at night—with breaks only for meals and silent walks. Over the first few days, I thought I would go crazy. I would either fall asleep from years of not getting enough sleep or my mind would race from one topic to another as I reviewed every experience of my past, planned how to improve my business, and wondered what I was doing sitting in a meditation hall while everyone else I knew was out enjoying life.

On the fourth day, an unexpected and wonderful thing happened. My mind became quiet and I moved into a place from which I could just witness everything that was occurring around me without judgment or attachment. I was aware of sounds, sensations in my body, and a profound sense of inner peace. Thoughts still came and went, but not at the same pace or of the same kind. The thoughts were deeper—what we might call insights, deeper understandings, and wisdom. I saw connections I had never seen before. I understood my motivations, fears, and desires at a deeper level. Creative solutions to problems that I had been facing in my life came into my consciousness.

I felt relaxed, calm, aware, and clearer than I had ever felt before. Gone were the pressures to perform, to prove myself, to explain myself, to measure up to some external standard, to meet the needs of others. Instead there was a deep sense of my self and my purpose in life. When I focused on my deepest, most heartfelt goals and desires, solutions would come pouring into my mind—clear thoughts and images of the steps I would need to take, the people I would need to talk to, and the ways to transcend any obstacles I might encounter. It was truly magical.

What I learned from this experience was that all the ideas I needed to complete any task, solve any problem, or achieve any goal were all available inside me. I have used this valuable insight ever since.

REGULAR MEDITATION WILL DEEPEN YOUR INTUITION

The regular practice of meditation will help you clear out distractions and teach you to recognize subtle impulses from within. Think of parents sitting on a bench on the edge of a playground filled with children laughing and yelling at each other. In the midst of all this noise, the parents can pick out their own child's voice from all the other voices on the playground.

Your intuition works the same way. As you meditate and become more spiritually attuned, you can better discern and recognize the sound of your higher self or the voice of God speaking to you through words, images, and sensations.

The intellect has little to do on the road to discovery.
There comes a leap in consciousness, call it intuition or what you will,
and the solution comes to you, and you don't know how or why.

ALBERT EINSTEIN
Physicist and winner of the Nobel Prize

THE ANSWERS LIE WITHIN

When Mark Victor Hansen and I were nearing completion of our first *Chicken Soup for the Soul*® book, we still did not have a title for it. Because Mark and I both meditate, we decided to "inquire within." Every day for a week, we asked our internal guidance for a bestselling title. Mark went to bed every night repeating the phrase "mega-bestselling title" and would awaken every morning and immediately go into meditation. I simply asked God to give me the best title for the book, and then I would sit with my eyes closed in a state of relaxed expectancy, waiting patiently for an answer to come.

On the third morning, I suddenly saw a hand write the words *chicken soup* on a blackboard in my mind. My immediate reaction was, *What does chicken soup have to do with our book?*

I heard a voice in my head respond, *Chicken soup is what your grandmother gave you when you were sick as a child.*

But this book isn't about sick people, I thought.

People's spirits are sick, my inner voice replied. *Millions of people are depressed and living in fear and resignation that things will never get better. This book will inspire them and uplift their spirits.*

During the remaining minutes of that meditation, the title evolved from *Chicken Soup for the Spirit* to *Chicken Soup for the Soul* to *Chicken Soup for the Soul: 101 Stories to Open the Heart and Rekindle the Spirit.* When I first heard *Chicken Soup for the Soul,* I got goose bumps. I have since learned that giving me goose bumps is one of the ways my intuition tells me I am on track.

Ten minutes later, I told my wife, and she got goose bumps, too. Then I called Mark and he got goose bumps. We were onto something right, and we all knew it.

Over the last 20 years, Chicken Soup for the Soul® has become a brand responsible for more than $2 billion in sales of books and many licensed products including pet food and greeting cards.

HOW YOUR INTUITION COMMUNICATES WITH YOU

Your intuition can communicate with you in many ways. You may get a message from within as a vision or a visual image while you are meditating or dreaming. I often get images while I am lying in bed after I first wake up, while I'm meditating or getting a massage, or while sitting in a hot tub or taking a shower. It can come in a flash out of the blue or it can be a long, unfolding image like a movie.

Your intuition may speak to you as a hunch, a thought, or a voice actually telling you *yes, no, go for it,* or *not yet.* It might come as one resounding word, a short sentence, or a complete lecture. You may find you can dialogue with the voice for clarification or more information.

You may also receive a message from your intuition through your physical senses. If the message is one of *watch out* or *be careful,* you may experience it as a chill, the creeps, a sense of restlessness, discomfort in your gut, constriction in your chest, tightness or pain in your head, even a sour taste in your mouth. A positive or "yes" message might come in the form of goose bumps, a dizzy feeling, warmth, a sense of opening or expansiveness in the chest, a sense of relaxation, a feeling of relief, or a letting go of tension.

You may also experience intuitive messages through your emotions, such as a feeling of uneasiness, concern, or confusion. Or when information is of a positive nature, you may experience a feeling of joy, euphoria, or profound inner peace.

Sometimes it is just a sense of knowing. How many times have you heard someone say, "I don't know how I knew; I just knew" or "I knew it in my heart" or "in the depth of my soul"?

An indicator that the message is truly from your intuition is that it will often be accompanied by a sense of greater clarity, a feeling of *rightness* about the answer or the impulse. Another indicator that the message you are receiving is a correct one is an accompanying feeling of passion and excitement. If you are considering a plan of action or a decision, and it leaves you feeling constricted, drained, bored, or enervated, that's a clear message saying *Don't go there.* On the other hand, if you feel expansive, energized, and enthusiastic, your intuition is telling you to go ahead.

INTUITIVE ANSWERS CAN COME ANYTIME

Your most valuable intuitive wisdom may also come through the many forms of informal meditation we engage in every day, such as sitting by a waterfall, watching the ocean, staring at the clouds or the stars, sitting under a tree, staring into a fire, listening to inspiring music, jogging, doing yoga, while praying, listening to a bird sing, taking a shower, driving on the freeway, watching a child play, or writing in a personal journal.

Intuition isn't mystical.
DR. JAMES WATSON
Nobel laureate and codiscoverer of DNA

You can even do informal meditation in an abbreviated way during the middle of a hectic day. When you need help making a decision, take time to pause, take a deep breath, reflect on the question, and allow the intuitive impressions to come to you. Pay attention to any images, words, physical sensations, or emotions you experience. Sometimes you will find that intuitive insights will immediately come into your awareness. Other times, they may come later in the day when you least expect it.

THE QUICK COHERENCE® TECHNIQUE

One of the simplest yet most powerful techniques I've learned (and now teach in all my workshops) is the Quick Coherence® Technique developed by the Institute of HeartMath in Boulder Creek, California. It's the fastest technique I've found to bring yourself into that relaxed and centered state from which you can access the higher dimensions of your consciousness, and therefore make better decisions and determine more effective solutions to whatever problems you might be facing.

Coherence is a term researchers use to describe a psychophysiological state in which your nervous, cardiovascular, hormonal, and immune systems are all working together efficiently and harmoniously. Doc Childre and Deborah Rozman of the Institute of HeartMath explain it this way:

> Research has found that the pattern of your heart rhythm reflects the state of your emotions and nervous system dynamics. For example, when you are feeling tense, irritable, impatient, frustrated, or anxious, your heart rhythm shifts into a disordered and incoherent pattern, like the diagram below. No wonder you can't calm your mind in this state.

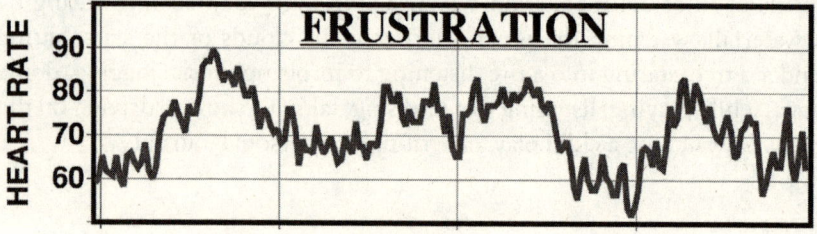

© Copyright 1998-2005 Institute of HeartMath Research Center

Your heart signals "incoherence" to the brain, which inhibits your higher brain functions and triggers a stress response. You can't perceive as clearly, and old emotional issues can start coming to the surface.

You can use the Quick Coherence technique to bring your heart rhythms into coherence and enable your brain to synchronize with your heart's coherent rhythm. Start by learning how to shift into a heart-focused, positive emotional state through three simple steps.

THE STEPS

1. **Heart Focus:** Focus your attention in the area of your heart, in the center of your chest. If you prefer, the first couple of times you try it, you can place your hand over the center of your chest to help keep your attention in the heart area.
2. **Heart Breathing:** As you focus on the area of your heart, breathe deeply but normally and imagine your breath is coming in and going out through your heart area. Continue breathing with ease until you find a natural inner rhythm that feels good to you.
3. **Heart Feeling:** As you continue to breathe through the area of your heart, recall a positive feeling, a time when you felt good inside, and try to re-experience the feeling. It could be feeling appreciation for the good things in your life, or the love and care you feel for a family member, close friend, or a pet. This is the most important step.

The next step is to take this technique and make it a habit. We recommend you do this by picking certain times of the day when you can give yourself a guilt-free three to five minutes to focus on your heart—the start of your day, right before lunch, and just before bed. When you find yourself waiting in line, instead of getting aggravated, you can use the time to practice the technique. You'll be amazed at how different your experience of waiting can be, and instead of draining your energy by focusing on the negative, you'll be using the time to recenter and charge. The more you practice, the more quickly heart coherence will emerge and be easier to sustain.

Once you start using this powerful centering tool, you may want to see for yourself how it affects your physiology. To help you do that, HeartMath has developed the emWave (emotion-wave) technology that actually tracks your coherence level using lights, sounds, and visuals, training to help you increase coherence for longer periods. There is both a simple-to-use handheld device and a smartphone app available.* Using this technology can quickly lead you to periods of high coherence, a state that many people who meditate spend years trying to achieve.

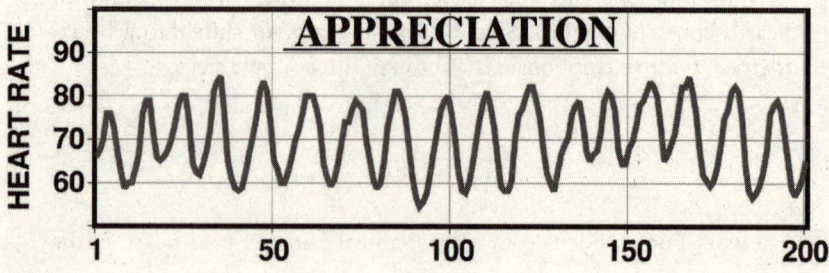

© Copyright 1998-2005 Institute of HeartMath Research Center

ASK QUESTIONS

Your intuition can also provide you with the answers to anything you need to know. Ask questions that begin with "Should I . . ." and "What should I do about . . . ?" and "How can I . . . ?" and "What can I do to . . . ?" You can ask your intuition questions such as

- Should I take this job?
- What should I do about the lack of morale in the company?
- What can I do to increase sales?
- Should I marry this person?
- What can I do to lower my time in the marathon?
- How can I achieve my ideal weight?
- What should I do next?

THE SWAY TEST

An easy way to get a clear yes or no answer from your intuition is to simply ask your body. I discussed *somatic decision-making*—"the sway test"—in Principle 6: "Use the Law of Attraction" but it's also a powerful technique for accessing your intuition.

In the field of energy psychology, the sway test is based on the theory

---

*Both can be purchased at the HeartMath store at heartmath.org or on Amazon.

that your body and mind have vast intelligence—not only your entire lifetime's worth of knowledge, responses, emotions, and goals (whether you remember them or not) but also innate knowledge about what is best for you. Just as a plant will grow toward the sun, the human body will incline toward what is best for it. When you ask *your* body questions about what's right for *you,* it will lean backward or forward in response to your queries.

I started using the sway test to ask questions about specific foods, supplements, sleep, and exercise. Then I used it for questions related to my relationships. Now I use it as part of all my decision making.

I've put complete instructions for the sway test online at jackcanfield.com/tsp-resources.

WRITE DOWN YOUR ANSWERS

Whenever you access your intuition, make sure to immediately write down any impressions you receive. Intuitive impressions are often subtle and therefore "evaporate" very quickly, so make sure to capture them in writing as soon as possible. Recent research in neuroscience indicates that an intuitive insight—or any new idea—*not* captured within 37 seconds is likely never to be recalled again. In seven minutes, it's gone forever. As my buddy Mark Victor Hansen likes to say, "As soon as you think it, ink it!" Make sure you always have your smartphone or a memo pad with you so you can record any intuitive insights or ideas that emerge.

TAKE IMMEDIATE ACTION

Pay attention to the answers you receive and act on the information as quickly as possible. When you act on the information you receive, you'll find that you get more and more intuitive impulses. After a while you will be living in the flow. It will all seem easy and effortless as the wisdom comes to you and you simply act on it. As you learn to trust yourself and your intuition more, it will become automatic.

Experts agree that your intuition works better when you trust it. The more you demonstrate faith in your intuition, the more you will see the results of it in your life.

I strongly encourage you to listen to your intuition, trust it, and follow it. Trusting your intuition is simply another form of trusting yourself, and the more you trust yourself, the more success you will have.

Remember, it's not what you think of; it's what you write down and take action on that counts.

SHE LISTENED AND TOOK ACTION

Madeline Balletta is a very spiritual person. For her, inquiring within means talking to God . . . and listening to His answers.

Madeline's life—and her own success path—were dramatically changed when she and her fellow church members prayed for a solution to her fatigue and heard the words *fresh royal jelly*. Not understanding this clear directive, she investigated and discovered that royal jelly was the food substance worker bees fed to the queen in their hives—a wholesome and highly nourishing liquid that was just starting to be distributed in England as a nutritional supplement.

After taking royal jelly for a time, Madeline started to get better. And soon, she began to pray about whether royal jelly was meant to do more than just help her.

Start a company was the response to her prayers. And so Madeline did.

Today, Bee-Alive is a multimillion-dollar company that has distributed nutritional products containing royal jelly to hundreds of thousands of people nationwide. And through it all, Madeline has prayerfully asked for guidance and listened attentively to the answers.

"I believe God gave me the vision, the inspiration, the strength, and the courage to see it all through," said Madeline.

For example, by her second year in business, Madeline's marketing efforts had produced few results. In fact, with only $450 left in her checking account, her accountant advised that she fold up shop and move on. Madeline returned from that meeting, locked herself in her room, and "cried and prayed and cried and prayed." On the third day, Madeline received the word *radio*, and decided to bet the farm—her remaining $450—on 10 radio commercials that cost $45 apiece. Within days she was making steady sales again. Impressed by her passionate commitment to her product, the radio station eventually interviewed her on one of their talk shows, and by the time she returned home from that interview, recording artist Pat Boone had called asking about royal jelly and how it might help his daughter Debbie. A few months later, Boone called back to tell her how pleased he was with the effects of the royal jelly. When he said, "If there's anything I can ever do for you, I'd be glad to," Madeline asked him to record three radio commercials. Boone agreed—and soon Bee-Alive was on 400 radio stations across America selling millions of dollars' worth of product.

What might happen when you inquire within? For Madeline Balletta, praying, listening quietly, and acting on what she heard meant the development of a successful company serving hundreds of thousands of satisfied customers, as well as the creation of an unimaginable lifestyle for her and her family.

BE MINDFUL

In addition to inquiring within and regularly accessing your intuition, successful people also maintain a state of *mindfulness*. They know that mindset matters—a lot.

Dawa Tarchin Phillips, a mindfulness research specialist at the University of California Santa Barbara, defines *mindfulness* as "bringing one's complete attention to the present experience on a moment-to-moment basis." It means "paying attention in a particular way, on purpose, in the present moment and nonjudgmentally."

When you use the principles in this book to focus on your future, it's also imperative that you stay rooted in the present, that you take action and maintain a growth-oriented mindset. Cultivating the skill of mindfulness will help you stay focused on doing those things that will get you to where you want to be.

For Dawa's complete tutorial on becoming more mindful, present, and self-supporting as you implement *The Success Principles,* visit jackcanfield.com/tsp-resources. Scroll down to Principle 47 and click on the appropriate link.

PART FOUR

Create Successful Relationships

Personal relationships are the fertile soil from which all advancement, all success, all achievement in real life grows.

BEN STEIN
Writer, actor, and game show host

PRINCIPLE 48

BE HEAR NOW

Listen a hundred times. Ponder a thousand times. Speak once.

SOURCE UNKNOWN

There's a big difference between *hearing*—that is, simply receiving communication—and truly *listening,* which is the art of paying thoughtful attention with a mind toward understanding the complete message being delivered. Unlike simply *hearing* someone's words, listening requires maintaining eye contact, watching the person's body language, asking for clarification, and listening for the unspoken message.

In the news-reporting industry, journalists are trained in the art of active listening—an interview technique in which reporters listen and understand so well, they're able to ask intelligent, more in-depth questions about the information being delivered. Active listening is how good news stories are developed—and how many of us can improve our relationships, too. Not surprisingly, it also helps ensure accuracy and fairness, two of the most important hallmarks of a journalist—and two important qualities of any relationship.

LISTENING PAYS OFF

Marcia Martin is an executive coach. One of her clients, a senior vice president at a major bank, asked her if she could help him make his team meetings more powerful. He complained that his direct team wasn't really operating the way he wanted it to in their meetings. They didn't bring the right things to the meeting, they weren't focused on the right things, and they didn't present properly.

When Marcia asked him what he did in his meetings and what the problems were, he said he always started off his meetings by telling them what the purpose of the meeting was, what he felt their breakdowns were, and what he wanted them to do. By the time he finished describing his meetings, she could tell the whole meeting was him just spitting out instructions to his team members.

Marcia told him, "I would advise you to start your meeting with just one sentence: 'The purpose of this meeting is for me to find out from you what you feel is going on in each of your departments, what you feel the breakdowns are, and what you need from me.' And then you should be quiet and just let them talk and talk and talk until they have totally talked themselves out. If they stop talking, just say, 'Well, what else?' and let them talk some more."

She explained that his people probably hadn't had a chance to really empty out their feelings, their viewpoints, their suggestions, or their questions. He was packing them with too much information and all of his opinions, and he wasn't really listening. She told him to allow two hours for the meeting and not to say anything during that whole time. He was just to listen, write down notes, and nod his head—be present and be interested, but not speak.

Three days later, he pulled Marcia aside to tell her that he'd just had the most fantastic, powerful meeting he'd ever experienced in his life. He had done exactly what she'd suggested—and had listened in a way that he had never listened before. As a result, his team members had talked and talked and talked, and he had learned more about what his people were going through, what his people needed, and what to do for them in that one meeting than he had in all of his previous executive experience.

ARGUE LESS AND LISTEN MORE

A New York photographer I once met traveled all over the world doing expensive location shoots for big-name clients like Revlon and Lancôme. At one point he shared with me how he would give clients exactly what they had asked for, then be mystified when they didn't like the end result. Even if it were the pyramids in Egypt, he said, they'd ask him to shoot it over.

It did no good to become defensive or argue with the clients, even though he had followed their specifications perfectly. Instead, he eventually learned—after losing several lucrative accounts—that all he had to do was say, "So let me see if I've got this right. You want more of this and less of that? Correct? Okay, I'll go reshoot it and bring it back so you can see if you like it."

In other words, he learned to argue less with the people who were paying the bills and to listen more—responding and adjusting to their feedback until *they* were satisfied.

BE *INTERESTED* RATHER THAN INTERESTING

Another way people fail to listen carefully is to be too concerned with being interesting themselves, rather than being *interested* in the person they're listening to. They believe the route to success is to constantly talk—showing off their expertise or intelligence with their words and comments.

The best way to establish rapport with people and to win them over to your side is to be truly interested in them, to listen with the intention of really learning about them. When the person feels that you are really interested in getting to know them and their feelings, they will open up to you and share their true feelings with you much more quickly.

Work to develop an attitude of curiosity. Be curious about other people, what they feel, how they think, how they see the world. What are their hopes, dreams, and fears? What are their aspirations? What obstacles are they facing in their lives?

If you want people to cooperate with you, to like you, or to open up to you, you must be *interested* . . . in them. Instead of focusing on yourself, start focusing on others. Notice what makes *them* happy or unhappy. When your thoughts are more on others than on yourself, you feel less stress. You can act and respond with more intelligence. Your production level increases and you have more fun. Additionally, when you are *interested,* people respond to your interest in them. They want to be around you. Your popularity increases.

A POWERFUL QUESTION

During my year of attending Dan Sullivan's "Strategic Coach Program,"* he taught me one of the most powerful communication tools I have ever learned. It is one of the most effective ways to establish rapport and create a feeling of connection with another person. I have used it in both my business and personal life. It is a series of four questions:

1. If we were meeting three years from today, what has to have happened during that three-year period for you to feel happy about your progress?
2. What are the biggest dangers you'll have to face and deal with in order to achieve that progress?

---

*For information on the "Strategic Coach Program" or Dan Sullivan's excellent books and audio programs, go to strategiccoach.com.

3. What are the biggest opportunities that you have that you would need to focus on and capture to achieve those things?
4. What strengths will you need to reinforce and maximize, and what skills and resources will you need to develop that you don't currently have in order to capture those opportunities?

About one week after I had learned these questions, I was meeting with my sister Kim, who is the coauthor of all of our early *Chicken Soup for the Teenage Soul* books. I didn't feel like we were making much progress in getting connected, so I decided to try these new questions I had just learned and then really listen.

When I asked her the first question, it was as if I had magically opened a locked door. She proceeded to tell me about all of her hopes and dreams for her future. I think she must have talked for at least 30 minutes without interruption. Then I asked the second question. Off she went for another 15 minutes. I didn't say one word. Then I asked the third and fourth questions. Over an hour later, she stopped. She was grinning from ear to ear and looked unusually calm and relaxed. She smiled at me and said, "That's the best conversation I think we've ever had. I feel so clear and focused. I know exactly what I need to go and do now. Thank you."

It was amazing. I hadn't said a word—except for asking the four questions. She had taken herself through a process of clarification with those questions. She hadn't clearly addressed them before, and doing it with me had brought her great clarity and relief. I felt very connected to my sister, and she felt very connected to me. Up until then, I think I would have had a tendency at some point to jump in and tell her what I thought she should do, interrupting her own process of self-discovery by not listening.

Since that time I have used those questions with my wife, my children, my staff, my corporate clients, my coaching clients, prospective seminar participants, and numerous potential business partners. The results are always magical.

IT'S YOUR TURN

Take the time today to write those four questions on an index card or in your smartphone or tablet and carry it with you. Practice each day asking someone these questions over lunch or dinner. Start with your friends and your family members, too. You will be surprised how much you will learn and how much closer you will feel afterward.

Use these questions with every potential business client or business colleague. Once they have answered, you'll know whether or not there is a basis for a business relationship. You'll know whether or not your products and services can help them achieve their goals. If you find they don't want to answer these questions, then they are not people you want to do business with. They are either unaware of their future and can't think ahead, which will make it hard for you to help them—or they are unwilling to tell you the answers, which means there is no trust present and no basis for a relationship.

One final suggestion: Make sure to take yourself through the same four questions either alone on a piece of paper or verbally with a friend or mastermind partner. It's a valuable exercise.

PRINCIPLE 49

HAVE A HEART TALK

Most communication resembles a Ping-Pong game in which people are merely preparing to slam their next point across; but pausing to understand differing points of view and associated feelings can turn apparent opponents into true members of the same team.

CLIFF DURFEE
Creator of the Heart Talk process

Unfortunately, in too many business, educational, and other settings, there is never an opportunity for feelings to be expressed and heard, so they build up to the point that people have no capacity to focus on the business at hand. There is too much emotional static in the space. It's like trying to put more water into a glass that is already full. There is nowhere for it to go. You must first pour out the old water to make room for the new.

It's the same with emotions. People can't listen until they have been heard. They first need to get whatever is bothering them off their chest. Whether you are someone who has just come home from work, a parent looking at your child's report card with all Cs, a salesperson attempting to sell a new car, or a CEO overseeing the merger of two companies, you first need to let the other people speak about their needs and wants, hopes and dreams, fears and concerns, hurts and pains, before you talk about yours. It opens up a space inside of them so they're able to listen and take in what you have to say.

WHAT IS A HEART TALK?

A Heart Talk is a structured communication process in which eight agreements are strictly adhered to. It creates a safe environment for a deep level of communication to occur—without the fear of condemnation, unsolicited advice, interruption, or being rushed. It's also a powerful tool used to surface and release any unexpressed emotions that could otherwise get in the way of people being totally present to deal with the business at hand. It can be used at home, in business, in the classroom, with sports teams, and in religious settings to develop rapport, understanding, and intimacy.

WHEN TO USE A HEART TALK

Heart talks are useful

- Before or during a staff meeting
- At the beginning of a business meeting where two new groups of people are coming together for the first time
- After an emotionally stimulating event like a merger, a massive layoff, a death, a major athletic loss, an unexpected financial setback, or even a tragedy such as the terrorist attacks of September 11, 2001
- When there is a conflict between two individuals, groups, or departments
- On a regular basis at home, in the office, or in the classroom to create a deeper level of communication and intimacy

HOW TO CONDUCT A HEART TALK

A Heart Talk can be conducted with any size group of between two and ten people. You'll want to break a group larger than ten into several smaller groups, because if the group is larger than that, the trust and safety factors tend to diminish, and it can also take up too much time to complete.

The first time you conduct a Heart Talk, start by explaining that there is value in occasionally using a structure for communication that guarantees a deeper level of listening. The structure of a Heart Talk creates a safe, nonjudgmental space that supports the constructive—rather than the destructive—expression of feelings that, if left unexpressed, can block teamwork, synergy, creativity, innovation, and intuition, which are vital to the productivity and success of any venture.

GUIDELINES FOR A HEART TALK

Start by asking people to sit in a circle or around a table. Introduce the basic agreements, which include these:

- Only the person holding "the heart" is allowed to talk.
- You don't judge or criticize what anyone else has said.
- You pass the heart/object to the left after your turn, or say "I pass" if you have nothing to say.
- You talk only about how you feel.
- You keep the information that is shared confidential.
- You don't leave the Heart Talk until it's declared complete.

Keep passing the heart/object around the circle—multiple times if necessary—to ensure participants have more than one opportunity to share. If you have plenty of time, a Heart Talk completes naturally when the heart makes a complete circle without anyone having something to say.

Ask the group to agree to the guidelines, which are very important to make sure that the talk does not deteriorate and lose its value. Because no one is supposed to talk except for the person holding the object, it is often best to wait until the completion of the talk to remind people about certain agreements that need more attention. Another option is to have the agreements written down on paper or a whiteboard and to merely point to them if someone is getting too far off-track. Go around the group at least once—with everybody getting one turn—or set a time frame (say 15 minutes to 30 minutes; longer for more emotionally intense issues) and keep going around the group until the time runs out or nobody has anything more to say.

You can use any object to pass around—a ball, a paperweight, a book, anything that can be seen by the other participants. I have seen everything from a stuffed animal (a hospital staff), a baseball (a college baseball team), and a football helmet (a state championship football team) to a Native American talking stick (on a corporate river rafting trip). I actually prefer to use one of the many stuffed red velvet hearts that are available on Amazon* because they remind everyone that what we are hearing is coming from

---

*For more complete information, visit jackcanfield.com/tsp-resources. You can also obtain a copy of the *Heart Talk Book*. A bright-red card-stock heart is inserted in each book, with the key agreements printed on the back side for an easy reminder before having a Heart Talk. If you are an educator, there is also a complete classroom curriculum guide on this subject entitled *More Teachable Moments*.

the other person's heart—and that we are trying to get to the heart of the matter at hand.

RESULTS YOU CAN EXPECT FROM A HEART TALK

You can expect the following results from a Heart Talk:

- Enhanced listening skills
- Constructive expression of feelings
- Improved conflict resolution skills
- Improved abilities to let go of resentments and old issues
- Development of mutual respect and understanding
- Greater sense of connection, unity, and bonding

One of the most valuable uses of the Heart Talk for me was in a weeklong training that I was conducting for 120 school administrators in Bergen, Norway. We were about to start our afternoon session when someone announced that one of the workshop participants had been killed in an automobile accident during the lunch break. There was massive shock and grief in the room. It would have been impossible to proceed with the scheduled agenda, so I divided the participants into groups of six and taught them the guidelines for a Heart Talk. I told them to just keep passing the heart around until everyone in the group said "I pass" twice in a row, meaning that there was nothing else to be said.

The groups talked and cried for over an hour. People talked about their grief, their own sense of mortality, how precious and fleeting life really is, how scary life can sometimes be, and how you need to live in the moment because your future is never guaranteed. We then took a short break and were able to proceed with the scheduled activities. Whatever emotions there were had been expressed and heard. The group was once again ready to focus on the subject I was there to teach.

A HEART TALK SAVES THE FAMILY BUSINESS

James owned a small family business that had supported him and his family for years. His wife and two sons, both married with children, also worked as employees in the company. At least once a week, they would all gather together for a large meal, and James would do his best to unify this growing family. James hoped that when he retired, the family business would survive and continue to provide a living for everyone in the extended family.

Though it looked like an excellent plan on the surface, there had always been rivalry and competition between the two sons, and when both their wives started working in the business, things started coming apart at the seams. Resentments over little things were pushed down to supposedly keep the peace, but they would resurface later in sarcastic comments and unexpected outbursts of anger. When the two sons actually threw a couple of punches at each other, James realized they all needed to talk and clear the air. But he was afraid that the situation could become even more explosive unless there were some powerful ground rules present—so he decided to use the structure of a Heart Talk.

Sitting in a large circle after their weekly family meal, the group was unusually quiet, not knowing what to expect. James started by getting everyone to agree to the six rules and the structure of the talk. At first the heart was passed without much to say. The second time around one of the sons expressed his anger, and when the heart reached the other son, even greater hostility surfaced—yet it was clear no one was going to violate the guidelines, stomp out of the room, or throw something.

It wasn't an easy talk, and there were times you could tell everyone would have preferred any other activity—even if it were doing the dishes. But as the heart kept going around the circle, everyone began to have the experience that he or she had been heard, and the hostility began to dissipate. Then one of the son's wives started crying and shared that she was at her wit's end. With all the friction in the family and in the business, she couldn't take it anymore. She said that something had to change. At that moment, something released, and there wasn't a dry eye in the group. As the heart continued around and around, the sadness was soon replaced by an acknowledgment of their love for each other and the things they were grateful for.

Though it will never be known for sure, James believes that that Heart Talk was most likely the key thing that saved his business, his family, and his sanity.

PRINCIPLE 50

TELL THE TRUTH FASTER

When in doubt, tell the truth.

MARK TWAIN
Author of several classic American works of fiction, including
Tom Sawyer and *The Adventures of Huckleberry Finn*

Most of us avoid telling the truth because it's uncomfortable. We're afraid of the consequences—making others feel uncomfortable, hurting their feelings, or risking their anger. And yet, when we don't tell the truth, and others don't tell us the truth, we can't deal with matters from a basis in reality.

We've all heard the phrase that "the truth will set you free." And it will. The truth allows us to be free to deal with the way things are, not the way we imagine them to be or hope them to be or might manipulate them to be with our lies.

Telling the truth also frees up our energy. It takes energy to withhold the truth, keep a secret, or keep up an act.

WHAT HAPPENS WHEN YOU TELL THE TRUTH?

In my four-day advanced seminar, I often do a process called Secrets. It's a very simple exercise where we spend an hour or two telling the group our secrets—those things we imagine that if others knew, they surely wouldn't like us or approve of us. I invite participants to simply stand up and tell the group whatever it is they've been hiding and then sit down.

There is no discussion and no feedback, just sharing and listening. It starts out slowly as people test the water with "I cheated on my eighth-grade math exam" and "I stole a penknife from the hardware store when I was fourteen years old." But as people begin to realize that nothing bad is happening to anyone, people eventually open up and talk about deeper, more painful issues.

After there are no more secrets to come out, I ask the group if they feel any less loving or accepting toward anyone in the group. In all these years, I have never had anyone answer yes.

Then I ask, "How many people feel relieved to have gotten this off their chest?"

Everyone says that they do.

And then I ask, "How many of you feel closer to the other people in the group?" and again all of the hands go up. People realize that the things they've been hiding aren't so horrible, but in fact are usually shared by at least a few others in the group. They are not alone but rather are part of the human community.

But most astounding is what people report over the next few days.

Lifelong migraines disappear. Spastic colons relax and medication is no longer needed. Depression lifts and aliveness returns. People actually look years younger and more vital. It's quite amazing. One participant actually reported losing five pounds of excess weight over the ensuing two days. He had indeed released more than just some withheld information.

This example tells us that it takes a lot of energy to hold back our truth, and that energy, when it is released, can be used to focus on creating greater success in all areas of our lives. We can become less cautious and more spontaneous, more willing to be our natural selves. And when this happens, information that is vital to making things work and to getting things done can be shared and acted on.

WHAT DO YOU NEED TO SHARE?

In every area of our lives, the three things that most need to be shared are resentments that have built up, the unmet needs and demands that underlie those resentments, and unexpressed appreciations.

Underneath all resentments are unfulfilled needs and desires. Whenever you find yourself resenting someone, ask yourself, *What is it that I am wanting from him that I am not getting?* And then make the commitment to at least ask for it. As we have talked about earlier, the worst that you'll get is a no. You just might get a yes. But at least the request will be out in the open.

One of the most valuable practices and yet the hardest to do for most people is telling the truth when it is uncomfortable. Most of us are so worried about hurting other people's feelings that we don't share *our* true feelings. We end up hurting ourselves instead.

TELLING THE TRUTH PAYS DIVIDENDS

Shortly after I created the Foundation for Self-Esteem to take my work to the nonprofit world of education, prisons, social services, and other at-risk populations, my director, Larry Price, discovered a request for a proposal that had been issued by the Los Angeles County Office of Education. It turns out that more than 84% of the people going through the county's welfare-to-work orientation program never returned after the first day to start the job-training portion. The county knew it needed an orientation program that would give people hope and motivate them to complete their job training and create a better life for themselves and their families.

We knew we could design a program that met the county's specifications in their request for proposals, but we also knew it would not include enough contact hours and reinforcement to produce the results that the county was hoping for. It was clear that the way the county had envisioned the program just wouldn't work.

Eager to land the $730,000 contract and provide the foundation with badly needed operating funds, however, we decided to create an extensive proposal and worked for months crafting a beautiful presentation. The night before it was due, we even stayed up all night finalizing, printing, and collating the numerous copies that were to be submitted.

It must have been a good proposal, because we were selected as one of the three finalists and were called into the county offices for a live interview and final presentation.

I can still remember standing in front of the county offices saying to Larry, "You know, I'm not sure I want to win this competition. No matter how good a program we put together, the way they want it structured can't possibly give them the results they want. I think we should tell them the truth. How were they to know how it needs to be structured? They're not the motivation experts. How could they ask for something they didn't fully understand?"

Our fear was that the county officers would feel somehow judged or criticized and award the contract to someone else. It was a huge risk, especially with the dollar figure involved. But we decided to tell the truth.

The reaction of the county officers surprised us. After listening to our point of view, they decided to hire us anyway *because we were willing to tell the truth.* After analyzing what we said, they agreed and felt we were the only ones who correctly understood the situation they were dealing with.

The results were so fantastic that eventually the program we developed—the GOALS Program—was adopted by 19 other county welfare programs, plus organizations in 22 other states like the Housing and Urban Development Authority, Head Start, and as a prerelease program for San Quentin and several other prisons. So far, more than 900,000 people have graduated from the program.

THERE'S NO "PERFECT TIME" TO TELL THE HARD TRUTH

As I discovered with the Los Angeles County Office of Education, telling the truth was the difference between winning that contract and losing it. We could have compromised our integrity, but we decided instead to tell the truth sooner rather than later.

Learning to speak your truth sooner is one of the most important success habits you will ever develop. In fact, as soon as you start asking yourself the question *I wonder when would be the best time to tell the truth,* that's actually the best time to do so.

Will it be uncomfortable? Probably. Will it create lots of reactions? Yes. But it is the right thing to do. Get into the habit of telling the truth faster. Ultimately, you want to get to the point where you say it as soon as you think it. That's when you become totally authentic. What you see is what you get. People will know where you stand. You can be counted on to speak your mind.

"I DON'T WANT TO HURT THEIR FEELINGS"

A lot of times people use the excuse that they don't want to hurt another person's feelings. This is always a lie. If you ever catch yourself thinking this, what's really happening is that you're protecting yourself from your own feelings. You're avoiding what you will feel when they get upset. It is the coward's way out, and it simply delays having all your cards on the table.

This includes telling the kids that you are getting a divorce, that the family is moving to Texas because Daddy got a new job, that you are going to have to lay off some staff members, that you aren't going to be taking a family vacation this year, that you have to put the family pet to sleep, that you aren't going to be able to deliver the order by the date you promised, or that you lost the family nest egg in a bad stock deal.

Hiding the truth always backfires. The longer you withhold it, the more disservice you do to yourself and to the others involved.

YOU WON'T WANT TO HEAR THIS, BUT . . .

I don't want any yes-men around me. I want everybody to tell me the truth even if it costs them their jobs.

SAMUEL GOLDWYN
Cofounder of Metro-Goldwyn-Mayer (MGM) Studios

Marilyn Tam was working as a divisional manager overseeing the operations of 320 stores for Miller's Outpost when a friend told her Nike was planning to open their own concept stores and CEO Phil Knight was interested in hiring her to oversee the project. Nike was frustrated because sports shoe stores like Foot Locker weren't displaying their clothing apparel in a way that properly portrayed Nike's lifestyle image. Because Marilyn thought that working for Nike would be a great opportunity, she did some research prior to her meeting by visiting a number of different stores that carried Nike apparel so that she would be ready to make a proposal to Phil about how to create a store Nike would be proud to present to the world.

As she did her research, she discovered two things: The footwear was good. It was functional, durable, and priced well. But the apparel was a disaster. It was inconsistent in quality, sizing, and durability, and it was not integrated or color coordinated. She found out later that Nike's clothing line had been an afterthought in response to consumer demand for more Nike logo apparel. It had not been thought out in a coordinated way. Nike had simply gone out and bought stock goods and just put its own label on them. The company bought apparel from different manufacturers without any consistent standards in size, quality, or color. It was not an image that was really reflective of the brand.

Marilyn's dilemma was that her desire to work for Nike was in conflict with her professional judgment about the products. She was afraid that if she told Phil that the product wasn't consistent with the brand image and shouldn't be in stores, she wouldn't get the job.

When she finally met with Phil Knight in Oregon, the initial conversation about the potential of the new store concept was exciting. But as the conversation unfolded, Marilyn became more and more uncomfortable because she knew she needed to tell him the truth about the quality of the merchandise and her belief that the stores would fail if they went ahead without first creating a standardized and integrated product line. But she hesitated because she feared that, in his haste to get the stores up and running, he'd just find someone else to do it. After two hours, she finally spoke up and told Phil that the Nike shoes were great, but if they were going to do a concept store based on apparel, she thought the stores would fail because the products would not reflect what Nike stood for.

Just as she feared, her disclosure ended the conversation rather quickly. She flew back to California wondering if she had done the right thing. She felt that she had probably lost any chance of getting a job there, but she also felt good about having told the truth.

Two weeks later, Phil Knight called her and told her he had reconsidered what she said, had done his own research on the quality of the merchandise, and agreed with her assessment of the situation. He offered her the job as the first vice president of apparel and accessories. He told her, "You come, fix the goods; then we open the stores."

As you probably know, the rest is history. Though the decision to wait held up the opening of the Nike stores by about two years, the apparel division has had huge growth, and the concept stores have helped Nike continue to expand and take even greater hold on the American imagination.*

A FORMULA FOR HAVING CRUCIAL CONVERSATIONS

Conversations like the one Marilyn Tam had with Phil Knight are definitely uncomfortable and difficult, but the people who master the art of these difficult but crucial conversations are the ones who advance the furthest in their careers. If you need to have a crucial conversation, the kind where emotions run high and opinions vary greatly, there are some guidelines that can help you.

The first one is to stop scaring yourself in advance of the conversation by escalating the actual facts into something truly frightening. Most people presuppose what the other party will do when they hear about the matter.

---

*I highly recommend Marilyn's inspirational book *How to Use What You've Got to Get What You Want* (New York: SelectBooks, 2004). In it, she shares her extraordinary life and the principles of success she has learned from her birth into a traditional family in Hong Kong to her meteoric rise through the executive ranks of the international business world with such world-class companies as Aveda, Reebok, and Nike.

This process of telling ourselves a story and attaching feelings to what's happened takes mere nanoseconds.

If you need to have a crucial conversation, but stop yourself by saying, *I'm afraid of how they'll react* or *I don't know how to begin,* realize that the issue you're failing to address is probably not going to go away—no matter how much you ignore it. In these situations, it's helpful to have a formula that not only steps you through the conversation but also helps both of you determine a solution.

1. To begin, determine your motivation for having the conversation, whether it's merely to express yourself and get something off your chest—or to eventually solve a problem.
2. Make sure to schedule enough time to have the conversation.
3. Plan your conversation in advance by crafting a clear message that keeps you on track. Start with the facts of what *actually* happened or is happening versus the story you may have made up in your head. How will you report the facts of the situation? Be sure to separate the actual facts from the feelings you've attached to the situation or the event.
4. After reporting the facts, ask the other person, "How do you see this?" What do *they* think the impact is? Oftentimes we presuppose or imagine some horrible reaction or consequence without knowing what the other person's actual experience of the situation is.
5. Ask the other party what they would like to do to resolve the matter—if in fact you are looking for resolution. Sometimes simply expressing yourself might be your goal.
6. If you decide to resolve the issue, agree on and document what actions you will both take, by when you will take them, and how you will follow up with each other.★

OVERCOMING THE FEAR OF JUDGMENT

Sometimes we don't tell the truth faster because we're afraid of being judged by others. We think we're not good enough, that our opinions are odd, or that something very real is "wrong with us"—so we don't divulge

---

★ Two valuable resources are *Difficult Conversations,* revised edition by Douglas Stone, Bruce Patton, Sheila Heen, and Roger Fisher (New York: Penguin, 2010) and *Crucial Conversations,* updated second edition, by Kerry Patterson, Joseph Grenny, Ron McMillan, and Al Switzler (New York: McGraw-Hill, 2011).

what's going on, explain why we can't participate, admit how we messed up, reveal why we can't donate, or express how our viewpoint is simply different.

Perhaps we've even been judged previously, after tentatively offering an explanation, so we hesitate to open ourselves up to judgment again. Unfortunately, this kind of withholding takes up a lot of energy. It requires us to monitor our conversations, plan all our actions, remember who was told what, and constantly formulate polite explanations for our "situation."

Imagine instead the freedom of simply stating your reasons and moving on. That kind of self-confidence is powerful and impressive—and few people will judge you for that kind of forthrightness.

When Charlie Collins was nine years old, he was diagnosed with macular degeneration. By the age of 13 he was declared legally blind. As a result of being unable to see anything but dim shapes, colors, and areas of light, Charlie struggled through high school, tried college but flunked out twice, and started drinking and taking drugs. After moving back in with his parents and working a series of whatever odd jobs he could get, Charlie eventually started his own company—Vision Dynamics—which supplies products and services to people living with low-vision blindness so they can lead independent and happy lives. But even with his ensuing business success and successful marriage, Charlie had low self-esteem and still considered himself "that dumb blind guy."

Looking to boost his self-esteem, Charlie found my audio album *Maximum Confidence* on the Internet. Later he discovered two of my audiobooks: *The Aladdin Factor* and *The Power of Focus*. For the next two years he listened to the audiotapes over and over. That's when he decided to attend a three-day seminar with me. Here's the rest of the story in his words.

> I was so impressed with what I was learning from Jack Canfield that in early 2008, I found myself sitting in the first row at a three-day seminar, hearing the man speak live.
>
> A few weeks earlier, when I'd registered for the program, I hadn't told anyone I was vision-impaired. Now, surrounded by more than 300 smart, successful people, I tried to hide my disability. I thought these people might feel sorry for me or look down on me.
>
> It wasn't a problem the first day. I took copious notes, writing with a big black Sharpie—the only way I could see what I was writing—until the lady to my right asked me to please use a different pen because the fumes from the Sharpie were bothering her. I didn't want to tell her why I needed to use that particular type of pen, so I took out a ballpoint pen and pretended to use it.

The next day, the hiding thing came to a head. I arrived for the morning meeting and saw our name badges laid out on a table outside the door. I couldn't see the writing on them at all. I looked around to make sure no one was watching me and then bent down with my nose an inch from the badges, trying to find mine and straightening up whenever I heard someone approach—which was every 30 seconds or so.

After a few minutes of this, I was panicked, ready to run back to my hotel room, skip the meeting, and hide until it was time for my flight back to Connecticut.

The doors were about to close when I had an idea. The next person who walked up to the table was a woman. "Excuse me," I said. "I left my glasses in my room. My name's Charlie. Can you point out my badge to me?" She smiled and handed it to me. I thanked her, my heart pounding, and sprinted into the meeting room.

At the first break, I walked up to the stage and introduced myself to Jack. We began talking, and for some reason, I told him about my experience with the name badges. After the break, I sat down in my chair, ready for more, when I heard Jack say, "Somebody please give Charlie the microphone." Then he asked me to stand up.

"Hi, Charlie," Jack said. "I want you to take a look around at all the people in the room. Now tell them what you told me at the break."

I was angry! How could he expose me like that! How could he make me tell everyone my secret? But I did it. And as I spoke, I could feel more and more power flowing inside me. At the end of my story, people clapped!

Jack said, "So, Charlie, I think you get it: You need to stop living your life this way. As of right now, you're no longer going to allow that legal blindness to run your life." Then he looked around the room and asked, "Is there anybody here who would say no if Charlie approached them and asked for help?"

The room went nuts. Everyone was calling out, "I'd help him!" "I'd love to help!" "Of course I'd help him!"

Jack continued, "Human beings like to help each other. That's what we're here for, to serve and help each other—and all of us need help at certain times. All you have to do is tell the truth and ask. Now do you believe that, Charlie?"

To my surprise, I did.

For the rest of the seminar, Charlie had a great time. While he felt somewhat vulnerable, he also was more open, authentic, and empowered than he'd ever been before. His transformation eventually led Charlie to what he believes is his true calling: being a motivational speaker who inspires others to look beyond life's challenges.

At the same time that his company sells items that make life easier for people with impaired vision, Charlie himself is able to inspire and empower them through personal-growth workshops and classes—a unique approach that has helped his business flourish year after year. Also, Charlie travels around the country talking to groups, who are both sighted and blind, about how we can all overcome our "blind spots." Thanks to telling the truth faster, he is living his authentic life-purpose—teaching people how to genuinely "see" again.

PRINCIPLE 51

SPEAK WITH IMPECCABILITY

Impeccability of the word can lead you to personal freedom, to huge success and abundance; it can take away all fear and transform it into joy and love.

DON MIGUEL RUIZ
Author of *The Four Agreements**

For most of us, our words are spoken without consciousness. We rarely stop to think about what we are saying. Our thoughts, opinions, judgments, and beliefs roll off our tongues without a care for the damage or the benefits they can produce.

Successful people, on the other hand, are the master of their words. They know that if they don't take dominion over their words, their words will take dominion over them. They're conscious of the thoughts they think and the words they speak—both about themselves and others. They know that to be more successful, they need to speak words that will build self-esteem and self-confidence, build relationships, and build dreams—words of affirmation, encouragement, appreciation, love, acceptance, possibility, and vision.

To speak with impeccability is to speak from your highest self. It means that you speak with intention and with integrity. It means that your words are in alignment with what you say you want to produce—your vision and your dreams.

---

*I wish to express my gratitude to Don Miguel Ruiz, author of *The Four Agreements,* for the insights on the impeccability of the word contained in this chapter. For more information, I strongly encourage you to read *The Four Agreements* (San Rafael, CA: Amber-Allen Publishing, 1997).

YOUR WORD HAS POWER

When you speak with impeccability, your words have power not only with yourself but also with others. To speak with impeccability is to speak only words that are true, that uplift, and that affirm other people's worth.

As you learn how to speak with impeccability, you'll discover that words are also the basis of all relationships. How I speak *to you* and *about you* determines the quality of our relationship.

WHAT YOU SAY *TO OTHERS* CREATES A RIPPLE EFFECT IN THE WORLD

Let no corrupt communication proceed out of your mouth,
but that which is good to the use of edifying,
that it may minister grace unto the hearers.

EPHESIANS 4:29
(King James version of the Bible)

Successful people speak words of inclusion rather than words of separation, words of acceptance rather than words of rejection, and words of tolerance rather than words of prejudice.

If I express love and acceptance to you, you will experience love for me. If I express judgment and contempt for you, you will judge me back. If I express gratitude and appreciation for you, you will express gratitude and appreciation back to me. If I express words of hatred toward you, you will most likely hate me back.

The truth is, your words put out a certain energy or message that creates a reaction in others—a reaction that is usually returned to you multiplied. If you are rude, impatient, arrogant, or hostile, you can expect negative conduct to be returned to you.

Everything you say produces an effect in the world. Everything you say to someone else produces an effect in that person. Know that you are constantly creating something—either positive or negative—with your words.

Always ask yourself, *Is what I am about to say going to advance the cause of my vision, mission, and goals? Will it uplift the hearer? Will it inspire, motivate, and create forward momentum? Will it dissolve fear and create safety and trust? Will it build self-esteem, self-confidence, and a willingness to risk and take action?* If not, find words that will, or keep silent.

STOP LYING

As with negative conduct, when you lie, you not only separate yourself from your higher self but you also run the risk of being found out and eroding others' trust even more.

With the *Chicken Soup for the Soul*® series, we had a policy that except for poems and stories that were clearly parables or fables, all the stories we printed in *Chicken Soup* books were true. This was important to us because if the story was inspiring, we wanted readers to be able to say, *If they can do it, then I can do it, too.*

Occasionally, we found out that a contributor had fabricated a story—simply made it up. Every time we learned that, we ended up not using any more of that writer's stories. We no longer trusted such writers. Their word was no longer impeccable.

In reality, lying is the product of low self-esteem—the belief that you and your abilities are somehow not enough to get what you want. It is also based on the false belief that you can't handle the consequences of people knowing the truth about you—which is simply another way of saying *I am not enough.*

WHAT YOU SAY *ABOUT* OTHERS MATTERS EVEN MORE

If we look back through history, all the world's highest and most respected beings and spiritual teachers have warned us against gossip and judgment of others. It's because they knew how damaging untruth really is. Wars have been started over words. People have been killed because of words. Deals have been lost because of words. Marriages have been destroyed because of words.

Not only that, but gossip and judgment affect you, too, because you end up releasing a poison into the river of energy that is set up to bring you that which you truly want.

When you speak ill of another to anyone else, it may temporarily bond you to that other person, but it creates a lasting impression in the other that you are the kind of person who gossips negatively about others. That other person will always be wondering—even if unconsciously—when you will turn that verbal poison against them. It will erode their sense of deep trust in you.

Even without any words being spoken, others can pick up your negative, judgmental, and critical energy toward them. Then, what you say about others has a way of finding its way back to the person you are talking about. Many times, people who care about me will call to say that someone I know has said something negative about me. What does that do to my relationship with them? It creates a subtle crack.

Additionally, I have had to learn the hard way that when I gossip about another person, it (1) brings me down in the moment, (2) focuses my attention on what I *don't* want in my life—rather than creating more of what I *do* want, and (3) literally wastes my breath. I've learned that I could be using my mental and verbal powers to create more of what I *do* want by focusing the power of my words on abundance instead.

To speak with more impeccability when addressing others,

- Make a commitment to be impeccable in your speech when talking to others.
- Make an effort to appreciate something about every person you interact with. Look for their positive aspects.
- Make a commitment to tell the truth, as best you can, in all of your interactions and dealings with others. Make a commitment to do it for one day, then two days in a row, then a whole week. If you falter, start over. Keep building that muscle.
- Make it the intention of every interaction with others that you uplift them in some small way. Notice how you feel when you do that.

Often, we use words in a damaging way not because we are bad people but simply because we are not paying attention. No one ever taught us how powerful words really are.

IDLE GOSSIP

I learned how powerful idle gossip is during my first year of teaching high school. On the first day of school, I walked into the teachers' lounge before school started. One of the older teachers approached me and said, "I see you have Devon James in your American history class. I had him last year. He is a real terror. Good luck!"

You can imagine what happened when I walked into class and saw Devon James. I was examining his every move. I was waiting for him to show signs of the terror he was promised to be. Devon didn't have a chance. He was already typecast. I already had an image of him before he ever opened his mouth. No doubt I was even sending him a sort of unconscious signal: *I know you are a troublemaker.* That is the definition of *prejudice*—prejudging a person before you ever really get a chance to know them.

I learned never to let another teacher—or anyone, for that matter—tell me what someone else was going to be like before I met the person. I learned to rely on my own observations. I also learned that if I treated all people with respect and signaled them through my speech and actions that I had high expectations for them, they almost always lived up to that positive expectation.

The biggest cost of gossiping, of course, is that it robs you of a clear mind. People who are impeccable see the world more clearly. They think more clearly and thus can be more effective in their decisions and actions. In *The Four Agreements,* Don Miguel Ruiz likens the process of gossiping to releasing a computer virus into your mind, causing it to think a little less clearly every time.

Here are some practical ways to stop yourself and discourage others from gossiping:

1. Change the subject.
2. Say something positive about the other person.
3. Walk away from the conversation.
4. Keep quiet.
5. Clearly state that you no longer want to participate in gossiping about others.

CHECK YOUR THOUGHTS AND YOUR FEELINGS

How do you know when you have been impeccable with your words? When you feel good, happy, joyful, calm, and at peace. If you're not feeling these things, check your thoughts, your self-talk, and your verbal and written communication with others.

When you begin to be more impeccable with your words, you will begin to see changes happening in all areas of your life.

PRINCIPLE 52

WHEN IN DOUBT, CHECK IT OUT

There may be some substitute for hard facts,
but if there is, I have no idea what it can be.
J. PAUL GETTY
One of the richest men in America and author of *How to Be Rich*

Too many people waste valuable time and precious resources wondering what other people are thinking, intending, or doing. Rather than just asking them for clarification, they make assumptions—usually assuming against themselves—and then make decisions based on those assumptions.

Successful people, on the other hand, don't waste time assuming or wondering. They simply check it out: "I'm wondering if . . ." or "Would it be okay to . . . ?" or "Are you feeling . . . ?" They are not afraid of rejection, so they ask.

PEOPLE ALWAYS IMAGINE THE WORST WHEN THEY DON'T KNOW WHAT IS TRUE

What's the fundamental problem with assuming anything? It's that people are usually the most afraid of that which they don't know. Instead of checking into things, they assume facts that may not exist, then build prejudices around those assumptions. They make bad decisions based on these assumptions, on rumors, or on other peoples' opinions.

Consider the difference when you know all the facts—the *actual* facts—about a situation, person, problem, or opportunity. Then you can make decisions and take actions on the basis of what is real rather than what you are making up.

I remember a seminar I once conducted where one attendee—sitting in the back of the room—looked like he just didn't want to be there. He looked hostile and withdrawn. He had his arms crossed over his chest. He had what looked like a permanent scowl on his face and looked like he hated everything I had to say. I knew if I wasn't careful, I'd end up focusing on him and his apparent hostility, to the detriment of everyone else in the room.

As you can imagine, no speaker wants to hear that an audience member was forced to come to the seminar by his boss or that he is unhappy with the material or—even worse—that he dislikes the speaker himself. Given this participant's body language, it would have been easy to assume one of these things to be the case.

Instead, I checked it out.

I approached him during the first break and said, "I can't help but notice you don't look like you're in a really good space. I was wondering if maybe the workshop's not working for you. Or maybe you were sent here by your boss against your will and you really don't want to be here. I'm just really concerned."

At that point, his entire demeanor shifted. He said, "Oh no. I'm loving everything you're saying. But I feel like I'm coming down with the flu. I didn't want to stay home and miss this, because I knew how good it would be. It's taking every ounce of my concentration just to be here, but it's worth it because I'm getting so much out of it."

Wow. If I hadn't asked, I could have ruined my whole day assuming the worst. How many times do *you* make assumptions—good or bad—without checking them out?

Do you assume without checking when a special project is due that all parties will deliver on time? Do you assume without checking that what you're providing is what everybody needs? Do you assume without checking at the end of a meeting that everyone is clear on who is responsible for getting which action items done by which date?

Imagine how much easier it would be to *not* assume—and instead say, "John, you're going to complete the report by next Friday. Right? And Mary, you're going to get a quote from the printer by Tuesday at five. Right?"

WE USUALLY HESITATE THE MOST WHEN IT MIGHT BE BAD NEWS

It's usually when we assume the worst that we don't want to check it out. We're simply afraid of what the answer might be. If I arrive home from work and my wife has a scowl on her face, it's easy to assume that she's mad at me. And though I could start walking around on tiptoes, thinking I've done something wrong and anticipating a blowup, imagine how much better it would be for our relationship if I simply said, "You don't look happy. What's going on?"

The moment you begin to check it out, two things happen.

First, you find out the real facts. Did you really do something wrong—or did she just get a nasty phone call from her sister that you don't know about? Second, you have the option to do something about it—to help her shift her mood—if you know what is really going on.

This goes the same for things that might improve your quality of life. Perhaps you assume there's no way to get a ticket to the rock concert at this late date or that you'll never be accepted into that arts program or that you can't afford that antique buffet that would look great in the dining room.

It's so much simpler just to ask. Check it out, using phrases such as *"I'm wondering if . . ."* and *"Would it be okay if . . ."* and *"Are you feeling . . ."* and *"Is there a possibility of getting . . ."* and *"What do I have to do in order to . . ."* and *"What would have to happen for you to be able to . . ."* and so on.

DO YOU MEAN . . . ?

Another way to check out assumptions is to use a technique I teach couples that can help improve communication in your relationships. I call it the "Do You Mean" technique.

Let's say that my wife asks me if I would be willing to help her clean out the garage on Saturday.

"No," I say.

Now, my wife could instantly assume, *Jack's mad at me. He doesn't care about my needs. He doesn't care that my car no longer fits in the garage,* and so on. But with the "Do You Mean" technique, she assumes nothing but *asks* what I'm really thinking instead.

"Jack, do you mean that you're not ever going to help me with this task, that you want me to do it all myself?"

"No, I don't mean that."

"Do you mean that you would rather be doing something else?"

"No, I don't mean that either."

"Do you mean that you're busy Saturday and you have something else planned that I don't know about?"

"Yes, that's exactly what I mean. I'm sorry I hadn't told you yet. It slipped my mind."

Sometimes, people don't immediately tell the reasons behind their answers. They just say no, with no explanation for their position. Men are more likely to respond like this. Whereas women will often give you all kinds of reasons why their answer is no; men more often will just give you the bottom line, not the details. Asking "Do you mean . . . ?" will get you a lot more clarity, so that you aren't left wondering what is really going on.

CHECKING IT OUT
CONTRIBUTES TO YOUR SUCCESS

Checking out your assumptions improves your communication, your relationships, your quality of life, and most especially your success and productivity in the workplace. You start getting better results. You don't show up with parts missing. You don't make assumptions about what people were going to do that they didn't do. Whenever you have the inkling that Barbara's not going to finish that on time, you call Barbara. You check it out.

W. Edwards Deming, the brilliant systems expert who helped post–World War II Japan manufacture automobiles, electronics, and other goods better than almost any other country on the planet, once said the first 15% of any project is the most important. This is where you need to get clear, gather data, check things out.

For example, when you get into a business relationship, you determine in the beginning—in the first 15%—how you'll work together, how you'll resolve conflicts, what the exit strategy is if someone wants to leave, what the criteria are for determining if one of the people is not living up to his or her side of the bargain, and so on. Most of the conflicts that arise later in relationships are because people made erroneous assumptions without checking them out. They failed to get clear up front on their agreements.

SPACE BETWEEN THE RULES

Of course, the 15% rule also applies to any personal goal you might pursue as well. Remember bestselling author Tim Ferriss, who once won the national kickboxing championship with just six weeks of training? The story behind that story is that he didn't assume *anything* about the rules of kickboxing but instead checked them out thoroughly. He learned from his research that if you threw your opponent out of the ring twice in one round, you won the match.

Now, in kickboxing, most people think of kicking and boxing. Ferriss, on the other hand, was a wrestler by training. So he told his coach, "Don't teach me how to knock someone out. Teach me how to throw my opponent out of the ring while not getting knocked out myself." That's how he won the championship. He determined the difference between what the rules *actually* were and what people *assumed* the rules were.

In life, there are a lot of instances where there is space to maneuver between the rules. If you don't ask and simply assume you can't accomplish something, it may be that you *could* have easily succeeded through some loophole or other hidden fact that is revealed only when you research it—when you *check it out*.

PRINCIPLE 53

PRACTICE UNCOMMON APPRECIATION

There is more hunger for love and appreciation in this world than for bread.

MOTHER TERESA
Winner of the Nobel Peace Prize

I have yet to find a man, however exalted his station, who did not do better work and put forth greater effort under a spirit of approval than under a spirit of criticism.

CHARLES M. SCHWAB
First president of the U.S. Steel Corporation

A recent management study revealed that 46% of employees leaving a company do so because they feel unappreciated; 61% said their bosses don't place much importance on them as people, and 88% said they do not receive acknowledgment for the work they do.

I've never known anyone to complain about receiving too much positive feedback. Have you? In fact, just the opposite is true.

Whether you are an entrepreneur, manager, teacher, parent, coach, or simply a friend, if you want to be successful with other people, you must master the art of appreciation.

Consider this: Every year, a management consulting firm conducts a survey with 200 companies on the subject of what motivates employees. When given a list of 10 possible things that would most motivate them, the employees always list *appreciation* as the number one motivator. When asked to rank-order that same list, the managers and supervisors ranked *appreciation* number eight. This is a major mismatch.

THE FIVE LANGUAGES OF
LOVE AND APPRECIATION

We have found that each person has a primary and secondary language of appreciation. Our primary language communicates more deeply to us than the others. Although we will accept appreciation in all five languages, we will not feel truly encouraged unless the message is communicated through our primary language.

GARY CHAPMAN AND PAUL WHITE
Coauthors of *The 5 Languages of Appreciation in the Workplace*

When I wrote the first edition of this book in 2005, I talked about how it was valuable to make a distinction between three kinds of appreciation—auditory, visual, and kinesthetic. These are the three different ways the brain takes in information, and everybody has a dominant type they prefer. Auditory people need to hear it, visual people need to see it, and kinesthetic people need to feel it. For example, if you give visual feedback to an auditory person, it doesn't have the same effect as verbal feedback. The auditory person might say, "He sends me letters, cards, and emails, but he never takes the time to pick up the phone or walk over here and tell me face-to-face."

Visual people, on the other hand, like to receive something they can see and perhaps even tape to their cubicle, put on their bulletin board, or hang on their refrigerator. They feel appreciated when they receive letters, cards, certificates of appreciation, plaques, trophies, pictures, and gifts—things they can see that will help keep the memory of it around forever. You can usually tell these people by their walls, bulletin boards, and refrigerators. They are covered with reminders that they are loved and appreciated.

Kinesthetic people need to feel it—a hug, a handshake, a high five, a pat on the back, a back rub, going for a walk together, going out dancing, or taking time to play a sport together.

While the auditory-visual-kinesthetic distinction is a useful one, relationship counselor Gary Chapman has created a model of the Five Love Languages that is a very useful further refinement of how people need different forms of communication to feel fully appreciated and loved. Chapman first noted the importance of this distinction in his work with couples, but has evolved it to include communicating with children, adult children, teenagers, people in the military, and people at work.*

WHAT ARE THE FIVE LOVE LANGUAGES?

Words of Affirmation. If this is someone's primary love language, they feel most cared for when you are open and expressive in telling them how wonderful you think they are, how much you appreciate them and what they do, and sharing words of encouragement expressing your belief in their talents and abilities.

Quality Time. If someone's love language is quality time, they need you to be fully present and engaged with them when you are talking with them or engaging in the activity at hand, no matter how trivial. While my wife, Inga, is a very kinesthetic person—she majored in physical education, was a massage therapist and a physical trainer, taught skiing and yoga, and loves to go hiking, swimming in the ocean, body surfing, and dancing—her primary love language is quality time, not physical touch as I originally thought.

When I am with her, she wants my full attention with the TV off, not looking at my computer or my iPhone, giving her full eye contact and actively listening and responding to what she is saying. When she returns from a session with her spiritual teacher, she always comments on how present he is, how deeply he listens to her, and how much she feels seen and heard by him. She loves to sit by our pool and have long conversations. She loves to go on long walks together with me or one of her close friends, and she can easily spend an hour on the phone with her sister talking about family members.

Receiving Gifts. If someone's primary love language is receiving gifts, you need to give them a gift for them to feel loved and appreciated. "Daddy, what did you bring me?" Receiving gifts is the primary love language of Patty Aubery, the president of the Canfield Training Group. If I bring her back a gift from one of my travels, she knows that I was thinking about her and took the time to buy her something meaningful. It can be as simple as a bottle of melatonin when I learned she was having trouble sleeping at night

---

*For a thorough exploration of the five love languages, I recommend you read *The 5 Love Languages: The Secret to Love That Lasts* by Gary Chapman (Chicago, IL: Northfield Publishing, 2009) and *The 5 Languages of Appreciation in the Workplace: Empowering Organizations by Encouraging People* by Gary Chapman and Paul White (Chicago, IL: Northfield Publishing, 2012).

or a case of Kirin Free, her favorite nonalcoholic beer that I learned about when we were eating lunch at Nobu, a Japanese restaurant in Malibu. Or it can be as expensive as the Rolex watch I bought her when we sold one of our companies that she helped build.

Acts of Service. If someone's love language is acts of service, doing something for them makes them feel appreciated. It could be watching the kids so they can go to the gym, washing the dishes without being asked, bringing them breakfast in bed, running an errand for them, or volunteering to help them out on a project.

Physical Touch. This love language is just like it sounds. A warm hug, a kiss, snuggling, holding hands, a massage, and sexual intimacy will make them feel most loved. In the work setting, an appropriate hug, a firm handshake, a pat on the back, a high five, a fist bump, or a one-minute shoulder massage works. I have also given gift certificates for pedicures and foot massages to staff and friends whose love language is physical touch.

One of the key things to remember with all of this is that your own primary love language may not be the primary love language of the person you want to appreciate. If you appreciate someone in the wrong language, whether it is your wife or daughter at home or an employee or coworker at work, it is like speaking French to a person who speaks only Chinese. The message doesn't get through.

Also remember that everyone has a secondary love language as well. While my primary love language is physical touch, I also respond to words of affirmation and gifts. Inga also loves acts of service, and my business partner Patty also loves words of affirmation.

So if you want to be a real pro at delivering uncommon appreciation, you'll want to learn which kind of feedback makes the most impact on the person to whom you are delivering it. Here are three quick ways to help you determine someone else's love language.

1. *Observe the person's behavior around others.* One of the easiest ways to determine a person's love language is to watch how they interact with others. Most people speak in their own love language, so how they behave offers clues as to what's most important to them. How do they respond in a social setting? Are they a hugger? If so, then physical touch could be their primary language. Are they always the first one to give a compliment? In that case,

words of affirmation may be their love language. Look for patterns.
2. *Listen to what they most often complain about.* The things that bother them about other people are important clues. If they say, "My husband went on a vacation and didn't bring anything back for me," or if they brighten up every time they receive a gift, then receiving gifts might be their primary love language.
3. *Pay attention to their requests.* Listen to what they ask of you. People will often reveal their love language through little hints, like saying, "Bring me home a surprise from your business trip," "Give me a hug!" or "I need you to turn off the TV when I'm talking to you."

At some level, I think we all like to receive gifts, acts of kindness, and words of affirmation, but if words of affirmation is not your primary language, it won't register as deeply as your primary one, so, as with all things, you have to experiment to see what works.

HANG IN THERE UNTIL YOU GET IT RIGHT

I once took a couples workshop with Dr. Harville Hendrix, the coauthor of *Getting the Love You Want: A Guide for Couples,* in which he told the story about learning exactly how his wife wanted to be told she was loved and appreciated. Because she always gave other people flowers as gifts of appreciation, he figured that was what she would also want. So one day he sent her a dozen roses. When he came home from work, he was expecting to get what he called his reward—a big, gracious thank-you from his wife.

When he walked in, she didn't even mention it. When he asked her if she had received the roses, she said yes. "Didn't you like them?" he asked.

"Not particularly."

"I don't understand. You always give other people flowers. I thought you loved flowers."

"Not really that much."

"Well, what do you like to get?"

"Cards," she replied.

Okay, he thought. So the next day he went to the card store and bought her a huge, oversize Snoopy card with a funny inscription inside and placed it where she would find it during the day. That night when he came home, he was once again expecting his reward.

No reward. He was so disappointed. He asked, "Did you find the card?"

"Yes."

"Didn't you like it?"

"Not really."

"Well, why not? I thought you liked to get cards."

"I do, but not funny cards. I like the kind of cards that you get at the art museums that have a piece of beautiful art on the front and then a really sweet and romantic message on the inside."

Okay.

The next day he went to the Metropolitan Museum of Art and bought a beautiful card and wrote a sweet, romantic inscription on the inside. The next day he placed it where his wife would find it. When he returned home, she met him at the door and smothered him with kisses and appreciation for the perfect card.

Out of his commitment to make sure that she knew he loved her, he finally found the perfect medium for his message.

APPRECIATION AS A SECRET OF SUCCESS

Another important reason for being in a state of appreciation as often as possible is that when you are in such a state, you are in one of the highest vibrational (emotional) states possible. When you are in a state of appreciation and gratitude, you are in a state of abundance. You are appreciating what you do have instead of focusing on and complaining about what you don't have. Your focus is on what you have received, and you always get more of what you focus on. Because the Law of Attraction states that like energy attracts like energy, you will attract more abundance—more to be thankful for. It becomes an upward-spiraling process of ever-increasing abundance that just keeps getting better and better.

Think about it. The more grateful people are for the gifts we give them, the more inclined we are to give them more gifts. Their gratitude and appreciation reinforces our giving. The same principle holds as true on a universal and spiritual level as it does on an interpersonal level.

KEEPING SCORE

When I first learned about the power of appreciation, it made total sense to me. However, it was still something that I forgot to do. I hadn't yet turned it into a habit. A valuable technique that I employed to help me lock in this new habit was to carry a 3" × 5" card in my pocket all day, and every time I acknowledged and appreciated someone, I would place a check mark on the card. I would not allow myself to go to bed until I had appreciated 10 people. If it was late in the evening and I didn't have 10 check marks, I would appreciate my wife and children, I would send an e-mail to several staff people, or I would write a letter to my mother or my stepfather. I did whatever it took until it became an unconscious habit. I did this every single day for six months—until I no longer needed to carry the card to remind me.

With today's technology, you can also set up reminders in your smartphone or computer calendar—anything that keeps you on track.

TAKE TIME TO APPRECIATE YOURSELF, TOO

David Casstevens, formerly of the *Dallas Morning News,* tells a story about Frank Szymanski, a Notre Dame center in the 1940s, who had been called as a witness in a civil suit in South Bend, Indiana.

"Are you on the Notre Dame football team this year?" the judge asked.

"Yes, Your Honor."

"What position?"

"Center, Your Honor."

"How good a center?"

Szymanski squirmed in his seat, but said firmly, "Sir, I'm the best center Notre Dame has ever had."

Coach Frank Leahy, who was in the courtroom, was surprised. Szymanski had always been modest and unassuming. So when the proceedings were over, he took Szymanski aside and asked why he had made such a statement. Szymanski blushed.

"I hated to do it, Coach," he said. "But, after all, I was under oath."

I want you to be under oath for the rest of your life and own the magnificent being you are, the positive qualities you have, and the wonderful accomplishments you have achieved.

PRINCIPLE 54

KEEP YOUR AGREEMENTS

Your life works to the degree you keep your agreements.
WERNER ERHARD
Founder of EST Training and the Landmark Forum

Never promise more than you can perform.
PUBLILIUS SYRUS
A Latin writer of maxims in the first century BC

It used to be that one's word was one's bond. Agreements were made and kept with a minimum of fanfare. People thought carefully about whether they could deliver on their promises before agreeing to anything. It was that important. Today, keeping one's agreements seems to be a hit-or-miss affair.

THE HIGH COST OF NOT KEEPING YOUR AGREEMENTS

In my seminars, I ask participants to agree to a list of 15 ground rules that include things like being on time, sitting in a different chair after every break, and no alcoholic beverages until after the training is over. If they will not agree to play by the ground rules, I do not allow them to take the training. I even have them sign a form in their workbook that says, "I agree to keep all these guidelines and ground rules."

On the morning of the third day, I ask everyone who has broken one of the ground rules to stand up. We then look at what we can learn from the experience. What becomes apparent is how casually we give our word—and then how casually we break it.

But what's even more interesting is that most people know they are going to break at least one of the guidelines *before agreeing to them*. And yet they agree to them anyway. Why? Most people want to avoid the discomfort of questioning, challenging, or asking for an exception to the rules. They don't want to be the focus of attention. They don't want to risk confrontation of any kind. Others want to take the training without really following, challenging, or asking for an exception to the rules, so they appear to agree, but they don't really intend to follow through.

The real problem is not that people give and break their word so easily; it's that they don't realize the psychological cost of doing so.

When you don't keep your agreements, you pay both external and internal costs. You lose trust, respect, and credibility with others—your family, your friends, your colleagues, and your customers. And you create messes in your own life and in the lives of those who depend on you for getting things done—whether it's showing up on time to leave for the movies, getting a report done on time, delivering needed parts to a customer, or cleaning the garage.

After a few weeks of not following through on your promise to take the kids to the park on the weekend, they begin not to trust you to keep your word. They realize they can't count on you. You lose authority with them. Your relationship deteriorates. The same thing happens in business.

EVERY AGREEMENT YOU MAKE IS WITH YOURSELF

More important, every agreement you make is ultimately with yourself. Even when you are making an agreement with someone else, your brain hears it and registers it as a commitment. You are making an agreement with yourself to do something, and when you don't follow through, you learn to distrust yourself. The result is a loss of self-esteem, self-respect, and self-confidence. You lose faith in your ability to produce a result. And you weaken your sense of integrity.

Let's say that you tell your spouse you're going to get up at 6:30 in the morning and exercise before going to work. But after three days of hitting the snooze alarm, your brain knows better than to trust you. Of course, *you* may think sleeping late is no big deal, but to your subconscious mind it is a very big deal. When you don't do what you say you will, you create confusion and self-doubt. You undermine your sense of personal power. It's ultimately not worth it.

YOUR INTEGRITY AND SELF-ESTEEM ARE WORTH MORE THAN A MILLION DOLLARS

When you realize how important your integrity and self-esteem really are, you will stop making casual agreements just to get someone off your back. You won't sell your self-esteem for momentary approval. You won't make agreements you don't intend to keep. You will make fewer agreements, and you will do whatever it takes to keep them.

To illustrate this in my seminars, I ask attendees, "If you knew you would get a million dollars if you made it to the end of the seminar without breaking one ground rule, could you have done it?" Most agree that they could have.

Often there is still one holdout who says, "No way. I just couldn't do it. I'm not responsible for the traffic jam I encountered on the way to the seminar this morning." Or "How am I supposed to be on time when my ride was late picking me up?"

I then ask, "What if the person whom you love most in the world would have to die if you didn't keep all the ground rules for the training? Would you have done anything differently then?"

Now the person who says the traffic made them late finally gets it and acknowledges, "Oh, yes. If my son's life were at stake, I wouldn't even have left this room. I would have slept on the floor in the conference room rather than take the risk of being late."

Once you realize how important keeping your word is, you realize you have the ability to do it. It's simply a matter of realizing the cost of not keeping your word. If you want more self-esteem, self-confidence, self-respect, personal power, mental clarity, and energy, then you'll make keeping your word more important. If you want to have the respect and trust of others, which is critical to accomplishing anything big and important in life (including making a million dollars), then you will take keeping your agreements more seriously.

SOME TIPS ON MAKING AND KEEPING AGREEMENTS

Here are some tips for making fewer agreements and for keeping the ones you make.

1. **Make only agreements that you intend to keep.** Take a few seconds before making an agreement to see if it is really what you *want* to do. Check in with yourself. How does your body feel

about it? Don't make an agreement just because you are looking for someone's approval. If you do, you'll find yourself breaking these commitments and ultimately losing their approval.

2. **Write down all the agreements you make.** Use a calendar, daily planning book, notebook, smartphone, tablet, or computer to record all of your agreements. In the course of a week, you might enter into dozens of agreements. One of the big reasons we don't keep our agreements is that with the daily press of all of our activities, we forget many of the agreements that we have made. Write them down, and then review your list every day. As I have stated before, a new finding from brain research is that when we don't write something down or make some effort to store it in long-term memory, the memory can be lost in as little as 37 seconds. You may have great intentions, but if you forget to do what you agreed to do, the result is the same as your *choosing* not to keep your agreements.

3. **Communicate any broken agreement at the first appropriate time.** As soon as you know you are going to have a broken agreement—your car won't start, you are caught in traffic, your child is sick, your babysitter can't make it, your computer crashes—notify the other person as soon as possible, and then renegotiate the agreement. This demonstrates respect for others' time and their needs. It gives them time to reschedule, replan, make other arrangements, and limit any potential damage. If the first appropriate time is after the fact, still let them know that you have a broken agreement, clean up any consequences, and decide whether to recommit to the agreement.

4. **Learn to say no more often.** Give yourself time to think it over before making any new agreements. I used to write the word *no* in yellow highlighter on all my calendar pages as a way to remind myself to really consider what else I would have to give up or not give my attention to if I said yes to something new. It made me pause and think before I added another commitment to my life.

THE RULES OF THE GAME

One of the most powerful trainings I ever took was Money & You®, created by Marshall Thurber and now run by DC Cordova of Excellerated Business Schools®. It radically changed how I related to money, business, and relationships.

Everything that you want to accomplish requires relationships—with your friends, family, staff, vendors, coaches, bosses, board of directors, clients, customers, partners, associates, students, teachers, audience, fans, and others. For those relationships to work, you need to set up what my friend John Assaraf calls "the rules of engagement"—what Marshall Thurber, DC Cordova, and the other folks at Excellerated Business Schools call "the rules of the game."

How are we going to play together? What are the ground rules and guidelines for the relationship going to be? Marshall taught us the following guidelines, which I have endeavored to live by ever since. If you and all the people you interacted with were to agree to the following rules, your level of success would soar.

1. Be willing to support our purpose, values, rules, and goals.
2. Speak with good purpose. If it doesn't serve, don't say it. No making people wrong, justifying, or defending.
3. If you disagree or do not understand, ask clarifying questions. Don't make the other person wrong.
4. Make only agreements you are willing and intend to keep.
5. If you can't keep an agreement, communicate as soon as practical to the appropriate person. Clear up any broken agreement at the first appropriate opportunity.
6. When something is not working, first look to the system for corrections and then propose a system-based solution to the person who can do something about it.
7. Be responsible. No blaming, no defending, no justifying, and no shaming.

IF YOU'RE NOT EARLY, YOU'RE LATE

One of the implied agreements in our culture is to be on time. It is an expression of respect. More people have lost credibility, trust, sales, business, jobs, money, and even relationships because of being late.

Anthony Bourdain, famed chef, host of CNN's *Anthony Bourdain: Parts Unknown,* and author of *Kitchen Confidential,** had a mentor who was a no-nonsense "bully, yenta, sadist, and mensch" named Bigfoot, who had a rule in his kitchen: Arrive 15 minutes early for your shift. The first time

---

**Kitchen Confidential: Adventures in the Culinary Underbelly* by Anthony Bourdain (London: Bloomsbury Publishing, 2000); updated edition (New York: Ecco, 2007).

Anthony was only 14 minutes early, he was advised that the next time it happened, he'd be sent home and lose the shift. And the next time after that, he'd be fired. Anthony was never late again for any job, and he instituted the same policy in his own legendary kitchens.

Remember, if you're not early, you're late. So make sure to plan an adequate amount of time to get ready, leave, and travel to whatever appointments, commitments, meetings, and jobs you have. Being on time is one of the most important habits you can develop for success.

UPPING THE ANTE

If you want to really up the ante in terms of keeping your commitments to yourself, you can use this technique that Martin Rutte taught me. Set up consequences—such as writing a large check to a person or an organization that you don't like or shaving off all of your hair—that are greater than the payoffs you get for not keeping your word (such as the comfort and safety of not taking a risk). The cost of having to deliver on the consequences would be too expensive not to follow through on the commitment.

Martin used this technique to motivate himself to follow through on his commitment to learn how to dive off a diving board. To make sure that he wouldn't back out of his commitment, he declared to his friends that if he didn't learn to dive by a certain date, he would write a check for $1,000 to the Ku Klux Klan. Because Martin is Jewish, that would have been more painful than confronting his fear of diving. So as challenging as it was for him, Martin learned how to dive.

What is so important in your life that you don't want to give yourself an out? Make a public declaration of a consequence that you would find painful to pay, and you'll use the power of motivating yourself to take the action that you say you want to take, but on which you have been procrastinating.

PRINCIPLE

55

BE A CLASS ACT

In every society, there are "human benchmarks"—certain individuals whose behavior becomes a model for everyone else—shining examples that others admire and emulate. We call these individuals "class acts."

DAN SULLIVAN
Cofounder and president of the Strategic Coach

I've already mentioned my friend and colleague Dan Sullivan, the creator of "The Strategic Coach Program." One of the groups he coaches is for high-achievers earning over $1 million a year. Though I routinely earn many times that, I still seek out coaches of Dan's caliber to help me fine-tune my success skills, so I joined Dan's coaching group in Chicago.

While I was in the program, Dan taught me a success principle that works for so many of the super-achievers I've met and studied that I'm surprised I didn't recognize it earlier as an important discipline we should all come to master.

Simply stated, it's "Be a class act."

That's it. Strive to become the kind of person who acts with class, who becomes known as a class act, and who attracts other people with class to his or her sphere of influence.

The sad truth in society today is that there don't seem to be as many class acts around as there used to be. I think everyone would agree that actors Jimmy Stewart and Paul Newman were class acts. Tom Hanks is a class act. Kate Middleton, Princess of Wales, and Maria Shriver are class acts. So are Denzel Washington and Garth Brooks. Coretta Scott King and former president of South Africa Nelson Mandela were both class acts. Herb Kelleher, cofounder and then CEO of Southwest Airlines, was a class act.

But how can you differentiate yourself as a class act in a world where most people are unconscious and "unspecial"? The answer is that you have to consciously work at it. Strive to free yourself from the many fears and anxieties that diminish the imagination and ambition of most people. Instead, operate outside the world of conventionality in your own world of expansion, creativity, and accomplishment. I'd like to suggest Dan Sullivan's model of class act behavior as a guide to up-leveling your own thinking and behavior.*

- **Live by your own highest standards.** Class acts liberate themselves by establishing personal standards of thinking and behavior that are more demanding and exacting than those of conventional society. These standards are consciously *chosen,* established, and applied.
- **Maintain dignity and grace under pressure.** You can do this three ways: (1) Remain imperturbable in the face of chaos. (2) Maintain a calmness that gives courage. Your calmness gives others hope that things will turn out all right. (3) Develop and express the quality of certainty. The greatest twentieth-century example of this characteristic of a class act was Winston Churchill—who in World War II almost single-handedly saved Western civilization from defeat at the hands of Nazi Germany, by his ability to stay calm and provide confident and courageous leadership that focused the resolve of both the British and the Americans.
- **Focus and improve the behavior of others.** Because a class act individual is a good role model, other people around them begin thinking and acting at a level that surprises both themselves and others. Someone who best exemplifies this third characteristic of a class act is Larry Bird, the great all-star, Hall of Fame basketball player who played on three championship teams with the Boston Celtics. To a person, the other players on those teams have said they were able to play at such a high level only because of Larry Bird's example and leadership.
- **Operate from a larger, inclusive perspective.** Because class acts are in touch with their own humanity, they have a deeper understanding and compassion for the humanity of others. They feel inextricably linked to others, are compassionate about human failures, and are courteous in the midst of conflict.

---

*This is adapted from the work of Dan Sullivan, the founder of The Strategic Coach. I strongly encourage you to check out his coaching program, his books, and audio programs. You can learn more at strategiccoach.com.

- **Increase the quality of every experience.** Class act individuals have the ability to transform seemingly insignificant situations into something enjoyable, meaningful, and memorable because of their conscious thinking and actions. They are creators rather than merely consumers, and they constantly enrich the lives of others by introducing greater beauty, significance, uniqueness, and stimulation into every experience. How you are treated at a Ritz-Carlton or a Four Seasons Hotel is a good example of this characteristic.
- **Counteract meanness, pettiness, and vulgarity.** The hallmarks of this characteristic are courtesy, respect, appreciation, gratitude, and generosity of spirit. One of my favorite examples of this characteristic of a class act is Pat Riley, the former coach of the Los Angeles Lakers and the New York Knicks and current president of the Miami Heat. What makes him a class act in my mind is his grace in the face of loss off the court. When Pat was coaching the Miami Heat in the NBA playoffs against the New York Knicks, he invited the entire opposing team and its coach to his home for a barbecue and personally spoke to each player, congratulating all for a great season and wishing them the best. Though Pat could have been competitive and aggressive, he acted instead in a way that elevated and acknowledged others. That's a class act.
- **Take responsibility for actions and results.** Class act individuals are accountable when others hide; they tell the truth about their failures; and they transform defeats into progress.
- **Strengthen the integrity of all situations.** Class act individuals are always establishing and achieving larger goals that require them to constantly grow and develop, and they're always adding increasing value to the world, too.
- **Expand the meaning of being human.** Class act individuals approach everyone, including themselves, uniquely, and as a result constantly find new ways to make life better for themselves and others. In pushing boundaries for themselves, they do the same for others by giving them new freedom to express their uniqueness at home, at work, and in the world.
- **Increase the confidence and capabilities of others.** Class acts are energy creators rather than energy drainers. Class acts build confidence in themselves by consciously choosing their governing ideals and by creating structures that support the fulfillment of their aspirations and capabilities. These new structures also

support others by creating safe and stimulating environments that encourage greater creativity, cooperation, progress, and growth.

In giving me the above list, Dan taught me a lot about what it truly means to be a class act. But more important, he taught me the benefits of being recognized as a class act by others.

HOW TO BECOME KNOWN AS A CLASS ACT

When people mention the great former UCLA basketball coach John Wooden, who won 10 NCAA Championships in a 12-year period, they agree that he was a class act. Wooden became known as a class act because, frankly, he acted like one. He took time to acknowledge others, and he conducted himself with an eye toward improving and expanding the world. He communicated to people, "You're special. You count."

One of the hardest parts of any coach's job is making the final cut—deciding who makes the team and who doesn't. Most coaches just post a list of who made the team on a bulletin board in the gym. You either made it or you didn't. But showing his deep respect and love for all people, Wooden did it differently. Instead of simply posting a list of names on the wall, Coach Wooden sat down with each player, one at a time, and told them what other sports at UCLA he felt they could be successful at. He shared what he saw as their strengths, discussed their weaknesses, and—on the basis of their strengths—identified what they could do to improve their athletic careers. He took the time to acknowledge their strengths and boost their self-esteem, leaving prospective athletes motivated and encouraged rather than feeling emotionally devastated.

When you choose to live by a higher set of standards, you get to watch people respond enthusiastically toward you. Soon, you'll notice the effect that it evokes: "Wow, that's someone I want to be friends with, be in business with, and be connected with."

WHY BEING A CLASS ACT HELPS YOU SUCCEED

In fact, that's one of the major benefits of being a class act: People want to do business with you or become involved in your sphere of influence. They perceive you as successful and someone who can expand their possibilities. They trust you to act with responsibility, integrity, and aplomb.

Perhaps that's why the easiest way to spot class acts is by looking at the people class acts attract. Look at the people they do business with, the people they socialize with. Class acts tend to attract people who are at the top of their game.

Have you taken a good look lately at your friends, your colleagues, your partners, clients, and contacts? Are they class acts? If not, consider that disparity as a mirror reflecting your status back to you. Make the decision now to re-create yourself as a class act, and see what kind of people you start attracting. Do fewer things, but do them better. Raise the quality of your attitude and change your behaviors for the better.

At my office, for example, when we noticed we were using disposable paper cups, we switched to using glassware, improving the quality of our office environment and sending a message to our staff, clients, and guests that we think highly of them.

Similarly, my wife and I used to throw several parties a year that frankly weren't all that great. Now, we throw one or two big parties every year, but we create it as an event that nobody can forget. People enjoy gourmet food in an elegant setting with an array of interesting and important guests and entertainment. Everyone feels privileged, esteemed, nurtured, and loved.

This is not to say that we never have a pizza and beer out by the pool with our closest friends and family, but when it comes to business and our larger social network, we continually strive to be class acts.

In the last several years, we have started conducting four-day high-end luxury retreats limited to 24 people who want to take their lives, their careers, and their businesses to the next level. We hold them in private villas and five-star hotels in exotic vacation destinations like Maui; Bali; Dubai; Florence, Italy; and Santa Barbara, California. We serve fine wines and gourmet food prepared by world-class chefs, and we greet people the first night with special gifts. We take people on excursions like sunset cruises in Maui, cocktail receptions at private beach clubs in Santa Barbara, and wine-tasting or dining out at the top restaurants in Florence and Dubai. In addition to providing a breakthrough training experience, we do everything we can to make the retreat an extraordinary personal experience as well.

CLASS ACTS TEACH OTHERS TO TREAT THEM WITH ESTEEM

Of course, the first person you should treat with dignity, respect, and esteem is yourself. My friend Martin Rutte is a class act. He always dresses well, eats well, and conducts himself at all times with refinement and style. In addition, he treats everyone around him with love, dignity, and respect.

Consequently and by example, he's taught everyone around him to also treat him well—simply because he treats himself and others with such thoughtfulness and care.

If you're sloppy, always late, and don't care how you conduct yourself, you're going to be met with people who treat you in a sloppy, always-late, don't-care manner.

When I know Martin's coming to visit, my first reaction is to make sure we have a good bottle of wine, some fresh fish, some simple but exceptional vegetables, and fresh raspberries for dessert, because that's how Martin has "trained" me to treat him.

If a head of state, the pope, or the Dalai Lama were coming to visit your home, wouldn't you have the housecleaners in there for a week? Wouldn't you buy the best food? Well, why don't you do that for yourself? You're just as important as they are!

The bottom line is that certain people command a certain level of respect not only because of how they treat others but, more important, because of how they treat themselves. When you establish a higher level of personal standards, not only do you get better treatment from those around you, but suddenly you also begin attracting others with the same elevated standards. You get invited to places where those standards exist. You get to enjoy the activities that people in the upper echelons enjoy. All by becoming a class act.

PART FIVE

Success and Money

There is a science of getting rich, and it is an exact science, like algebra or arithmetic. There are certain laws which govern the process of acquiring riches, and once these laws are learned and obeyed by anyone, that person will get rich with mathematical certainty.

WALLACE D. WATTLES
Author of *The Science of Getting Rich*

PRINCIPLE 56

DEVELOP A POSITIVE MONEY CONSCIOUSNESS

There is a secret psychology to money. Most people don't know about it. That's why most people never become financially successful. A lack of money is not the problem; it is merely a symptom of what's going on inside you.

T. HARV EKER
Multimillionaire and author of *Secrets of the Millionaire Mind*

Like everything else I've discussed in this book, financial success also starts in the mind. You have to first decide what you want. Next, you have to believe it's possible and that you deserve it. Then you must focus on it by thinking about it and visualizing it as if it were already yours. And finally, you have to be willing to pay the price to get it—with disciplined effort and perseverance over time.

But most people never get to even the first stages of accumulating wealth. Too often, they are limited by their own beliefs about money and by the question of whether or not they deserve it.

IDENTIFY YOUR LIMITING BELIEFS ABOUT MONEY

To become wealthy, you'll need to surface, identify, root out, and replace any negative or limiting beliefs you may have about money. Though it may seem odd that anyone would have a negative predisposition toward wealth, we often have limiting beliefs buried deep in our subconscious that we picked up in our childhood. Perhaps when you were young, you heard phrases like

Money doesn't grow on trees.
There's not enough money to go around.

It's selfish to want a lot of money.
You have to have money to make money.
The rich get richer and the poor get poorer.
You have to work too hard to get money.
Money is the root of all evil.
People with money are evil, selfish, and unethical.
Rich people are greedy and dishonest.
You can't buy happiness.
The more money you have, the more problems you have.
If you are rich, you can't be spiritual.

These messages from early childhood can actually sabotage and dilute your later financial success, because they subconsciously emit a vibration that can cancel out your conscious intentions.

What did your parents, grandparents, teachers, religious leaders, friends, and coworkers teach you about money as you were growing up and as a young adult?

My father taught me that rich people got rich by exploiting the working classes. He constantly told me he wasn't made of money, that money didn't grow on trees, and that money was hard to come by. One Christmas my father decided to sell Christmas trees. He rented an empty lot, worked hard every night from Thanksgiving to Christmas Eve, and just broke even after a month of hard labor. As a family, we were left with the belief that no matter how hard you work, you never get ahead.

Wealth Brings Pain and Misery

There are many other limiting decisions you can make about money that can keep you from making or enjoying the amount of money you deserve or want. For example:

Anne was in her midthirties when she attended one of my seminars in Australia. She had inherited a lot of money, but she hated it. She was ashamed of her wealth, hid it, and wouldn't spend it. When the subject of money came up in the seminar, she began screaming about how money had destroyed her family. Her father, who had made a lot of money, was never home. He was either out working hard to make money or out jet-setting around the world spending it. As a result, her mother drank excessively, causing constant fighting and screaming in their household. Not surprisingly, Anne's childhood had been a miserable experience. But instead of identifying her father's greed and workaholism as the actual cause of her pain, Anne had decided as a child that money was the culprit. Because childhood decisions made during times of intense emotional upset tend to stay with us longer—and actually grow stronger over time—Anne had retained her negative beliefs around money for more than 20 years.

It's Not Okay to Make More Money Than My Father

Scott Schilling, an executive coach and international sales trainer, was attending one of my seminars where we were working on identifying and releasing limiting beliefs.

When I took the participants through a deep process to discover a limiting belief that might be keeping them stuck financially, Scott remembered the day he was 18 and had just finished his first month as a life insurance agent—earning a commission check of $1,856. His father, who was in his forty-sixth year with the same insurance company and only one month away from retirement, received his own paycheck that day—for $1,360.

Scott said, "When I showed my check to my father, he never said a word, but the look on his face told me he was deeply hurt. I thought, *How could I do that to my dad? How could I make such a great and noble man question himself and his value?*"

Scott had made a subconscious decision that day not to earn more money than his father—in order to avoid causing his father the shame and embarrassment Scott imagined he felt that day 25 years earlier. But less than a month after releasing this decision in my seminar, Scott told me he received a contract to do a week's worth of sales training for a fee equal to one fifth of his previous year's total salary.

Since then, Scott has gone on to become the national sales director for several companies, generating nearly $25 million in sales from the platform for one of them, and developing a training program for another one that grew their sales from $8 million to $100 million in 5½ years.

Becoming Rich Would Violate the Family Code

I grew up in a working-class family. My father was a florist and he worked "for the rich." Somehow the rich were not to be trusted. They stepped on the little people. They took advantage of the common worker. To become rich would have meant becoming a traitor to my family and my class. I didn't want to become one of the "bad guys."

If I Become Wealthy, I Will Be a Burden

Tom Boyer is a business consultant who felt like he had hit a plateau in terms of his income. With some brilliant assistance from my friend and trainer Gay Hendricks, he discovered a childhood decision had put a cap on his success.

Tom grew up in a middle-class family in Ohio. While they never wanted for food or basic necessities, his father made lots of financial sacrifices so that Tom could pursue his dream of playing the clarinet.

While he started out playing on his dad's old metal clarinet, Tom soon graduated to a Leblanc, a very middle-of-the-road wooden instrument. When he began to really excel, his clarinet teacher, Mrs. Zielinski, went to Tom's parents and said, "Your son has real talent. He deserves a very, very fine instrument. He deserves a Buffet clarinet." In 1964, a Buffet cost $300, which is about $1,500 today. And though that was a lot of money to Tom's family, nevertheless, it was agreed that Mrs. Zielinski would pick out the clarinet that was to be Tom's Christmas present.

On Christmas morning Tom went downstairs, unwrapped the package, opened the case, and discovered the beautiful clarinet with its polished grenadilla wood body and bright shiny silver keys, sitting in its regal blue velvet case. It was the most beautiful thing he'd ever seen.

But when Tom turned to thank his parents, he didn't even get the thank-you out of his mouth before his mom said, "We never would've been able to afford that if your sister had lived." (Tom's sister Carol had suddenly died of encephalitis when he was seven years old.)

In that moment Tom took on the subconscious belief that the greater a success he became, the greater a burden he would be to those who love him—not only financially but emotionally.

With Gay Hendricks's help, Tom realized that this subconscious belief had held him back from attaining the level of success he consciously wanted. He had convicted himself of the crime of being a burden, and was now punishing himself by not allowing himself the level of success he truly deserved.

The present state of your bank account is nothing more than the physical manifestation of your previous thinking. If you sincerely wish to improve your results in the physical world, you must change your thoughts, and you must change them IMMEDIATELY.

BOB PROCTOR
Author of *The Power to Have It All* and a featured teacher in the movie *The Secret*

THREE STEPS TO TURN AROUND YOUR LIMITING BELIEFS ABOUT MONEY

You can change your childhood programming by using a simple yet powerful three-step technique that replaces your limiting beliefs with more positive and empowering ones. While this exercise can be done on your own, it's usually more powerful—and definitely more fun!—to do it with a partner or a small group of people.

1. **Write down your limiting belief.**
   Money is the root of all evil.

2. **Challenge, make fun of, and argue with the limiting belief.** You can do this by brainstorming a list of new beliefs that challenge the old ones. The more outrageous and fun you make them, the more powerful the resulting shift in your consciousness will be.

   Money is the root of all philanthropy.
   Money is the root of great vacations!
   Money might be the root of evil for someone who is evil, but I am a loving, generous, compassionate, and kind person who will always use money to create good in the world.

   You can even write out your new money beliefs on 3″ × 5″ index cards and add them to your stack of affirmations to be read out loud with enthusiasm and passion every day. This daily discipline will go a long way toward helping you manifest success in the area of money.

3. **Create a positive turnaround statement.** Create a new statement that is the opposite of the original belief. You want this "turnaround statement" to be one that sends shivers of delight through your body when you say it. Once you have it, walk around the room for a few moments repeating the new statement out loud with energy and passion. Repeat this new belief

several times a day for a minimum of 30 days and it will be yours forever.* Try one like

When it comes to me, money is the root of love, joy, and good works.

Remember, ideas about financial success never form by themselves! You have to keep thinking the thoughts that build the "thought form" of prosperity. You have to take time each day and focus on thoughts of prosperity and images of financial success. When you intentionally focus on these thoughts and images, they will eventually crowd out the limiting thoughts and images and begin to dominate your thinking. If you want to accelerate reaching your financial goals, you need to practice saying positive money affirmations every day. Here are a few more that I have used with great success:

- God is my infinite supply, and large sums of money come to me quickly and easily for the highest good of all concerned.
- I now have more money than I need to do everything I want to do.
- Money comes to me in many unforeseen ways.
- I am making positive choices about what to do with my money.
- Every day, my income increases whether I am working, playing, or sleeping.
- All my investments are profitable.
- People love to pay me money for what I most love to do.

Remember, you can plant any idea into the subconscious mind by repetition of thought infused with positive expectancy—and the intensely felt emotion associated with already having it.

USE THE POWER OF RELEASING TO ACCELERATE YOUR MILLIONAIRE MINDSET

Whenever you are doing your money affirmations—or any affirmation, for that matter—it is not uncommon to become aware of competing thoughts

---

*Strong emotions actually facilitate the growth of thousands of new microscopic hairlike filaments on the ends of the dendrites of the neurons in your brain. These little dendrite spiny protuberances actually create more connections in the brain that will support the installment of the new belief and the creative fulfillment of your new financial goals. It's not magic; it's brain science!

(objections), such as *Who are you kidding? You're never going to be rich. How many times do I have to tell you? You have to have money to make money.* When this occurs, first write down the competing thought and any negative feelings it creates. Then you can close your eyes and release the thought and any negative emotions that accompany it using the Sedona Method or tapping therapy.

The Sedona Method, created by Hale Dwoskin, is another simple but powerful technique for releasing limiting beliefs. I am a big fan of this methodology and I teach it in my workshops. I also recommend you take a Sedona Method Class, purchase the *Sedona Method Home Study* audio program, watch the movie *Letting Go,* or read Hale's book, *The Sedona Method.*★

We've put a complete tutorial to the Sedona Method's basic releasing questions at *The Success Principles* website: jackcanfield.com/tsp-resources. Scroll down to Principle 56 and click on the link.

VISUALIZE WHAT YOU WANT AS IF YOU ALREADY HAVE IT

Remember to also include money in your daily visualizations, seeing all your financial goals as already accomplished. See images that affirm your desired level of income such as paychecks, rent checks, royalty checks, dividend statements, and people handing you cash. See images of your ideal bank statements, stock reports, and real estate portfolios. See images of the things you would be able to buy, do, and contribute to if you had already met all of your financial goals. Make sure to add the kinesthetic and olfactory dimensions to your visualization—feel the smooth texture of the world's finest silk against your skin, feel the relaxation of a luxurious massage in the world's finest spas, and smell the fragrance of your favorite cut flowers filling your home or the delicate scent of your favorite imported perfume. Next, add in the auditory dimension such as the sound of the surf on the beach in front of your vacation home or the gentle hum of the finely tuned engine of your new Porsche.

Finally, remember to add in the feeling of appreciation and gratitude you would feel if you already had these things. This feeling of abundance is part of what will actually attract more abundance to you. This is a critical part of the process that people often leave out.

Constantly fill your mind with images of what you want and picture yourself already having them.

★*The Sedona Method* by Hale Dwoskin (Sedona, AZ: Sedona Press, 2003). For more information on workshops, audio programs, the movie *Letting Go,* and other resources on the Sedona Method, go to sedona.com.

Make sure you also include your words and images of your financial goals on your Vision Board (see pages 117–18).

Another technique I've found helpful in visualizing a wealthy lifestyle is taught by Esther and Jerry Hicks in their book *Ask and It Is Given*. Find a beautiful box and put a label on it that reads "Whatever is contained in this box . . . IS!" Then begin clipping pictures, ads, and other images of those things you want to bring into your life. Place each clipping in the box and feel the feeling of owning it, using it, and enjoying it.

PRINCIPLE 57

YOU GET WHAT YOU FOCUS ON

If you don't put a value on money and seek wealth, you most probably won't receive it. You must seek wealth for it to seek you. If no burning desire for wealth arises within you, no wealth will arise around you. Having definiteness of purpose for acquiring wealth is essential for its acquisition.

DR. JOHN DEMARTINI
Self-made multimillionaire, consultant on financial and life mastery, and author of *The Breakthrough Experience* and *Riches Within*

It's been said that in life, you get what you focus on. This rule applies to getting a new job, building a business, winning an award—but most especially to acquiring money, wealth, and a rich lifestyle.

YOU MUST *DECIDE* TO BE WEALTHY

One of the first requirements of becoming wealthy is to make a conscious decision to do so.

When I was in graduate school, I made the decision to become wealthy. Though I didn't quite know at the time what that meant, "being wealthy" seemed as if it would provide many of the things I wanted in life—the ability to travel to attend any workshops I wanted, to buy the books I wanted, to support the causes I cared about, and to have all the resources I needed to accomplish my goals and underwrite my hobbies. I wanted to be able to do whatever I wanted, whenever I wanted, wherever I wanted, for as long as I wanted.

If you want wealth, too, you must decide now from the deepest place in your heart to have wealth in your life—without yet worrying about how or if it's possible or not.

NEXT, DECIDE WHAT *WEALTHY* MEANS TO YOU

Do you know how much wealth you want? Some of my friends want to retire as millionaires, whereas others want to retire with $30 million or even $100 million. Two friends want to become megarich because of the philanthropic ability it would give them. There is no right financial goal to have. But you do have to decide what *you* want.

If you haven't yet determined your vision from Principle 3: "Decide What You Want"—including defining what your financial goals are—take time to do so now. Make sure to include written goals like these:

I will have a net worth of $ _____ by the year _____.
I will earn at least $ _____ by December 31st next year.
I will save and invest $ _____ every month.
A new financial habit I will develop starting now is _____.
To become debt free, I will _____.
I will be debt free by _____.

FIND OUT WHAT IT COSTS TO FINANCE YOUR DREAM LIFE . . . NOW AND LATER

When creating wealth in your life, remember that there is the life you want to live now and the life you want to live in the future.

The life you are currently living is the result of the thoughts you have thought, the choices you have made, and the actions you have taken in the past. The life you live in the future will be the result of today's thoughts, choices, and actions. To get the kind of life you want one to two years from now, as well as the kind of lifestyle you want when you "retire," you need to calculate and decide exactly how much money you'll need to live the lifestyle of your dreams. If you don't know, research how much it would cost you to do and buy everything you want over the course of the next year. This could include rent or mortgage, food, clothes, medical care, automobiles, utilities, education, vacations, recreation, insurance, savings, investments, and philanthropy.

For each category, visualize those items or activities in your life, then write down what you would need to spend to get them. Imagine eating in fine restaurants, driving your dream car, going on your dream vacation—even refurbishing your home or moving into a new one. Don't let your mind tell you that these things are impossible or crazy. For the moment, just do the research and find out exactly what it will cost to fund your dream life—whatever that is.

GET REAL ABOUT YOUR RETIREMENT

Determine, too, how much you'll need to maintain your current or upgraded lifestyle once you retire and stop working. Though I don't ever plan to stop working, if retirement is in your plans, Charles Schwab suggests that for every $1,000 in monthly income you'll want during retirement, you'll need to have $230,000 invested when you stop working. If you have $1 million invested with a 6% yield, that will give you a taxable income of about $4,300 a month.

Whether that's enough will depend on a number of factors, such as whether your house is paid for, how many people you'll be supporting, how much you will be receiving from Social Security, and what level of lifestyle you expect to live. At any rate, today $4,300 a month may not be enough to support the abundant lifestyle you may be envisioning for yourself. If you are hoping to travel and have an active life, it may not even be adequate. With inflation, it may be less than adequate.

BECOME MINDFUL ABOUT YOUR MONEY

Most people are unconscious when it comes to their money. For instance, do you know your net worth—your total assets minus your total liabilities? Do you know how much money you have in savings? Do you know exactly what your fixed and variable monthly expenses are? Do you know the total amount of debt you are carrying and the amount of money you are spending a year on interest payments? Do you know if you are adequately insured? Do you have a financial plan? Do you have an estate plan? Do you have a will? Is it up to date?

If you want to be financially successful, you have to become conscious. Not only do you have to know precisely where you are, but you also need to know exactly where you want to go and what's required to get you there.

Step 1: Determine Your Net Worth

If you don't know your net worth, you can

1. Work with an accountant or a financial planner to calculate it.

REAL LIFE ADVENTURES by Gary Wise and Lance Aldrich

According to your latest figures, if you retired today, you could live very, very comfortably until about 2 p.m. tomorrow.

2. Use one of the many free techniques on the Internet.
3. Purchase some software, such as Personal Financial Statement, which is available at myfinancialstatement.com.

Step 2: Determine What You Need to Retire

Next, calculate what your financial needs will be when and if you retire. Be aware that retirement by its very nature requires that you be financially independent. A good financial planner can tell you how much in savings and investments would be required to produce enough in interest, dividend, rental, and royalty income to live your current or future lifestyle without having to work.

Financial independence frees you up to pursue your passions, travel, engage in philanthropic endeavors and service projects—or do whatever you wish.

Step 3: Become Aware of What You're Spending

The number one problem in today's generation and economy is the lack of financial literacy.

ALAN GREENSPAN
Former chairman of the Federal Reserve Board

Most people aren't aware of what they really spend in a month. If you've never tracked your expenditures, start by writing down all your normal *fixed* monthly expenses such as your mortgage or rent, your car payment, any other installment or loan payments, insurance bills, cable bill, Internet provider, health club, and so on. Then go back over the last six to twelve months and calculate *average* monthly expenditures that fluctuate—utilities, phone bills, food bills, clothing expenditures, auto maintenance, medical expenses, and so on.

Finally, keep a record for one month of *everything* you spend money on during that month, no matter how big or small—from gas for your car to coffee at Starbucks. Add up everything at the end of the month so that you are consciously aware—rather than unaware—of what you're spending. Check off those items you must pay for and those things you have discretion over. This exercise will make you aware of what you're currently spending and where you could cut back if you chose to.

Step 4: Become Financially Literate

We were not taught financial literacy in school. It takes a lot of work and time to change your thinking and to become financially literate.

ROBERT KIYOSAKI
Coauthor of *Rich Dad, Poor Dad* and creator of the Cash Flow Game

Not only should you stay conscious around money by reviewing your financial goals every day and tracking your spending every month, but I recommend that you also proactively learn about money and investing by reading at least one good financial book every month for the next year. I recommend you read two really good resources written by my friend Phil Town: *Rule #1: The Simple Strategy for Successful Investing in Only 15 Minutes a Week!* and *Payback Time: Making Big Money Is the Best Revenge!* For additional resources, go to the "Suggested Reading and Additional Resources for Success" section at jackcanfield.com/tsp-resources.

Another way to become financially literate is to seek out professionals who can teach you the money skills you'll need to grow a healthy financial future. You can invest your money in stocks and bonds, which pay you in dividends and interest, or you can invest in income-producing real estate, which pays you in positive cash-flow from rental income that is greater than your mortgage payments.

Like most baby boomers in their midfifties, Mark and Sheila Robbins were locked into the employee mindset. They didn't talk about creating a life of wealth and abundance. They just worked hard—Sheila for 35 years as a flight attendant for United Airlines, and Mark as the manager of a car dealership—and put money in their 401(k) accounts.

After losing about half of their retirement funds in a declining stock market, they decided there had to be a better way. That's when they joined a financial services organization and started taking the courses they offered. As a result of reading the *Rich Dad, Poor Dad* books and playing the Cash Flow Game, their conversations began to include the language of money and their minds embraced the idea of becoming real estate investors. They sought out a realtor who specialized in the types of properties they were interested in, and over the summer they went shopping. Only one short year later, they had 15 single-family rental properties worth over $2 million, all of which were generating positive cash flow.

If that weren't enough, they also now own their own successful Chrysler/Dodge/Jeep dealership, and another home-based business. Because they were willing to take the time and money to invest in their financial education and implement the principles they learned, their lives have dramatically changed and will never be the same again.

PRINCIPLE 58

PAY YOURSELF FIRST

You have a divine right to abundance, and if you are anything less than a millionaire, you haven't had your fair share.

STUART WILDE
Author of *The Trick to Money Is Having Some!*

In 1926, George Clason wrote a book called *The Richest Man in Babylon*—one of the great success classics of all time. It's the fabled story of a man named Arkad, a simple scribe who convinces his client, a money lender, to teach him the secrets of money.

The first principle the money lender teaches Arkad is: "A part of all you earn must be yours to keep." He goes on to explain that by first putting aside at least 10% of his earnings—and making that money inaccessible for expenses—Arkad would see this amount build over time and, in turn, start earning money on its own. Over an even longer time, it would grow into a lot, because of the power of compound interest.

Many people have built their fortunes by paying themselves first. It's as true and effective today as it was in 1926.

A TELLING STORY

As easy as this 10% formula is, I'm always shocked at how unwilling people are to hear it. Not too long ago, I was taking a limo from the airport back to my home in Santa Barbara. The 28-year-old limo driver, after realizing who I was, asked me to share with him some principles of success he could apply to his own life. When I told him he should invest 10% of every dollar he earned, and then keep reinvesting the dividends, I could tell the information was falling on deaf ears. He was looking for a get-rich-quick scheme.

But though opportunities that can earn you money faster are always something to look for, I believe your future must initially be built on the solid bedrock of a long-term investment plan. The earlier you start, the more quickly you can build your safety net of a million dollars.

Sit down with a financial planner—or go to one of the myriad sites on the Internet where you can enter the amount of your current net worth and your financial goals for retirement—then calculate how much you need to save and invest from this point forward to achieve your goal amount by the time you retire.*

THE EIGHTH WONDER OF THE WORLD

Compound interest is the eighth natural wonder of the world and the most powerful thing I have ever encountered.

ALBERT EINSTEIN
Physicist and winner of the Nobel Prize

---

*A number of websites will help you calculate what's required to reach your financial goals—whether you want to determine how much is needed to fund your retirement, calculate how much mortgage you can afford, or estimate how much wealth you'll amass through saving and investing. Search "online financial calculators" in your Internet browser to see what's currently offered.

If you are new to the idea of compound interest, here's how it works: If you invest $1,000 at a 10% rate of interest, you'll earn $100 in interest and at the end of the first year have a total investment of $1,100. If you leave both your original investment and the earned interest in the account, the next year you'll earn 10% interest on $1,100, which is $110. The third year, you'll earn 10% on $1,210—and so on, for as long as you leave it there. At this rate, your money would actually double every seven years. That's how it eventually turns into a huge amount over time.

Of course, the best news is, time is your friend when it comes to compound interest. The sooner you start, the greater the result. Consider the following example: Mary starts investing at age 25 and stops when she reaches 35. Tom doesn't start investing until the age of 35 but keeps investing until he retires at 65. Both Mary and Tom invest $150 per month, with a rate of return of 8% per year compounding interest. But look at the surprising result when they both retire at age 65. Mary invested only $18,000 over 10 years and ended up with $283,385, whereas Tom contributes $54,000 over 30 years and ends up with only $220,233. The person who contributed for only 10 years has more than the person who invested for 30 years but started later! The sooner you start saving, the longer you have for compounding interest to work its powerful magic.

MAKE SAVING AND INVESTING A PRIORITY

The world's most aggressive savers make investing money as central a part of their money management as they do paying their mortgage.

To get in the habit of saving *some* money every month, immediately take a predetermined percentage of your paycheck and put it in a savings account that you don't allow yourself to touch. Keep building that account until you've saved enough to move it into a mutual fund or bond account or to invest it in real estate—including the purchase of your own home. The amount of money that is wasted paying rent without building any equity in a home is a tragedy for many people.

Investing just 10% or 15% of your income will help you eventually amass a fortune. Pay yourself first, then live on what is left. This will do two things: (1) it will force you to start building your fortune, and (2) if you still want to buy more or do more, it will force you to find ways to earn more money to afford it.

Never dip into your savings to fund your bigger lifestyle. You want your investments to grow to the point that you could live off of the interest, if necessary. Only then will you be truly financially independent.

HE PAID HIMSELF FIRST

Dr. John Demartini is a chiropractor who now conducts seminars for other chiropractors on how to grow themselves personally and their practices financially. He is one of the wealthiest and most abundant people I know—in spirit, friends, and adventure, as well as in money. John told me:

> When I first got into practice years ago, I paid everybody first and took whatever was left over. I didn't know any better. Then I noticed that people who had only been working for me less than six months were all getting paid on time. I realized that their pay was fixed and mine was variable. That was kind of crazy. The most important person—me—was the one under the stress, while the others had all the stability. I decided to turn that around and pay myself first. I paid my taxes second, my lifestyle budget third, and my bills fourth.
>
> I arranged for *automatic* withdrawals, and they've completely changed my financial situation. I don't waver. If bills pile up and money doesn't come in, I don't stop the withdrawals. My staff is forced to find a way to book more seminars and collect more money. Under the old system, if they didn't book or collect, it was on my back. But now, it's the other way around. If they want to get paid, they figure out ways to make more money.

THE 50/50 LAW

Another rule John suggests is that you never spend more than you save. John puts 50% of every dollar he earns into savings. If he wants to increase his personal expenditures by $45,000, he first has to earn an additional $90,000. Let's say you want to buy a car for $40,000. If you can't put an extra $40,000 into savings, you don't buy the car. Either buy a cheaper car, make do with what you have right now, or go out and make more money. The key is that you don't raise your lifestyle until you've earned the right to raise it by putting the same amount into savings. If you *do* raise your savings by $40,000, you know you've earned the right to raise your lifestyle by that same amount.

The 50/50 Law will get you rich very quickly. It was the core of billionaire Sir John Marks Templeton's strategy for building wealth.

DON'T TELL ME YOU CAN'T DO IT!

Most people wait to start saving until they have some extra money lying around—a comfortable surplus. But it doesn't work like that. You have to start saving and investing for the future *now!* And the more you invest, the sooner you will reach financial independence. Sir John Marks Templeton, mutual fund pioneer and philanthropist, started out working for $150 a week as a stockbroker. He and his wife, Judith Folk, decided to invest *50% of their income in the stock market while still making tithing a priority.* That left the two of them only 40% of his income to live on. But by his death in 2008, John Templeton was a billionaire! He kept the practice up his whole life and later in life gave away $10 for every dollar he spent to individuals and organizations that support spiritual growth.

WHO WANTS TO BE A MILLIONAIRE?

According to government figures, in 1980 there were 1.5 million millionaires in the United States. By 2000, there were 7 million. By 2024, there were 24.5 million (and 62.5 million worldwide, with that number expected to climb to 86 million by 2027). It has been estimated that 1,700 people in America become millionaires every single day. With a little planning, self-discipline, and effort, one of these millionaires can be you.

MILLIONAIRE DOESN'T MEAN "CELEBRITY"

Although you might think—judging from Taylor Swift, Brad Pitt, Rihanna, Michael Jordan, and Oprah Winfrey—that most millionaires are celebrities, the truth is more than 99% of millionaires are hardworking, methodical savers and investors.

These folks typically make their fortune in one of three ways: from entrepreneurship, which accounts for 75% of all the millionaires in the United States; as an executive at a major corporation, about 10% of millionaires; or as a professional practitioner (doctor, lawyer, dentist, certified public accountant, architect). Additionally, about 5% become millionaires through sales and sales consulting.

Indeed, most U.S. millionaires are regular folks who worked hard, lived within their budgets, saved 10% to 20% of all their income, and invested it back into their businesses, real estate,* and the stock market. They are the people who own the dry cleaning business, the car dealership, the restaurant chain, the bread company, the jewelry store, the cattle ranch, the trucking company, and the plumbing supply store.

However, people from any walk of life can become millionaires if they learn the discipline of saving and investing and start early enough. You've no doubt heard of Oseola McCarty of Hattiesburg, Mississippi, who had to drop out of school in the sixth grade to take care of her family. She eventually spent some 75 years of her life washing and ironing other people's clothes, lived a frugal lifestyle, and saved what she could from the little money she made. In 1995, she donated $150,000, the bulk of her $250,000 life savings, to the University of Southern Mississippi to provide scholarships for needy students. And here's the interesting part: Had Oseola invested her savings, which is estimated to have been about $50,000 in 1965, in an S&P 500 index fund, which had earned on average 10.5% a year, her money would have grown to not $250,000, but $999,628—virtually a million dollars, four times as much.[†]

HOW TO BECOME AN "AUTOMATIC MILLIONAIRE"

The simplest way to implement the pay-yourself-first plan is to have a plan that's totally "automatic"—that is, set up so a percentage of your paycheck is automatically deducted and invested as you direct.

Financial planners will tell you, from their extensive experience with hundreds of clients, that very few—if any—follow through with a plan to pay themselves first, if it is not automatic. If you're an employee, check with your company to see if they have self-directed retirement accounts such as 401(k) plans.

You can arrange for the company to automatically deduct your contribution to the plan from your paycheck. If it's deducted before you receive your check, you'll never miss it. More important, you won't have to

---

*Most analysis reports that about 90% of millionaires become millionaires by investing in real estate.
[†]See "The Oseola McCarty Fribble" by Selena Maranjian, September 5, 1997, on the Motley Fool website at https://www.fool.com/Fribble/1997/Fribble970905.htm.

think about your investments—you won't have to exercise self-discipline. It doesn't depend on your mood swings, household emergencies, or anything else. You make the commitment once and it's done. Another advantage of these kinds of plans is that they are free of most taxes until you withdraw the money. So instead of having 70¢ working for you, you have an entire dollar working for you—compounding year after year.

Some companies will even match a portion of your contribution. If you work for such a company, get on board *now!* Check with the employee benefits office of your company and find out how to sign up. When you do, make sure to make the largest percentage contribution you are allowed by law, but at least 10%. If you absolutely cannot bring yourself to do 10%, then do the largest percentage you can. After a few months, reassess and then see if you can't increase it. Get creative about where you can cut costs and how you can increase your income through other sources.

If you don't have a company retirement plan, you can open an individual retirement account (IRA) at a bank or a brokerage firm. With an IRA, you make a financial contribution of up to $7,000 a year ($8,000 if you're 50 or older). Ask the bank, the brokerage firm, or a financial advisor to help you decide if you want a traditional IRA or a Roth IRA. The paperwork to start an IRA takes about the same amount of time as opening a checking account. And to keep it automatic, you can arrange for an automatic deduction from your checking account.

For a much more detailed explanation of how to benefit from an automatic investment program, I strongly recommend that you read *The Automatic Millionaire: A Powerful One-Step Plan to Live and Finish Rich,* by David Bach. For those of you older than 40, read David's *Start Late, Finish Rich.* David has done a superb job of providing you with everything you need to know, as well as a host of resources for putting these recommendations into action—even including phone numbers and websites so you can do all of this from the comfort of your own home.

BUILD ASSETS RATHER THAN LIABILITIES

Rule One. You must know the difference between an asset and a liability and buy assets. Poor and middle class acquire liabilities, but they think they are assets. An asset is something that puts money in my pocket. A liability is something that takes money out of my pocket.

ROBERT T. KIYOSAKI
Coauthor of *Rich Dad, Poor Dad* and creator of the Cash Flow Game

Far too many people run their financial lives by their expenditures and whims. For most people, their "investment" model looks like this:

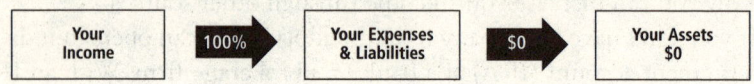

But take a look at how wealthy people approach their investments. They take the money they earn and invest a large portion of it in income-producing assets—real estate, small businesses, stocks, bonds, gold, and so on. If you want to become wealthy, follow their lead. Start approaching your financial activities like this:

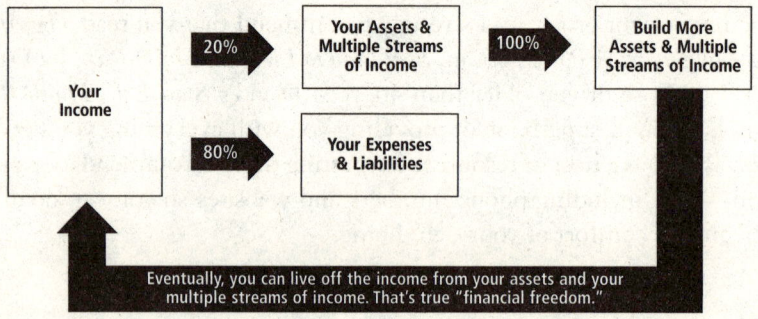

ONCE YOUR NEST EGG STARTS TO GROW

As your money begins to grow, you'll want to educate yourself further about the best way to invest your money. Eventually, you'll probably want to find a good financial advisor. The way I found mine was to ask successful friends who they used, then listen for the same name to come up more than once or twice. That's exactly what happened.

It's best to go with a certified financial planner (CFP), which is an instant signal of credibility, but not necessarily a guarantee. To start, ask people like you if they can recommend a planner. If possible, you want to find a planner with successful experience advising clients in the same stage of life as you. If you don't have friends who are using a financial advisor or you don't get anyone that several people agree on, a good place to go is the National Association of Personal Financial Advisors at napfa.org. These planners are fee-only, which means their only revenue comes from their clients. They accept no commissions at all and pledge to act in their clients' best interests at all times. (A planner who earns money based on commission rather than a flat hourly rate could have an incentive to steer you in a particular direction.) In many respects, NAPFA standards meet or surpass the requirements needed for a CFP credential.

One final word about building an investment portfolio. Be sure to protect it with appropriate insurance—including professional liability insurance if you are self-employed and a prenuptial agreement that acknowledges the financial resources you're bringing to the marriage.

PRINCIPLE 59

MASTER THE SPENDING GAME

*Too many people spend money they haven't earned,
to buy things they don't want,
to impress people they don't like.*

WILL ROGERS
American humorist, actor, and writer

Make no mistake. Earning millions per year, living in an expensive home, experiencing a rich and luxurious lifestyle—plus building a high net worth through extensive investments—should be everyone's financial goal. Along the way, however, it should *also* be your goal to become intelligent about how you spend your money.

Today the amount of consumer debt amassed by the average household is staggering. Add to that consumer debt a mortgage payment, car payment, and student loan payment—not to mention daily groceries and other necessities purchased on credit cards—and it's easy to see why most people *never* achieve the net worth and luxury lifestyle they dream about. They commit what little money is left over each month toward paying off past purchases rather than toward investing for their future lifestyle. They're heavily in debt today—and they'll stay in debt over their lifetime—simply because they spend more money than they make.

Successful people, on the other hand, have mastered the spending game. They live below their means. They pay less for what they need. And they figure out how to accomplish what they want to do while spending as little as possible.

HOW MUCH DID YOU SPEND LAST YEAR?

*Ask yourself if what you're buying is a need or a want.
There is a big difference.*

DAVE RAMSEY
Author of *The Total Money Makeover*

Spending too much can wreak havoc with your financial goals. It keeps you in debt, prevents you from saving as much as you could, and turns your focus to consumption, rather than to wealth creation and accumulation.

If you can't seem to curb your spending, try this exercise. Go through every closet, drawer, and cabinet in your house and take out everything you haven't used in the past year. This includes clothes, shoes, jewelry, utensils, consumer electronics and appliances, blankets, craft supplies, sporting equipment, games, toys, auto accessories, and tools—anything and everything you spent money on *but didn't use in the last year*. Gather it all together in one place, such as your living room, family room, or garage. Then add up the price you paid for each and every item.

I've encountered people who found expensive clothes with the tags still attached, shopping bags containing housewares they never unboxed, and expensive tools and equipment they literally used once, perhaps three or four years ago.

The truth is that with the exception of tuxedos, evening gowns, ski boots, and snorkel gear you may use only once every few years, you probably never really needed all those things in the first place. You didn't use them in the last year, and yet you spent money on them. When you add up what these items cost, you may find the total will be more than your current credit card debt.

START PAYING CASH FOR VIRTUALLY EVERYTHING

One way to curb spending is to start paying cash for everything. Cash is more immediate. It makes you think about what you're buying. You'll probably find yourself spending less than you would if you used credit cards. Every potential purchase will be considered more carefully, "necessary" incidentals will become less necessary, and large purchases will probably be put off, forcing you to think about how you can make do without them.

REDUCE THE COST OF YOUR RICH LIFESTYLE

Another way to master the spending game is to live the lifestyle you want yet pay a whole lot less for it. I know many people who do this all the time yet still maintain an aggressive saving and investment program, with a few simple changes in the way they spend and buy.

Let's look at a few examples.

A woman I know regularly purchases $685 season tickets to the opera for just $123. She sees the same world-class tenors, hears the same thunderous music, and hobnobs with the same art patrons as those who pay more to be there—but she gets her tickets at 82% off what other people pay. How does she do it? When the mailing for season ticket subscribers arrives in March, she selects the operas she wants to see, disregards those she doesn't like, and sends in her payment with instructions for her "Design-Your-Own" series—simply assuming the order will be accepted (which, of course, it always is). Because she is perfectly happy to sit in the balcony, she gets an entire season's worth of "champagne" experiences for less than the cost of a month's worth of gas for her car.

Another friend is a collector of vintage cars—not just any cars, but convertible Cadillacs. He buys them in January when no one would ever think of purchasing a convertible and saves literally tens of thousands of dollars off the cost of his purchases. As a result of this strategy and other savvy purchasing ideas, he can afford to own several rental properties and put the positive cash flow they produce into saving himself rich.

Another woman I know likes to wear expensive designer fashions but feels morally bound to purchase them at the consignment store, where she selects from racks and racks of virtually new or never-been-worn cast-offs, paying pennies on the dollar to look like a movie star.

Other people barter for goods and services, ask for discounts even when they're not offered, ask how they can buy the item cheaper, call four or five vendors and take bids for the same identical item, shop at ultra-budget stores for the things that don't matter so that they can spend more on the ones that do. In short, they routinely squeeze every dime they can out of the cost of living the extravagant lifestyle they want.

To these people—who are all aggressive savers—living this kind of lifestyle on as little money as possible has become a game.

WHAT WILL MAKE YOU TRULY HAPPY?

That man is richest whose pleasures are the cheapest.

HENRY DAVID THOREAU
Author, poet, and philosopher

Financial mentor Todd Tresidder recommends that you add up the cost of all the unnecessary "stuff" you've been spending money on and compare that amount to what you *could be spending that money for*—either building a rainy day fund, enjoying rich and rewarding life experiences, or paying for things that are much more critical to your happiness. Wouldn't an exotic vacation, a virtual assistant, interesting educational or personal growth opportunities—or the ability to pursue global philanthropy—make life more enjoyable and inspire you to achieve even greater financial success?

David Bach, bestselling author of *Start Late, Finish Rich,* calls this prudent strategy the "Latte Factor"—the idea that if you eliminate small but unnecessary daily expenses, such as that $4.00 cup of morning coffee from the gourmet coffee shop or buying lunch every day or hitting the mall for retail therapy, you could redirect the savings into investments that would help achieve your financial goals. While these purchases might seem small, it always surprises people how quickly they add up to substantial savings.

RECONSIDER WHETHER YOU REALLY NEED THAT STUDENT LOAN

Today in America, the student loans that have yet to be repaid add up to more than the total credit-card debt for all American households *combined*. Nearly one trillion dollars have been borrowed for tuition, books, and living expenses, but have yet to be paid back. Some students graduate with $200,000 or more in debt—hampering their ability to buy a house, get married, start a business, travel, or even pursue a career they love. Instead, they're faced with moving back home, curtailing their future plans, and taking whichever job pays the most—even if it's not what they studied for in the first place.

Not only that, but experts suggest that the ease of obtaining a student loan has actually caused universities to inflate their tuition and fees—knowing the costs will be easily met by students who are willing to borrow to get an education. And most lenders will tell you that a substantial portion of student loan money is spent on lifestyle expenses, rent, and other day-to-day expenses that don't necessarily contribute to a student's education.

But before you say, "Without a student loan, I can't go to college!" ask yourself whether you really need that loan (or need one that is quite so large). Can you go to a community college the first two years and live at home to cut costs? Can you live inexpensively in the dorms versus renting and furnishing an apartment or house? Can you become an excellent candidate for merit-based scholarships by doing internships in your field, becoming active in industry groups, creating a substantial résumé and curriculum vitae—then researching less well-publicized scholarships available through private family foundations?

Graduating with as little debt as possible should be the goal of every college student.

TAKE STEPS NOW TO BECOME DEBT FREE

Another big part of mastering the spending game is to simply get out of debt. Stop paying high credit card interest rates and assume a less consumerist lifestyle.

It's amazing that as a population, we've amassed as much personal debt as we have. Credit card, mortgage, and auto payments are staggering for many people. Savings and financial security suffer. If this is your situation, take steps now to start living life debt free using these strategies:

1. **Stop borrowing money.** As simple as this may sound, borrowing money is one of the main reasons why people don't get out of debt. While they're paying down existing debt, they're still using their credit cards, taking out new loans, and so on. This is madness. Why? Because the cost of borrowing is actually more staggering than most people know. The numbers below show you how much you actually pay when you purchase an item with borrowed money.

Amount borrowed	$10,000
Interest rate	10%
Months financed	60 months
Total interest paid	$3,346.67
Total interest as a percentage of item purchased	33.5%

If you wouldn't pay $13,346 for the item you've just borrowed $10,000 for, find a way to pay cash for it, purchase a similar item for less money, or decide whether you really need that item at all.

2. **Don't get a home equity loan to pay off credit card debt.** When you "consolidate" all your monthly payments into a lower-rate loan, you actually make your situation worse. Why? Because you start back at the beginning of the amortization scale where interest is the highest portion of each month's payment. At the beginning of any loan, very little of your new monthly payment goes to pay down the principal, whereas the consumer loans you were paying on before may have had most or even all of your monthly payment going toward reduction of the principal.

3. **Pay off your smallest debts first.** When you pay off your smallest debt first, you achieve a major success breakthrough—even if it doesn't seem that way. For one thing, you experience a huge boost in your self-esteem whenever you accomplish any goal. Why not start with the smallest goal that's the easiest to achieve?

4. **Slowly increase your debt payments.** Once you've paid off a smaller debt, simply take the monthly payment you were making on that debt and use it to increase your payments on your next debt. For example, if by paying $300 a month on your credit card you reduce your balance to zero, take that same $300 next month and add it to the amount you would normally make on your car loan. This saves you thousands of dollars in interest by paying off your car loan early, plus it keeps you from expanding your lifestyle by that $300 a month.

5. **Pay off your home mortgage and credit cards early.** Many mortgage lenders offer what's called a biweekly mortgage. That means you pay half your monthly mortgage amount every other week, instead of making one big payment at the beginning of the month. Because these loans often reamortize with every payment, it has the effect of turning a 30-year mortgage into a 23-year loan. This results in staggering savings on mortgage interest and gets you out of debt faster than you ever thought possible. If your lender doesn't offer such a loan, why not make

one extra payment a year or pay a small extra sum on your own every month? It will still reduce the number of years on the loan and save you years' worth of interest. You can also use the same technique to make extra payments on your credit cards.

THE POWER OF FOCUS

As you commit to becoming debt free and saving more, you'll encounter an almost miraculous force working in your life. As you change your focus from spending and consuming to enjoying the things you already have and putting money aside, you'll progress at an almost unexplainable rate.

Even if you don't believe you'll survive every month, once you commit to a debt-reduction and savings plan, you'll be surprised at your ability to manage and arrive at your goal faster than you had planned.

You may go through a profound transformation. You'll see your values and priorities change. Suddenly, you'll measure your success in terms of debts paid off rather than goods purchased. And as your investment portfolio grows, you'll begin to weigh *all purchases* against your goal to be financially secure and debt free.

Regardless of where you are in life—even if you're in what appears to be a hopeless situation—stay the course and allow this miracle to accelerate you to your goal.

PRINCIPLE 60

TO SPEND MORE, FIRST MAKE MORE

*Whatever may be said in praise of poverty,
the fact remains that it is not possible to live a
really complete or successful life unless one is rich.*

WALLACE D. WATTLES
Author of *The Science of Getting Rich*

In the final analysis, there are really only two ways to end up with more money for investing or additional luxuries—either spend less money in the first place or simply make more of it. Personally, I'm a fan of making more. I would rather make more and have more to spend than to always be denying myself things I want for some distant future gain.

The fact is that making more money means you can both invest more *and* spend more on the things you want—travel, clothes, art, concerts, fine food, quality medical care, world-class entertainment experiences, quality transportation, education, hobbies, and all sorts of time- and labor-saving devices and services.

This is common sense.

HOW TO MAKE MORE MONEY

The first step to making more money is to decide how much more you want to make. I've talked extensively about using the power of affirmations and visualization to see yourself as already in the possession of that money. Not surprisingly, story after story exists in the world about super-rich individuals who have used these daily habits to bring more abundance into their lives.

The second step is to ask yourself, *What product, service, or additional value can I deliver to generate that money?* What does the world, your employer, your community, fellow businesspeople, fellow students, or your customers need that you could provide?

Finally, the third step is simply to develop and deliver that product, service, or extra value.

MORE MONEY IDEA #1: BECOME AN INTRAPRENEUR

Today, many of America's smartest companies are cultivating entrepreneurship among their employees and executives. If one of these companies is your employer—or if you can convince your boss to give you a percentage of the newfound money you generate from overlooked areas of revenue, you can almost instantly increase your income.

Perhaps your employer has a customer list that it isn't selling additional goods and services to. Perhaps your work group is so good at managing projects, its members have extra time that they could "hire out" to other departments for extra pay. Maybe there's a piece of machinery, a vendor relationship, an overlooked marketing idea, or other unusual asset your employer isn't using to full advantage. You can create a plan to turn this asset into cash and approach your employer with a proposal to work on the asset-maximizing project off-hours for extra pay. It may even garner you a well-deserved promotion.

Janet Switzer's book *Instant Income: Strategies That Bring in the Cash for Small Businesses, Innovative Employees, and Occasional Entrepreneurs* details an entire plan for going into business with the boss—including a checklist for finding hidden income opportunities, a script for negotiating a deal with your employer, recommended compensation models, strategies that will help you generate newfound revenue, and even a comprehensive implementation guide for executing your plans.

MORE MONEY IDEA #2: FIND A NEED AND FILL IT

I never perfected an invention that I did not think about in terms of the service it might give others. . . . I find out what the world needs, then I proceed to invent it.

THOMAS A. EDISON
America's most successful inventor

Many of the most successful people throughout history have identified a need in the marketplace and provided a solution for it, yet most of us have never asked what's needed—or even what's possible.

If your dream is to earn more money—either with your own business or in addition to your job—identify a need that isn't being met and determine how to meet it.

Whether it's starting a website for a particular group of collectors, providing a unique education for people who need rare or unusual skills, or developing new products or services to address emerging trends you see in society, there are always needs you can find to create a business or a service around. Many of these former "met needs" are inventions and services we now take for granted. But the fact remains that people discovered something they needed in their own life or stumbled on the needs of others, then created the gadgets and services we enjoy today:

- The Baby Jogger was invented by a man who wanted to go jogging but had child care responsibilities. What he created for himself was soon in demand by nearly everyone who saw it.
- eBay, the world's largest online auction service, was born in 1995 when founder Pierre Omidyar engineered a way to help his fiancée trade PEZ candy dispensers.
- Avon decided that its direct-selling approach was ideal for the newly emerging Russian democracy, where Avon representatives could not only act as personal beauty consultants to Russian women who were unaccustomed to wearing cosmetics but could also serve as delivery outlets at a time when retail infrastructures were practically nonexistent.
- Internet dating services were invented when smart entrepreneurs matched the desires (and busy schedules) of single people with the computer technology that was sitting in front of them 8 to 12 hours a day.
- After 26-year-old Nicholas Woodman's marketing company called FunBug failed in 2002, he decided to travel around the world surfing. In an effort to capture his surfing activities on film, he attached a 35mm camera to the palm of his hand with a rubber band. Seeing that amateur photographers like him, who wanted to capture quality action photos of their activities, had difficulties because they could not get close enough to the action or were unable to purchase quality equipment at affordable prices, he was inspired to found GoPro. His solution was to develop a belt that would attach the camera to the body. He and

his future wife financed the business by selling shell necklaces from their car—paying $1.90 in Bali and selling them for $60 in California—eventually combining the proceeds with money borrowed from his mother and father. The original cameras he developed have evolved into a compact waterproof digital camera that supports Wi-Fi, can be remotely controlled, and is affordable to the average action sports enthusiast. In 2004, he made his first big sale when a Japanese company ordered 100 cameras at a sports show. Sales have doubled every year since, and in 2012, GoPro sold 2.3 million cameras. That same year, a Taiwanese contract manufacturer purchased 8.88% of the company for $200 million, which set the market value of the company at $2.25 billion, making Woodman, who owned the majority of the stock, a billionaire at the age of 38.

- In the 1970s, a German forest ranger made an interesting discovery. Caught in an avalanche, he owed his survival to the dead game he was carrying on his shoulders, since it allowed him to remain on the surface of the snow. Experiments with voluminous canisters and balloons followed, and the idea for the avalanche airbag was born. In 1980, Peter Aschauer, after a firsthand experience with an avalanche, acquired the patent, founded the company ABS Peter Aschauer GmbH, and started to develop a system that allowed avalanche victims to gain a sufficient increase in volume within seconds, without obstructing their ability to move. Since 1991, the documented survival rate for airbag-equipped skiers in avalanches has been 255 out of 262, or 97%. The company eventually grew to sell in 25 countries, and in 2023, they reported total sales of $293 million.

What need could you identify? Need is literally everywhere you look. It doesn't matter whether you are a college student seeking a summer income, a housewife wanting to earn an extra $1,000 a month to make ends meet, or an entrepreneur looking for the next big business opportunity—there is always a need that could be your opportunity to make some serious money.

A Fresh Idea Makes Mike Milliorn a Multimillionaire

Mike Milliorn was a salesman for a label company who needed to make a few more dollars a month. One of his biggest customers was the TGI Friday's restaurant chain, a sophisticated operation looking for a fail-safe way to mark their stock and ensure that employees used the oldest perishable foods first—a process called food rotation. Before meeting Mike, they used masking tape and markers, or they bought colored dots at an office supply store and posted a chart on the wall that said "Red dot equals Wednesday."

Their biggest problem? The adhesive didn't stick in their walk-in coolers. So Mike invented Daydots for food rotation—a fail-proof system of colored dots with the day of the week imprinted right on the cold-temperature label.

He realized that if TGI Friday's needed the dots, other restaurants probably needed them, too. He began marketing Daydots to as many restaurants as he could economically afford to reach.

Like most people with a new idea, Mike kept his day job. "With three kids, a mortgage, and two car payments, it was too big of a risk to quit and devote full time to Daydots. I had zero money, so I had to figure out how to take my idea to market economically and without quitting my job. That's where the mail-order idea came up."

Mike produced a simple one-page flyer that explained the Daydots system and financed it with a $6,000 loan against his wife's Chevy station wagon—then mailed it to the handful of restaurants for which he could afford the postage. He got just enough orders from that first mailing to encourage him to do another mailing, then another. For four years, he and his wife kept their day jobs and worked out of their house.

Today, Mike's company mails 3 million catalogs a year and prints over 100 million Daydots a week. Mike saw a need, and—with the help of his wife, kids, and employees—he worked diligently to fill it.

Daydots has even evolved into a manufacturer and distributor of food safety products—as well as cold-temperature, dissolvable, and "Super-Removable" dots and labels.

Thirteen years later, Mike was approached by a $4 billion Fortune 500 company that purchased Daydots for tens of millions of dollars. What started out as a simple enterprise to earn a few extra dollars to "get his kids through school" ended up earning Mike enough to do all that—and more. Mike Milliorn noticed a need and found a creative, economical way to fill it.

The Possibilities Are Endless

Think of all the companies that are now household names that grew out of someone recognizing a need and figuring out how to fill it, many of which were created in the past ten years: Zoom, DoorDash, Beyond Meat, Uber, Lyft, and Airbnb, just to name a few.

Do you see something you want or need in your life that could become a business? What about a need, longing, or aspiration in the lives of others around you?

Is there something that needs to be provided, solved, addressed, or eliminated? Is there something you find annoying that could be alleviated if there were some gadget or service to solve that particular problem? Do you share a common goal or ambition with others in your industry or social circle that you could achieve if only someone provided a system or process for achieving it? Do you enjoy certain activities that could be made even more enjoyable with a new invention or service?

Look at your own life and ask what is missing that would make it easier or more fulfilling.

MORE MONEY IDEA #3: THINK OUTSIDE THE BOX

When Dave Liniger, founder and CEO of RE/MAX, was a successful young real estate agent, like everyone else he grumbled about paying 50% of his commissions to the broker whose office he worked in. Experienced and an out-of-the-box thinker, he began to look for an alternative—a better way to sell homes and keep more of what he earned at the same time.

Not long after, Dave happened upon a simple, independent rent-a-desk real estate office that—for $500 a month—provided a desk, a receptionist, and limited other services to real estate agents who were experienced enough to find their own customers and do their own marketing. Like Dave, these agents didn't need the backing of a big-name entity to be successful. But unlike more professionally managed real estate brokerages, the rent-a-desk idea didn't offer outstanding management, a large brand name, lots of offices, and the ability to share expenses across thousands of agents.

Why not create a hybrid? Dave mused. *Why not create a firm that offers more independence to agents, that lets them keep more than 50% of their sales commission but still provides more support than going it alone?*

Real Estate Maximums—RE/MAX for short—was born. And since its inception in 1973, because of Dave's commitment to the vision and his dogged determination not to give up during the very challenging first five years, RE/MAX has become the fastest-growing, largest network of real estate agents in the world, with more than 140,000 agents in more than 110 countries who share overhead, enjoy expense control, and are part of a bigger entity but who also remain independent enough to determine their own advertising budget and decide how much of their income they want to keep after their expenses.

Because Liniger's out-of-the-box idea was backed up with hard work, perseverance, and passion, and because it met a need for thousands of real estate agents, the dream has grown into an almost billion-dollar-a-year business.

How far might you go if you were willing to do some out-of-the-box thinking and then take action?

MORE MONEY IDEA #4: START A BUSINESS ON THE INTERNET

As an income generation specialist, Janet Switzer works with countless Internet entrepreneurs, helping them earn more money from their online businesses. Today, an Internet business is one of the easiest to start and operate—even while you keep your current job. You can find a need and fill it for a very narrow market, yet still reach thousands and even millions of people with that special interest all over the world.

Today, services abound that give you a platform for selling anything you make, find, or can do for others. Online shopping platforms like eBay, Etsy, Shopify, and others let you set up a storefront and sell items you've made or acquired—whether it's antiques, electronics, used books, or something else—paying a small percentage of each sale.

The free website Craigslist, on the other hand, lets you advertise virtually any item for sale—from garden plants to household items to clothing, even real estate and vehicles—all at no charge. It's the world's biggest yard sale. You provide your contact information so buyers can contact you directly—and there are even apps to alert buyers when a specific item is posted by a seller.

If you set up your own website and subscribe to a shopping cart service, you can sell and accept credit cards for payment at your own site. This is where your expertise becomes valuable—selling ebooks, audio courses, training materials, specialized reports or directories, how-to information, and other *knowledge products* that are downloadable—meaning you never have to ship a single box or send an envelope.

Additionally, the good news is the Internet is now a mature marketplace. Hundreds of other websites, newsletters, and clubs already have visitors, subscribers, and members who could be perfect prospective customers for you, once you offer a percentage to the other website owner, or affiliate.

Once you learn how to market on the Internet, you can also market other people's products online. A man in Florida approached his local jeweler and asked him if he had ever thought about selling his jewelry on the

Internet. The jeweler replied that he had thought about it but had never had the time to get around to actually doing it. He offered to build the website and drive traffic to it for a percentage of the profits. The jeweler readily agreed. It was a win-win for both of them.

Shane Lewis, a medical student in Virginia, decided to create an Internet business to cover the cost of supporting his family while he was attending medical school at George Washington University. With the help of StoresOnline.com, he looked around for a product he could market and found a rapid urine drug test that parents and others could use to administer drug tests with immediate results. When this book was first published in 2005, Shane was making well over $100,000 a year from this and two other drug- and alcohol-testing products. He told me back then, "My first month I only had a few orders, but by the third month we were doing really well and exceeded my initial goals. Today we earn enough for my wife to stay home with our children while I attend school. Thanks to our Internet business, we are virtually debt free and no longer have to rely on student loans to make ends meet."

MORE MONEY IDEA #5:
JOIN A NETWORK MARKETING COMPANY

There are more than 2,500 companies in the world (1,000 in the United States) who sell their products and services through network marketing—certainly one or more you can get passionate about. From health and nutrition products to cosmetics, cookware, toys, educational materials, and phone services—even low-cost legal and financial services—there is something for everyone. A little research on the Internet will yield a host of opportunities. You can visit the websites of the Direct Selling Association at dsa.org for an extensive list of companies.

Tony and Randi Escobar decided to join forces with Isagenix, a newly created network marketing company specializing in nutrition for life, internal cleansing, weight loss, and skin care products. They had a passion for health and wellness, the desire to succeed, a love for people, a love of the products, and a commitment to work hard.

Tony, an Australian immigrant who had been working in the copper mines of Arizona only a few short years before, and his wife—who were facing bankruptcy just prior to their joining Isagenix—created an income of nearly $2,000,000 a year in less than two years. Although the speed at which they achieved this level is exceptional, millions of people are adding thousands of dollars a month to their incomes by participating in network marketing companies—and many are becoming millionaires. In fact, it has been reported that network marketing has produced over 100,000 millionaires since the mid-1990s in the United States alone! It's also reported that 20% of all new millionaires have come from network marketing.

Because many network marketing companies do not last, make sure you get solid advice about the company and its products before you get involved. Find a company that has been around for a while and has a great reputation. Try the products and make sure you love them. If you are passionate about the product and passionate about people, you can make a lot of money through the leverage that building a downline provides you. There are very few businesses where you can capitalize on such a huge opportunity for such a small financial investment.*

MONEY FLOWS TO VALUE

Wherever you decide to put your energies, the key is to become more valuable to your current employer, customers, or clients. You do that by getting better at solving their problems, delivering products, and adding services that they want and need.

You may need to get more training, develop new skills, create new relationships, or put in extra time. But the responsibility for getting better at what you do and how you do it is totally yours. Always seek out opportunities for more training and self-development. If you need an advanced degree or some kind of certification to move up in your chosen trade or profession, quit talking about it and go get it.

CREATE MULTIPLE SOURCES OF INCOME

The best way to enjoy greater income *and* develop economic security in your life is to create several sources of income. This protects you from any one of those sources—usually your job—from drying up and leaving you without any cash flow. I have always had several sources of income. Even

---

*If you choose to pursue network marketing as a career or as a source of supplemental income, read the following books to quickly learn the important basics. I consider these must-reads: *Your First Year in Network Marketing* by Mark Yarnell and Rene Reid Yarnell (Roseville, CA: Prima Publishing, 1998), *Secrets of Building a Million Dollar Network Marketing Organization: From a Guy Who's Been There Done That and Shows You How to Do It, Too* by Joe Rubino (Charlottesville, VA: Upline Press, 1997), and *GoPro–7 Steps to Becoming a Network Marketing Professional* by Eric Worre (Wichita, KS: Network Marketing Pro, 2013).

when I was a therapist in private practice, I also gave speeches, ran workshops for educators, wrote magazine articles and books, and had a mail-order bookstore.

You, too, can find all kinds of additional ways to make money if you merely start looking for them. You can work up from simple ways such as hauling trash with your truck on the weekends, tutoring someone, or giving music lessons to investing in rental properties, consulting, or marketing on the Internet.

There are endless possibilities for multiple income sources. If you are a voracious reader, you could create a website that includes reviews of the books you have read, with links to Amazon, which will pay you an affiliate fee, a percentage of every book that is sold through your link. You also receive a percentage of any other purchases they might make on Amazon while they are there. I know one blogger who makes an average of $2,500 a month doing this. You can sell something on eBay. You can buy and sell art. One of my friends whose main source of income is professional speaking loves Oriental art. Twice a year, he travels to China and Japan and purchases art very inexpensively. He keeps what he likes and sells the rest for a handsome profit to a growing list of collectors he has cultivated. His travel and his own art is in essence free, plus he makes a handsome profit off the art that he sells. I know the principal of a private school who does the same thing during his summer vacation with antique Chinese furniture, which he then sells out of his home and garage.

My sister, Kimberly Kirberger, is best known as the coauthor of 11 books in the *Chicken Soup for the Teenage Soul* series. But she is also someone who understands the importance of multiple streams of income. When she was in her twenties her hobby was stringing beads, but by the time she was 35 she started designing more upscale jewelry and turned her hobby into another source of income. She created Kirberger Designs and quickly became known for her one-of-a-kind pieces—and it didn't take long before they were being sold in Nordstrom and Barneys, as well as a host of boutiques around the country.

IF YOU'RE EMPLOYED FULL-TIME, YOU CAN STILL MAKE MORE MONEY AS AN OCCASIONAL ENTREPRENEUR

If you're employed and you love your job (including the steady paycheck), but you just want to earn a few thousand dollars on the side several times a year, there are strategies you can use to become what Janet Switzer calls an "occasional entrepreneur." In her book *Instant Income,* Janet details short-term, minimum-commitment, hassle-free projects that are less involved than maintaining a part-time business year-round.

For example, there are online services like Upwork that will link you up with people who are looking to outsource various services. If you do any kind of creative work—like writing or graphic design, putting together PowerPoint presentations—or if you could use your expertise to advise a small business on a specific project they want to pursue, these services will give you a platform to discuss your skills, showcase samples of your work, bid for projects, and even get paid by the party who is hiring you.

Occasional entrepreneurship also lets you pursue your passion. Like the college professor who writes articles for hire ... the aerospace manager who sells Native American crafts at weekend powwows ... or the stay-at-home mom who runs a podcasting website for other stay-at-home moms, it lets you make money in ways that don't feel like work.*

What kinds of occasional opportunities does Janet recommend?

Consulting. If you have knowledge or expertise that others don't, you can earn a superb income as an occasional consultant. To best market yourself, first determine who needs what you know and which niche markets they belong to. Then target your online content to reach these buyers (more about this later in the section "Success in the Digital Age"). Articles, your blog, free reports, and free assessment tools at your website are good ways to familiarize potential clients with your specific expertise.

Service Provider. Thousands of people offer services on an occasional basis—whether it's professional organizing, tax preparation, party planning, interior decorating, weed clearing, grant writing, holiday gift-buying for corporations, magic acts, or one of the hundreds of other types of services that consumers and businesses will pay for. Almost anything you love to do—that is also bothersome or time-consuming to others—can be turned into an occasional service earning instant income. The key to marketing yourself as a service provider on an occasional basis is to approach *other* providers from whom these consumers and businesses are already buying, and negotiate a referral.

Retail and Manufacturing. These work well when you're selling highly specialized one-of-a-kind items that you enjoy making and that you can sell at a very high price—such as unique jewelry, intricate model ships, hand-tied fishing flies, couture clothing, and other limited-manufacture

---

*For a list of the 13 criteria Janet looks for in an ideal occasional entrepreneurship opportunity—as well as ways to minimize the hassle factor and a checklist of marketing strategies you can use—pick up Janet's book *Instant Income*. Get her free *Instant Income 10-Day Turnaround* guide at instantincome.com.

items. Use your own website or a service like Etsy to feature your products and sell worldwide.

AN IMPORTANT DISTINCTION

When you are building multiple sources of income, do your best to focus on creating sources that require very little time and money to start and operate. Your ultimate goal is to set things up so that you're free to work when and where you want—or to take time off to pursue leisure. Too many scattered streams mean that you run the risk of losing your main source of income.

The two best resources I know for really understanding and mastering multiple sources of income are *Multiple Streams of Income: How to Generate a Lifetime of Unlimited Wealth,* second edition, and *Multiple Streams of Internet Income: How Ordinary People Make Extraordinary Money Online,* both by Robert G. Allen.

And remember to apply everything you have learned so far to creating multiple sources of income. Make it part of your vision and your goals, visualize and affirm that you are making money from your multiple income sources, start reading books and articles about it, and talk with your friends about it. Based on the Law of Attraction, you will start attracting all kinds of opportunities and ideas. Then just act on the ones that feel most right for you.

PRINCIPLE 61

GIVE MORE TO GET MORE

*Bring the full tithes into the storehouse,
that there may be food in my house;
and thereby put me to the test, says the Lord of hosts,
if I will not open the windows of heaven for you
and pour down for you an overflowing blessing.*

MALACHI 3:10
(Revised standard version of the Bible)

Tithing—that is, giving 10% of your earnings to the work of God which can include charities and other nonprofits, as well as your church, synagogue, or mosque—is one of the best guarantees of prosperity ever known. Many of the world's richest individuals and most successful people have been devout tithers. By tithing regularly, you, too, can put into motion God's universal force, bringing you continual abundance.

Not only does it serve others but it serves you as the giver, too. The benefits cross all religious boundaries and serve those of every faith—because the simple act of giving both creates a spiritual alliance with the God of abundance, and fosters the mindset of love for others. Tithing proves in a compelling way that abundant wealth is something God wants for His children. In fact, He created a world where the more successful you are, the more wealth there is for everyone to share. An increase in wealth for an individual almost always represents an increase in wealth for society at large.★

★See *God Wants You to Be Rich: How and Why Everyone Can Enjoy Material and Spiritual Wealth in Our Abundant World* by Paul Zane Pilzer (New York: Fireside, 1997).

THE TITHING PLAN THAT
CHICKEN SOUP COOKED UP

Tithing has certainly played a huge part in my success and the success of the *Chicken Soup for the Soul®* series. Ever since the first book in the series, Mark and I tithed a portion of the profits to nonprofit organizations that were dedicated to healing the sick, feeding the hungry, housing the homeless, empowering the disempowered, educating the uneducated, and saving the environment.

Along with our publisher and coauthors, we've given away millions of dollars to more than 100 organizations including the Red Cross, the YWCA, and the Make-A-Wish Foundation. Since 1993 we've planted over 250,000 trees at Yellowstone National Park with the National Arbor Day Foundation, underwritten the cost of building homes for the homeless with Habitat for Humanity, fed the hungry of the world with Feed the Children, and prevented thousands of teen suicides through Yellow Ribbon International. We feel so blessed by all that we have been given that we want to give back. We also strongly believe that everything we give away comes back multiplied many times over.

We also tithe a portion of our personal income to our churches and other spiritual missionary and service organizations that uplift humanity through doing spiritual and humanitarian work.

One of the most exciting projects we've been involved in was the distribution of 100,000 free copies of *Chicken Soup for the Prisoner's Soul* to people incarcerated in U.S. prisons. The book was never intended for distribution in the general population, but it was so successful that soon we received thousands of requests from family members, correctional officers, and prison ministries to make copies of the book available for them. What started out strictly as a philanthropic endeavor turned into another successful *Chicken Soup* book in the bookstores—and another example of how good works come back to you multiplied.

THERE ARE DIFFERENT TYPES OF TITHING

There are two different kinds of tithing. *Financial tithing* is best explained as contributing 10% of your gross income to the organization from whence you derive your spiritual guidance or whose philanthropic work you want to support.

Time tithing is volunteering your time to serve your church, temple, synagogue, mosque, or any charity that could use your help. There are currently more than one million charities just in the United States alone that need volunteers. Think about what organizations you could volunteer your time and expertise to.

HIS LIFE TURNED AROUND AS SOON AS HE STARTED TITHING

Nature gives all, without reservation, and loses nothing; man or woman, grasping all, loses everything.

JAMES ALLEN
Author of *Path of Prosperity*

Robert Allen, bestselling author of *Nothing Down* and *The One Minute Millionaire*, didn't always tithe. But after he'd lost everything and was down to zero, he said to himself, *Wait a second. I've had so much money in my life. I'm supposed to be the guru who teaches people how to become rich. Where's it all gone? I must have done something wrong.*

Eventually Bob worked his way back to prosperity. But along the way, he learned a valuable lesson: *Either I believe in tithing,* he said to himself, *or I don't. If I believe it, I'm going to tithe every week. I'm going to figure out what our income is that week and write my check that week.*

As he became a dedicated tither, suddenly a whole new world opened up for him. Though his debts were almost insurmountable, he became more grateful for what he had. Soon, new opportunities started flowing to him. Today, Bob says, he has so much opportunity it would take him 10 lifetimes to tap into it all. He believes it's that way for all dedicated tithers.

But even more telling than his own story is how he inspires others to tithe. He recalls one woman who approached him and complained, "My husband and I can't tithe. We can barely make our mortgage payment. Our lifestyle costs us $5,000 a month. There's not enough money left over at the end of the month."

Bob admonished her, saying, "You don't tithe because you want to get something. You tithe because you've already gotten it. You're so blessed already, there's no way in the world you'll be able to repay it. There are six billion people on the face of the Earth who would give their left lung to trade places with you. You tithe out of the gratitude you feel for the unbelievable blessings and lifestyle you have."

Bob never expects a thing when he tithes, because he now realizes the windows of heaven have already been opened to him. He tithes because he's already received the blessings.

KEEPING IT ALL IN PERSPECTIVE

When you let go of trying to get more of what you don't really need, it frees up oceans of energy to make a difference with what you have.

LYNNE TWIST
Author of *The Soul of Money*

As my friend Lynne Twist writes in her book, *The Soul of Money,* it's important to consciously examine your relationship with money and to remember that while money can be helpful in many aspects of your life, the goal of amassing wealth for the sake of wealth can lead to greed—a very destructive force to yourself, your relationships, and the environment. She wisely cautions that the quest for abundance that most people get caught up in usually results in a never-ending pursuit of "more."

So often we think of abundance as the point at which we'll know we've really "arrived." But abundance will actually remain elusive as long as we believe we'll find it by owning or buying some excessive amount of something.

True abundance, on the other hand, does exist. It flows from what Lynne calls *sufficiency*—having *enough.*

"Abundance," Lynne says, "is a fact of nature. It's a fundamental law of nature that there is enough. But even that *enough* is finite—leading to our current situation where, in our quest for more, we're consuming parts of the environment at a faster rate than it can renew and replenish itself."

Luckily, *enough* is a place you can arrive at easily and dwell in happily. And once you've arrived there, it's time to transcend your fear of scarcity—both now and in the future—and use the excess you have to make a difference in the world in whatever areas you are drawn to.

The age-old maxim that money can't buy happiness is ultimately true. While earning money and keeping score can at times be exciting and sometimes even necessary, it's incredibly important not to lose sight of the bigger picture—that the size of your income, your bank account, and your collection of stuff is not what ultimately creates the amount of fulfillment you experience in your life.

MAKING A DIFFERENCE

Tom, a neighbor of mine who likes to contribute quietly, loves to travel for business. He is a member of the Directors Guild of America, and at one time his contract required him to travel first class wherever he went in the world. The comfortable seat, great food, attention, and drinks were a nice perk added to a film shoot schedule. He became accustomed to all these benefits, and they became a normal part of his agenda for each job.

One trip, however, took Tom to New Zealand for filming. When he landed, he asked the production manager how much a coach-class ticket cost, as he was considering bringing one of his sons over. The production manager told him the coach-class ticket was $1,800. The first-class ticket he had just flown over on had cost $7,700! He was a little stunned, as he never considered there would be such a big disparity in prices.

At first, Tom thought that if he sat in coach on future flights and had the film company pay him the difference in fares, he would have nearly $6,000 more. His mind raced to all the things he could buy for himself with that $6,000; motorcycles, trips, and many other goods ran through his mind.

Then a lightbulb went off in Tom's mind. He thought about the kids he had met through the years who couldn't afford to go to college. Tom thought that with $6,000, surely he could cover some tuition. At this turning point, Tom made a pledge to himself. He would no longer fly first class. He would fly coach class and have the difference given to him to donate to a worthy cause. The first time he did it, he paid the college tuition for a boy for the year. He was astounded. He realized that by sacrificing a small amount of comfort on a flight, he gave someone not only a year's worth of tuition, but possibly a whole new direction in life.

Then, some curious things began to happen. Tom was still meeting interesting people in coach class. The other people Tom worked with asked him why he wasn't sitting in first class with them. When he told them what he was doing with the money, some of them started to do the same. His business increased, too. Was it because he was doing something good, or just coincidence?

Tom is still flying coach and giving the difference in fares to scholarship funds and land preservation charities. He learned that small steps and seemingly small amounts of money can have a major impact on the direction of someone's life. With that knowledge, Tom's coach-class seat is a little more comfortable!

Tom's story is a beautiful illustration of the impact of moving from abundance to sufficiency and the impact it can have in the world.

CORPORATE GIVING

Corporations, too, can reap the rewards of giving back. William H. George, the chairman and CEO of Medtronic, revealed to a Minneapolis conference on philanthropy how his company had committed to giving 2% of their pretax profits. Although these "tithes" amounted to only $1.5 million in the beginning, the company's continuous growth streak enabled them to boost their total giving to more than $400 million—with $17 million given in one year alone.

Perhaps the most impressive recent acts of giving have been MacKenzie Scott's $5.6 billion in grants to more than 500 charities, and Chuck Feeney's goal to give away his entire $8 billion fortune and go broke in his lifetime. However, you don't have to be a corporation or super-wealthy to give back to the community. Any contribution, whether it is in time or in money, will make a difference to the recipients and to you, both in the good feelings you'll experience and in the expanded flow of abundance streaming into your life.

SHARE THE WEALTH

Money is like manure. If you spread it around it does a lot of good. But if you pile it up in one place it stinks like hell.

JUNIOR MURCHISON
Founder of the Dallas Cowboys football team

When you engage others in your success—when you share the wealth with them—more work gets done, greater success is achieved, and ultimately everyone benefits more. The key to the success of the *Chicken Soup for the Soul®* series was our decision to involve more coauthors in the process. Though Mark and I each received smaller royalties—30 or 40¢ a book instead of 60¢—it allowed us to complete more titles, get more media coverage, and sell more books. There is no way the two of us could have compiled, edited, written, and promoted more than 200 books by ourselves.

What started out as the collaboration of two authors and two assistants grew to a staff of twelve people with two editors, several consulting editors, two editorial assistants, a permissions specialist, a marketing director, a licensing director, a new-projects director, several assistants, and a group of 100 coauthors and almost 10,000 contributors, including over 100 cartoonists. We always did our best to fairly compensate everybody involved. Our staff salaries have been higher than normal for the publishing industry, and we have a generous pension plan and an equally generous bonus plan for our employees. All of our staff members get six weeks of vacation time every year. We have paid out over $4 million in permissions fees to contributors and donated millions of dollars to charity. It is our firm belief that this willingness to share the wealth has produced more financial abundance than we could have ever produced on our own. Trying to hang on to it all would have just constricted the flow of money.

PRINCIPLE 62

FIND A WAY TO SERVE

It is one of the beautiful compensations of this life that no man can sincerely try to help another without helping himself.

RALPH WALDO EMERSON
American essayist and poet

The greatest levels of contentment and self-satisfaction are experienced by those who have found a way to serve others. In addition to the true inner joy that is created by serving others, it is a universal principle that you cannot serve others without it coming back multiplied to yourself.

DECIDE WHAT IS IMPORTANT TO *YOU*

Take some time to determine what causes and groups of people are important to you. What issues call out to you? What organizations make your heart sing? Do you care about housing the homeless, promoting the arts, protecting the abused, healing the addicted, providing education, feeding the hungry, or supporting our veterans?

If you love art and think that the schools are woefully lacking in art education, you might decide to volunteer to raise funds for art supplies, volunteer to teach an art class, or become a docent at your local art museum. If you were an only child or really missed having your father or mother around, you might want to volunteer for Big Brothers or Big Sisters. Perhaps you love animals and would rather help find homes for abandoned pets. If you love books, you could volunteer to read a book for the Recording for the Blind & Dyslexic.

VOLUNTEER YOUR SKILLS

There are many nonprofit organizations that could use your business skills—management, accounting, marketing, volunteer recruitment, fund-raising, and so on.

If you have organizational talent, consider working on charitable events. If you can easily convince others of the value of your cause, consider becoming a fund-raiser for local charities who need your help. If you are a skilled executive, consider serving on the board of a nonprofit organization.

YOU'LL GET MORE THAN YOU GIVE

When you volunteer, you will get back a whole lot more than you give. Research on volunteerism shows that people who volunteer live longer, have stronger immune systems, have fewer heart attacks, recover from heart attacks faster, have higher self-esteem, and have a deeper sense of meaning and purpose than those who don't volunteer. The research also shows that people who volunteer in their younger years are more likely to end up in more prestigious and higher-paying jobs than their nonvolunteering counterparts. Volunteering is a powerful way of networking and often leads to business and career opportunities, not to mention more friendships.

Volunteering is also a way to develop important success skills. Many large corporations have come to realize this and actually encourage their employees to volunteer. Many companies, such as SAFECO and the Pillsbury Company, have actually built volunteerism into their employee development programs and have made it part of their annual review process.

Many prospective employers also report that when they are interviewing candidates for hire, they now look to see if the candidates have engaged in volunteer work. So volunteering your time could well have a positive payoff by helping you land a future job.

Additionally, one of the keys to success is building a huge network of relationships, and volunteering lets you meet all kinds of people you would never meet otherwise. Better yet, they're often the people—or the spouses of the people—who make things happen in your profession and in your community.

UNEXPECTED CAREER AND BUSINESS REWARDS

Dillanos Coffee Roasters has a policy of sponsoring a Child Fund International child for every employee in the company. As a way to give back to the countries that make their business possible, they sponsor children only in coffee-growing countries from which they buy beans, such as Guatemala, Colombia, and Costa Rica. Dillanos pays the $35 monthly sponsorship fee, and the individual employees correspond with their child, send birthday and Christmas gifts, and maintain a relationship with the child. In addition to making a difference in the world, the sponsorship program has proven to be a great boost for employee morale.

And while the motivation to sponsor these children was purely philanthropic, it has also had a positive impact on the company's bottom line. All the pictures of the children they sponsor are posted along the wall of one of the hallways in the company. A prospective client was being given a tour of the company and asked about the origin of the pictures. When it was explained that the pictures were of children being supported by the company through ChildFund International, the woman was so touched that before she even tasted Dillanos's coffee, she decided that she wanted to do business with a company that cared so much for children and for their employees.

SERVICE ALWAYS COMES BACK MULTIPLIED

Serving others can also consist of focusing your company's mission on producing products and services that are beneficial to mankind. Sir John Marks Templeton studied more than 10,000 companies over a 50-year period and discovered that the best long-term results flowed to those who focused on providing increasingly beneficial products and services.

"Whatever one does," Templeton said, "he first should ask, *In the long run, is this really useful to the public?* If so, he is serving as a minister. I think those in business can assure each other that if one tries to give his best when serving the community, his business will not languish but prosper."★

Think about the possibility that when you choose to do work that uplifts and serves, that brings people "increasingly beneficial" products and services, when your efforts are focused on giving rather than getting, then you are going to eventually receive back more than you have given.

As Zig Ziglar, one of America's greatest teachers of success principles,

---

★Excerpted from *Religion and Liberty* (November–December 2000, volume 10, number 6), a publication of the Acton Institute for the Study of Religion and Liberty.

was fond of saying, "You can get anything in life you want if you will just help enough other people get what they want."

The world responds to givers more positively than to takers. We naturally want to support the givers. Simply stated, givers get.

THE ROAD TO FULFILLMENT

Kenneth Behring was a very wealthy man who appeared numerous times on the annual Fortune 500 and Forbes 400 lists of the wealthiest people in America, with an estimated net worth of $495 million. Growing up poor in Wisconsin, he earned his first money delivering newspapers, cutting lawns, caddying, and as a teenager, working in a lumberyard and in a retail store. After high school, he sold used cars and eventually opened his own new and used car dealerships. By the age of 27 he was a millionaire. He then moved to Florida and began a second career as a real estate developer. He founded and built Tamarac, Florida, and later moved to California, where he developed Blackhawk, one of the most exclusive residential communities in the United States.

When I met him and heard him speak at the International Achievement Summit in Chicago, Illinois, he talked about how his quest for a happy life had gone through four stages. He called the first stage "More Stuff." In the early days of getting started, he wanted all the basic stuff—a car, a house, a business that was growing and expanding. He thought if he had these things, he would be happy . . . but he wasn't.

He called the second stage of his life "Better Stuff." He thought if he had a big mansion, a more expensive car, a private jet (a huge DC-9), a yacht, and exotic vacations, he would be happy . . . but he wasn't.

He called the third stage of his life "Different Stuff." He thought perhaps he had been buying the wrong kind of stuff. So Ken started buying classic cars—expensive ones. He eventually owned over 100 of them, and even opened an automotive museum to display what had become the world's largest classic car collection. Still looking for the thing that would make him happy, he decided to join with his partner Ken Hofmann and buy the NFL's Seattle Seahawks football team. He figured if he owned a professional football team, he could sit in the owners' box with his friends, and mingle with the players on the field and in the locker room, and this would bring him happiness . . . but it didn't.

The fourth stage of his life began when a friend asked Ken if on his way back from a trip to Africa in his private plane, he wouldn't mind stopping in Romania to deliver six wheelchairs to a hospital there. During that trip Ken was transformed by the experience of lifting an elderly man, who had lost his wife and then suffered a stroke, into a wheelchair. The man started to cry, and Ken found himself touched at a deeper level than he had ever been touched before. He felt more gratitude and joy than he had ever experienced before.

Inspired by that experience, he came home and founded the Wheelchair Foundation, which provides free wheelchairs for people with physical disabilities in developing nations unable to afford one. As of 2023, the Wheelchair Foundation had given away over 1,175,000 wheelchairs in 157 countries around the globe.

One year, Ken had the experience of delivering a wheelchair to a frail 11-year-old boy in Mexico City who was disabled and blind. The boy wanted to thank him, so Ken bent down and took his hands so the boy would know where he was. Through tears and an interpreter the young boy said, "I can't see you now, but I will see you in heaven, and I will thank you one more time." Kenneth said he was touched so deeply he was unable to answer him. Then he told us, "That was the first time in my life I felt pure joy."★

Make sure you, too, find a way to serve.

For it is in giving that we receive.

ST. FRANCIS OF ASSISI

★Kenneth E. Behring published a memoir called *Road to Purpose: One Man's Journey Bringing Hope to Millions and Finding Purpose Along the Way,* which is a very inspiring book.

PART SIX

Success in the
Digital Age

PRINCIPLE 63

MASTER THE TECHNOLOGY YOU NEED

Technology is supposed to make our lives easier, allowing us to do things more quickly and efficiently. But too often it seems to make things harder, leaving us with fifty-button remote controls, digital cameras with hundreds of mysterious features, and cars with dashboard systems worthy of the space shuttle.

JAMES SUROWIECKI
Business and finance columnist at *The New Yorker* magazine

Since the first edition of *The Success Principles* was written, a digital revolution has created a tidal wave of change that has deeply transformed the world we live in. The driving force of this revolution over the last 20 years has been a 98% reduction in the cost of computing and Internet connections—driven by technology upgrades that get more powerful every year. And this trend is expected to accelerate.

Twenty years from now, computers will be roughly a million times faster, a million times smaller, and a thousand times cheaper than they were when they were first invented. New technologies like 3-D printing, robotics, self-driving cars, nano-materials, artificial intelligence, and computational biology—all considered "exponential technologies" that merge the digital world into the physical world—will enable us to enjoy more abundance by generating more breakthroughs in the next two decades than we have experienced over the last two hundred years.

Thousands of high-flying start-ups will be launched, creating millions of new high-paying jobs. In fact, it is likely that humanity will eventually develop the ability to meet and exceed the basic needs of every man, woman, and child on the planet. Planetary abundance is within our grasp.

When I think about creating abundance, it's not about creating a life of luxury for everybody on this planet; it's about creating a life of possibility.

PETER DIAMANDIS
Author of *Abundance: The Future Is Better than You Think,* chairman of the
X PRIZE Foundation, and chairman of Singularity University

What's so exciting—but also daunting—is that anyone connected to the Internet has access to more information than ever before in history, but this kind of access has also created a problem: There's so much information that Mitch Kapor, the inventor of the Lotus 1-2-3 spreadsheet, said, "Getting information off the Internet is like taking a drink from a fire hydrant."

Because of this acceleration, the rules for success have changed.

In the digital age, the knowledge required to become super-successful—which used to take years to acquire—is not only within everyone's reach, it's immediate and plentiful. In fact, it's almost overwhelming. There are literally millions of websites, videos, and e-learning resources out there to help you succeed.

Because of this overwhelming amount of resources and information, succeeding in the digital age now requires a more diligent approach to time management, information management, and life management. All this new technology is definitely exciting, but if you are not careful, you can drown in it. It's very easy to get lost in hours of mindlessly surfing the Web going from one interesting website, YouTube video, and Facebook post to the next—but if you're not careful, you can end up lost in a rabbit hole of fascinating but irrelevant information. Information is useful, but it is the information you *actually act on* that makes a difference to your success.

THE LOW-INFORMATION DIET

In his breakthrough book *The 4-Hour Workweek** Tim Ferriss addresses the information overload that now exists and advocates going on a low-information diet. Just as with our food—where most of us eat too many calories and calories of no nutritional value—we are consuming too much information, and usually it's of no real value. Most of the information we

---

**The 4-Hour Work Week* (make sure you get the expanded and updated version) by Tim Ferriss (New York: Crown, 2009) is the best book I know on how to take advantage of the technological revolution without being victimized by it. I strongly urge you to read it. It is full of valuable information and more than 100 apps, websites, and online tools that can make your work more efficient and your life much easier.

are exposed to in newspapers, magazines, books, on television and the Internet is too time consuming, usually negative, mostly irrelevant to your goals, and typically outside of your ability to influence or change.

Tim recommends that all your reading, except when reading fiction for pleasure, be reading with a purpose. Just as when I am working on this book, even though I am writing mainly from my own experience, when I do need to check out some information from another author's book, I read only the parts that are immediately relevant to what I am writing about. It's easy to get hooked and start reading things just because they are interesting.

The same is true for surfing the Internet. When looking for a piece of information on the Huffington Post, it was hard not to open up other articles on "3 Gross Things Lurking in Your Ice Cubes," "4 Benefits of Soaking Up Some Sun," and "Wall Street's Secret Weapon: Congress." These are all interesting and tempting topics, but totally off-purpose for finishing the book. It's so easy to get unconsciously trapped into reading random articles and blogs—with each one leading you to other articles that are equally interesting. You have to exercise discipline.

Tim goes on to recommend a one-week media fast—no newspapers, magazines, audio books, or non-music radio. No news websites. No television at all except for one hour of pleasure viewing each evening. No reading of books except for one hour of fiction. And no Web surfing at the desk unless it is necessary to complete a work task for that day. He recommends that if you need to get your news fix, do it at your lunch break by asking a friend or the waiter, "Anything important happening in the world? I couldn't get the paper today."

Finally, he recommends developing the habit of asking yourself the question, "Will I definitely use this information for something immediate and important?" If the answer is no on either count, don't consume it.

I recently went on a one-week media fast, and while I was nervous at first without my daily dose of CNN, the Huffington Post, and a slew of magazines I regularly read—*Bloomberg Business Week, Fast Company, Success, Psychology Today,* and *Science of Mind*—I found I had lots more time to work on my highest priority goals, go for walks with my wife, exercise, meditate, and play my guitar. As a result, I canceled a number of other travel, food, and news magazines that were piling up in my office and my home.

Steve Pavlina, the author of *Personal Development for Smart People,* recommends trying on new behaviors for a minimum of 30 days. What if you didn't watch television for a month? Or didn't watch the news for a month? Or didn't read a newspaper or magazine for a month? Every one of my students who have experimented with this informational detox program has reported amazing breakthroughs in both happiness and productivity. I encourage you to try it.

IT'S A PERFECT TIME TO THRIVE

In addition to bringing us knowledge and connections, the digital age has endowed us with a vast array of technological devices and self-improvement tools that help make us smarter, help us never miss an appointment, let us research and work with coaches, find mentors and partners, and learn new skills. There are over a million apps for your smartphone that teach just about anything you want to learn. And there are dozens of apps that help you develop a success mindset. It's an amazing time to be alive and a perfect time to thrive.

Technology is no longer something to be feared—it's something powerful we can use to get what we want in life. Unfortunately, many people feel technology is too daunting for them or that they're too old to understand it or that it's actually "cool" to be techno-averse. Just like the early nineteenth-century Luddites—English textile workers who protested against newly developed labor-saving machinery—many people today have chosen the path of protest over the path of progress.

In Principle 31: "Embrace Change," I said there are two types of change—*cyclical* and *structural*—and that tackling new things can bring you better circumstances, more money, greater free time, or other benefits you didn't originally expect. The digital age isn't just *cyclical change* that will somehow correct itself. We are living in an age of deep and pervasive *structural change*—the kind where there is no going back (and the kind of change that can sweep you away if you resist it). Embracing it and leveraging it, on the other hand, can accelerate your success.

Of course, the good news is that there's really nothing out there that is over your head. Everything you need to use to create greater success can be learned and mastered. But how do you choose among the vast array of devices, platforms, portals, websites, services, software programs, and other offerings in this magnificent new era? More important, how can we master our use of each tool so that we get all the benefits—and none of the overwhelm?

It's time to put some policies in place and take control of our technology.

TAKE CONTROL OF YOUR TECHNOLOGY

One of the best pieces of advice I've ever gotten from a digital lifestyle expert is that *technology shouldn't drive your success*. In other words, your good ideas should come first, with technology simply supporting the rollout of your good idea. You don't need to have every device available simply because it's available. What you should be asking is, *How can I better manage my email when traveling?* Or *How can I put my artwork online so that gallery owners can commission showings?* Then go find the technology that supports that good idea.

Łukasz Jakóbiak had the idea to launch his own television show and ended up creating one of the most popular shows in Europe—*from his 20-square-meter apartment in Warsaw, Poland*. He couldn't afford the studio rental and expensive equipment that would be required to produce his own show—let alone negotiate the distribution rights with major television networks as a start-up project with no track record.

What he did have was a laptop, an Internet connection, and a small apartment—one of thousands of capsule apartments built by the Polish government as part of an affordable housing initiative.

When Łukasz interviewed me as part of a media tour I was doing in Eastern Europe, I was surprised at the quality of the finished show, appropriately named *20m²*. Yet, initially, I had my doubts when I arrived for the taping and saw Łukasz's living space that contained a bed, a tiny kitchen, lighting equipment, and two iPhones perched on small tripods in front of two kitchen chairs.

For years Łukasz edited the show himself on his laptop and "broadcast" it on the Internet—which was perfect for the millions of viewers who were watching independently produced TV shows on mobile devices instead of watching big network productions sitting in their living room.* Łukasz had found a way to use technology to support his good idea. Eventually he went on to interview Bradley Cooper, Zac Efron, Woody Allen, Brian Tracy, and a host of European stars, musicians, and politicians. As a result of the success of his show, he began being invited to close to a hundred inspirational talks a year, including one where he spoke to nearly 30,000 people along with Nick Vujicic.

---

*You can find Łukasz's show *20m²* on YouTube by typing *20m2 lukasza* in the search field. If you look, you can even watch his interview with me (*20m2 lukasza odcinek 101*), which is in English with Polish subtitles. The rest of his shows are in Polish. Most recently Łukasz had a spiritual awakening that he beautifully portrays in his YouTube video *Autograph of Love*, which has subtitles in English. It is well worth watching.

Take a moment and think about other ways you can take control and use technology to your advantage.

Divide Your Use of Technology Among Different Devices

One of the challenges of the technological revolution is that most devices are now designed to do multiple things. We can check our email, send a text, surf the Internet, call people, and take pictures with our smartphones. We can also attend a class, make videos, watch TV, and read ebooks with our tablets. Our laptops and desktop computers will do even more.

But one thing I've noticed about all this functionality is that, because we *can* perform all sorts of tasks on many different devices, we now tend to multitask randomly, on any device within reach, at all times of the day (and night), almost without thought to prioritizing what we're doing—versus simply focusing on accomplishing specific tasks that are central to our success. The result is that our technology has started to create chaos in our lives rather than simply being a tool. The other drawback to all this "instant" functionality is that it has created the expectation that people will get an instant response from you to all their most pressing issues.

I'd like to propose the radical notion *instead* that you divide your use of technology among your multiple devices—and use them for their intended purpose in a deliberate, focused way. When you are working at your job or business—creating documents, producing spreadsheets, writing your blog, doing projects, initiating emails to people—use your desktop or laptop computer. This "heavylifting" of work-related creation is what it was intended for. When you turn off creation and want to "consume" information—meaning read books, check your social networking sites, surf the Internet, flip through magazines, watch videos—turn on your tablet because *consumption* is what it was intended for. And smartphones? They're for *communicating* with people—calling, texting, using WhatsApp, Instagramming, and sending impromptu photos.

The benefits of this "divide your use" philosophy is not only that it lets you focus on the task at hand, but it also lets you be more present with the people you're interacting with. If you've ever been on the phone with someone while they're Skyping, surfing, and texting—you know how disconnected you feel from them and how disinterested they appear about the matter at hand.

If you think you could never give up your mobile devices—even for a few hours while you sit at your desktop computer focusing on your future—consider how much more productive you could truly be without the distractions of multiple devices ringing, chiming, and popping . . . alerting you to dozens of things that frankly can wait until later.

Use the Bookmarks Toolbar for Your Most Important Web Sites

Even with predictive browser windows that pop-down a list of choices every time you start typing, you would be surprised at the "mental minutes" you spend every week typing the addresses of your favorite websites. Programming these URLs into your browser's bookmarks toolbar is a tremendous timesaver.

For Security, Use a Password Manager and Always Log Out

Similarly, spending time searching for passwords or maintaining an up-to-date printed list or trying to remember (or create) new passwords is one of the most frustrating annoyances of the digital age for most people. And that doesn't begin to approach the time spent finding the login URLs and usernames of accounts you've created all over the Internet.

For time saving—and security—a password manager will remember your websites, bring up the correct login webpage (usually different from the home page), create high-security passwords that are strings of letters and numbers a rocket scientist couldn't remember, and automatically fill in your username and passcode every time you need to log in to an online service, membership site, social media page, or other destination.

Once you're finished at a password-protected website, be sure to prevent identity theft, hacking of your passcodes, and session hijacking (cookie theft) by getting in the habit of always logging out. The time required to clean up problems once your private information has been stolen is enormous, and if you were logged in to a site that has your financial details, watch out. Avoid this major headache by always logging out of online services—don't just close the browser window.

Use Cloud Applications to Mirror Your Devices for Safety and Ease of Reinstatement

While cloud storage—uploading your files to an Internet-based "hard drive" with companies like Dropbox, Google Drive, and Apple's iCloud—was a major paradigm shift for our time, it has become a major timesaver and safety feature for millions of people.

Instead of storing your files on a desktop or laptop computer, cloud storage lets you store your documents, photos, movies, apps, and other files via a service that utilizes the entire Internet infrastructure to find space for them. While it started as a way to store memory-intensive files such as music, photos, and movies, it has now become a total storage solution for companies and individuals alike.

By uploading your work files to the cloud, you can access them anytime from anywhere—as long as you have an Internet connection. Many people are buying laptops with smaller hard drives, and then using the cloud to store the majority of their files. While it does seem scary to put a service provider and potentially unreliable technology in charge of your important data, the cloud has numerous benefits, so long as you develop some rules about what you'll store in the cloud and what—absolutely—must remain private, residing on your own computer at home or the office.

You can either store your files in their entirety on the cloud—using Dropbox, for example, as your main hard drive—or you can store files on your own hard drive, but back up to a cloud-based service for peace of mind. While automatic backup software has been around for years, most people either don't program it or they don't connect it to a storage unit. A colleague of mine once had their office broken into and lost every single workshop handout, marketing campaign, product artwork, manuscript draft, and other files when their seven computers were stolen. But because they had backed up all their files onto *both* a physical storage drive and the cloud, they were able to reinstate their business within a day of purchasing new computers.

Acknowledge That You Have No Privacy with Digital Materials and Information

One of the reasons people were squeamish about cloud storage in the beginning is privacy—plain and simple. Are my files hackable? Will the service provider be able to read my financial statements? Can someone else download or divert my files as I'm uploading them? These were all legitimate questions. But while cloud storage is password-protected and has many safety measures in place, be aware that the digital age comes with one major downside: You can have no expectation of 100% privacy on the Internet. As daily news stories tell us, hackers can copy your passcodes from websites where you've created accounts. Emails can be grabbed and read enroute. Photos can be lifted from your Facebook page and posted elsewhere in the blink of an eye—as can any digital file of any kind.

My advice is to approach your digital lifestyle with the premise that nothing is private, and become very careful about what you post, upload, email, or say in the online world. Of course, 100% privacy is available to those organizations that require it, but it's currently expensive. Be advised and be careful.

One organization of which I have been on the Board of Advisors for is MeWe—a social networking platform like Facebook that has privacy and safety as its underlying premise.* MeWe currently has over 20 million users worldwide and more than 600,000 interest groups, and is committed to giving their users control, protecting their data, and providing a great

---

*You can read more about how MeWe's privacy works—and create a profile page—at mewe.com.

user experience. MeWe contains no ads, no targeting, and no newsfeed manipulation. It is available on iOS, Android, and desktop in more than 20 languages and over 200 countries worldwide. Check it out.

Contain the Sprawl of Monthly Charges

One final way to take control of the technology in your life is to contain the cost of ongoing services you've signed up for. Countless millions of people still pay (via automatic credit card charges) for services long ago forgotten. But a regular review of your credit card statement will give you a list of services you need to cancel or reevaluate—especially if newer, less expensive options are now available.

This is particularly important if you're a business owner and someone else does your accounting. A friend who owns an advertising agency recently saved nearly $1,500 *a month* by canceling services the agency had signed up for years ago. That's nearly $18,000 a year—money that surely could be put to better uses.

Find People to Teach You and Learn Quickly

No one person can know everything about the digital lifestyle, and training courses and technical support services abound for every activity. So don't be worried that you have to master every activity. Choose those activities you need to use in order to pursue your goals, get someone to help you learn them—then master them quickly and move on.

DO A SEVEN-DAY TECHNOLOGY TURNAROUND

Just as I recommend that you make a list of irritations and annoyances (see Principle 28: "Clean Up Your Messes and Your Incompletes" on page 250), you should create a separate list of your technology annoyances. Once you've compiled your list, you can begin to tackle the cleanup process (or hire someone to do it). Completing a technology turnaround could take seven days—*or less*—if you focus on the process.

We've put a comprehensive checklist of seven days' worth of clean-up activities at jackcanfield.com/tsp-resources. Scroll down to Principle 63 and click on the link.

CONSIDER REDUCING TIME ON YOUR CELL PHONE AND YOUR EMAIL

Today, a lot of people have taken a "drastic" approach to regaining control of their life: They've given up their cell phones and their email. The technological revolution was supposed to make our lives easier. But nearly three decades after email became popular and cell phones became affordable for everyone, most of us are inundated with nonessential e-mail (not to mention spam).

Many businesspeople I know spend three to four hours a day just answering email. I used to be one of them. Now my assistant opens my email messages and brings me only the important ones (about five per day) to respond to.

Some can't even go shopping, out to dinner, or on vacation without their cell phones going off—not once but several times. This trend is growing worldwide. I still carry a cell phone, but I only turn it on if I am expecting an important call or if I need to make outgoing calls.

Because they provide instant communication, cell phones and email also create the expectation of an instant response. People who have your cell phone number know they can instantly reach you for help with their immediate needs. Email messages are delivered within minutes—so people expect you to respond equally fast. When you distribute your cell phone number and private email address (especially if you receive emails on your smartphone), you give others implied permission to make these demands upon you. But imagine how much more time and control over your life you would have if you didn't have to react to all of these immediate needs or read dozens of nonessential email messages every day.

Recently, I had lunch with four top people in a major publishing firm. They were all complaining about how overwhelmed they were by the amount of email they were getting—as many as 150 messages a day—and most of them were being generated right inside the company.

When I asked them how much of it was essential to their job, the answer was maybe 10% to 20%. When I asked why they didn't just tell people to take them off of their general distribution list, they said they were afraid of hurting people's feelings. It seemed they would rather suffer than solve the problem. Think about the consequences of not telling the truth and changing things. If they could cut out even half of the unwanted e-mail messages, they would save 90 minutes per workday, freeing up time for more important work and allowing them to go home at a reasonable time. That would add up to 375 hours, or just over nine 40-hour workweeks a year. That's more than two months of valuable time. Isn't that worth a few people being upset for a few days?

SUCCESS IN THE AGE OF AI

In the rapidly evolving landscape of technology, one tool stands out as a game changer for achieving success—artificial intelligence (AI). Just as the internet revolutionized access to information and global connectivity, AI is transforming how we approach tasks, solve problems, and make decisions. Whether you're an entrepreneur looking to streamline your business processes, a student aiming to enhance your learning, or a professional seeking to maximize productivity, AI offers unprecedented opportunities to elevate your success.

AI technology is advancing at an astonishing pace. According to a report by McKinsey, AI has the potential to create an additional $13 trillion in economic activity by 2030, boosting global GDP by about 1.2% annually. This rapid development is not just limited to a few niche areas; AI's applications are expanding into virtually every aspect of our lives. From personalized learning platforms that adapt to individual students' needs to sophisticated business analytics that provide real-time insights, AI is becoming an integral part of our daily operations and decision-making processes.

One of the most compelling aspects of AI is its ability to handle a diverse range of tasks with remarkable efficiency. For example, AI-powered virtual assistants can manage your schedule, send reminders, and even draft emails, freeing up valuable time for more strategic activities. In the medical field, AI is being used to analyze patient data and assist in diagnosing diseases with greater accuracy than ever before. A study by the *Journal of the American Medical Association* found that AI algorithms could diagnose skin cancer with a success rate of 95%, compared to 86.6% by dermatologists. This level of precision and efficiency is being replicated across industries—from finance to customer service—making AI an indispensable tool for success.

Moreover, the integration of AI into our lives is not just a fleeting trend but a profound shift in how we operate. As Sundar Pichai, CEO of Alphabet Inc., remarked, "AI is one of the most important things humanity is working on. It is more profound than, I don't know, electricity or fire." This statement underscores the transformative potential of AI, highlighting its capacity to revolutionize our world in ways we are only beginning to understand.

While the following information on AI and how it can be used mentions various programs and resources available, please note that AI resources are proliferating and evolving at lightning speed. By the time you read this, much may have changed. Make sure to take the time (or work with an AI expert who will) to stay up on the rapidly changing field.

I have asked Mike Koenigs, the AI expert I trust the most, to share some insights on how you can use AI to accelerate your success in your life and business.

USE AI TO ACCELERATE YOUR SUCCESS
BY MIKE KOENIG

You don't have to worry about AI taking your job, but you do need to worry about someone using AI taking your job.

PETER DIAMANDIS
Founder of the XPrize and author of *Abundance* and *Bold*

If you're not already using AI in your life and business, now is the time to start. And if you are, there are ways to accelerate your ability to leverage AI as a powerful tool. This isn't just about adopting new technology; it's about cultivating the right mindsets that will make AI an indispensable asset in your journey toward success.

To begin, let's talk about what I call "AI money mindsets." These mindsets are crucial for understanding how to use AI to boost your productivity and, ultimately, your profitability. For instance, a number of the tools that I use personally have also helped *business owners* increase their revenue by 20% to 100% in just one month. That's a phenomenal amount of extra money for most business owners. But here's the best part: a simple 20% increase in revenue can often *double the profitability* of a business, because you don't need to add more people, equipment or overhead. This kind of 5X or 10X thinking is what I call the Millionaire, Billionaire, and Trillionaire Mindsets.

When I speak to audiences of high-level business owners—such as Tony Robbins's Platinum Partners, members of Dan Sullivan's Strategic Coach program, or Peter Diamandis's Abundance 360 community—I know these individuals are already doing well. But when I show them some of the latest AI tools available, suddenly those revelations are a game-changer. For instance, one of my favorite demonstrations is translating a video into five or six different languages in just minutes. Imagine taking a video, like one from Beachbody's P90X (a client of mine), and using a tool like HeyGen to translate it into Spanish, French, Portuguese, Arabic, and

Chinese—all while keeping the voice characteristics and lip movements perfectly synchronized. The audience is always amazed because it opens up the possibility of doing business with anyone in the world, regardless of language barriers.

This demonstration drives home the point that AI can help you communicate globally—expanding your reach and your impact. Or imagine being able to "speak" to every Spanish, French, Portuguese, Italian, Chinese, Hindi, German, and Japanese person with your podcast or book? How could that expand your business?

But it doesn't stop there. I also share how I use AI tools in my own writing process. For instance, while writing this section for *The Success Principles*, I used what I call an "application stack." Over the years, I've written 19 books, but my last one was completed in record time—just two weeks from start to finish. Here's how I did it: I started by creating an outline, then launched an application called Otter.ai, which does real-time voice transcription and also creates summaries of the content. At the same time, I used another program called TheOasis, which not only records and transcribes but also generates emails, presentation summaries, quotes, and even custom content. Finally, I employed a tool called CastMagic, which can take any content—like podcasts, YouTube videos, or sales calls—and turn it into newsletters, YouTube timestamps, and lead magnets. It's basically an automated marketing assistant.

The best part is, when you combine these various AI tools, you can take verbal ideas and transform them into a complete book chapter or product *simply by talking*.

Once I have the transcript of my spoken words, I can turn that into a complete email marketing sequence or product launch campaign that can produce tens or even hundreds of thousands of dollars in a single weekend. Then, I bring in another application called ChatHub.gg or Poe.com, which allows me to run six different AI programs simultaneously. Each program offers unique insights, and by using all six, I can refine and perfect the output.

ACCESS TO A GENIUS WHO KNOWS EVERYTHING

Imagine having a single genius who knows virtually everything ever captured by humans, for just $20 per month. Who wouldn't want that kind of resource! But that's exactly what OpenAI's ChatGPT service offers. When it's combined with ChatHub—a platform that lets you run multiple AI chat services at one time—you can compare ChatGPT's answers to information you get from Google's Gemini, Anthropic's Claude, Perplexity, Bing, and Groq (the fastest AI platform available). I use these tools to turn any transcript into comprehensive content, such as a book chapter, by combining the best elements from each AI model. This process, which I refer to as "refinement prompting," allows me to create high-quality content quickly and efficiently. It's like having six genius writers working at once. In fact, this is exactly how I wrote this chapter. I spoke it into Otter.ai on my iPhone, then used Claude.ai to rewrite it in a voice that's engaging and tailored to the reader. In less than five minutes, my spoken words were transformed into a first draft, ready for me to reframe in my own style, saving me hours of writing time.

AMPLIFY YOUR CAPABILITIES AND CREATE EVEN MORE VALUE

The future of creating value lies in using AI as a "Capability Amplifier" or a creative muse. Imagine a world where you no longer have to expend mental energy on trivial, mundane tasks. AI is ready and willing to take on the boring work, freeing you to focus on what truly matters—innovation, creativity, and the synthesis of ideas.

Of course, AI in its present form may not excel at generating original content, but it is an exceptional first-draft partner. It can generate derivative content, offering a wealth of options that your human brain can then refine, select, and perfect. This collaboration between human creativity and AI efficiency is where true value is created.

In fact, in a world where information is no longer scarce, the real value comes from what you do with it. Knowledge itself has become more accessible than ever, but the ability to combine that knowledge with human judgment, style, and creativity remains uniquely powerful. Those who can skillfully apply information, synthesize insights, and combine technology with storytelling and marketing will continue to be the highest value producers—whether as artists, engineers, creators, or innovators.

This isn't the first time technology has reshaped the world. Look back to the early days of industrialization. Farmers, who didn't understand the benefits of crop rotation, once scattered seeds haphazardly until 1760 when Jethro Tull invented a seed planter that revolutionized farming, increasing productivity tenfold. Those who embraced this new technology prospered, while those who resisted it were left behind. The same pattern emerged with the invention of spinning wheels and cotton gins. Industrialists who adopted these tools created immense wealth, while those who feared and resisted the technology found themselves out of work. History shows that those who cling to the status quo and resist innovation are often left behind.

The lesson is clear: instead of fearing AI, embrace it as a powerful tool for growth. Poor principles and limited thinking keep people stuck in place, but AI can accelerate learning and help you break free from those limitations. Just as industrialization created millionaires and the internet revolution created billionaires, AI has the potential to create the world's first trillionaires.

We are on the brink of a new era. The names of the first AI-driven trillionaires may not yet be known, but they will emerge from those who understand how to use AI as a force multiplier—a tool that amplifies human capability and creativity to unprecedented levels. The question is, will you be among them?

Businesses that embrace AI are not just adapting to the future— they are actively shaping it. The companies that leverage AI effectively will set the pace and lead their industries.

GINNI ROMETTY
Former CEO of IBM

COULD YOU BECOME THE NEXT AI MILLIONAIRE, BILLIONAIRE, OR EVEN TRILLIONAIRE?

Imagine becoming the next AI millionaire—someone who taps into the incredible potential of artificial intelligence to create unprecedented value. According to recent research, AI is set to make a significant number of people wealthy, as those who embrace it will gain a competitive edge. This isn't just about technology; it's about leveraging AI as a "Capability Amplifier" or creative muse. The mundane tasks? AI handles those. You get to focus on what truly matters—creating, innovating, and scaling your success.

Sam Altman, the CEO of OpenAI, said, "There's a running bet in Silicon Valley right now for by what year there will be the first one-person billion-dollar company." This quote highlights the transformative power of AI and how it's revolutionizing the landscape of wealth creation.

Let's explore the Millionaire, Billionaire, and Trillionaire Mindsets and understand why they are crucial for your success:

The Millionaire Mindset

The Millionaire Mindset is about recognizing that you can use affordable, off-the-shelf tools to increase your efficiency, intelligence, and create simple automations in your business. These tools can make your copywriting and marketing more efficient and effective with just a few copy-paste prompts. My team and I have developed over 30 playbooks that solve practically every problem a business owner might face—whether it's writing courses and content, handling HR, drafting legal agreements, or providing customer service and support. We've transformed these insights into several businesses and products, including a 90-day training program that covers each of these areas. Without AI, we couldn't have created these products as quickly as we did.

One example of applying the Millionaire Mindset is through our Fractional AI Services, which help business owners figure out how to use AI to automate or solve challenges. In just two-hour sessions, we help identify big opportunities or solve significant problems, often delivering between $15,000 to $100,000 in value. For instance, many business owners struggle with customer service, copywriting, or content creation. We use a tool that can import various forms of content—like podcasts, videos, and social media posts—and create a smart AI that speaks in the voice of the brand or founder. This AI, costing just a few hundred dollars a month, can do the work of one to three employees. That's the Millionaire Mindset at work—using accessible tools to create significant value and efficiency in your business.

The Billionaire Mindset

The Billionaire Mindset takes it a step further by creating additional automations and removing key people from day-to-day operations. For example, we worked with one client who was a holistic and peptide doctor with a unique approach to attracting new patients. Instead of the standard 14 to 20 blood markers most doctors evaluate, he offered an extensive blood test that analyzed 94 unique markers—completely free as a way to get new patients. This deep analysis allowed the doctor and his team to create highly customized healthcare plans, including nutritional supplements, peptides, and even stem cell treatments that spanned 6 to 12 months.

However, there was a challenge. Each blood test required about four hours to evaluate, then produce a custom report. To scale his business, the doctor would need to add $60,000 to $70,000 per month in additional team members and dedicate significant time to training them on his unique process. It was a bottleneck that threatened to limit his growth.

Recognizing this, our team is using AI to build a software product that will evaluate the blood tests and generate comprehensive reports in less than five minutes. When asked about his biggest challenge in scaling his business, the doctor identified the time-consuming process of reading blood tests and building reports as the main obstacle. He shared that, if he had a tool like the one we're building, he could triple the number of patients his practice could add without needing to hire more staff. This alone would increase the profitability of his business by tenfold.

So imagine this doctor, who was generating $5 million in revenue, now scaling his business to $15 million without the cost of more overhead. That kind of profitability boost is a perfect example of the Billionaire Mindset in action. It's not just about making a billion in revenue, but about creating a new business model that delivers exponential growth in service capabilities, profitability, and the overall value of the business. A company generating $300 million in revenue could become a billion-dollar company overnight. Or a smaller company could grow steadily to one day be valued at $1 billion on Wall Street.

The Trillionaire Mindset

Taken a step further, AI could also generate the kind of ancillary income streams that could eventually combine to become one of the leading companies in the world—a perspective I call the Trillionaire Mindset.

For instance, what if this holistic doctor took the software product that enabled him to triple his own patient load (thereby increasing his profitability by 10 times) and packaged it as a solution for other holistic doctors? If the software was capable of adding $2 million to $5 million per year in revenue to other practices, charging $10,000 or more per month for it would be completely reasonable. And if just 100 doctors' offices subscribed to the software, it would generate a million dollars a month in recurring revenue for our client: that's $12 million annually just by sharing the software with other holistic doctors! In the venture-capital world, a business like this—with that kind of high profit margin—could easily be valued at 10 to 20 times its revenue, resulting in a business worth $120 to $240 million for our client.

And how might a *trillion-dollar company* be created? By also selling the software to *other* kinds of doctors, medical facilities, labs and hospital systems . . . by marketing the software to subscribing practices and networks around the world . . . by identifying patterns and trends in patient data, leading to new medical discoveries or the development of new treatment protocols, which could be patented and sold . . . by developing complementary products, such as patient-facing apps, wearables, or personalized supplement lines, thereby creating an entire ecosystem of services and products that work together, driving up customer retention and lifetime value . . . or even by diversifying into non-medical uses, all of which could combine to create a trillion-dollar valuation in the investment sector for the doctor's now-behemoth software and services company.

In the final outcome, the intellectual property and software could ultimately be worth more than the original medical practice itself. That's The Trillionaire Mindset at work—turning innovation into a scalable, high-value enterprise.

Are you ready to adopt the mindset of the future: using AI to amplify your capabilities, handle the mundane tasks, and allow you to focus on innovation and growth? By adopting these mindsets, you can position yourself to be at the forefront of this new era of wealth creation.

EMBRACE CHANGE AND START EXPERIMENTING

We've said that creating a future filled with immense value starts with a shift in mindset. By asking yourself the right questions, you can unlock opportunities that may have seemed out of reach before:

- What are the recurring challenges in your industry?
- How can AI and automation be the key to solving these problems, boosting productivity and profitability?
- Can you build a solution that not only benefits your business but can also be packaged and sold as a subscription service to others in your industry?
- What impact would that have on your business and its potential valuation?

These questions are the gateway to transforming how you think and operate in this AI-driven world. I challenge you to take the first steps by exploring these ideas and implementing them in your business. If you need guidance, there are resources available to help you on this journey. My book, *AI Accelerator for Entrepreneurs,* offers a deeper dive into these concepts. You can find it at DigitalCafe.ai/jc. Additionally, you can access recordings, webinars, and a list of the latest tools I'm using at MikeKoenigs.com/FreeAI.

Remember, the key is to start experimenting with AI tools today. Don't worry about making mistakes—AI is here to help, not hinder. It's like having a tireless partner who's always ready to work, never complains, and can turn your ideas into reality. The future belongs to those who embrace an abundant, creative mindset and can leverage AI to make their dreams come true while helping others along the way.

PRINCIPLE

64

BRAND YOURSELF WITH AN ONLINE PERSONA*

Personal branding online is not about you; it's about your content. How do you become someone worth talking to, or even better, worth talking about?

MATTHEW CAPALA
Author of *Away with the Average,* adjunct professor at New York University, and founder of SearchDecoder.com

Every day, millions of Internet users go online with little to no thought of the portrait they paint about themselves in the digital world. They make inflammatory comments on controversial blogs. They tweet meaningless messages about their personal life. They post questionable photos on their Facebook page. They upload videos of their hobbies, parties, vacations, and friends alongside professional clips at YouTube—never considering what this haphazard collection of information portrays about them. While much of this content can be removed, much more stays on the Internet as permanent, public content that can be searched instantly by a potential employer, investor, bank loan officer—even a first date.

Successful people, on the other hand, carefully manage their online persona. They post only information that will contribute positively to the image they present to the world. Even when they are voicing their opinions and bringing their personality to the Internet, they think about the impact it will have. They have mastered the art of appearing competent, authori-

---

*This chapter is a result of a major collaboration between my coauthor Janet Switzer, Moses Ma, and myself. Moses is my go-to guy for what is innovative in the world of technology—especially as it relates to breakthrough success, personal growth, and accelerated business development. He is the managing partner of FutureLab Consulting—a venture accelerator and strategic consulting company located in San Francisco, California.

tative, respected—someone worth listening to—wherever they are found online.

What does your online presence say about you?

Just as major consumer brands carefully craft what is said about their products and services, you too can turn yourself into a "brand" that is carefully developed, managed, and maintained online. Even if your current "life project" is just to clean up a local park, get a big promotion at work, win the regional track meet, become president of your local garden club, or something else that's not business related, you can still develop an online presence that inspires others to want to help you, gets people excited about participating in your goals, and advances your cause, whatever it may be. This principle is not just for businesspeople anymore. In fact, with the powerful impact of social media, *personal branding* as a success tool has grown rapidly and is now within reach of everyone.

PERSONAL BRANDING ISN'T JUST FOR CELEBRITIES

While many people think that personal branding is just for celebrities, the reality is that Facebook, LinkedIn, Pinterest, Google+, Tumblr, Instagram, and YouTube make it possible for each and every one of us to become a brand. And as a brand, we can leverage the same strategies used by these celebrities or corporate brands to appeal to others. We can build brand equity just like them. Of course, once you begin to define your personal brand, you'll see important benefits. For one thing, personal branding requires you to be crystal clear on what you want to achieve and helps you set goals to get there. It helps you create visibility and presence, which attracts people who can help you achieve your goals (and achieve them more quickly). But it also empowers you. It puts you in control of the business of you. And having a strong personal brand makes you resilient to what's going on in the world. Strong corporate brands, for example, are successful despite challenges and downturns in the economy because they stand for something unique. The same thing goes for you . . . if you choose to differentiate yourself with a brand!

Fortune 500 companies know that over 80% of their market value resides in their "intangible assets"—including their brand and other intellectual capital. This same statistic holds true for personal branding. Your "market value" is 80% based on the brilliance of your thoughts and the strength of your personal brand image in the world. As such, wealth can flow from your valuable personal brand.

So what are the steps to creating your own personal brand online?

STEP ONE: DECIDE WHO YOU WANT TO BE

If you're a career professional hoping to move up the ladder or even become a CEO or C-level executive one day, you should know that many of the top candidates you'll be competing against are already online with content that depicts them as competent, forward-thinking, and in-demand—in other words, a good investment for some smart company. Many corporate executives are even writing books, joining the speaking circuit, securing media interviews, participating in industry events—even hiring publicists and marketing agencies. They know that, in a competitive hiring situation, the job candidate who has off-the-charts presence in their field will be seen as bringing more to the company once they are hired.

If you're a small-business owner or consultant, being online with the right message is even more important since there are dozens (if not hundreds) of other companies your potential customer can spend money with—and these competitors are already online with professional websites, authoritative articles, smart marketing, and social media profiles that tell prospects they're a safe bet to spend money with.

Even non-profits are in competition with other causes for donor dollars, so online branding is important. And if you're an emerging musician, dancer, athlete, or young author, who knows what exciting dimension an online presence could add to your future?

To develop an online persona or "brand" that will advance your career, business or cause, start distributing content that positions you as someone who can benefit a potential employer, customer, investor, or donor, or inspire a future mentor, coach, or sponsor.

Determine the Market You Want to Reach

If you created a network of 100,000 people—all of whom could help your career or connect you with new opportunities—who would you want those 100,000 people to be? Alternatively, what categories of people will benefit the most from your knowledge, expertise, or opinions? Do they work in your industry, have an interest in your field of study, or are they random consumers who have the same hobby, decorating ideas, fashion sense, or entertainment preferences that you do?

You don't have to hold a Ph.D. or be a recognized media personality to have a following or build your expert persona online. Even if you're a college student, stay-at-home mom or corporate employee with big plans for your future, you can still bring useful information and insights to others who find value or enjoyment in following your "work."

Since you'll eventually be nurturing this following with ongoing advice and updates, be sure you're targeting the market you are most passionate about and which will provide the greatest benefit for your future. This process of choosing your market is even more critical if you own a business or consulting practice.

As part of the process of determining the market you want to reach, be sure to take a moment and Google yourself. Is this what you want people to see? Next, Google your top "competitor" by name. What do the search results tell you?

Start a Blog and Build a Website

Blogging is probably the best way to hone your brand online. Writing your thoughts, sharing your experiences, and helping people when they bring up a question or comment about a blog post will help you build confidence in your personal brand—but also build awareness of you and your brand on the Internet. For one thing, Google loves blogs and, once you are listed on Google, they will immediately index (make appear in its search engine) any article you post—this happens within minutes. Not only that, but you can begin to earn credibility and trust among your followers. Starting a blog is so easy that you can get going with just a few clicks.

One of the easiest blog platforms to start with is WordPress. You can choose a colorful theme, add an About page for your biography, easily upload pictures from royalty-free photography sources around the Internet, and manage blog commenting privileges. WordPress is so easy to use—and has developed so many plug-ins (or add-on features)—that people now use it to build entire websites. While it's not just for blogs anymore, it still remains the easiest blog platform to use. Not only that, it's been around long enough so that there are countless WordPress freelancers who can help you start up. To find one of these, post your blog project on Upwork, or, for super low-cost help, try Fiverr—a website that represents freelancers all over the world who will do small jobs for just $5.

As part of the process of setting up your blog, consider creating a buzzword, phrase, or actual trade name that can be tied to your real name. For example, searching the trade name "Success Principles" will show my name connected to that phrase on thousands of webpages across the Internet. My marketing team, headed by Lisa Williams, has worked very hard to create this outcome over the years. We now effectively "own" this phrase. Before "Success Principles," my buzzword phrase or trade name was *Chicken Soup for the Soul*®.

Of course, once you start your blog, it's time to think about how a website might benefit you. A website can feature pages in addition to your blog that describe products or services you have for sale, detail how to hire you for consulting work, provide forms where people can opt in for a free guide or other samples of your work (so you have their email address for future marketing), and generally represent you to the public as an authority in your field. If you're an artist or photographer, you can feature a gallery of your artwork. If you own a restaurant, you can feature coupons for new customers. If you're a corporate executive, you can feature information on your speaking availability and topics. And if you own a business, your website can generate actual sales for you 24 hours a day—all over the world, if you choose.

Create Key Social Media Profiles

With your blog and website in place, you now have a destination for your social media followers—a place to send people where they can find out how to work with you (or buy from you). Your blog shares your knowledge and perspectives on your profession or industry, and your website offers solutions.

Social media is where you connect, share links, and network. It isn't where you overtly sell. Once you send prospects from social media to your blog—through sharing a hook and a link to your latest blog articles—each article should close with a link to that part of your website that offers ways to work with you or buy something from you.

These days, if you claim to be an authority on any subject and you aren't featured on at least Facebook and LinkedIn, you're not considered a "real" expert. Knowing that, it's simple to start or upgrade your Facebook page to begin positioning yourself as a go-to source for information, help, and advice related to your personal brand. You can post short videos about useful topics. You can write short advice pieces on a single subject. You can survey your followers, run contests, let them in on your latest project—and even advertise to get more people into your "network."

LinkedIn is an even more important social networking site if you are a career professional or business owner. Now with more than 774 million members worldwide (up from just 8.5 million in 2007), it's literally the world's largest professional network—so not only does it provide opportunities to connect with people who can help your business, it's the ideal recruitment platform for new clients and customers.

Depending on your personal branding and the advice or information you'll be distributing, other social networking sites you may want to use are Google+, Pinterest, YouTube—plus the many thousands of sites dedicated to specific themes or subject matter.

Post Regularly

Of course, once you launch your social networking profiles, you'll want to post regularly. Nothing looks worse than having large gaps in your posts. It makes you look inattentive and unprofessional—even though you may have nothing important to say for weeks or months. Some experts recommend that if you're not able to maintain your social media pages that you disable them for a time until you can return to them.

Building a brand takes diligence and effort—so stay active and connected. After all, connecting is what social media is for.

Limit Unrelated Personal Content that Could Detract from Your "Brand"

Finally, consider limiting your personal and non-career material that shows up online—or at least limit it to social media pages that are private for your family and friends only. Unless your lifestyle, family activities, romantic relationships, parties, vacations, and other aspects of your personal life are part of your brand, keep these matters private via social media groups that allow you to restrict who sees what you share. Throwing your private life open to the world by posting personal photographs, opinions, tweets, and details about your downtime activities will detract from your brand—and gives your followers permission to judge you and maybe even a reason to question your expertise. Be real, be personable online—but keep most of your private life private.

STEP TWO: MAKE SURE YOUR ONLINE CONTENT ADVANCES YOUR "BRAND"

Incredible but true, more than a billion names are searched on Google every day[*]—almost the entire population of the United States and Europe combined. Even more important, the *Washington Post* reports that 75% of human-resources professionals are required to research job applicants online—with a whopping 70% having rejected job candidates in the past following such searches. What was their biggest factor in deciding not to hire someone? Provocative photographs posted by the job candidate on their own social networking page *or even on the pages of their friends*. The trend has become such a career-killer for young professionals that one university actually purchased reputation management services for every graduating senior—where online experts search out and delete questionable content.

---

[*] A Pennsylvania State University study found that, of the approximate 6 billion Google searches performed per day, about 30% of them—or 1.8 billion searches—were for someone's name.

Today, what you say and do online has the power to affect your professional future. So what can you do to transmit your online persona in a way that advances your brand and builds rapport with your market—just as successful people do?

Live Your Brand

Moses Ma, coauthor of *Agile Innovation: A Revolutionary Approach to Accelerate Success, Overcome Risk, and Engage Everyone,* recommends that you live your brand—meaning to actually be, think, breathe, and eventually manifest the ideals that you seek.

Most people simply come up with a few words to slap on their social network profile. To be truly successful, you need to manage your thoughts, be conscious in how you act, and be aware of how you are received by your friends, partners, clients, prospects, vendors, colleagues . . . everyone on the Web. If you're branding yourself as someone who is good at something, try to be helpful, informative, insightful—not only for the clients who are paying, but for everyone. Share some of your "secret sauce" wherever you post, comment, or upload. If you're innovative, demonstrate that. If you're a great coach, don't just include testimonials; offer some coaching through your blog.

Unleash Your Participation

The Internet provides an amazing opportunity to engage with others. Don't just sign up and lurk around. Get involved in conversations, be genuinely interested in what people do, and help others if you have a fact, contact name, idea, or something else that would be valuable. Contribute to the community, and give before you take. You not only should follow and comment on others' blog posts to give them encouragement, but also make an effort to participate on social media, too—following people and posting tidbits of information. Get good enough at it so you know what a hashtag and HootSuite are. Let your handle, avatar, and wallpaper express your personal brand.★

Cultivate Your Online Presence

Nothing is worse than dealing with someone who talks only about themselves at a party or who glazes over when you're responding. The Internet is no different. To be "present" online means to be more interested in other

---

★An *avatar* is the screen name, picture, or graphic you've chosen that represents you (or your alter ego) when posting online, commenting on blogs, gaming, or participating in virtual worlds.

people than you are in advancing your own message—who they are, what makes them tick, what makes them happy, and what excites them. Even on a chat board, you should be fully present when you read what others are saying. Once you feel empathy, you will want to help them get what they want, and that is the way to build the helpful, insightful, wise, and "value" aspect of your personal brand.

Command Positivity

There are a lot of negative, critical, sarcastic, and cynical people online. Don't be one of them. Your positive energy and attitude is like a ship carrying you across a sea of online activity and helping you navigate your online journey. Don't just float aimlessly like a life raft—be the captain of your ship, steering it toward your goals with purpose and positivity.

Positivity starts with being friendly, loving, and caring. Make an effort to be polite to everyone you meet or are seen by online, and it will put your offline reputation in a good light, too. So don't just be nice to prospects; be nice to *everyone*. Make an effort to appreciate something about every person you interact with online. Make an effort to uplift them in some small way.

I'm reminded of the week I spent in Bermuda for a meeting of the Transformational Leadership Council. As several of us were boarding a local bus for dinner on the other side of the island, a young man who worked in the kitchen of our hotel boarded at the last minute and—with no other seats available—took a seat next to Reverend Michael Beckwith, one of the teachers featured in *The Secret,* a star of his own upcoming movie, and largely heralded as one of America's most popular spiritual thinkers. While Michael *could* have sat in silence next to the hotel worker, he instead struck up a spirited conversation with the young man—exhibiting the same enthusiastic interest and friendliness to him that he had exhibited with the other high-level "important" participants at the TLC meeting.

I believe that I should treat people like I want to be treated.
That means any online effort requires serious, relentless
mutual commitment to the people involved with that effort.

CRAIG NEWMARK
Founder of Craigslist

Craigslist founder Craig Newmark explains this kind of online "presence" as a permanent listening/action cycle. You ask for community feedback, you do something about it, and you repeat . . . forever. This was Craig's formula for building a community website to "connect the world for the common good" that surpassed eBay in traffic in 2010 with over 50 billion page views per month. Your personal brand and this energy of positivity—or lack of it—radiates around you much like an energy field, so be sure that you have genuinely positive energy at your core before you go online. That means that even on your worst days, even after life-draining meetings, and even with a lifetime of potential baggage . . . allow your core to shine. Speak with impeccability, use empowering words when you post, always respect other viewpoints in a controversy, assume that other people have the best intentions (even if they don't), and be a person of integrity—both online and off.

Radiate the Energy of Success

Inspire people by sharing your success stories. Share inspiring quotes, articles, or books you've read. Help others by revealing your way to success. Don't keep everything for yourself. Not only do people learn through stories; sharing in this way humanizes you and helps them see what's possible for their lives.

Share Your "Why"

According to Simon Sinek, the *New York Times* bestselling author of *Start with Why,* "People don't buy WHAT you do; they buy WHY you do it."

Why did you decide to start sharing information as an expert in your area? Why do you approach your work in the way that you do? What keeps you excited every day in your career path or field of study? Your "why" should be the single most powerful, clear, positive idea that comes to mind whenever anyone thinks of you. It's what you stand for—the values, capabilities, and attitude that people associate with you whenever they see you on the Web or whenever others refer to you.

By defining your personal why first, you'll have interested and open-minded listeners when you describe what you are doing, how you are doing it, why others should be interested—and what you have to offer.

Forge Deeper Relationships

While the Internet can be a very transient, anonymous place—with people dropping in for a few minutes but never staying long enough to get connected—you, on the other hand, have the ability to forge long-lasting relationships, simply by approaching your online time with deeper relationships as your goal. The Web now gives you the chance to build a powerful support team, connect with potential mentors, create a mastermind group—or simply develop supportive friendships in chat rooms, forums, and membership sites with people who are on the same path as you. Once you've established a connection, feel free to ask for what you want and need.

But similarly, be someone who is approachable for help by others. Give before asking. Follow the conversation and offer help in context with the discussions and communities where you find yourself.

In his book *Jab, Jab, Jab, Right Hook,* author and social media expert Gary Vaynerchuk explains that, for years, marketers crafted two different approaches to selling online: (1) high-impact campaigns designed to knock sales out of the park (the "right hook"), and (2) patiently nurturing relationships with customers over time (the "jab"). Now because of social media, he says, the winning combination of jabs and right hooks has changed—requiring online marketers to create content that is specific to the communities and conversations within individual social media platforms. The only way to appear engaged on all these different platforms is to . . . be engaged! Get out there and forge strong and meaningful relationships with those who need your help and are more likely to speak up on your behalf and tell others about you. It doesn't matter how many friends you have on Facebook or how many people follow you on Instagram. What matters is how strong and resilient those relationships turn out to be.

Upload Photos and Videos

People online relate best to other people—not words or images. So get out of your shell and start taking more photos and filming more short videos of your work, your interests, your advice, and your customer interactions.

As humans, our brain function is naturally drawn to faces, motion, and sound. Susan Weinschenk, Ph.D. (who consults to companies like Walmart, Amazon, Best Buy, and Disney) uses brain science to predict, understand, and explain what motivates people and how they behave.* She says there are four reasons why online video is compelling and persuasive:

1. The *fusiform face area* of the brain forces us to pay attention to faces—so we connect more readily with what's being said. Additionally, this part of the brain also processes emotions, so viewers often achieve an emotional connection with both the message and the person delivering it.
2. The human voice conveys rich information. In fact, just the tone of voice you use to deliver your message will impact what

---

*http://www.blog.theteamw.com/2013/01/22/4-reasons-why-online-video-is-compelling-persuasive

viewers hear. So be careful to convey enthusiasm, authority, even excitement—depending on the response you want from viewers.
3. Emotions are contagious. Due to the human-to-human interaction that video provides, video helps you communicate excitement and passion for a topic in a way that the written word simply can't convey.
4. Movement grabs attention. Over the course of human evolution, our brain has become programmed to pay attention to movement in our peripheral line of vision. That means we listen to any message when movement is attached to it.

And finally, Susan advises: Video testimonials are social validation on steroids. They combine social proof, brain syncing, and emotional content . . . you just can't beat this for converting someone to your line of thinking.

One of my top students, Mykola Latansky, who is originally from Kyiv, Ukraine, and currently lives in Edinburgh, Scotland, is the number-one Russian speaker teaching the success principles. He posts to his video blog (or vlog) every day. Before he started doing this he was attracting 50 or 60 people to his trainings. Now, because of the engaging nature of the vlogs and how viral they have become, he attracts 600 or more participants and has grown his business to an over a million-dollar-a-year enterprise.

STEP THREE: MONITOR YOUR ONLINE PERSONA AND CLEAN UP ANY NEGATIVE INFORMATION

One of the hottest trends, especially for entrepreneurs and small businesses, is "reputation management"—the monitoring, correcting, and enhancing of online information about you and your business. And whether this information takes the form of reviews on consumer sites . . . photographs of you in dubious situations . . . posts or videos you have uploaded . . . third-party blogs featuring you or your business name . . . or even someone infringing on your trademarked product name, online content about you and your business can be inspiring, informative, or downright embarrassing.

Not surprisingly, a whole new crop of service providers has emerged to help you manage your online reputation—whether you own a business, are graduating from college and launching your career, or recently decided to take up a worthy cause. Even personal relationships that have ended or former business relationships that turned sour can be managed or minimized online through reputation management.

But before you hire a professional service, there are things you can do on your own. We've put an entire tutorial and checklist online to help you through the process, including a list of reputation management companies that can eventually take over the process from you when the time comes. Visit jackcanfield.com/tsp-resources. Scroll down to Principle 64 and click on the link.

SUPPRESS YOUR PAST IF YOU CAN, ALONG WITH MALICIOUS CONTENT ABOUT YOU

Of course, if there's something terrible in your past that you cannot have removed (and you're now a person of integrity and impeccability who truly wants to make a new start)—or if you've been a victim of online harassment or hazing—you should take advantage of "right to be forgotten" privileges that let you petition to have "inadequate, irrelevant or excessive" information about yourself hidden on Google. Nearly 12,000 people completed petitions the first day they were available—after the European Union's Court of Justice decision compelled Google to make the service available. Google quietly rolled out this option in the United States in 2022, and many social media platforms now have mechanisms in place to remove malicious content.*

BRAND YOURSELF WITH A TED TALK

Perhaps the penultimate experience for personal branding is to give a TED talk or a TEDx talk. Since its start in 2009, TEDx events have been held in 167 countries at an average rate of eight per day. If you haven't yet discovered TED Talks, go to TED.com, click on the "most viewed" tab, and watch a few to get started and later on click the "explore the whole library" tab.

I do my best to watch one TED talk a day. All the talks are by people who are geniuses and leaders in their field who have presented talks at the TED Conferences over the past years. Here are some of my favorite top-rated TED Talks. You can find them all on YouTube.

- Sir Ken Robinson: Do Schools Kill Creativity?
- Tony Robbins: Why We Do What We Do
- Dan Pink: The Puzzle of Motivation

---

* https://www.oif.ala.org/google-quietly-rolls-out-the-right-to-be-forgotten-mechanism-in-the-us

- Brené Brown: The Power of Vulnerability
- Jill Bolte Taylor: My Stroke of Insight
- Simon Sinek: How Great Leaders Inspire Action
- Dan Gilbert: The Surprising Science of Happiness
- Angela Lee Duckworth: The Key to Success? Grit.

VISUALIZE YOURSELF GIVING A TEDX TALK

TED CEO and curator Chris Anderson shares what it takes to create a truly compelling TED talk:

> When we first experimented with giving away TED talks on the Web, our main concern was that no one would watch. Why would you sit through an 18-minute lecture when there's a whole world of hilarious cat videos to be explored? To our astonishment, the talks started to go viral, and it happened because our speakers were tapping into something amazing and primal: In certain circumstances an idea resident in a human mind can resonate with the same insight and excitement felt by the originator.
>
> For this little miracle to happen, it needs all the help it can get. The ignition of curiosity. Clarity. Humor. The stripping out of needless jargon. And yes, in some cases, an emotional connection to the speaker is a valuable ingredient. You learn more from people you care about. We appear to have found an approach that appeals, in our 18-minute format.
>
> But can you share something worthwhile in 18 minutes? Definitively, unequivocally yes. The Gettysburg address made history in a ninth of that time. Martin Luther King's "I have a dream" speech? Sixteen minutes.
>
> Our instructions to speakers include: Substance matters more than performance; personal connection may be good, emotional manipulation is not; and there is no formula. Give the talk in your own way.

And that's a perfect recipe to maintaining your personal brand: When you share, blog, or comment . . . always remember that substance matters, that personal connection matters, that you must be true to yourself in every way.

Here's a powerful visualization: See yourself giving a TED talk someday—or something similar to it because that's where we're heading, so do whatever it takes to give that speech. This might mean figuring out what you want to say. It might mean getting some training in public speaking and developing onstage presence. It might mean putting yourself out there, getting rejected, getting feedback, getting better, and finally getting it right.*

When you have something truly worth sharing with the entire world—something that you are absolutely passionate about—it'll be given a chance to happen.

THE SECRET SAUCE OF DIGITAL SUCCESS IS PASSION

In closing, the secret sauce for branding yourself successfully in the digital age is passion. It's all about finding your own voice, finding your own way, finding a kind of creativity that you can call your own. It means allowing your intuition and inner brilliance to lead you—like an unseen hand—to your own path, in defiance of accepted norms or current trends. Passion is something within you that provides the continual enthusiasm, focus, and energy you need to succeed. But unlike feel-good motivation derived from external sources, true passion has a more spiritual nature. It comes from within. And it can be channeled into amazing feats of success.

You can absolutely succeed and thrive in the digital age.

Don't tell yourself you're too old or too techno-challenged. Get outside your comfort zone and gain confidence with all things digital. The only barrier today is your own belief.

Jimmy Wales, the founder of Wikipedia, once said, "Imagine a world in which every single person on the planet is given free access to the sum of all human knowledge." That world is today. The sum of all human knowledge is there for you—like an ocean of information and data. It's up to you whether you want to stand on the beach or learn how to swim.

---

*There are now three really good books on how to give a TED Talk. Even if you never give a TED Talk, and you just want to become a better speaker, these books are invaluable: *Talk Like TED: The 9 Public-Speaking Secrets of the World's Top Minds* by Carmine Gallo (New York: St. Martin's Press, 2014), *How to Deliver a TED Talk* by Jeremy Donovan (New York: McGraw-Hill Education, 2014), and *How to Deliver a Great TED Talk* by Akash Karia (self-published, 2012).

PRINCIPLE

65

USE SOCIAL MEDIA IN A WAY THAT ENHANCES YOUR REPUTATION

The Internet has been the most fundamental change during my lifetime and for hundreds of years. It's the biggest thing since the invention of writing.

RUPERT MURDOCH
Former chairman and CEO of News Corp and 21st Century Fox

Over the years, a lot of businesspeople, sales professionals, and consultants have questioned whether social media really works to create more customers. It's consumer-oriented. It's mass-market. And while some people say it's the only thing they use to market their business, others say it's a lot of time spent for not much return.

Frankly, the reality has probably been somewhere in between.

Today, however, social media has finally hit the tipping point where—instead of seeing a lot of interest but not many takers—we're now seeing millions of followers convert into "buyers" (whatever that term may mean for you). If you're using social media and the Internet to advance your expertise and enhance your personal brand, this has great relevance for you—whether you own an actual business, are involved in a charitable cause, have an idea for a new social movement, or are working to build your career. Not only that, but social media has matured now to offer new ways to connect—so it's easier than ever to reach out to the right kinds of prospects.

HOW TO GET FOLLOWERS TO STAY ENGAGED WITH YOU

What's the most powerful aspect of social networking for advancing your personal brand? Attracting followers who will stay engaged with you and your message—then pass on your information to friends, colleagues, and their own fans. To reach that goal, you'll want to maintain an ongoing presence on the most popular social media sites. And, today, the biggest site out there is Facebook—with 3 billion users around the world.

Of course, we've already recommended that you maintain a *private* Facebook page for sharing personal information and photographs with close friends and family. But you can also create a Facebook page for your business, career, or cause—or create a Facebook group to discuss your work or cause with a unique cadre of followers with whom you identify.

Once you do that, you can use a number of strategies recommended by Facebook to increase your visibility, engage better with your fans, and improve your chances of being shown in Facebook's News Feed—a continuously updated list of stories from people and Pages that an individual Facebook user follows on Facebook. Not only can an individual user adjust their settings of which types of posts they want to receive on their news feed, but Facebook uses its own formula to determine which posts get used. Popularity of posts is one factor in the algorithm.

So be interesting, be engaging, be helpful, and create each post in a way that people will want to hear more. This requires more than just product announcements. What does Facebook recommend to better engage your fans?

1. Use "rich media" in combination with written words. Rich media such as photos and videos are known to get more attention and help your message stand out. Posts of about 100 to 250 words are recommended, as are lifestyle-type images. Try sharing photos of people living your recommendations or using your product.
2. Increase engagement with your Facebook posts by creating a two-way conversation between you and your followers. Post a quote, a video, or an idea and ask followers to share their thoughts, feedback or their own stories about what they've seen. On my Facebook Fan Page, a short article will generate 10 to 20 comments in response, while a cool quote I've found or short video from me will inspire over 1,600 comments. Big difference. Also, posting information that shows you listened to the feedback helps create further engagement with your followers and builds loyalty.
3. If you own a business, share discounts and promotions that are exclusive to Facebook followers. Always include a clear call-to-action with the exact steps to take to redeem the voucher or coupon or discount code—plus always tell when the promotion will end in order to create a sense of urgency. You can drive readers directly to a page on your website to improve online sales.

4. Provide access to exclusive information. Janet Switzer uses this to launch her clients on Facebook or provide a boost where they need to get more followers. She broadcasts an email to the client's list (and lists owned by helpful colleagues or endorsers) offering a special report or other item of interest—then asks them to "Like Us on Facebook" in order to get the report. Similarly, you can make people who are already followers feel special by sharing exclusive product news, contests, and events. This boosts loyalty with people who are already followers, but also drives online sales. You can do individual giveaways—or a 10-day series of giveaways.
5. Tie your Facebook posts to current events or other things that are trending and top-of-mind—including news stories, holidays, and consumer trends. Reply in a timely way to comments on your page. The faster you reply, the more likely fans will engage with you in the future.
6. Plan a calendar of Facebook activity—even if it's just a calendar of those ideas you want to talk about each week or each month. This will help you stay on track with posting on a regular basis, but also ensure that your content is well planned, interesting, and that you don't miss using Facebook for major business events and news. How frequently should you post? That's really determined by trial and error—find a frequency that works for you and your followers.
7. Once you find a frequency that works, write your posts in batches ahead of time and schedule them to be posted at specific times by clicking on the clock icon of your Page's sharing tool. You can also schedule your posts to appear when most of your fans are online. To find out when this is, visit your Page Insights and go to the posts tab. Scheduling posts is a great time manager.
8. Target posts to specific demographics within your fan base. If some posts are meant for specific groups of people, you can manage these posts in your Page's sharing tool by clicking on the target icon at the bottom-left corner and selecting Add Targeting. Facebook compiles information like gender, relationship status, educational status, interests, age, location, and language from your followers and will carve out a specific group for you using those details.
9. Create posts in such a way that they drive readers to your website. For me, this is the ultimate value of Facebook, because—as sometimes happens—Facebook can limit the connection between you and your fans at any time. But once these followers

have migrated over to your website to opt-in to your email list, you control the communication with those names. And don't be nervous about reports that no one is using email any longer—or that people are solely using Facebook for email. That may be true for younger populations, but it's not true for business-oriented, older demographics. To create links from Facebook to your website, go to your Page's sharing tool, enter the website address or URL where you want to send people, then hit Enter.

10. Check the performance of individual posts to see where you can improve. You can see what's working by going to the Page Insights area. This also will help you better understand your followers and create Facebook content that continually engages them.

SHE MASTERED THE POWER OF SOCIAL MEDIA AND BECAME A GLOBAL PHENOMENON

In the early years of her career, long before Taylor Swift became a global pop sensation, she was just a young girl with a dream and a guitar. The world had yet to witness the powerhouse that she would become, and social media was still in its infancy. However, Swift recognized the potential of these platforms as powerful tools to connect with fans, even when she was far from becoming a household name.

Back in the mid-2000s, Taylor Swift was a budding country artist trying to make her mark in a highly competitive industry. Armed with her raw talent and an unwavering determination, Swift turned to social media to create a personal brand that would set her apart. She began by sharing snippets of her life, thoughts, and of course, her music on platforms like MySpace and, later, the emerging giant Facebook.

Swift's approach was authentic and relatable. She engaged with her small but growing fan base by responding to comments, sharing behind-the-scenes glimpses of her journey, and even occasionally dropping personal anecdotes. This genuine connection resonated with her audience, and her followers felt like they were a part of her story, not just spectators.

As her career started to gain momentum, Swift's social media strategy evolved. With the release of her breakthrough album, *Fearless*, she leveraged platforms like Twitter and Instagram to connect on a deeper level with fans. She began sharing more polished content, showcasing not only her musical talents but also her evolving style and personality. The shift was subtle yet significant, as Swift navigated the fine line between staying relatable and embracing the glamor associated with the music industry.

The turning point came when she transitioned from country to pop music with the release of the album *1989*. This move could have alienated some of her original fan base, but Swift's adept use of social media ensured a smooth transition. She utilized platforms strategically, teasing snippets of the new sound, engaging in conversations with fans about the change, and even playfully addressing rumors and speculations.

As Taylor Swift ascended to global stardom, her social media habits underwent another transformation. With millions of followers, she had to balance maintaining her personal connection with fans while navigating the complexities of fame. Swift became more deliberate in her content, using platforms not just for personal expression but also as a strategic tool for her brand. She shared professionally curated photo shoots, collaborated with influencers, and aligned herself with social causes that resonated with her audience.

What truly sets Swift apart in the realm of social media, however, is her ability to mobilize her fan base for real-world impact. She strategically uses platforms like Instagram and Twitter (now X) to announce tour dates, create anticipation for new releases, and most notably, encourage fans to attend her concerts. A study by QuestionPro calculated that, in 2023, Swift fans spent around $5 billion on travel, food, hotels, tourist activities, and other local expenditures while attending her concerts. U.S. Travel Association put that estimate at over $10 billion.* This revelation goes beyond the realm of just music and social media; it's a testament to the significant economic contribution that Swift's fan base brings to local communities.

Today, Swift's posts are not just promotional; they're a call to action. She engages fans by sharing their stories, creating personalized connections, and fostering a sense of community among her followers. Whether it's through exclusive content, limited-time offers, or interactive challenges, Swift ensures that her social media presence is not just about herself but also about the vibrant community that surrounds her.

Taylor Swift's journey from a young country singer to a global pop icon is intricately woven with her mastery of social media. She didn't let the platforms change her; instead, she adapted and evolved, always staying true to the authenticity that initially drew fans to her. Today, as she continues to dominate the music industry, Swift's social media prowess remains a key factor in her ability to not only connect with fans but also drive substantial economic impact through her concerts. It's a testament to the enduring power of a well-crafted personal brand in the age of social media.

---

*https://www.ustravel.org/news/taylor-swift-impact-5-months-and-5-billion

TREAT YOUR FOLLOWERS THE WAY YOU WOULD LIKE TO BE TREATED

Authenticity is the key to keeping social media friends, fans, and followers engaged. Be humble—let others talk about you. Never be selling. Protect your reputation so that it's as golden offline as it is online. Avoid giving out your own political, religious, or medical views—unless your personal branding is based on those subjects.

Learn how to brag in a way that gets people to cheer you—not envy you. *Humblebragging* is the annoying technique of telling people how fantastic your life is, while interjecting self-effacing humor or fake "woe is me" claims. Jean Twenge, a psychology professor at San Diego State University and coauthor of the book *The Narcissism Epidemic: Living in the Age of Entitlement,* says "Bragging alone makes you sound like a narcissist," Twenge says. "Humblebragging makes you sound like a narcissist who is also being deceptive." It's normal to want to share the awesome things that happen. Share the good stuff, but share it sparingly, and remember your audience.

And if controversy is not typically part of your subject matter? Don't engage in online combat over others' controversial viewpoints, but instead diffuse them using the *Feel Felt Found* social persuasion technique—typically used by salespeople and advocated[*] by Wired.com: "Wow, I totally see why you FEEL that water legislation is a real threat. I FELT concerned for my property values, too! But then I FOUND this article about how we're not getting the whole story from either corporate interests or our state legislators...."

USE THE SOCIAL MEDIA THAT'S APPROPRIATE FOR YOUR SUBJECT MATTER AND CAREER

If you're an actress, Facebook and Instagram will help you manage your fans. But if you're a bank president or a Supreme Court judge, Pinterest and Facebook's consumer-focus simply aren't for you. For most professionals and corporate employers building their career, LinkedIn is the ideal professional networking platform for you, but—by contrast—it's difficult to get respected on LinkedIn if you are a professional clown, mime, or comedian. Professional practitioners and small-business owners should check into the many social media platforms specifically for your industry.

One word of advice, by the way: Do *not* participate in any schemes to

---

[*] https://www.wired.com/2014/06/connected-world

"buy" friends from dubious companies who claim they'll add thousands of Facebook fans for a fee.

LINKEDIN IS THE MAIN PLATFORM FOR BUSINESS PROFESSIONALS

If you're a corporate employee or a business owner selling products and services that businesspeople need, LinkedIn will help you represent yourself as an authority in your field.

To create your profile, decide how you want to represent yourself and whom you want to attract as customers, clients, or supporters. While this may seem basic, you'd be surprised how many people add information to their LinkedIn profile that doesn't really serve their recruitment effort. For instance, if you're now an executive coach or management consultant, do we really need to know that you studied yoga or became a certified massage therapist in 1994?

Also, remember that LinkedIn profiles are about specific people, not companies. So if you own a business, choose someone to be the face of the company on LinkedIn—if it's not you—or decide which multiple employees will be listed. (Most corporate employees have a LinkedIn profile anyway.)

Once you decide, create as complete a profile as possible using good marketing strategies.* Use LinkedIn's email feature to add contacts that align with your skills and experience—from a wide range of companies. This starts your "tree" or physical network, which will allow you to expand your contacts exponentially. Next, reach out to your contacts and ask for a recommendation—this serves as a "testimonial" on your profile. (You don't need a lot. Try to get four or five at minimum.)

Once you've built your profile and started seeking recommendations, it's time to get recognized as an expert. To do this, start participating in LinkedIn groups. LinkedIn has fostered all kinds of groups of like-minded people in similar fields, areas of expertise, or lines of work. You can participate in these groups and become known among others in the group who could be potential clients or customers for you. Find group(s) of professionals that match your interests or industry—then from the group's main page, you can share links and start discussions. It's a great way to make new professional contacts.

---

*For detailed information on how to write a powerful LinkedIn profile, visit Janet Switzer's blog at janetswitzer.com/blog.

These days, there's so much more to do on LinkedIn that can build your personal brand, including publishing articles based on your expertise. And while LinkedIn is not the only marketing method available to you (though it's one that many people solely rely on), it can bring you new connections, new recognition, and new business. And like Facebook, it's someplace you need to be found in order to look legitimate.

One final reason to upgrade or start a profile at LinkedIn is that Google's love affair with LinkedIn will get your website ranked higher, too. Here's why: LinkedIn lets search engines like Google view and rank the data in LinkedIn profiles. As part of your LinkedIn profile, you should always list your website or blog (along with descriptive copy that helps the search engines find them). Google gives LinkedIn profiles a fairly high ranking when it comes to returning search results for end users. (Hint: Be sure to set your LinkedIn profile preferences to "Full View" so your website/blog shows up in the publicly viewable profile.)

PRINCIPLE

66

USE THE EXPONENTIAL POWER OF CROWDFUNDING

Coauthored with Moses Ma★

Crowdfunding is nothing new. What most people don't know is that the Statue of Liberty was crowdfunded. What's different today is that you have access to so many more people than you otherwise would.

ERICA LABOVITZ
Director of Marketing at Indiegogo

In Success Principles 17, 18 and 19, you learned that you should "Ask! Ask! Ask!"; "Reject Rejection"; and "Use Feedback to Your Advantage." Well, there's a perfect place to practice all three of these principles—crowdfunding, which is the collection of funds through small contributions from many people over the Internet in order to finance a project, venture, or initiative.

This exciting way to get your vision off the ground achieved a tipping point in America with the passage of the Jumpstart Our Business Startups (JOBS) Act signed by President Obama—which reduces the regulatory burden on emerging companies and makes it easier for them to go public. These crowdfunding platforms have helped fund everything from startups, film and music projects, nonprofits, and all types of small businesses in between—as well as helping individuals and small groups raise money for things like college tuition, medical bills, sports teams, and volunteer trips.

Crowdfunding websites have helped people all over the world raise

---

★Moses Ma is my go-to guy for what is happening and what is innovative in the world of technology. He is the coauthor of *Agile Innovation: A Revolutionary Approach to Accelerate Success, Overcome Risk, and Engage Everyone* (New York: Wiley, 2014).

money—growing exponentially from $89 million in 2010 to $5 billion in 2013 to more than $113 billion in 2020. Growth is expected to double every year, and more than a million individual campaigns have been established globally so far. Recently, the World Bank commissioned a study on how crowdfunding would grow, and their most conservative estimates predict that it will grow into a $93 billion investment market by 2025.

WHAT IT TAKES TO WORK THE CROWD

If you're looking at how to run a crowdfunding campaign, it's good to learn from a winner. One of the most successful crowdfunding campaign ever was for the Pebble Watch, a customizable watch that could display messages and alerts from your iPhone or Android smartphone, as well as run a variety of apps. The founder, Eric Migicovsky, failed to raise enough money through traditional venture capital sources, so Pebble Technology launched a Kickstarter campaign on April 11, 2012, with an initial fund-raising target of $100,000. Backers spending $115 would receive a Pebble Watch when they became available ($99 for the first 200), effectively preordering the $150 Pebble at a discounted price.

Within two hours of going live, the project met the $100,000 goal, and within 6 days, the project had become the most funded project in the history of Kickstarter up to that point, raising over $4.7 million with 30 days still remaining in the campaign. On May 10, Pebble Technology announced they were limiting the number of preorders, and on May 18, funding closed with $10,266,844 pledged by 68,928 people. Pebble's early record has since been bested by everything from blockchain launches to novels to the Christian television series *The Chosen*.

So, if you're looking to go out and give crowdfunding a try, here are some principles that helped the Pebble become successful. These are all things you can do by yourself, and for next to nothing in terms of cost.

1. Use the Power of Storytelling. As humans, we feel first and think second. And the best way to evoke an emotional response is to tell a great story—and to do it on video. So if you want to crowdfund, think of yourself as in the movie business. Kickstarter reports that projects including a video get successfully funded 50% of the time, while those without are only 30% likely to fund their project. Projects that include a video raise significantly more money, too.

The surprising thing is that those videos that have helped raise the most funds are not the ones that go hog wild on Hollywood production values. The videos that work the best are modest and direct, and simply say, "This is me, and I'm not hiding anything." More important, they allow you to present your passion honestly.

Check out Pebble's video. It honestly expresses that they don't have the money to shoot a professional commercial. It's rough at the edges and clearly homemade, but it exudes an adorable quality of earnestness and sheer likeability that no advertising agency could match with a $200,000 production budget.

No one will want to invest in something that doesn't pique their curiosity. Photos and text aren't enough to tell the full story—you must go deeper and connect your future customers with the people and personalities behind the product. And you must do so in an authentic way. I think we accomplished all of this with our video, which featured our entire team and was shot at our corporate headquarters—better known as my apartment at the time—in about a month.

ERIC MIGICOVSKY
Founder and CEO of Pebble Technology

Remember, donors and venture capitalists never invest in an idea; they invest in a person. *You.* When describing yourself or your idea, use simple and clear language that gives an honest and concise portrayal of who you really are, as a real person. And more important, show that your passion is real and worth supporting.

2. Execute Flawlessly. Having a great idea for a campaign is one thing; executing it is another matter entirely. Once you have your story down, the most important thing for your campaign is to reach more people. So get out there and beg your friends to participate, bloggers to write about your campaign, and, most important, get testimonials from everyone you can to include on your campaign page. When you look at Pebble's campaign page, you'll see that it offers a plethora of quotes right at the top, from people and organizations endorsing it, including the celebrity author who invented "cyberspace"—William Gibson. Plus, the site offers a media kit for bloggers with very compelling materials for creating viral articles.

The secret sauce for a successfully funded Kickstarter project is frequent and managed updates. If you talk to anyone who's run a campaign, they'll tell you that spikes in funding follow major updates. Seeing updates makes people relate to you as a person, makes it believable that the project will get completed, gives people something to share with others, and keeps you in their mind space.

3. Build and Reward Your Community. Just as you wouldn't embark on a major expedition into the wilderness all by yourself, it's really important to build a team for crowdfunding. You need a solid core team of hard workers who can help manage daily promotion, thanking donors, and other essential but time-consuming tasks. Once that core team is set, then get out there and beg every friend and family member to actively champion your cause, or at least cheer you on by making a contribution and sharing the news about your campaign with everyone they know. Get out there on Instagram and Facebook. Do what it takes.

The three most important keys to succeeding with crowdfunding are *community, community,* and *community*. It is vital to "pre-rally" a large group of people who are eager to commit the minute the crowdfunding campaign goes live. I call this technique "rumble, lightning, thunder." You have to start with a rumble, before the campaign starts, and sign up hundreds of people to commit the instant you launch. It's a lot like a book getting released—if the initial sales are strong, its success is a self-fulfilling prophecy. It's important to gather your instant liftoff community before you launch. And when you launch, you have to execute like lightning. Flawlessly. Without a hiccup. If you're fast out of the gate, the bloggers will invariably report about you. You go to the top of the "what's hot" list. Herd behavior sets in and it's all to your benefit. That's the thunder stage, when the herd starts stampeding toward your campaign.

Next, you need to reward your community. This is pretty obvious to most people already, but if you're kickstarting a product, having the product included in one of the reward levels is crucial. It's one of the main reasons for most backers giving their money to most projects. Still, it's amazing how many campaigns forget to do this.*

---

*For a good sense of how to create reward levels that work, check out the rewards at Pebble's Kickstarter page: https://www.kickstarter.com/projects/getpebble/pebble-time-awesome-smart-watch-no-compromises.

> *Kickstarter's mission is to help bring companies to life through a community of supporters. We wouldn't be here without the close to 70,000 people who believed in our product. It's all about giving the people what they want—without them, none of this would be possible.*
>
> ERIC MIGIKOVSKY

Finally, don't be shy . . . get out there and engage people. This is the time to learn how to collect no's with style and panache. If you study the Pebble campaign page, they do this really well.

4. The Birth of a Brand. A campaign on a crowdfunding site is sort of like a newborn baby—it's a beautiful thing. And part of the beauty is to see the birth of your brand. And the essence of your brand is trust. So what you need to do is communicate on multiple levels your credibility and your expertise. This is something the Pebble team pulled off seamlessly.

When watching your video and reading your project description or updates, it's important to answer over and over that you can do it, that you will do it, that there is no way in the world that you won't do it. Keep expressing gratitude for the people on your team who have the skills to make it happen. The key is to have your audience empathize with you.

5. Ask Nicely and Be Grateful. This seems obvious, but you'd be surprised how many campaigns never ask for the money. They describe the need. They exhibit passion. But there's no call to action. Be sure to add language that tells people what actions they can take to help your campaign. And when you ask, ask nicely.

Finally, thank every one of your supporters, contributors, and donors at least twice. And not just for a successful campaign, thank them profusely so they'll sign up for the next campaign.

WHERE TO FIND A CROWD

The combination of all of these five factors is what made the launch of the Pebble watch one of the most successful Kickstarter launches of all time. Ready to give it a try? Here are seven sites to check out to find the one that's best for you.

Kickstarter is the 800-pound gorilla in crowdfunding, originally designed and built for creative arts, but many technology entrepreneurs now use the site. Some have raised tens of millions of dollars. Check out the Kickstarter campaign for the "Coolest Cooler," which had only $50,000 as their original goal and had raised over $10,056,281 from 48,141 people (at the time I wrote this) to underwrite production of a beverage cooler for the beach that has a built-in battery powered rechargeable blender for making margaritas or smoothies, a waterproof Bluetooth speaker, a USB charger, an LED lid light, wide rolling tires, and several other cool features. You can learn a lot from this campaign.

Indiegogo allows you to raise money for absolutely anything, using an optional "keep what you raise" model in addition to the standard all-or-nothing funding approach. My favorite Indiegogo success story is Solar Roadways Inc., a startup company in Sandpoint, Idaho, whose goal is to replace current petroleum-based asphalt roads, parking lots, and driveways with road panels made from recycled materials and incorporating photovoltaic cells that generate renewable energy that may be used by homes and businesses. They raised over $2 million for their project.

Fundable is another major crowdfunding platform that offers both rewards-based campaigns (where backers are able to pledge money to start-ups in exchange for rewards or preorders of the goods that businesses will produce) and equity-based campaigns (where accredited investors—those investors with a net worth of at least $1 million—are able to invest in start-ups on the equity portion of the platform for small businesses). A startup called TuneGo—which is a new platform to support independent artists in the music industry in building their careers, publishing and distributing their music, and getting radio play for their music—raised $774,000 on Fundable.

GoFundMe is a personal fund-raising website that has helped thousands of people raise millions of dollars for causes like school tuition, sports teams, medical bills, volunteer trips, business ideas, special events, and travel expenses. My favorite GoFundMe success story is 13-year-old Chandra Starr's. Chandra and her mother were once homeless, but after finding stability, housing, and steady work, Chandra set out to collect a million pennies—$10,000—in order to feed the homeless in her community by building vegetable gardens. She surpassed her goal by $4,500.

StartSomeGood is great for early-stage social good projects that are not yet 501(c)(3) registered nonprofits. It even offers human advice, coaching, and feedback on your campaign. One of the features at their site is a free five-part email course called Crowdfunding 101. A nonprofit in Los Angeles called the Do Good Bus wanted to take their bus on the road with the band Foster the People and visit 22 cities with the intention of involving young people in working with at-risk youth, music education, gardening, and soup kitchens. With 680 contributions ranging from $1 to over $10,000 they raised $101,781 to fund their trip. In Dallas, the Do Good Bus prepared more than 8,500 meals at a food bank. At the Austin City Limits Festival, they worked with local Do-Gooders to raise $12,981 toward purchasing equipment for firefighters battling overwhelming wildfires in Texas. Due to a matching contribution, more than $25,000 went toward that cause.

"Yeah, my dad started a crowdfunding project to pay us NOT to practice."

All of these sites are making great things happen for real people every day, advancing the arts, entrepreneurship, and philanthropy in myriad ways.

CAINE'S ARCADE

When I was researching crowdfunding, I came across an inspirational story that I simply must share. In the summer of 2011, nine-year-old Caine Monroy spent the summer building an arcade out of old cardboard boxes and everyday objects in the front of his father's auto parts store, which was more like a warehouse, in East Los Angeles. The "arcade" consisted of all kinds of ingenious games that Caine designed and built himself, including a ticket and prize redemption system using his old toys like Hot Wheels cars as the prizes. (You have to watch the video "Caine's Arcade" on YouTube to get the full scope of this boy's monumental and creative accomplishment.)

The only problem was that because of the store's location and the fact that most of its business was fulfilling orders online, the arcade had no customers until on the last day of summer, when Nirvan Mullick, a filmmaker, came to the auto parts store to buy a door handle for his car. Intrigued by the arcade, he bought a $2 "Fun Pass" and became Caine's first customer. Impressed with the boy's creativity, optimism, and perseverance, Mullick organized a crowd of more than a hundred of his friends and followers on Facebook to surprise Caine by all showing up as customers at his arcade. Mullick captured the whole event on film and later released an 11-minute documentary, "Caine's Arcade," on Vimeo and YouTube. It immediately went viral with more than one million views the first day.★

In 2012, Mullick created a crowdfunded scholarship fund for Caine with the initial goal of raising $25,000—but $60,000 was raised on the first day, and $170,000 the first week. With more than 19,000 individual donors, the total fund reached $240,000 with the ultimate goal being $250,000.

And that's not all. Caine, who was only 12 years old at the time, was invited to speak at the USC Marshall School of Business, the Lions International Festival of Creativity in Cannes, France, and ultimately he spoke at TEDxTeen hosted by Chelsea Clinton. And after he and Mullick spoke in Denver at the 2013 Colorado Innovation Network Summit, Caine was offered a full scholarship to attend Colorado State University.

Inspired by Caine, Nirvan created the Imagination Foundation, whose

---

★ So far Caine's Arcade has had more than 10 million views on YouTube and Vimeo.

mission is to create "a world where creativity and entrepreneurship are core social values nurtured in schools, homes and communities everywhere; where all children are taught to be creative thinkers and doers, and encouraged to make their very best ideas happen." One of their main projects is the annual Global Cardboard Challenge where kids of all ages are invited to build anything they can dream up using cardboard, recycled materials, and imagination—and then come together to share what they have created and play on October 11, the anniversary of the day Mullick surprised Caine with a hundred customers at his arcade. In the first two years, more than 100,000 kids in 50 countries participated in the Cardboard Challenge.*

---

*You can learn more about the foundation and the Cardboard Challenge by visiting imagination.org.

PRINCIPLE 67

CONNECT WITH PEOPLE WHO CAN EXPAND YOUR VISION

*Facebook was not originally created to be a company.
It was built to accomplish a social mission—
to make the world more open and connected.*

MARK ZUCKERBERG
Founder of Facebook

What's the most powerful aspect of the Internet today? Its ability to connect you to millions upon millions of people who can share your passion, support your vision, give you advice, and show up to help you achieve your dream. In fact, never before in the history of mankind has there been a resource like it—one that puts the achievement of your loftiest goals within reach.

Of course, your job is to *use* this tool to achieve what you want—then expand your thinking to enroll and positively impact even more people in initiatives that will improve their lives. Alone you may not have had that power in the past, but with the Internet and current technology, pursuing social good—as well as your own objectives—should be an important goal of every success-principled person.

CONNECT LIKE-MINDED PEOPLE TO SUPPORT YOUR GOALS THROUGH CROWDSOURCING

When we published the very first *Chicken Soup for the Soul®* book, little did we know that it was one of the very first crowdsourced books in history. Dozens of people gave us content in the form of individual stories, poems, and cartoons for the book. It was so successful that the entire *Chicken Soup* series of books was compiled using this method. At one point, we had hundreds of professional writers and everyday people contributing stories for future books we wanted to produce. It's a model that not only worked—but it became even easier with the connecting power of the Internet.

What is crowdsourcing and how can it help you to pursue your goals? Merriam-Webster.com* defines *crowdsourcing* as "the practice of obtaining needed services, ideas, or content by soliciting contributions from a large group of people, and especially from the online community, rather than from traditional employees or suppliers."

Start wide, expand further, and never look back.
ARNOLD SCHWARZENEGGER
Actor, philanthropist, body builder, film producer, and former governor of California

If you're a would-be author but can't write well or can't get started, crowdsourcing can help you complete your manuscript. In fact, *Rich Dad Poor Dad* author Robert Kiyosaki crowdsourced his recent book *Conspiracy of the Rich* by posting the Introduction online, then inviting his millions of existing readers to comment and provide their ideas about the remainder of the book's topics. Not only was it great market research about what people really needed in a financial book, but also, as part of the commenting process, contributors had to register and agree that Robert could use any of their comments and ideas in the remaining chapters of the book.

"I have a germ of an inkling of a notion, but I will need ten million dollars to develop it into an abstraction of a vision of a concept."

---

*See https://www.merriam-webster.com/dictionary/crowdsourcing.

If you're an entrepreneur with a great idea to provide a unique service in cities around the world—but can't deliver the service yourself or don't want to—there are incredible success stories of businesses that have been launched by recruiting others to deliver the services for you. Uber is the popular smartphone app that will find you a rideshare in major cities by texting private drivers for you. In other words, no single company supplies all those drivers—the services are crowdsourced and the app even helps you find the car's exact position on the street outside your location.

Other businesses have been launched by crowdsourcing services from thousands of individual providers, then simply building a website portal to link buyers of these services with the service providers themselves. One of my favorites is Fiverr—a website that represents freelancers all over the world who will do small jobs for just $5. And the online freelance marketplace Upwork connects graphic artists, writers, programmers, and other creative professionals around the world with businesses who need seasoned workers but who want to outsource the work instead of hiring an employee. Upwork charges the providers a small percentage of each transaction and, in 2022, booked $4.1 billion worth of projects through its website without providing any of the creative services itself.

GET HELP WITH YOUR PROJECTS THROUGH VIRTUAL ASSISTANTS OR RUN YOUR ENTIRE COMPANY VIRTUALLY

One of the truly life-changing aspects of the digital age is that the Internet gives talented people the ability to work from anywhere—as long as they have a computer and an Internet connection. Not only has this created a massive shift in how, when, and where people work; it has given rise to an entire virtual workforce that includes remote workers, flex-time workers, outsource vendors, and virtual assistants.

If you own a consulting business in New York, for example, you can hire a marketing director in Texas, an after-hours answering service in Iowa, a personal assistant in Maryland, and a bookkeeper in Ohio—all in addition to your regular employees *or even in place of them.*

The concept of a "virtual business"—where every worker lives and works remotely—has been around for several years, but the digital age has made these businesses more manageable and more productive than ever before. You can now hold video staff meetings with your entire team—for free—using Zoom. You can instantly transfer files while talking or messaging at no cost on Skype. And for a few dollars a month, you can rent a virtual phone system that will route inbound calls to your company's individual "departments"—even though your workers live in several different cities. Hire a voiceover artist on Fiverr to record your phone greetings and routing prompts, and your virtual company will sound as professional as your biggest competitor across town.

What's truly exciting about the virtual-assistant model is that the Internet also makes it possible for people in more developed economies to hire part-time workers in other countries like Romania, India, and the Philippines—paying them rates that are excellent hourly wages in those countries but that are a fraction of what comparably trained professionals would earn in more developed countries. It's not uncommon for MBA-level accountants, veteran programmers, and smart research assistants to charge only between $20 and $35 per hour for first-rate work.

BUILD A VIRTUAL MASTERMIND GROUP

Today, the Internet allows you to build a mastermind group much more easily because now your reach is global—and your ability to check references, get referrals, and find the right mastermind group members is unlimited.

There has never been a better time to build a mastermind group. And with technology like Zoom, Google Hangouts, and GoToMeeting, you can hold a mastermind group meeting—where everyone participates via video—with group members from all over the world. Not only that, but technology makes it inexpensive to use compared to the long-distance phone call fees of the past. Plus you can share documents, slides, photos, and other information while you interact.

If you lead seminars or workshops (or you're thinking about it), check out MaestroConference. You can run a live seminar online for groups up to 5,000 people or up to 2,000 screen share users. You can subdivide them into partners or small discussion groups, and you can listen in on their conversations just as you would if you were walking around a room in a regular classroom setting. People can ask questions by digitally raising their hands, and you can spontaneously call on whomever you want. Or you can pre-screen written questions and save time by not answering irrelevant ones. It's just like a live seminar. Plus, Maestro offers top-notch personalized training in how to use the system.

AFTERWORD

EMPOWER YOURSELF
BY EMPOWERING OTHERS

*Many people die with their music still in them.
Why is this so? Too often it is because they are always getting
ready to live. Before they know it, time runs out.*

OLIVER WENDELL HOLMES
Former U.S. Supreme Court justice

The key to success is to take what you have learned (or relearned) in this book and put it into action. You can't do everything at once, but you can begin. There are 67 principles in this book. If you're not careful, that could feel a bit overwhelming to you. So here is all you have to do:

Go back to Section I and start working through each principle one at a time, in the order they are presented—take 100% responsibility for your life and your success, clarify your life purpose, decide what you want, set specific and measurable goals for all the parts of your personal vision, break them down into specific action steps you can take, create affirmations for each one of your goals, and begin the practice of visualizing your completed goals every day. If you're smart, you'll also enroll someone to be your accountability partner, or you'll start a mastermind group to do these first steps with you.

Then begin *taking action* on your most important goals *every day except your Free Days.* Pay the price by doing whatever it takes, ask for whatever you need with no expectation or fear of rejection, ask for and respond to feedback, commit to never-ending improvement, and persist in the face of whatever obstacles may come up. Now you're up *and running* toward the completion of your major goals.

Next, to build and maintain momentum, create a program for cleaning up your incompletes, work on transforming your limiting beliefs, pick a habit to work on developing for the next quarter, commit to reading one of the books in "Suggested Reading and Additional Resources for Success" (and then another and another), and purchase a motivational audio program to listen to in your car or when you are exercising. Then schedule a vacation with your spouse or some friends, and enroll in a personal development seminar to be completed sometime in the next six months. Start saying no to the people and things that distract you from your major goals, and find a mentor or hire a coach to advise you and keep you on track.

Finally, work on developing your money consciousness. Make sure you set up a procedure for automatically investing 10% *or more* of every paycheck in an investment account, and some portion of your time and money to your religious or favorite nonprofit organization. Analyze and cut back on your spending, and begin figuring out how to make a fortune rather than a living by becoming more valuable to your employer or your clients.

You can't do everything at once. But if you keep adding a little progress every day, over time you will have built a whole new set of habits and self-disciplines. Remember, anything valuable takes time. There are no overnight successes. It took me years to learn and implement all of the principles in this book. I have mastered some and am still working on mastering others.

Though it will take you some time, it shouldn't have to take you as long as it took me. I had to discover all of these principles on my own over a period of many years and from many different sources. I am passing them all on to you in one large package. Take advantage of my having gone before and blazed a trail for you. Everything you need is here to take you to the next level.

Granted, there are things you'll need to learn that are unique to your specific situation, profession, career, and goals that are not covered in this book, but the fundamental principles needed to succeed in *any* venture or line of work have been covered throughout the preceding chapters. Make the commitment to start now and get on with using them to create the life of your dreams.

PRECESSIONAL EFFECTS

Scientist, inventor, and philosopher Buckminster Fuller talked about the *precessional effects* that issue from just getting started—that by being "in motion" on your own goals, you can end up serving humanity. Fuller explained precession by pointing out that the honeybee's seemingly primary objective is to obtain nectar to make honey, but while going after the nectar, the honeybee is unwittingly involved in a much bigger purpose. As it flies from flower to flower in search of more nectar, it picks up pollen on its wings and thus ends up cross-pollinating all the rooted botanicals in the world. It's an unintended by-product of the bee's nectar-seeking activity. You can also think of yourself as a speedboat moving through the water. To the sides of you and behind you is a wake of activity caused by the sheer force of your forward motion. Life is like that, too. As long as you are actively in motion in the pursuit of your goals, you will create precessional effects that will turn out to be far more important than you initially were capable of understanding or intending. You just begin, and the path of opportunities just keeps unfolding in front of and to the side of you.

None of the wealthy and successful people I know (both my closest friends and the more than 90 people I interviewed for this book) could have possibly planned or predicted the exact sequence of events that unfolded over the courses of their lives. They all started with a dream and a plan, but once they started, things unfolded in unexpected ways.

Look at my own example. Mark Victor Hansen and I never predicted that *Chicken Soup for the Soul*®, the title of our first book, would evolve into a brand name and would become a household phrase in North America and numerous other countries around the globe. Nor could we have ever predicted that we would have a line of Chicken Soup for the Pet Lover's Soul™ dog and cat foods, a line of greeting cards, a television show, a syndicated column, or a syndicated radio show. All of these things just evolved out of our initial commitment to write a book and be of service.

When Dave Liniger decided to leave the biggest real estate agency in Denver and start his own agency, he had no idea that 40 years later his company, RE/MAX, would become the largest real estate agency in the United States, a billion-dollar business with 140,000 agents in 110 countries around the world.

Carl Karcher started with a rolling hot dog stand in downtown Los Angeles. As he made a little money, he bought another one and then another one until he could buy a real restaurant. That one restaurant evolved into Carl's Jr.

When Paul Orfalea opened a single copy shop to serve local college students, little did he know it would evolve into a chain of over 1,800 Kinko's stores and net him $116 million when he later sold it to FedEx.

All of these people may have had a set of goals and a detailed plan as best as they could conceive it at the time, but each new success opened up new unforeseen possibilities. If you just aim in the direction you want to go, start, and keep moving forward, all kinds of unforeseen opportunities will grow out of that forward motion.

AN OLYMPIC DREAM TURNS INTO A PROFESSIONAL SPEAKING CAREER

When Ruben Gonzalez finally realized his dream of competing in the winter Olympics for the third time, he returned home to Texas, where his 11-year-old neighbor reminded him of his promise to be his show-and-tell story at the local elementary school. After Ruben regaled Will's fifth-grade class with the tales of his struggles to achieve his Olympic dream, Will's teacher asked Ruben if he would be willing to address an assembly of the whole school. So Ruben stayed for another hour and talked to all 200 kids.

At the end of his talk, several teachers told him that they often hired speakers to come speak to the kids, and he was easily better than anyone they had previously hired. They told him that he had a natural gift as a speaker. Encouraged by this feedback, Ruben began calling up other schools in the Houston area, and soon had so many bookings that he quit his job as a copier salesman.

Everything went well until June when, to Ruben's surprise, school let out for the summer and there were no more speaking engagements until the fall. Spurred on by the need to feed himself and his wife, Ruben began calling up local businesses. Little by little, he established a toehold in the corporate world around Dallas and, as word grew about his incredibly motivating talks, Ruben's career took off. Just under two years later, Ruben made as much money in the first two months of the year as he had made all year in his previous job as a copier salesman.

Placing 35th in the world in luge, a sport most people have never even heard of, was a step toward a career as a world-class speaker, but it was not something he was planning when he was plummeting down the ice track at 90 miles an hour at the U.S. Olympic Training Center in Lake Placid, New York. It was one of those precessional effects that Buckminster Fuller was talking about.

GO GET STARTED!

No amount of reading or memorizing will make you successful in life.
It is the understanding and application of wise thought that counts.

BOB PROCTOR
Author of *You Were Born Rich* and a teacher in *The Secret*

I have done my best to give you the principles and the tools you need to go and make all of your dreams come true. They have worked for me and for countless others, and they can work for you as well. But this is where the information, motivation, and inspiration stop, and the perspiration (provided by you) begins. You and you alone are responsible for taking the actions to create the life of your dreams. Nobody else can do it for you.

You have all of the talent and the resources you need to start right now and eventually create anything you want. I know you can do it. You know you can do it . . . so go out there and do it! It's a lot of fun as well as a lot of hard work. So remember to enjoy the journey!

Everyone who got to where they are had to begin where they were.

RICHARD PAUL EVANS
Bestselling author of *The Christmas Box*

EMPOWER YOURSELF BY EMPOWERING OTHERS

I also want to suggest that you give several copies of this book to your teenage and college-age children, to your employees, team members, and managers. You'll be amazed at how radically you can change a family, a team, or a business simply by having everyone using the same success principles at the same time.

The greatest gift you can give anyone is a gift of empowerment and love. What could be more loving than helping people you care about get free from their limiting beliefs and ignorance about success—and empowering them to create the life they truly want from the depths of their soul?

So many people in the world currently live in a state of resignation or despair. It is time to turn that around. We all have the power within us to create the life we want, the life we dream about, the life we were born to live. We all deserve to fulfill our full potential and manifest our true destiny. It is our birthright, but it must be claimed. It must be earned through hard work, and part of that work is first learning and then living by the time-tested and ageless principles that are guaranteed to bring about our desired results. Most of us did not learn these principles in school, and only a few of us learned them at home.

They have been passed down from person to person by mentors, trainers, successful entrepreneurs, teachers, coaches, and more recently, in books, seminars, and audio programs. Now you have the core of those principles in your hands. First use them to liberate your own life—and the lives of those whom you care about most and whose activities most impact your life.

What if all members of your family gave up complaining, took full responsibility for themselves and their lives, and started creating the lives of their dreams? What if all employees in your company practiced these principles? What if all members of your softball team approached life this way? What if all the high school students in the United States knew these principles and put them into practice in class, on the playing field, and in their social lives? What if all men and women in prison were to learn these valuable principles before they were released back into society? It would be a very different world.

People would take 100% responsibility for their lives and the results they produce or don't produce. They would be clear about their visions and their goals. Nobody would fall victim to the criticism and abuse of others. People would keep their agreements. Everyone would persevere in the face of hardship and challenge. Men and women would band together in teams to support each other to become all that they could be. People would ask for what they need and want and feel free to say no to the requests of others when it is not right for them to respond with a yes. People would stop whining and complaining and get on with creating the life that they want. People would be doing the work they love and would therefore be of greater joyful service to others. People would tell the truth and listen to each other with compassion because they know that peace, joy, and prosperity flourish when they do.

In short, the world would work!

The greatest contribution you can make to the world is to grow in self-awareness, self-realization, and the power to manifest your own heartfelt dreams and desires. The next greatest thing you can do is to help others do the same. What a wonderful world it would be if we were all to do that.

It is my intention that this book would contribute to creating that kind of world. If it does, I will have fulfilled my purpose of inspiring and empowering others to live their highest vision in a context of love and joy in harmony with the highest good of all concerned.

If you would thoroughly know anything, teach it to others.

TYRON EDWARDS
American theologian

TEACH THESE PRINCIPLES TO OTHERS

One of the most powerful ways to learn anything is to teach it to others. It forces you to clarify your ideas, confront inconsistencies in your own thinking, and more closely walk your talk. But most important, it requires you to read, study, and speak the information over and over again. The resulting repetition reinforces your own learning.

One of the great benefits to me of researching and teaching the principles of success is that I am constantly reminding myself about the principles and how important it is to use them. As my staff members read the chapters of this book as I finished them, it helped all of us recommit to the ones we were not fully implementing. And whenever I conduct seminars around the world, I find I become more diligent in implementing the principles in my own life.

Think about whom you might teach these principles to. Could you teach a seminar at your church? Offer a class at the local high school or community college? Teach a seminar at work? Facilitate a six-week study group that meets once a week over lunch? Lead a discussion group with your family?

If you would like to, go to jackcanfield.com/tsp-resources and click the "join the team" tab to download the free "Success Principles Facilitator's Guide" for leading a six-session course that teaches the basic principles of this book to others.

You don't have to be a master of these principles to lead a discussion group or a six-session workshop. You just have to be willing to read the directions out loud. The study guide will tell you everything you need to say and do to lead a productive mini-workshop and help people implement the principles at work, at school, and at home.

We are also actively involved in training thousands of people to teach the success principles in highly interactive and experiential workshops and trainings. In addition to our live two- and three-week trainings (spread out over the course of a year) held in the United States, we also have a complete Success Principles Train-the-Trainer Home Study Course available. Both programs lead to becoming a Certified Canfield Success Principles Trainer. Our ultimate goal is to have one million people teaching these principles, strategies, methods, and techniques in corporations, small businesses, schools, universities, governments, nonprofit organizations, churches, and public seminars by 2030. We are already well on our way to accomplishing this goal, and we would love to have you join us. For more information, visit jackcanfield.com.

Imagine a family, group, club, religious group, office, sales team, or company where the people were all working together to support each other in actively living these principles. The results would be miraculous. And you could be the person who makes that happen. If not you, then who? If not now, then when?

WHEN YOU LIFT UP OTHERS, THEY WILL LIFT YOU UP

And here's another major benefit—the more you help other people succeed in life, the more they will want to help you succeed. You might wonder why all the people who teach success strategies are so successful. It's because they have helped so many people get what they want. People naturally support those who have supported them. The same will be true for you.

One of my spiritual teachers once taught me to be a student to those above me, a teacher to those below me, and a fellow traveler and helpmate to those on the same level. That's good advice for all of us.*

HELP US START A MOVEMENT

If you think you're too small to have an impact, try going to bed with a mosquito in the room.

ANITA RODDICK
Founder of the Body Shop, with 3,000 stores in more than 80 countries, and a prominent human rights activist and environmentalist

I envision a world where all people are inspired to believe in themselves and their abilities and are empowered to reach their full potential and realize all their dreams. I want these principles taught in every school and university and practiced in every small business and large corporation.

I have trained other trainers and speakers, developed curricula for schools,† created video-based training programs for welfare programs and

---

*If you are interested in deepening your own understanding of these principles and learning how to teach these principles in the form of an interactive workshop, you might also want to attend my Breakthrough to Success three-day training. It will accelerate your own growth and teach you valuable leadership skills and instructional methods. For more information, go to jackcanfield.com.

†See *Self-Esteem in the Classroom: A Curriculum Guide,* by Jack Canfield. Available in the store at jackcanfield.com.

corporations, written books, created audio and video programs,* conducted seminars and online courses, and developed coaching and telecoaching programs† for the general public. I've created a syndicated column, helped produce a television series, developed a YouTube channel, created the Jack Canfield Podcast, and appeared on more than 1,000 radio and television programs sharing these ideas with others.

I'd love to have you join me in spreading the word. If you'd like to be part of the Success Principles Team, visit jackcanfield.com and click on the Trainings tab at the top of the page. Scroll down and choose either the Success Principles ADVANCED Certification or the Success Principles Online Certification. You'll see more information about how to become a certified trainer in these powerful success principles. You can also explore these opportunities more fully with one of our staff by calling (805) 563-2935.

TRANSFORM YOURSELF FOR SUCCESS!
ATTEND "BREAKTHROUGH TO SUCCESS"
JACK CANFIELD'S PREMIER TRAINING EVENT

Your ideal life is so much closer than you think. Through this powerful live-training program, thousands of people around the world have achieved their loftiest dreams—from becoming bestselling authors to launching new businesses, doubling their incomes, tripling their time off, funding new charities, becoming the top salesperson, and so much more. In just three days, you'll get crystal clear about what you want, get help overcoming the obstacles that have been holding you back, write a step-by-step plan to take your life to the next level—then learn how to kick that plan into high-gear action! Visit BreakthroughtoSuccess.com for information.

GET SUPPORT AS YOU APPLY THESE PRINCIPLES!
DISCOVER JACK CANFIELD PERSONAL COACHING

It doesn't matter if your goals are to be the top salesperson in your company, become a leading architect, score straight As in school, buy your dream home or double your income—the principles and strategies are the

---

*For a complete listing of my books, audio and video programs, seminars, and coaching programs, go to jackcanfield.com and jackcanfield.com/tsp-resources.

†For a free introduction to coaching (to determine if the Canfield Coaching Program is right for you), go to jackcanfield.com/coaching.

same, but they must be applied! Jack has trained and mentored a team of coaches in the Success Principles to provide you with the personal support, objectivity, and constructive feedback you need to achieve success. With the support of your coach, you can learn to apply the powerful principles from this book. Visit jackcanfield.com/coaching for a free introduction to coaching.

JOIN THE NEXT GENERATION OF HUMAN-POTENTIAL TRAINERS AS A SUCCESS PRINCIPLES QUALIFIED INSTRUCTOR!

Jack Canfield's Train the Trainer program is professional development training where Jack personally trains you to become certified to teach the Success Principles using the "Jack Canfield Methodology" of experiential learning and the holistic model of growth and development. Together with a group of no more than 100 students, you'll be empowered to bring his Success Principles to the world—the same principles outlined in this book. Jack will help you become a dynamic success trainer and equip you with the skill set, content, exercises, workshop design, training tools, and mindset necessary to get results! Attend live trainings or study in the convenience of your home or office. Visit canfieldtrainthetrainer.com.

JACK CANFIELD PRIVATE MASTERMIND RETREATS

If you've ever wanted to get Jack's personal help in creating the meaningful, fulfilling, and exciting life you deserve, these small-group retreats held in exclusive locations like Maui; Bali; Dubai; Tuscany, Italy; and Santa Barbara, California, offer a tranquil, transformational environment while giving you the personalized support you need to awaken the next phase of your life. If selected to participate, you'll join a high-caliber group of self-aware achievers who have invested years in their personal and professional growth, rising to the top of their professions. If you've ever wanted Jack to focus on your biggest dreams and to meet other leaders who share your commitment to unlimited success, this is your chance. *By application only.* Limited to 25 participants. For more information, visit jackcanfield.com and click on the Trainings tab or call (805) 563-2935 to talk to one of our staff.

Take your success to the next level . . .

Download
The Success Principles
FREE SUCCESS TOOLS™

at jackcanfield.com/tsp-resources

FREE One-Year Planning Guide . . . to help you plan your activities, to-do list, action items, success reading, time-management schedule, and more. Includes page after page of colorful daily checklists, notes pages, goal-setting pages, reading lists, personal journal entries, inspirational and thought-provoking messages from Jack and Janet . . . and more.

FREE Victory Log . . . for your three-ring binder or other victory log format. These letter-size pages are colorful, inspiring, and designed to empower you with daily successes you create. When times are tough, remind yourself how successful you really are—with your own Victory Log pages designed to coordinate with *The Success Principles*.

FREE Mastermind Strategy Guide . . . designed specifically for mastermind groups, this free strategy guide helps your group with activities, ideas, and thought-provoking messages that can help any group break through to a higher level of success!

BRING THE POWER OF CHANGE TO YOUR ORGANIZATION: *THE SUCCESS PRINCIPLES* KEYNOTE, WORKSHOP, AND TRAINING

Positive and profound changes are the result when your employees, managers, members, and students experience *The Success Principles* in a live group workshop, training, or keynote.

Not only will your team be inspired and motivated to achieve greater success but they'll also learn how to up-level all their mindsets, actions, relationships, and strategic alliances.

The Success Principles Keynote, Workshop, or training will empower them with strategies that make them more productive with less effort . . . that help put more money in their paychecks . . . that help them function better within their workgroups . . . and that help them respond more effectively and productively to everyday events.

The Success Principles Keynote, Workshop, and training includes success tools, plus highly customized program materials, for each participant. Long-term training or remote training can also be designed for your organization. *The Success Principles* Keynote, Workshop, and training is ideal for groups such as

- Independent sales professionals
- Small-business owners
- Managers and executives
- Trade association memberships
- Corporate workgroups and new hires
- Work-at-home employees and telecommuters
- Students and educators
- School business officials and administrators
- Nonprofit employees and managers
- Professional practitioners and their staffs
- Employees facing layoff or transfer
- Government employees
- Military and civilian personnel

To learn more, go to jackcanfield.com and click on the Hire Jack tab.

YOUR EMPLOYEES AND MEMBERS BENEFIT WHEN YOU PURCHASE *THE SUCCESS PRINCIPLES*™ 30-DAY AUDIO PROGRAM IN QUANTITY...

Now your employees, managers, members, and students can experience this revolutionary system for accomplishing any goal, living any dream, and becoming successful in any area when you purchase *The Success Principles*™ 30-day Audio Program in bulk. You'll enjoy substantial discounts off the regular retail price—plus your team will discover powerful new habits that bring astonishing opportunities and extraordinary results.

Let *The Success Principles* give your group the day-by-day written exercises that will help them incorporate these new attitudes and behaviors into their compelling new lives. Then, watch as unexplained benefits come their way ... important new contacts approach them with opportunities ... and the world opens its bounty and riches to them—all because they, too, have made the journey through exercises and success principles like these:

- Articulating your unique appeal so the world's resources will gravitate toward you
- Accessing powerful mentors and friends who'll open doors for you as you seek success
- Saying no to the good so you'll have room in your life to say yes to the great
- Completing past projects, relationships, and hurts so that you can embrace the future
- Telling the truth sooner to save you from disaster as you move forward to success
- Changing the outcome of any event, simply by changing your reaction to it
- Preparing and being instantly ready when opportunity comes knocking
- Using the unique time management system that ensures you'll have more time to focus on success-producing activities

To purchase *The Success Principles*™ *30-Day Journey Audio Program,* **visit jackcanfield.com/store. To arrange for an in-house workshop, call (805) 563-2935.**

SUGGESTED READING AND ADDITIONAL RESOURCES FOR SUCCESS

You are the same today as you'll be in five years except for two things, the books you read and the people you meet.

CHARLIE "TREMENDOUS" JONES
Member of the National Speakers Hall of Fame

As you may remember, I recommend that you read something educational, motivational, or inspirational every day—20 minutes a day minimum, an hour a day preferred. Below is a short list of some of my books to get you started. I have also listed the books that I have found most useful in my success journey (almost 200 of them) on the companion website at jackcanfield.com/tsp-resources. There are enough books there to keep you busy for several years.

I suggest you read through the list on the website, see which books jump out at you, and start with those. Follow your interests and you'll find that each book you read will lead you to other books.

There is also a list of audio programs I suggest you listen to—and several training programs conducted by others that I encourage you to attend. There are even two success-oriented summer camps I recommend for your kids.

We constantly update this list with the best new resources that I discover.

Here is a short list of my books that focus on success. They are all available for purchase online at jackcanfield.com, Amazon, Barnes and Noble, and Books-A-Million, as well as many of your local bookstores.

The Aladdin Factor: How to Ask for and Get Anything You Want in Life by Jack Canfield and Mark Victor Hansen (New York: Berkley, 1995).

Jack Canfield's Key to Living the Law of Attraction: A Simple Guide to Creating the Life of Your Dreams by Jack Canfield and Dee Dee Watkins (Deerfield Beach, FL: Health Communications, 2007).

Chicken Soup for the Soul: Unlocking the Secrets to Living Your Dreams by Jack Canfield and Mark Victor Hansen (Cos Cob, CT: Chicken Soup for the Soul Publishing, 2012).

Coaching for Breakthrough Results: Proven Techniques for Making Impossible Dreams Possible by Jack Canfield and Peter Chee (New York: McGraw-Hill, 2013).

The Power of Focus: How to Hit Your Business, Personal and Financial Targets with Absolute Certainty, 10th Anniversary Edition by Jack Canfield, Mark Victor Hansen, and Les Hewitt (Deerfield Beach, FL: Health Communications, 2011).

The Success Principles Workbook: An Action Plan for Getting from Where You Are to Where You Want to Be by Jack Canfield with Brandon Hall and Janet Switzer (New York: William Morrow, 2020).

Tapping Into Ultimate Success: How to Overcome Any Obstacle and Skyrocket Your Results by Jack Canfield and Pamela Bruner (Carlsbad, CA: Hay House, 2012).

ABOUT THE AUTHORS

Jack Canfield, known as America's #1 success coach, is a bestselling author, professional speaker, trainer, and entrepreneur. He is the founder and chairman of The Canfield Training Group, which trains entrepreneurs, educators, corporate leaders, sales professionals, and motivated individuals in how to expand their vision and accelerate the achievement of their personal and professional goals.

As the creator of the beloved *Chicken Soup for the Soul®* series and the driving force behind the development and sales of more than 200 *Chicken Soup for the Soul®* books, with 100 million copies sold in the United States (and 500 million worldwide in 51 languages), Jack is uniquely qualified to talk about success.

Jack is a graduate of Harvard, holds a master's degree in psychological education from the University of Massachusetts, and has three honorary doctorates. Over the past 50 years, he has been a psychotherapist, an educational consultant, a corporate trainer, and a leading authority in the areas of self-esteem, breakthrough success, and peak performance.

The first edition of *The Success Principles* has sold nearly a million copies in 41 languages around the globe. Jack's other bestselling books—*The Success Principles for Teens, The Power of Focus, The Aladdin Factor, Dare to Win, You've Got to Read This Book!, The Key to Living the Law of Attraction, Coaching for Breakthrough Success,* and *Tapping into Ultimate Success*—have sold millions of copies and have launched complementary multimedia programs, coaching programs, and corporate training programs to enthusiastic individuals and corporations.

Jack holds a Guinness World Record title for having seven books on the *New York Times* bestsellers list on the same day (May 24, 1998). He also achieved a Guinness World Record title for the largest book signing (held for *Chicken Soup for the Kid's Soul*).

Jack is also the founder of The Foundation for Self-Esteem, which has provided self-esteem resources and trainings to social workers, welfare recipients, and human resource professionals. Jack wrote and coproduced the GOALS Program, a video-based training program to help people in California transition from welfare to work, which has helped more than 800,000 people get off welfare.

Jack has appeared on more than 1,000 radio and television programs, including *Oprah, Oprah's Super Soul Sunday, The Montel Williams Show, Larry King Live,* the *Today* show, *Fox & Friends,* the *CBS Evening News,* the *NBC Nightly News,* and

CNN's *Talk Back Live,* and on PBS and the BBC. Jack is a featured teacher in 19 movies, including *The Secret, The Truth, The Opus, Choice Point, The Tapping Solution,* and *The Keeper of the Keys.*

Jack has conducted more than 2,500 trainings, workshops, and seminars—and has presented and conducted workshops for more than 500 corporations, professional associations, universities, school systems, and mental health organizations in all 50 states and 50 countries. His clients include Microsoft, Federal Express, Siemens, Campbell's Soup Company, Virgin Records, Sony Pictures, General Electric, Sprint, Merrill Lynch, Hartford Insurance, Johnson & Johnson, Coldwell Banker, Northrop, RE/MAX, Keller Williams, UCLA, YPO, the U.S. Department of the Navy, and the Children's Miracle Network.

Jack has been inducted into the National Speakers Association Speakers Hall of Fame and the Coaches Hall of Fame, is a recipient of the Rotary Club's Paul Harris Fellowship, was awarded the Golden Plate Award from the National Achievement Summit, and received the Chancellor's Medal from the University of Massachusetts. He was twice named Motivator of the Year from *Business Digest* magazine, received the Speaker of the Year Award from the Society of Leadership and Success, and is a recipient of the National Leadership Award from the National Association for Self-Esteem.

To find out more about Jack's Breakthrough to Success Trainings, Train-the-Trainer Program, Coaching Programs, and audio and video programs, or to inquire about hiring him as a speaker or trainer, you can contact his office at

The Canfield Training Group, P.O. Box 30880, Santa Barbara, CA 93130
Phone: (805) 563-2935 and (800) 237-8336; fax: (805) 563-2945
Email: info@JackCanfield.com
Websites: jackcanfield.com, canfieldtrainings.com, canfieldcoaching.com

Janet Switzer exemplifies the personal achievement and professional accomplishment that comes from applying these proven principles of success.

At age 19, she began her professional career as a campaign specialist for a member of the United States Congress, and by age 29 had built an international publishing venture with over $10 million in assets.

Today she's the revenue strategist of choice for many of the world's top celebrity entrepreneurs. Her high-profile clients have included Jack Canfield; motivational speaker Les Brown; underground business icon Jay Abraham; and tapping-therapy psychologist Dr. Roger Callahan, among many others.

She's the *New York Times* bestselling coauthor and marketing strategist behind *The Success Principles*—the number one self-help classic published in 41 languages. She is also the number one bestselling author of *Instant Income: Strategies That Bring in the Cash for Small Businesses, Innovative Employees, and Occasional Entrepreneurs.*

For over 30 years, Miss Switzer has been at the forefront of helping business owners learn, grow, and profit. Her books, newsletters, and training courses are read and used by entrepreneurs in more than 80 countries. She has counseled thousands of companies and solo entrepreneurs on the systems and strategies that bring reliable, predictable cash flow. And she has traveled to nearly every continent speaking to entrepreneurs, independent sales professionals, corporate employees, and industry association members.

She has been a widely published journalist and is a former columnist with Nightingale-Conant's *AdvantEdge* magazine and *Training Magazine*. A popular media personality seen by more than 75 million viewers, she has been featured in the *Wall Street Journal, USA Today*, the *New York Times, Time, Entrepreneur Magazine,* and *Speaker Magazine* and on MSNBC and the ABC Radio Network.

Miss Switzer's consulting division helps establish revenue-generation campaigns and new business units for authors, speakers, coaches, and niche-market experts.

Visit janetswitzer.com.

ACKNOWLEDGMENTS

This book, like everything else I have created in my life, is the result of a huge team effort. I extend my deepest gratitude and thanks to the following:

Janet Switzer, without whose Herculean efforts this book would never have been completed. Thank you for your incredible support, deep insights, and long days spent in the original conception of this book, coauthoring a world-class book proposal, distilling my endless production of written words down into a manageable manuscript, contributing exciting and valuable new content to the revised edition, bringing your business perspective to this book for my entrepreneurial readers, and creating such an amazing marketing plan for reaching millions of people with the message of this book over the last two decades. You have been a trusted advisor and incredible strategist for my career for more than 30 years. You are truly awesome!

Patty Aubery, former president of Chicken Soup for the Soul Enterprises and current president of the Canfield Training Group. Thank you for "making" me write this book and for bringing Janet Switzer into our organization almost 35 years ago, as well as introducing me to Bonnie Solow, who helped make this book possible. Also for your persistence in enrolling PEI, our coaching company, convincing them that my message was worth the risk. Your commitment to leveraging the Canfield brand to transform millions of lives and your determination to create the next generation of transformational leaders continuously stretch me. You are living proof that the principles in this book work if you work the principles. Words can never convey how much I appreciate your support in bringing out the best in me.

Jeff Aubery, for living without your wife as she worked on this book and on the Train-the-Trainer Home Study Program at the same time. You are an amazing man and father.

Steve Hanselman, who was the editor and publisher at HarperCollins for the first edition of this book and who urged me to publish this revised edition. Thanks for your boundless energy, your beautiful spirit, and your dedication to educating and uplifting the world through the written word.

Bonnie Solow, my literary agent for this project. You are more than an agent. You were there every step of the way with your editorial insights, emotional support, enthusiastic encouragement, and authentic friendship. I admire your integrity, your professionalism, your commitment to excellence, your sincere desire to make a difference, and your love for life.

Peter Hubbard, executive editor at HarperCollins, who championed the tenth anniversary revision of this book. I deeply appreciate your support of this project.

All those talented individuals at HarperCollins who were instrumental in the creation of this book, especially Nick Amphlett, Andrew DiCecco, Rachel Meyers, Diane Shanley, Nyamekye Waliyaya, Dale Rohrbaugh, Onalee Smith, and Katie Steinberg.

Deborah Feingold, who took the cover photograph for this book.

All the staff at the Jack Canfield Companies, without whose help this book could not have been completed. Especially Russell Kamalski, chief operating officer at the Canfield Training Group. Thanks for your calm, easygoing demeanor, which helps keep it all together in the midst of the tornado-like frenzy we often find ourselves in. You're a true gentleman.

Jesse Ianniello, for all of your endless hours of transcribing the hundreds of interviews I recorded for the original manuscript, and for taking on the huge in-house assembly job required to complete the *10th Anniversary Edition*—on top of your regular role as vice president of training. You consistently make the difficult look easy. You are a true wonder.

Andrea Haefele-Ventim, who is not only our old soul but kept us all grounded and took over so many of the training- and product-development tasks of the company while I was working on this book. You proved how much can be accomplished over the Internet and Skype by doing it all from Hawaii after moving there with your husband. Your ability to stay calm and centered along with your sense of humor is greatly appreciated.

Veronica Romero, my executive assistant, who has kept my life in order with very little support from me during the last month of being buried under the weight of this project. Thanks for scheduling all of my interviews and for overseeing getting all of the necessary permissions for this book. Thanks for keeping my travel, my speaking career, and me alive and well during this time. Your tireless efforts, your attention to detail, and your commitment to excellence are awesome. I appreciate you so much!

Jocelyn Kuhn, for keeping me up to speed on all the new books, podcasts, and other developments in the human potential movement and for helping with some of the research for this *20th Anniversary Edition* of *The Success Principles*.

Donna Bailey, for looking after me in so many areas of my life, especially making sure we stay on budget so that we always have enough money to do the things we need to do.

Teresa Collett, for managing to coordinate all my speaking engagements and keeping all of our clients happy for the last twenty-eight years, especially while I was rewriting this book.

Lisa Williams, my marketing director, who oversees all our Internet presence, for constantly advancing this work and for being the caretaker of my message, and for your work in soliciting new success stories for this (and the earlier) revised edition. Your tireless dedication to the mission is amazing.

Lexi Wagner, for all your support in the marketing department as well as social media. I so appreciate your technological expertise and your "whatever you need" and "whatever it takes" attitude.

Alice Doughty-Refauvelet, for your enthusiasm, your creativity, and your ability to do just about anything we put in front of you.

Jody Schwartz, for your complete and total focus on filling our flagship training, Breakthrough to Success and Train the Trainer. Your enthusiasm is contagious!

Dwain Jeworski, for making yourself available to us as our trusted resource around the digital age, as well as all of your marketing brilliance and genuine willingness to do whatever it takes to support me and the company on so many levels, beyond the Success Principles.

All of my family for their love, support, and understanding during what has been unquestionably the greatest professional challenge of my career. Thanks for understanding the long hours that were required to finish this project on time. I love and appreciate you all so much. Inga, my wife, whom I adore for how much she understands me and what I am about, and for her unceasing love, support, humor, and encouragement. Christopher, my now 34-year-old son, for putting up with my obsession around this book. I hope our trips to Europe and Africa made up for some of the time lost during the writing of the first edition. Riley and Travis, my two stepchildren, who are courageously pursuing their dreams and who always keep it interesting. Thanks for being so supportive. Oran and Kyle, my two older sons, now we have more time to focus on family and Ozzie, my first grandson.

Janet's family, for their support, understanding, and good humor in the face of missed vacations and endless book-related dinner conversation. To her parents, Les and Beverly, who showed Janet early on the meaning of success and who fostered an atmosphere of achievement in their home. And most especially, thanks to Janet's niece, Brianne, who not only reflects how children learn to be successful but is also a gentle reminder that the most important thing is to enjoy it.

PERMISSIONS

We acknowledge the many publishers and individuals who granted us permission to reprint the cited material:

Doug Wittal. Reprinted with permission.
Justin Bendel. Reprinted with permission.
Natalie Peace. Reprinted with permission.
Elvin Slew. Reprinted with permission.
Pavel Popiolek. Reprinted with permission.
Heather O'Brien Walker, author of *Don't Give Up. Get Up!* And creator of the HELP Philosophy helpfulspeaker.com.
Akshay Nanavati. Reprinted with permission.
Lewis Pugh. Reprinted with permission.
Forrest Willett. Reprinted with permission.
John Calub. Reprinted with permission.
© Randy Glasbergen glasbergen.com
Charles Rodrigues. ©1991 Tribune Media Services. Reprinted with permission.
Raj Bhavsar. Reprinted with permission.
Julie Marie Carrier, interviewed by author.
Pat Williams, interviewed by author.
Arnold M. Patent. Reprinted with permission.
Dave Liniger, interviewed by author.
Monty Roberts, interviewed by author.
Logan Doughty. Reprinted with permission.
Timothy Ferriss, interviewed by author.
Ruben Gonzalez, interviewed by author.
Jason W. McDougall. Reprinted with permission.
Peak Performers by Charles A. Garfield, Ph.D. Reprinted with permission.
Catherine Lanigan. Reprinted with permission.
Buddy Hickerson. ©Tribune Media Services. Reprinted with permission.
Daniel Amen, M.D., Director of Amen Clinics, Inc. and author of *Change Your Brain, Change Your Life*.
© Reprinted with special permission of King Features Syndicate.
Stuart Lichtman, interviewed by author.
C.K. Kumaravel. Reprinted with permission.

Brian Tracy. Reprinted with permission.
Les Hewitt. Reprinted with permission.
DC Cordova. Reprinted with permission.
T. Harv Eker, interviewed by author.
Anthony Robbins. Reprinted with permission.
Copyright © 1994 Stephen Rebello. Originally published in *MovieLine Magazine*, July 1994. All Rights Reserved. Reprinted by arrangement with Mary Evans, Inc.
Joseph Newberry. Reprinted with permission.
© The New Yorker Collection 1998 William Haefeli from cartoonbank.com. All Rights Reserved.
Peter Vidmar. Reprinted with permission.
Heather O'Brien Walker, author of *Don't Give Up. Get Up!* And creator of the HELP Philosophy helpfulspeaker.com.
John Assaraf, interviewed by author.
Kabir Khan. Reprinted with permission.
Trisha Jacobson. Reprinted with permission.
Sergio Sedas Gersey, Ph.D., award winning author of *Intentional Possibilities.*
cartoonstock.com. Reprinted with permission.
Jack Bierman. Reprinted with permission.
© 1990 Thaves. Reprinted with permission. Newspaper dist. By NEA, Inc.
Jana Stanfield, interviewed by author.
Peter H. Douglas. Reprinted with permission.
Michael T. Kelley, interviewed by author.
Dr. John DeMartini, interviewed by author.
Tom Boyer, interviewed by author.
Dr. Christine Carter—a sociologist and the author of *The Sweet Spot: How to Find Your Groove At Work and Home*—says that . . .
Wyland. Reprinted with permission.
Gordon Weiske. Reprinted with permission.
Marshall Thurber, interviewed by author.
Sylvia Collins. Reprinted with permission.
Dale and Donna Hutcherson. Reprinted with permission.
Chad Pregracke. Reprinted with permission.
Lisa Nichols. Reprinted with permission.
Jeff Olson. Reprinted with permission.
Charles Coonradt. Reprinted with permission.
Michael Walsh, interviewed by author.
Excerpted from "Don't Burn Out." This article was originally published in the May 2000 issue of *FAST COMPANY,* © 2000 by FAST COMPANY. All Rights Reserved.
Debbie Macomber, *New York Times* bestselling author. Reprinted with permission.
Jaroldeen Edwards. Reprinted with permission.
David J. Morris, interviewed by author.

Steve Beers. Reprinted with permission.
Dan Sullivan. Reprinted with permission.
Martin Rutte is at martinrutte.com. Reprinted with permission.
David Babb. Reprinted with permission.
Sharon Worsley. Reprinted with permission.
Sid Simon, Professor Emeritus, Psychological Education, University of Massachusetts. Reprinted with permission.
Skip Barber, interviewed by author.
Les Brown, interviewed by author.
© 1996 Tedd Goff
Elaine Fosse. Reprinted with permission.
Kyle Canfield. Reprinted with permission.
Rafe Esquith. Reprinted with permission.
Diana von Welanetz Wentworth. Reprinted with permission.
© Leo Cullum from cartoonbank.com All Rights Reserved.
Raymond Aaron, interviewed by author.
© The New Yorker Collection 1993 Robert Mankoff from cartoonbank.com. All Rights Reserved.
Kathleen Seeley. Reprinted with permission.
Lisa Miller. Reprinted with permission.
Jason Ryan Dorsey, bestselling author, *Graduate to Your Perfect Job*
Miriam Laundry and I CAN Company. Reprinted with permission.
Jean MacDonald. Reprinted with permission.
Ivan R. Misner Founder of BNI & Sr. Partner of Referral Institute.
jilldouka.com. Reprinted with permission.
Burt Dubin, Creator, Speaking Success System, speakingsuccess.com. Reprinted with permission.
David Babb. Reprinted with permission.
The changing heart rhythm graphic maintains a copyright with the Heart Math Research Center. HeartMath.org.
Madeline Balletta, interviewed by author.
Pat Boone. Reprinted with permission.
Dawa Tarchin Phillips. Reprinted with permission.
Marcia Martin O'Hagan, interviewed by author.
Kim Kirberger. Reprinted with permission.
Cliff Durfee, interviewed by author.
Larry Price, executive director, Foundation for Self Esteem. Reprinted with permission.
Marilyn Tam, interviewed by author.
Charlie Collins, charliecollinsinternational.com.
Don Miguel Ruiz. Reprinted with permission.
Dr. Harville Hendrix. Reprinted with permission.
The Dallas Morning News, September 10, 1985, pg. 1b. Reprinted with permission.
Scott Schilling, interviewed by author.

Real Live Adventures © 1993 GarLanco. Reprinted with permission of UNIVERSAL PRESS SYNDICATE. All rights reserved.
J. Mike Milliorn, interviewed by author.
Ira and Linda Distenfield, interviewed by author.
Shane Lewis, autosplit.com. Reprinted with permission.
Tony and Randi Escobar. Reprinted with permission.
Robert Allen, interviewed by author.
Tom, Jack's neighbor. Reprinted with permission.
Kenneth E. Behring. Reprinted with permission.
Excerpted from *Religion and Liberty,* November/December 2000, vol. 10, number 6, a publication of the Acton Institute for the Study of Religion and Liberty. Reprinted with permission.
crowdfundingheros.com. Reprinted with permission.
Moses Ma. Reprinted with permission.

INDEX

$2.00 Game, 14
4-Hour Workweek, The (Ferriss), 44, 231, 504–5, 504*n*
9/11 terrorist attacks (2001), 113, 214, 265
15% rule, 424, 463
18/40/60 Rule, 58
"20 Things I Love to Do" lists, 33–34
50/50 Law, 464–65
80/20 Principle, The (Koch), 339*n*
100 Ways to Enhance Self-Concept in the Classroom (Canfield), 107, 372
1001 Ways to Market Your Book (Kremer), 221
"2020 Vision," 36

Aaron, Raymond, 333–34
abundance, 461, 492, 493, 514
Abundance (Diamandis), 504
Abundance Now (Nichols), 200
Academy of Achievement, 163–64
accountability, 257, 341; of leaders, 344–45
accountability partners, 295, 379
Achievers Coaching Program, 94, 355
Achievers Focusing System, 94
acknowledgment, as step to forgiveness, 260–61
acting out desired future (acting as if), 125–34
actions: bias for, 139–40; inspired, 68, 70–71. *See also* taking action
active listening. *See* listening, active
acts of service, as love language, 429
Adams, Brian, 220
adrenaline, 152, 158
advisors, 332–33, 340

affirmations, 102–7; of forgiveness, 263–66; guidelines for effective, 102–5; how to use, 105; of love, 428, 429; money and, 452–53, 477; power of, 106–7; for vibrational match, 72–73
Agile Innovation (Ma), 528
agreements, 433–38; being on time, 437–38; integrity and self-esteem and, 435; making and keeping, 435–36; with yourself, 434
AI. *See* artificial intelligence
AI Accelerator for Entrepreneurs (Canfield), 520–21
"AI money mindsets," 514–15
"Ain't It Awful" Club, 233–35
Aladdin Factor, The (Canfield and Hansen), 177–78, 310, 412, 571
Alcoa, 183
Alcoholics Anonymous, 10
Alford, Steve, 166
Ali, Muhammad, 141–42
Allen, James, 275, 281, 491
Allen, Robert, 24*n*, 97, 353, 488, 491–92
Allen, Woody, 364, 507
Alphabet Inc., 513
alpha brain waves, 248
Altman, Sam, 517
altruism. *See* tithing; volunteerism
always-or-never thinking, 278
Amazon, 310, 402, 486, 531
Amen, Daniel, 58, 277, 277*n*
Anderson, Chris, 534
Anderson, Walter, 267
anger, 196, 197, 257, 282, 283
Anheuser-Busch, 183
ante, upping the, 438

anxiety, 263–64
Apollinaire, Guillaume, 160
application stacks, 515
applied kinesiology, 50–51
appreciation, 426–32; five languages of, 427–30; of leaders, 352; through meditation, 73–74; score card, 431–32; as secret of success, 431
Appreciation Game, 279
artificial intelligence (AI), 513–21; amplifying capabilities and creating more value, 516–17; Billionaire Mindset, 518–19; embracing change and experimenting, 520–21; Millionaire Mindset, 517; OpenAI's ChatGPT, 515–16, 517; success in the age of, 513–14; Trillionaire Mindset, 519–20
As a Man Thinketh (Allen), 275, 281
Aschauer, Peter, 480
Ash, Mary Kay, 147, 220
ask (asking), 176–84; everything to gain by, 182; fear of, 176–77; for feedback, 197–98; intuition and, 388; for money, 182–83; rules for, 177–79; starting today, 184; for upgrade, 180–81. *See also* questions
Ask and It Is Given (Hicks), 94n, 454
Assaraf, John, 120, 232–33, 234, 437
assets, financial, 457, 468
assumptions, 421–25; bad news and hesitation, 422–23; "Do You Mean" technique, 423–24; space between rules, 424–25
attention, paying, 18–19
attention units, 251, 252, 254
attitude, for belief in oneself, 48
attraction law. *See* Law of Attraction
Attwood, Janet and Chris, 29
Aubery, Patty, 180–81, 364
audio programs, motivational, 307–10
auditory appreciation, 427
authenticity, 344, 539
automatic deductions, 467, 468
automatic investing, 466–67, 558
"automatic millionaire," 466–67

Automatic Millionaire, The (Bach), 467
Automatic Negative Thoughts (ANTs), 277–78, 277n
automatic withdrawals, 464
automation, 518–19, 520
avatars, 528, 528n
Avon, 479
Awaken the Giant Within (Robbins), 218, 358
awkward stage, 175

Baby Jogger, 479
Bach, David, 467, 473
Bach, Richard, 44, 126, 275
Back Roads (O'Dell), 187
bad news and hesitation, 422–23
Balletta, Madeline, 390–91
Barber, Skip, 302
bartering, 472
Baumgartner, Felix, 358–59
Baylando Records, 312
Beach Activities of Maui, 160–61
Beatty, Melody, 149
Beckwith, Michael, 529
Bee-Alive Company, 390–91
Behring, Kenneth, 499–500, 500n
belief in oneself, 48–58; affirming, 67–68; attitude for, 48–49; choice of, 49–50; lack of college and, 57–58; negative thinking as impediment to, 50–53; never too late, 53–55; never too young, 55–57; others' opinions as impediment to, 52–53, 58; "You gotta believe" attitude, 43–44
belief in one's own potential, 42–47, 67–68
beliefs, limiting. *See* limiting beliefs
Bench, Doug, 277–78
Bendel, Justin, xx
Bennis, Warren, 341
Bestseller Blueprint, 373
Better Life Day, 378–79
Bhavsar, Raj, 19–22
bias for action, 139–40
Bierman, Jack, 140–41
Billionaire Mindset, 518–19
bio-entanglement physics, 62–63
biographies, 301

Black Enterprise (magazine), 185
Blakely, Sara, 346–47
blame, 4–5, 10–11, 14
Blanchard, Ken, 194, 221, 296, 323, 351, 373
Bledsoe, Jaylen, 57
blogs (blogging), 525–28, 543
Bogguss, Suzy, 149
"bold asking" exercise, 176–77
Bono, 501
bookmarks toolbar, 509
Boone, Pat, 390–91
Booth, Leo, 323
Borten, Craig, 217–18
Bourdain, Anthony, 437–38
Boxer, Barbara, 6
Boyer, Tom, 449–50
Boyle, Susan, 53
Bradbury, Ray, 150
Bradley, Bill, 166
Bragg, Paul, 162
brainstorming, 220, 290, 377, 451
brain waves, 60–61
brakes, releasing the, 97–108, 304
branding. *See* personal branding
Brause, Diane, 33
breakthrough goals, 79–80
"Breakthrough to Success" training, 29, 305–6, 565
Breitman, Patti, 338
Brin, Sergey, 191
Bristol, Claude, 291
Brown, Brené, 534
Brown, Les, 302–3, 354
Bryant, Paul "Bear," 168
Buddha, 60
budgets (budgeting), 457–60. *See also* expenditures
Buffer Days, 326, 328
Bunch, Jim, 359
burning coals, walking on, 51
Burt Dubin Speaking Success System, 381
Buzan, Tony, 91*n*
Byrne, Rhonda, 75, 94*n*

Callahan, Roger, 159, 159*n*, 263–66, 263*n*
Calub, John, xxv–xxvii
Canfield, Inga, 243, 428, 429
Canfield, Kyle, 312
Canfield Coaching program, 370–72, 565–66
Capability Amplifier, 516–17
Capala, Matthew, 522
Cardillo, Donna, 247
Carnegie, Andrew, 76, 374
Carrey, Jim, 82–83, 102
Carrie (King), 190–91
Carrier, Julie Marie, 25
Carroll, Pete, 13
Carter, Christine, 168
Carter-Scott, Chérie, 32–33
Carver, George Washington, 5
Cash Flow Game, 460
cash payments, 471–72
Casstevens, David, 432
CastMagic, 515
casual-contact networks, 361–62
catastrophic predicting, 279–80
caving in, 196, 197
cell phones. *See* smartphones
certified financial planners (CFPs), 469
change: through affirmations, 102–7; complaining vs., 12–14, 14; embracing of, 272–74, 506; improvement and, 205–6; in response to events, 7–8
Change Your Brain, Change Your Life (Amen), 277*n*
Chaplin, Charlie, 142
Chapman, Gary, 427–28, 428*n*
ChatGPT, 515–16, 517
ChatHub, 515
Chee, Peter, 350*n*, 373
Cheney, Dick, 57–58
Chicken Soup for the African American Soul (Canfield et al.), 200
Chicken Soup for the Gardener's Soul (Edwards), 222–23
Chicken Soup for the Prisoner's Soul (Canfield et al.), 490
Chicken Soup for the Soul (Canfield et al.), 24, 36, 66, 71, 80, 82, 119, 140, 151, 187–88, 221–22, 262, 373, 384, 417, 490, 494–95, 553–54, 559
Chicken Soup for the Soul Cookbook (Canfield et al.), 323

Chicken Soup for the Teenage Soul
(Kirberger), 398, 486
child, inner, 242, 244–45
Child, Julia, 53
child care, 327
Child Fund International, 498
childhood programming, 30–31, 288–89, 451–52
childlike ego, 244–45
Childre, Doc, 386–87
choice, 5–10; belief in oneself and, 49–50; personal responsibility and, 5–10, 14–15
Chopra, Deepak, 46, 67, 94*n*
Christmas Box, The (Evans), 561
chunking down, 90–94; doing first things first, 93; mind mapping, 91–93; planning next day night before, 93–94
Churchill, Winston, 60, 187, 440
Clark, Wesley, 35
Clason, George, 461
class acts, 439–44
Claude.ai, 516
Clinton, Bill, 164, 219
closure, and Cycle of Completion, 250–51
cloud applications, 509–10
clues, seeking out, 95–96
clutter, 252–53, 254, 255
coaches (coaching), 368–73; Canfield program, 370–72, 565–66; inner coach, 275, 282–87; other to take leadership role, 349–51; purpose of, 368, 369; types of, 368–69; for writers, 372–73
Coaching for Breakthrough Success (Canfield and Chee), 350*n*, 373, 572
Coach Yourself to Success (Miedaner), 255
college: lack of degree, 57–58; student loans, 473–74
Collier, Robert, 221
Collins, Charlie, 412–14
Collins, Jim, 336, 338
Collins, Sylvia, 179–80
Colvin, Geoffrey, 168–69, 169*n*
Come As You'll Be Party, 127–34
comfort zone, 97–108

commitments, 296–98; to improvement, 205–8; of leaders, 344–45. *See also* agreements
compassion, 258
complaints (complaining), 12–14; $2.00 Game, 14; to wrong person, 14
complete delegation, 320–22
completion, 250–55; checklist for, 253–54; cycle of, 250–51; four D's of, 252; in household environment, 252–53; sense of, 245–46
completion consciousness, 251
compound interest, 223, 462–63
con artists, 321–22
conditioning, 48, 307
conferences, 301–2
consequences, 438; creating vs. allowing of, 14–15; of habits, 292–93; as result of response to events, 7–8
considerations, 84–86
Conspiracy of the Rich (Kiyosaki), 554
consulting, 487
consumer debt, 470
contact lists, 364
Context-Based Learning, 130, 131
conversations, formula for having, 410–11
Coolidge, Calvin, 216
Coonradt, Charles, 209, 209*n*
Cordova, DC, 24*n*, 95, 436–37
core genius, 319–23, 324–25, 330
corporate giving, 494
counseling, business, 356
Couples, Fred, 126–27
courage, 162, 165–66
Courage to Be Yourself, The (Thoele), 335
courtesy, 440–41
Cousteau, Jacques-Yves, xxix
Cowboy Leadership (Douglas), 155
Cox, Marty, 224–25
Coyle, Daniel, 169*n*
Craig, Gary, 263–64, 264*n*
Craigslist, 483, 529–30
CRA Management Group, 355
creating outcomes, 14–15
creating wealth. *See* wealth creation
creative muse, 516
credibility stage of relationship, 362

credit cards, 470, 474, 475–76, 511
Crichton, Michael, 173
critical drivers, 210
Cromwell, Oliver, 207
crowdfunding, 544–52; of Caine Monroy, 551–52; list of sites, 548–51; of Miriam Laundry, 367; of Pebble Watch, 545–48; principles to use, 545–48
crowdsourcing, 553–55
crucial conversations, 410–11
Crucial Conversations (Patterson, ed.), 411*n*
Cycle of Completion, 250–51
cyclical change, 273–74, 506

Daggett, Tim, 113–14
daily irritants, 254–55
Daily Success Focus Journal, 243–44
daily to-do lists, 91, 93, 94
Dallas Buyers Club (movie), 217–18
Dantzig, George, 51
Daydots, 481
daydreaming, 66–67
debt reduction, 474–76
DeGeneres, Ellen, 33, 56
delegation (delegating responsibility), 252, 319–21; to support team, 330–34; total focus process for, 330–31
deliberate practice, 168–69
Demartini, John, 161–63, 300, 455, 464
Deming, W. Edwards, 424
denial, 267–71; action vs., 271; based on fear, 270; reasons for, 268–69
determination. *See* persistence
Diamandis, Peter, 504, 514
Difficult Conversations (Stone, ed.), 411*n*
"Difficult or Troubling Situation" exercise, 350–51
digital age, 503–12; taking control, 507–11. *See also* artificial intelligence; Internet; online persona; smartphones; social media
digital privacy, 510–11, 533
dignity, 439–44
Dillanos Coffee Roasters, 224–25, 498
Directors Guild of America, 493
Direct Selling Association, 484–85

"divide your use" philosophy, 508
Doby, Danielle, 236
Do Good Bus, 549–50
"Do it now," 141–42
"don't do" policies, 336
Don't Give Up, Get Up! (Walker), 118
Dooner, John, 302
Dorsey, Jason, 356–57
Double Your Income Doing What You Love (Aaron), 333
Doughty, Logan, 39–41
Douglas, Peter, 153–55
Douka, Jill, 378–79
"Do You Mean" technique, 423–24
dreams, 146–49; belief in one's own potential, 42–47; of high achievers, 35–36; intentional daydreaming, 66–67; living someone else's, 31–32; never giving up on, 216–20; vision boards and goal books for realizing, 119–20; of wealth, 447, 456–57
dream-stealers, 36–37
drug addiction, 39, 265
Dubin, Burt, 381
Duckworth, Angela Lee, 534
Durfee, Cliff, 400
Dwoskin, Hale, 453, 453*n*
Dyer, Wayne, 10, 94*n*, 224
Dynamic Laws of Prosperity, The (Ponder), 59

E + R = O (Event + Response = Outcome), 6–7, 16, 267, 273
early childhood programming, 30–31, 288–89, 451–52
Eat That Frog! (Tracy), 93
eBay, 479
Eckhart, Meister, 73
Edison, Thomas, 374–75, 376, 478
education, 496; investing in team's, 304–6; passion for teaching, 312–13. *See also* college; learning
Edwards, Jaroldeen, 222–23
Edwards, Tyron, 562
eidetic visualizers, 118
Einstein, Albert, 61, 99, 109, 383, 462
Eker, T. Harv, 447

INDEX

elephant, 98
Eller, Stevie and Karl, 163–64
Ellison, Larry, 57
email, 334, 507–8; better habits with, 294; privacy concerns, 510; security concerns, 509
embracing change, 272–74, 506
emergencies, and Free Days, 326
emergency brakes, 97, 304
Emerson, Ralph Waldo, 60, 311, 496
Emotional Freedom Technique (EFT), 264, 264n, 287
emotional negativity, 234
empowerment, 561–62
endorphins, 277
energy and thoughts, 60–63
entanglement, 62–63
entheos, 311
enthusiasm, 311–15; developing, 313–14; maintaining, 314–15; for teaching, 312–13
entitlement, sense of, 3, 539, 542
Entrepreneurial Time System, 324–29
Ephesians, 416
Erhard, Werner, 37, 433
Escobar, Tony and Randi, 484–85
Esquith, Rafe, 312–13, 313n
Evans, Janet, 167
Evans, Richard Paul, 561
evening review, 248
events, responding to, 7–8; changing response, 7–8; creating outcomes, 14–15; giving up blame, 10–11; giving up complaining, 12–14; past choices and, 9–10
Everhart, Angie, 190
exceeding expectations, 224–27
Excellerated Business Schools, 24n, 436–37
excuses, giving up, 5–7, 14
exit strategy, 424
expectancy theory, 42–43
expectations, exceeding of, 224–27
expenditures, 470–76; debt reduction, 474–76; eliminating small expenses, 473; paying with cash, 471–72; reducing costs, 472; student loans, 473–74; tracking, 459, 471, 558

experiencing fear and taking action anyway, 152–64
expertise, primary area of, 319–23
external yellow alerts, 16
extra mile, 224–27
eye contact, 243, 395
eye on the prize, 247–49

Facebook, 522, 523, 526, 537–42, 551, 553; appropriate use of, 541–42; authenticity on, 541; creating key profiles, 526; forging deeper relationships, 530–31; keeping followers engaged, 537–40; posting regularly, 527; privacy concerns, 510
failure: dealing with, 220; fear of (failing forward), 142–44; feedback and, 203–4
failure experience, 203–4
family code, and money, 449
Fantasized Experiences Appearing Real (FEAR), 155–56
Fast Company (magazine), 211, 328, 369
fear, 152–64; acceptance of, 153–55; of asking, 176–77; in denial, 270; of failure (failing forward), 142–44; fantasizing to overcome, 155–56; getting rid of, 156–59; goal-setting and, 84–86; imagined outcomes and, 155–56; of judgment, 411–14; as phobia, 159; positive uses of, 153–55; reasons for, 152–53; replacing physical sensations of, 157; scaling down the risk, 158–59; self-talk and, 282, 283–84; taking a leap of faith, 160–63; Total Truth Process and, 256, 257; using memory for relief of, 157–58
Fearless: A Woman's Guide to Personal Self-Protection (Doughty), 41
feedback, 17–18, 194–204; accuracy of, 202; asking for, 197–98; on course, off course, 195; failure and, 203–4; leaders and, 344; listening to, 202; as on-the-job training, 150–51; patterns in, 202–3; response to, 196–97;

in showing appreciation, 426, 429–30; types of, 194–95; weekly ritual, 199–200
Feed the Children, 490
"Feel Felt Found" technique, 541
Feel the Fear and Do It Anyway (Jeffers), 128, 152*n*
Feeney, Chuck, 494
Feinstein, Dianne, 6
Ferriss, Tim, 44–45, 231, 373, 424–25, 504–5, 504*n*
financial assets, 457, 468
financial goals, 452–53, 456–57, 461–62, 462*n*, 471
financial literacy, 459–60
financial planners, 457, 458, 462, 466, 469
financial planning, 457–60; determining net worth, 457, 462; tracking spending, 459. *See also* expenditures; investing money; retirement
financial temperature, 99–101
financial tithing, 490. *See also* tithing
Firestone, Harvey, 375, 376
Five Love Languages, 427–30
Five-Minute Phobia Cure, 159
Fiverr, 334, 525, 555, 556
Flag Is Up Farms, 37
Florida, Richard, 348
focus: Daily Success Focus Journal, 243–44; on money and wealth, 455–60, 476; negative, 278–79; positive, 247–49, 279; on success, 237–46; total focus process, 330–31; on vision, 36–37
Focus Days, 324–25, 328
focusing regimen, 247–48
Folk, Judith, 465
Fonda, Jane, 53
Forbes, B. C., 213
Forbes, Malcolm S., 319, 321
Ford, Arielle, 253*n*
Ford, Eileen, 190
Ford, Henry, 50, 374–75, 376
forgiveness, 258, 259–61; affirmations of, 263–66; moving on and, 259; steps to, 260–61

Fosse, Elaine, 308–9
Foundation for Self-Esteem, 407–8
Four Agreements, The (Ruiz), 415, 415*n*, 419
Four Seasons hotels, 227
Francis of Assisi, Saint, 500
Free Days, 326–29, 557
Freelancer, 334, 334*n*
Fritz, Robert, 36
Frost, David, 216, 217*n*
FTD (Florists' Telegraph Delivery), 272, 274
Fujimoto, Shun, 165–66
Fuller, Buckminster, 36, 143, 202, 558
full moon, 297–98
Fundable, 549
fusiform face area, 531

Gallagher, Sean, xx
Gallozzi, Chuck, 205
Game of Work, The (Coonradt), 209, 209*n*
Gandhi, Mahatma, 60, 219, 342, 346
Garson, Greer, 322
Gates, Bill, 6, 36, 57, 346
Gelb, Michael J., 380
generative AI. *See* artificial intelligence
George, William H., 494
Gersey, Sergio Sedas, 129–30
Getting the Love You Want (Hendrix), 430–31
Getty, J. Paul, 292, 421
Gibson, William, 546
gifts, 428–29
Gilbert, Dan, 534
Givens, Charles J., 269
giving up, 5–7, 216–17
Gladstone, William E., 142
Gladwell, Malcolm, 168, 169*n*
Glamour (magazine), 190
goals, 30–41; acknowledgment of, 34; acting as if achieved, 125–34; action plan for, 90–94; active approach to, 135–44; affirmations and, 106–7; breakthrough, 79–80; carrying in your wallet, 82; chunking down of, 90–94; clarifying of, 34–39; demands of others vs., 335–40; early

childhood programming vs., 30–31; fear of failure vs., 142–44; financial, 452–53, 456–57, 461–62, 462*n*, 471; good ideas vs., 78; improvement and, 206; making a living and, 26–27; motivation in pursuit of, 147–49; moving towards, 221–22; power of, 87–89; practice towards, 168–69; purpose of, 31–34; rereading three times a day, 81–82; Rule of 5 and, 221–23; setting. *See* goal-setting; taking action toward, 135–44, 149–50, 557; taking first steps toward, 145–46; using failure in achievement of, 142–44; visualization and, 111–12; waiting vs., 135–44. *See also* vision
Goals Books, 82, 83, 120
goal-setting, 76–89; action plan, 91–94; clarifying aims in, 78; considerations, fears, and roadblocks, 84–86; creating breakthrough, 79–80; mastery as aim of, 79, 86–87; multiple goals in, 83–84; power of, 76–78; specificity in, 79; writing yourself a check, 82–83
goals lists, 81, 83–84
GOALS (Gaining Opportunities and Life Skills) Program, 238, 408
God, 24, 46, 67, 79, 87, 106, 142, 311, 375, 380, 383, 390, 489
Goethe, Johann Wolfgang von, xxix
GoFundMe, 549
going the extra mile, 224–27
Goldwyn, Samuel, 409
Gonzalez, Ruben, 137–39, 560
Good to Great (Collins), 336, 338
good vs. great opportunities, 338, 340
Good Will Hunting (movie), 172
Google, 191, 523, 525, 527
Google Drive, 509
Google Gemini, 516
Google Hangouts, 377, 378, 556
GoPro, 479–80
gossip, 418–19
GPS (Global Positioning System), 34–35, 67

Graduate to Your Perfect Job (Dorsey), 357
gratitude: of leaders, 352; vibrational match through, 73–74
Graves, Earl G., 185
gravity, 12, 59
Gray, John, 95, 221, 373
greed, 492
Greene, Brian, 61, 61*n*
Greenspan, Alan, 459
Greven, Alec, 56
grudges, 260
Guber, Peter, 347
guilt, about saying no, 337, 338
guilt-tripping, 280
Guinness World Records, 54, 119, 366–67

Habitat for Humanity, 490
habits, 292–95; changing of, 293–95; consequences of, 292–93; self-destructive, 6–7, 292–95. *See also* limiting beliefs
Haddock, Doris, 54
Hamilton, Scott, 136
Hammerstein, Oscar, 216
Hammond, Darrell, 218–20
Hansen, Mark Victor, 36, 66, 75, 80, 82, 119, 151, 177, 186, 187–88, 200, 221–22, 323, 384, 389, 559, 571–72
Harrison, Steve, 373
Hatch, Connie, 338
Health Communications, Inc., 188
Healy, Kent, 365
Heart Talk, 400–404; guidelines for, 402–3; how to conduct, 401; results, 403; when to use, 401
Heart Talk Book (Canfield), 402*n*
Hemingway, Ernest, 173
Hendricks, Gay, 95, 449–50
Hendrix, Harville, 430–31
Hesburgh, Theodore, 346
Hewitt, Les, 94, 352, 355–56, 571
HeyGen, 514–15
Hicks, Esther and Jerry, 72, 73, 74, 75, 94*n*, 454
high achievers, 35–36, 93–94, 213, 330
high intention, 163–64
High Performers International, 210
Hill, Napoleon, 4, 42, 43, 374–75

Hilton, Conrad, 381
Hobart Elementary School, 312–13
hobbies, 38, 169, 486
Holland, Isabelle, 259
Holmes, Oliver Wendell, 557
Holtz, Lou, 12, 83
home equity loans, 475
home mortgages, 475–76
hopes, never giving up on, 216–20
Hour of Power, 124
Howard, Ron, 321
How to Be Rich (Getty), 421
How to Get What You Really, Really, Really, Really Want (Dyer), 10, 224
How to Say No Without Feeling Guilty (Breitman and Hatch), 338
How to Talk to Girls (Greven), 56
How to Think Like Leonardo da Vinci (Gelb), 380
How to Use What You've Got to Get What You Want (Tam), 410n
Hreljac, Ryan, 56–57
human-potential training, 304, 566
humblebragging, 541
Hunt, John, 330
hurt, 84, 253, 257, 259–61, 408–9
Hutcherson, Donna and Dale, 182
Huxley, Aldous, 267

"I am" affirmations, 102, 103–4
I CAN Believe in Myself (Laundry), 366–67
"I can't" thinking, 50–52
ideal day, 249
ideal life, vision of, 34
idle gossip, 419
If Life Is a Game, These Are the Rules (Carter-Scott), 32–33
Imagination Foundation, 551–52
impeccability, in speech, 415–20
improvement, 205–8; deciding on what, 206; pace of change and, 205–6; skipping steps, 207; slight edge and, 208; in small increments, 206
improvement opportunities, 195, 285, 287
Income Builders International, 101–2
income enhancement. *See* money-making ideas
income sources, multiple, 485–88

incompleteness, 250–55
Indiegogo, 549
individual retirement accounts (IRAs), 467
industrialization, 516–17
information overload, 504–5
inner child, 242, 244–45
inner coach, 275, 282–87
inner critic, 275, 282–87
inner global positioning system, 34–35, 67
inner guidance system, 26–27
"innernet," 249
"inquire within." *See* intuition; meditation
Inside Edge, 323
"inspired actions," 68, 70–71
Instant Income (Switzer), 70–71, 478, 487n
integrity, personal, 344–45, 435
intentional thoughts, 63, 65, 66–67
Intention Experiment, The (McTaggart), 62, 63n
interests vs. commitments, 296–98
internal psychological thermostat, 99–101
internal yellow alerts, 16
International Achievement Summit, 163–64, 499
International Youth Foundation, 189
Internet, 503–52; connecting with people, 553–56; dating services, 479; low-information diet, 504–6; security concerns, 509; start-up businesses, 483–84; taking control of, 507–11. *See also* crowdfunding; online persona; social media; websites
intrapreneurs, 478
intuition, 260, 380–91; asking questions, 388; communicating with you, 384–85; meditation to access, 382–84; Quick Coherence Technique, 386–88; sway test, 71, 388–90
inventory, of major successes, 239–40
investing money, 463–67; automatic programs, 466–67, 558; building assets, 468; 50/50 Law, 464–65; millionaire mentality, 465–67
IRAs (individual retirement accounts), 467

Israel-Hamas War, 113
It's a Grind Coffee Houses, 224
"It's not against you; it's for me," 338
"I want" lists, 33

Jab, Jab, Jab, Right Hook (Vaynerchuk), 531
Jack Canfield Personal Coaching, 370–72, 565–66
Jack Canfield Private Retreats, 443, 566
Jack Canfield's Key to Living the Law of Attraction, 571
Jack Canfield's Key to Living the Law of Attraction (Canfield et al.), 75
Jacobson, Trisha, 131–33
Jakóbiak, Łukasz, 507, 507*n*
Jamal, Azim, 124
James, Devon, 419
James, Henry, xxxv
James, William, 229
Jeffers, Susan, 128, 152, 152*n*, 323
Jobs, Steve, 346
Johnson, Jimmy, 163
Johnson, Spencer, 194
Jolley, Elizabeth, 54
Jonathan Livingston Seagull (Bach), 44, 126, 275
Jones, Charlie "Tremendous," 571
Jönsson, Olof, 62
Jordan, Michael, 166
journal writing, 69–70, 73, 203; Daily Success Focus Journal, 243–44
joy, 24, 26–27, 65*n*, 73, 103–4, 256–57
Judge, Aaron, 321
judgment, 418–19; fear of, 411–14
Jumpstart Our Business Startups (JOBS) Act, 544
Jung, Carl, 60
"just do it." *See* taking action
"just say no!" *See* saying no

kaizen, 205
Kapor, Mitch, 504
Karcher, Carl, 559
keeping one's word, 433–38
Keller, Helen, 317
Kelley, Mike, 160–61
Kennedy, John F., 36, 87, 272, 342, 346
Kersey, Cynthia, 192

Kettering, Charles F., 125
Keynote Concerts, 149
Khan, Kabir, 120–24
Khosla, Vinod, 211–12
Kickstarter, 545–49
Kim Phuc, Phan Thi, 262
kinesiology, 50–51
kinesthetic appreciation, 427–28
King, Martin Luther, Jr., 36, 66, 146, 219, 534
King, Stephen, 174, 190–91
Kingsolver, Barbara, 188
Kinko's, 148, 559
Kirberger, Kimberly, 398, 486
Kitchen Confidential (Bourdain), 437
Kittinger, Joseph, 358–59
Kiyosaki, Robert, 366, 459, 460, 468, 554
Klein, Helen, 54–55
Knight, Phil, 409–10
Koch, Richard, 339*n*
Kohl, David, 77–78
Kraus, Stephen, 76, 76*n*
Kremer, John, 221
Kriegel, Otis, 139–40
Kroc, Ray, 53–54, 141
Kumaravel, CK and Veena, 87–89, 89*n*

labeling, 280–81
Labovitz, Erica, 544
language translation, 514–15
Lanigan, Catherine, 52–53
L.A. Parent (magazine), 140–41
Latansky, Mykola, 532
"Latte Factor," 473
Laundry, Miriam, xx, 366–67
Law of Attraction, 59–75, 126; appreciation and, 73–74, 431; asking for what you want (step 1), 63–67; believing you'll get what you want and taking action (step 2), 67–68; constant state of vibration, 63; energy and our thoughts, 60–63; receiving what you want using vibrational match (step 3), 72–74; recommended books about, 75; taking "inspired actions," 68, 70–71; visualization and, 66–67, 109*n*
Law of Attraction, The (Hicks), 72, 74, 75

leaders (leadership), 341–52; accountability of, 344–45; coaching others to take role of, 349–51; gratitude of, 352; listening for possibility, 347–49; strengths and weaknesses of, 342–44; support team. *See* support team; vision of, 346–47

Leadership Secrets of Jesus, The (Murdock), 232

Leahy, Frank, 432

leaning into it, 145–51; creating momentum, 145; dreams, 146–47; starting now, 149–50; starting without seeing whole path, 146; underlying motivations, 147

leap of faith, 160–63

learning, 299–310; being teachable, 302; human-potential training as sources for, 304; investing in team's education, 304–6; from motivational masters, 307–10; as preparation for opportunity, 302–3; reading as tool to, 300–301; television and streaming time vs., 299–300

Learning Strategies Corporation, 50, 300–301

letting go, 256–66; being teachable, 302; forgiveness and, 259–66; Total Truth Process for, 256–58

Levi Strauss & Co., 240

Lewis, Shane, 484

liabilities, financial, 468. *See also* expenditures

Lichtman, Stu, 85

Life Lessons for Mastering the Law of Attraction (Canfield et al.), 75

life purpose, 23–29; finding of, 24–28; inner guidance system and, 26–27; personal statements of, 24; staying on, 28–29

life purpose exercise, 27–28

Life Purpose Guided Visualization, 29

limiting beliefs, 288–91; about money, 447–52; Law of Attraction and, 68; overcoming, 6–7, 290–91; self-talk endless loop, 98–99; sources of, 288–89

Lincoln, Abraham, 135

Liniger, Dave, 35, 482–83, 559

LinkedIn, 523, 542–43; appropriate use of, 541–42; creating key profiles, 526

listening, active, 395–99; arguing vs., 396; to feedback, 202; four questions exercise for, 397–99; hearing vs., 395; interest in person, 397; as love language, 430; for possibility, of leaders, 347–49

lists: "20 Things I Love to Do," 33–34; for completion, 253–54; daily to-do, 91, 93, 94; forgiveness, 261; of goals, 81, 83–84; "I want," 33; mind mapping, 91; stop-doing, 336; success, 239–40; technology annoyances, 511

Little, Rick, 189

Live Your Dreams (Brown), 302–3

Loggins, Kenny, 149

Lombardi, Vince, 233

lottery, 101, 142

Louganis, Greg, 167

love, 258, 289, 416, 430–31; "20 Things I Love to Do" lists, 33–34; capable and worthy of, 289; Five Love Languages, 427–30; inner-critic to inner-coach process for, 282, 284; money follows doing what you, 322–23

low attachment, 163–64

low-information diet, 504–6

Lucado, Max, 48

Lucas, George, 164

lying (lies), 417

Ma, Moses, 522*n*, 528, 544*n*

Mabet, Susan, 192–93

Macauley, Ed, 166

McCain, John, 164

McCarty, Oseola, 466

McConaughey, Matthew, 217–18

MacDonald, Jean, 364–66

McDonald's, 53–54, 141

McDougall, Jason, 45–46

McGraw, Tug, 43–44

McKeown, Les, 343

Macomber, Debbie and Wayne, 215

McTaggart, Lynne, 62, 63, 63n
MaestroConference, 556
Magic of Believing, The (Bristol), 291
Magic of Thinking Big (Schwartz), 83
Make-A-Wish Foundation, 490
Managing the Obvious (Williams), 211
Mandela, Nelson, 260, 346, 439
Man Who Listens to Horses, The (Roberts), 36–37, 37n
market, and personal brand, 524–25
Martin, Marcia, 395–96
Mary Kay Cosmetics, 147, 220, 364–66
mastermind groups, 374–77, 556
masterminding, 374–79
mastermind meetings, 377
mastery, as aim of setting goals, 79, 86–87
Matthews, Gail, 76, 76n
Maw, Jeanette, 68–70
Maxwell, John, 208
meanness, 441
measurable goals, 76, 79, 90, 557
media fasts, 505
meditation: to access intuition, 382–84; appreciation and gratitude through, 73–74; evening review, 248; informal, 385–86; on life purpose, 29
Medtronic, 494
memory, for relief of fear, 157–58
mentors, 353–58: acting on advice of, 356–57; making contact with, 354–56; purpose of, 353–54; returning the favor, 357
Michelangelo, 35, 165
micromanagement, 320
Microsoft, 6, 57
Miedaner, Talane, 255
Migicovsky, Eric, 545–48
Miller, Lisa, 355
Millionaire Cocktail Party, 127
Millionaire Mindset, 101, 134, 452–53, 517
millionaires, 95, 465–67; becoming automatic, 466–67; building assets, 468. *See also* money-making ideas
Million Dollar Forum, 101–2
Million Dollar Habits (Ringer), 293

Milliorn, Mike, 480–81
mindfulness, 391; about money, 457–60
Mind Map Book, The (Buzan), 91n
mind mapping, 91, *92*, 93
"mind movies," 116–17
mind-reading, 280
mindsets: "AI money mindsets," 514–15; apps for developing, 506; Billionaire, 518–19; Millionaire, 101, 134, 452–53, 517; Trillionaire, 519–20
Mirror Exercise, 242–44
misery, and wealth, 448–49
Misner, Ivan, 360–64, 361n
Mississippi River Beautification and Restoration Project, 183
mistakes as opportunities for learning, 142–44
Mitchell, Edgar, 62
momentum, 145–47, 174
money affirmations, 452–53
Money and You Training, 95, 436–37
money consciousness, 447–54
money-making ideas, 477–88; 482-by thinking outside the box, 483; becoming an intrapreneur, 478; five ideas, 478–85; Internet start-ups, 483–84; by joining network marketing companies, 484–85; by meeting needs, 478–82; occasional entrepreneurs, 486–88
money management. *See* expenditures; financial planning
Monroy, Caine, 551–52
monthly charges, 511
Morris, David, 224–25
mortgages, home, 475–76
Mother Teresa, 66, 311, 342, 426
Motivating the Teen Spirit, 200
motivation, 147–49
motivational masters, 307–10
moving on, and forgiveness, 259
Moyer, Jane, 328
Mullick, Nirvan, 551–52
Multiple Streams of Income (Allen), 488
Multiple Streams of Internet Income (Allen), 488
Murchison, Junior, 494
Murdoch, Rupert, 536

INDEX

Murdock, Mike, 232
Murphy, Joseph, 288

Nanavati, Akshay, xxi
Nantz, Jim, 126–27
Narcissism Epidemic, The (Twenge), 541
Nardelli, Bob, 368
NASA, 119–20, 174, 216
National Association of Personal Financial Advisers, 469
National Association of Professional Organizers (NAPO), 255, 255n
Naturals Unisex Salon and Spa, 88–89
Naval Sea Systems Command, 273
negative expectations, 43
negative feedback, 194–95
negative focus, 278–79
negative labels, 280–81
negative outcomes, and fear, 155–56
negative thoughts (images), xxiii, 275–87; effect on body, 276–77; as impediment to belief in oneself, 50–53; inner-critic to inner-coach process for, 282–87; Law of Attraction and, 66–67, 68, 72; limiting beliefs and, 288–91; releasing the brakes and, 97; Total Truth Process for, 256–58; types of, 278–81
networking, 359–67; opportunities everywhere for, 359, 364–66; tips for successful, 364; VCP Process for, 360–64; volunteering and, 497
network marketing companies, 484–85, 485n
net worth, 9–10, 457, 462
Newberry, Joe, 108
New England Center for Personal and Organizational Development, 151, 239
Newmark, Craig, 529–30
Next Principle, 189
Nichols, Lisa, 200–201
Nicklaus, Jack, 1, 110
Nike, 409–10
Nikken, 366–67
no, saying. *See* saying no

"no exceptions rule," 296–97
No Matter What (Nichols), 200
Nordstrom, 227
Nothing Down (Allen), 491

Obama, Barack, 6
obstacles: in goal-setting, 84–86; persistence in face of, 213–20
occasional entrepreneurs, 486–88
Ochs, Nola, 54
O'Dell, Tawni, 187, 216
off course, 195
Oklahoma (musical), 216
Olson, Jeff, 208
Olympic athletes, 113–15, 137–39, 165–66, 167, 560
Omidyar, Pierre, 479
on course, 195
One Minute Manager, The (Blanchard), 194, 221, 296, 351
One Minute Millionaire, The (Allen), 97, 353, 491
online persona, 522–35; content advancing "brand," 527–32; deciding who you want to be, 524–27; monitoring and cleaning up, 532–33; suppressing past and malicious content, 533; TED talks, 533–35
online security, 509
online summits, 302
online video, 531–32
on-the-job training, 150–51
OpenAI's ChatGPT, 515–16, 517
opportunities: failures as, 142–44, 220; good vs. great, 338, 340; inspired actions at, 68, 70–71; for networking, 359, 364–66; preparation for, 302–3
Orfalea, Paul, 559
organizers, professional, 255, 255n
Ortner, Nick, 263–64, 264n
Otter.ai, 515, 516
outcomes, 7–8; creating vs. allowing of, 14–15; as result of response to events, 7–8
Outliers: The Story of Success (Gladwell), 168, 169n

out-of-the-box thinking, 482–83
overcoming limitations, 97–108

Page, Larry, 191
pain, 165–66; wealth and, 448–49
Panero, Hugh, 214
Pareto Principle, 339
Parker-Follett, Mary, 349
Party, Come As You'll Be, 127–34
passion, 311–15; developing of, 313–14; digital success and, 535; maintaining of, 314–15; for teaching, 312–13
Passion Test, 29
Passion Test, The (Attwood), 29
password managers, 509
past, personal: acknowledging success in, 237–46; choices in, 9–10; in early childhood programming, 30–31; letting go of, 256–66; money consciousness and, 447–54
Patent, Arnold M., 27n
Path of Least Resistance, The (Fritz), 36
Path of Prosperity (Allen), 491
patterns, in feedback, 202–3
Pavlina, Steve, 505–6
paying attention, 18–19
Peace, Natalie, xx
Peale, Norman Vincent, 217, 354
Peary, Robert, 216
Pebble Watch, 545–48
Peck, M. Scott, 173
Peoplemaking (Satir), 201
Peres, Shimon, 164
performance critics, 285–87
Perot, H. Ross, 213, 216–17
perseverance, 137–39, 185–93, 213–20, 221–23
persistence, 178–79, 213–20
personal advisors, 332–33, 340
personal branding, 522–35; content advancing "brand," 527–32; deciding who you want to be, 524–27; monitoring and cleaning up online persona, 532–33; suppressing past and malicious content, 533; TED talks, 533–35
personal coaches. *See* coaches

Personal Development for Smart People (Pavlina), 505–6
personal development training, 304
personal integrity, 344–45, 435
personalizing, 281
personal past. *See* past, personal
personal responsibility, xxiii, 3–22; blame and, 10–11, 14; choice and, 5–10, 14–15; complaining and, 12–14; excuses and, 5–7, 14; outcomes and, 7–8; paying attention, 18–19
Peter, Laurence J., 250
pettiness, 441
Phelps, Michael, 167
Phillips, Dawa Tarchin, 391
phobias, 159; Five-Minute Phobia Cure, 159; Tapping Therapy, 263, 265–66
PhotoReading Course, 300–301
physical sensations of fear, 157
physical touch, 429
Piazza, Ignatius, 189–90
Pichai, Sundar, 513
Pillsbury Company, 497
Pilzer, Paul Zane, 489n
Pink, Dan, 533
Pinterest, 241, 523, 526, 541
placebo effect, 43
planning next day night before, 93–94
Plass, Leo, 54
Platinum Partners, 514
Poe.com, 515
Poisonwood Bible, The (Kingsolver), 188
Poitier, Sidney, 6
poker chip theory, 238–39
polygraph (lie-detector) tests, 276–77
Ponder, Catherine, 59
Popiolek, Pavel, xx–xxi
positive emotions, 72, 128, 352, 452, 452n; "imprinted" in subconscious mind, 133–34
positive expectations, 43–44, 59, 67–68, 452
positive feedback, 194–95
positive focus, 247–49, 279
positive thoughts (thinking): effect on body, 277; inner-critic to inner-coach process for, 282–87; Law of

Attraction and, 63–67, 66–67, 72; talking to yourself like a winner, 281
positive turnaround statements, 451–52
positivity, 529, 530
Powell, Colin, 256
Power of Focus, The (Canfield), 24, 352, 412, 571
power of releasing to accelerate millionaire mindset, 452–53
power of words, 416
Power of Your Subconscious Mind (Murphy), 288
Power to Have It All, The (Proctor), 450
Poynter, Dan, 221
practice, 166–69, 207; persistence and, 213–20
prayer, 390–91
precessional effects, 558–59
Pregracke, Chad, 182–83
prejudices, 416, 419, 421
Price, Larry, 407
price, paying the, 165–75; building momentum, 174; doing whatever it takes, 170–72; finding out, 175; going through awkward stage, 175; practice, 166–69; putting in the time, 173; temporary pain and, 165–66
Primerica, 42
Principle 24: Exceed Expectations (Peace), xx
privacy, digital, 510–11, 533
procrastination, 93, 293
Proctor, Bob, 152, 450, 560
professional organizers, 255, 255n
profitability, 514, 519; stage of relationship, 363–64
prosperity, 72, 452, 489, 491
public service. *See* volunteerism
Publilius Syrus, 433
Pugh, Lewis, xxi
purpose in life. *See* life purpose
push-ups, xxxii

quality time, 428
quantum entanglement, 62–63
Quantum Field, 249
quantum leap, 79
quantum mechanics, 61
questions, 176–84; assumptions vs., 421–25; for basic releasing exercise, 452–53; fear in asking of, 176–77; most valuable, 198–200; rules for asking of, 177–79
Quest program, 189
Quick Coherence Technique, 386–88
quitting, 196, 217–18
quit waiting, 135–44

Ramirez, Mary Alice, 183
Rampage of Appreciation, 73–74
Ramsey, Dave, 471
reading, 300–301; suggested, 571–72
"Ready, aim, fire!", 140–41
recession, 8–9
re-creating same experience over and over, 98–99
Red Cross, 490
Referral Institute, 361n
referrals, 226, 359, 360, 361, 363
regret, 257
rejection, 185–93; cases, 187–93; famous examples of, 190–91; fear of, 176–77; myth of, 185–86
Rejections of the Written Famous (Spizer), 214
relationships: creating successful, 395–444; networking and stages of, 360–62; on social media, 530–31
Relatively Famous Records, 149
"release the brakes," 97–108, 304
RE/MAX, 35, 482–83, 559
"Remember, You Are Raising Children, Not Flowers!" (Canfield), 140
remorse, 257
reputation management, 532–33
requests, 14, 63–64, 282, 283–84
resentment, 257, 259, 260, 273, 349, 403, 404, 406
Resnick, Robert, 6
responses: to events, 7–8; negative outcomes and, 155–56
responsibility: delegation of. *See* delegation; personal. *See* personal responsibility
retail and manufacturing, 487–88

reticular activating system (RAS), 109–11, 125
retirement (retirement accounts), 466–67; automatic contributions for, 466–67; financial literacy and, 459–60; financial planning for, 457, 458
retreats, 301–2, 443, 566
rewards, of inner child, 244–45
Rich Dad, Poor Dad (Kiyosaki), 366, 459, 460, 468, 554
Richest Man in Babylon, The (Clason), 461
"rich media," 537
"right to be forgotten" privileges, 533
Riley, Pat, 441
Ringer, Martha, 255*n*
Ringer, Robert J., 293
Ripa, Kelly, 265
ripple effect, 416
risk, 12, 13, 153–54; fear of taking, 176–77, 180–81; progress and, 160–63; scaling down, 158–59
Ritz-Carlton hotels, 101–2, 227, 441
roadblocks, 84–86. *See also* obstacles
Road Less Traveled, The (Peck), 173, 221
Robbins, Anthony "Tony," 24*n*, 51, 95, 158, 218, 321, 323, 358, 514, 533
Robbins, Mark and Sheila, 460
Roberts, Monty, 24*n*, 36–37, 37*n*
Robertson, Anna Mary (Grandma Moses), 54, 237
Robinson, Jackie, 6
Robinson, Ken, 533
Rocky (movie), 142, 339–40
Roddick, Anita, 564
Rogers, Will, 470
Rohn, Jim, xxxii, 3, 86, 231, 300
Rometty, Ginni, 517
Roosevelt, Theodore, 382
Rosenblum, Jack, 202–3
Ross, Percy, 176
Ross, Ryan, 55–56
Rowling, J. K., 191
Rozman, Deborah, 386–87
Ruiz, Don Miguel, 415, 415*n*, 419
Rule of 5, 221–23
rules of the game, 95, 436–37

Ruskin, John, 135
Rutte, Martin, 253, 438, 443–44

SAFECO, 497
Sanders, Colonel Harland, 187
Satir, Virginia, 201, 281
Saturday Night Live (TV series), 219
saving money, 100–101. *See also* investing money
saying no, 335–40; difficulty in, 337–38; to good in favor of great, 338, 340; guilt about, 337, 338; techniques for, 338–39
schedules (scheduling), 328–29; being on time, 437–38; daily to-do list, 93
Scheele, Paul R., 50, 300–301
Scheinfeld, Robert, 94*n*, 249
Schilling, Scott, 449
Schneider, John, 149
Schwab, Charles M., 426, 457
Schwartz, David, 83
Schwarzenegger, Arnold, 120, 554
Science of Getting Rich (Wattles), 68, 445, 477
Scolastico, Ron, 221–22
SCORE (Service Corps of Retired Executives), 356
scorekeeping, 209–12; appreciation and, 431–32; critical drivers in, 210; at home, 211–12; measurement, 210
Scott, MacKenzie, 494
Secret, The (Byrne), 75, 94*n*
Secret, The (movie), 59, 62–63, 74, 75, 108, 115, 161
Secret of the Ages, The (Collier), 221
Secrets process, 405–6
Sedas, Sergio, 378–79
Sedona Method, 453, 453*n*
Seeley, Kathleen, 342*n*
See You at the Top (Ziglar), 310
Seidler, Gary, 188
selectiveness, 234–35
self-awareness, of leaders, 343–44
self-confidence, 48, 130, 131, 134, 238–41, 289, 415. *See also* belief in oneself
self-criticism, 275–87; inner-critic to inner-coach process for, 282–87; negative thoughts in, 275–81; stomping the ANTs, 277

self-destructive habits, 6–7, 292–95. *See also* limiting beliefs
self-esteem, 435; of class acts, 443–44; Foundation for Self-Esteem, 407–8; lying as product of low, 417; poker chip theory of, 238–39
self-fulfilling prophecy, 49
self-image, 97, 99, 100–101
self-improvement, 205–8; deciding on what, 206; pace of change and, 205–6; skipping steps, 207; slight edge and, 208; in small increments, 206
self-talk, 98–99, 115, 275, 281; changing with affirmations, 102
self-talk endless loop, 98–99
Serebriakoff, Victor, 49–50
service providers, 487
serving others. *See* volunteerism
Seven-Day Technology Turnaround, 511
Seven Spiritual Laws of Success, The (Chopra), 46, 67, 94n
sharing the wealth, 489–95
Sharp, Billy, 348–49
Sherman, Harold, 61–62
Shimoff, Marci, 373
Shinn, Florence Scovell, 106
Simon, Sid, 297–98
Sinek, Simon, 530, 534
Situational Coaching Model, 373
Sitzman, Nick, 276
skepticism, xxv–xxvii, xxxi
slight edge, 208
Slight Edge, The (Olson), 208
Small, Adam, 359
Small Business Administration, U.S., 356
smartphones, 507–8; apps, 506; goals and affirmations, 81, 106; GPS on, 34, 65; memo pad, 389; reducing time spent on, 512
Smith, Manuel J., 338
social media, 536–42; appropriate use of, 541–42; connecting with people, 553–56; creating key profiles, 526; engaging followers, 536–39; forging deeper relationships, 530–31; limiting unrelated content, 527; posting regularly, 527; respecting followers, 541; suppressing past and malicious content, 533; uploading photos and videos, 531–32. *See also* Facebook; online persona; personal branding
Solar Roadways Inc., 549
somatic decision-making, 71, 388–89
Soulmate Secret, The (Ford), 253n
Soul of Money, The (Twist), 492
Southwest Airlines, 439
space between rules, 424–25
spam, 512
Spanx, 346–47
Speaker's Sourcebook, The (Van Ekeren), 276n
speaking, with impeccability, 415–20
specificity: of goals, 78–79; of questions, 177–78
spending money. *See* expenditures
Spielberg, Steven, 172, 191, 222
Spizer, Joyce, 214
Sports Illustrated, 43, 138
staff members, 331–32, 408–9, 563. *See also* support team
Stallone, Sylvester, 142, 189, 339–40
Stanfield, Jana, 146–49, 149n
Starr, Chandra, 549
Start Late, Finish Rich (Bach), 467, 473
StartSomeGood, 549–50
Start with Why (Sinek), 530
Stein, Ben, 30, 393
Stern, Isaac, 169
Stevens Corporation, 381
Stone, W. Clement, xxx, 4–5, 82, 106, 141, 234, 299–300
stop-doing lists, 336
storytelling, 147, 516, 545–46
Strand Prophecy, The (Winner), 57
Strategic Coach Program, 321, 324, 397, 397n, 439, 514
streaming time, 299–300
Street Kid's Guide to Having It All, The (Assaraf), 234
strengths, of leaders, 342–44
stress, 263–65, 352
structural change, 273–74, 506
"structural tension," 81
stuck, 98–99

student loans, 473–74
success: appreciation and, 431; "Breakthrough to Success" training, 29, 305–6, 565; Daily Success Focus Journal, 243–44; focusing on and celebrating, 237–46; leaving clues, 95–96; poker chip theory of, 238–39
successful people, surrounding yourself with, 231–36
success inventory, 239–40
success lists, 239–40
Success Principles Keynote, Workshop, and Training, 569
Success Principles Team, 565
success rallies, 301–2
success symbols, 241–42
Success System That Never Fails (Stone), 4–5
Success Through a Positive Mental Attitude (Hill), 4
sufficiency, 492
Sullivan, Dan, 227, 321, 321*n*, 324, 397, 439, 440, 514
superachievers, 35–36, 93–94, 213, 330
support team, 330–34; education of, 304–6; leader coaching of, 349–51; leader listening for possibility and, 347–49; leader's vision and, 346–47; personal advisors, 332–33, 340; trust in, 333–34
Surowiecki, James, 503
Suu Kyi, Aung San, 346
sway test, 71, 388–90
Swift, Taylor, 539–40
Switzer, Janet, 70–71, 210*n*, 325, 355, 364, 478, 483, 486–87, 487*n*, 538
SWSWSWSW ("some will, some won't; so what–someone's waiting"), 186
Szymanski, Frank, 432

Tagore, Rabindranath, 145
taking action, 135–44, 557; bias of successful people for, 139–40; denial vs., 271; "Do it now," 141–42; experiencing fear and, 152–64; failing forward, 142–44; leaning into, 149–50; nothing happens unless, 136–39; "Ready, aim, fire!" 140–41; talk is cheap, 137
Talent Code, The (Coyle), 169*n*
Talent Is Overrated (Colvin), 168–69, 169*n*
Tam, Marilyn, 409–10, 410*n*
Tapping Into Ultimate Success (Canfield and Bruner), 24, 264, 287, 287*n*, 571
Tapping Therapy, 98, 263–66, 287
Taylor, Jill Bolte, 534
teaching, passion for, 312–13
Teach Like Your Hair's on Fire (Esquith), 313*n*
technology, 503–12; low-information diet, 504–6; taking control of, 507–11. *See also* artificial intelligence; Internet; online persona; smartphones; social media
TED talks, 533–35, 535*n*
television time, 299–300
Tell to Win (Guber), 347
Templeton, John Marks, 465, 498
Teresa, Mother, 66, 311, 342, 426
TGI Friday's, 480–81
TheOasis, 515
There Are No Shortcuts (Esquith), 313*n*
Thigpen, Peter, 240
Think and Grow Rich (Hill), 42, 43, 374–75
thinking outside the box, 482–83
Thoele, Sue Patton, 335
Thoreau, Henry David, 473
Thought Field Therapy (TFT), 263–64
thoughts: energy and, 60–67. *See also* Law of Attraction; negative thoughts; positive thoughts
Thoughts Through Space (Wilkins and Sherman), 61–62
Thurber, Marshall, 175, 436–37
Thurman, Howard, 323
time, putting in the, 173
time management: being on time, 437–38; delegating responsibility and, 319–21; Entrepreneurial Time System, 324–29; support team, 330–34; vacation time, 327–28, 329. *See also* schedules
Time Present, Time Past (Bradley), 166

time tithing, 490–91. *See also* volunteerism
tithing, 465, 489–95; types of, 490–91
to-do lists, 91, 93, 94
total focus process, 330–31
Total Truth Letter, 256–58
Total Truth Process, 256–58, 261
Town, Phil, 459
toxic people, 234–35, 349
Tracy, Brian, 23, 93, 242, 342
Train-the-Trainer Program, 155, 197, 243, 266, 305–6, 366
Tresidder, Todd, 473
Trick to Money Is Having Some!, The (Wilde), 461
Trillionaire Mindset, 519–20
Troup, John, 167
True, Herbert, 179
Trump, Donald, 56, 220
trust, in support team, 333–34
truth, 405–11; Total Truth Process, 256–58, 261
TuneGo, 549
turnaround statements, 451–52
Tutu, Desmond, 164
Twain, Mark, 90, 156, 405
twelve-step programs, 10
Twenge, Jean, 541
Twist, Lynne, 492
Twitter, 539, 540

Uber, 481, 555
Ueberroth, Peter, 161
Ultimate Game of Life, 359
United States Capitol attack (2021), 113
universities. *See* college
Unlimited Power (Robbins), 95
Unstoppable Foundation, 192–93
Upwork, 334, 334*n*, 487, 525, 555

vacation time, 327–28, 329
Van Ekeren, Glen, 276*n*
Vaynerchuk, Gary, 531
VCP Process, 360–64
Vegso, Peter, 188
vibrational match, 72–74
vibrational states, 63, 431
victim stories, 5–7, 19–21
victory logs, 240–41

video programs, motivational, 307–10
video testimonials, 532
Vidmar, Peter, 113–15
Vietnam War, 216–17, 262
virtual assistants, 334, 513, 555–56
"virtual businesses," 555–56
virtual mastermind groups, 556
virtual summits, 302
visibility stage of relationship, 361–62
vision, 34–39; Achievers Focusing System for, 94; connecting with people and expanding, 553–56; of high achievers, 35–36; of ideal life, 34; inner global positioning system, 34–35; of leaders, 346–47; sharing of, 39; staying focused on, 36–37. *See also* goals
vision boards, 119–20, 454; how to, 119–20; of Jack Canfield, xxvii, 119; of John Assaraf, 120; of Justin Bendel, xx; of Kabir Khan, 121, 122–23; of Raj Bhavsar, 20–21; using printed pictures, 118–19
vision exercise, 37–39
visual appreciation, 427–28
visualization, 109–24; in acquiring wealth, 447, 453–54, 456–57, 477; adding sounds and feelings, 112; brain function and, 109–11; cases, 113–18, 120–24; emotion in, 113; giving a TEDx talk, 534–35; how to use, 105; of ideal day, 249; intentional daydreaming, 66–67; in performance enhancement, 110–11; printed pictures in, 118–19; process of, 111–12; starting now, 124
volunteerism, 490–91, 496–500; receiving more than you give, 497; unexpected career and business rewards, 499; your skills, 497
vulgarity, 441

waiting vs. goals, 135–44
Wales, Jimmy, 535
Walker, Heather O'Brien, xxi, 115–18
Wallack, Melisa, 217–18
wallet card, of goals, 82
Walsh, Mike, 210

wants, 32–33, 258; inner global positioning system, 34–35; "I want" list, 33; Law of Attraction and, 65–66, 67
Washington, Denzel, 6, 439
Watson, James, 385
Wattles, Wallace D., 68, 445, 477
weaknesses, of leaders, 342–44
wealth creation, 477–88; making money, 478–85; multiple sources of income, 485–86; pain and misery, 448–49; sharing of, 489–95; visualization in, 447, 453–54, 456–57, 477
Wealth Without Risk (Givens), 269
websites: bookmarks toolbar, 509; building, 525–26; security concerns, 509; virtual assistants, 334, 513, 555–56. *See also* personal branding; *and specific websites*
weekly ritual: feedback, 199–200
Weinschenk, Susan, 531
Weiske, Gordon, 170–72
Wentworth, Diana von Welanetz, 322–23
Wepner, Chuck, 141–42
Weston, Simon, 262
"whatever," 32
When I Say No, I Feel Guilty (Smith), 338
White, Paul, 427–28, 428*n*
Whole Foods, 309
"why" of what you do, 24–26, 530
Wilcox, Frederick, 160
Wilde, Stuart, 461
Wilkins, Hubert, 61–62
Willett, Forrest, xxii–xxv
Williams, Arthur L., 42
Williams, Lisa, 525

Williams, Pat, 26
Williams, Rick and Tyler, 211
Williams, Serena, 81–82
Williams, Venus, 58
Wilson, Kemmons, 307
Winfrey, Oprah, 33, 74, 173, 216, 235, 465
Winner, Brianna and Brittany, 57
Winters, Jonathan, 136
Wittal, Doug, xx
Wooden, John, 299, 442
Woodman, Nicholas, 479–80
Woods, Tiger, 33
words: of affirmation, 428; focusing on what you want, 65–66; impeccability in, 415–20; power of, 416
workaholics, xxx, 269, 332, 448
World Trade Center attacks (2001), 113, 214, 265
worry, 58, 64, 67, 276
Worsley, Sharon, 266
Wyland, 169–70, 233

yellow alerts, 15–16, 267–68
yellow notebook, 32–33
Yellow Ribbon International, 490
You Can Have It All (Patent), 27*n*
"You gotta believe" attitude, 43–44
Young, Cliff, 46–47
Young, Whitney M., Jr., 302
Young Entrepreneurs Organization, 232
YWCA, 490

Ziglar, Zig, 310, 498–99
Zmeskal, Kim, 167
Zuckerberg, Mark, 57, 553